# ENCYCLOPEDIA OF CAPITAL PUNISHMENT

# ENCYCLOPEDIA OF CAPITAL PUNISHMENT

## Mark Grossman

ABC-CLIO

Santa Barbara, California
Denver, Colorado
Oxford, England

Library of Congress Cataloging-in-Publication Data
Grossman, Mark.
Encyclopedia of capital punishment / Mark Grossman.
p. cm.
Includes bibliographical references and index.
1. Capital punishment—Encyclopedias. 2. Capital punishment—History—Encyclopedias. 3. Executions and executioners—Encyclopedias. 4. Executions and executioners—History—Encyclopedias. I. Title.
HV8694.G76 1998
364.66'03—dc21 98-21248
CIP

ISBN 0-87436-871-5

04 03 02 01 00 99 10 9 8 7 6 5 4 3 2

ABC-CLIO, Inc.
130 Cremona Drive, P.O. Box 1911
Santa Barbara, California 93116-1911

Typesetting by Letra Libre

This book is printed on acid-free paper ♾.

Manufactured in the United States of America.

*To my parents, Larry and Lois,*
*who remain my staunchest supporters;*
*to my cousin, Jane Morrin;*
*and to the memories of Hans and Sophie Scholl,*
*who gave up their young lives in the fight to end tyranny*
*in Germany in 1943*

CONTENTS

The death penalty has since time immemorial fascinated the public. Before they were barred in the twentieth century, public executions—hangings, beheadings, burnings at the stake—attracted enormous crowds. And since the introduction of Hammurabi's Code, the first set of rules for a nation-state to set forth an official death penalty, capital punishment has always been controversial. From the beginning, leaders of nations have been caught in the debate over its use. During his reign, William the Conqueror resisted the usage of capital punishment but instead resorted to torture. He wrote, "We forbid . . . that anyone be hanged or otherwise put to death, for any offense whatsoever. But . . . his eyes may be put out, his feet cut off, or his testicles, or his hands; and in such manner only as to allow the rest of his body to go on living." William did, however, put some people to death, and invented just for them a new form of death by execution—beheading by sword. The first man to suffer this punishment was Waltheof, the Earl of Huntington, Northampton, and Northumberland, in 1076.

From Socrates willingly drinking the hemlock handed to him by his jailers, to Jesus' crucifixion, to the burning of Joan of Arc at the stake, to the guillotining of France's King Louis XVI, to the electrocution of murderer William Kemmler, to the gas-chamber execution of Chinese killer Gee Jon, to the firing squad execution of Gary Gilmore, to more recent executions, nations and states have reserved their harshest penalties for lawbreakers, but others have come under the "point of the blade" as well. Followers of Jesus, among them Paul the Apostle and Pope St. Stephen I, and others persecuted for their religious beliefs, were martyred with the use of capital punishment. In ancient Israel, persons sentenced to death suffered either stoning, burning at the stake, strangling by a cord, or death by sword. The Soviets, as well as other Communist countries, used show trials and purges to cleanse the nation of undesirables, political opponents, or dissidents. The Nazis in the years before and during World War II sent thousands of dissidents, among them Dietrich Bonhoeffer and Hans and Sophie Scholl, to their deaths for opposing the regime. Recently, Nigeria executed the Ogoni activist Ken Saro-Wiwa, in the face of world condemnation, under the pretense that he had conspired to murder three rival Ogoni chiefs; the evidence was thin at best, however, and Saro-Wiwa had spoken out against the environmental destruction by Shell Oil in his Ogoni homeland.

The debate over capital punishment, in the United States particularly, has taken a back seat to the arguments over the various social reform movements that have captured the nation's attention—slavery, civil rights, women's suffrage. Those who argued against the death penalty in the eighteenth and nineteenth centuries were regarded as crackpots and troublemakers. Through the first half of the twentieth century, opponents of capital punishment held little sway over public opinion, although a decline in the number of executions began in the 1930s. During that decade, 1,667 executions took place; in the 1940s that number fell to 1,284. In the 1950s, 717 people were executed, and only 191 from 1960 until Jose Luis Monge died in Colorado's gas chamber on 2 June 1967, the last man put to death before the states instituted a moratorium on the use of the death penalty. It was the notable executions of Caryl Chessman (1960), a man many thought was innocent or did not deserve a death sentence, and Barbara Graham (1955), a woman who, despite her brutal crime, attracted sympathy for her plight, that turned public opinion against capital punishment. By the 1960s, the death penalty was losing its firm national support.

When the U.S. Supreme Court, in the landmark case of *Furman v. Georgia* (1972), outlawed the sentence of death as arbitrary, the states worked for the next several years to fashion a death statute that could pass constitutional muster. The Court found that the state of Georgia's scheme fit that bill with its decision in *Gregg v. Georgia* (1976). However, the reimposition of the ultimate penalty, and the public's demand for swift justice, has not resulted in a torrent of executions: from the firing-squad execution of Gary Gilmore in 1977 until the completion of this work only 437 men and 3 woman were put to death, an average of about 13 per year. But that pace is quickening. Recent Supreme Court decisions are limiting appeals by death-row convicts. States that have never had executions are beginning the process, and states that had been bastions of opposition to the penalty, such as New York, have passed statutes reimposing capital punishment.

But this book is not only about the death penalty in the United States. The arguments that led to the abolition of capital punishment in England are examined here in a speech by John Stuart Mill in the British House of Commons, as well as two cases that many argue sounded the death knell for the noose in England: those of Ruth Ellis and James Hanratty. A comprehensive look at the nations that have abolished capital punishment, and the dates on which abolition occurred, is included as well.

The subject of the death penalty and the way it has been carried out has always intrigued me. Years before I began writing this book, I had collected, through my many travels across the United States, newspapers and books with that theme in mind. For this work, I traveled to Great Britain to research that nation's relationship with capital punishment, visiting graves of executed people and execution sites. As well, I utilized the archives of universities and libraries in the United States, England, Australia, and Canada to gain some insight into works of literature, many of them hundreds of years old, spread throughout the world.

To stand before what seems to be such bloody history is indicative of the love I have not only of history but of the role of famous people in it. That's why I included in this work famous persons who were executed—to discuss capital punishment and ignore those who suffered from its effects would, in my estimation, diminish the book. Although I am a partisan on the subject of capital punishment, I have tried not to let any bias seep into the text. If any can be detected, I duly apologize. The lives and writings of those who campaigned for and against the death penalty are examined, but there is no editorial comment on the positions taken by activists on either side of the issue. Nor is there an all-encompassing essay on the reasons for capital punishment and the arguments against it, though I do examine particular approaches in some entries. The reasons why various states use the death penalty and why some persons oppose it and others support it are not explored at any great length, though again, I do present the theories of some well-known advocates and opponents of the death penalty.

The criteria utilized in selecting the entries were simple: I wanted to represent, through the biographies of persons, those whose cases were most famous. Of the thousands of Christian martyrs, I chose only a few, because most of them were burned at the stake and to include more than a few would seem redundant. As far as the other entries, I decided to include every major mode of capital punishment in the history of the world, though some obscure methods may have escaped my attention. The ground rules for the book were essentially that persons included must have been legally executed and that the execution must have been carried out, or at least sanctioned, by the state. However, I did include several people outside these rules (the reasoning for this is explained in the text); for example, prominent advocates or opponents of capital punishment, and the history of lynching is included. Any errors of fact or interpretation are my own.

I would like to thank the following people and institutions for their work in helping to make this work a reality: the staff, particularly of the newspaper reading room, of the Chicago Public Library (the Harold Washington Center), where I began the work on this book five years ago; Tom Metzger in the Office of Public Affairs of the United States Bureau of Prisons, for his help in obtaining a listing of those executed by the Federal Government; the folks at the Maricopa County Library, Phoenix, Arizona (particularly Bill, Steve, and Barbara), who endured years of my research and frenetic interlibrary loan requests; the staff of the Arizona State Law Library, Phoenix, for withstanding my scurrying around for obscure law cases and articles in their wonderful institution; the staff of the microforms and newspapers section of the Hayden Library at Arizona State University, Tempe; the dedicated folks of the Main Reading Room of the British Library, London; the friendly people, include the Yeoman Warders, at the Tower of London, where I got a chance to see up close the spot where Lady Jane Grey and Catherine Howard, among others, met their ends, and where Sir Walter Raleigh was imprisoned while he wrote his *History of the World;* the staff of the University of London; the incredible staff of the Public Record Office, Chancery Lane, London (they asked me to add that their collections will be moving at the end of 1996 out to Kew); the great people at the British Library Newspaper Library in Colindale, England, for their expertise while I was at their fine facility in handling my requests for obscure British journals and newspapers; the staff of the Main Reading Room at the Library of Congress, as well as the Newspaper Reading Room and the Law Library of that institution; the staff of American University, Washington, D.C.; the staff of the Lauinger Library, Georgetown University, Washington, D.C.; the fine people at the Natural Resources Library at the Interior Department, Washington, D.C. (their collections can be used for just about any sort of research, even on capital punishment); the staff of the New York Public Library; the staff of the Nicholas Murray Butler Library, Columbia University; the folks at the Bobst Library, New York University; the staff of the library at the Frances Perkins Labor Department Building, Washington, D.C.; the National Archives staff, particularly Katherine Collado of the Congressional Research Center; L. Kay Gillespie, professor of sociology at Weber State University at Ogden, Utah, for loaning me his important work on Utah's condemned, and for his material on blood atonement; Melanie Grace, Tourism Director at the Civil War Village at Andersonville, Georgia, for assisting me on the entry on Henry Wirz and the monument to him at the site of the infamous Civil War prison; the staff of the Malcolm A. Love Library at San Diego State University, California; the folks at the American Civil Liberties Union in Washington, D.C., as well as the staff of the NAACP Legal Defense and Education Fund, Inc., whose publications helped me to form a clearer picture of their efforts to end capital punishment; the staff of the Los Angeles Public Library; the staff of the University of Queensland Library, Queensland, Australia; the staff of the Alexander Library, the State Library of Western Australia; the staff of the Trinity College Library, Cambridge, England; and the folks at Westminster Abbey in London, particularly the elderly gentlemen who let me spend some time early one morning at the grave of Major John André, before the Abbey opened, and take some notes.

## A-6 Murderer

See Hanratty, James

## Abolition of Capital Punishment, World Statistics on

Since 1781, most of the world's nations have abolished capital punishment, starting with the Austro-Hungarian Empire and continuing through the 1996 abolition of capital punishment in Spain. The nations and states where the use of the death penalty has been ended, with the year of abolition, are listed in the table below.

**Abolition of Capital Punishment**

| *Nation/State* | *Date of Abolition or Abandonment* |
|---|---|
| Austria-Hungary | 1781 |
| Lichtenstein[2] | 1798[1] |
| San Marino | 1848 |
| Belgium | 1863[2] |
| Venezuela | 1863 |
| Romania | 1864 |
| Portugal | 1867 |
| Holland | 1870 |
| Costa Rica | 1880 |
| Netherlands[3] | 1886[4] |
| Nicaragua | 1892[1] |
| Ecuador | 1897 |
| Norway[3] | 1905[4] |
| Uruguay | 1907 |
| Colombia | 1910 |
| Panama | 1915 |
| Austria[5] | 1919 |
| Sweden[3] | 1921 |
| Argentina | 1922 |
| Australia, Queensland[6] | 1922 |
| Dominican Republic | 1924 |
| Surinam | 1927[1] |
| Denmark[3] | 1930 |
| Mexico | 1931 |
| Iceland | 1940 |
| Switzerland[3] | 1942 |
| India | 1944 |
| Italy[3] | 1944 |
| Australia, Federal[6] | 1945 |
| Brazil[6] | 1946 |
| Soviet Union[7] | 1947 |
| West Germany | 1949 |
| Finland[3] | 1949 |
| Nepal[6] | 1950 |
| Greenland | 1954 |
| Israel[8] | 1954 |
| Australia, New South Wales[6] | 1955 |
| Honduras | 1957 |
| Netherlands Antilles[6] | 1957 |
| Bolivia | 1961 |
| New Zealand[6] | 1961 |
| Monaco | 1962 |
| Great Britain[6] | 1965 |
| Northern Ireland[6] | 1966 |
| Canada[6] | 1967 |
| Austria | 1968 |
| Australia, Tasmania[6] | 1968 |
| Vatican City | 1969 |
| France | 1981 |
| Gambia[9] | 1993 |
| Mauritius[10] | 1995 |
| South Africa[11] | 1995 |
| Ukraine | 1995 |
| Spain[12] | 1996 |

1. Date of de facto abandonment of capital punishment.
2. Excludes one execution.
3. Allows for the death penalty in time of war.
4. Executed Nazi collaborators at the end of World War II.
5. After it was split in two following World War I, Austria abolished capital punishment but reinstated it at the start of World War II.
6. Retained the death penalty for extraordinary civil offenses.
7. Reinstated in 1950 for certain offenses.
8. Executed Nazi war criminal Adolf Eichmann in 1960.
9. Abolished capital punishment in 1993 but reinstated it in 1995.
10. When the parliament of Mauritius decided on 3 August 1995 to abolish capital punishment, it tipped the balance among the nations of the world: 98 have abolished the death penalty, 97 have not.
11. The death penalty was held unconstitutional by the South African Supreme Court on this date, though it was not abolished until the new constitution was signed in December 1996.
12. The Spanish senate voted to abolish the use of capital punishment in its military penal code, ending the death penalty in the nation as a whole.

## Alban, Saint (?–?)

English protomartyr put to death during the reign of the Roman Emperor Diocletian (284–313) for refusing to worship pagan gods. (A protomartyr [from the Greek: *proto,* meaning "first" or "foremost"] is defined as "the first martyr in any cause"; the name was originally given to Saint Stephen.)

Saint Alban was probably born in the city of Verulamium (now St. Albans), Hertfordshire, England. Religious persecution was severe under Diocletian, and one of the citizens he persecuted was a priest whom St. Alban harbored and thereby protected from torture. According to historian John Delaney, "Alban was so impressed by the priest [that] he was converted to Christianity, changed clothes with the priest, and was mistakenly arrested as the priest because he was wearing his clothes." Refusing to convert back to the pagan faith, Alban was beheaded, but not before he allegedly performed several miracles along the path to his execution. One of these was making a spring of clear water leap forth from the foot of Holmhurst Hill in Verulamium, allowing him to quench his thirst before he was executed. A Roman soldier converted by Alban's piety and refusal to renounce his faith was also beheaded. Alban's feast day for the Roman Catholic Church is 22 June; for the Anglican Church, 17 June.

However, the story of Alban is nearly impossible to substantiate, and many historians doubt its authenticity. Constantius of Lyons first wrote of the martyr in a biography of Saint Germanus of Auxerre in the fifth century, telling of Germanus's claim that he visited the tomb of St. Alban and that "the intercession of the blessed martyr St. Alban procured a smooth passage" for him and for his companions on their return home. He does not specify where the tomb is located, though, and it has never been found. Still, Alban is considered by the church to be a saint.

**References:** *The Abbey of Saint Alban. Some Extracts from Its Early History and a Description of Its Conventual Church* (London: George Bell, 1851), 8; Delaney, John J., *Dictionary of Saints* (Garden City, NY: Doubleday, 1980), 35; Thurston, Herbert J., and Donald Attwater, eds., *Butler's Lives of the Saints,* 4 vols. (Westminster, MD: Christian Classics, 1988), 2:612–13.

## *Aldridge v. United States* (283 U.S. 308, 75 L.Ed. 1054, 51 S.Ct. 470 [1931])

U.S. Supreme Court decision, holding that juries must be asked about their feelings about racial prejudice and capital punishment when chosen to sit on a jury, or a resulting death sentence from that jury may be overturned.

Petitioner Alfred Scott Aldridge, a black man, had been convicted in the Supreme Court of the District of Columbia of murder in the first degree and sentenced to death for killing a white policeman. During the jury selection process, Aldridge's lawyer, James Francis Reilly, attempted to ask the prospective jurors if they had any racial bias toward a black defendant accused of murdering a white policeman. However, the judge refused to allow this question; he also prevented Reilly from questioning the prospective jurors about their feelings on capital punishment. An all-white jury was seated. Aldridge appealed both the conviction and death sentence to the U.S. Supreme Court; arguments were heard on 16 March 1931.

About a month later, on 20 April 1931, the Court handed down its decision. Speaking for an 8–1 court (Justice James McReynolds issued a strong dissent), Chief Justice Charles Evans Hughes struck down Aldridge's conviction and death sentence because they violated his right to a fair trial. Hughes wrote: "The argument is advanced on behalf of the government that it would be detrimental to the administration of the law in the courts of the United States to allow questions to jurors as to racial or religious prejudices. We think that it would be far more injurious to permit it to be thought that persons entertaining a disqualifying prejudice were allowed to serve as jurors and that inquiries designed to elicit the fact of disqualification were barred. No surer way could be devised to bring the processes of justice into disrepute."

## American Civil Liberties Union Capital Punishment Project

Leading American civil liberties organization, dedicated, among other objectives, to ending capital punishment for all crimes in the United States. Established by such notables as civil libertarian Roger Baldwin, Felix Frankfurter (later an associate justice on the U.S. Supreme Court), and activist Helen Keller, the organization was founded during the anticommunist "Red Scare" of the early 1920s and came to defend Communists, labor activists, and Nazis in their attempts to speak freely in an increasingly hostile nation. Today the ACLU takes the position that "in all circumstances, the death penalty is unconstitutional under the Eighth Amendment, and that its discriminatory application violates the Fourteenth Amendment." The ACLU fights the death penalty in state and federal courts through its Capital Punishment Project (CPP).

The CPP consistently files amicus curiae ("friend of the court") briefs with the U.S. Supreme Court in cases involving capital punishment questions. In recent years, however, with pressure from conservatives to shorten time for appeals and speed up executions, the efforts of the CPP have become less successful. Once headed by famed anti–death penalty activist Henry Schwarzchild, the group is currently headed by activist Diann Rust-Tierney and headquartered in Washington, D.C. The CPP publishes the *ACLU Abolitionist,* a newsletter dedicated to informing its members about current capital punishment issues.

Another ACLU-inspired group, the National Coalition to Abolish the Death Penalty (NCADP), of which Schwarzchild was a founding member, now operates as an independent group with headquarters in Washington, D.C.

**See also:** National Coalition to Abolish the Death Penalty; Schwarzchild, Henry.
**References:** "The Death Penalty," ACLU Briefing Paper No. 8, 1996, 1; Donohue, William A., *The Politics of the American Civil Liberties Union* (New Brunswick, NJ: Transaction Books, 1985), 266–69; Walker, Samuel, *In Defense of American Liberties: A History of the ACLU* (New York: Oxford University Press, 1990), 359.

## *An American Tragedy*

1925 novel by American author Theodore Dreiser (1871–1945), based on the murder case of Chester Gillette, who had murdered his girl friend in a lake in New York state in 1906, and which exemplified the continuing American debate on capital punishment. Dreiser had been a reporter at Gillette's trial, and his novel appeared some time after the criminal had been executed.

In the novel, Dreiser demonstrates his contempt for the rich Gillette and for the social system in general. Dreiser portrayed Clyde Griffiths, the protagonist, as a poverty-stricken youth determined to rise above his social status at any cost—even killing a beautiful young woman who, as in the Gillette case, was carrying his baby. The novel was the basis of a 1931 film of the same title, directed by Josef von Sternberg and starring Phillips Holmes as the murderer, and a 1951 remake, entitled *A Place in the Sun,* starring Montgomery Clift as Griffiths.

References: Alexander, Charlotte A., *Theodore Dreiser's* An American Tragedy (New York: Monarch Press, 1965); Maltin, Leonard, ed., *Leonard Maltin's 1996 Movie and Video Guide* (New York: Plume Books, 1995), 36, 1019.

## Amnesty International

Premier international association dedicated to ending capital punishment in every nation, awarded the 1977 Nobel Prize Peace for its efforts to "protect the human rights of prisoners of conscience."

Prior to 1960, prisoners in many nations had little or no recourse when their human rights were violated. In that year, a lawyer in London, Peter Berenson, read with dismay of two Portuguese students arrested and jailed for raising a toast to freedom in a nation that had none at the time. He placed an advertisement entitled "The Forgotten Prisoners" in the 28 May 1961 *London Observer,* in which he wrote, "Open your newspaper any day of the week and you will find a report from somewhere in the world of someone being imprisoned, tortured or executed because his opinions or religion are unacceptable to his government." With this advertisement Berenson launched what he called an "Appeal for Amnesty," and from the ensuing campaign, he founded Amnesty International.

Amnesty International recruits human rights advocates from around the world to pressure governments through letter-writing campaigns and publicity to free political prisoners and protect human rights protesters. Its goals are straightforward: the freedom of all prisoners of conscience, fair and free trials for all prisoners who call themselves political prisoners, and the abolition of capital punishment, which the group decries as cruel and inhuman torture. Its first director was Irish human rights advocate Sean MacBride, who was awarded the Nobel Peace Prize in 1974. Its world headquarters are located in London, and its American division, Amnesty International USA, has offices in several cities, including New York, Washington, D.C., and Atlanta.

References: Abrams, Irwin, *The Nobel Peace Prize and the Laureates: An Illustrated Biographical History, 1901–1987* (Boston: G. K. Hall & Co., 1988), 219–21; Amnesty International, *Report on Torture* (New York: Farrar, Straus & Giroux, 1975); Larsen, Egon, *A Flame in Barbed Wire* (New York: W. W. Norton, 1979); Power, Jonathan, *Amnesty International: The Human Rights Story* (New York: McGraw-Hill, 1981).

## André, John (1751–1780)

English military officer hanged for spying on the American army during the American Revolutionary War. Born in London on 2 May 1751, André was tutored at private schools in Geneva. With his social standing, he was able to purchase a commission as a second lieutenant in the Royal Welsh Fusiliers. When the American Revolution broke out, he was at St. John's, Quebec, where he was taken prisoner when the town was captured by the rebels. André was treated poorly, and he grew to hate the American rebellion and all that it stood for. Exchanged in November 1776, he joined the British army, then in New York City, under the command of Major General Charles Grey and Sir Henry Clinton. Promoted to the rank of captain, André was named in 1777 as an aide to Grey. He participated in the brutal extermination of American troops in Paoli, Pennsylvania, and it was this experience, as well as his reports of the American force he had witnessed when a prisoner, that brought him to the attention of Clinton. He was later promoted to adjutant general, with the rank of major.

While in Philadelphia he befriended a young lady named Margaret Shippen, an American with British sympathies. By 1779, she had married the American general Benedict Arnold, who, influenced by spies sent by André, had decided to turn against the Americans and hand over a vital fort that he was in charge of to André and his troops. André sailed from New York City upstate on board the *Vulture,* then moved inland and met Arnold, who gave him the plans to West Point and its environs as well as a pass under the name John Anderson, which guaranteed André's safe passage back to British lines. However, on his return, André was stopped by three American militiamen, who searched him, found the plans and notes from Arnold, and turned him over to the American army. Arnold, hearing of the capture and fearing for his safety, quietly crossed over to the British lines.

General George Washington, upon hearing of Arnold's actions, convened a court of inquiry to hear charges against André. It found André guilty of treason, not spying, and sentenced him to death. On the day before his execution, André wrote to General Washington requesting that he die a spy's death before a firing squad: "Sympathy towards a soldier will surely induce your Excellency and a military tribunal, to adapt the mode of my death to the feelings of a man of honor. Let me hope, Sir, that if aught in my character impresses you with esteem towards me, if aught in my misfortune marks me as the victim of policy and not of resentment, I shall experience the operation of these feelings in your breast, be informed that I am not to die on a gibbet."

At noon on 2 October 1780, André was executed at Tappan. A Dr. Thacher, who was a witness to the execution, preserved the "particulars" of the event in his journal, a portion of which is reprinted here:

> Major André walked from the stone house, in which he had been confined, between two of our subaltern officers, arm in arm; the eyes of the immense multitude were fixed on him, who, rising superior to the fear of death, appeared as if conscious of the dignified deportment which he displayed. . . . It was his earnest desire to be shot, as being the mode of death most conformable to the feelings of a military man, and he had indulged the hope that his request would be granted. At the moment, therefore, when suddenly he came in view of the gallows, he involuntarily started backward, and made a pause. "Why this emotion, sir?" said an officer by his side. Instantly recovering his composure, he said, "I am reconciled to my death, but I detest the mode."
>
> While waiting and standing near the gallows, I observed some degree of trepidation; placing his foot on a stone, and rolling it over, and choking in his throat, as if attempting to swallow. So soon, however as he perceived that things were in readiness, he stepped quickly into the wagon, and at this moment appeared to shrink, but instantly elevating his head with firmness, he said, "I will be but a momentary pang"; and taking from his pocket two white handkerchiefs, the provost marshal with one pinioned his arms, and with the other, the victim, after taking off his hat and stock, bandaged his own eyes with perfect firmness, which melted the hearts, and moistened the cheeks, not only of his servant, but of the throng of spectators. The rope being appended to the gallows, he slipped the noose over his head, and adjusted it to his neck, without the assistance of the executioner. Colonel Scammell now informed him that he had an opportunity to speak if he desired it. He raised the handkerchief from his eyes, and said, "I pray you bear me witness, that I meet my fate like a brave man." The wagon being now removed from under him he was suspended and instantly expired.

On 10 August 1821, upon the orders of the Prince of York, André's remains were exhumed from the spot in Tappan where they had been deposited after his execution and moved to Westminster Abbey in London on 28 November 1821, where they remain to this day. In 1879 a monument was erected on the site of his execution, with a tablet that reads in part: "His death, though according to the stern code of war, moved even his enemies to pity and both armies mourned the death of one so young and brave." A journal of American military movements that André kept from 1777 to 1778 was discovered in England in 1902 and published as *André's Journal.*

**See also:** Hale, Nathan.

**References:** *Andreana: Containing the Trial, Execution, and Various Matter Connected with the History of Major John André, Adjutant General of the British Army in American, A.D. 1780* (Philadelphia: Published by Horace W. Smith, 1865); *The Encyclopedia Americana International Edition,* 30 vols. (Danbury, CT: Grolier, 1996), 1:821–22; Garnett, Richard, "André, John" in Sir Leslie Stephens and Sir Sidney Lee, eds., *The Dictionary of National Biography,* 10 vols., 12 supplements (Oxford, England: Oxford University Press, 1917–1993), 1:397–98; Hatch, Robert McConnell, *Major John André: A Gallant in Spy's Clothing* (Boston: Houghton Mifflin, 1986); Lossing, Benson John, *The Two Spies: Nathan Hale and John André, by Benson John Lossing, LL.D. Illustrated with pen-and-ink sketches by H. Rosa. Anna Seward's Menody on Major André* (New York: D. Appleton & Company, 1886); *Proceedings of a Board of General Officers Held By Order of his Excellency General Washington, Commander-in-Chief of the Army of the United States of America, Respecting Major John André, Adjutant General of the British Army, September 29, 1780* (Philadelphia: Printed by Francis Bailey in Market Street, 1780); Smith, Joshua Hett, *An Authentic Narrative of the Causes Which Led to the Death of Major André, Adjutant-General of His Majesty's Forces in North America, To Which is Added a Monody on the Death of Major André by Miss Seward* (London, England: Printed for Mathews and Leigh, 1808); "The Trial of Major John André for Being a Spy, Tappan, New York, 1780" in John D. Lawson, ed., *American State Trials: A Collection of the Important and Interesting Criminal Trials Which Have Taken Place in the United States, from the Beginning of our Government to the Present Day,* 17 vols. (St. Louis, MO: F. H. Thomas Law Book Company, 1914–36), 6:464–85.

## Anticapitalpunishmentism

This term for those who argue against capital punishment on any ground was coined by Canadian writer Bernard Lande Cohen in his 1970 work, *Law without Order: Capital Punishment and the Liberals.* As part of his critique of anticapitalpunishmentism, he writes: "The movement for mitigating the horrors and frequency of the death penalty has a distinguished record. In our own time, its underlying motivation has become powerfully entrenched throughout the greater part of the free world. And yet in face of the acquired absolutism of this campaign, I challenge its dogmatic assumptions, whose logical imperfections are obvious."

Cohen definitely sides with those who favor capital punishment. He writes: "The state has a duty to protect itself and its citizens not only from foreign enemies, but from the domestic variety as well. There are occasions when to forestall anarchy and chaos, the choice is between killing or being killed." But he also insists that "the right of a government to take the life of any of its subjects ought to be subject to the strictest review in all instances," arguing that "no matter how deserving of death an offender might be, and how little deserving of pity, it would be entirely wrong to inflict any torture upon him, or any form of death that is of an exceptionally painful nature."

**Reference:** Cohen, Bernard Lande, *Law without Order: Capital Punishment and the Liberals* (New Rochelle, NY: Arlington House, 1970), 17, 33–34.

## Aram, Eugene (1704–1759)

British scholar hanged fourteen years after committing a heinous murder for profit in England, which made his case a very prominent one at the time.

Born in Ramsgill, Yorkshire, in September 1704, Aram was largely self-educated and supported himself by teaching school. In his spare time he did research into philology and became adept at mastering European languages; he worked on the manuscript of one of the first major works on the subject. By all accounts, Aram was brilliant and an asset to his community. However, the disappearance of his good friend Daniel Clark in 1746 set off suspicions, but no concrete evidence was discovered. Thirteen years later, a skeleton was found, and when it was identified as Clark's, Aram became the number one suspect. In court, he defended himself with knowledge and grace, but the evidence amassed against him led a jury to find him guilty. On 6 August 1759, Aram faced the hangman's noose in York for his crime, having evaded justice for more than a decade. In 1832, British author and historian Edward Bulwer-Lytton published his 3-volume novel *Eugene Aram,* a fictionalized study of the Aram case. Bulwer-Lytton's work was one of the first to turn a true crime into a successful novel. Later, he changed his mind as to Aram's guilt, finding him to be innocent of the crime, and a subsequent edition released in 1851 illustrated this change of heart. English poet Thomas Hood also wrote of the case in his poem "The Dream of Eugene Aram."

**References:** Nash, Jay Robert, *Encyclopedia of World Crime,* 4 vols. (Wilmette, IL: CrimeBooks, Inc., 1990), 1:141–42; Watson, Eric R., *Eugene Aram: His Life and Trial* (Glasgow and Edinburgh, Scotland: William Hodge, 1913).

## Argyll, Archibald Campbell, First Marquess and Eighth Earl of (1598–1661)

Scottish statesman, great-grandson of the Fifth Earl of Argyll, a supporter of Mary, Queen of Scots, and high chancellor of Scotland, executed for his collaboration with Oliver Cromwell in the British invasion of his native Scotland.

A Puritan, Argyll became chief of the powerful clan Campbell upon his father's death in 1638, and he soon dominated the Scottish political and religious scene. He was also the leader of the Scottish armed force known as the Covenanters (for which he was nicknamed "The Master-Fiend Argyll"), and at the outbreak of the first phase of the English Revolution he forced Charles I to submit to the demands of the Scottish Parliament. In 1645 Argyll and his forces were defeated at Inverlochy by Scottish Royalist nobles led by James Graham, first marquess of Montrose, who would himself face the headsman's ax. After the execution of Charles I in 1649, Argyll invited Charles's son, Charles II, to Scotland and crowned him king of Scotland at Scone in 1651. In 1660, upon the restoration of the Stuart dynasty to the English throne in the person of Charles II, Argyll was arrested on a charge of having collaborated with Commonwealth leader Oliver Cromwell in the latter's invasion of Scotland in 1650. Argyll was tried by the Scottish Parliament, convicted, and beheaded.

Thomas Finlayson Henderson, a biographer of Argyll, wrote of his final day:

> His last words on the scaffold were "I am free from any accession by knowledge, contriving, counsel, or any other way to his late majesty's death." [After the execution] his body was carried to St. Magdalene Chapel in the Cowgate, thence to Newbattle Abbey, and after a few weeks to the burial place of family on the Holy

Loch. His head was exposed on the west end of the tollbooth, on the same spike previously occupied by that of Montrose; but in May 1664 there came "a letter from the king to the council, commanding them to take down Argyll's head that it might be buried with his body, which was done quietly in the night time."

**See also:** Argyll, Archibald Campbell, Ninth Earl of Argyll; Montrose, James Graham, First Marquess of.

**References:** Adam, Frank, *The Clans, Septs, and Regiments of the Scottish Highlands* (Stirling, Scotland: Johnson & Bacon, 1984), 206; Donnachie, Ian, and George Hewitt, *A Companion to Scottish History: From the Reformation to the Present* (New York: Facts on File, 1989), 31; Henderson, Thomas Finlayson, "Campbell, Archibald" in Sir Leslie Stephens and Sir Sidney Lee, eds., *The Dictionary of National Biography,* 10 vols, 12 supplements (Oxford, England: Oxford University Press, 1917–1993), 3:771–81.

## Argyll, Archibald Campbell, Ninth Earl of (1629–1685)

Scottish nobleman, son of the eighth earl, put to death, as his father was, for allegedly conspiring with British authorities to invade Scotland. During the second phase of the English Revolution, Argyll fought for Charles II against Oliver Cromwell at Dunbar, Scotland, in 1650. After the restoration of the Stuarts to the throne in the person of Charles II, Argyll increasingly criticized the government. Subsequently, he was arrested for treason and his estates were seized. He escaped to the Netherlands dressed as Lady Sophia Lindsay, his step-daughter, where he joined the conspiracy to capture the English throne for James Scott, Duke of Monmouth. Argyll led an invasion of Scotland in support of Monmouth in 1685, but he was captured and beheaded without a trial. During his execution he was so calm and composed that the scene became the subject of the painting *Argyll's Last Sleep*. Afterward his head was mounted on a steel spike, as was his father's, and his headless remains were interred at Inverary.

**References:** Adam, Frank, *The Clans, Septs, and Regiments of the Scottish Highlands* (Stirling, Scotland: Johnson & Bacon Books Limited, 1984), 206; Airy, Osmund, "Campbell, Archibald" in Sir Leslie Stephens and Sir Sidney Lee, eds., *The Dictionary of National Biography,* 10 vols., 12 supplements (Oxford, England: Oxford University Press, 1917–1993), 3:781–91; Donnachie, Ian, and George Hewitt, *A Companion to Scottish History: From the Reformation to the Present* (New York: Facts on File, 1989), 31–32.

## Arnold of Brescia (c.1100–1155)

Italian reformer martyred by the church for what they considered his heretical ideas.

Little is known of Arnold of Brescia's life (including his full name), except that he was born in Brescia in northern Italy on the Garza River. After studying at Paris under Peter Abelard, he became an Augustinian monk and began a sustained attack on the worldliness of the church, advocating radical church reforms, including a life of poverty for the clergy and the abandonment of wealth and temporal power by the church. He also rejected the idea of the confession of one's sins to a priest. In 1139 the Second Lateran Council condemned these views, and Pope Innocent II ordered Arnold exiled and his books burned. He also fell out of favor with Abelard, who condemned him at the Council of Sens in 1140. Fearing for his life, Arnold began a long journey into exile, first settling in Zurich, and then in northern Italy.

In either 1145 or 1146, Pope Eugene III allowed Arnold to return to Rome. As soon as he returned, however, Arnold began to agitate for reduced papal power and for a senatorial form of government in Rome. Pope Adrian IV, who had become pope in 1154, placed the city on an interdict until the heretic was arrested. Arnold fled the city a second time, but he fell into the hands of Frederick Barbarossa, who delivered him to Adrian's representatives. Arnold was returned to Rome, condemned as a heretic, and burned at the stake in the Piazza del Popolo. His ashes were then unceremoniously dumped into the Tiber River to prevent them from being venerated as sacred objects.

In the introduction to her little-known work *Arnold of Brescia, a Dramatic Poem,* composed in the middle of the nineteenth century, Sophia Skelton wrote, "Arnold of Brescia is a name which appears to be little known in England; yet as one of the first reformers he is more justly entitled to be remembered in this Protestant country than even the great Martin Luther, for he ventured to raise the standard of liberty in Rome itself, in the very face of the Pope, and the fiery stake of the martyr was his reward."

**See also:** Savonarola, Girolamo.
**References:** Law, M. D. and M. Vibart Dixon, man. eds., *Chambers' Encyclopaedia,* 15 vols. (London: International Learning Systems Corporation Limited, 1970), 1:650; Skelton, Sophia, *Arnold of Brescia, a Dramatic Poem* (London: Simpkin, Marshall, 1866).

## "The Arraignment of John Selman"

English manuscript, 1612, which described the final moments of the life of one John Selman, executed "neere Charing-Cross" in London on 7 January 1612. The pamphlet quotes Selman's final words as he stood on the scaffold:

> "I Am come (as you see) patiently to offer up the sweet, and deare sacrifice of my life, a life, which I have gracelessly abused, and by the unruly course thereof, made my death a scandall to my kindred and aquaintance; I have consumed fortunes gifts in riotous companies, wasted my good name in the purchase of goods unlawfully gotten, and now ending my daies in too late repentence, I am placed in the rancke of reprobates, which the rusty canker of time must needs turne to oblivion. I stand here as shames example, ready to bee spewed out of the Common wealth. I confesse, I have knowne too much, performed more, but consented to most. I have bin the only corruption of many ripe witted youth, and leader of them to confusion. Pardon me God, for that is now a burthen to my conscience, wash it away sweet Creator, that I may spotlesse enter into thy glorious kingdome." Whereupon being demanded, if he would discover any of his fraternity, for the good of the Common wealth or not: Answered, that he had already left the names of divers notorious malefactors in writing behind him, which he thought sufficient. So he requested the quietnes of conscience that his soule might depart without molestation. For (quoth he) I have deserved death long before this time, and deservedly now I suffer death. I offence I dye for, was high presumption, a fact done even in the Kings Maiesties presence, even in the Church of God, in the time of devine Service, and the celebration of the Sacred Communion, for which if forgivenes may descend from Gods tribunall Throne, with penitence of hart I desire it,' all which being spoken, he patiently left this world for another life.

**Reference:** *The Arraignment of John Selman, who was executed neere Charing-Cross the 7. of January, 1612, for a Fellony by him committed in the Kings Chappell at White-Hall upon Christmas day last, in presence of the King and divers of the Nobility* (London: W. H. for Thomas Archer, 1612), 16–17.

## *Auto-da-Fé*

From the Portuguese for "Act of Faith," this ceremony was involved during the execution of those condemned by the Inquisition. Voltaire wrote of such an act in his famed work *Candide.* It involved a procession of those condemned to die through the streets of a town or village led by Dominican friars; the condemned were separated from others by a great cross and forced to wear pointed caps as well as garments called *san benito*s *(a san benito,* or, as some sources call it, a *sanbenito,* is "a Spanish garment resembling a scapular and either of yellow with red crosses for the penitent or of black cloth with painted devils and flames for the impenitent condemned to an auto-da-fé"), which were inscribed with their purported crimes. Marched slowly to the place of execution, the victims would be turned over to secular authorities to be put to death. Before priests and monks, effigies of the condemned were paraded, as well as the bones and body parts of former victims.

British writer Basil Montagu quotes a work describing *auto-de-fé* that took place in Madrid 1680 in presence of King Charles II, his queen, and her mother. It contains the 50-page sermon preached before the execution of the criminals "and a catalogue of the nineteen unhappy persons who were burnt alive, of the thirty-two who were burnt in effigy, and of the seven who were whipped, together with an account of their crimes, and of the sixty who were condemned, some to temporary, and some to perpetual imprisonment, some to banishment, and some to the galleys."

> Their Majesties were present during the whole time the sentences were pronouncing, which was from eight in the morning till half past nine in the evening, when they retired, without having tasted any refreshment during the whole day; neither had the Inquisitors nor Judges. At half past nine fire was put to the scaffold, which was sixty foot square, and seven feet high, and the nineteen martyrs were burnt. Six of these were women, and twelve men, who were condemned for Judaising, and one renegade Spanish pirate, because he would not abjure his faith in Mahomet; they consisted of three rag-merchants, a slop-seller, an innkeeper, a soldier, two snuff-dealers, a pedlar, a strolling silver-smith, and three vagabonds; the women were all of the like respectable professions. All their goods were confiscated, and the Spanish account says that ten of them had none. The formula observed by the Holy Tribunal of the Inquisition in delivering the criminals out of its custody is thus: We must and hereby do surrender the body of N. N. to justice and the secular power; more especially to M. M., Chief Magistrate of this City, and to his assistants, whom we charge and affectionately pray (as much as lies in their power) to proceed with pity and tenderness.—The criminals were burnt alive, shewing no small signs of impatience, rage and despair, and by nine next morning all were reduced to ashes.

**Reference:** "The Auto-de-fé of Spain" in Basil Montagu, ed., *The Opinions of Different Authors Upon the Punishment of Death, Selected By Basil Montagu, Esq. of Lincoln's Inn* (London: Printed for Longman, Hurst, Rees, and Paternoster Row, 3 volumes, 1809–13), 3:250–51.

## The Bab (Mirza Ali Muhammad, 1819 or 1820–1850)

Islamic religious leader and prophet put to death by Islamic religious authorities because his teachings, known as Babism, threatened the civil order of their societies. Followers of the Bab were called Babis; they addressed Mirza Ali Muhammad as *awwal man amana* ("the first believer").

Mirza Ali Muhammad was the son of a tradesman in Shiraz, Persia (now Iran). Orphaned at an early age, he came under the care and supervision of his maternal uncle, Agha Sayyid Ali. He was selected to be a tradesman like his father, but he soon turned to religion instead. He was led by the Islamic thinker Sayyid Kazim Rashti, who, as head of the religious movement known as the Shaykhis, searched for the Mahdi, or the true prophet of the Islamic religion. Sayyid Kazim died in 1843, but his student Mirza Ali Muhammad carried on his studies.

On 23 May 1844, at Shiraz, Mirza Ali proclaimed himself the Bab ("the gate" in Persian) and the precursor of the Imam Mahdi. (With that declaration, Mirza Ali was in fact claiming to be a reincarnation of one of the prophets of Islam, equal to the prophet Mohammed.) He also declared that exactly 19 years after he had showed himself, an even greater manifestation of prophets would appear. To aid in this work, the Bab composed his holy book, *The Bayan* ("Revelation") to rival the Koran. To challenge what they saw as corruption within the Shi'ite religion, a group of 18 Babi disciples called the *Hurufat al-Hayy* ("The Letters of the Living") took up arms to spread their faith.

Those whom the Bab opposed did not see any danger in his movement, until the accession of Nasir al-Din as shah of Persia (1831–1896) in 1848. He began violent persecutions of the Babis, and they, in turn, began a brutal two-year civil war to win their religious freedom. The insurrection was put down with great severity and the Bab was taken prisoner by the forces of the shah. Although he had not ordered the revolt or taken part in it, the Bab was arrested for treason against the state. The shah then decided that to end the threat of Babism, its leader must be put to death. As Bab biographer A. Mausani notes:

> The Bab was secured with the same ropes as his disciples to a pillar in the courtyard of the barracks at Tabriz, and the Christian regiment of the Bahaduran, commanded by Sam Khan, fired. The first shot, according to the descriptions even in Muslim sources and others hostile to the reformer, merely severed the ropes, leaving the Bab completely free. Khan, terrified, refused to reopen fire, and consequently another firing squad was detailed. On 9 July 1850, about midday, the Bab paid for preaching his doctrine with his life. The mangled body was thrown into a ditch in the town, and after many vicissitudes (disinterred by the Babis, hidden for several years at Tehran), it was removed on the order of Baha' Allah to Akka, where it now rests in a large mausoleum on the slopes of Mount Carmel.

After the Bab's execution, the leadership of his sect was split between his half-brother Mirza Hussein Ali, who took the name Bahaullah ("Splendor of God"), and a follower who took the name Subh-i-Ezel ("The Dawn of Eternity"). This schism led to the breakup of the sect. Bahaullah's followers later founded the spiritual movement known as the Baha'i, one of the leading faiths in the Islamic world.

**References:** Mausani, A., "Bab, The" in Sir Hamilton Alexander Rosskeen Gibb, J. H. Kramers, E. Lévi-Provençal, and J. Schacht, eds., *The Encyclopedia of Islam,* 8 vols., 1 supplement, 1 index (Leiden, the Netherlands: E. J. Brill, 1960–1979), 1:833–35; Wigoder, Geoffrey, *They Made History: A Biographical Dictionary* (New York: Simon & Schuster, 1993), 54–55.

## Babington, Anthony (1561–1586)

English conspirator involved in a plot to rescue the imprisoned Mary Stuart, Queen of Scots, before she was executed, an act for which he paid with his own life.

Born in Dethick, Derbyshire, in October 1561, Anthony Babington served briefly as a page to Mary, Queen of Scots, during her imprisonment by the English in Sheffield. He founded in 1580 a society for the defense of Jesuit missionaries in England. In 1586, Babington, with the aid of John Ballard, a Jesuit, entered into a Catholic conspiracy to murder Queen Elizabeth I, thus removing the Protestant threat to the English throne and freeing Mary from her captivity. He exchanged letters with Mary approving of the proposed assassination; however, the letters fell into the hands of Sir Francis Walsingham, Elizabeth's secretary, who had Babington and his accomplices arrested. They were found guilty of treason and beheaded on Tower Hill in London. The letters were also used against Mary as evidence that she was a threat to Elizabeth and led to her beheading in February 1687.

According to one Babington biographer, Sidney L. Lee,

> A great crowd collected to see the conspirators die. Babington declared from the scaffold that no private ends had influenced him, but that he honestly believed himself engaged in "a deed lawful and meritorious." Ballard suffered first, and Babington witnessed his barbarous death. According to an eyewitness he showed to the last "a signe of his former pride" by standing, instead of praying on his knees, "with his hat on his head as if he had been but a beholder of the execution" . . . [Babington] followed Ballard, and underwent diabolical tortures. He was still alive when taken down from the gallows and exclaimed, "Parce mihi, Domino Jesu" while the executioner was using the knife upon him.

**See also:** Mary Stuart, Queen of Scots.
**References:** Lee, Sidney L., "Babington, Anthony" in Sir Leslie Stephens and Sir Sidney Lee, eds., *The Dictionary of National Biography,* 10 vols., 12 supplements (Oxford, England: Oxford University Press, 1917–1993), 1:780–83; Nash, Jay Robert, *Encyclopedia of World Crime,* 4 vols. (Wilmette, IL: CrimeBooks, Inc., 1990), 1:204; Pollen, John Hungerford, *Mary Queen of Scots and the Babington Plot* (Edinburgh, Scotland: T. and A. Constable, Ltd., for the Scottish History Society, 1922); Smith, Alan Gordon, *The Babington Plot* (London: Macmillan, 1936).

## Ball, John (?–1381)

English priest who "combined the teaching of ecclesiastical heresy with that of social reform"; prominent in the English Peasants' Revolt (also known as Wat Tyler's Rebellion) over the imposition of the poll tax on the peasants of England, activities for which he was put to death.

Though the date of Ball's birth is uncertain, his biographer, James Gairdner, claims that Ball was a preacher for twenty years when he was put to death and assumes that he was at least 40 years old when he died. A disciple of John Wyclif (or Wycliffe), he spoke openly and frequently of the liberty and equality of all persons, thoughts that at the time were considered heresy. Jailed many times for short periods for his speeches,

Ball was summoned before a church court as early as 1366 for teaching a view of property derived from the teachings of Wyclif. It asserted that the rights of lordship and possession depended specifically on divine grace. Excommunicated, Ball faced a long prison term. After he was freed by rebels in 1381, he preached the violent overthrow of the privileged classes, using as his text the famous line: "When Adam delved and Eve span, Who then was the gentleman?" After the Peasants' Revolt collapsed in June 1381, Ball was captured, tried, and convicted of treason. King Richard II, the subject of some of Ball's utterances, attended his execution at St. Albans on 15 July 1381. Ball was hanged and, while still alive, drawn and quartered. The four torn pieces of Ball's body were then sent to four different villages in England to be publicly exhibited.

**See also:** Tyler, Wat (or Walter).

**References:** Bird, Brian, *A Colchester Rebel: A Short Study of John Ball, sometime parochial chaplain at St. James' Church, Colchester, and Leader of the Peasant's Revolt in 1381* (Colchester, England: Privately Printed, 1981); Gairdner, James, "Ball, John" in Sir Leslie Stephens and Sir Sidney Lee, eds., *The Dictionary of National Biography,* 10 vols., 12 supplements (Oxford, England: Oxford University Press, 1917–1993), 1:993–94; Law, M. D., and M. Vibart Dixon, man. eds., *Chambers' Encyclopaedia,* 15 vols. (London: International Learning Systems Corporation Limited, 1970), 2:71.

## *Barefoot v. Estelle* (463 U.S. 880 [1983])

Supreme Court decision holding that a Texas law that allowed for the submission to a jury of the question of whether a defendant convicted of a capital crime might possibly commit further acts of violence in the future, to allow jury members to decide whether or not to impose the death penalty, was constitutional. On 14 November 1978, Thomas Andy Barefoot was convicted of the capital murder of a police officer in Bell County, Texas. A death-penalty hearing was then held, and, under Texas law, two psychiatrists testified that Barefoot's "reputation for lawlessness" and criminal career led them to believe that he would commit further crimes in the future. The jury, after deliberating, returned with a recommendation of death. Barefoot appealed to the Texas Court of Criminal Appeals on the grounds that the use of psychiatry at a criminal proceeding to determine the matter of a criminal's future conduct was "so likely to produce erroneous sentences that their use violated the Eighth and Fourteenth Amendments," and that since the psychiatrists had not personally examined Barefoot, their observations were reversible error. The court rejected all of these arguments (*Barefoot v. State,* 596 S. W. 2d 875), and Barefoot's execution date of 17 September 1980 was set. On 29 June of that year, the U.S. Supreme Court issued a stay, but the Texas court rejected a petition for certiorari, and the date was reset. Barefoot then appealed to the U.S. District Court for the Western District of Texas and the U.S. Circuit Court of Appeals for the Fifth Circuit, both of which ruled against him. Barefoot then sued W. J. Estelle, Jr., the director of the Texas Department of Corrections, and the case went to the U.S. Supreme Court. Arguments were heard before the Court on 26 April 1983.

On 6 July of that same year, Justice Byron White spoke for a 6-3 court (Justices Thurgood Marshall, William Brennan, and Harry Blackmun dissented) in holding that the Texas law allowing for the psychiatric testimony was constitutional. Justice White wrote, "The suggestion that no psychiatrist's testimony may be presented with respect to a defendant's future dangerousness is somewhat like asking us to disinvent the wheel. In the first place, it is contrary to our cases. If the likelihood of a defendant's committing further crimes is a constitutionally acceptable criterion for imposing the death penalty, which it is, (*Jurek v. Texas,* 428 U.S. 262 [1976]), and if it is not impossible for even a lay person sensibly to arrive at that conclusion, it makes little sense, if any, to submit that psychiatrists, out of the entire universe of persons who might have an opinion on the issue, would know so little about the subject that they should not be permitted to testify. In *Jurek,* seven Justices rejected the claim that it was impossible to predict future behavior and that dangerousness was therefore an invalid consideration in imposing the death penalty." After explaining the reasoning in that earlier case, Justice White concluded, "In sum, we affirm the judgment of the District Court. There is no doubt that the psychiatric testimony increased the likelihood that petitioner would be sentenced to death, but this fact does not make that evidence inadmissible, any more than it would with respect to other relevant evidence against any defendant in a criminal case. At bottom, to agree with petitioner's basic position would seriously undermine and in effect overrule *Jurek v. Texas*. . . . Petitioner conceded as much at oral argument. . . . We are not inclined, however, to overturn the decision in that case."

On 30 October 1984, Thomas Barefoot was put to death by lethal injection.

**Reference:** Text of case at 463 U.S. 880, at 896, 906.

## Bartholomew, Saint

See Crucifixion

## Beccaria, Cesare Bonesana, Marchese di (1735? 1738?–1794)

Italian author, economist and reformist best known for his *Trato del Delitti e delle Pene* ("Treatise [or Essay] on Crime and Punishments," 1764; reprinted, 1767), one of the first works to oppose state-sanctioned capital punishment.

Beccaria was the son of a Milanese Italian aristocrat and, because of his social status, received much of his early education at a Jesuit school in Parma. He later attended the University of Pavia, where he received a law degree in 1758. He supplemented his education by reading such works as Montesquieu's *Persian Letters* and soon began writing his own tracts.

Beccaria joined the reform movement that swept across Europe during the Enlightenment and soon became known for his work on criminal and penal reform. His mentor, Count Pietro Verri, solicited Beccaria in 1763 to undertake a study of criminal law in Italy. The following year, his landmark work, *Trato del Delitti e delle Pene,* appeared and was praised as one of the finest works of its kind. One biographer describes it as "the first succinct and systematic statement of principles governing criminal punishment. Although many of the ideas expressed were familiar, and Beccaria's indebtedness to such writers as the French philosopher Montesquieu is clear, the work nevertheless represents a major advance in criminological thought." For the first time,

> a major literary figure questioned the use of capital punishment: The useless profusion of punishments, which as they never made men better, induces me to inquire, whether the punishment of *Death* be really just or useful in a well governed state? *What right, I ask, have men to cut the throats of their fellow creatures?* . . . Did any one ever give to others the right of taking away his life? Is it possible, that in the smallest portions of the liberty of each, sacrificed to the good of the public, can be contained the greatest of all good, life? If it were so, how shall it be reconciled to the maxim which tells us, that a

man has no right to kill himself? Which he certainly must have, if he could give it away to another.

But the punishment of death is not authorised by any right. . . . It is therefore a war of a whole nation against a citizen, whose destruction they consider as necessary, or useful to the general good.

The death of a citizen *cannot be necessary, but in one case*. When, though deprived of liberty, he has such power and connections as he may endanger the security of the nation; when his existence may produce a dangerous revolution in the established form of government. But even in this case, it can only be necessary when a nation is on the verge of recovering or losing its liberty; or in times of absolute anarchy, when the disorders themselves hold the place of laws. But in a reign of tranquility . . . there can be no necessity for taking away the life of a subject.

Although Beccaria's name is little remembered except by historians and researchers, his ideas and work strongly impacted the anti–capital punishment movement. His work led Jeremy Bentham and Sir Samuel Romilly to press the government to restrict the use of death as a punishment in England; Emperor Joseph of Austria, impressed by Beccaria's argument, prohibited the death penalty in that country; and the criminal codes of Russia and Sweden were altered to eliminate the death penalty. In the United States, several state legislatures in the nineteenth century, contemplating an end to capital punishment, utilized Beccaria's arguments.

Although Beccaria was only in his twenties when his *Treatise* appeared, he never published another major work. In 1768, a chair of political philosophy in his name was established at the University of Milan.

**References:** Beccaria, Cesare, *Trato del Delitti e delle Pene* (An Essay on Crimes and Punishments) (London: J. Almon, 1767); Goetz, Philip W., ed.-in-Chief, *The New Encyclopedia Britannica,* 22 vols. (Chicago: Encyclopedia Britannica, Inc., 1995), 2:27–28; Montagu, Basil, ed., *The Opinions of Different Authors Upon the Punishment of Death, Selected By Basil Montagu, Esq. of Lincoln's Inn,* 3 vols. (London: Longman, Hurst, Rees, and Paternoster Row, 1809–1813) 1:18–27.

## Becker, Charles (1870–1915)

He was a police lieutenant in New York City, known for his vicious but effective crackdowns on gambling and vice in that city. Yet few knew that Becker was behind much of the corruption in the city. When his power was challenged by a leading gambler, Becker ordered his murder, a crime for which Becker paid with his life in the electric chair.

Born in 1869 to a family of German immigrants in New York City, Becker attended local schools. The city at that time was filled with immigrants with few skills who jammed and crowded the slums and ghettos of the Lower East Side, and it was there that Charles Becker became known as "the crookedest cop who ever stood behind a shield." In the 1890s, a young writer named Stephen Crane witnessed an angry Becker pummel a prostitute for refusing to pay her protection money; Crane later used the scenario in his classic work, *Maggie: A Girl of the Streets*.

Becker eventually rose to become a lieutenant and assistant to Commissioner Rhinelander Waldo, and although Waldo was politically corrupt, Becker did him one better: as head of the police special crimes bureau, he used his influence to demand payoffs from some of the city's most notorious gamblers, vice operators, and prostitutes. To back him up, Becker employed underworld thugs, including "Billiard Ball" Jack Rose, Harry Vallon, and "Bridgey" Webber.

By 1912, one gambler, Herman "Beansie" Rosenthal, began to refuse to pay Becker protection money. Becker retaliated by using police muscle to close down Rosenthal's gambling parlor. In retaliation, Rosenthal went to New York district attorney Charles S. Whitman and told him of Becker's activities. Whitman, suspecting Becker and looking for an arrest that could catapult him to the New York governor's mansion, summoned a grand jury to hear Rosenthal's charges against Becker. Becker, angered at this challenge to his power, ordered some of his thugs to hit Rosenthal once and for all. On 21 July 1912, several of these men, including Rose, accosted Rosenthal outside the Hotel Metropole on 43rd Street and shot him to death.

Whitman was stunned, but soon he had Becker and his associates arrested for the murder. Rose turned state's evidence, for which he received a life sentence; four men were ultimately captured, convicted, and electrocuted for the Rosenthal hit: Jacob Seidenschner (a.k.a. "Whitey Lewis"), Harry Horowitz (a.k.a. "Gyp the Blood"), Louis Rosenberg (a.k.a. "Lefty Louie"), and Frank Cirofici (a.k.a. "Dago Frank").

On 7 October 1912, Becker's trial, before Judge John W. Goff, opened in Manhattan with Whitman, the district attorney, handling the prosecuting personally. The first, and key, witness against Becker was Rose, who claimed on the stand that Becker himself had ordered Rose to "just stop [Rosenthal] so that he will not bother anybody any more for all time." According to Rose, Becker added, "I don't want him beat up. I could do that myself. . . . Have him murdered, cut his throat, dynamited, or anything."

Judge Goff cut off much of the questioning by Becker's attorneys, making an acquittal increasingly unlikely. On 30 October 1912, Becker was found guilty. But because of the judge's conduct, the New York State Court of Appeals threw out the verdict and ordered a new trial. This second prosecution opened on 2 May 1914. This time Whitman de-emphasized Rose's testimony and relied on that of James Marshall, a black man on Becker's payroll. On 22 May 1914, Becker was again convicted and sentenced to death for ordering Rosenthal's murder.

As Charles Whitman had predicted, the trial and conviction of Charles Becker propelled him to the governor's mansion. His election on 3 November 1914 forced Becker, who had run out of appeals, to beg for a pardon from the man who sent him to death row in the first place. But even a tear-filled visit from Becker's wife, Helen, did not sway Whitman.

In his final hours before he was put to death on 30 July 1915, Becker, who was described as "unnerved," composed a note that he had prepared to read before his execution, but which was found after his death. It read:

> Gentlemen: My dying declaration:
>
> I stand before you in my full senses, knowing that no power on earth can save me from the grave that is to receive me. In the face of that, in the teeth of those who condemn me, and in the presence of my God and your God, I proclaim my absolute innocence of the foul crime for which I must die. You are about to witness my destruction by the State, which is organized to protect the lives of the innocent.
>
> May Almighty God pardon every one who has contributed in any degree to my untimely death. And now, on the brink of my grave, I declare to the world that I am proud to have been the husband of the purest, noblest woman that has ever lived, Helen Becker. This acknowledgment is the only legacy I can leave her.
>
> I bid you all goodbye. Father, I am ready to go.
>
> CHARLES BECKER

At 5:49 A.M., Becker sat in the electric chair in Sing Sing and was put to death. *The New York Times* reported that although he walked to the chair bravely, he nonetheless broke down as he was strapped in. After his body was removed from the chair, a small photograph of his wife, affixed to his shirt, slid out onto the floor, and it was published in the newspapers the next day. When he was buried two days later, his widow had affixed a plate to the coffin: "Charles Becker, Murdered July 30, 1915, by Governor Whitman." Before the body could be lowered into the ground, however, Whitman had officials at the funeral rip the plate off the coffin on the grounds of criminal libel.

Although Becker's guilt has never seriously been in doubt, anti–capital punishment advocates Hugo Adam Bedau and Michael Radelet list Becker, as well as Frank Cirofici, among the persons they believe were innocent and unjustly executed. They report that Warden Osborne of Sing Sing Prison believed Becker to be innocent, but no firm evidence has ever turned up. However, with the evidence presented by crime historian Jay Robert Nash, Becker's guilt seems to have been more than enough to send him to the chair.

**References:** "Becker Dies in the Chair, on the Verge of a Collapse, But Protesting His Innocence," *The World* (New York), 2 August 1915, 5; "Becker Unnerved Goes to Chair; His Bonds Slip," *The New York Times,* 31 July 1915, 1; Bedau, Hugo Adam, and Michael L. Radelet, "Miscarriages of Justice in Potentially Capital Cases," *Stanford Law Review, 40* (November 1987), 95–96; Christianson, Stephen G., "Charles Becker Trials: 1912–14" in Edward W. Knappman, ed., *Great American Trials* (Detroit: Visible Ink Press, 1994), 262–66; Delmar, Vina, *The Becker Scandal: A Time Remembered* (New York: Harcourt, Brace & World, 1968); "Egoism of Becker Led Him to Murder," *The New York Times,* 31 July 1915, 3; *People v. Becker* (215 N.Y. 126, 109 N.E. Reporter 127 [1915]); Root, Jonathan, *The Life and Times of Charlie Becker: The True Story of a Famous American Murder Trial* (London: Secker & Warburg, 1961); "Schepps Tells of Becker Plot," *New York Journal,* 15 October 1912, 1; "The Strong-Arm Man and the Songbird" in *Crime and Punishment: The Illustrated Crime Encyclopedia,* 28 vols. (Westport, CT: H. S. Stuttman, Inc., 1994), 1:225–32; Sullivan, Harold W., *Trial By Newspaper* (Hyannis, MA: The Patriot Press, 1961), 21–38.

## Bedau, Hugo Adam (1926– )

American professor, staunch advocate of the abolition of capital punishment. Born in Portland, Oregon, on 23 September 1926, Bedau attended local schools, then earned a bachelor's degree at the University of Redlands (California) in 1949, a master's degree at Boston University in 1951, and a Ph.D. from Harvard University in 1961. Since 1953, Bedau has taught at numerous universities, including Dartmouth, Princeton, Harvard (where he was a visiting fellow in 1967), and Tufts University, where he currently is Austin Fletcher Professor of Philosophy.

An outspoken adherent of the abolition of capital punishment, Bedau is considered one of the national leaders in this area. Besides his numerous writings on the subject, which include the anthology *The Death Penalty in America* (1964), "Capital Punishment in Oregon, 1903–1964" (1965), and "Death Sentences in New Jersey, 1907–1960" (1965), he is a past chairman of the National Coalition for the Abolition of the Death Penalty. In 1987, with death penalty opponent Michael Radelet, Bedau issued a report that appeared in the *Stanford Law Review* under the title "Miscarriages of Justice in Potentially Capital Cases," in which the two argued that 20 innocent men had been put to death in the United States since 1900 and that 21 others had come close to the death chamber before being spared in one way or another. Utilizing court records and newspaper accounts, the writers reasoned that the error feared by all—that an innocent man could be put to death—had occurred.

**References:** Bedau, Hugo Adam, "Capital Punishment in Oregon, 1903–1964," *Oregon Law Review,* 45:1 (December 1965), 1–39; "Bedau, Hugo Adam," in Clare D. Kinsman and Mary Ann Tennenhouse, eds., *Contemporary Authors: A Bio-Bibliographical Guide to Current Writers in Fiction, General Nonfiction, Poetry, Journalism, Drama, Motion Pictures, Television, and Other Fields* 151 vols. (Detroit: Gale Research, Inc., 1962–96), 9-12:66; Bedau, Hugo Adam, ed., *The Death Penalty in America* (New York: Oxford University Press, 1982); Bedau, Hugo Adam, and Michael L. Radelet, "Miscarriages of Justice in Potentially Capital Cases," *Stanford Law Review,* 40 (November 1987), 21–172; Berger, Raoul, "Death Penalties and Hugo Bedau: A Crusading Philosopher Goes Overboard," *Ohio State Law Journal,* 45:4 (1984), 863–81.

## Beheading

Method of capital punishment, whereby a criminal's head is sliced apart from the body, utilizing an axe or sword. The technique is different from guillotining.

Historian John Laurence wrote of this form of capital punishment:

> Among the earliest records we find mention in the Ancient Laws of China of beheading as the prescribed mode of capital punishment. In early Egypt and Assyria the axe was used. . . . It is a remarkable commentary on human psychology that it should have been thought throughout the ages to be more honorable to have one's head cut off than to have one's neck broken. The axe and the sword were the instruments of capital punishment from the earliest times, and we find Xenophon, at the end of the second book of the Anabasis, stating that beheading was the most honorable form of death. The sword, too, was considered to be a less degrading instrument than the axe. The Romans, like the Greeks, considered beheading honorable. An offender was tied to a stake previous to decapitation and whipped with rods. The actual decapitation was carried out with the axe or the sword, and the condemned placed his head upon a block placed in a pit dug for the purpose. Caligula, according to Suetonius, employed a soldier, who had the reputation for his skill as a headsman, specially to decapitate prisoners chosen at random from the gaols.

According to English historians John L. Rayner and G. T. Crook, the Romans used beheading as a military punishment; it was called *decollatio.* A block, called a *cippus,* was placed before a hole or pit dug for the criminal's head to fall into. Before the execution was carried out, the criminal was tied to a stake and whipped with strong rods, then dragged to the *cippus* and held down. His head was cut off with a single stroke (early executions are said to have been messy affairs and got cleaner with experience) of an axe or a sword.

In England, this method was repeated, except for the infliction of whipping. Beheading has been called the punishment for nobles (hanging is considered a traitor's death), and it is not uncommon to read of persons of high social standing in England going to what many today consider a grotesque death with grace and understanding toward the system.

**See also:** Guillotine.

**References:** Laurence, John, *A History of Capital Punishment* (New York: The Citadel Press, 1960), 1, 28; Rayner, John L., and G. T. Crook, eds., *The Complete Newgate Calendar,* 5 vols. (London: Privately Printed for the Navarre Society Limited, 1926), 2:321.

## *Bell v. Ohio* (438 U.S. 637, 57 L.Ed. 2d 1010, 98 S.Ct. 2977 [1978])

U.S. Supreme Court decision in which it was held that a sentencer, namely a trial judge, must not be precluded by a state law "from considering, as a mitigating factor, any aspect of a defendant's character or record and any aspect of the offense that the defendant proffered."

Willie Lee Bell was 16 years old when he joined a friend in robbing, kidnapping, and then murdering an elderly man. Convicted by a three-judge panel (instead of a jury) of aggravated murder and the additional charge of kidnapping, Bell told the court that he had been under the influence of drugs for three years before the murder and that he had acted out of fear of his friend. The judges chose to ignore these mitigating circumstances and, as per state statute, sentenced Bell to death. Both the Court of Appeals of Ohio and the Supreme Court of Ohio affirmed the sentence. Bell then appealed to the U.S. Supreme Court, which heard arguments in the case on 17 January 1978.

On 3 July of that same year, the Court handed down decisions in both *Bell* and a companion case, *Lockett v. Ohio*. Speaking for seven members of the court (Justice William H. Rehnquist dissented, and Justice William Brennan did not participate), Chief Justice Warren Burger held that the state statute that called for a mandatory death sentence for an aggravated murder with at least one of seven aggravating circumstances was unconstitutional. In the short opinion, Chief Justice Burger wrote:

> Bell contends that the Ohio death penalty statute violated his rights under the Eighth and Fourteenth Amendments because it prevented the sentencing judges from considering the particular circumstances of his crime and aspects of his character and record as mitigating factors. For the reasons stated in *Lockett v. Ohio*, . . . we have concluded that "the Eighth and Fourteenth Amendments require that the sentencer, in all but the rarest kind of capital case, not be precluded from considering *as a mitigating factor*, any aspect of a defendant's character or record and any of the circumstances of the offense that the defendant proffers" . . . We also concluded that "[t]he Ohio penalty statute does not permit the type of individualized consideration of mitigating factors that is required by the Eighth and Fourteenth Amendments." We therefore agree with Bell's contention.

**See also:** *Lockett v. Ohio.*

## Bentley, Derek William (1933–1953)

British youth put to death in 1953 in a famous case in which he participated in, but did not commit, the murder of an English police officer. Born on 30 June 1933, Bentley grew up in the East End of London during World War II. When he was four he apparently fell on his head, causing some degree of brain damage and epilepsy. This fact would later become a major element in his case for clemency.

On 2 November 1952, Bentley hooked up with a friend, Christopher Craig, and went out for a night of breaking and entering into stores. Craig gave Bentley a knife, while he carried a .45 Colt revolver, known in England as a .455 Eley. They broke into Barlow & Parker's, a confectionary shop in the Croydon section of south London. They were spotted, and before they could escape the police surrounded the building. The two boys tried to hide, but a police officer spotted them and demanded that they surrender. He made his way to the roof, and tackled Bentley. The 19-year-old broke from the officer's grip and said, "Let him have it, Chris." Craig shot the officer, but he recovered. Another officer, PC Sidney Miles, had gotten the keys to the front door of the building and made his way up the stairs. He broke open the door to the roof and was instantly shot dead by Craig. Craig himself refused to surrender, and when he ran out of ammunition he jumped from the roof, breaking his spine, breastbone, and left wrist.

The two boys went on trial at London's Old Bailey courthouse on 9 December 1952, both charged with murder. Bentley, though he had not fired the fatal shot, was subject to the death penalty; Craig, under age at 16, could not be hanged even though he was the most responsible. The trial hung on whether the phrase "Let him have it" meant that Craig should hand over the gun to the officer or shoot him. The Crown argued precedent, a 1940 case that held that "where two persons engage in the commission of a crime with a common design of resisting by violence arrest by an officer of justice, they have a common design to do that which will amount to murder if the officer should be killed in consequence of resistance. If, therefore, an officer of justice is killed in such circumstances, both persons are guilty of murder." Lord Goddard, the trial judge, instructed the jury that if they found both boys had acted together in a criminal enterprise that ended in murder, they were equally guilty. On 11 December the jury returned after just 75 minutes with two verdicts of guilty. Craig was jailed "at the pleasure of the Queen," while Bentley was sentenced to death.

The time between the trial and the date of Bentley's execution was a mere month. The argument of whether or not to grant clemency raged in Parliament. In the House of Commons, Labour MPs Reginald Thomas Paget and Samuel Sydney Silverman demanded that Home Secretary David Maxwell Fife commute the sentence on the grounds that Bentley was too young and was incompetent to stand trial either from low intelligence or epilepsy, and that there may have been a "scintilla" of doubt as to his guilt. Home Secretary Fife decided that Bentley should be made an example of, and he refused to entertain any motions for clemency. On 28 January 1953, Bentley was hanged at Wandsworth Prison in London. In 1953, soon after Bentley's execution, Paget and Silverman published their arguments in a work entitled *Hanged—and Innocent?* Christopher Craig was imprisoned until 1963.

Following his execution, Bentley's family took action to clear his name. After his parents died in the 1970s, his sister, Iris, carried on the fight, writing a popular book on the subject. She died in January 1997, and the fight was left to Derek Bentley's brother and niece. In 1997 the Home Office, which reopened the case, passed it on to the Criminal Cases Review Commission (CCRC), destined to release its findings in 1998 or 1999 and possibly grant Bentley a posthumous pardon.

**References:** Bentley, Iris, with Penelope Dening, *Let Him Have Justice* (London: Sidgwick and Jackson, 1995); Fido, Martin, *The Chronicles of Crime: The Infamous Felons of Modern History and Their Hideous Crimes* (Boston: Little, Brown, and Company, 1993), 220; Montgomery Hyde, Harford, *The Trial of Craig and Bentley,* Notable British Trials Series (London: William Hodge and Co., 1954); Paget, Reginald Thomas, and Samuel Sydney Silverman, *Hanged—and Innocent?* (London: Victor Gollancz, 1953).

## Beria, Lavrentii Pavlovich (1899–1953)

Russian politician, head of the NKVD, the Soviet secret police, during the reign of Joseph Stalin, and put to death by Nikita Khrushchev for allegedly plotting against the new Soviet government that took power after Stalin's death.

Beria was born in Merkheuli, in the Sukhumi region of Soviet Georgia (now an independent nation), on 29 March 1899. He was trained as an architectural engineer, but his life changed in 1917 when he joined the Bolshevik party. A rising star in the Soviet system,

Beria became a low-level Communist party official in the Georgian and Caucasian regions in 1931; three years later he was named to the Central Committee of the Communist Party. In 1935 he published "On the History of the Bolshevik Organizations in Transcaucasia," an article that extolled the virtues of Stalin's rule in the Georgian Communist Party before he became the leader of the nation. During Stalin's massive purges of party officialdom in the 1920s and 1930s, Beria escaped any punishment and became one of Stalin's closest advisors. In 1936, he was brought to Moscow to become the chief assistant to Nicolai Yezhov, then head of the Soviet secret police. Two years later, Yezhov fell out of favor with Stalin and was arrested and shot, and Beria was named to head the NKVD. In this role, he oversaw the massive purges of those whom the Stalin regime saw as "enemies of the people" from 1938 to 1953.

While Stalin was alive, Beria was protected from any retribution from the Soviet apparatus he had helped to purge. But in 1953, Stalin died. Historian Michael Florinsky writes, "In the unsettled situation following Stalin's death Beria's power apparently became a menace to Stalin's successors. Beria was accused of having been a British agent since 1919, of plotting to seize power, of subverting farm collectivization, and sponsoring nationalist feeling among Soviet minorities." He was secretly tried for these crimes and found guilty. Details of his execution remain a mystery. Some sources report that he was shot along with six of his aides in December 1953, after a quick trial in which he was swiftly condemned; others claim that he was put to death in the spring of 1953 during a tumultuous session of the Politburo. The records of his ultimate fate may remain sealed in the Russian archives for a long time.

Lavrentii Beria, who had played such a critical role in the formation of the modern Soviet police state, was soon written out of Soviet history. Soon after Beria's death, readers of the *Great Soviet Encyclopedia* were issued razor blades, ordered to cut the article on Beria out of their copies and replace it with one on the Bering Strait. Even today, his name is rarely mentioned in Russia.

**References:** Florinsky, Michael T., ed., *McGraw-Hill Encyclopedia of Russia and the Soviet Union* (New York: McGraw-Hill Book Company, Inc., 1961), 65–66; Goetz, Philip W., ed.-in-Chief, *The New Encyclopedia Britannica,* 22 vols. (Chicago: Encyclopedia Britannica, Inc., 1995), 2:130–31; Warth, Robert D., "Beria, Lavrentii Pavlovich" in Joseph L. Wieczynski, ed., *The Modern Encyclopedia of Russian and Soviet History,* 58 vols., 1 supplement (Gulf Breeze, FL: Academic International Press, 1977–95), 4:36–39; Wittlin, Thaddeus, *Commissar: The Life and Death of Lavrenty Pavlovich Beria* (London: Angus and Robertson, 1973).

## Berns, Walter Fred, Jr. (1919– )

American supporter of capital punishment known for his 1979 work on the subject, *For Capital Punishment: Crime and the Morality of the Death Penalty.*

Born in Chicago, Illinois, on 3 May 1919, Berns attended local schools then graduated from the University of Iowa in 1941. After completing graduate studies at the London School of Economics and Political Science (1949–1950), he earned first a master's degree from the University of Chicago in 1951, then a Ph.D. from that same institution in 1953. He subsequently taught at Louisiana State University in Baton Rouge, Yale University, Cornell University, and Georgetown University. Since 1979, he has been a visiting professor in lectures at Georgetown.

In his landmark work on the death penalty, Berns argues that society has failed in instilling the rational fear that should be created from the imposition of capital punishment because prisons of today emphasize deterrence or rehabilitation when their true mission is punishment, plain and simple. The failure of prisons to carry out their true mission results in importance being placed on the criminal rather than the crime. Berns argues that society must have the will to "demand that criminals be paid back, and that the worst of them be made to pay back with their lives." Berns explains that today's death penalty cannot be considered a deterrent because the punishment is not meted out regularly and consistently.

Berns is also the author of *Constitutional Cases in American Government* (Crowell, 1963), *Taking the Constitution Seriously* (Madison Books, 1987), and *After the People Vote: A Guide to the Electoral College* (AEI Books, 1992).

**References:** Berns, Walter, *For Capital Punishment: Crime and the Morality of the Death Penalty* (New York: Basic Books, 1979); "Berns, Walter F." in Louis Filler, *A Dictionary of American Conservatism* (Secaucus, NJ: Citadel Press, 1988), 47; "Berns, Walter Fred" in Frances C. Locher, ed., *Contemporary Authors: A Bio-Bibliographical Guide to Current Writers in Fiction, General Nonfiction, Poetry, Journalism, Drama, Motion Pictures, Television, and Other Fields,* 151 vols. (Detroit: Gale Research, 1962–96), 101:54–55.

## Bhutto, Zulfikar Ali (1928–1979)

Pakistani leader and strongman put to death by his rival, Mohammed Zia ul-Haq, for allegedly murdering a political opponent, an execution that shocked the world.

Bhutto, the son of an aristocratic family, was born on his father's estate near Larkana, 200 miles northeast of Karachi, on 5 January 1928. His father was Sir Shahnawaz Khan Bhutto, a politician in the colonial British government that ruled India before it was partitioned into India and Pakistan in 1947. Zulfikar Bhutto attended schools in Bombay before going to the United States, where he graduated with honors from the University of California at Berkeley with a degree in political science. He then attended Christ College at Oxford, England, practiced law in London and lectured at the University of Southampton before returning to Pakistan in 1953.

Bhutto became close to several national leaders, including Major General Iskander Mirza, who served as president from 1956 to 1958, and General Mohammad Iyub Khan, who was the leader of a coup against Mirza in 1958. Mirza, impressed with Bhutto's intellect, sent him back to the United States as a member of the Pakistani delegation to the United Nations in 1957. Following the 1958 coup, Bhutto returned to Pakistan as Khan's minister of commerce. Five years later, Bhutto became the foreign minister.

However, Bhutto began to veer to the left politically (he felt China was his country's best ally) and saw Khan's pro-American, pro-Western stance as a hindrance to the country's prosperity. In 1965, after Pakistan fought a war with India over the disputed Kashmir region, Bhutto criticized Khan's policy toward the United States and resigned. He became a founder of the Pakistan People's Party, which called for a nationalist Islamic socialism and denounced General Khan as a dictator. Bhutto was detained in 1968 for a short time but released. The Ayub Khan government was overthrown in a coup, but Bhutto refused to participate in elections called for by the new government. The war over East Pakistan, which resulted in the formation of Bangladesh, and the continuing conflict with India led the new president, Agha Yahya Khan, to name Bhutto as his foreign minister and call for aid from the United Nations. Agha Khan then resigned, making Zulfikar Ali Bhutto, on 20 December 1971, the president of Pakistan.

To calm the nation, Bhutto instituted martial law, which lasted until 1974. During that time, he placed Agha Khan under house arrest, nationalized some of the nation's economic industries, worked toward the redistribution of land, and angered some by imposing restrictions on the use of money by the nation's wealthy. In 1974, he returned the nation to civilian rule, resigned the presidency, and instead took the prime minister's position as well as several other cabinet positions for himself.

Opposition to his rule grew. General Mohammad Zia ul-Haq led a coup against Bhutto on 5 July 1977 and put the former leader under arrest for the murder of a political opponent, Nawab Ahmed Khan. On the testimony of his former deputy of security—testimony many believe to be coerced—Bhutto was found guilty of murder on 18 March 1978 and sentenced to be hanged. After his appeals were denied, and despite the appeals of leaders around the world calling for mercy, Bhutto was executed on 4 April 1979 along with the four men convicted of participating in the political murder.

Pakistan was shocked by the execution; crowds in the city of Rawalpindi cried "Death to Zia and Zia's Children!" Bhutto's daughter, Benazir, returned to Pakistan from exile in Europe in 1986. In August 1988, President Zia's plane was blown up in midair by unknown persons, killing Zia as well as the U.S. ambassador to Pakistan. In the November elections that same year, Benazir Bhutto was elected Prime Minister, the first woman to hold that post in a Muslim nation.

**References:** "Bhutto Hanged in Pakistan for Murder Plot," *The New York Times*, 4 April 1979, 1; "Pakistan Stunned by Bhutto Execution," *The Washington Post*, 5 April 1979, A1; "Pakistan Without Mr. Bhutto," *The Washington Post*, 5 April 1979, A18; Schofield, Victoria, *Bhutto: Trial and Execution* (London: Cassell, 1979); Taseer, Salmaan, *Bhutto: A Political Biography* (London: Ithaca Press, 1979).

## The Bible on Capital Punishment, Position of

For at least three centuries, during the time that capital punishment has become such a controversial issue, people on both sides of the debate have utilized the Bible to support their respective arguments and justify that God supports or denies the right of society to put persons to death.

The portion of the Bible most often cited by those who support capital punishment is Genesis 9:6, which says, "Whoso sheddeth man's blood, by man shall his blood be shed: for in the image of God made he man." In Numbers 35:30 and 31, the Bible reads, "Whoso killeth any person, the murderer shall be put to death by the mouth of witnesses: but one witness shall not testify against any person to cause him to die" and "Moreover ye shall take no satisfaction for the life of a murderer, which is guilty of death: but he shall be surely put to death." The Bible also commands, "Thou shalt not avenge, nor bear any grudge against the children of thy people" (Leviticus 19:18) and, in the name of God himself, "To me belongeth vengeance and recompense" (Deuteronomy 32:35).

The leading authority in the debate on the Bible's teachings regarding capital punishment was the Rev. George Barrell Cheever (1807–1890), who spent much of the late nineteenth century battling the anti–death penalty crusade and sought to have states retain their capital punishment statutes. In his *Punishment by Death: Its Authority and Expediency* (New York: John Wiley, 1849), Cheever explains:

> The argument from Scripture[,] in favour of capital punishment, is plain and powerful. . . . [It] commences with the ordinance against bloodshed communicated to Noah; this being the first instance of divine legislation with the punishment of death annexed as its sanction. Taken with the context, it reads thus: "And surely your blood of your lives will I require; at the hand of every beast will I require it, and at the hand of man; at the hand of every man's brother will I require the life of man. Whoso sheddeth man's blood, by man shall his blood be shed: for in the image of God made he man."

In the reply to these arguments, those against capital punishment contend that while the Bible does support death for murderers, it also condones slavery and punishments that are not now considered humane by a civilized society; such as a sentence of death for one who curses his mother and father. Marvin Bovee lays out these arguments in *Christ and the Gallows; or, Reasons for the Abolition of Capital Punishment* (New York: Masonic Publishing Company, 1869), where he writes:

> It is scarcely possible to estimate the importance which is attached to the above text [Genesis 9:6] by that portion of the religious public which maintains the gallows as a Divine institution. No toy in the hands of a child was ever held in higher esteem than is this same passage of Scripture by those theologians who possess so peculiar a reverence for the gallows. One can hardly realize that the text referred to has so important a bearing upon the question under discussion, until it is observed that so many prominent *divines* tenaciously cling to it as the great bulwark of defense for the law of capital punishment. And it will be further noticed that no other passage in the Bible is regarded of sufficient force, in the discussion of the question, as to merit repeated quotations in maintenance of the death penalty. It is this text which is so often cited in lyceum debates; so frequently quoted in legislative halls, and so often thundered from pulpits and platforms in the defense of the "barbarous law." It is the grand capstan around which coils the hangman's rope. "It is," as a distinguished theologian declares it, "the citadel, commanding and sweeping the whole argument."

**See also:** Bovee, Marvin Henry; Cheever, the Rev. George Barrell.
**References:** Bovee, Marvin Henry, *Christ and Gallows; or, Reasons for the Abolition of Capital Punishment* (New York: Published for the Author by the Masonic Publishing Company, 1869), 290–91; *Punishment By Death: Its Authority and Expediency* (New York: John Wiley, 1849), 123–24.

## Blackmun, Harry Andrew (1908– )

American jurist, Associate Justice of the United States Supreme Court (1970–94), an early supporter of capital punishment who changed his attitude during his final years on the court.

Born in Nashville, Illinois, on 12 November 1908, to a struggling family, he moved when a child to St. Paul, Minnesota, a state with which he would be identified for the rest of his life. He attended local schools, then graduated magna cum laude from Harvard in 1929 and received his law degree from the Harvard Law School three years later. After serving as a law clerk for a judge on the U.S. Circuit Court for the Eighth Circuit for a year, Blackmun joined a private law firm in Minneapolis, where he worked until 1950. In that year, he became the resident counsel of the Mayo Clinic in Rochester, Minnesota.

In 1959, President Dwight D. Eisenhower named his fellow Republican Blackmun to a seat on the circuit court for the eighth circuit, where he became noted for judicial restraint and a conservative approach toward the law. Although considered a moderate on civil rights and civil liberties issues, he was nonetheless strictly conservative on fiscal and criminal matters. Blackmun sat on this court until 1970. In that year, President Richard M. Nixon attempted twice to fill the U.S. Supreme Court seat vacated by Justice Abe Fortas; Nixon's first two nominees, circuit judges Clement F. Haynsworth, Jr., and G. Harrold Carswell, were both defeated in the Senate. The president then turned to the little-known Blackmun, who fit the bill.

Appointed on 14 April 1970, Blackmun was approved by the Senate, 94–0, and sworn in on 9 June by his good friend and fellow Minnesotan Chief Justice Warren Burger. Although noted in his first years for his authorship of the majority opinion in the controversial abortion case, *Roe v. Wade,* Blackmun was, as a whole, more conservative than widely believed. In both 1972 (*Furman v. Georgia*) and in 1976 (*Gregg v. Georgia*), Blackmun sided first with the minority and then with the majority in finding that the death penalty did not violate the constitutional ban on cruel and unusual punishments. In such cases as *Spaziano v. Florida* (in which he wrote the majority opinion), allowing for the override by a judge of a jury's recommendation of a life sentence in a capital case, Blackmun sided squarely with the pro–capital punishment faction of the Court. His moderate course on civil rights issues commanded respect from both the conservative and liberal members of the Court.

However, on 18 November 1993, shortly after his 85th birthday, Blackmun appeared on ABC's *Nightline* to voice his growing uneasiness with capital punishment. He told interviewers Ted Koppel and Nina Totenberg, "I'm not sure the death penalty . . . is fairly administered. I think it comes close to violating the Equal Protection Clause of the Constitution. . . . I haven't taken that position yet, but I'm getting close to it." He also voiced concerns he had expressed as part of his dissent in *McCleskey v. Kemp* (1987), in which the majority held that racial statistics that tended to show that blacks were more likely to get a death sentence in Georgia could not be used without proof that discrimination was involved in every case. He said that there are "disturbing statistics that come in when one considers race. . . . And, of course, some people can rationalize that to their satisfaction. But there it stands, and I'm bothered by it." And although he felt the Constitution did not specifically ban capital punishment, he added, "It always bothers me. These cases are wretched."

Blackmun's clearly upsetting decision whether or not to vote against the use of capital punishment was settled in one of his last cases on the court, *Callins v. Collins* (1994). In his stinging, personal dissent, he wrote:

> Twenty years have passed since this Court declared that the death penalty must be imposed "fairly, and with reasonable consistency, or not at all" . . . and, despite the efforts of the states and courts to devise legal formulas and procedural rules . . . the death penalty remains fraught with arbitrariness, discrimination, caprice and mistake. . . . Experience has taught us that the constitutional goal of eliminating arbitrariness and discrimination from the administration of death . . . can never be achieved without compromising an equally essential component of fundamental fairness: individualized sentencing. . . .
>
> From this day forward, I no longer shall tinker with the machinery of death. For more than 20 years I have endeavored—indeed, I have struggled—along with a majority of this Court, to develop procedural and substantive rules that would lend more than the mere appearance of fairness to the death penalty endeavor. Rather than continue to coddle the Court's delusion that the desired level of fairness has been achieved and the need for regulation eviscerated, I feel

morally and intellectually obligated simply to concede that the death penalty experiment has failed. It is virtually self-evident to me now that no combination of procedural rules or substantive regulations ever can save the death penalty from its inherent constitutional deficiencies. The basic question—does the system accurately and consistently determine which defendants "deserve" to die?—cannot be answered in the affirmative. It is not simply that this Court has allowed vague aggravating circumstances to be employed, . . . and vital judicial review to be blocked. The problem is that the inevitability of factual, legal, and moral error gives us a system that we know must wrongly kill some defendants, a system that fails to deliver the fair, consistent, and reliable sentences of death required by the Constitution.

**See also:** *Spaziano v. Florida.*
**References:** Blackmun opinion in *Bruce Edwin Callins, Petitioner v. James A. Collins, Director, Texas Department of Criminal Justice, Institutional Division* (127 L.Ed. 2d 435 [1994]), at 436–39; "Blackmun Reevaluating His Death Penalty Stand," *The Washington Post,* 19 November 1993, A4; Gest, Ted, et al., "Life After Blackmun," *U.S. News & World Report,* 18 April 1994, 28–30; Greenhouse, Linda, "Justice Blackmun's Odyssey: From Moderate to a Liberal," *The New York Times,* 7 April 1994, 1; "Second Thoughts," *The Economist,* 5 March 1994, 26.

## Blackstone, Sir William (1723–1780)

English jurisprudence writer, author of the four volume *Commentaries on the Laws of England* (1765–69), considered one of the major classics on the writing of the law and which discussed capital punishment as it was applied in English law in the eighteenth century.

Blackstone was born in London on 10 July 1723 and raised by an older brother after both parents died. He entered Oxford University at the age of 15 after attending a private boarding school. Three years later he began the study of the law. In 1746 he was called to the bar, but his law practice was a dismal failure and he was forced to work as a bursar at Oxford. He published his first work on the law in 1750, and eight years later was named to the post of professor of common law at Oxford, the first man to be so named. His lectures there became the most important in the history of English law. Elected to a seat in the lower house of the English Parliament in 1761, he was named solicitor general to the queen two years later.

In 1765, Blackstone composed the first volume of his monumental *Commentaries on the Laws of England,* a landmark work that to this day is still used by legal scholars. In the *Commentaries,* Blackstone points out the importance of the juvenile criminal's ability to distinguish right from wrong in deciding whether or not the death penalty is justified:

> By the law as it now stands, and has stood at least since the time of Edward the Third [1327–77], the capacity of doing ill, or contracting guilt, is not so much measured by years and days as by the strength of the delinquent's understanding and judgement. . . . Thus a girl of thirteen has been burned for killing her mistress; and one boy of ten, and another of nine years old, who had killed their companions, have been sentenced to death, and he of ten years actually hanged; because it appeared upon their trials that the one hid himself, and the other hid the body he had killed, which hiding manifested a consciousness of guilt, and a discretion to discern between good and evil. And there was an instance in the last century where a boy of eight years old was tried at Abington for firing two barns; he was found guilty, condemned, and hanged accordingly. Thus, also, in very modern times, a boy of ten yeas old was convicted on his own confession of murdering his bed-fellow, there appearing his whole behavior plain tokens of mischievous discretion; and as

the sparing this boy merely on account of his tender years might be of dangerous consequence to the public, by propagating a notion that children might commit such atrocious crimes with impunity, it was unanimously agreed by all the judges that he was a proper subject of capital punishment. But, in all such cases, the evidence of that malice which to supply age ought to be strong and clear beyond all doubt and contradiction."

Blackstone completed work on the last volume of the *Commentaries* in 1769. Knighted for his lifetime of contributions to the study of the law, Blackstone died on 14 February 1780 at the age of 56 and was buried in Wallingford.

**Reference:** Blackstone, Sir William (W.N. Welsby and John L. Wendell, eds.), *Commentaries on the Laws of England: In Four Books; with an Analysis of the Work*, 4 vols. (New York: Harper & Brothers, 1857), 4:19–20.

## Blood Atonement

Religious belief utilized in capital punishment in which a convict's blood must be shed during execution to "atone' before Christ for his sins.

L. Kay Gillespie of Weber State University in Utah, who has written extensively on this subject, describes the origins of the belief:

> Utah is unique in that the state's practice of allowing the condemned his choice of execution stems from a religious doctrine: only through choosing a method of execution which results in blood being "spilled" (or shed) can the condemned hope to receive forgiveness in the next life. The existence and evolution of this belief—known in Mormon theology as "blood atonement"—is complex.
>
> . . . . The punishment prescribed [by the first territorial legislature] for first-degree murder was execution with the condemned allowed to choose among firing squad, hanging, or beheading.
>
> Mormon leaders believed that Jesus' blood did not forgive murderers, who could personally "atone" for their sin only by offering their own blood. Brigham Young, for example, maintained, "There are sins that men commit for which they cannot receive forgiveness in this world, or in that which is to come, and if they had their eyes open to see their true condition, they would be perfectly willing to have their blood spilt upon the ground, that the smoke thereof might ascend to heaven as an offering for their sins; and the smoking incense would atone for their sin; whereas, if such is not the case, they will stick to them and remain upon them in the spirit world." Young's counselor Jedediah M. Grant agreed: "I say, that there are men and women that I would advise to go to the President immediately, and ask him to appoint a committee to attend to their case; and then let a place be selected, and let that committee shed their blood." On another occasion he argued, "Brethren and sisters, we want you to repent and forsake your sins. And you who have committed sins that cannot be forgiven through baptism, let your blood be shed . . . before God as an atonement for your sins."

**Reference:** Gillespie, L. Kay, *The Unforgiven: Utah's Executed Men* (Salt Lake City, UT: Signature Books, 1991), 12–14.

## Boiling to Death

Little-used method of capital punishment, utilized mainly to stun the victims before they were hanged on the gallows. The first use of this technique may have come soon after 1531, when it was made legal by King Henry VIII of England. According to crime historian Robert Nash, "The first culprit killed under the new law, a cook accused of attempting to poison the Bishop of Rochester's household, was publicly boiled to death in a cauldron suspended from an iron tripod over a pile of burning logs. Another boiling death, of a servant who had poisoned her mistress, took place the same year, and a third, another servant, was boiled to death in 1542. Edward VI repealed the law in 1547 and substituted hanging or burning" at the stake.

**Reference:** Nash, Jay Robert, *Encyclopedia of World Crime,* 4 vols. (Wilmette, IL: CrimeBooks, Inc., 1990), 4:3285.

## Boleyn, Anne (1507–1536)

Queen of England, second wife of Henry VIII, put to death by her husband because she could not produce a male heir.

She was born in 1507, the daughter of Sir Thomas Boleyn (also spelled Bullen and Bouleyne), Henry VIII's ambassador to France. Traveling with her sister, Mary, to France, she remained in that nation in the court of Claude de France, the wife of Francis I, as one of her attendants. In 1521, she returned to England to become the lady of honor to Queen Catherine of Aragon, Henry's first wife. Soon she became the object of Henry's advances and was most likely his mistress when the king sought to annul his marriage to Catherine. When the Pope refused to consider an annulment or divorce, Henry broke from the Catholic Church and formed the Anglican Church, which gave him his desired divorce. (The refusal of John Fisher, Bishop of Rochester, to affirm the annulment or the establishment of the Anglican Church led to his own execution in 1535.)

In January 1533, Henry secretly married Anne Boleyn. That September, Anne gave birth to the child who would one day reign as Queen Elizabeth I; however, Henry was angered that Anne could not produce a male heir, and their separation began. Henry next turned to Anne's lady of honor, Jane Seymour. In order to marry Jane, Henry accused Anne of infidelity with several men before her marriage to him; to make Anne appear more hideous to the public, many accounts produced at the time and some years later distorted her appearance; one, by a historian named Sanders in 1585, claimed that Anne had a large tumor on her neck and a sixth finger on her right hand. Another account claimed that she had three breasts, a consequence of her dabbling with witchcraft.

Anne was brought to trial on a charge of treachery. In a reprint of an old English account, *The Trial and Execution of Ann Boleyn, 1536,* editor and English historian C. H. Williams recounts,

> There was no precedent for the trial of an English Queen for treason. Anne Boleyn was arraigned before a Court of Peers. After her sentence Archbishop [Thomas] Cranmer held an ecclesiastical court at Lambet and pronounced her marriage to Henry null and void on the ground that there had been a previous contract of marriage with the earl of Northumberland, although this was denied by the earl. This had not been known at the time of Anne's marrige to Henry, but she confessed it to the Archbishop.

English historian Charles Wriothesley wrote in 1875:

> The Friday following [her trial], being the 19th day of May, 1536, and the 28th year of King Henry the VIIIth[,] at eight of the clock in the morning, Anne Boleyn, Queen, was brought to execution on the green within the Tower of London. . . . On a scaffold made there for the said execution the said Queen Anne said thus; Masters I here humbly submit me to the law as the law hath judged me, and as for mine offences, I here accuse no man, God knoweth them; I remit them to God, beseeching him to have mercy on my soul, and I beseech Jesu save my sovereign and master the King, the most godly, noble, and gentle Prince that is, and long to reign over you; which words

were spoken with a goodly smiling countenance; and this done she kneeled down on her knees and said: To Jesu Christ I commend my soul; and suddenly the hangman smote off her head at a stroke with a sword; her body with the head was buried in the Chapel within the Tower of London, in the quire there, the same day at afternoon, when she had reigned as Queen three years lacking 14 days, from her coronation to her death.

Historian Retha M. Warnicke relates that another account has Anne saying to the group assembled to see her die,

> Good Christen people, I am come hether to dye, for according to the lawe, and by the law I am judged to dye, and therefore I wyll speake nothynge agaynst it. I am come hether to accuse no man, nor to speake any thyng of that, whereof I am accused and comdempned to dye, but I pray God save the king and send him long to reygne over you, for a gentler not a more mercifull prince was there never; and to me he was ever good, a gentle and soveraygne lorde. And if anye person wyll medle of my cause, I require them to judge the best. And thus I take my leve of the worlde and of you all, and hertely desyre you all to praye for me. O Lorde have mercy on me, to God I commende my soule.

According to eyewitnesses at the scene, after her head was cut off, Anne's lips continued to move, and her eyes continued to blink, for several minutes. After these motions stopped, her head was tucked under her arm, and she was buried in the St. Peter-ad-Vincula, a chapel on the grounds of the Tower of London.

**References:** Ives, E. W., *Anne Boleyn* (Oxford, England: Basil Blackwell, 1986); Strickland, Agnes, *Lives of the Tudor Princesses, Including Lady Jane Grey and Her Sisters* (London: Longmans & Co., 1868); Warnicke, Retha M., *The Rise and Fall of Ann Boleyn: Family Politics at the Court of Henry VIII* (New York: Cambridge University Press, 1989), 3; Williams, C. H., ed., *English Historical Documents, 1485–1558* (London: Eyre & Spottiswoode, 1967), 723; Wriothesley, Charles, ed., *A Chronicle of England During the Reigns of the Tudors*, 2 vols. (London: The Camden Society, 1875), 1:36–38.

## Bonhoeffer, Dietrich (1906–1945)

German theoretician whose vocal opposition to the Third Reich led to his execution by the Germans in the Flossenbürg concentration camp in 1945.

Born in Breslau, Germany, on 4 February 1906, he was the son of Karl Bonhoeffer, a psychiatrist who attempted to have Hitler committed in the 1930s as insane; Dietrich's brother, Klaus, was also involved in the Hitler resistance and was shot in 1945. Dietrich Bonhoeffer's early education was supplemented by his service as a curate in Barcelona from 1927 to 1929, and as an auditor at the Union Theological Seminary in New York in 1930. In 1931 he returned to Germany and was a student chaplain in Berlin.

In the 1930s, many Christians inside Germany secretly opposed Hitler and the German Third Reich. In 1934, many of these evangelicals formed the group known as The Confessing Church to openly oppose the German government. Bonhoeffer, in his role as a critic of the Nazis, became the movement's representative in the city of Finkenwalde. Of the Confessing Church's members, Bonhoeffer was its most outspoken. In 1936, the Nazis forbade him to teach; by 1941 he had been likewise banned from preaching and publishing. Yet he continued to write, at one point writing that Hitler was the Antichrist and that he should be gotten rid of.

In 1939 Bonhoeffer slipped out of Germany and met with anti-Hitler forces in England, where he attempted to raise support for outside resistance to the Nazis. In 1942, through his brother-in-law, Hans von Dohnányi, he was able to meet again with British representatives in Sweden. Yet because the Allies suspected that he was a plant, his pleas for assistance were met with skepticism. On 5 April 1943, he was arrested by the Gestapo on the pretense that he had been using his church office to further a political career. A little more than a year later, on 20 July 1944, other plotters attempted to assassinate Hitler, and Bonhoeffer, who had been sent to the Flossenbürg concentration camp, was accused of being part of the plot and rearrested. Following his court-martial by the SS, he was hanged on 9 April 1945 along with Admiral Wilhelm Canaris and Hans Oster, two German officials involved in the actual attempt on Hitler's life.

After the war, Bonhoeffer's notes on his opinions were published as *Auf dem Wege zur Freiheit* ("The Way to Freedom"). The notes that he took during his year in prison were published in 1951 as *Widerstand und Ergebung* ("Opposition and Resignation") and translated in two volumes with the titles "Prisoner for God" and "Letters and Papers from Prison." In 1996, on the fifty-first anniversary of his execution, attempts to rehabilitate him were finally successful when a German court ruled that his conviction and execution had been illegal.

**References:** Bethge, Eberhard (ed. with English translation by John W. De Gruchy), *Bonhoeffer, Exile and Martyr* (New York: Seabury Press, 1979); Bethge, Eberhard (ed. with English translation by Rosaleen Ockenden), *Bonhoeffer, an Illustrated Introduction in Documents and Photographs* (London: Fount Paperbacks, 1979); Niebuhr, Gustav, "Undoing the Legacy of Nazi Courts," *The New York Times,* 11 February 1996, E6; Taylor, James, and Warren Shaw, *The Third Reich Almanac* (New York: World Almanac, 1987), 62–63; Zentner, Christian, and Friedemann Bedüftig, eds., *Encyclopedia of the Third Reich,* 2 vols. (New York: Macmillan, 1991), 1:98.

## *Booth v. Maryland* (482 U.S. 496, 107 S.Ct. 2529, 96 L.Ed. 2d 440 [1987])

U.S. Supreme Court case that held that the introduction of victim impact statements (VISs) violated the Eighth Amendment to the United States Constitution.

Defendant John Booth was convicted in the circuit court of Baltimore, Maryland, of the murders of two people. As part of the presentencing report, the state included a victim impact statement, which described the opinions of the victims' families and how the murders were affecting them, as well as personal characteristics of the murder victims themselves. The court rejected the defendants' petition to disallow introduction of the VIS, and with it the jury sentenced Booth to death. The Maryland court of appeals upheld the death sentence, ruling that the introduction of the impact statement did not inject "an arbitrary factor" into Booth's sentence.

The case was argued before the U.S. Supreme Court on 24 March 1987, and the Court handed down its decision on 15 June. Speaking for a 5–4 majority, Justice Lewis Powell (Chief Justice William H. Rehnquist and Justices Byron White, Sandra Day O'Connor, and Antonin Scalia dissented) held that the introduction of the VIS was a violation of the Eighth Amendment and thus a sentence of death arising from it was struck down. Justice Powell wrote:

> The formal presentation of this information by the State can serve no other purpose than to inflame the jury and divert it from deciding the case on the relevant evidence concerning the crime and the defendant. As we have noted, any decision to impose the death sentence must "be, and appear to be, based on reason rather than caprice or emotion." *Gardner v. Florida,* . . . The admission of these emotionally charged opinions as to what conclusions the jury should draw from the evidence clearly is inconsistent with the

reasoned decisionmaking we require in capital cases.

In his dissent, Justice White wrote:

> The affront to humanity of a brutal murder such as petitioner committed is not limited to its impact on the victim or victims; a victim's community is also injured, and in particular the victim's family suffers shock and grief of a kind difficult to imagine for those who have not shared a similar loss. Maryland's legislature has decided that the jury should have the testimony of the victim's family in order to assist it in weighing the degree of harm that the defendant caused and the corresponding degree of punishment that should be inflicted.

*Booth* and a later impact-statement case, *South Carolina v. Gathers,* were overturned by the 1991 decision of *Payne v. Tennessee.*

**See also:** *Gardner v. Florida; Payne v. Tennessee; South Carolina v. Gathers.*

## Bovee, Marvin Henry (1827–1888)

Nineteenth-century American reformer who worked to abolish capital punishment in the United States and whose *Christ and the Gallows; or, Reasons for the Abolition of Capital Punishment* (New York: Published for the Author by the Masonic Publishing Company, 1869) was one of the leading works directed toward that aim.

Little is known of Bovee's life. He was born in Amsterdam, New York, on 5 January 1827. What little education he received was obtained in Amsterdam, and in 1843 he moved with his father (there is no indication of what became of his mother) to Eagle, Wisconsin. He was elected to the state Senate in 1853, where he became the first man to introduce a bill outlawing capital punishment in the state. After his bill passed, making Wisconsin the second state in the Union to do away with the death penalty (Michigan was the first in 1846), he worked on and was successful with similar legislation in Illinois. Eventually Bovee's work carried him to New York, Minnesota, Iowa, and many other states where capital punishment was either abolished or modified.

In his only work on capital punishment, *Christ and the Gallows,* Bovee printed his "Enunciation of Principles," which included the following statement: "Penalties which do not contemplate the reformation of the criminal, are not punishment, but cruelties." His work includes not only his thoughts and writings on capital punishment as punishment, but ideas for reforms and the comments of others, mainly anti–death penalty writers, on the subject. As for Bovee himself, he spent 1884 on the campaign trail, speaking on behalf of presidential candidate Grover Cleveland who, as the sheriff of Buffalo, New York, was one of the most pro–death penalty officials in the nation.

Bovee died in Whitewater, Wisconsin, on 7 May 1888.

**References:** Bovee, Marvin Henry, "Christ and the Gallows; or, Reasons for the Abolition of Capital Punishment" (New York: Published for the Author by the Masonic Publishing Company, 1869), frontispiece; Wilson, James Grant, ed., *Appletons' Cyclopedia of American Biography,* 7 vols. (New York: D. Appleton and Company, 1888–1901), 7:31.

## Breaking on the Wheel

Method of capital punishment marked by torturous and agony-filled suffering on a wooden wheel while the condemned is stretched and has his or her limbs broken (by the executioner) with a metal rod or pole.

Crime historian Jay Robert Nash writes, "First used in Germany and France, it featured a large oak wheel placed in the center of town where the prisoner was led. Stripped to a loin cloth, the prisoner was tied to the wheel with his wrists and ankles extending over the rim. An executioner first smashed the arms and legs with an iron bar so that the pulverized bones fitted around the outside of the wheel, and then he wheeled the culprit around town. Finally, the executioner would strike the man solidly on the rib cage with the iron bar and death came soon after."

The first apparent victim of the wheel was Saint Catherine, a fourth-century victim of religious persecution in Egypt. (The wheel was nicknamed the "Catherine Wheel" after her.) Ironically, however, she did not die on the wheel, which broke. Also famed for being broken on the wheel was the French Jean Calas, suspected but later cleared of murdering his son. One less-famous but important victim of the Catherine Wheel was Johann Reinhold von Patkul (1660–1707), a Livonian nobleman (Livonia is now a district of Latvia) who was broken on the wheel in Kazimierz, Poland, for being a traitor to the reign of Augustus II, elector of Saxony and King of Poland.

**See also:** Calas, Jean; The Catherine Wheel.
**References:** Abbott, Geoffrey, *Lords of the Scaffold: A History of the Executioner* (London: Robert Hale, 1991), 148–55; "The Burial of the Living" in *Crime and Punishment: The Illustrated Crime Encyclopedia,* 28 vols. (Westport, CT: H. S. Stuttman, 1994), 4:489; Nash, Jay Robert, *Encyclopedia of World Crime,* 4 vols. (Wilmette, IL: CrimeBooks, Inc., 1990), 4:3287.

## Brennan, William Joseph, Jr. (1906–1997)

American jurist, U.S. Supreme Court Associate Justice (1956–1990), and firm opponent of capital punishment.

Born in Newark, New Jersey, on 25 April 1906, Brennan was the second of eight children, the son of Irish immigrants. He attended local schools and received his bachelor's degree from the Wharton School of Finance at the University of Pennsylvania in 1928. He then went to the Harvard University Law School, where one of the faculty was Felix Frankfurter, later a Supreme Court justice himself. (Years later, when asked about Brennan's impact on the Court, Frankfurter remarked, "I always wanted my students to think for themselves, but Brennan goes too far.")

After earning his law degree at Harvard in 1931, Brennan began to practice law in Newark, specializing in labor law. During World War II he served in the army, then returned to his practice before being nominated in 1949 for a judgeship on the New Jersey Superior Court. The following year he was named to the appellate division of the state superior court, and finally in 1952 to the New Jersey state supreme court.

On 15 October 1956, U.S. Supreme Court Justice Sherman Minton retired due to ill health. President Dwight D. Eisenhower turned to the 50-year-old Brennan to replace Minton. Only Senator Joseph McCarthy voted against Brennan's confirmation, which occurred on 16 October. In his 34 years on the Court, one of the longest tenures in history, Brennan became ensconced in the liberal wing of the Court along with fellow judicial activists Thurgood Marshall, Potter Stewart, Earl Warren, and John Paul Stevens. Among Brennan's decisions were his arguments in *Baker v. Carr* (1962), which upheld the "one man, one vote" doctrine; *New York Times Company v. Sullivan* (1964), allowing for an unencumbered press free from government intrusion; and *Lemon v. Kurtzman* (1971), where, as the only Roman Catholic on the Court, he argued for the strict separation of church and state. Because of these rulings, Eisenhower called Brennan's appointment "the biggest damnfool mistake I ever made."

Yet Brennan's most consistent, and persistent, arguments were against capital punishment. In all death penalty cases that came before the Court, Brennan voted against its imposition. In 1985 he wrote, "The calculated killing of a human being by the state involves, by its very nature, an absolute denial of the executed person's humanity." In an article for *The New York Times* in 1996, entitled "What the Constitution Requires," Brennan wrote:

> One area of law more than any other besmirches the constitutional vision of human dignity. My old friend Justice Harry Blackmun called it the "machinery of death." It is the death penalty.
>
> The statistics paint a chilling portrait of racial discrimination on death row. Yet the ultimate problem is more fundamental. The barbaric death penalty violates our Constitution. Even the most vile murderer does not release the state from its obligation to respect dignity, for the state does not honor the victim by emulating his murderer. Capital punishment's fatal flaw is that it treats people as objects to be toyed with and discarded. But I refuse to despair. One day the Court will outlaw the death penalty. Permanently.

On 20 July 1990, at age 86 and in failing health, Brennan announced his retirement from the Court. He was replaced by David Souter, a moderate. Brennon died almost exactly seven years later, on 24 July 1997.

**References:** Brennan, William J., Jr., "What the Constitution Requires," *The New York Times,* 28 April 1996, E13; Greenhouse, Linda, "Brennan, Key Liberal, Quits Supreme Court; Battle for Seat Likely," *The New York Times,* 21 July 1990, 1; Greenhouse, Linda, "William Brennan, 91, Dies; Gave Court Liberal Vision," *The New York Times,* 25 July 1997, 1; "Liberal Brennan Played Key Role," *The Miami Herald,* 21 July 1990, 17A; Mello, Michael, *Against the Death Penalty: The Relentless Dissents of Justices Brennan and Marshall* (Boston: Northeastern University Press, 1996); Stewart, David O., "Justice William J. Brennan Jr.: A Life on the Court," *ABA Journal,* 77:2 (February 1991), 62–64; Tribe, Laurence H., "Justice William J. Brennan Jr.: Architect of the Bill of Rights," *ABA Journal,* 77:2 (February 1991), 47–51.

## Brown, Edmund Gerald ("Pat") (1905–1996)

American politician, liberal governor of California (1959–67), noted for his muted reluctance to capital punishment, shown most notably in his hesitancy to sign the death warrant for Caryl Chessman, an objection that blossomed into complete opposition at the end of his life.

Born in San Francisco of Irish and German ancestry, Brown attended local school. He received a law degree from the San Francisco College of Law in 1927 and read the law in the office of a blind attorney for whom Brown became a confidant. In 1928 Brown made his first try at office, running as a Republican for the state assembly. He lost, but the political bug was in his blood, and although he switched parties in the overwhelmingly Republican state, he was elected San Francisco district attorney in 1943. As D.A., he cracked down on that city's notorious dens of prostitution, gambling, and illegal abortion. Although he was defeated in 1946 for state attorney general, he ran again four years later and won, the only Democrat that year to win a state-wide election.

As attorney general, Brown was noted for his investigation of the State Liquor Administration as well as his crackdown on illegal narcotics and organized crime. He held the post until 1950. Eight years later, he opposed Republican senator William F. Knowland for the governorship. Brown ran on a platform of "bread and butter issues"—those problems facing average families. Promising to clean up labor unions, Brown won by more than a million votes out of five million cast. As governor, from 1959 to 1967, he oversaw the establishment of the State Water Project, a large irrigation scheme that made California an agricultural giant; supported the passage of a fair housing law (which was overturned by a referendum but upheld by the courts); and created the state's Master Plan for Higher Education, which outlined the state collegiate system that has become one of the nation's best. Brown's one later regret was that he did not do more during his time as governor to oppose the death penalty. At the time, however, he allowed 36 people (including notables Caryl Chessman and Barbara Graham) to be executed in the gas chamber, while commuting the sentences of 23 others.

In 1962, Brown defeated former presidential candidate Richard Nixon for the governorship but was defeated in 1966 by another rising Republican star, Ronald Reagan. Although many believe that Reagan won because voters felt Brown had been too "soft" on growing Vietnam War protests and social unrest (including the Watts riots of 1965), Brown himself seemed to believe that his handling of the Chessman case in the end soured voters on his administration.

After leaving office, as the *Los Angeles Times* explained, "a second life began for Pat Brown." Through the careers of his son, Edmund G. "Jerry" Brown, Jr. (who served two terms as California governor) and his daughter, Kathleen Brown (who served as state treasurer and lost a bitter battle to become governor in 1994), Pat Brown remained a social activist. In 1989, in what may be called his *mea culpa*, "Public Justice, Private Mercy: A Governor's Education on Death Row," Brown wrote, "The naked, simple fact is that the death penalty has been a gross failure. Beyond its horror and incivility, it has neither protected the innocent nor deterred the wicked." Brown further explained that he believed that as evil as Chessman was, someone should have stepped forward to help him, and Brown regretted that he had not done so.

Edmund Brown was 90 years old when he died of a heart attack at his home in Beverly Hills, California, on 16 February 1996.

**See also:** Chessman, Caryl Whittier.

**References:** Brown, Edmund, with Dick Adler, *Public Justice, Private Mercy: A Governor's Education on Death Row* (New York: Weidenfeld & Nicolson, 1989); "Brown, Edmund G(erald)" in Charles Moritz, ed., *Current Biography 1960* (New York: H. W. Wilson, 1960), 55–57; Rainey, James, and Larry Gordon, "Pat Brown's Death Marks Passing of Era," *Los Angeles Times,* 18 February 1996, A1, A24; Reinhold, Robert, "Edmund G. Brown is Dead at 90; He Led California in Boom Years," *The New York Times,* 18 February 1996, 1.

## Brown, John (1800–1859)

American abolitionist hanged for his role in the raid on Harper's Ferry, Virginia (now in West Virginia) to free slaves and start a revolution against the slave states.

Brown was born in Torrington, Connecticut, on 9 May 1800, the son of Owen Brown, a radical abolitionist. John Brown grew up in Hudson, Ohio, but did not attend school. As a result, he was forced to work at a variety of jobs, including surveyor, sheep raiser, and land speculator. In 1842, facing increasing debts and unable to properly care for his 12 children, he declared bankruptcy.

Because of his stern upbringing and the religious and moral lessons he learned from his father, John Brown was radically opposed to slavery. He was a member of the Underground Railroad, opening his home in Richmond, Pennsylvania, as early as 1825 as a secret way station for runaway slaves. In 1834, he helped form an association in Pennsylvania to educate free black youths. He planned for the settlement of former slaves in Ohio and for a time worked on a free black settlement in North Elba, New York, that belonged to abolitionist and friend Gerrit Smith.

By the early 1850s, however, Brown became obsessed with ending slavery at any cost. With the passage of the Kansas-Nebraska Act in 1854, allowing those territories to enter the Union as free or slave states depending on how their citizens voted, Brown traveled to Kansas and began a land war to drive slave owners out and preserve the area for abolitionism. In October 1855, he joined five of his sons, who were already in Kansas, at Osawatomie, and led the radical antislavery faction known as the "Free State" forces.

Yet Brown's main focus was not Kansas; instead, through the aid of abolitionists in Massachusetts, he was getting ready to lead an armed insurrection in Virginia, arming freed slaves and murdering slave owners. During periods of quiet in Kansas, he worked tirelessly to funnel guns and ammunition to Virginia. In 1858, using the alias Shubel Morgan, he helped 11 slaves escape in a foray into Missouri; moving them to Ontario, the group established the Free Government of Virginia and Maryland, designated Brown as commander-in-chief, and drafted a constitution that ended slavery. With this document in hand, Brown and his followers rented a farm near Harper's Ferry, Virginia (now in West Virginia), near a state ammunition arsenal, for the purpose of fomenting his revolution.

On the night of 16 October 1859, the men attacked various farms in Harper's Ferry. Entering the village, Brown and his men met fierce resistance from troops there, led by Col. Robert E. Lee. Trapped in a warehouse, Brown and his men were quickly surrounded and captured. As he was being arrested, Brown said, "I want you to understand, gentlemen . . . that I respect the rights of the poorest and weakest of colored people, oppressed by the slave system, just as much as I do those of the most wealthy and powerful. That is the idea that has moved me, and that alone." Then, he forewarned his captors, "You had better—all you people at the South—prepare yourselves for a settlement of that question that must come up for settlement sooner than you are prepared for. . . . this negro question I mean—the end of that is not yet."

Many newspapers in the South denounced the raid as a plot by radical Republicans in the North to dictate social policy in the South; and while many northerners decried Brown's violent tactics, others publicly or secretly applauded his courage. Taken to Charles Town, Brown was put on trial for his life for treason against the Commonwealth of Virginia, for conspiring with slaves in rebellion, and for murder. Wounded during the raid, Brown lay on a cot in the courtroom during his entire three day trial, which began on 27 October. Andrew Hunter, prosecutor, demanded that Brown be "arraigned, tried, found guilty, sentenced and hung, all within three days." Apparently the jury sided with Hunter; 45 minutes after retiring, they pronounced Brown guilty on all three counts. On 2 November, he was sentenced to be hanged in one month's time.

On 2 December 1859, Brown was taken from the Charles Town jail, placed in a cart, and removed to a gallows that had been specially built for his execution. He left this scribbled note: "Charlestown, Va. 2 December, 1859. I John Brown am now quite CERTAIN that the crimes of this guilty land will never be purged away; but with Blood. I had as now think, vainly flattered myself that without very much bloodshed, it might be done."

Commanding the troops from the Virginia Military Institute guarding the execution site was Thomas Jackson, later known for his heroics during the Civil War as "Stonewall" Jackson; also in the crowd was a young actor, John Wilkes Booth, who less than six years hence would make history himself.

The reporter for *The New-York Times* described the execution:

> I visited the field in which the gallows had been erected at an early hour this morning. The day was very fine and the air warm. All strangers were excluded from the town. Indeed, no railroad trains were allowed to enter during the entire day.
>
> The gallows was erected at 71/2 o'-clock, and all preparations for the execution immediately completed. The reporters who had secured the privilege of being present were allowed to enter soon after.
>
> On being summoned, Brown appeared perfectly calm and collected. He took formal leave of each of his fellow prisoners, and gave each one a quarter of a dollar as a token of remembrance. . . .
>
> He rode to the scaffold in an open wagon, seated upon his own coffin.
>
> At the gallows Brown was still perfectly cool. He made no remarks. As soon as he had mounted the scaffold the cap was put and drawn over his face.
>
> He was not standing on the drop. The Sheriff told him to get upon it. Brown said, "I cannot see—place me on it, and don't keep me waiting." He stood upon the drop nine minutes and a half when it fell. He suffered but little. After three minutes, there were no convulsions, or indications of life. At the end of twenty minutes his body was examined, and he was reported dead.

Among Southerners, Brown's death was greeted with applause and the hope that abolitionists would now stop meddling in the Southern way of life. In the North, however, Brown was remembered as a martyr and even compared to Jesus Christ. The Rev. George Barrell Cheever, a supporter of capital punishment, nonetheless denounced Brown's execution and called him the first martyr of the "Anti-Slavery Crusade." Brown's body was taken to North Elba, New York, where it was laid to rest. Within two years Americans would be marching off to fight John Brown's war, and from the lips of the northern troops would come the words, "John Brown's body lies a-mould'ring in the grave, but his soul goes marching on."

**References:** "Affairs at Charles Town. Final Preparations for the Execution. Arrests of Northern Editors. Increased Excitement," *The New-York Times,* 2 December 1859, 1; Christianson, Stephen G., "John Brown Trial: 1859" in Edward W. Knappman, ed., *Great American Trials* (Detroit: Visible Ink Press, 1994), 133–37; "Execution of John Brown. His Interview With His Wife. Scenes at the Scaffold. Profound Feeling Throughout the Northern States," *The New-York Times,* 3 December 1859, 1; Hinton, Richard Josiah, *John Brown and His Men* (New York: Funk and Wagnalls, 1894); "John Brown's Execution," *The New-York Times,* 2 December 1859, 6; National Park Service, *John Brown Raid* (Washington, DC: Office of Publications, National Park Service, U.S. Department of the Interior, 1976); Renehan, Edward J., Jr., *The Secret Six: The True Tale of the Men Who Conspired With John Brown* (New York: Crown Publishers, 1990); "The Virginia Insurgents. Affairs at Charles Town. Preparations for the Execution of Brown. Facts, Documents and Letters," *The New-York Times,* 1 December 1859, 1.

## Bruno, Giordano (1548–1600)

Italian philosopher burned to death at the end of the sixteenth century for holding heretical beliefs.

Born Filippo Bruno in the village of Nola, near Naples, Italy, Bruno entered the Dominican order at the age of 15, where he took the name he became famous with. While in the monastery, he developed heretical views, reading the works of Plato and Hermes Trismegistus (a prophet from the time of Moses who wrote the *Corpus Hermeticum*), both of whose views were controversial in their own times, and felt that Jesus was part of heaven, where persons would go after a good life. After 13 years at the monastery, he fled to Rome but was targeted by the Inquisition. Thus he left the Dominicans and went to France to lecture on various religious ideas. From 1583 to 1585 he lived at the residence of the French King Henry III's ambassador to England, Michel de Castelnau. There, Bruno wrote several works, including "Cena de le Ceneri" (The Ash Wednesday Supper), "De l'Infinito, Universo e Mondi" (On the Infinite Universe and Worlds), "De la causa, principio e uno" (Concerning the Cause, Principle, and One), and "Spaccio de la bestia trionfante" (The Expulsion of the Triumphant Beast), all published in 1584. In the first, he explained the theory of the Polish astronomer Copernicus; in the final work, he called for a religious and moral reform in the world.

When, after wandering for 16 years, Bruno returned to Rome, he was betrayed by a friend and arrested by agents of the Inquisition. He was charged with the denial of Christ's divinity, the mythical character of the Holy Writ, the belief in universal salvation at the end of time, and the salvation of the fallen angels. Quickly tried, he was found guilty and ordered to prison for seven years; there he remained, unrepentant. In 1600, he was brought once again before the judges of the Inquisition and asked if he recanted any of his beliefs. He refused, even when threatened with death by burning. Standing before the court, Bruno told the judges as they prepared to sentence him to death, "You perhaps pronounce sentence against me with a fear greater than that with which I receive it."

On the morning of 17 February 1600, after eight days of torture in which he repeatedly refused to recant his beliefs, the 51- or 52-year-old Bruno was taken to a square in Rome called the Campo dei Fiori. As British historian J. Lewis McIntyre relates from the work of one of the Company of St. John the Beheaded, also known as the Company of Mercy and Pity, which accompanied the condemned to the place of execution:

> With all charity our brethren exhorted him to repent, . . . but he remained to the end in his accursed obstinacy, his brain and intellect seething with a thousand errors and vanities. So, persevering in his obstinacy, he was led by the servants of justice to the Campo dei Fiori, there stripped, bound to a stake, and burnt alive, attended always by our Company chanting the litanies, the comforters exhorting him up to the last point to abandon his obstinacy, but in it finally he ended his miserable, unhappy life."

Historian Arthur Imerti reports that as the flames rose to him, Bruno "was shown an image of Christ, from which he averted his gaze."

In 1603, all of Bruno's works were put on the Index, the Church's listing of banned books, and Bruno was relegated to the pantheon of the forgotten. Although historians speculate that Bruno was put to death for his belief in Copernicanism, this has never been substantiated, because the records of his trial are missing from the archives on file with the Catholic Church. French historian Paul Henri Michel speculates that they were accidentally burned between 1815 and 1817, when they were moved from Paris (where Napoleon had had them housed) back to Rome.

**References:** Bruno, Giordano (Arthur D. Imerti, ed. and trans.), *The Expulsions of the Triumphant Beast* (New Brunswick, NJ: Rutgers University Press, 1964), 64; Goetz, Philip W., ed.-in-Chief, *The New Encyclopedia Britannica,* 22 vols. (Chicago: Encyclopedia Britannica, Inc., 1995), 2:580–81; Horowitz, Irving Louis, *The Renaissance Philosophy of Giordano Bruno*

(New York: Coleman-Ross, 1952); McIntyre, J. Lewis, *Giordano Bruno* (London: Macmillan and Co., Limited, 1903), 96; Michel, Paul Henri (R.E.W. Madison, trans.), *The Cosmology of Giordano Bruno* (Paris: Hermann, 1973), 18; Paterson, Antoinette Mann, *The Infinite Worlds of Giordano Bruno* (Springfield, IL: Charles C. Thomas, 1970); Yates, Francis A., "Bruno, Giordano" in Charles Coulston Gillespie, ed.-in-Chief, *Dictionary of Scientific Biography,* 4 vols. (New York: Charles Scribner's Sons, 1980–90), 1:359–44.

## Buchanan, Dr. Robert Williams (1862–1895)

His was likely the most notable trial of the last decade of the nineteenth century: Dr. Robert Buchanan was tried and found guilty for the poisoning murder (by a morphine overdose) of his wife and was put to death in the electric chair for his crime.

Buchanan was born in Halifax, Nova Scotia, in 1862, and at a young age became an apothecary's clerk. He then studied medicine in Scotland, where he received his doctoral degree and medical license. He returned to Halifax and married Anna Patterson, and they moved to New York in 1887. Apparently Buchanan was not a very good doctor, for his practice failed and he lived in poverty. In 1890 he sued his wife for divorce, which was granted that same year. At the same time, he met and married Annie Sutherland, a rich widow and a brothel owner, although he told friends that she was his housekeeper and not his wife. Within a month of their marriage he had convinced his second wife to transfer all of her holdings to his name in case of her early death. Within a year, however, she desired to return to her hometown of Newark, New Jersey, and asked Buchanan for her property back and a divorce.

On 21 April 1892, on the day that she was to return to Newark, and four days before Buchanan was to sail for Scotland, Annie Sutherland took ill. A doctor was called who administered some medication, and she stabilized. Later, a nurse witnessed Buchanan give his wife an injection, although she could not see what it was. Within a short time the second Mrs. Buchanan was in a coma, and she soon died. One of her physicians, a Dr. McIntyre, put on her death certificate that the cause of death was cerebral hemorrhage, and she was buried without an official autopsy.

Buchanan returned to Nova Scotia, where he remarried his first wife. According to crime writer Oliver Cyriax, "A tip-off from a suspicious partner of Annie [Sutherland] alerted the *New York World*. A reporter [Isaac White] interviewed Dr. McIntyre, who vouchsafed that the prime symptom of morphine poisoning [which some had suspected] was lacking; the pupils of Annie's eyes, which would have contracted to pin-points with an overdose, were normal."

What no one knew was that Buchanan had followed the case of one Carlyle Harris, a 19-year-old medical student who had murdered his wife with morphine. Exposed by the pin-point pupils of his victim's eyes, Harris was convicted of murder and executed in New York's electric chair on 8 May 1893. Through his medical training, Buchanan was aware that a mix of the chemical atropine with a morphine injection would mask the reaction in the eyes and make for the perfect crime.

Although Buchanan had given the cemetery officials strict orders not to let his wife's body be disturbed, White, the reporter, arranged for it to be exhumed and autopsied while Buchanan was out of the country. Atropine was discovered (although some sources note that it was belladonna, which like atropine masks the effects of morphine) as well as morphine, and an arrest warrant went out for the doctor.

He had returned from Nova Scotia to wrap up some business, and he was forewarned that the police were coming for him, but he was arrested before he could leave his Greenwich Village apartment.

In court, Buchanan rejected the prosecution's findings that Annie was poisoned and that he was her killer. However, witnesses were found who heard Buchanan brag about being able to mask the effects of morphine poisoning, and, in an important court decision, the prosecution was allowed to poison a cat in the court with morphine and then utilize atropine to disguise the effects. The cat died, but the point was proven and Buchanan, who took the stand and was brutally attacked by the prosecution, was found guilty and sentenced to die. His first wife tried to save his life but failed. On 1 July 1895, he was put to death in the electric chair in New York's Sing Sing Prison. A reporter for *The World,* the paper that had led to his downfall, wrote: "Rats and murderers when trapped usually die game. Buchanan died game. With his teeth tight shut and his eyes cast down he waited for death without a word. His bare leg trembled slightly as the wet electrode touched the flesh, and his fingers twitched."

Buchanan's case is lightly treated (a similar character poisons his wife using a similar method) in John Dickson Carr's 1946 work, *The Sleeping Sphinx.*

**References:** "Buchanan Put To Death; Two Electrical Shocks Needed to End the Wife-Poisoner's Life," *The New York Times,* 2 July 1895, 9; Cyriax, Oliver, *Crime: An Encyclopedia* (London: André Deutsch Ltd., 1993), 55; "Dr. Buchanan Killed; Justice, So Long Delayed by Law, Done to the Wife Murderer at Last," *The World* (New York), 2 July 1895, 1; Nash, Jay Robert, *Encyclopedia of World Crime,* 4 vols. (Wilmette, IL: CrimeBooks, Inc., 1990), 1:529–31.

## *Buchanan v. Angelone* (U.S. Supreme Court, No. 96-8400, 1998)

Supreme Court decision holding that a judge did not have to supply a jury with mitigating factors in a death-penalty case so that the jury could choose a life sentence over a recommendation of death.

Douglas Buchanan was convicted in the 1987 deaths of his father, stepmother, and two young stepbrothers in Naola, Virginia. The court then held a death-penalty hearing in which the jury was presented with both aggravating and mitigating factors, including two full days of psychiatric and other testimony as to Buchanan's troubled family background and mental and emotional problems. As the *Washington Post* later noted, "The jury instructions, however, did not order jurors to consider the mitigating evidence in its deliberations. It told them, rather, to consider 'all the evidence' and decide whether the prosecution had proven that the crime had been vile enough to warrant death." In fact, the court refused the defendant's request "to give four additional instructions on particular statutory mitigating factors and a general instruction on the concept of mitigating evidence." The jury returned a verdict of death, the trial court imposed that sentence, and the Virginia Supreme Court affirmed it. Buchanan then sued Ronald Angelone, the director of the Virginia Department of Corrections, for habeas corpus relief. The Federal District Court denied Buchanan this relief, and the Fourth Circuit affirmed that decision. The U.S. Supreme Court agreed to hear the case, and arguments were heard on 3 November 1997.

On 21 January 1998, Chief Justice William H. Rehnquist spoke for a 6-3 court (Justices Steven Breyer, John Paul Stevens, and Ruth Bader Ginsburg dissented) in holding that "the absence of instructions on the concept of mitigation and on particular statutorily defined mitigating factors did not violate the

Eighth and Fourteenth Amendments." He concluded, "The instructions here did not violate these constitutional principles. This conclusion is confirmed by the context in which the instructions were given. The court directed the jurors to base their decision on 'all the evidence' and to impose a life sentence if they believed the evidence so warranted, there was extensive testimony as to Buchanan's family background and mental and emotional problems, and counsel made detailed arguments on the mitigating evidence. Because the parties in effect agreed that there was substantial mitigating evidence and that the jury had to weigh that evidence against Buchanan's conduct in making a discretionary decision on the appropriate penalty, there is not a reasonable likelihood that the jurors understood the instructions to preclude consideration of relevant mitigating evidence."

**References:** Text of decision; "The Court and the Death Penalty," *Washington Post*, 26 January 1998, A22.

## Bundy, Theodore Robert (1946–1989)

American serial murderer put to death in Florida's electric chair in 1989.

Born illegitimate on 24 November 1946, in Burlington, Vermont, Bundy was the product of a broken home. His mother married his foster father when he was still a youngster, and Bundy took his name. (It has been rumored that his maternal grandfather was also his father.) Bundy was an extremely bright youngster and showed his intelligence by going to law school. He also joined the Republican party. Yet in his spare time he began to exhibit the signs that modern criminologists view as the first indications that a person may become a serial murderer: Bundy had a fixation with knives and tortured and killed small animals. He later also admitted that it was at this time that he began to experiment with hard-core pornography, which he later blamed for the horrible route his life was about to take.

Starting in the late 1960s, young women who fit a particular description—tall, slender, with shoulder-length brown hair—began to vanish mysteriously from the Seattle area. Yet the first recorded abductions attributed to Bundy started in 1974. At this time, a handsome young man named Ted with his arm in a cast was seen approaching young women on the street and asking for help to his car. One girl was brutally attacked and smashed in the head with a blunt instrument; she was left in a coma by her attacker. Soon, eight women were missing from the Washington-Oregon area.

At this same time, however, many knew Ted Bundy to be an outgoing, intelligent young man who held a job, attended college, had a girlfriend, and worked hard at becoming a political insider. When some of the bodies of the missing girls turned up, police were baffled by the lack of clues. Witnesses came forward to report that a young man going by the name of Ted and driving a yellow Volkswagen had used the same excuse to get them into his car right around the time of the disappearances. The Washington state police initiated the "Ted" search, but no suspect turned up.

Then, suddenly, the abductions stopped, and police were again baffled. Bundy, however, had moved his collegiate studies from Washington to Utah. It was there that a wave of murders began in earnest, and a young man in a cast was seen with the victims prior to their vanishing. On 8 November 1974, however, the spree came to a halt, when a young girl lured into a yellow Volkswagen escaped after being tied up, jumped from the moving car, and was left for dead. Nine months later, Salt Lake City police arrested a young man in a yellow Volkswagen and found handcuffs and other incriminating evidence in his car. The man arrested was Theodore Robert Bundy, a 29-year-old law student. The victim identified Bundy, and he was placed on trial for kidnapping. He asked for a trial by the judge, but he was found guilty and sentenced to 1–15 years in prison.

By this time, police agencies from Washington to Utah to Colorado were searching their books of unsolved crimes and comparing Bundy's modus operandi with cases of other missing girls. In 1977, Bundy was extradited to Colorado to stand trial for the murder of a girl in Snowmass. Soon after being sent to Colorado for trial, Bundy mysteriously escaped; captured eight days later, he escaped again on 30 December 1977. A local Colorado reporter remembered Bundy asking him which states at the time had capital punishment. He was told one of them was Florida.

On the night of 15 January 1978, a masked man broke into the house of the Chi Omega sorority on the grounds of Florida State University in Tallahassee and savagely murdered two young girls in their beds. On 9 February of that same year, a young 12-year-old girl vanished from her classroom in Jacksonville; when her body was later found, evidence indicated that she had been molested and strangled. Bundy was arrested on 16 February 1978 using the name Chris Hagen, but when questioned begged the officers to kill him. Later he admitted that he was the fugitive Ted Bundy. Quickly tried for the murders of the two college students and the young girl, Bundy was found guilty and received two death sentences in July 1979 and February 1980. He fought the convictions for the next decade, using every legal device to put off his execution.

By the end of 1988, Bundy had run out of appeals. He then issued a challenge to Florida governor Bob Martinez: spare his life, and he would confess to every murder he was suspected of and help authorities to find the missing girls. Martinez refused, set Bundy's execution date, and allowed police from agencies across the nation to question the mass killer. In a series of recorded interviews, Bundy showed where he had dumped several bodies, but he could not account for them all; in the end, although he claimed to have killed more than 30 girls, authorities believe the number to be nearer to 50 and perhaps as high as 100. Days before his scheduled execution, Bundy gave an interview in which he claimed that his life of crime was due to his experiences with hard-core pornography, and he warned others to avoid these materials at any cost. Skeptics noted that Bundy could not possibly have had contact with such materials, which were hard to come by when he was growing up.

Authorities reported that Bundy spent his last night weeping. Weak to the point that he was almost carried in to the death chamber, he went to his death quickly. Reporters said that his last words were "Give my love to my family and my friends."

**References:** Ayresworth, Hugh, *The Only Living Witness* (New York: Linden Press, 1983); Ayresworth, Hugh, *Ted Bundy: Conversations With a Killer* (New York: New American Library, 1989); Evans, Colin, "Theodore Robert Bundy Trials: 1976 & 1979" in Edward W. Knappman, ed., *Great American Trials* (Detroit: Visible Ink Press, 1994), 652–56; Gaute, J.H.H., and Robin Odell, *The New Murderers' Who's Who* (New York: International Polygonics, Ltd., 1989), 69; Larsen, Richard W., *Bundy: the Deliberate Stranger* (New York: Pocket Books, 1986).

## Burning at the Stake

Method of capital punishment in which the condemned is tied to a wooden stake, surrounded by flammable material (usually faggots or sticks of wood) assembled into a pyre, which is then lit afire and allowed to burn until the victim is consumed.

Crime historian Jay Robert Nash writes: "Fire as a method of killing people has been used through the ages. Two thousand years before Christ, King Hammurabi of Babylonia decreed burning as a punishment for anybody who destroyed a neighbor's possessions by arson. Assyrians used it as an instrument of terror in their conquest of Israel. French and Spanish inquisitors broadened and refined the ordeal. And in North America, the Puritans stoically burned 'witches' while across the woods Indians war-danced around a pyre containing whites."

Historian Geoffrey Abbott describes a particular incident:

> Over the years flames claimed the lives of at least fifty-three men and eleven women [in England], one victim being John Rogers, vicar of St. Sepulchre's Church, Newgate. He had been sentenced to death on the orders of Queen Mary for preaching forbidden sermons outside St. Paul's Church. . . . Arriving at Smithfield, he was tied to a stake, probably by the hangman Stumpleg, and the faggots were ignited. It is not known whether he was granted the merciful privilege sometimes conceded to martyrs, of having a small bag of gunpowder hung around his neck in order to speed his demise and so reduce his suffering but, like the others, he died bravely.

Considered one of the most painful forms of capital punishment save drawing and quartering, such famous people as Girolamo Savonarola, Arnold of Brescia, the protomartyr Patrick Hamilton, and the Blessed Edmund Campion have suffered a cruel death from it.

**See also:** Arnold of Brescia; Auto-da-Fe; Calas, Jean; Campion, Edmund, Blessed; Hamilton, Patrick; Savonarola, Girolamo.

**References:** Abbott, Geoffrey, *Lords of the Scaffold: A History of the Executioner* (London: Robert Hale, 1991), 167–68; Nash, Jay Robert, *Encyclopedia of World Crime*, 4 vols. (Wilmette, IL: CrimeBooks, Inc., 1990), 4:3286.

## Bywaters, Frederick Edward Francis (1902?–1923), and Edith Jessie Graydon Thompson (1894?–1923)

British murderer and murderess executed for their role in the murder of Percy Thompson, Edith Thompson's husband. The case was a cause célèbre when the two were tried in London's Old Bailey court in 1923.

Percy Thompson, a mild-mannered fellow, married Edith Jessie Graydon in 1914, when she was only 20. In 1921, they went on holiday to the Isle of Wight with a friend, Frederick Bywaters, a 19-year-old steward who had been known to the Graydon family for some time. On their return to London, Bywaters moved in with the couple, and he and Edith began a year-long romance unbeknownst to her husband. Their letters reflected boundless love for each other—a young, impressionable man of nearly 20 desperately in love with an unhappily married older woman of 28.

On 4 October 1922, as Percy and Edith returned home to their London flat from a movie, Bywaters jumped out of the dark and attacked Percy, stabbing him to death before fleeing into the night. Edith claimed at first that Percy had said he was ill and that he had collapsed and died before help could arrive. An autopsy, however, showed Percy Thompson's violent death, and after a bloody knife was found in a nearby storm drain five days after the crime, and a neighbor told police that Bywaters had been carrying on an affair with the widow, Bywaters and Edith Thompson were arrested.

Edith claimed to have had no knowledge of what Bywaters had intended to do, and Bywaters to the end supported her story, taking full responsibility for the crime. At trial, however, Edith's cold demeanor on the stand and the introduction of the incriminating letters to her young lover damned her as well. The two were found guilty, and their appeals for clemency were dismissed. Bywaters told jailers and friends, "I swear she is completely innocent. She never knew that I was going to meet them that night. . . . For her to be hanged as a criminal is too awful. She didn't commit the murder. I did. She never planned it. She never knew about it. She is innocent, absolutely innocent. I can't believe that they will hang her."

But on 9 January 1923, at the same hour, 9 A.M., that Bywaters was hanged at London's Pentonville Prison, at Holloway Prison, Thompson, in a state of total collapse, had to be carried to the gallows, setting off a firestorm of protest in England about whether a woman should be put to death at all. In any case, Thompson became the first woman hanged in Britain since 1908, and, with the execution of Ruth Ellis in 1955, one of the last.

Her counsel later said of Edith Thompson, "She was a vain woman and an obstinate one. Also her imagination was highly developed, but it failed to show her the mistake she was making [in testifying]. . . . In short, Mrs. Thompson was hanged for immorality."

**References:** "Do Something Desperate, Darling" in *Crime and Punishment: The Illustrated Crime Encyclopedia,* 28 vols. (Westport, CT: H. S. Stuttman, 1994), 4:458–65; Dudley, Ernest, *Bywaters and Mrs. Thompson* (London: Odhams Press, 1953); Frederick Bywaters/Edith Thompson Criminal Records, Public Record Office, Kew, England; Young, Filson, ed., *Trial of Frederick Bywaters and Edith Thompson* (Toronto: Canada Law Book Company, Ltd., 1923).

## Calas, Jean (1698–1762)

French execution victim whose probable innocence of the crime for which he died led many notables of the time, including the French writer Voltaire, to call for an end to capital punishment.

Calas was born in Lacabarède, France, on 19 March 1698. A Huguenot and cloth merchant, he toiled in anonymity until 1761. On 13 October of that year, his eldest son, Marc-Antoine, was found hanged in his father's warehouse. Because rumors swirled that his son was considering converting to Catholicism, Calas, a Protestant, was suspected of murdering him. His entire family was arrested, and he was put on trial. The Parlement of Toulouse, sitting as a court of justice, found against him by a vote of eight to five and condemned him to be broken on the wheel and then burned to death at the stake.

On 9 March 1762 the sentence was carried out. However, even from the beginning, doubts about his guilt were voiced. After his death, the philosopher Voltaire looked into the case and felt that a great injustice had been committed. In his 1763 work, *Traité sur la tolérance* ("Treatise on Tolerance"), Voltaire documented how Calas's son had committed suicide. With Voltaire's assistance, Calas's widow petitioned the courts to review the case, and on 9 March 1765, exactly three years to the day that he had been put to death, 50 French judges found that Calas's son had committed suicide and that he had been wrongfully put to death. The case, one of the best known in European law, led to the abolishment or the curtailment of the death penalty in many European countries soon after.

**References:** Jones, David A., *History of Criminology: A Philosophical Perspective* (Westport, CT: Greenwood Press, 1986), 5; Nixon, Edna, *Voltaire and the Calas Case* (London: Gollancz, 1961).

## Campion, Edmund, Blessed (1540–1581)

English Roman Catholic Jesuit priest and martyr, put to death for refusing to recant his religion.

Born in London and educated at Oxford, Campion left that university when he could not reconcile with Anglicanism. He traveled to Ireland in 1569, to Douay, France, in 1571, and finally to Rome; there he entered the Society of Jesus in 1573, where he was ordained a priest five years later. In 1580, he and Robert Persons were the first Jesuits to be sent to England. Campion was at liberty for only a year, spending his time lecturing on Roman Catholicism and producing many converts to the cause. His Latin thesis in pamphlet form defending his religion and denouncing Anglicanism, *Decem rationes* ("Ten Reasons"), caused a sensation when he released it to the public during a service in St. Mary's, Oxford, on 27 June 1581.

That same year he was arrested while preaching at Lyford Grange and thrown into the Tower of London. But he refused to recant his beliefs before Queen Elizabeth herself, even if his life were spared. Nor did torture on the rack get him to recant. Tried for sedition (on the trumped up charge that he was conspiring to overthrow the queen) and convicted, he was executed by drawing and quartering at Tyburn on 1 December 1581. Editors Herbert J. Thurston and Donald Attwater wrote, "On the scaffold . . . Edmund publicly prayed for [the queen]: 'Your queen and my queen, unto whom I wish a long reign with all prosperity.'" As he was torn apart, his blood splashed onto the garments of a witness, Henry Walpole, who was so moved by the sight that he became a Jesuit and later suffered a similar martyrdom for his religion. Campion was beatified in 1886 and canonized by Pope Paul VI in 1970 as one of the Forty Martyrs of England and Wales. Campion Hall on the campus of Oxford University in England is named for him.

**References:** Campion, Leslie, *The Family of Edmund Campion* (London: Research Publishing Company, 1975); Cooper, Thompson, "Campion, Edmund" in Sir Leslie Stephens and Sir Sidney Lee, eds., *The Dictionary of National Biography,* 10 vols., 12 supplements (Oxford, England: Oxford University Press, 1917–1993), 3:850–54; Law, M. D., and M. Vibart Dixon, man. eds., *Chambers' Encyclopaedia,* 15 vols. (London: International Learning Systems Corporation Limited, 1970), 2:808; Thurston, Herbert J., and Donald Attwater, eds., *Butler's Lives of the Saints,* 4 vols. (Westminster, MD: Christian Classics, 1988), 4:468.

## Casement, Sir Roger David (1864–1916)

British consular official and Irish nationalist executed on a charge of treason for his part in the Easter Rebellion of 1916.

According to a statement delivered to the British court that would sentence him to death, Casement was born in the village of Kingstown, in County Dublin, on 1 September 1864 to Protestant parents. After a common school education, he went to Africa in 1892 as a traveling commissioner in the Nigeria Coast Protectorate but soon entered the British consular service. He eventually served as the British consul at Lourenço Marques in 1895, at Luanda in 1898, and at Boma in 1900. In 1903, he was sent to investigate human rights abuses in the Upper Congo among workers who collected rubber from trees there; Casement's report bitterly condemned their treatment. Two years later he was sent to Brazil, where he served as British consul at Santos, Pará, and general consul at Rio De Janeiro. In 1910, he again investigated human rights abuses, this time among the rubber workers of the Peruvian Amazon Company. For this work, he was knighted in 1911.

After a distinguished career in the service of the British, Casement returned to Ireland. In the years after the turn of the century, he had quietly become an ardent Irish nationalist, opposed to the British influence in his homeland. He subsequently joined extremist groups, among them the Sinn Fein (Irish: "We Ourselves" or "Ourselves Alone"), which advocated complete independence for the Irish island. In 1914, with the outbreak of World War I, Casement went to Germany via the United States and solicited financial assistance as well as further German help in defeating the British and thus liberating his country. While in Berlin he composed *The Crime Against Europe,* a 1914 work that denounced Britain's rule in Ireland.

Historian W. J. Maloney, who collected Casement's writings and documents relating to his treason case, comments on the work: "This is perhaps the most famous of Casement's writings. It is recorded in the British Blue Book 'Documents Relating to Sinn Fein.' British commentators have regarded it as Casement's crime against England. To the Irish it was a startling incursion into foreign policy, a field strange to them, where they followed with misgivings. As Casement tells in the preface, this book comprises a series of articles written at intervals between August 1911 and December 1913."

In Germany, Casement's attempt to recruit an Irish brigade from among Irish prisoners of war held by the Germans was unsuccessful. Convinced Germany would send little aid, he returned to Ireland by German submarine, hoping to postpone the rebellion until a more propitious time. Instead, he was captured by the British, tried in London for treason, and hanged on 3 August 1916. Prior to his execution, diaries in his handwriting appeared; they showed that Casement had committed many homosexual acts, and all sympathy for his plight to spare him from the hangman's noose ended. Although many who sided with him claim that the diaries are clever forgeries, experts familiar with his handwriting and style of penmanship declare them to be authentic, and they were deposited in the Public Record Office in London in 1958.

In February 1965 Casement's body was returned to Ireland, and following a state funeral attended by Irish president Eamon de Valera, he was interred in Glasnevin Cemetery in Dublin. The Garden of Remembrance in Parnell Square, Dublin, in the shape of a cross, is dedicated to those who died in the struggle for Irish independence, including Casement.

**References:** Copy of Casement's manuscript, "The Crime Against Europe," and official transcript of *In the High Court of Justice, King's Bench Division: Rex v. Sir Roger David Casement* in the W. J. Maloney Historical Papers, records on Sir Roger Casement, New York Public Library; "Execution of Casement," *The Times* (London), 4 August 1916, 4; Gwynn, Denis, *The Life and Death of Roger Casement* (London, England: J. Cape, 1930); Gwynn, Denis, *Traitor or Patriot: The Life and Death of Roger Casement* (New York: J. Cape and H. Smith, 1931); Inglis, Brian, *Roger Casement* (London: Hoffer and Stoughton, 1973); Noyes, Alfred, *The Accusing Ghost; or, Justice for Casement* (London, England: Gollancz, 1957); Reid, B. L., *The Lives of Roger Casement* (New Haven, CT: Yale University Press, 1976); Sawyer, Roger, *Casement: The Flawed Hero* (London: Routledge & Kegan Paul, 1984); Singleton-Gates, Peter, *The Black Diaries: An Account of Roger Casement's Life and Times With a Collection of His Diaries and Public Writings* (Paris, France: Olympia Press, 1959).

## The Catherine Wheel

Method of capital punishment; a device utilized for torture and named after Saint Catherine of Alexandria, who flourished in the fourth century in Alexandria, Egypt, and was its first victim. In its use, the condemned is strapped to a wheel, which is lowered onto another with sharp metallic spikes projecting outwards; as the victim is dropped, the blades disembowel him or her until death occurs.

Saint Catherine, an Egyptian theologian, protested the persecution of Christians under the Roman Emperor Maxentius. Maxentius had 50 noted scholars argue with her over religious philosophy, but instead she convinced them of her arguments, and Maxentius had them each put to death. For Catherine, he reserved the most brutal treatment: she was tied to a wooden wheel and lowered onto spikes. However, according to legend, the wheel broke, the blades were thrown aside, and Catherine was spared this brutal death. Angered that he could not kill her, Maxentius had Catherine beheaded. Legend further relates that as her head was sliced off, milk instead of blood flowed from the trunk.

The Catherine Wheel, or models based on it, were used on the European continent during the Middle Ages. In France, the wheel had on it the cross of St. Andrews; in Germany an iron bar was used to break the arms and legs of the condemned to facilitate further torture and accelerate death.

**See also:** Breaking on the Wheel.
**References:** Abbott, Geoffrey, *Lords of the Scaffold: A History of the Executioner* (London: Robert Hale, 1991), 148–55; Nash, Jay Robert, *Encyclopedia of World Crime*, 4 vols. (Wilmette, IL: CrimeBooks, Inc., 1990), 4:3287.

## Cavell, Edith Louisa (1865–1915)

British nurse executed by the German army for rescuing Allied soldiers in occupied Belgium during World War I.

Born in Swardeston, Norfolk, England, on 4 December 1865, Cavell was the eldest daughter of the Rev. Frederick Cavell, the vicar of Swardeston, and his wife Louisa Sophia Cavell. She entered the nursing profession in 1895, when she began studies at the London Hospital. Two years later she became the head of emergency typhoid services at a special typhoid hospital in Maidstone. Over the next eight years she worked in London hospitals, including two infirmaries.

In 1906, a Dr. Depage requested that she work at the Berkendael Institute at Brussels, where she was appointed the first matron and where, according to one source, "she improved the standard of nursing." Cavell worked at the hospital until August 1914, when the tides of World War I swept German troops into Belgium in preparation for the invasion of France. At first, the Germans allowed Cavell to remain at her post, attending as she did to the medical care of both German and Allied soldiers. Later, when the Allies were forced to leave behind many of their wounded during the evacuation of Belgium, Cavell became part of the clandestine route to freedom for them after their recovery. They were at times sheltered in the Berkendael Institute, where Cavell, funded with money from a wealthy Belgian named Phillipe Baucq, aided them.

The Germans became suspicious of her, and on 5 August 1915 she was arrested with other nurses and placed in the prison at St. Giles. She had been warned that arrest was imminent, but had told a friend, "Escape for me is futile and unthinkable." When told by the German authorities that 35 other nurses and aid workers had been arrested with her, she quickly confessed that she was the brains of the operation, taking full responsibility. As she later wrote in a letter from her cell, "Had I not helped, they would have been shot."

Cavell was placed on trial and, with four other Belgians, including Baucq, found guilty of aiding and abetting the enemy and sentenced to death. Yet at the same time there began a massive propaganda campaign in England to call attention to the fact that a woman was being put to death. Attempts by British as well as American diplomats to intercede with the German authorities failed, and the sentence was carried out on the morning of 12 October 1915. Cavell biographer Pamela Bright writes, "At her trial, she had worn a plain blue dress and dreary hat reserved for Sundays rather than her uniform, as this might have compromised both her school and her profession, but on the day of her execution she put these aside for uniform. She was ready at five o'clock in the morning, but it was six before the German guards came for her. They drove her to the *Tir National* [a Belgian national rifle range]. When her turn came, she was led to the post, tied tightly to it and had her eyes bandaged. Also led forward at the same time was Phillipe Baucq."

When both had been prepared, Cavell spoke her last words: "Standing, as I do, in the view of God and eternity, I realize that patriotism is not enough. I must have no hatred or bitterness towards anyone." Two volleys then rang out, and thus it was that Edith Cavell met her death. A cartoon later popular in England shows a fainting Cavell, clad in her nurse's attire, being dispatched by a single shot from a German officer's gun after the firing squad refused to execute a woman—but it was in fact a myth. Her body was returned to her homeland, and she was buried in Norwich next to the Norwich Cathedral.

At the memorial service in London, held just after her execution, one speaker rose and, holding a wreath, yelled to the crowd, "Who will avenge the death of this splendid English woman?" However, no one in the German high command or government was ever prosecuted after the end of the war. Years later, a statue in Cavell's memory was situated at St. Martin's Place near Trafalgar Square in London, and Mount Edith Cavell, an 11,000 foot peak in Jasper National Park in Alberta, Canada, bears her name. Executed by the Germans as a traitor, she nonetheless became a martyr to the Allied powers, and her death, while militarily proper (spies and others caught helping the enemy can be shot in time of warfare), was a political and psychological blunder on the part of the Germans. It allowed the Allies to brand the Germans as fiends, and it increased recruitment in England.

**References:** Bright, Pamela, "Nurse Cavell" in Peter Young, ed.-in-Chief, *The Marshall Cavendish Encyclopedia of World War I*, 11 vols., 1 index (New York: Marshall Cavendish, 1986), 1:800–04; Clowes, Peter, "A Fanatically Selfless Sense of Duty Drove nurse Edith Cavell to Harbor Allied Soldiers Behind Enemy Lines" *Military History, 13:3* (August 1996), 18, 73–74; Gascoigne, Bamber, *Encyclopedia of Britain* (New York: Macmillan Publishing Company, 1993), 119; Ginsburg, Benedict William, "Cavell, Edith Louisa" in Sir Leslie Stephens and Sir Sidney Lee, eds., *The Dictionary of National Biography,* 10 vols., 12 supplements (Oxford, England: Oxford University Press, 1917–1993), 2:100–01; Goetz, Philip W., ed.-in-Chief, *The New Encyclopedia Britannica,* 22 vols. (Chicago: Encyclopedia Britannica, Inc., 1995), 2:974; Ryder, Rowland, *Edith Cavell* (New York: Stein and Day, 1975).

## Ceausescu, Nicolae (1918–1989)

Romanian dictator executed with his wife Elena Petrescu Ceausescu for "grave crimes" against the Romanian people, who finally rose up against him and his *Securitate* (security force), which had held them in virtual slavery for over 20 years.

Ceausescu was born in the village of Scornicesti, Romania, on 26 January 1918. During his youth he was a leading member of the Romanian Communist Youth movement and was imprisoned twice (in 1936 and 1940) for his Communist activities. In 1939 he married Elena Petrescu (1919–1989). While in prison, Ceausescu befriended and became an intimate of fellow Communist Gheorghe Gheorghiu-Dej, who after the end of World War II led Romania in a Communist revolution and went on to become the head of the country (1952–1965). Near the end of the war, Ceausescu escaped from prison and served as secretary of the Union of Communist Youth (1944–1945). In the postwar Romanian government, he served as agriculture minister and then as deputy minister of the Romanian Armed Forces. When Gheorghiu-Dej took office in 1952, his compatriot Ceausescu became one of the most powerful men in the nation, with a seat in the Romanian Politburo and on the Secretariat. With Gheorghiu-Dej's death in March 1965, Ceausescu became the head of the Romanian Communist party, serving as first secretary. Four months later, he consolidated his power within the party when he was named general secretary and, in December 1967, he was named president, effectively controlling all major government posts.

Ceausescu's rise to power began a 24-year reign of terror against the Romanian people that was exceptional even for Eastern Europe (except for nearby Albania). Although he remained a strong friend of the Soviet Union in this period, he was also staunchly independent, meeting with Western leaders and criticizing Soviet moves such as the Soviet invasions of Czechoslovakia in 1968 and Afghanistan in 1979. However, his secret police, the *Securitate,* became the most hated in the world. Dissension was abolished, and Elena Ceausescu served, along with other members of the Ceausescu family, in the government. Hatred of the family grew as the years passed.

On 17 December 1989, a small demonstration against the faltering Romanian economy by people in the small village of Timisoara (pronounced Tim-ish-wara) escalated into a full-blown revolution. Ceausescu ordered his *Securitate* troops to fire on the demonstrators if they did not disperse; when the troops followed these orders, killing an unknown number of people, the survivors began to fight the government troops with unaccustomed ferocity. Dissidents in the capital of Bucharest, buoyed by the resistance and fierce fighting, took to the streets and began to call for an end to the Ceausescu dictatorship.

When Ceausescu, long isolated from the people, stepped onto the balcony of the presidential palace to deliver his annual Christmas address to the people below, he was surprised to hear heckling, jeering, and calls for his overthrow. Panicked, Ceausescu called in more *Securitate* troops to fight the people in the streets and restore order. Army soldiers, once loyal, turned on the government and battled with the *Securitate* in the streets. When the protesters reached the presidential palace, Ceausescu and his wife fled through an underground tunnel to a helicopter, which flew them to one of his vacation chateaus. It was there that the Romanian army, once devoted to the Ceausescus, turned on them and put them under arrest.

Brought before a tribunal consisting of army leaders, Ceausescu and his wife were found guilty of committing "grave crimes" against the Romanian people, led into a courtyard, and shot. Bucharest Radio confirmed that the Ceausescus had been executed by firing squad during the Christmas holiday. The announcer intoned, "Oh, what wonderful news on this Christmas evening. The Anti-Christ is dead." Thus, Nicolae Ceausescu became the only Eastern European dictator to be put to death by his own people with the collapse of the former Soviet Union and communist rule in Europe.

**References:** Behr, Edward, *Kiss the Hand You Cannot Bite: The Rise and Fall of the Ceausescus* (New York: Villard Books, 1991); Fischer, Mary Ellen, *Nicolae Ceausescu and the Romanian Political Leadership: Nationalism and Personalization of Power* (Saratoga Springs, NY: Skidmore College, 1983); Goetz, Philip W., ed.-in-chief, *The New Encyclopedia Britannica,* 22 vols. (Chicago: Encyclopedia Britannica, Inc., 1995), 3:1; *Nicolae Ceausescu: Builder of Modern Romania and International Statesman* (Oxford, England: Pergamon, 1983); Powers, Charles T., "Ceausescu: Despotism Turned to Madness," *The Miami Herald,* 24 December 1989, 1C, 4C; "Romanian Dictator Executed: Ceausescu, wife shot after trial," *The Miami Herald,* 26 December 1989, 1.

## Charles Stuart, King of England (1600–1649)

King of Great Britain and Ireland (1625–49), and the key player in the English Civil War, which toppled him from the throne and cost him his life.

Born on 19 November 1600 at Dunfermline, Scotland, he was the second son of James I of England (also James V of Scotland) and Anne of Denmark, and grandson of Mary Stuart, Queen of Scots. Named as the Duke of York in 1605, Charles became heir to the English throne upon the death of his older brother Henry Frederick in 1612. Charles was betrothed to Henrietta Maria, the daughter of Henry IV of France, whom he married after taking the throne upon his father's death in 1625.

Almost from the beginning of his reign, Charles ruled with an iron hand, believing that Parliament had limited powers and he was in charge of the nation's affairs and finances. When Parliament refused to grant him the monetary resources necessary to raise an army against France, he dissolved it. A second Parliament was just as quickly dissolved. In 1628, short of supplies, Charles was forced to call a third Parliament. After granting the king the reserves he requested, the members drew up the "Petition of Right," a statement of Parliament's constitutional claims, which Charles signed in protest. In it, he promised never again to raise money without the consent of the Parliament, not to imprison anyone for refusing to pay an illegal tax, and not to dissolve Parliament under martial law. However, when a fourth Parliament in 1629 refused to go along with Charles's attempt to levy taxes, he dissolved it. By 1634, Charles once again needed funds for the military and, without the consent of Parliament, levied a tax on ships, first from seaports and later from inland counties. Resistance to this policy sowed the seeds for later insurrection.

When Charles tried to force Scotland to accept the doctrines of the Church of England, those opposed to the policy, called Covenanters, raised an army that defeated Charles's army and forced him to sign the Treaty of Berwick in 1639. His coffers exhausted, Charles was forced to call a fifth Parliament in 1640, but when members began to compile letters of grievance before they would grant tax raises, Charles dissolved it and prosecuted some of the members. Raising money for another army that he sent into Scotland to subdue the Covenanters (which was badly defeated in what is known as the Second Bishop's War), Charles called a Parliament that is noted in history as the Long Parliament. It sat, regardless of Charles's desires, for twenty years. One of its key accomplishments was the drawing up of the document known as the "Grand Remonstrance" (22 November 1641), which enumerated Charles's past faults, explained the reforms achieved by the Long Parliament, and listed the members' outstanding grievances against the king. In June 1642, the Long Parliament was angered further by Charles's rejection of its demands for reform (known as the "Nineteen Propositions"), which then precipitated the outbreak of wholesale rebellion against the crown.

This insurrection, known as the English Civil War (1642–1645), saw the Royalist forces confront those backing the Parliamentarians at the battles of Edge Hill, Marston Moor, where Oliver Cromwell helped defeat the king's army, and Naseby, where Charles's forces were routed. The king then surrendered to the Scottish and was turned over to the Parliamentarians. Although he escaped for a time, he was recaptured on the Isle of Wight and charged with high treason. The House of Lords refused to participate in the trial, but the House of Commons set up a court to try the king. Brought before a tribunal of 67 judges on 20 January 1649, Charles denied the court's authority to try him for anything. Found guilty of treason against the people, he was sentenced to be beheaded.

On 20 January 1649, Charles was led from his cell in the Tower of London to the area outside the walled fort where men were executed (women were executed inside the walls of the Tower). In his "account of the Execution of Charles I," editor and historian James Harvey Robinson relates Charles's last moments on the scaffold:

> To the executioner he said, "I shall say but very short prayers, and when I thrust out my hands—"
>
> Then he called to the bishop for his cap, and having put it on, asked the executioner, "Does my hair trouble you?"

and the executioner desired him to put it under his cap, which as he was doing by the help of the bishop and the executioner, he turned to the bishop and said, "I have a good cause, and a gracious God on my side."

The bishop said, "There is but one stage more, which, though turbulent and troublesome, yet is a very short one . . . It will carry you from earth to heaven . . . to a crown of glory . . . "

Then the king asked the executioner, "Is my hair well?"

And taking off his cloak and George [the Order of the Garter, bearing the figure of St. George], he delivered his George to the bishop . . .

Then putting on his doublet and being in his waistcoat, he put on his cloak again, and looking upon the block [where he would place his head], said to the executioner, "You must set it fast."

THE EXECUTIONER: "It is fast, sir."

KING: "It might have been a little higher."

EXECUTIONER: "It can be no higher, sir."

KING: "When I put out my hands this way, then . . . "

Then having said a few words to himself, as he stood with hands and eyes lifted up, immediately stooping down he laid his neck upon the block; and the executioner, again putting his hair under his cap, his Majesty, thinking he had been going to strike, bade him, "Stay for the sign."

EXECUTIONER: "Yes, I will, as it please your Majesty."

After a very short pause, his Majesty stretching forth his hands, the executioner at one blow severed his head from his body; which being held up and showed to the people, was with his body put into a coffin covered with black velvet and carried into his lodging.

His blood was taken up by divers persons for the different ends; by some as trophies of the villainy, by others as relics of a martyr.

He was buried a week later in the Royal Chapel of St. George at Windsor Palace.

Ten days after Charles was executed, his alleged diary was published under the title *Eikon Basilike* [Greek: "The Royal Image"]: *The Pourtraicture of His Sacred Majestie in His Solitudes and Sufferings*, although some years later John Gauden, the Bishop of Worcester, claimed to have written it himself. At the time of its release, however, John Milton was commissioned by Parliament to answer it, which he did with his *Eikonoklastes* [Greek: "Imagebreaker"] (1649).

Charles's death was the beginning of constitutional monarchy in England. His eldest son, Charles, was crowned Charles II in 1660 in what has been called the Restoration and reigned until 1685. The men who signed Charles's death warrant have been referred to in history as "regicides." Among these men are Edward Whalley, John Dixwell, Thomas Pride, and William Goffe. After the Restoration of the Stuart dynasty through Charles II, many of those who had sentenced Charles to death were hunted down and themselves executed; three, including Oliver Cromwell and William Bradshaw, who had died in the intervening years, were exhumed, hung at Tyburn (the main place for executions) in London, and nailed to a bridge for their bodies to decay. A statue of Charles I atop his horse is situated near that of Admiral Horatio Nelson in Trafalgar Square in London.

**References:** Ashley, Maurice, *The Battle of Naseby and the Fall of King Charles I* (New York: St. Martin's Press, 1992); Bennett, Martyn, *The English Civil War, 1640–1649* (London, England: Longman Group Limited, 1995), 8–16; Donaldson, Norman, and Betty Donaldson, *How Did They Die?* (New York: St. Martin's Press, 1980), 64–65; Gardiner, Samuel Rawson, "Charles I" in Sir Leslie Stephens and Sir Sidney Lee, eds., *The Dictionary of National Biography,* 10 vols., 12 supplements (Oxford, England: Oxford University Press, 1917–1993), 4:67–84; Perrinchief, Richard, *The Royal Martyr: or,* *the Life and Death of King Charles* (London: Printed by J. M. for R. Royston, Bookseller, 1676); Robinson, James Harvey, ed., *Readings in European History,* 2 vols. (Boston: Athenaeum, 1906), 2:244–45; The trial of "Charles Steward (Stuart)" is covered in some length in Hamilton, William Douglas, ed., *Calendar of State Papers, Domestic Series, of the Reign of Charles I. 1648–49 (including undated Petitions, etc.), Preserved in Her Majesty's Public Record Office* (London, England: Her Majesty's Stationary Office, 1893), 350–53; and Nalson, John, *A True Copy of the Journal of the High-Court of Justice for the Tryal of King Charles I. Taken by J. Nalson, LL.D., Jan. 4, 1683* (Dublin, Ireland: Printed for R. Gunne, 1731).

## Cheever, the Rev. George Barrell (1807–1890)

American clergyman and reformer, noted nineteenth century advocate for capital punishment.

Born in Hallowell, Maine, on 17 April 1807, he was the son of Nathaniel Cheever, a bookseller, and Charlotte (nee Barrell) Cheever. He graduated from Bowdoin College in 1825 and took a divinity degree from the Andover Theological Seminary in 1830. Eight years later he became the pastor at the Allen Street Presbyterian Church in New York City, and from 1846 to 1867 was the pastor of the Church of the Puritans in that same city. During this period he was noted for antislavery diatribes to his parishioners; from 1845 to 1846 he edited the New York *Evangelist,* a religious newspaper, and he later wrote for the New York *Observer* and New York *Independent,* two now-defunct religious dailies.

With the end of the Civil War, Cheever turned his attentions toward other reform movements. His chief target was the movement against capital punishment, which was called the antigallows movement. A lively and forceful speaker who debated many of his opponents, Cheever became the leading advocate of the death penalty in the United States during the last half of the nineteenth century. According to one of his biographers, historian Frederick T. Persons, Cheever wrote 23 volumes, 50 pamphlets, and uncounted speeches. Among these is the little known 1846 work "A Defense of Capital Punishment." In his better known work, *Punishment By Death: Its Authority and Expediency* (1849), Cheever reproduces his argument from a debate with capital punishment opponent John O'Sullivan:

> I have shown that this penalty is necessary for the restraint of crime and the protection of society, I shall now show that the proposed abolition of it is unjust and inhuman to the last degree. It is a policy, the cruelty and barbarism of which is susceptible of a perfect demonstration. It introduces the element of inhumanity into the very education of society. Your jurisprudence is a most important part of your education for the community. It trains the common conscience. But in the abolition of this penalty, you occasion a general degradation of the moral sense; you teach that there is no difference between the guilt of murder, and that of mere forgery and stealing. You lessen man's estimate of the sacredness of human life, and you are unconsciously training men's passions for the cruelty of murder. You degrade the whole subject and science of morals. . . . You take away the strong security of your police, and you expose the lives of your jail-keepers to imminent hazard. . . . Who indeed, what public servant, either in this city [New York] or in London, would dare plunge into the recesses of crime to ferret out the villain, if the strong fear of this penalty did not go before him?"

A prolific writer and speaker on many issues of his day, Cheever died almost anonymously in Englewood, New Jersey, on 1 October 1890.

**See also:** The Bible on Capital Punishment, Position of.

**References:** Cheever, George B., *Punishment By Death: Its Authority and Expediency* (New York: John Wiley, 1849), 280–81; Persons, Frederick T., "Cheever, George Barrell" in Dumas Malone, et al., eds., *Dictionary of American Biography,* 10 vols., 10 supplements (New York: Charles Scribner's Sons, 1930–95), 2:48–49.

## Chessman, Caryl Whittier (1921–1960)

His was the case that most likely led to the abolition of capital punishment in the United States in the 1960s and 1970s, but he did not live to see it.

Chessman, a distant relative of John Greenleaf Whittier, was born in St. Joseph, Michigan, on 27 May 1921, the only son of Serl Whittier Chessman, a laborer, and Hallie (nee Cottle) Chessman. His father was a failure who could not support his family, and Caryl turned to a life of crime at an early age. Arrested at age 16, he was sent to a reformatory. Over the years, he served time for assault and armed robbery. However, he had an IQ of 136, and in prison he taught shorthand and became an accomplished writer.

In January 1948, the 27-year-old Chessman was released from California's Folsom Prison. Just six weeks into his parole, he was arrested in Los Angeles as the suspected Red Light Bandit, who had utilized the red light of a police car to accost several woman and force them to perform sex acts on him. Several witnesses identified him as the bandit, a wire (used for tying up his victims) and a gun were found in his possession, and he confessed, although he later claimed that the confession was exacted under torture. Chessman was charged with 18 felonies.

About 15 years earlier, after the 1932 kidnapping of Charles Lindbergh, Jr., California had enacted the "Little Lindbergh" law, which mandated the death penalty for those who kidnapped a person and forced him or her to commit violent acts. Chessman was charged with crimes under the "Little Lindbergh" law, making him subject to death in the gas chamber.

When his trial began in April 1948, Chessman decided to represent himself; Judge Charles Fricke tried to dissuade him, to no avail. During questioning, Chessman swaggered and inflamed the jury against him. When he tried to show inconsistencies in some of the witnesses' testimonies, they named him in court as the bandit. After only three days of deliberations, the jury found Chessman guilty of 17 counts and recommended death. The following month, the court reporter died, leaving many of his court notes untranscribed. At sentencing, Chessman asked for a new trial, as the court record was unusable, but the judge declined and sentenced him to death.

Chessman served a total of 12 years on death row, at that time a record. From his cell in San Quentin, he pumped out detailed legal analyses and appeals that to this day impress legal scholars for their legal thought and precision. His first appeal argued that he deserved a new trial based on the shoddy transcript; Judge Fricke claimed that a transcript prepared by the reporter's family was sufficient. The U.S. Supreme Court agreed in 1949. Starting in 1952, Chessman received the first of eight stays of execution from various courts; each time, the U.S. Supreme Court vacated them.

During his years on death row, Chessman began to write several books, including *Cell 2455 Death Row: A Condemned Man's Own Story.* Chessman also became a celebrity. Leaders from around the world stepped forward to call for leniency, and two million people signed a petition. According to historian Carl Sifakis: "Protests came from all levels of society. Millions of persons in Brazil, 2.5 million in Sao Paulo alone, and thousands more in Switzerland, signed petitions pleading for his life. The Queen of Belgium made a special plea for Chessman, as did Aldous Huxley, Pablo Cassals, Eleanor Roosevelt, Dr. Karl Menninger, Arthur Koestler, Andre Maurois, and François Mauriac. Added to those names were Max Ascoli, Harry Elmer Barnes, Ray Bradbury, Norman Corwin, William Inge, Norman Mailer, Dwight MacDonald, Clifford Odets, Christopher Isherwood, Carey McWilliams, Billy Graham, Harry Golden and Robert Frost."

California governor Edmund "Pat" Brown originally refused a stay but changed his mind on the advice of his son, later governor and presidential candidate Jerry Brown. Brown ordered a 60-day stay to allow Chessman to appeal further. On 5 May 1960, however, with all stays exhausted, Brown refused to intervene further. As Chessman was led from his cell into the gas chamber, his lawyers were obtaining a record ninth stay, this time from federal judge Louis E. Goodman. Goodman instructed his secretary to call San Quentin and order a halt to the execution. But as she dialed the number, she missed a digit, and called the wrong number. By the time she had confirmed the correct number and phoned the prison, the pellets of cyanide gas had already been dropped. Goodman turned to Chessman's attorneys and simply said, "It's too late."

Chessman had walked unaided into the gas chamber. He was strapped down, and pellets of cyanide gas were dropped into a vat of acid below his seat. In a prearranged signal with a newspaperwoman, he began to shake his head violently, the sign that he was suffering. After holding his breath, he succumbed to the fumes. Within a minute, he was dead. The news of his execution brought riots around the world, and attacks on U.S. embassies in several nations were reported.

Those who opposed Chessman's execution argued that Chessman was innocent; that he was denied a fair trial; that 12 years on death row constituted cruel and unusual punishment, forbidden by the Constitution. In "The Caryl Chessman Case: A Legal Analysis," an article that appeared in the *Minnesota Law Review* in 1960, the authors argued that "Chessman was accorded all of his rights under the law, that the complexity of the legal issues did not warrant twelve years of litigation, and that judicial indecision was the principal factor which accounted for the years of delay." Actor Alan Alda portrayed Chessman in the 1977 television movie, *Kill Me If You Can*.

**See also:** Brown, Edmund Gerald ("Pat").

**References:** Ames, Walter, "Chessman Denies Guilt as He Dies" *Los Angeles Times,* 3 May 1960, 1; Averbach, Albert, and Charles Price, eds., *The Verdicts Were Just: Eight Famous Lawyers Present Their Most Memorable Cases* (Rochester, NY: Lawyer's Cooperative Publishing Co., 1968); Evans, Colin, "Caryl Chessman Trial: 1948" in Edward W. Knappman, ed., *Great American Trials* (Detroit: Visible Ink Press, 1994), 431–34; Fisher, Galen R., "Chessman, Caryl Whittier" in Dumas Malone, et al., eds., *Dictionary of American Biography,* 10 vols., 10 supplements (New York: Charles Scribner's Sons, 1930–95), 6:110–12; Largo, Andrew O. comp., *Caryl Whittier Chessman, 1921–1960: Essay and Critical Bibliography* (San Jose, CA: Bibliographic Information Center for the Study of Political Science, 1971); Note, "The Caryl Chessman Case: A Legal Analysis," *Minnesota Law Review,* 44:5 (April 1960), 941; Sifakis, Carl, *The Encyclopedia of American Crime* (New York: Facts on File, 1982), 142.

## Childers, Robert Erskine (1870–1922)

English-Irish writer and revolutionary, member of the Irish Republican Army, executed by the British by firing squad for treason against England. Childers's biographer Jim Ring wrote of him that he "was a man around whom legends gather and myths cling."

Born in London on 25 June 1870, he was the son of Robert Caesar Childers, a scholar who served as secretary to the governor of Ceylon (now Sri Lanka), and Anna (nee Barton) Childers, the offspring of an Irish family with a long history in that nation. Erskine Childers was but six years old when his father, a professor at University College in London, died. When his mother died a few years later, he was raised by an aunt and uncle in Ireland. Thus he came to know and love Ireland and become intertwined with its history and fate.

Childers was educated at Haileybury College and Trinity College in Cambridge. A first cousin of the English politician Hugh Childers, he served as a clerk in the English House of Commons from 1895 to 1910, during which time he served with the British Army in South Africa during the Boer War. Yet something inside of Childers demanded that he help his adopted homeland. In 1914, he used his yacht to transfer rifles he had surreptitiously purchased in Germany to Ireland, landing near Dublin.

During World War I he again served in the British Army as an intelligence officer, but his desire to aid in the fight for the freedom of Ireland burned inside him. His wife, Molly, was an American with strong pro-Irish sympathies. Together, after the war, they called for a free Ireland; in 1921 Childers was elected as a member of the Dáil Éireann, the free Irish Assembly, representing County Wicklow; that year he served as the secretary of an Irish delegation that included Michael Collins and went to London to negotiate the freedom of Ireland. A treaty was arranged, which left much of the northern part of Ireland in the hands of the British.

Childers went back to Dublin and denounced the treaty; when it was accepted, he, along with Irish statesman Eamon de Valera, walked out of the Dáil with their followers in protest. Childers then joined the Irish Republican Army (IRA), which began a bloody and protracted guerrilla war against the protreaty activists (including Collins, who was assassinated) and the British. During this time, Childers carried a revolver given him by a friend; when he was captured by the British in his home where he had been hiding, he was tried not for treason but for carrying an illegal weapon. Court-martialed in Dublin by a court he refused to recognize, he was found guilty on 17 November 1922 and sentenced to be shot within seven days.

Before his death, Childers was photographed outside the prison-house; he stares bleakly into the camera, emaciated from his experiences in fighting the British as well as his captivity. Biographer Jim Ring writes, "Childers faced death with absolute equanimity and indomitable courage. In a sense he welcomed death. Alive, it was clear that he could not do more for the cause; his life was the last contribution that he could make to Irish freedom." On 24 November 1922, he was taken from his jail cell to Beggar's Bush, in County Dublin, placed before a firing squad, and put to death; before the shots rang out he shook the hands of every member of the firing squad. Ring adds that, "marched to the wall by the officer in charge, he was saluted, and left alone to face the guns. No mask or blindfold concealed the scene from his eyes—the grey granite square, the firing squad, the rifles. To the squad he called, 'Take a step or two forwards, lads. It will be easier that way.'" Childers was only 52 years old when he died.

The London *Daily Sketch* led the next morning's edition with a large headline: "ERSKINE CHILDERS EXECUTED IN DUBLIN," accompanied by the pitiful last photo of the rebel. His son, Erskine Childers, Jr., became one of the most respected Irish politicians of the twentieth century. He served as president of Ireland and died in 1996.

**References:** Boyle, Andrew, *The Riddle of Erskine Childers* (London: Hutchinson, 1977); Cox, Tom, *Damned Englishman: A Study of Erskine Childers (1870–1922)* (Hicksville, NY: Exposition Press, 1975); "Erskine Childers Executed in Dublin," *London Daily Sketch,* 25 November 1922, 1; Foote, Timothy, "'No Revolution ever Produced a Nobler or Purer Spirit,'" *Smithsonian,* 25:8 (November 1994), 158–79; Jeffares, A. Norman, "Childers, (Robert) Erskine" in John M. Reilly, ed., *Twentieth-Century Crime and Mystery Writers* (New York: St. Martin's Press, 1985), 163–64; Ring, Jim, *Erskine Childers* (London: John Murray, 1996), 288–89; Wilkinson, Burke, *The Zeal of the Convert* (Gerrards Cross, England: Colin Smythe, 1978), vii; Williams, Basil, "Childers, Robert Erskine" in Sir Leslie Stephens and Sir Sidney Lee, eds., *The Dictionary of National Biography,* 10 vols., 12 supplements (Oxford, England: Oxford University Press, 1917–1993) 3:180–82; Young, John N., *Erskine H. Childers, President of Ireland: A Biography* (Gerrards Cross, England: Colin Smythe, 1985), 1–2.

## *Coker v. Georgia* (433 U.S. 584, 53 L.Ed 2d 982, 97 S.Ct. 2861 [1977])

U.S. Supreme Court decision that held that a death sentence given for the crime of rape violated the prohibition on the application of cruel and unusual punishments found in the Eighth Amendment to the United States Constitution.

Ehrlich Anthony Coker, a lifelong criminal, escaped from a correctional institution in Georgia where he was serving life sentences for murder, rape, kidnapping, and aggravated assault, as well as other offenses. During his flight, he raped a woman and committed an armed robbery. Captured, he stood trial and was convicted. Georgia law allowed the death penalty for rape when the following aggravating circumstances were involved: (1) the crime was committed by a person previously convicted of a capital felony; (2) it was committed during the commission of another capital felony; and (3) it was outrageously or wantonly vile, horrible, or inhuman in that it involved torture, depravity of mind, or aggravated battery to the victim. The jury, in the sentencing hearing, held that Coker fit all three aggravating circumstances and sentenced him to death for the rape. On appeal, the Georgia Supreme Court affirmed both the verdict and the sentence of death. Coker appealed to the U.S. Supreme Court, which heard arguments in the case on 28 March 1977 and delivered an opinion on 29 June of that same year.

Justice Byron White, representing a plurality, held that the death sentence for the rape conviction violated the cruel and unusual punishments clause of the Eighth Amendment of the U.S. Constitution. Joined in his opinion by Justices Potter Stewart, Harry Blackmun, John Paul Stevens, William Brennan, and Thurgood Marshall (Chief Justice Warren Burger and Justice William H. Rehnquist dissented), White wrote:

> We have concluded that a sentence of death is grossly disproportionate and excessive punishment for the crime of rape and is therefore forbidden by the Eighth Amendment as cruel and unusual punishment. We do not discount the seriousness of rape as a crime. It is highly reprehensible, both in a moral sense and in its almost total contempt for the personal integrity and autonomy of the female victim and for the latter's privilege of choosing those with whom intimate relationships are to be established. Short of homicide, it is the "ultimate violation of self." . . . Rape is without doubt deserving of serious punishment; but in terms of moral depravity and of the injury to the person and to the public, it does not compare with murder, which does involve the unjustified taking of human life.

Chief Justice Burger answered:

> Unlike the plurality, I would narrow the inquiry in this case to the question actually presented: Does the Eighth Amendment's ban against cruel and unusual punishment prohibit the State of Georgia from executing a person who has, within the space of three years, raped three separate women, killing one and attempting to kill another, who is serving prison terms exceeding his probable lifetime and who has not hesitated to escape confinement at the first available opportunity? Whatever one's view may be as to the State's constitutional power to impose the death penalty upon a rapist who stands before a court convicted for the first time, this case reveals a chronic rapist whose continuing danger to the community is abundantly clear.

## Colquhoun, Patrick (1745–1820)

Scottish jurist and writer, author of *A Treatise on the Police of the Metropolis* (1800), which discussed capital punishment as it was inflicted at that time in England. Born in Dumbarton, Scotland, on 14 March 1745, Colquhoun received much of his education there. His commercial interests dominated the early part of his life. It was not until 1789, for an unknown reason, that he and his family moved to London, where he was appointed a justice in the newly established police system. He then proceeded to write a series of pamphlets on social problems. His most famous was "A Treatise on the Police of the Metropolis" (1800), in which he discussed the methods of police work and punishment in England at that time, including the increase in the use of capital punishment:

> In the course of the present century, several of the old sanguinary modes of punishment have been either, very properly, abolished by acts of parliament, or allowed, to the honour of humanity, to fall into disuse: such as *Burning alive, (particularly women) cutting off hands or ears, slitting nostrils, or branding the hand or face;* and among the lesser punishments, fallen into disuse, may be mentioned the *ducking-stool.* The punishment of death for felony (as has already been observed) has existed since the reign of Henry I. [1100–35] nearly 700 years.—Transportation is commonly understood to have been first introduced, anno 1718, by the act of the 4th George I, cap. 11; and afterwards enlarged by the Act 6th of George I. c. 23, which allowed the court a discretionary power to order felons who were by law entitled to their clergy, to be transported to the American plantations for seven or fourteen years, according to circumstances.
>
> Since that period the mode of punishment has undergone several other alterations; and many Crimes which were formerly considered of an inferior rank, have been rendered capital . . . 1. CRIMES punishable by the Deprivation of Life; and where, upon the conviction of the Offenders the sentence of Death must be pronounced by the Judge. Of these, it has been stated, the whole, on the authority of Sir William Blackstone, including all the various of the same offence, is about 160 in number.

Colquhoun wrote several other pamphlets, including "Treatise on the Functions and Duties of a Constable" (1803), but none had the impact of his 1800 work, which was reprinted six times in the first decade of the nineteenth century and received a positive comment from the king. Colquhoun died in Westminster on 25 April 1820 at the age of 75.

**References:** Colquhoun, Patrick, *A Treatise on the Police of the Metropolis, Explaining the Various Crimes and Misdemeanors which are at Present felt as a Pressure Upon the Community, and Suggesting Remedies for their Prevention, by a Magistrate* (London: Joseph Mawman, 1800), 436–37; Espinasse, Francis, "Colquhoun, Patrick, LL.D." in Sir Leslie Stephens and Sir Sidney Lee, eds., *The Dictionary of National Biography,* 10 vols., 12 supplements (Oxford, England: Oxford University Press, 1917–1993), 4:859–60.

## The Condemned Sermon

Little is known of the rite known as the condemned sermon exhorted to those who were put to death in the eighteenth and nineteenth centuries.

In 1824 two murderers, John Thurtell and Joseph Hunt, were put to death in a famous British double execution. A record of the condemned sermon preached on that occasion still exists, citing Corinthians II:10 as its basis: "We must all appear before the judgement-seat of Christ, and every one may receive the things done in his body, according to that he hath done, whether it be good or bad." The chaplain spoke these words: "Let this present season of Advent constrain us all to look carefully and steadily to our last great account; and seeing now, with our own eyes, the awful spectacle before us, where human justice is about to vindicate the violation of her laws, let us lift up our hearts to higher views, and raise our thoughts from earthly to heavenly subjects. Let us argue thus: If the day of God's judgment be so dreadful at a distance, that I can hardly now bear the very thought of it, from the recollection of my sins, how insupportable will the thought itself be, when it certainly does come?"

**Reference:** *The Trial of John Thurtell and Joseph Hunt for the Murder of Mr. William Weare, in Gill's Hill Lane, Herts, Before Mr. Justice Park, on Tuesday, the 6th, and Wednesday, the 7th January, 1824, with the Prayer, and the Condemned Sermon, that was Preached Before the Unhappy Culprits; Also, Full Particulars of the Execution[s]* (London: Printed by and for Hodgson & Co., 1824), 88–90.

## Corday D'Armont (or D'Armans), Marie-Anne Charlotte (1768–1793)

French female revolutionary beheaded for the assassination of Jean Paul Marat, himself a revolutionary and a leader of the French Revolution.

Born to a noble family (she was a descendant of the French playwright Pierre Corneille) in the town of Saint-Saturnin in the Normandy region of northern France, on 27 July 1768, she attended a convent school near Caen. There, she became caught up in the controversy over the May 1793 expulsion of the Girondists, a radical sect, from the French Convention that had replaced the Parliament. Corday, under the influence of such Girondists as Charles Barbaroux, blamed the newly instituted French revolutionaries Robespierre and Danton for the Girondists' exclusion but held Jean Paul Marat, the leader of the revolutionary press, responsible.

Disguising herself as a sympathizer of Marat's cause, she obtained an interview with him at his home in Paris on 13 July. Marat, who was suffering from a horrible skin disease and was bathing to ease the pain, saw her in his bathroom. She told him that several men from Caen were conspiring to return the Girondists to power; when Marat asked for their names, she made up fictitious names. As Marat declared that he would have all of them guillotined at once, Corday drew from her bosom a large knife and drove the blade into Marat's heart. Marat called for his aides, who grabbed Corday and forced her to the ground as Marat slid into unconsciousness and death.

At her trial, Corday admitted her deed and hailed all who murdered tyrants in the name of freedom. But she denied that she was tied in any way to a conspiracy to topple the French government. Even so, her conviction was but a formality; on 17 July she faced the guillotine bravely, having struck what she claimed was a blow for liberty. The scene of the assassination was later depicted by French painter Jacques Louis David.

**References:** Cher, Marie, pseud [Scherr, Marie], "Charlotte Corday and Certain Men of the Revolutionary Torment" (New York:

D. Appleton, 1929); Goetz, Philip W., ed.-in-Chief, *The New Encyclopedia Britannica,* 22 vols. (Chicago: Encyclopedia Britannica, Inc., 1995), 3:624; Paxton, John, *Companion to the French Revolution* (New York: Facts on File, 1988), 57; Stone, D., "Corday D'Armans, Marie-Ann Charlotte" in Samuel F. Scott and Barry Rothaus, eds., *Historical Dictionary of the French Revolution, 1789–1799,* 2 vols. (Westport, CT: Greenwood Press, 1985), 1:248.

## Cost of Capital Punishment

In his dissenting opinion in *Furman v. Georgia,* Justice Thurgood Marshall wrote, "When all is said and done, there can be no doubt that it costs more to execute a man than to keep him in prison for life."

Arguments over the costs involved in carrying out the death penalty have been at the forefront of the capital punishment controversy. Proponents of capital punishment argue that cost cannot be considered as part of the judicial equation when justice is being sought; advocates against the death penalty utilize numbers to illustrate their argument that it costs society far more to execute a single inmate than to house that offender for life. The only major study done to date on this subject is by Margot Garey in the summer 1985 edition of the *University of California at Davis Law Review.* Alan Blakley wrote in 1990, "While many people talk about the costs, few have attempted to qualify them. It seems to be 'common knowledge' that the death penalty costs more than life imprisonment, but few people can say why." Garey seems to pinpoint this issue: "Because of constitutional requirements and the diligence of attorneys in capital cases, death penalty litigation is a long, expensive process." Examining the entire judicial process, from arrest to execution, Garey discovers that because the U.S. Supreme Court has certified that the sentence of death requires great industry and patience in the application of sentence, it requires far more scrutiny than does any other punishment. Costs begin to accrue in dealing with evidence, pretrial motions, trial, verdict, sentence, and appeals. (In most criminal cases there is usually a plea, without a jury trial. All capital cases require a jury trial because the jury must render the death sentence if there is a guilty verdict.) In many death-penalty trials, there may be a change of venue order, sequestration of jurors during the *voir dire* process (in which the jury is selected through intense questioning) and trial, and additional funds set aside by both prosecution and defense for expert testimony. Garey calls this phase "super due process," in which the defendant's every constitutional right is defended to a higher degree. If effective counsel is not provided, an appeals court will strike down the death sentence; this adds to the costs.

In 1985, the Supreme Court held that if the defendant's sanity during the commission of the crime is at question, he or she must be allowed a state-provided psychiatrist. After conviction, there is a sentencing phase, in which more care is taken to ensure that the punishment is just. Appeals, usually running more than a decade, follow as courts carefully examine the written record of the trial and investigate possible legal errors that could overturn the death sentence or return the defendant for retrial.

In its decision in *Furman,* the Supreme Court explained that although it did not find the death penalty itself to be unconstitutional, it did observe that its mechanisms made its then current application unconstitutional. The system set up in the wake of *Furman,* found to be constitutional in 1976 in *Gregg v. Georgia,* ensures that constitutional safeguards of the highest magnitude are in place, regardless of cost, if society wants to continue to execute persons that deserve the sentence of death.

**References:** Blakley, Alan F., "The Cost of Killing Criminals," *Northern Kentucky Law Review,* 18:1 (Fall 1990), 61–79; Garey, Margot, "The Cost of Taking a Life: Dollars and Sense of the Death Penalty," *University of California at Davis Law Review,* 18:4 (Summer 1985), 1221–70; Marshall opinion in *Furman v. Georgia,* 408 U.S. 238 (1972), at 358; Nakell, Barry, "The Cost of the Death Penalty," *Criminal Law Bulletin,* 14:1 (January 1978), 72–80.

## Courvoisier, Benjamin (1817?–1840)

Swiss-British servant put to death in the mid–eighteenth century for the murder of his employer. The publicity surrounding his execution demonstrated the popularity of public executions during the nineteenth century and earlier.

Little is known of Courvoisier; according to crime historian Jay Robert Nash, he was born in Geneva in 1817 and emigrated to London when just nineteen years old. After a series of odd jobs, he was hired as a servant by Lord William Russell. On 6 May 1840, a maid came home to find the house torn asunder and Lord Russell lying dead in a bedroom, his throat slit. A search of the premises found valuables belonging to the lord in Courvoisier's possession and several pieces of clothing smeared with blood. Courvoisier was arrested and tried at London's Old Bailey courtroom in May 1840. Despite further evidence that he stole a silver crest from Lord Russell and left it with a friend for safekeeping, Courvoisier shouted his innocence. The court, however, found him guilty and sentenced him to death. On 6 July 1840, two months after Lord Russell was murdered, Courvoisier faced the hangman's noose in a public execution (considered one of the greatest public events of the nineteenth century) at London's Newgate Prison. The *Times* of London reported on it the following day:

> The scaffold was raised at a very early hour in the morning, and by 6 o'clock the crowd collected in front, and filling all the adjacent places from which any view of the apparatus of death could be obtained, was immense. The people were pressed together in the compactest mass, and we believe it to be a moderate calculation when we state that 20,000 persons at least must have witnessed this memorable execution. So great, indeed, was the anxiety felt to procure a favourable station, that some hundreds of individuals had taken up their position in front of the debtor's door of the Old Bailey [courthouse and prison] so soon as 10 o'clock on Sunday night [the execution took place on a Monday], cheerfully exposing themselves to the inconvenience of standing in the open air during the whole of the night, in order that their curiosity might be fully gratified in the morning. The windows of the neighbouring houses were all occupied by spectators, who in most instances had paid a pretty high fee for their places, whilst others who had less money to spare, but more nerve, ascended to the roofs, and perched themselves in the most precarious situations. Among the crowd there was a considerable sprinkling of females and boys, and the number of manservants present was remarkable, as evincing the fearful interest taken in the culprit's fate to the class to which he had belonged. In the long interval between the assembling of the multitude and the hour of execution, a few incidents, such as the futile attempts of some daring individuals to attain an enviable eminence without the ceremony of paying, or the tossing about of a stray hat or bonnet, occasionally excited bursts of merriment, but in general the demeanour of the mob was decent and proper for the solemn occasion which had drawn them together.
>
> A numerous body of city police was on the spot in front of the scaffold and dispersed through the crowd, and their conduct and arrangements for the preservation of order were in every respect commendable. At five minutes to 8 o'-clock the dismal sound of the prison bell struck upon the ear, and immediately the vast multitude uncovered. This was a

moment of intense excitement; it was impossible to behold the mob, with their heads all bared, and their eyes all eagerly directed towards the gallows, without the deepest feeling of awe, and the spectacle thus exhibited was enough in itself to have struck terror to the heart of the miserable felon, whose ignominious fate rendered him the sole gaze of such an immense mass of human beings. At two minutes after 8 o'clock, Courvoisier ascended the steps, and advanced, without looking round him, to the centre of the platform, followed by the executioner, and the Ordinary of the prison, the Rev. Mr. Carver. On his appearance a few yells of execration escaped from a portion of the crowd; but the general body of the people, great as must have been their abhorrence of his atrocious crime, remained silent spectators of the scene which was passing before their eyes. The prisoner's manner was marked by an extraordinary appearance of firmness. His step was steady and collected, and his movements free from the slightest agitations or indecision. His countenance was indeed pale, and bore the trace of much dejection, but it was at the same time calm and unmoved. While the executioner was placing him on the drop, he slightly moved his hands (which were tied down in front of him, and strongly clasped one within the other) up and down two or three times; and this was the only visible symptom of any emotion or mental anguish which the wretched man endured. His face was then covered with the cap, fitting so closely as not to conceal the outlines of his countenances, and the noose adjusted. During the operation he lifted up his head and arised his hand to his breast, as if in the action of fervent prayer. In a moment the fatal bolt was withdrawn, the drop fell, and in this attitude the murderer perished. He died without any violent struggle. In two minutes after he had fallen his legs were twice slightly convulsed, but no further motion was observable, excepting that his raised arms, gradually losing their vitality, sank down from their own lifeless weight. After hanging one hour, the body was cut down and removed within the prison.

One of the witnesses to the execution was British writer William Makepeace Thackeray, who, until that time, had been a strong supporter of capital punishment. Horrified as he watched Courvoisier strangled to death by the noose, Thackeray wrote one of the most enduring pieces of anti–death penalty literature, "Going to See a Man Hanged," which appeared in an obscure British magazine that same year.

**See also:** Thackeray, William Makepeace.
**References:** "The Execution of Courvoisier," *The Times* (London), 7 July 1840, 6–7; "The Execution of François Courvoisier for the Murder of Lord William Russell, Opposite the Debtor's Door this Day" (London: Seven Dials, 1840); Nash, Jay Robert, *Encyclopedia of World Crime,* 4 vols. (Wilmette, IL: CrimeBooks, Inc., 1990), 1:800; Rayner, John L., and G. T. Crook, eds., *The Complete Newgate Calendar,* 5 vols. (London: Privately Printed for the Navarre Society Limited, 1926), 5:296–304; *Report of the Trial of Courvoisier for the Murder of Lord William Russell, June 1840* (London: Chiswick, 1918).

## Crippen, Hawley Harvey (1862–1910)

American doctor who died on the gallows in England for the murder of his wife, one of the most famous English capital-punishment cases of the twentieth century.

Crippen received his M.D. at the Hospital College at Cleveland, Ohio, and went to England in 1883. He was apparently married in New York to a woman known only as Bell, who died in either 1890 or 1891, and in 1893 he met Cora Turner, who was 17 years old and was "living under the protection of another man." Crippen found her attractive, took pity on her, and helped her escape from the violent relationship to Jersey City, New Jersey, where the two were married that same year. They moved from place to place to avoid her old lover.

In about 1900 Crippen went to England alone to look for a home for the two of them. When he returned to the United States, he found that his wife had been seeing an "American music-hall artist" named Bruce Miller, and Crippen confirmed the budding romance when he found letters to his wife from Miller signed "with love and kisses to Brown Eyes." Crippen took his wife to England, and, according to him, "her manner towards him had entirely changed." Miller followed the two to England and continued to see Cora, now living under the name Belle Crippen, or her stage name, Belle Elmore, without Dr. Crippen's knowledge. At the time, Crippen worked days and nights at the Bethlehem Royal Hospital for the Insane in London. In 1906 or 1907, he met and hired as his personal assistant Ethel Le Neve, who was 27 (he was 48), and subsequently began a three-year affair with the young typist who worked in his office.

There is no evidence to suggest on what date Crippen decided on his plan to do away with his troublesome wife and install his lover Ethel as the new Mrs. Crippen. On 1 January, he ordered five grains of hyoscin from the pharmacy he dealt with, Lewis & Barnes. Nine days later, the drug was delivered to the store, and Crippen picked it up. (It had taken so long to get the order because such a large dose of hyoscine was not easy to obtain.) According to Roger Kershaw, who itemized the papers of the Crippen case located in London's Public Record Office, "Cora Crippen was last seen alive on 31 January 1910." Crippen then sat down and typed several letters to friends of his wife, claiming that she had to return to America because of the "illness of a near relative." A few weeks later, on 20 March, however, Crippen himself wrote to one of her friends and said that Cora had "double pleuro-pneumonia" and that she was near death. Six days after that letter, an ad appeared in a local London newspaper, *The Era,* which claimed that Crippen's wife had died in California on 23 March. There was no funeral, but before the death announcement a young woman identified as Ethel Le Neve started living in the Crippen home, wearing Mrs. Crippen's jewelry. Friends of Mrs. Crippen asked Scotland Yard to investigate. Chief Inspector Walter Dew appeared at the address, 39 Hilltop Crescent, London, and asked Crippen if he could look around. Crippen claimed that his wife had run off with another man, and that he was still in shock from the matter. When Dew returned the next day, suspicious, he discovered that Crippen and Le Neve had packed and left for Brussels the night before.

Five days after first speaking with Crippen, Dew returned to the residence with other officers and conducted a thorough search. Under several bricks in the coal cellar in the basement he discovered human remains. An alert was then issued for Crippen's arrest. At that time, he was on the *Montrose,* a ship bound from Brussels to Canada. Dew radioed the captain and inquired whether a man and woman fitting Crippen and Le Neve's description were on board. Informed that a man looking like Crippen was with a young boy, Dew ordered their arrest; it was discovered that Le Neve was traveling as Crippen's son. Taken to Quebec, the two were extradited back to London in the first case of radio helping to capture murder suspects.

On trial in London's Old Bailey courthouse, Crippen's solicitor was Sir Alfred Tobin, who later defended British murderer George Ball. At trial, a doctor, Augustus Joseph Pepper, of London University, testified that the remains in the house had been there from four to eight months, and that they had been dismembered by a person expert in dissection. Although the evidence was all circumstantial, it was more than enough to convict the erstwhile doctor of killing his wife. According to the indictments calendar, Crippen was found guilty of "murder . . . on the coroner's Inquisition," and, with his appeal dismissed, was hanged at Pentonville Prison on 23 November 1910. He did not confess to anything; instead, he asked that a picture of Ethel Le Neve be placed on his chest before he was buried. His former mistress, cleared of all charges, sailed for America at the hour of Crippen's execution; she remained forgotten until shortly before her death in the 1970s, when she was tracked down by a reporter who desired to hear her side of the story. That she never fell out of love with Crippen was still apparent; yet as to his guilt, Le Neve was insistent: her lover was innocent, innocent enough to sacrifice his life for hers.

**References:** *Central Criminal Court Calendar of Indictments, from 28th April 1908 to 20th July 1914;* Cullen, Tom, *Crippen: The Mild Murderer* (London: Bodley Head, 1977); Cullen, Tom, *The Mild Murderer: The True Story of the Dr. Crippen Case* (Boston: Houghton Mifflin, 1977); Dr. Hawley Harvey Crippen Criminal Records, Public Record Office, London; "Execution of Crippen," *The Times* (London), 24 November 1910, 4; Graham-Campbell, R. F., ed., *Central Criminal Courts Sessions Paper. First Session, held November 16th 1909, and Following Days. Minutes of Evidence, Taken in Shorthand, by George Walpole Shouthard, Writer to the Court* (London: George Walpole, 1910), 712–72; Kershaw, Roger, "General Memorandum: Dr. Hawley Harvey Crippen," Public Record Office, London, England; Young, Filson, ed., *Trial of Hawley Harvey Crippen* (Toronto: Canada Law Book Company, Ltd., 1923).

## Crucifixion

Utilized in biblical times as a mode of torture and capital punishment, the act of crucifixion ("to crucify") started mainly with the Roman system of justice. Rome used it from the beginning of the republic until the fourth century, though Roman citizens were exempt from the punishment by law. The Emperor Constantine abolished crucifixion in the fourth century in memory of the Passion of Jesus Christ.

The process of crucifixion was simple. The condemned was first flogged mercilessly to bring on a loss of blood and weakness, and a cross was erected on a hill or at a high point for the sake of witnesses. The victim was then attached to the cross with leather cords, or in some cases with nails through the hands or wrists. The victim's feet were also nailed to the cross, allowing the victim to breathe but prolonging agony (it is impossible to take a breath while hanging on a cross without using the feet to brace the body). The victim was then left to hang there until dead. (Although many surmise that Jesus was nailed through the palms of his hands, modern historians now believe that the nails were placed through his wrists, a stronger and more easily accessible portion of the hand.) A normally healthy victim could survive one or two days, although some lasted for a week, finally expiring from thirst or blood poisoning from the nails. In some cases, the victim's legs or knees were broken to bring about a quicker death.

There is no evidence to suggest when or why a cross was first used, although it fits the shape of the human body quite well. However, according to criminal historian John Laurence, "there were [several types of crosses]: the *crux immissa,* consisting of four arms; the *crux commissa,* consisting of three arms; and the *crux decussata* or St. Andrew's Cross, the proper Greek cross, being in the form of the Greek letter chi. There was also the three-sided cross, like an association goal post, to which the victim was hanged by one leg and an arm."

Many persons, famous and not, were victims of crucifixion. Aside from Jesus and the two criminals who were put to death next to him, St. Bartholomew, an apostle and son of Tolmai, whom St. John called in the Bible "an upright Israelite," was put to death by crucifixion for preaching the word of God. Flayed (lashed with a whip) alive, he was crucified upside down. Spartacus, the leader of a massive slave revolt, and his followers were crucified on crosses left alongside a road as a lesson to others.

**See also:** Dismas and Gestas; Jesus Christ.
**References:** Laurence, John, *A History of Capital Punishment* (New York: The Citadel Press, 1960), 221–22; Nash, Jay Robert, *Encyclopedia of World Crime,* 4 vols. (Wilmette, IL: CrimeBooks, Inc., 1990), 4:3286.

## Cruel and Unusual Punishments, Historical Ban on

In his majority opinion in the landmark U.S. Supreme Court decision *Gregg v. Georgia,* Justice Potter Stewart writes at length on the history of the ban on cruel and unusual punishments in the Western world:

> The phrase first appeared in the English Bill of Rights of 1689, which was drafted by Parliament at the accession of William and Mary. . . . The English version appears to have been directed against punishments unauthorized by statute and beyond the jurisdiction of the sentencing court, as well as those disproportionate to the offense involved. . . . The American draftsmen, who adopted the English phrasing in drafting the Eighth Amendment, were primarily concerned, however, with proscribing "tortures" and other "barbarous" methods of punishment. . . . In the earliest cases raising Eighth Amendment claims, the Court focused on particular methods of execution to determine whether they were too cruel to pass constitutional muster. The constitutionality of the sentence of death itself was not at issue, and the criterion used to evaluate the mode of execution was its similarity to "torture" and other "barbarous"' methods.

In his majority opinion in *Thompson v. Oklahoma,* in which the U.S. Supreme Court struck down death sentences for those convicted of crimes committed before the age of 16, Justice John Paul Stevens wrote, "The authors of the Eighth Amendment drafted a categorical prohibition against the infliction of cruel and unusual punishments, but they made no attempt to define the contours of that category. They delegated that task to future generations of judges who have been guided by the evolving standards of decency that mark the progress of a maturing society."

**See also:** *Furman v. Georgia; Gregg v. Georgia; Thompson v. Oklahoma.*
**References:** Granucci, Anthony F., "'Nor Cruel and Unusual Punishments Inflicted:' The Original Meaning," *California Law Review,* 57:4 (October 1969), 839–65; Majority opinion in *Gregg v. Georgia* (428 U.S. 153, at 872–73, 49 L.Ed. 2d 859, 96 S.Ct. 2909 [1976]); Majority opinion in *Thompson v. Oklahoma* (487 U.S. 815, 101 L.Ed. 2d 702, 108 S.Ct. 2687 [1988]), at 2691.

## Curtis, Newton Martin (1835–1910)

American politician, opponent of capital punishment.

Born at De Peyster, New York, on 21 May 1835, Curtis was educated in the common schools of his hometown, at the Gouverneur Wesleyan Seminary, and by a private tutor. With the onset of the Civil War, Curtis joined Company G of the 16th New York Infantry, where he was commissioned a captain. During the war, he served with the armies of the Potomac and the James; he was brevetted a brigadier general for his service at the Battle of Derby Town Road, 27 October 1864, and was awarded a congressional medal for his role in the capture of Fort Fisher, in Southport, North Carolina. He served in the New York Assembly from 1884 to 1890, and in the latter year was elected to the U.S. House of Representatives.

Curtis served in the House from 1891 to 1897. He attempted—on two occasions—to introduce bills to "abolish the punishment of death and substitute therefor imprisonment for life" to the committee on the judiciary, but they were never reported out of committee. The introduction of these two bills may have been Curtis's only two actions in the House.

In a speech that he delivered on the House floor on 9 June 1892, and which was subsequently published as a pamphlet, "To Define the Crime of Murder," Curtis argued that

> the individual has the natural right to protect himself from assault and death, and all codes protect him in the proper exercise of the right of self-defense. So has the state the right to employ its forces in protecting the individual from violence, and society from the acts of the unbridled and vicious. The individual, at the moment of attack, may employ all means at hand to save his life until rescued; and the state, in defense of the individual, its peace and tranquility, can go as far in maintaining its authority as civilized nations, in the exercise of just and equal laws, have ever gone. Although an individual may use every means for his protection when menaced and in imminent peril, he can not, under the fiction of self-defense, carry it to the destruction of his assailant when the assailant is unarmed and in keeping of the police. Nor can a state find judicious warrant for going beyond the disarming and confining of a disorderly person. A single step beyond the line of safety is one step in the direction of society where brute force, not reason, rules.

Curtis's only full-length published work seems to be *From Bull Run to Chancellorsville: The Story of the Sixteenth New York Infantry, Together with Personal Reminiscences"* (New York: G. P. Putnam's Sons, 1906), although a speech that he delivered in London, entitled "General Curtis on the Death Penalty" was published by the Howard Association in London in 1876. Curtis died on 8 January 1910 at the age of 74.

**References:** *Congressional Record: Containing the Proceedings and Debates of the Fifty-Second Congress, First Session* 23:2 (Washington, DC: Government Printing Office, 1892), 1578; *Congressional Record: Containing the Proceedings and Debates of the Fifty-Second Congress, First Session* 23:3 (Washington, DC: Government Printing Office, 1892), 2071; Curtis, Newton M., *To Define the Crime of Murder* (Washington, DC: Government Printing Office, 1892), 9–11; "Curtis, Newton Martin" in *National Cyclopedia of American Biography,* 57 vols., supplements A-L (New York: James T. White & Company, 1898–1972), 4:328–29; MacLear, Anne B., "Curtis, Newton Martin" in Dumas Malone, et al., eds., *Dictionary of American Biography,* 10 vols., 10 supplements (New York: Charles Scribner's Sons, 1930–95), II:618–19.

## Czolgosz, Leon (1873–1901)

American anarchist, assassin of President William McKinley at the Pan-American Exposition in Buffalo, New York, in 1901, and put to death for his crime.

Born in Detroit, Michigan, in 1873, Czolgosz (pronounced Chol-gosh) was of Polish-German ancestry. Nothing is known of his life except that while working as an ironworker in Detroit in the 1890s he became an anarchist, attending meetings under the alias Fred Nieman. When a radical murdered Italy's King Humbert I on 29 July 1900, Czolgosz became fascinated with the idea of an anarchist assassination. He purchased a pistol and made his way to Buffalo, where the 1901 Pan-American

Exposition was taking place, a display at which President William McKinley, just reelected to his second term, was to appear and greet the crowds.

On 6 September, as McKinley met the line of well-wishers who wanted to shake his hand, a small, unassuming man with his right hand heavily bandaged approached the president. McKinley stepped forward to greet him and was shocked as a shot rang out from the bandaged hand. It struck a button on McKinley's jacket and bounced away, but a second shot hit the president's abdomen. Police knocked the assassin down, as the president whispered, "Be easy with him boys." Czolgosz answered, "I done my duty."

On 14 September, McKinley slipped into a coma and died. Just nine days later, Czolgosz was put on trial; he refused to help his attorneys and did not question the evidence against him. He did not even appear upset when he was found guilty of murdering the president of the United States and sentenced to death.

On 29 October 1901, less than eight weeks after shooting McKinley and six weeks after the president had succumbed to his wounds, Leon Czolgosz was strapped into the electric chair at New York's Auburn Prison. The work *American State Trials* contains this description of Czolgosz's execution:

> As Czolgosz entered the room he appeared calm and self-possessed, his head was erect and his face bore an expression of defiant determination. The guards, one on either side, quietly and quickly guided him to the fatal chair, the binding straps were rapidly adjusted to his arms, legs and body, and the head and electrodes were quickly placed *in situ* and connected with the wire which was to transmit the lethal current through his body. These preliminaries occupied about one minute. Czolgosz offered no resistance whatever, but during the preparations addressed himself to the witnesses in a clear, distinct voice in the following language: "I killed the President because he was an enemy of the good people—the good working people. I am not sorry for my crime." At this moment, everything being in readiness, the Warden signalled the official electrician in charge of the switch, who immediately turned the lever which closed the circuit and shot the deadly current through the criminal's body, which was instantly thrown into a state of tonic spasm involving apparently every fibre of the entire muscular system. At the same time, consciousness, sensation and motion were apparently abolished.
>
> Two electrical contacts were made, occupying in all one minute and five seconds. In the first contact the electromotive pressure was maintained at 1800 volts for seven seconds, then reduced to 300 volts for twenty-three seconds, increased to 1800 volts for four seconds and again reduced to 300 volts for twenty-six seconds—one minute in all. The second contact, which was made as a precautionary measure, but which was probably unnecessary, was maintained at 1800 volts for five seconds. That conscious life was absolutely destroyed the instant the first contact was made, was conceded by all of the medical witnesses present; also that organic life was abolished within a few seconds thereafter.
>
> Czolgosz was pronounced dead by the attending physicians and several of the other physicians present, after personal examination, in four minutes from the time he entered the room; one minute of this period was occupied in the preliminary preparations, one minute and five seconds in the electrical contacts, and the remainder of the time in examinations by the physicians to determine the fact of death.

After an autopsy in which it was found that Czolgosz had no apparent mental disease (his brain was normal), Czolgosz's body was placed into a standard prison coffin, and to avoid any part of him ever being stolen or used as a relic, six barrels of quicklime and a carboy of sulfuric acid, to destroy the body and the clothes it was wearing, were poured over him, and the lid was closed. He was then buried in the prison yard of Auburn Prison.

**References:** Christianson, Stephen G., "Leon Czolgosz Trial: 1901" in Edward W. Knappman, ed., *Great American Trials* (Detroit: Visible Ink Press, 1994), 225–27; Drimmer, Frederick, *Until You Are Dead: The Book of Executions in America* (New York: Windsor Publishing, 1990), 279–83; Lawson, John D., ed., *American State Trials: A Collection of the Important and Interesting Criminal Trials Which Have Taken Place in the United States, from the Beginning of our Government to the Present Day,* 17 vols. (St. Louis, MO: F. H. Thomas Law Book Company, 1914–36), 14:229–31; MacDonald, Carlos F., *The Trial, Execution, Autopsy, and Mental Status of Leon F. Czolgosz, alias Fred Nieman. By Carlos F. MacDonald, A.M., M.D. With a Report of the Post-Mortem Examination, by Edward Spitzka* (Baltimore: The Johns Hopkins Press, 1902); "President M'Kinley Shot!" *Buffalo Evening News,* 6 September 1901, 1; Sifakis, Carl, *The Encyclopedia of American Crime* (New York: Facts on File, 1982), 190; Wesley Johns, A., *The Man Who Shot McKinley* (South Brunswick, NJ: A. S. Barnes, 1970); "Whole Nation in Grief: President McKinley Passes Away Peacefully at 2:15 A.M., Surrounded by his Immediate Relatives," *The Chicago Daily News,* 14 September 1901, 1.

**Danton, Georges Jacques (1759–1794)**

French revolutionary put to death by his accomplices, most notably Maximilien Robespierre, during the French Revolution.

Danton was born in the commune of Arcis-sur-Aube on the Aube River, located about 17 miles north of the city of Troyes, France, on 26 October 1759. His father died when he was two, and he was raised by his mother. In 1773, he was admitted to the Oratorian School, where he became schooled in the classics. Seven years later he went to Paris to study law; he became a law clerk and, without getting a degree from a university, purchased one. After opening his own office, he married the daughter of a rich proprietor, who gave Danton the money to buy the office of advocate to the royal councils, where he became successful in court.

With the outbreak of the French Revolution in 1789, Danton became one of France's most eloquent spokesmen—an unexpected development, considering Danton's rather undistinguished background. His biographer Mona Ozouf wrote: "Danton, like Robespierre and Marat, was a creation of the Revolution. . . . Despite the diligence of his biographers in scouring his youth for early signs of future greatness, it is hard to see in their portraits of the young Danton a man with his course firmly set on the Revolution to come."

With fellow revolutionaries Maximilien Robespierre and Camille Desmoulins, Danton established the Cordelier's Club and became its most important leader. He also became a powerful speaker before the commune and the assembly, calling for a constitutional monarchy rather than no king at all. Danton was one of nine (later twelve) men who sat on the *Comite du Salut Public* (Committee of Public Safety) with Robespierre, which exercised brutal and ruthless dictatorial power during the French Revolution, sending thousands of people to the guillotine. Gradually, however, he began to clash with Robespierre, who demanded bloodshed rather than liberty.

As the Reign of Terror instituted by Robespierre intensified, Danton became a leading critic of the government. Yet even when notified that Robespierre was out to destroy him and had ordered his arrest for treason, Danton did not seem overly concerned, nor did he flee the country to safety. Placed on trial for his life with Desmoulins and others, he spoke until his voice gave out, calling for an end to the senseless executions. When Robespierre demanded an end to the trial, a verdict of guilty was returned, and the sentence of death passed. As he was being led away, Danton yelled to the court that Robespierre was next—that he would be going to the guillotine himself if he murdered Danton and his compatriots.

On the morning of 5 April 1794 Danton, Desmoulins, and their allies were led from jail to the gallows. As the tumbrels (small carts used to transport prisoners from the jail to the guillotine) moved toward the place of execution, the men could hear the crowd warming up for a total of 16 executions. Danton reputedly shouted, "Stupid clods! They'll shout 'Long live the Republic!' when the Republic no longer has a head!" Danton was forced to watch as all fifteen of his fellow defendants met their fate on *la guillotine*. When his turn came and he walked up the steps to the blade, he slipped on the blood of his compatriots. The executioner heard him whisper to his 16-year-old wife, Louise, "I shall never see you again, my darling!" Then, quickly, he added, "Come, Danton, no weakness!" To the executioner, he sighed, just before his end came, "Sanson, thou wilt show my head to the people; it is worth showing." When the knife slashed down, it was also the beginning of the end for Robespierre, who, as Danton had predicted, soon lost his own head.

**See also:** Desmoulins, Lucie Simplice Camille Benoist; Robespierre, Maximilien François Marie Isidore de.

**References:** Cher, Marie, pseud. [Scherr, Marie], *Charlotte Corday and Certain Men of the Revolutionary Torment* (New York: D. Appleton, 1929); Donaldson, Norman, and Betty Donaldson, *How Did They Die?* (New York: St. Martin's Press, 1980), 90–91; Hampson, Norman, *Danton* (New York: Holmes & Meier, 1978); Lytle, S., "Danton, Georges-Jacques" in Samuel F. Scott and Barry Rothaus, eds., *Historical Dictionary of the French Revolution, 1789–1799,* 2 vols. (Westport, CT: Greenwood Press, 1985), 1:283–90; Ozouf, Mona, "Danton" in François Furet and Mona Ozouf, eds., *A Critical Dictionary of the French Revolution* (Cambridge, MA: The Belknap Press of Harvard University Press, 1989), 213–23; Paxton, John, *Companion to the French Revolution* (New York: Facts on File, 1988), 61–62.

## Darrow, Clarence Seward (1857–1938)

American trial lawyer Clarence Darrow, noted for his outspoken opposition to capital punishment, is remembered for his defense of the McNamara Brothers, Leopold and Loeb, socialist Eugene Debs, labor leader "Big Bill" Haywood, and science teacher John T. Scopes.

Born near the town of Kinsman in northeastern Ohio on 18 April 1857, he was the son and the fifth of eight children of Amirus Darrow, a furniture maker and former preacher, and his wife Emily (nee Eddy) Darrow. Clarence went to local schools in Kinsman, attended Allegheny College in Meadville, Pennsylvania, for a year, then spent a year in law school at the University of Michigan. He was admitted to the Ohio bar in 1878.

As he practiced law in Kinsman and in other small Ohio villages, Darrow became more liberal in his thought, influenced by several economic tracts and a work by Illinois judge John Peter Altgeld. In 1887, Darrow went to Chicago, where he soon became an intimate of Altgeld. There he worked to gain reprieves for the Haymarket defendants, of which several were sentenced to hang. Although Darrow failed to save their lives, his reputation in socialist circles grew. He also worked to end corruption in the so-called Chicago Machine, which was ruled with an iron fist by the Democratic party.

In 1890, Darrow became the attorney for the Chicago & Northwestern Railway but retained his right to fight criminal cases. In 1894, he tried but failed to save the life of one Robert Prendergast, who had been convicted and sentenced to death for the murder of Chicago mayor Carter H. Harrison. Prendergast would be the first and last of Darrow's clients to be put to death. Darrow then defended labor leader Eugene V. Debs on the charge of conspiring to obstruct interstate commerce. Although Debs went to jail for contempt, Darrow became a leading labor attorney.

In 1906 and 1907, Darrow came to the defense of Western Federation of Miners head William "Big Bill" Haywood when he was accused with others of conspiring to murder Idaho Governor Frank Steunenberg with a bomb, and helped obtain an acquittal. In 1911 he was the legal advocate for the McNamara brothers, accused of destroying the

Los Angeles *Times* building with dynamite, but when the brothers pled guilty, Darrow himself was put on trial for perjury. An acquittal nonetheless left him injured in the minds of the labor movement, and Darrow's career in that area was over.

Perhaps Darrow's greatest period of lawyering came in the 1920s, when he became caught up in two of the biggest cases of that decade. He saved murderers Nathan Leopold and Richard Loeb from the electric chair in a stunning speech that earned him much enmity. He also defended teacher John T. Scopes during the infamous "Monkey Trial" in Tennessee in 1925 when the evolution vs. creationism debate started.

Because he seemed to defend those who otherwise would be headed for certain death at the hands of the state, Darrow was a staunch opponent of capital punishment for his entire life. In an article for *The Forum*, September 1928, Darrow wrote:

> Little more than a century ago, in England, there were over two hundred offenses that were punishable with death. The death sentence was passed upon children under ten years old. And every time the sentimentalist sought to lessen the number of crimes punishable by death, the self-righteous said no, that it would be the destruction of the state; that it would be better to kill for more transgressions rather than for less.
>
> Today, both in England and America, the number of capital offenses has been reduced to a very few, and capital punishment would doubtless be abolished altogether were it not for the self-righteous, who still defend it with the same old arguments. Their major claim is that capital punishment decreases the number of murders and hence, that the state must retain the institution as its last defense against the criminal. . . .
>
> . . . Behind the idea of capital punishment lie false training and crude views of human conduct. People do evil things, say the judges, lawyers, and preachers, because of depraved hearts. . . .
>
> If crime were really the result of wilful depravity, we should be ready to concede that capital punishment may serve as a deterrent to the criminally inclined. But it is hardly probable that the great majority of people refrain from killing their neighbors because they are afraid; they refrain because they never had the inclination. . . .
>
> Of course, no one will be converted to this point of view by statistics of crime. In the first place, it is impossible to obtain reliable ones; and in the second place, the conditions to which they apply are never the same. But if one cares to analyze the figures, such as we have, it is easy to trace the more frequent causes of homicide. The greatest number of killings occur during attempted burglaries and robberies. The robber knows that penalties for burglary do not average more than five years in prison. He also knows that the penalty for murder is death or life imprisonment. Faced with this alternative, what does the burglar do when he is detected and threatened with arrest? He shoots to kill. He deliberately takes the chance of death to save himself from a five-year term in prison. It is therefore as obvious as anything can be that death has no effect in diminishing homicides of this kind, which are more numerous than any other type.
>
> . . . Even now, are not all imaginative and humane people shocked at the spectacle of a killing by the state? How many men and women would be willing to act as executioners? How many fathers and mothers would want their children to witness an official killing? What kind of people read the sensational reports of an execution? If all right-thinking men and women were not ashamed of it, why would it be needful that judges and lawyers and preachers apologize for the barbarity? How can the state censure the cruelty of the man who—moved by strong passions, or acting to save his freedom, or influenced by weakness or fear—takes human life, when everyone knows that the state itself, after long premedita-

> tion and settled hatred, not only kills, but first tortures and bedevils its victims for weeks with the impending doom?
>
> . . . There is no doubt whatever that the world is growing more humane and sensitive and more understanding. The time will come when all people view with horror the light way in which society and its courts of law now take human life; and when that time comes, the way will be clear to devise some better method of dealing with poverty and ignorance and their frequent byproducts, which we call crime.

In his final years, Darrow retired to Chicago, where he succumbed to heart disease on 13 March 1938, one month shy of his eighty-first birthday. His remains were cremated and spread over the Jackson Park Lagoon near his home.

**References:** Ginger, Ray, "Darrow, Clarence Seward" in Dumas Malone, et al., eds., *Dictionary of American Biography,* 10 vols., 10 supplements (New York: Charles Scribner's Sons, 1930–95), 2:141–44; Weinberg, Arthur, *Clarence Darrow, Attorney for the Damned* (New York: Simon & Schuster, 1957); Weinberg, Arthur, and Lila Weinberg, eds., *Clarence Darrow: Verdicts Out of Court* (Chicago: Ivan R. Dee, Inc., 1963), 226–32.

## *Davis v. Georgia* (429 U.S. 122, 50 L.Ed. 2d 339, 97 S.Ct. 399 [1976])

U.S. Supreme Court decision in which it was held that the exclusion of a juror who had qualms about capital punishment from a capital case denied a defendant a fair jury representing a cross section of the community.

Curfew Davis was convicted of murder in a Georgia court; however, during the process of selecting a jury, a single potential juror was excluded because he or she could not say whether he or she would vote to recommend the penalty of death. The Supreme Court of Georgia affirmed both the conviction and sentence. The U.S. Supreme Court, however, agreed to hear the case *in forma pauperis* (permission given to an indigent person to proceed without liability for court fees or costs).

The decision handed down on 6 December 1976 was delivered *per curiam* (with no acknowledged author) but expressing the views of Justices William Brennan, Potter Stewart, Byron White, Thurgood Marshall, Lewis Powell, and John Paul Stevens (Chief Justice Warren Burger was joined in dissent by Justices William H. Rehnquist and Harry Blackmun). The Court overturned Davis's death sentence, holding that the exclusion of the single juror had denied him a fair trial. In the opinion, which runs a single page, the majority wrote: "Unless a venireman [potential juror] is 'irrevocably committed, before the trial has begun, to vote against a penalty of death regardless of the facts and circumstances that might emerge in the course of the proceedings, . . . he cannot be excluded; if a venireman is improperly excluded even though not so committed, any subsequently imposed death penalty cannot stand."

**See also:** *Gray v. Mississippi; Witherspoon v. Illinois.*

**Reference:** Definition of *in forma pauperis* from Black, Henry Campbell (Joseph R. Nolan and Jacqueline M. Nolan-Haley, editors), *Black's Law Dictionary: Definitions of the Terms and Phrases of American and English Jurisprudence, Ancient and Modern* (St. Paul, Minnesota: West Publishing Company, 1990), 779.

## *Dead Man Walking*

1993 book and 1996 motion picture written by Sister Helen Prejean, S. J., a nun who ministers to those about to be put to death in the Louisiana State Penitentiary at Angola. In the book, as well as the movie, Sister Prejean is shown counseling death row inmates and being with them until their deaths. "There is much pain in these pages," Prejean writes in the introduction to her book.

Prejean, a member of the order known as the Sisters of St. Joseph of Medaille, was born in Baton Rouge and currently serves as the national chairman for the National Coalition to Abolish the Death Penalty. She became involved in the issue of capital punishment when in 1982 she served as the spiritual advisor to Elmo Patrick Sonnier, a double murderer who was put to death in 1984. From her experiences with Sonnier (and others she has since counseled) came *Dead Man Walking*, the story of a nun's attempt to help a double murderer, Matthew Poncelet (considered a composite of all of the killers she has counseled), find himself before he is executed by lethal injection. For her work as Prejean, actress Susan Sarandon was awarded the 1996 Academy Award for best actress.

**Reference:** Prejean, Sister Helen, *Dead Man Walking: An Eyewitness Account of the Death Penalty in the United States* (New York: Random House, 1993).

## Death Penalty Information Center

American anti–capital punishment umbrella group consisting of various organizations that disseminate information on ways to end capital punishment in the United States. Founded in 1990 by John R. MacArthur, the publisher of *Harper's* magazine, the Death Penalty Information Center (DPIC) prepares reports and other material for courts and the media on issues relating to capital punishment.

The DPIC is located at 1606 20th Street N.W. in Washington, D.C. On its board of directors are some of the nation's leading voices against capital punishment, including Anthony Amsterdam, who argued *Furman v. Georgia* before the U.S. Supreme Court in 1972; David Bruck, who defended double-murderer Susan Smith and saved her from the death penalty; Steven Hawkins, national director of the National Coalition to Abolish the Death Penalty; and George Kendall, death penalty counsel for the National Association for the Advancement of Colored People Legal Defense and Education Fund (NAACPLDEF).

## Desmoulins, Lucie Simplice Camille Benoist (1760–1794)

French revolutionary executed by beheading during the French Revolution.

Born in Guise, Picardy, on 2 March 1760, Desmoulins studied at the Lyceé Louis-le-Grand and later read the law. By 1785 he was able to appear before the Parlement of Paris as an advocate, but a speech impediment prevented him from becoming a great speaker.

At about this time, the French people were beginning to rise up against the repressive conditions under King Louis XVI. Desmoulins published a pamphlet entitled "La philosophie du peuple français" ("The Philosophy of the French People"), which vaulted him to the top of the revolutionary movement.

When Louis XVI fired Jacques Necker, his popular minister of finance, for personal reasons, then called out the French army to arrest the revolutionaries, Desmoulins, taking up the sword, cried "To arms!" in the streets. Further radical pamphlets followed, which earned him the title *Procureur général de la Lanterne* (General of the streetlamp). In November 1789 he began publishing his radical journal, *Les Révolutions de France et de Brabant* (The revolutions in France and Brabant), which earned him the reputation of one of the country's greatest antimonarchy journalists. He supported, through his writings, his friends Maximilien François Marie Isidore de Robespierre and Georges Jacques Danton, both of whom were at the forefront of the revolution following the arrest of the royal family and the subsequent execution of the king. Yet as thousands of opponents of the regime were brought under the blade of the guillotine, Desmoulins began publicly to question the system that was exterminating French citizens and his role in its creation. His outspokenness in calling for just trials, social justice, and fairer sentences made him an enemy of the regime, particularly of his former ally Robespierre. When he denounced Robespierre and the Committee of Public Safety in a Dantonist newspaper, he, Danton, and their confederates were arrested. A short trial ensued, in which the outcome was predetermined, but the men fought for their lives by denouncing the trial as a farce. Found guilty of treason, Desmoulins and the others were sentenced to death. On 5 April 1794 he faced the guillotine, as did his comrade Danton. His wife, Lucile Desmoulins, who had been involved in antigovernment activity as well, was also arrested and suffered the same fate as her husband only eight days after he died.

**See also:** Danton, Georges Jacques; Robespierre, Maximilien François Marie Isidore de.

**References:** Censer, J., "Desmoulins, Lucie-Camille-Simplice" in Samuel F. Scott and Barry Rothaus, eds., *Historical Dictionary of the French Revolution, 1789–1799,* 2 vols. (Westport, Connecticut: Greenwood Press, 1985), 1:310–12; Saint-Beuve, Charles Augustin, *Portraits of Men* (Freeport, New York: Books for Libraries Press, 1972).

## Deterrence of Capital Punishment

See Gibbet; Murder Rates, Capital Punishment's Effect on; Retribution and Deterrence, Theory of

## Disemboweling or Disembowelment

See Drawing and Quartering

## Dismas and Gestas

Thieves crucified to death with Jesus, according to Biblical sources. Nothing is known of the pair except that they were thieves (Dismas is considered to have been the penitent one). Though the Bible does not identify either of them by name, apocryphal literature written since the Crucifixion has invented a number of names for both, most notably Dismas and Gestas. John 19 merely tells of the thieves' existence:

> "And they took Jesus and led *him* away. And he bearing his cross went forth into a place called the place of a skull, which is called in the Hebrew Gol'go-tha: Where they crucified him [Jesus], *and two others with him* [my emphasis], on either side one, and Jesus in the midst. And Pilate wrote a title, and put it on the cross. And the writing was, JESUS OF NAZARETH, THE KING OF THE JEWS. This title then [was] read [by] many of the Jews: for the place where Jesus was crucified was night to the city; and it was written in Hebrew, and Greek, and Latin. Then said the chief priests of the Jews to Pilate, Write not. The King of the Jews, but that he said, I am King of the Jews. Pilate answered, What I have written I have written."

A portion of the cross on which Dismas is said to have died is preserved at the Church of Santa Croce in Rome; he is the patron saint of those condemned to death.

**See also:** Jesus Christ.

## *Dobbert v. Florida* (432 U.S. 282, 53 L.Ed. 2d 344, 97 S.Ct. 2290 [1977])

U.S. Supreme Court case allowing for certain changes in state laws regarding the imposition of the death penalty without a defendant being subjected to *ex post facto* laws or a reversible death sentence.

Ernest John Dobbert, Jr., was convicted in a Florida court in the first and second degree murders of two of his young children and the torture of two other children. The jury, however, found that several mitigating factors existed and recommended a life sentence. The trial judge disagreed, overrode the jury's recommendation, and sentenced Dobbert to death. The Florida Supreme Court upheld the sentence.

Dobbert challenged the sentence on the change in a 1971 law, passed after he committed his crimes, which allowed trial judges, once bound by jury recommendations in capital cases, to override the recommendation and sentence a convicted defendant to death. Dobbert challenged this change in the law, claiming that it punished him for a crime committed before the law was passed. The U.S. Supreme Court heard arguments in the case on 28 March 1977.

On 17 June of that same year, the court held 6–3 (Justices William Brennan, Thurgood Marshall, and John Paul Stevens dissented) that Dobbert was not denied a fair trial because of the change in the law and that the sentence imposed on him by the judge would stand. Speaking for the majority, Justice William H. Rehnquist wrote,

> After our *Furman* [*Furman v. Georgia,* 1972, which struck down all death sentences in the United States] decision and its own decision in *Florida v. Sack,* the Florida Supreme Court resentenced all prisoners under sentence of death pursuant to the old statute to life imprisonment. . . . Petitioner argues that since his crimes were committed before our decision in *Furman,* the imposition of the death sentence upon him pursuant to the new statute which was in effect at the time of his trial denies him equal protection of the laws. But petitioner is simply not similarly situated to those whose sentences were commuted. He was neither tried nor sentenced prior to *Furman,* as were they, and the only effect of the former statute was to provide sufficient warning of the gravity Florida attached to first-degree murder so as to make the application of this new statute to him consistent with the Ex Post Facto Clause of the United States Constitution. Florida obviously had to draw the line at some point between those whose cases had progressed sufficiently far in the legal process as to be governed solely by the old statute, with the concomitant unconstitutionality of its death penalty provision, and those whose cases involved acts which could properly subject them to punishment under the new statute. There is nothing irrational about Florida's decision to regulate petitioner to the latter class, since the new statute was in effect at the time of his trial and sentence.

On 7 September 1984, Ernest Dobbert was put to death in Florida's electric chair, nicknamed "Old Sparky," the twenty-third person put to death since the Supreme Court held capital punishment to be constitutional in 1976.

**Reference:** Hough, Lloyd, "Witness to an Execution," *The Miami Herald,* 7 October 1984, 1E, 4E.

## Dodd, William (1729–1777)

British forger whose execution for what many considered a minor offense led to a "growth of public uneasiness" in England regarding the imposition of capital punishment in that country.

Born on 29 May 1728, Dodd was the son of the vicar of Bourne in Lincolnshire. He went to London, where he married and became a man of letters, publishing more than 50 works during his lifetime. In fact, according to historian John J. Burke, "The pattern of his activities in the 1750s and 1760s suggests that his design was to acquire fame and fortune with the fashionable and wealthy." By 1774, he had become involved in a scheme (with his wife's help) to bribe an official in order to obtain a trendy apartment in London. By 1777, Dodd was in poor financial shape, and to solve some of his pressing debts, he forged a signature on a bond belonging to Lord Chesterfield, a young man whom he had invited to live in his home. Arrested, Dodd was placed on trial and convicted of forgery. In those days of stern punishment by the English courts, Dodd was sentenced to death. Dodd then turned to Samuel Johnson, the revered writer, for help. (James Boswell's *Life of Johnson* chronicles Johnson's work to save Dodd from the hangman.)

As soon as it became apparent that the government would go through with Dodd's execution, Johnson sprang into action, securing more than 23,000 signatures to spare his life. Yet when the king denied clemency, Johnson composed a condemned sermon entitled "A Convict's Address to his Unhappy Brethren." The king made his decision on the advice of Lord Mansfield, who had executed two brothers, David and Robert Parreau, for a similar crime a year earlier, and who exclaimed, "If I pardon Dodd, I shall have murdered the Parreaus." Dodd was hanged at Newgate on 27 June 1777, at the age of 48. He begged the executioner to make the hanging go quickly. After he was hanged, an attempt was made to spirit his body away to be resuscitated, but the size of the crowd made such a move impossible. Dodd was buried at Cowley, Middlesex.

**References:** Burke, John J., Jr., "Crime and Punishment in 1777: The Execution of the Reverend Dr. William Dodd and Its Impact upon His Contemporaries" in William B. Thesing, ed., *Executions and the British Experience from the 17th to the 20th Century: A Collection of Essays* (Jefferson, NC: McFarland & Company, 1990), 59–75; Fitzgerald, Percy Hetherington, *A Famous Forgery: Being the Story of the 'Unfortunate' Doctor Dodd* (London: Chapman and Hall, 1865); Hill, G. B., and L. F. Powell, eds., *Boswell's Life of Johnson*, 6 vols. (Oxford, England: Clarendon Press, 1934–64), 3:139–40; Radzinowicz, Leon, *A History of English Criminal Law and its Administration from 1750*, 5 vols. (London: Stevens and Sons Limited, 1948–86), 1:451–72; Stephens, Sir Leslie, "Dodd, William" in Sir Leslie Stephens and Sir Sidney Lee, eds., *The Dictionary of National Biography*, 10 vols., 12 supplements (Oxford, England: Oxford University Press, 1917–1993), 5:1060–62.

## Dostoyevsky (or Dostoievsky), Fyodor Mikhailovich (1821–1881)

Russian writer known for his book *Crime and Punishment* (1866), and for *The House of the Dead* (1858), the latter of which recorded in a nonfiction form his life experiences with capital punishment of which he was nearly a victim.

Born in Moscow on 11 November 1821, he received his education there and at the Military Engineering Academy at St. Petersburg. Although he graduated in 1843 with the rank of sublieutenant, he resigned the following year upon the death of his father to become a writer. His first work, *Poor People,* appeared two years later, and he began to contribute articles to the Russian magazine *Annals of the Country.* In 1847, Dostoyevsky became involved with an underground anarchist group that opposed the Russian government. For his connection with the group he was arrested, tried, and condemned to death in 1849. While on the scaffold, awaiting his turn to be hanged, Dostoyevsky received a last-minute pardon that exiled him to Siberia for four years.

The years in Siberia were horrible for the young Russian writer, and in 1858 he told of this experience in his little-considered work *The House of the Dead*. His 1866 work *Crime and Punishment* was a frank examination of the Russian legal system. It also reflected, according to Geoffrey Wigoder, Dostoyevsky's "wrestling with the problem of the existence of God." It concerns a young student, Rodion Raskolnikov, who must deal with his conscience after committing a murder of a person he feels is evil and allowing another to confess. In strong dramatic fashion, Dostoyevsky deals with murder, then a capital offense in Russia, and how this young man is convinced that it is better for all if he confesses. The officials in charge reward him at the last moment for his courage and sentence him instead to eight years of hard labor in Siberia.

Dostoyevsky's later works, including *The Insulted and the Injured* (1867), *The Idiot* (1869), and *The Brothers Karamazov* (1881), are considered classics. Dostoyevsky died in St. Petersburg soon after the publication of *The Brothers Karamazov* on 9 February 1881.

**Reference:** Wigoder, Geoffrey, *They Made History: A Biographical Dictionary* (New York: Simon & Schuster, 1993), 173–74.

## Drawing and Quartering

Method of capital punishment, perhaps one of the most brutal, in which a prisoner was hanged until near death, torn down from the gallows, had his four limbs tied to two or four horses, and was then pulled apart as the horses ran off in different directions. Another part of the ritual was disembowelment. After he was hanged, while still alive, the culprit was dragged from the gallows, laid down on the ground, and his entrails were ripped from his body. Sometimes his genitals were also chopped off. Still alive after all this, the culprit was shown his entrails, before they were thrown on a fire and burned. At this point, the four limbs of the nearly dead victim were tied to two or four horses and he was pulled apart as the horses ran off in different directions.

The first man to suffer this punishment appears to have been William Maurice, the son of a nobleman, who was drawn and quartered in 1241 for piracy, although crime historian Jay Robert Nash contends that the first victim was actually the Welsh prince David in 1283. A notable victim was Sir William Wallace, the Scottish patriot. Nash also reports that the Statute of Treason, enacted by the English parliament in 1351, mandated that drawing and quartering was to be the official punishment of England.

One victim of the practice of drawing and quartering was Richard Fetherston, the Catholic martyr. The chaplain to King Henry VIII's Queen, Katherine of Aragon, and the tutor to their daughter, the future Queen Mary I, Fetherston objected to the Pope's granting of a small stipend to Katherine, who had been previously married to Henry's deceased older brother, Arthur. Because he refused to bow to his king, Fetherston was imprisoned with others who dissented in the Tower of London. On 30 July 1540, along with fellow dissenters Thomas Abell and Edward Powell, he was taken from the Tower, hanged, and, while still alive, disemboweled, beheaded, and then quartered with the use of four horses, which pulled apart his headless body.

Another victim of drawing and quartering was Robert-François Damiens, a Frenchman condemned for attempting to assassinate King Louis XV. During his execution in 1757, the horses failed to tear him apart because he was so muscular. Faced with this dilemma, the executioner made incisions in his limbs, which then were ripped from Damiens's body more easily. Damiens's was the last execution by drawing and quartering in France.

**References:** Laurence, John, *A History of Capital Punishment* (New York: The Citadel Press, 1960), 6; Nash, Jay Robert, *Encyclopedia of World Crime*, 4 vols. (Wilmette, IL: CrimeBooks, Inc., 1990), 2:3286; Spierenburg, Pieter, "The Body and the State: Early Modern Europe" in Norval Morris and David J. Rothman, eds., *The Oxford History of the Prison: The Practice of Punishment in Western Society* (New York: Oxford University Press, 1995), 49.

## Drug "Kingpins," Execution of, as Mandated in American Law

See Federal Death Penalty Act of 1994

## Duchesne, Père

See Hébert, Jacques-René

## *Dugger v. Adams* (489 U.S. 401, 103 L.Ed. 2d 435, 109 S.Ct. 1211 [1989])

U.S. Supreme Court case holding that even though the instruction to the jury that its sentencing recommendation of life or death was not binding on the court was mistakenly delivered to the seated jury rather than to the venire panel (the entire pool of potential jurors), that mistake was not an unconstitutional violation of a defendant's rights to a fair trial.

Aubrey Dennis Adams, Jr., was tried in 1978 in a Florida court for the murder of an eight-year-old girl. Florida law bound the judge to instruct the venire panel that if they found the defendant guilty, their sentencing recommendation may or may not be applied by the court. The judge failed to do this; however, as appeals courts as well as the Supreme Court later noted, the judge did make this instruction clear to each juror as they were selected to sit, even interrupting one counsel's questioning of a potential juror twice to explain the law. Defense counsel did not object to the judge's bending of the law. On 20 October 1978, Adams was convicted of first-degree murder. The jury recommended death, and the judge agreed, sentencing Adams to die in Florida's electric chair.

For several years of his appeals, Adams and his attorneys did not mention any challenge to the judge's error. However, on 11 June 1985, the U.S. Supreme Court struck down a conviction in *Caldwell v. Mississippi,* holding that a prosecutor's remark to the jury "tainted" the atmosphere for a fair trial. Adams then appealed both his conviction and death sentence under the "Caldwell doctrine." The U.S. District Court for the Middle District of Florida held that Adams did not have a suit under *Caldwell* and further that his action did not have merit. The circuit court for the eleventh circuit reversed, however, holding that the judge's failure to properly instruct the potential jurors, as per Florida law, tainted Adams's chances for a fair trial. The secretary of Florida's department of corrections, Richard L. Dugger, as well as the state attorney general, Robert Butterworth, appealed to the U.S. Supreme Court. Arguments were heard in the case on 1 November 1988.

Less than four months later, on 28 February 1989, Justice Byron White, speaking for a 5–4 court (Justices Harry Blackmun, William Brennan, Thurgood Marshall, and John Paul Stevens dissenting), held that Adams had no claim under *Caldwell:* "We believe that the Eleventh Circuit failed to give sufficient weight to a critical fact that leads us to conclude, without passing on the Court of Appeals' historical analysis, that *Caldwell* does not provide cause for respondent's procedural default. As we have noted, the decision in *Caldwell* is relevant only to certain types of comment—those that mislead the jury as to its role in the sentencing process in a way that allows the jury to feel less responsible that it should for the sentencing decision."

On 4 May 1989, less than two months after this decision was handed down, Aubrey Adams died in Florida's electric chair.

## Easter Rebellion (Ireland)

See Pearse, Padraic (Patrick) Henry

## *Eddings v. Oklahoma* (455 U.S. 104, 71 L.Ed. 2d 1, 102 S.Ct. 869 [1982])

United States Supreme Court case in which the court struck down a death sentence in which a state trial judge refused to consider the defendant's "family history and emotional disturbance" as mitigating factors in determining a sentence for a conviction of first-degree murder.

Monty Lee Eddings was 16 when he ran away from a juvenile facility and stole a car. Pulled over by an Oklahoma Highway Patrol officer, he reached for a gun he had stolen and killed the policeman with it. He was ordered to stand trial as an adult, and when he pleaded no contest to the charges, was convicted of first-degree murder. The state then proved three aggravating circumstances in the killing. The defense showed that Eddings had an "unhappy upbringing and emotional disturbance," which the judge considered but then sentenced Eddings to death anyway. On appeal, the Court of Criminal Appeals in Oklahoma upheld the death sentence, finding that the state had proved the three aggravating circumstances and that the judge had correctly considered the defendant's age, the only requisite he could follow by state law.

The U.S. Supreme Court heard arguments in the case on 2 November 1981 and handed down its decision on 19 January 1982. Holding for a 5–4 court (Chief Justice Warren Burger, joined by Justices Byron White, Harry Blackmun, and William H. Rehnquist, dissented), Justice Lewis Powell found that since the trial judge did not adequately consider each of Eddings's mitigating factors individually, the death sentence that he imposed violated the Eighth and Fourteenth amendments to the Constitution. Referring to *Lockett v. Ohio* (438 U.S. 586, 98 S.Ct. 2954, 57 L.Ed. 2d 973 [1978]), Justice Powell wrote:

> We now apply the rule in *Lockett* to the circumstances in this case. The trial judge stated that "in following the law," he could not "consider the fact of this young man's violent background." There is no dispute that by "violent background" the trial judge was referring to the mitigating evidence of Eddings' family history. From this statement it is clear that the trial judge did not evaluate the evidence in mitigation and find it wanting as a matter of fact, rather he found that *as a matter of law* he was unable even to consider the evidence. The Court of Appeals took the same approach. It found that the evidence in mitigation was not relevant because it did not tend to provide a legal excuse from criminal responsibility. Thus the court conceded that Eddings had a "personality disorder," but cast this evidence aside on the basis that "he knew the difference between right and wrong . . . and that is the test of criminal responsibility." Similarly, the evidence of Eddings' family history was of "use in explaining" his behavior, but it did not "excuse" the behavior. From these statements it appears that the Court of Criminal Appeals also considered only that evidence to be mitigating which would tend to support a legal excuse from criminal liability. We find that these limitations placed by these courts upon the mitigating evidence they would consider violated the rule in *Lockett*.

He added, "We are not unaware of the extent to which minors engage increasingly in violent crime. Nor do we suggest an absence of legal responsibility where crime in committed by a minor. We are concerned here only with the manner of the imposition of the ultimate penalty: the death sentence imposed for the crime of murder upon an emotionally disturbed youth with a disturbed child's immaturity."

## Eden, William (1745–1814)

British penal law reformer, supporter of capital punishment and its application. Historian Leon Radzinowicz writes of Eden's work:

> Eden agrees in principle with writers such as [the Rev. Martin] Madan and [the Rev. William] Paley, who defended the system of criminal law based on capital punishment, that deterrence is the main object of punishment. But, and here lies the important difference, Eden's doctrine may perhaps be called one of mitigated deterrence. The severity of penal laws should be controlled first by "natural justice" and secondly by "public utility." He rejects the thesis advanced by Madan and Paley that penalties of any degree of severity may be justified if they are effective in preventing a particular crime, and also disagrees with Paley and [Sir William] Blackstone that the severity of punishments should be increased in proportion to the ease with which the corresponding offences may be committed, or to the degree of temptation to commit them. Such a "perversion of distributive justice" must inevitably lead to the appointment of excessively and indiscriminately severe punishments, on the effectiveness of which Eden fully agrees with Montesquieu and [Cesare] Beccaria; like these two authors, he also insists that punishments should bear some proportion to the gravity of offences.

**References:** Radzinowicz, Leon, *A History of English Criminal Law and its Administration from 1750,* 5 vols. (London: Stevens and Sons Limited, 1948–86), 301–02.

## Eichmann, Adolf Otto (1906–1960)

As head of the Jewish section of the Nazi Gestapo during World War II, Adolf Eichmann oversaw and controlled the death machine that put to death some six million Jews during the Holocaust. After the war he fled to South America, but the Israeli government captured him, put him on trial in Israel, and executed him in 1961.

Eichmann was born on 19 March 1906 in Solingen, Germany, but grew up in Linz, Austria. Originally set to become a mechanical engineer, he instead dropped out of school and became a laborer. Sometime in the 1920s he became a friend of Ernst Kaltenbrunner, later head of internal security for the Nazis in Austria. This connection to a powerful Nazi helped Eichmann get a cushy job inside the Austrian wing of the Nazi party on 1 April 1932. After military training, Eichmann was named to the Security Service (SD) as administrator of Jewish emigration (*Judenferat*) with the rank of SS-Scharführer. From 1938 until 1939, he helped to deport 150,000 Jews from Austria. Named to the Reich Central Office for Jewish Emigration in Berlin, and later to the main office of the Reich Security, he helped move more than three million Jews from their homes inside Nazi-occupied Europe to Nazi death camps. Perhaps more than anyone else, he greased the wheels of the Nazi death machine.

As the Allies overran occupied territory in 1945, Eichmann fled Europe with some assistance from the Catholic Church and underground Nazis and settled down in Argentina, where he established a comfortable life under various aliases, including Richard Klement. He seemed to have avoided justice. However, in 1960, Israeli secret agents tracked him down and established a safe house on Garibaldi Street, and on 22 May 1960 grabbed him off the street and secretly flew him to Israel, stunning the world.

A year later, on 11 April 1961, Eichmann's trial began in Jerusalem. Seated in a glass booth to protect him from bystanders, he pleaded that he was only following orders to do what he did. In a sensational trial that lasted until 11 December, scores of witnesses pointed out Eichmann as the head of the mass deportation of Jews. Four days after the defense rested, Eichmann was found guilty of crimes against humanity for his role in the murders of more than six million Jews. Less than six months later, on 31 May 1962, Eichmann faced the hangman's noose at Israel's Ramle Prison. One source commented, "By his standards it was a humane death." The 1975 film *The Man in the Glass Booth,* starring Maximilian Schell, was partly based on his trial.

**References:** Fellows, Lawrence, "Eichmann Dies on Gallows for Role in Killing of Jews," *The New York Times,* 1 June 1962, 1, 2; Harel, Isser, *The House on Garibaldi Street: The first Full Account of the Capture of Adolf Eichmann, Told by the Former Head of Israel's Secret Service* (New York: Viking Press, 1975); Hausner, Gideon, *Justice in Jerusalem* (New York: Harper & Row, 1966); Lord Russell of Liverpool, *The Record: The Trial of Adolf Eichmann for the Crimes Against the Jewish People and Against Humanity* (New York: Alfred A. Knopf, 1963); Taylor, James, and Warren Shaw, *The Third Reich Almanac* (New York: World Almanac, 1987), 105; Zentner, Christian, and Friedemann Bedüftig, eds., *Encyclopedia of the Third Reich,* 2 vols. (New York: Macmillan, 1991), 1:226.

## Electric Chair

Method of execution adopted in the United States in the last decade of the nineteenth century and used strictly in that nation. The majority of executions since then have been done with electricity.

In the 1880s, a wave of reform swept the nation, and among the movements calling out for justice was the anti–capital punishment lobby. Adding to the existing pressure against hanging as punishment were a number of botched executions, and a state legislative commission in New York concluded that the noose should be abolished. At the same time, pioneer inventors Thomas Edison and George Westinghouse were battling over the proper currents to wire American businesses and homes. Edison's direct current (DC) and Westinghouse's alternating current (AC) were then looked at closely by the New York commission to determine whether electricity, a deadly power source, could be used to safely and humanely kill criminals on death row. Edison caught wind of the concept and sent an engineer, Harold Brown, around the United States showing the potential for an "electric chair." In Albany, after a horrible display in which he electrocuted an orangutan, Brown convinced the legislators to adopt the chair once and for all.

The first man set to die in the new instrument was William Kemmler, who had murdered his mistress and was sentenced to hang. Kemmler was seated in the wooden chair in New York's Auburn Prison on 6 August 1890, but what happened was unexpected. The current sent crashing through Kemmler's body was not sufficient to kill him—only to stun him and render him unconscious. As the moist pads cushioning the electrodes began to dry out, his flesh started to burn, and in a comatose state he began to foam at the mouth. It took several shocks to ultimately kill him, and many of the witnesses were horrified. The *World* of New York called Kemmler "the first electrocide."

Following Kemmler, almost a full year passed before the electric chair was utilized again; the scene had shifted from Auburn to Sing Sing prison at Ossining, New York. This time, four men were put to death on the same day: murderers Harris A. Smiler, James Slocum, Joseph Wood, and Subihick Jugigo. The *New-York Times* reported: "There was nothing about the executions of the horrible nature that shocked the country when Kemmler was made the first victim of the [electrocution] law. If the testimony of the score of witnesses is to be believed, the executions demonstrated the use of electricity for public executions to be practical whether or not it is humane. Although the Kemmler butchery, with all its terrible details, cannot be forgotten, against that one awful failure the advocates of the law now point with unconcealed pride to four 'successes.'"

The next execution, which also took place at Sing Sing, was of Martin D. Loppy, who had murdered his wife. As he walked to the death chamber on 7 December 1891, the 51-year-old Loppy needed assistance from prison officials and clergy. But his execution was remembered more for its horror than for Loppy's lack of courage. As the current was switched on, Loppy lunged forward, straining against the straps and forcing his long fingernails into his palms. After fifteen seconds, the current of 1,750 volts was turned off, and Dr. Carlos MacDonald, who would supervise the execution of presidential assassin Leon Czolgosz ten years hence and was here in the same capacity, saw at once that Loppy was not dead. The killer's windpipe opened and foam began to spew forth from his mouth. Again, the current was turned back on, and again Loppy groaned against the straps that held him, although he seemed to be unconscious as he did it. Suddenly, as the witnesses were watching, Loppy's left eyeball popped, and the aqueous humor, the liquid in the eyeball, dripped out and flowed down his face. Smoke began to rise as the burning electrode began to eat away at his skin. MacDonald ordered that the power be turned off, but still Loppy was not dead. For a third time, the current was turned back on, this time for 21 and a half seconds. By now, Loppy had expired.

Loppy's gruesome death did not stop the move toward further electrocutions. Such notables as wife murderers Carlyle Harris and Dr. Robert W. Buchanan went to their deaths in the chair at Sing Sing in the years before the turn of the century. Martha Place, the first woman to be electrocuted, was convicted of killing her step-daughter and attempting to murder her husband. Her case aroused great controversy: Should a woman suffer the same fate of electrocution as a man? Governor Theodore Roosevelt appointed a committee to look into whether Place deserved this ultimate of penalties. After thorough research, the committee reported that Place's crime made her eligible for death in the electric chair. She was put to death on 20 March 1899, the first woman to suffer death by electricity.

The new century did not dampen the nation's enthusiasm for cleaning out its death rows. Although the number of fouled up executions allowed for the introduction of the gas chamber, the firing squad, and, for some states, the return of the noose, the electric chair remained the leading instrument of death. Master Soviet spies Julius and Ethel Rosenberg died in the electric chair. But in the 1960s, executions became less and less numerous and were banned entirely (along with all other forms of capital punishment) by the U.S. Supreme Court in 1972. The chair did return to its place as a capital punishment tool after the Supreme Court lifted its ban on the death penalty in 1976; among the first to die in the United States under the new laws was John Spenkelink, a murderer who was put to death in Florida's "Old Sparky" in 1979. By the 1990s, however, as groups like the American Civil

Liberties Union sued to have the death penalty declared cruel and unusual punishment, states turned to lethal injection as a logical alternative.

The electric chair is usually a wooden device, though some are metal, with two legs in back and a single one in front. The routine of electrocution is simple: the criminal is escorted into the death chamber, unshackled, and bound to the chair with leather straps. The death warrant is read, and final words are requested. (There are almost never final words or ceremonial good-byes as depicted in the movies.) After a short period, in which connections are checked, the executioner throws a switch that sends a cycle of about 2,000 volts shooting into the prisoner, causing instantaneous death. (Such a shock destroys the vital functions of the brain that keep people alive; movements by the body afterward are muscle contractions.) After about a minute, the charge is lowered to 1,000 volts to end all muscle action in the body, until a doctor proclaims the prisoner to be dead. The skin can be burnt like seared meat, the hair singed, limbs may be frozen into place (as was the case with Ethel Rosenberg in 1953), or, in extreme cases, the victim may even catch fire (as with Jesse Tafero in the Florida electric chair in 1990). The electric chair has never been utilized outside the United States, and in many states as of this writing it is being replaced with lethal injection.

**See also:** Buchanan, Dr. Robert Williams; *In re Kemmler;* Kemmler, William Francis; Place, Martha Garretson Savacoli.

**References:** "Far Worse Than Hanging: Kemmler's Death Proves an Awful Spectacle," *The New-York Times,* 7 August 1890, 1, 2; "The First Electrocide: How Brutal Murderer Kemmler Was Killed at Auburn," *The World* (New York), 7 August 1890, 1; "Four Men Die By the Law: The Electric Current Does Its Deadly Work," *The New-York Times,* 8 July 1891, 1; "Gov. Hill's Sixth Victim: Scenes of Horror in Sing Sing Prison Death Chamber," *The New-York Times,* 8 December 1891, 1; "Kemmler's Death by Torture," *New York Herald,* 7 August 1890, 3; "Mrs. Place Electrocuted: Brooklyn Murderess Put to Death at Sing Sing Today," *New Haven Evening Register,* 20 March 1899, 1; Nicolai, Sandra, Karen Riley, Rhonda Christensen, Patrice Stych, and Leslie Greunke, eds., *The Question of Capital Punishment* (Lincoln, NE: CONtact, Inc., 1981), 74–75; "Seven Put to Death in Hour at Sing Sing; the Highest Number to Die There in a Day Since Electricity Was Adopted," *The New York Times,* 13 August 1912, 5; Sifakis, Carl, *The Encyclopedia of American Crime* (New York: Facts on File, 1982), 237–38.

## Ellis, Ruth Neilson (1926–1955)

Few murderers in the history of crime have elicited as much sympathy as Ruth Ellis in the days before she was hanged for the murder of her lover, David Blakely; at the same time, she seemed the last person to become a *cause celébré,* having committed a cold-blooded murder in front of several witnesses.

Ellis was a waitress and at times a nude model who had had untold numbers of lovers and as many abortions at a time when English society frowned on both. But her involvement with Blakely, an unsuccessful race car driver, was her ultimate undoing. He sometimes beat Ellis, then made up with her, and overall their relationship was unhealthy. In 1955 Blakely, after finding Ellis involved with another man, decided to leave her. Ellis suspected Blakely of an affair himself, and when he stood her up on Good Friday, she went in search of him the following morning. He had been with friends, he told her. She left him and went home. After several drinks on Easter Sunday, she again went in search of him, this time finding him outside the Magdala Pub in London. Confronting him, she pulled out a .38 caliber handgun and shot him. As he stumbled down the street, she fired again and again, emptying the gun into her former lover until he lay dead on the street.

On trial for her life, she was asked only one question on cross-examination by Christmas Humphreys, the queen's counsel: "Mrs. Ellis, when you fired that revolver at close range into the body of David Blakely, what did you intend to do?" She answered, "It is obvious that when I shot him I intended to kill him." The jury took only 14 minutes to return with a verdict of guilty of first-degree murder, and she was sentenced to death. A month went by between sentencing and the carrying out of the sentence, and in that time, Great Britain went through a spasm of self-doubt. Should a woman be hanged by a so-called civilized society? Her defenders included the writer Raymond Chandler, who wrote: "No other country in the world would hang this woman. . . . This thing haunts me and, so far as I may say it, disgusts me as something obscene. I am not referring to the trial, of course, but to the medieval savagery of the law."

On 13 July 1955, Ruth Ellis became the last woman to be put to death in Great Britain. Because Britain, unlike the United States, allows no press to report on executions, there is no eyewitness report of her death. But the *Daily Mirror* of London asked on its front page, "SHOULD HANGING BE STOPPED?" Ten years later, after a short moratorium, England ended capital punishment. Ruth Ellis had been one of the last to face the death penalty there. Twenty-seven years later her son, Andria, committed suicide. Ruth Ellis's story was dramatized in the 1985 British motion picture *Dance with a Stranger*, starring Miranda Richardson as Ellis.

**References:** Cyriax, Oliver, *Crime: An Encyclopedia* (London: André Deutsch Ltd., 1993), 109–10; Goodman, Jonathan, and Patrick Pringle, eds., *The Trial of Ruth Ellis* (Newton Abbot, England: David and Charles, 1974); Marks, Laurence, and Tony van den Bergh, *Ruth Ellis: A Case of Diminished Responsibility?* (London: Macdonald and Jane's, 1977).

## Engel, George

See Haymarket Martyrs Case

## Essex, Robert Devereux, Second Earl of (1566–1601)

English nobleman and soldier beheaded for treason against Queen Elizabeth I.

The eldest son of Walter Devereux, the first earl of Essex, and his wife Lettice Knollys, Robert was born at Netherwood, Herefordshire, on 19 November 1566. Robert was educated at Trinity College, Cambridge, and he was taken under the wing of Queen Elizabeth, whom his father had served by suppressing a rebellion in 1569 and by helping to capture and execute many Irish. In 1586, Robert Devereaux joined Robert Dudley, the Earl of Leicester, and served with great distinction under his command in Holland, particularly at the siege of the city of Zutphen, and, on returning to England the following year, was treated with great honor in Elizabeth's court. Upon Dudley's death in 1588 he became the queen's closest companion, yet two years later he infuriated her by secretly marrying the widow of Sir Philip Sidney, a daughter of one of the queen's former enemies. They eventually reconciled, and he served in military and naval expeditions for the Crown, notably the assault on Cádiz in Spain in 1596. However, on his return, the queen reprimanded him for not capturing enough Spanish territory or more Spanish treasure. Devereux retired as chancellor of the University of Cambridge in 1598.

That same year, he got into an argument while visiting with the queen; in their famous fight, she boxed him on the ear and bade him to "go and be hanged."

Another reconciliation followed, and he was called out of retirement to lead the British army as Lord Lieutenant in Ireland to suppress a rebellion there. Failing at that, he was accused by the queen's counselors of signing a humiliating peace; tried for treason, he was convicted but appealed to the queen and was pardoned.

Angered at the treatment he received at the hands of Elizabeth's advisers, particularly William Cecil, First Baron Burghley, and Sir Walter Raleigh, he set about forcing the queen to dismiss them from her court. Instead, a contingent of the queen's soldiers arrested Devereux and locked him in the Tower of London. After a second trial for treason, in which he was prosecuted by a former friend, Francis Bacon, he was sentenced to be beheaded, a punishment that the queen, after some hesitation (and recalling the first death warrant so that she could change her mind), approved. Devereux biographer Sidney L. Lee writes, "On Wednesday, the 25th [of February 1601], Essex, dressed in black . . . was led to the high court above Caesar's Tower, within the Tower precincts. About a hundred persons were present. Essex acknowledged the justice of his sentence, and asseverated [declared] that he died a protestant. After praying aloud his head was severed at three blows. [His tormentor] Cecil wrote that he 'suffered with great patience and humility.' Marshal Biron, who met with a similar fate soon afterwards, declared that he died more like a minister than a soldier."

**Reference:** Lee, Sidney L., "Devereux, Robert" in Sir Leslie Stephens and Sir Sidney Lee, eds., *The Dictionary of National Biography,* 10 vols., 12 supplements (Oxford, England: Oxford University Press, 1917–1993), 5:875–90.

## Executioners

Without the man dressed in black, standing before the crowd during a beheading, or in front of a small assemblage of witnesses for a hanging or electrocution, the execution would not take place. "The profession of headsman, hangman, lord high executioner, or by whatever other title he may have been known, is very ancient," writes historian John Laurence. Furthermore, it has always been cloaked in mystery.

Only before the twentieth century, and in nations other than the United States, were the identities of executioners known at all. The first man known to hold the post as official executioner was the famed Jack Ketch, or Jack Catch, although historian Oliver Cyriax claims that his real name was Richard Jacquet. Known for his savagery in carrying out executions, his position was preserved for most of his life by Judge George Jeffreys, Lord Chancellor of England; during his reign it was said that "while Jeffreys sits on the bench, Ketch on the gibbet sits." After Jeffreys's death, Ketch killed a woman and, in 1686, swung on the same gallows where he had seen so many off. Ketch's executioner was one John Price, who, ironically, later died on the same gallows himself. Afterwards, all British executioners were known by the name Jack Ketch.

British executioner William Calcraft, who worked in the nineteenth century, had a sign on his boot and shoe mending store that read, "Executioner to Her Majesty." One of the least famous of the British executioners was Sir Claude de Crespigny, who, using the name Charles Maldon or Maddon, helped execute three murderers in 1886, his one and only time in the hangman's role. However, the most famed of the English executioners were the members of the Pierrepoint family, including "Old" Harry Pierrepoint (1877–1922), his older brother Tom (1871–1955), and Tom's nephew Albert (1905–1992), who presided over the executions of 550 people in his career, including approximately 200 war criminals during World War II.

The French family named the Sansons is considered by historians to have been the most prestigious and prodigious to have held the title of official state executioner in France. Starting with Charles Sanson, appointed in 1688, and continuing until 1847, when Henru-Clement Sanson was dismissed for trying to sell the state guillotine, the family "reign" lasted for more than two centuries; it was Charles-Henri Sanson who was the executioner for Louis XVI, Danton, and Robespierre, in that order. After the dismissal of Sanson in 1847, the state used anonymous headsmen to conduct its executions.

In the United States, the executioner has usually been an anonymous local person who was paid a small sum to throw the switch or pull the handle. In the 1980s and 1990s, however, with the use of lethal injection, the executioner has become a nameless physician.

**References:** Christophe, Robert (Len Ortzen, trans.), *The Executioners: a History of the Sanson Family, Public Executioners from 1688 to 1847* (London: A Barker, 1962); Cyriax, Oliver, *Crime: An Encyclopedia* (London: André Deutsch Ltd., 1993), 85, 209, 356; Laurence, John, *A History of Capital Punishment* (New York: The Citadel Press, 1960), 86; Nash, Jay Robert, *Encyclopedia of World Crime, 4 vols.* (Wilmette, IL: CrimeBooks, Inc., 1990), 2:2678–79.

## *Ex parte Quirin et al.* (317 U.S. 1 [1942])

U.S. Supreme Court case deciding the fate of seven Nazi saboteurs who entered the United States to commit sabotage, and who were tried before a military commission established by the President of the United States, which convicted them and sentenced them to death. The case is officially titled *Ex parte Quirin, Ex parte Haupt, Ex parte Kerling, Ex parte Burger, Ex parte Heinck, Ex parte Thiel,* and *Ex parte Neubauer.* (It also contained the case of *United States ex rel. Quirin v. Cox, Brigadier General, U.S.A., Provost Marshal of the Military District of Washington, and Six Other Cases.)*

The seven men, all Nazi spies, were born in Germany and were at one time American citizens but returned to Germany between 1933 and 1941; all but petitioner Haupt resumed their German citizenship. After the declaration of war between the United States and Germany, the men were trained in sabotage at a school near Berlin, where "they were instructed in the use of explosives and in methods of secret writing." Joining with a German spy named George Dasch, they sailed from an occupied French seaport in a German submarine; once off the American coast, near Amagansett Beach on Long Island, they split into two groups.

On the night of 13 June 1942, the first group came ashore, armed with explosives, incendiaries, fuses, detonators, timing devices, and acids, and more than $90,000 for expenses. They changed from their German military uniforms into American civilian clothes and made their way to New York City. On 17 June, the rest of the group came ashore on a beach near Jacksonville, Florida, and scattered, eventually meeting up in Chicago. Little is known about how the men were apprehended, except that evidence was discovered on the New York beach by a Coast Guardsman. On 27 June, J. Edgar Hoover, director of the Federal Bureau of Investigation, announced that Dasch and the other seven men had been arrested.

On 2 July, President Franklin D. Roosevelt announced that he was creating a military commission to try the men on charges of espionage, sabotage, and conspiracy to commit both acts against the United States. On 8 July, five days after the charges were filed, the trial started at the Department of Justice building in Washington, D.C. The case was wrapped up on 20 July; that same day, the defendants (except Dasch) appealed to the U.S. Supreme Court to hear their writs of habeas corpus. The Court ordered itself into special session to hear arguments. These were held on 29 and 30 July; Col. Kenneth C. Royall, an army lawyer who had defended the men during their trial, argued their case before the Court, while Attorney General Francis Biddle carried the government's case.

On 31 July, just a day after the arguments, a per curiam opinion (an opinion without an identified author) expressing the views of a unanimous court, denied the defendants a motion of leave to file the writs of habeas corpus. In a separate opinion, authored by Chief Justice Harlan Fiske Stone, the court held unanimously that the military commission established to try the defendants was "in conformity to the laws and Constitution of the United States." Furthermore, Stone wrote:

> The detention and trial of petitioners—ordered by the President in the declared exercise of his powers as Commander in Chief of the Army in time of war and of grave public danger—are not to be set aside by the courts without the clear conviction that they are in conflict with the Constitution or laws of Congress constitutionally enacted. . . . Accordingly, we conclude that . . . his Order convening the Commission was a lawful order and that the Commission was lawfully constituted; that the petitioners were held in lawful custody and did not show cause for their discharge. It follows that the orders of the District Court should be affirmed, and that leave to file petitions for habeas corpus in this Court should be denied.

On 8 August 1942, six of the saboteurs, Neuhauer, Heinck, Thiel, Kerling, Haupt, and Quirin, all died in the electric chair in the District of Columbia jail in Washington. Fellow conspirators George Dasch and Ernest Peter Burger received prison sentences.

**References:** "Nazi Spies Caught Within Two Weeks," *The New York Times,* 9 August 1942, 34; "6 Nazi Spies Die: Clemency for Two; Executions in Capital Jail Carry Out Verdict of Army Commission," *The New York Times,* 9 August 1942, 1; "Sketches of Spies Bare Nazi System," *The New York Times,* 9 August 1942, 35.

## *Ex parte Spies* (123 U.S. 131 [1887])

U.S. Supreme Court decision in which four anarchists were put to death in Illinois for the murders of several policemen during a violent labor rally.

August Spies, the subject of this decision, was joined by fellow socialists Adolph Fischer, Albert Richard Parsons, and George Engel in challenging their convictions and death sentences for their roles in the brutal Haymarket Square riot in 1886 that left several policemen dead. After a trial in which their views came under closer scrutiny than the crimes that resulted from the riot they were accused of inciting, they were sentenced to be hanged. The U.S. Supreme Court decided to hear the issues in the case of *Ex parte Spies and Others,* also known as The Anarchists' Case, and arguments for a writ of error were heard on 24 October 1887.

On 2 November, less than two weeks later, Chief Justice Morrison Remick Waite held for a unanimous court in denying the defendants the writ of error they had been pursuing. In his lengthy opinion he examined each point raised by the defendants, then concluded, "Being of [the] opinion, therefore, that the federal questions presented by the counsel for the petitioners, and which they say they desire to argue, are not involved in the determination of the case as it appears on the face of the record, we deny the writ." On 11 November, nine days after this decision was handed down, the four men were put to death.

**See also:** Haymarket Martyrs Case for information on the people and events relating to this decision.

## Fawkes, Guy or Guido (1570–1606)

English conspirator, member of the infamous Gunpowder Plot to blow up Parliament and murder King James I of England, and put to death for his role in the conspiracy.

Born in York in April 1570, Fawkes was raised in the Protestant faith and received his education at a Protestant school in York. But when his mother married his stepfather, Dionis Baynbrigge (or Bainbridge), Fawkes turned to Roman Catholicism, and it was this turn of events that led to his horrible end.

Trained as a soldier, he left England in 1593 to join the Spanish army as a soldier of fortune, and he saw action at Calais when that French town fell to Spanish forces. But by 1605, Fawkes had become involved with several Roman Catholics who wanted their faith freed from the intolerance of the Protestant king, James I. The group, led by Robert Catesby, included Thomas Winter, Thomas Percy, John Wright, and Fawkes, and by the middle of 1605 they had decided that James should be murdered. They intended to blow up the Parliament building while he was there, and thus their conspiracy became known to history as the Gunpowder Plot. The conspirators rented a building near the Parliament building and left it up to Fawkes, the former soldier, to secure 36 barrels of gunpowder, which were hidden in the coal cellar in the basement.

Meanwhile Catesby, in order to get more support for what he perceived would be a panic after the king and most of the government was blown up, tried to recruit more conspirators. Among these was Francis Tresham, who warned his Catholic brother-in-law, Lord Monteagle, to avoid attending the meeting of the House of Lords on the day the king would visit, 5 November 1605. Monteagle alerted the government to the plot, and the cellar was

raided. Catesby, Percy, and two others were killed in the resistance, and Fawkes and his confederates were arrested. Evidence suggests that Fawkes was brutally tortured before he confessed his and the others' roles; comparisons between his signature before and after the arrest show a man who was brutally beaten.

At trial, the men claimed different reasons for their respective roles in the plot: Digby, speaking for the group, asserted that his motives were loyalty to his friends, religion, the fostering of an atmosphere of tolerance, and hatred of the laws against Catholicism that the men feared were soon to be promulgated. When Digby asked that he alone be punished but that his friends and family be spared, Lord Coke, presiding over the trial, quoted from the Psalm 109: "May his children be fatherless and his wife a widow. Let his children be carried about vagabonds and beg, and in one generation may his name be blotted out." The jury returned with a verdict of guilty and demanded that all be drawn and quartered. Fawkes, still suffering from the brutal beating he had received, asked only that a number of Jesuit priests, accused of being involved in the plot, be spared any punishment whatsoever. On 27 January 1606 Fawkes and his confederates were taken in a cold rain from Westminster Hall to the Tower of London, where they waited four days while the scaffold was constructed.

As they were taken from the Tower, they could see that beside the scaffold a butcher stood with knives ready to slice off their genitals and cut out their entrails, while a fire burned where they would be destroyed. Digby went first, and after him, Thomas and Robert Winter, John Grant, Bates, Ambrose Rookwood, Robert Keyes, and then Fawkes. The hangman's job during this form of execution is not to kill by hanging but to inflict the maximum amount of agony while keeping the subject alive to be drawn and quartered. Fawkes tried to cheat: he ran onto the scaffold and jumped off, attempting to break his neck, but he failed. When Fawkes was cut down, the butcher sliced off his genitals and removed his entrails, held them up before the dying man, and, declaring to the crowd that "this is the heart of a traitor," placed them in the fire. Finally, he used a sword to cut off Fawkes's head. John Winter, the last conspirator to die, was executed at Worcester's Red Hill on 7 April 1606.

The same month that the plotters met their fateful ends (January 1606) the Parliament established 5 November as a day of public thanksgiving for the salvation of the king. Yet every year on that date, England commemorates Fawkes's attempt with an air of celebration. As the children's poem relates,

> Please to remember the fifth of November
> The Gunpowder Treason and Plot
> I see no reason why the Gunpowder
> Treason
> Should ever be forgot.

**References:** Garnett, Henry, *Portrait of Guy Fawkes: An Experiment in Biography* (London: Hale, 1962); Goetz, Philip W., ed.-in-Chief, *The New Encyclopedia Britannica,* 22 vols. (Chicago: Encyclopedia Britannica, Inc., 1995), 5:571–72; *The History of Guy Fawkes and the Torrid Conspiracy of the Gun Powder Plot* (York, England: Printed by J. Kendrew, 1815?); Lathbury, Thomas, *Guy Fawkes; or, A Complete History of the Gunpowder Treason, A.D. 1605* (London: L. Parker, 1839); Loomie, Albert Joseph, *Guy Fawkes in Spain: The 'Spanish Treason' in Spanish Documents* (London: University of London Institute of Historical Research, 1971).

## Federal Death Penalty Act (FDPA)

American Congressional legislation enacted into law in 1994 as part of the Federal Crime Control Act of 1994. Signed into law by President Bill Clinton on 13 September of that year, it mandated the death penalty for 60 crimes never before covered in the federal statutes. This law supplemented the Anti-Drug Abuse Act of 1988, which allowed for the federal execution of so-called drug kingpins, leading figures in illegal narcotics traffic.

Cited as Title VI of the Crime Control Act, the FDPA mandates the death penalty for, among other offenses,

> any other offense for which a sentence of death is provided, if the defendant, as determined beyond a reasonable doubt at the hearing under 3593—(A) intentionally killed the victim; (B) intentionally inflicted serious bodily injury that resulted in the death of the victim; (C) intentionally participated in an act, contemplating that the life of a person would be taken or intending that lethal force would be used. . . . and the victim died as a direct result of the act; or (D) intentionally and specifically engaged in an act of violence, knowing that the act created a grave risk of death to a person . . . such that participation in the act constituted a reckless disregard for human life and the victim died as a direct result of the act.

The act also required death for specified crimes, such as the murder by an inmate serving a life sentence in a federal penitentiary; the murder of a federal law enforcement official; a drive-by shooting committed in the course of certain drug offenses; carjacking resulting in death; the foreign murder of American nationals; and murder by escaped federal inmates.

## Firing Squad

Method of execution in which the condemned is placed before an assemblage of shooters, tied down, and shot (usually in the heart) to death. The first man known to have suffered this death in the New World was George Kendall, one of the councillors of Virginia. Since then, many persons have been executed before the firing squad, including John Doyle Lee, a Mormon put to death for instigating the so-called Mountain Meadows Massacre of settlers heading west; Joe Hill, a labor organizer executed in 1915; Eddie Slovik, an American soldier put to death for desertion during World War II; and Gary Gilmore, the first man put to death following the Supreme Court's ruling in *Gregg v. Georgia* that the death penalty did not violate the Eighth Amendment to the Constitution. No woman, at least in the United States, has undergone this form of capital punishment.

The protocol involved in preparing a criminal for death before the firing squad is as complex and intricate as some other forms of capital punishment but requires more people. Prior to the execution, a five-man squad is chosen; four of them are given guns with live ammunition while a fifth is given a black round so that each can honestly say that he might not have fired the fatal round (although a blank does not create any recoil). This group is usually situated behind a white sheet with small holes cut in it for the rifles, some 10 to 20 feet from a chair (in Gilmore's case, an ordinary office chair) where the criminal will be seated.

After the criminal is tied down, a white patch is pinned over his heart, and, on a call, the squad fires at the patch. The criminal ultimately dies of heart failure, but the destruction of the central nervous system as well as other vital organs contributes to his end. There have been problems, however: Gilmore was hit in the heart with all four shots but took two minutes to die; in 1951 Elisio Mares, also executed in Utah, was hit in the chest but not the heart, and bled to death.

Except in rare cases, the firing squad is unique to the United States. Today, however, it is the main form of capital punishment in China, where forgers and others convicted of corruption are shot at point blank range in the back of the head, as are murderers and rapists.

**See also:** Gilmore, Gary; Hill, Joe; Lee, John Doyle; Slovik, Edward Donald.

**References:** Sifakis, Carl, *The Encyclopedia of American Crime* (New York: Facts on File, 1982), 237; Trombley, Stephen, *The Execution Protocol: Inside America's Capital Punishment Industry* (New York: Crown Publishers, 1992), 10–11.

## Fischer, Adolph

See Haymarket Martyrs Case

## Fisher, John, Saint, Bishop of Rochester (1459?–1535)

English prelate beheaded by King Henry VIII of England for refusing to consent to the annulment of Henry's marriage to Catherine of Aragon in violation of Church law.

Fisher was born the eldest son of Robert Fisher, a mercer (merchant), and his wife Agnes, at Beverley, in Yorkshire, probably in 1459. Little is known of his early life, except that he might have attended a religious school in the Rochester Cathedral. He later attended Michaelhouse, at Cambridge, under the tutelage of one William de Melton, where he received his bachelor of arts degree in 1487. Later a fellow of Michaelhouse, he was awarded a master's degree in 1491 and became the master, or president, of the college in 1497. In 1501, Fisher was named vice-chancellor of the university.

On 14 October 1504, Pope Julius II issued a bull electing Fisher as the See of Rochester. In this capacity he became a close confidant of English royalty, including kings Henry VII and Henry VIII. In 1533, when Henry VIII asked the pope to annul his marriage to Catherine of Aragon so that he could marry Anne Boleyn, the request was refused. Henry then established the Anglican Church, the first act of which was to grant the controversial annulment.

Fisher did not accede to the notion of royal supremacy over the pope and bitterly derided the establishment of the Anglican Church. For the next two years, Fisher was a thorn in Henry's side, refusing to accept as legal his marriage to Anne Boleyn or any child born to them. Summoned to London to take an oath of allegiance to the king, Fisher refused (as did his compatriot, Sir Thomas More). On 16 April 1535, the elderly Fisher was arrested and taken to the Tower of London, where he was soon joined by More.

The Act of Supremacy, passed in November 1534 by the Parliament, made those who refused to recognize the supremacy of the king guilty of treason. Yet Fisher, like More, refused to recant their belief that Henry was answerable to the pope in Rome. For Fisher's courage, Pope Paul III thought to send to him, through channels, a cardinal's hat. When hearing of this, Henry allegedly exclaimed, "Mother of God! He shall wear it on his shoulders, for I will leave him never a head to set it on."

Fisher was quickly tried for treason against the crown. Because no evidence existed of Fisher's actual intentions to overthrow the king, Henry had him admit before the court that the monarch was not supreme even though he was the head of the Anglican Church. Armed with this statement, the court found Fisher guilty and sentenced him to be beheaded. He was so frail that he had to be carried from his cell in the Tower of London to Tower Hill, where he was beheaded.

English writer Thomas Bailey, writing of Fisher's execution 230 years later, described Fisher's last words and his death:

> "Christian people, I am come hither to die for the faith of Christ's holy Catholick Church; and I thank God hitherto my stomach hath served me very well thereunto, so that yet I have not feared death: wherefore I desire you all to help and assist with your prayers, that at the very point and instant of death's stroke, I may in that very moment stand stedfast without fainting in any one point of the Catholick faith, free from any fear. . . . And I beseech Almighty God, of his infinite goodness to save the King and this realm; and that it may please him to hold his hand over it, and send the king good council." The executioner being ready, with a sharp and a heavy axe cut asunder his slender neck at one blow; which bled so abundantly that many wondered to see so much blood issue out of so slender and lean body.

British historian John Laurence wrote:

> Fisher . . . was executed on St. Albans Day, the 22nd of June, 1535. It is recorded, "The next day after his burying, the head, being parboyled was pricked upon a pole, and set high upon London Bridge, among the rest of the holy Carthusians' heads that suffered death lately before him. And here I cannot omit to declare unto you the miraculous sight of this head, which, after it had stood up the space of fourteen dayes upon the bridge, could not be perceived to wast[e] nor consume; neither for the weather which was then very hot, neither for the parboyling in hot water, but grew daily fresher and fresher, so that in this lifetime he never looked so well; for his

cheeks being beautified with a comely red, the face looked as though it had beholden the people passing by, and would have spoken to them; which many took for a miracle that Almighty God was pleased to shew above the course of nature in thus preserving the flesh and lively colour of his face."

Two weeks later, on 6 July 1535, More was beheaded on the same spot. Both men were canonized as saints by Pope Pius XI in 1935.

**See also:** More, Sir Thomas, Saint.

**References:** Bailey, Thomas, *The Life and Death of the Renowned John Fisher, Bishop of Rochester, who was Beheaded on Tower-Hill, the 22nd of June 1535, and in the 27th Year of the Reign of King Henry VII, Comprising the Highest and Hidden Transactions of Church and State in the Reign of King Henry the Eighth; with divers Moral, Historical and Political Animadversions upon Cardinal Wolsey, Sir Thomas More, and Martin Luther; with a Full Relation of Queen Katherine's Divorce, Carefully Selected from Several antient Records* (Dublin, Ireland: Printed for P. Lord, R. Fitzsimmons, and D. Kylly, Booksellers, 1765), 143–45; Laurence, John, *A History of Capital Punishment* (New York: The Citadel Press, 1960), 32–33; Mullinger, James Bass, "Fisher, John" in Sir Leslie Stephens and Sir Sidney Lee, eds., *The Dictionary of National Biography,* 10 vols., 12 supplements (Oxford, England: Oxford University Press, 1917–1993), 7:58–63; Roper, Thomas, and Thomas Bailey, *The Lives and Deaths of Sir Thomas More, KNT. Lord High Chancellor of England. And of John Fisher, Bishop of Rochester; who were both Beheaded in the Reign of H. VIII. Comprising the Highest and Hidden Transactions of Church and State, in the Reign of Henry the Eighth; with divers Moral, Historical, and Political Animadversions upon Cardinal Wolsey, Sir Thomas More, and Martin Luther; with a Full Relation of Queen Catherine's Divorce, and the Will of Henry the VIII; to which are added, Some Original Letters, refer'd to in the Work* (Dublin, Ireland: P. Lord, R. Fitzsimmons, and D. Kylly, Booksellers, 1765); Welsby, Paul A., *Saint John Fisher, Bishop of Rochester* (London: Church Literature Association, 1978).

## Frank, Hans

See Nuremberg War Crimes Defendants

## Frank, Leo

See Lynching

## Frick, Wilhelm

See Nuremberg War Crimes Defendants

## *Furman v. Georgia* (408 U.S. 238, 33 L.Ed. 2d 346, 92 S.Ct. 2726 [1972])

Landmark United States Supreme Court case that effectively declared that the imposition of capital punishment in the United States was violative of the Eighth Amendment's ban on cruel and unusual punishments because of the arbitrariness of sentencing.

William Henry Furman, a black man, was convicted of murdering a man while breaking into his house (he shot the deceased through a closed door to avoid discovery). He was 26 years old and had finished only the sixth grade in school. Prior to trial, he was committed to the Georgia Central State Hospital, where a psychiatric examination found that while he was not psychotic, he was "not capable of cooperating with his counsel in the preparation of his defense." Still, Furman was tried, convicted, and sentenced to death. Furman's conviction and death sentence were upheld by the Georgia Supreme Court (225 Ga. 253), and the U.S. Supreme Court agreed to hear the issues in the case. The companion cases of *Lucious Jackson, Jr., Petitioner, v. State of Georgia* and *Elmer Branch v. State of Georgia* (two cases where men of similar background had committed different crimes but had also been sentenced to death) were added to the arguments in *Furman*, heard by the Court on 17 January 1972.

On 29 June of that same year, the court handed down its decision: by a 5–4 vote, the justices struck down capital punishment nationwide, holding that "the imposition and carrying out of the death sentences in the present cases constituted cruel and unusual punishment, in violation of the Eighth and Fourteenth Amendments." Although five members voted to strike down the death penalty, their reasoning was not the same, and each wrote separate opinions. (The four members in the minority were Chief Justice Warren Burger, and justices Lewis Powell, Harry Blackmun, and William H. Rehnquist.) Justice William O. Douglas wrote:

> We cannot say from facts disclosed in these records that [Furman was] sentenced because [he was] black. Yet our task is not restricted to an effort to divine what motives impelled [the jury to sentence him to death]. Rather, we deal with a system of law and of justice that leaves to the uncontrolled discretion of judges or juries the determination whether defendants committing [such a crime] should die or be imprisoned. Under these laws no standards govern the selection of the penalty. People live or die, dependant on the whim of one man or of 12.

Justice William Brennan wrote:

> The primary principle is that a punishment must not be so severe as to be degrading to the dignity of human beings. Pain, certainly, may be a factor in the judgment. The infliction of an extremely severe punishment will often entail physical suffering. . . . Yet the Framers [of the Constitution] also knew "that there could be exercises of cruelty by laws other than those which inflicted bodily pain or mutilation" . . . Even though "there may be involved no physical mistreatment, no primitive torture" . . ., severe mental pain may be inherent in the infliction of a particular punishment. . . . In determining whether a punishment comports with human dignity, we are also aided by a second principle in the [cruel and unusual punishments] Clause—that the State must not arbitrarily inflict a severe punishment. This principle derives from the notion that the State does not respect human dignity when, without reason, it inflicts upon some people a severe punishment that it does not inflict upon others. Indeed, the words "cruel and unusual punishments" imply condemnation of the arbitrary infliction of severe punishments. And, as we . . . know, the English history of the Clause reveals a particular concern with the establishment of a safeguard against arbitrary punishments.

Justice Potter Stewart voted to strike down the death sentences not because he felt the death penalty as a whole violated the Eighth Amendment but because the capriciousness of the sentences violated it. He wrote:

> In this respect, I add only that past and present legislative judgment with respect to the death penalty loses much of its force when viewed in light of the recurring practice of delegating sentencing authority to the jury and the fact that a jury, in its own discretion, and without violating its trust or any statutory policy, may refuse to impose the death penalty no matter what the circumstances of the crime. Legislative "policy" is thus necessarily defined not by what is legislatively authorized but by what juries and judges do in exercising the discretion so regularly conferred upon them. In my judgment what was done in these cases violated the Eighth Amendment.

After this decision, state legislatures that wanted to retain capital punishment established a new set of rules that set a firm standard, in order to avoid arbitrary sentencing and meet strict constitutional scrutiny. The *Furman* decision, however, struck down the death sentences of all persons then on death rows across America, including Charles Manson, Sirhan Sirhan, and, in Georgia, William Henry Furman, the focus of the decision. Four years later, however, the Court found capital punishment to be constitutional under these new rules in *Gregg v. Georgia*. In 1984, William Furman was paroled; he is now a construction worker in Georgia.

**See also:** *Gregg v. Georgia*.

## *Gardner v. Florida* (430 U.S. 349, 561 L.Ed. 2d 393, 97 S.Ct. 1197 [1977])

A defendant's trial and sentencing in a capital case must satisfy *all* elements of the Due Process Clause of the Constitution to be upheld on appeal—so held the U.S. Supreme Court in this landmark case, decided in 1977.

Daniel Wilbur Gardner was convicted by a Florida jury of first-degree murder, but in the sentencing phase of the trial, which is required by state law, the jury found no aggravating circumstances to impose a death sentence and recommended life. The judge, however, after reading a presentencing report containing confidential information on the defendant that had not been furnished to him before the trial, overrode the jury's recommendation and sentenced Gardner to death. He held that the murder was "especially heinous, atrocious, or cruel, and that such aggravating circumstance outweighed 'the mitigating circumstance, to wit: none.'"

The Florida Supreme Court, after reviewing the record but not the issue of the confidential portion of the presentencing report, upheld the conviction and death sentence, and Gardner appealed to the U.S. Supreme Court. After arguments were heard on 30 November 1976, the Court handed down its decision on 22 March 1977. Speaking for a divided court unable to agree on a majority opinion, Justice John Paul Stevens held that the judge's imposition of a death sentence was invalid because it was based on information not available to the jury or the defendant prior to sentencing, a violation of the Due Process Clause. Justices Potter Stewart and Lewis Powell joined Stevens's opinion. Chief Justice Warren Burger concurred without an opinion; Justice Byron White concurred that allowing secret sentencing information "failed to meet the need for reliability in the determination that death was the appropriate punishment."

Dissenters were split into three camps: Justice William Brennan, who, while agreeing that the death sentence should be vacated, disagreed that the case should be remanded to the trial court because a death sentence could be reimposed; Justice Thurgood Marshall argued that the case invited the Court to strike down all state death penalty statutes, which he deemed to be cruel and unusual and a violation of the Eighth and Fourteenth Amendments; and Justice William H. Rehnquist disputed the striking down of the death sentence and asserted that since the Court had never before held certain sentencing procedures to be a violation of the Due Process Clause, it was wrong to do so now and thus make a punishment the Court had found to be constitutional to be unconstitutional.

## Garrote

Method of execution utilized almost exclusively in Austria as well as Spain before the latter nation abolished capital punishment in 1996. Many of the victims of the Spanish Inquisition suffered either the garrote or burning at the stake. Crime historian Robert Jay Nash reports that the garotte was used once in North America: in 1902, following the end of the Spanish-American War, four men were executed by this method in Puerto Rico. When photographs of the gruesome event appeared, the U.S. government was so embarrassed that the use of the garrote was declared illegal. Thieves used the garrote during a crime wave in London in the 1850s to rob innocent travelers.

Nash writes: "A comparatively modern mode of legal killing . . . garroting (called hanging in Austria) is an offshoot of the wheel, a torturous form of execution once popular in Germany and France. The simplest form of garrote is a double cord passed through a hole in an upright post. The loop of the cord goes around the victim's neck, the free ends are pulled, and the man dies of strangulation. Modifications led to an iron collar passed around the felon's neck and the upright post. A screw is passed through the collar and slowly tightened against the post until death ensues."

With Spain's abolition of capital punishment in 1996, the use of the garotte passed into history.

**References:** Byrne, Richard, *The London Dungeon Book of Crime and Punishment* (London: Little, Brown and Company, 1993), 119–20; Nash, Jay Robert, *Encyclopedia of World Crime,* 4 vols. (Wilmette, IL: CrimeBooks, Inc., 1990), 4:3286.

## Gas Chamber

Method of capital punishment utilized exclusively in the United States from 1924 until the present day, although it is currently being phased out as "cruel and inhuman punishment."

After World War I, many people, disgusted with the brutality of electrocutions and hangings, sought a better, more efficient method of executing prisoners. Pumping lethal gas into the prisoners' cells while they slept was considered, but preventing the gas from escaping into the rest of the prison presented a problem. Nevada became the first state to build a chamber in which the prisoner would be sealed and gas would be pumped in.

A chair, normally a metal seat, is housed inside the gas chamber. After the prisoner is brought in and strapped down, with a stethoscope attached to his or her chest, the door is closed and sealed. Beneath the chair is a pan filled with distilled water and sulfuric acid. When a small bag of 16 one-ounce pellets of cyanide is dropped into the pan, cyanide gas begins to rise. The prisoner breathes the fumes, and within minutes death comes. Through the stethoscope, a doctor outside the chamber monitors the prisoner's heartbeat until death is confirmed. A fan is then turned on, blowing the deadly gas out of the room, and the body is washed with liquid ammonia to clean away the last vestiges of cyanide. There is no evidence that this mode of death is painful, although witnesses have stated that some prisoners have strained against the straps and fought until the end for breath.

The first man to die in the chamber was a Chinese-American murderer named Gee Jon. The most celebrated gas chamber in the nation (recently phased out) was the one in San Quentin Prison in California. Among its victims were Barbara Graham; Burton W. Abbott, whose 1957 execution was stayed by Governor Goodwin Knight just as the lethal cyanide pellets had already fallen; Elizabeth Duncan, an elderly women put to death for arranging the death of her daughter-in-law; Caryl Chessman, convicted of being the Red Light Bandit, a notorious rapist whose case became a *cause celébré* around the world; and Aaron Mitchell, convicted of killing a law enforcement officer. Mitchell was the second to last man executed in the United States before a self-imposed moratorium in advance of the U.S. Supreme Court decision that the death penalty, as it was then applied, was unconstitutional. Other famous persons put to death in the gas chamber include kidnapper-murderers Carl Austin Hall and Bonnie Brown Heady, put to death in Missouri, and mass murderer John Gilbert Graham, executed in 1957 in Colorado for placing a bomb on his mother's plane, killing 44 people.

The gas chamber has been used only in a small number of states, including California, Arizona, Nevada, and Missouri. Currently, it is utilized in the states of Arizona, Maryland, Mississippi, and North Carolina.

**See also:** Chessman, Caryl Whittier; Jon, Gee.
**References:** Nash, Jay Robert, *Encyclopedia of World Crime,* 4 vols. (Wilmette, IL: CrimeBooks, Inc., 1990), 4:3284; Trombley, Stephen, *The Execution Protocol: Inside America's Capital Punishment Industry* (New York: Crown Publishers, 1992), 12.

## Gibbet

Method of displaying a condemned murderer's body after execution, utilizing a steel cage usually hung near the place of execution.

One aim of capital punishment has been to deter crime, and the practice of gibbeting served that aim by giving the general public a long-lasting visual impression of the consequences. According to crime historian Jay Robert Nash: "Usually in Britain a hanged prisoner was exhibited in an iron cage placed on a roadside. Another form of exhibiting the dead culprit was to throw the body into a cauldron of boiling tar to preserve it for a length of time. Then the body was taken out of the vat, placed in symbolic chains, riveted into a 'suit' of criss-crossing metal strips, and exhibited along a well-traveled road.

English historians John L. Rayner and G. T. Crook write of the "Origin of the Gibbet in England" in a 1927 work on the history of the Newgate, the London prison outside which public executions were held:

The gibbet was used in England for carrying into effect the final sentence of the law upon murderers, that their bodies might hang a dreadful warning to the passenger not to stray from the path of honesty; yet perhaps few have inquired into its origin.

The gibbet is of doubtful derivation. It is both an English word and a French word, implying the same meaning—"a post on which malefactors are exposed."

We find this punishment recorded in the Bible, Joshua 3:28, 29:

"And Joshua burnt Ai, and made it heap for ever, even a desolation unto this day. And the king of Ai he hanged on a tree until eventide: and as soon as the sun was down, Joshua commanded that they should take his carcase down from the tree, and cast it at the entering of the gate of the city, and raise thereon a great heap of stones, that remaineth unto this day."

Searching back farther into ancient history we find from Martinius, the learned etymologist, that this mark of the grossest infamy that can be inflicted on a criminal was not unknown to the Greeks. It is most probable, however, that we had the mode of punishment of the gibbet from the French at so early a period in the thirteenth century, when it was used here [in England], and known by that name.

In the year 1242, says the historian, Matthew of Paris, William de Maniocs, a knight, was judicially condemned and ignominiously put to death. He was brought from the Tower [of London] to that penal machine vulgarly called the gibbet, and after he had breathed his last was hung on one of the hooks (untorum), and being taken down after he was grown stiff, was bowelled; his bowels were burnt, and his body being divided into four parts, the quarters were sent to four cities. This evidently had the intention of exhibiting a terrible spectacle to the people, just as hanging a dead body in irons was meant to do. But it varies much from gibbeting; the gibbet, in this case, serving only as common gallows. . . .

The first gibbet used in England whereupon to expose criminals after death by hanging was in the reign of King Henry III., A.D. 1236.

**References:** Laurence, John, *A History of Capital Punishment* (New York: The Citadel Press, 1960), 57–58; Nash, Jay Robert, *Encyclopedia of World Crime,* 4 vols. (Wilmette, IL: CrimeBooks, Inc., 1990), 4:3286; Rayner, John L. and G. T. Crook, eds., *The Complete Newgate Calendar,* 5 vols. (London: Privately Printed for the Navarre Society Limited, 1926), 2:322–23.

## Gillette, Chester

See *An American Tragedy*

## Gilmore, Gary Mark (1940–1977)

American murderer, the first man put to death in the United States following the ten-year moratorium on capital punishment ended by the Supreme Court's ruling in *Gregg v. Georgia.*

Gilmore spent most of his life either in trouble or in jail being punished for it. He was born 4 December 1940 as Faye Robert Gilmore (a birth certificate records him as Faye Robert Coffin) in the back of his father's car in Texas, the son of Frank and Bessie Gilmore. He grew up in Portland, Oregon, the target of his father's physical abuse. When the family moved to Salt Lake City, he started on a life of crime, and after the family moved back to Portland, Gilmore became a neighborhood tough and dropped out of school at age 14. His involvement in a car theft ring opened his long criminal record.

Arrested a second time, he was sent to a boy's reformatory, where he spent most of the time in solitary confinement. After his release, he was arrested again and spent much of the next two years in jail. Arrested for statutory rape, he was sent to another prison. Released in 1961, he moved back with his parents. He was again arrested and while in jail tore his cell apart when he learned that his father had died of cancer. Again, he was put in solitary. The continuing experiences hardened him. He was again arrested for assaulting a man with a pipe, a crime that netted him $11; he was sentenced to 11 years in the Oregon State Penitentiary.

Gilmore was released in April 1976; only three months later, on 19 July, he killed a service station attendant during a robbery attempt in Orem, Utah. The following night, repeating the crime, he murdered a 25-year-old motel manager. Both men, married with children, had been shot twice in the back of the head. Gilmore, distraught over the breakup of his relationship with an unstable girl, was caught, convicted, and, in October 1976, sentenced to death. His sentence came just months after the U.S. Supreme Court had found the death penalty to be constitutional in the landmark case of *Gregg v. Georgia.*

On 8 November the Utah Supreme Court stayed the execution, which would have been the first following the national moratorium imposed by the states in 1967. The American Civil Liberties Union and other anti–death penalty groups saw Gilmore's execution as the opening salvo in a rush to empty America's death rows. But by this time, Gilmore had spent 18 of his 37 years in reformatories and prison, and he had had enough. He fought his own lawyers and the American Civil Liberties Union for the right to die a quick death by firing squad. When the U.S. Supreme Court agreed that he wanted to die, they removed all stays from his execution order.

On the morning of 17 January 1977, Gilmore was led from his cell on death row to a vacant cannery located on the grounds of the Utah State Prison, tied to a beat-up office chair, and read his execution order. A black corduroy hood was placed over his head; the five marksmen, seated 10 feet away behind a canvas curtain, fired at a black target with a white circle pinned on his chest, and Gilmore died. After his organs were harvested for use, he was cremated, and his ashes were sprinkled over a small area in Utah.

Gilmore's story was dramatized in Norman Mailer's novel, *The Executioner's Song,* which was later made into a television miniseries.

**References:** Evans, Colin, "Gary Mark Gilmore: 1976" in Edward W. Knappman, ed., *Great American Trials* (Detroit: Visible Ink Press, 1994), 657–58; Gillespie, L. Kay, *The Unforgiven: Utah's Executed Men* (Salt Lake City, UT: Signature Books, 1991), 149–51; Nash, Jay Robert, *Encyclopedia of World Crime,* 4 vols. (Wilmette, IL: CrimeBooks, Inc., 1990), 2:1314–15; Sifakis, Carl, *The Encyclopedia of American Crime* (New York: Facts on File, 1982), 283.

## *Godfrey v. Georgia* (446 U.S. 420, 64 L.Ed. 2d 398, 100 S.Ct. 1759 [1980])

U.S. Supreme Court case in which it was held that a state statute that allowed for the death penalty for the committing of crimes that were "outrageously or wantonly vile, horrible or inhuman in that it involved torture, depravity of mind, or an aggravated battery to the victim" was unconstitutionally vague and a violation of the Eighth and Fourteenth Amendments to the U.S. Constitution.

When Robert Franklin Godfrey had marital problems, he believed that his mother-in-law was involved in his wife's failure to reconcile. He took a shotgun over to the mother-in-law's house, where he found his wife and shot her to death, then killed his mother-in-law with a single shotgun blast to the head. Godfrey was convicted by a Georgia court of two counts of murder. The trial court found no mitigating circumstances to lessen any penalty against him; furthermore, a state statute required a death sentence, since Godfrey's crime was "outrageous or wantonly vile." The Supreme Court of Georgia upheld the death sentence, and the U.S. Supreme Court decided to hear the case. Arguments were heard by the Court on 20 February 1980.

On 19 May 1980, the Court, by a 6–3 vote (Chief Justice Warren Burger was joined in dissent by justices Byron White and William H. Rehnquist) struck down Godfrey's death sentence and the state statute as "unconstitutionally vague." Speaking for the majority, Justice Potter Stewart wrote:

> The validity of the petitioner's death sentences turns on whether, in light of the facts and circumstances of the murders that Godfrey was convicted of committing, the Georgia Supreme Court can be said to have applied a constitutional construction of the phrase "outrageously or wantonly vile, horrible or inhuman in that [they] involved . . . depravity of mind . . ." We conclude that the answer must be no. The petitioner's crimes cannot be said to have reflected a consciousness materially more 'depraved' than that of any person guilty of murder. His victims were killed instantaneously. They were members of his family who were causing his extreme emotional trauma. Shortly after the killings, he acknowledged his responsibility and the heinous nature of his crimes. These factors certainly did not remove the criminality from the petitioner's acts. But as was said in *Gardner v. Florida,* 430 U.S. 349, [at] 358, 51 L.Ed. 2d 393, 97 S.Ct. 1197, it is of vital importance to the defendant and to the community that any decision to impose the death sentence be, and appear to be, based on reason rather than caprice or emotion. . . . That cannot be said here. There is no principled way to distinguish this case, in which the death penalty was imposed, from the many

cases in which it was not. Accordingly, the judgment of the Georgia Supreme Court insofar as it leave standing the petitioner's death sentences is reversed, and the case is remanded to that court for further proceedings.

## Graham, Barbara Elaine Wood (1923–1955)

American murderess, one of only a handful of women executed in the United States in the twentieth century.

Graham was born Barbara Elaine Wood in Oakland, California. Her mother was sent to a reformatory, so Barbara was raised by neighbors. Although she received little education (later in life she attended a business college and took a few courses), many considered her quite bright. At age 14 she was sent to the same reformatory her mother went to because of a growing criminal career. Yet her crimes were petty ones, such as an arrest for vagrancy and lewd conduct in public as well as a prostitution conviction in 1944 that sent her to jail for several months. In San Francisco, she hooked up with members of organized crime, obtaining work as a call girl. Her conviction for perjury in 1947 again found her imprisoned.

After her release, she married for the third time and moved with her new husband to Seattle, where in 1951 she met Henry Graham. She ran away with him and later married him, taking his name as her own. Graham started Barbara on hard drugs, and in this state she met Emmett Perkins, a small-time hood who hired Barbara as a waitress in his gambling parlor. On the night of 9 March 1953, Barbara, Perkins, another hood named Jack Santo, and two others, broke into the home of a widow in Burbank who was rumored to have $100,000 in her house. As Perkins and Santo ransacked the house, Graham beat the 62-year-old woman mercilessly in the head with the butt of her gun. Perkins and Santo tied the woman up afterwards, and although a coroner found that she had died of strangulation, he concluded that she would have succumbed to the injuries Graham had inflicted on her.

At trial, one of the assailants, John True, testified that it was Graham who had attacked the elderly woman. Graham declared her innocence, but a police spy planted in her cell recorded her agreeing to pay $25,000 if a phony alibi could be established. Confronted with this evidence, Graham admitted her role in the widow's murder. On 22 September 1953, after a six-week trial, Graham, Perkins, and Santo were convicted of first-degree murder and sentenced to death. (Perkins and Santo, who both had long criminal records dating back to 1924, were also sentenced to death in a separate case for the murder of a grocer and his entire family.)

As with the case of Caryl Chessman, which was going on at the same time, Barbara Graham's case became a *cause célèbre:* many did not want to see a woman put to death, even if she had committed a heinous murder. Pleas to the governor and higher courts went nowhere. Finally, on 3 June 1955, Barbara Graham took the long walk to her death. Originally scheduled for death at 10 A.M., she was given a short stay by the governor, Goodwin Knight, who allowed her lawyers to continue to appeal. The delay, however, caused Graham great torment as she sat by the death chamber waiting to see if she was to die.

As some 40 newsmen, police, and guards gathered to witness Graham's impending execution, a second delay was delivered by Governor Knight. Graham asked solemnly, "Why do they torture me? I was ready to go at 10 o'clock." Finally, at 11:15 A.M., an hour and fifteen minutes after her torment started, Warden H. O. Teets informed her that her last stay had been lifted and the execution would proceed. As she entered the apple-green gas chamber, built in 1937, her last words were, "Good people are always so sure they're right." She had been wearing on her upper face a linen mask for most of that morning; at her insistence, Warden Teets allowed her to die with it on. "I don't want to have to look at people," she explained.

One of the guards told her to breathe deeply once the gas pellets were dropped. She agreed, and the door was closed. At 11:34 the pellets were dropped; at once, spectators reported, Graham's head drooped, and she seemed to lose consciousness almost immediately. Seven minutes later she was declared dead. Three hours later, after her body had been removed, her cohorts, Santo and Perkins, were strapped into the same chamber and put to death; it was California's first triple execution since three men were put to death on 2 March 1945.

In their editorial on the execution, which appeared the following day, the *Los Angeles Times* opined:

> Barbara Graham was a depraved woman. If the death penalty is justifiable, her swift execution would have been justifiable.
>
> But her execution was a hideous thing—a disgusting, permanent smear on the record of this State.
>
> California has loaded its Criminal Code with little props for human dignity; it forbids cruel and unusual punishments; it created the gas chamber as the gentlest way of death; it screens its victims' last agonies from the general gaping public.
>
> Yet, with all its mercies and humanities, California let lawyers, judges and officials run Barbara Graham through a grisly death routine that prolonged her execution for more than an hour and a half.
>
> We shudder and creep over the stories of the barbarous Chinese Communists who lead their prisoners back and forth between their cells and the firing squad. And then we read of the same rite being performed outside the gas chamber at San Quentin, by Californians to a Californian.
>
> Let's hope that judges and officials consult their consciences, and the State Bar issue some sort of encyclical to the membership to prevent another execution from becoming an event more suited to a Roman arena.

In 1958, Hollywood glamorized Graham's case in *I Want to Live!* starring Susan Hayward as Graham, a role for which she won the Best Actress Oscar. The movie implies that Santo and Perkins were guilty and that Graham was an innocent woman framed for murder; that scenario makes for a good film, but the evidence suggests otherwise. Lindsay Wagner resurrected the role in the 1983 television movie of the same name.

**References:** "Babs, Santo, Perkins Gassed After Delays," *Los Angeles Times,* 4 June 1955, 1; "Barbara Graham Dies in San Quentin Today," *Los Angeles Times,* 3 June 1955, 1; Nash, Jay Robert, *Encyclopedia of World Crime,* 4 vols. (Wilmette, IL: CrimeBooks, Inc., 1990), 2:135–56; "Shameful Bungling in California," *Los Angeles Times,* 4 June 1955, 8.

## Gray, Judd

See Snyder, Ruth May Brown

## *Gray v. Mississippi* (481 U.S. 648, 95 L.Ed. 2d 622, 107 S.Ct. 2045 [1987])

U.S. Supreme Court case in which it was held that the exclusion of a juror "not irrevocably committed" to voting for the death penalty was reversible error in a capital sentencing case and could strike down a death sentence.

In 1982, David Randolph Gray was indicted in Harrison County, Mississippi, for the stabbing death of a man whom he was attempting to kidnap. During the jury selection, prosecutors removed a prospective juror who they believed could not sentence a man to death, though she said that she could. After being convicted and sentenced to death, Gray appealed on the grounds that the removal of the juror was in violation of the Supreme Court's 1968 decision in *Witherspoon v. Illinois,* which held that persons could not be removed from a jury even if they did not believe in the death penalty. The Mississippi Supreme Court affirmed the conviction and sentence, holding that the exclusion of the juror did not taint the trial because several other jurors who expressed reservations about capital punishment were not removed. The U.S. Supreme Court granted certiorari, and arguments were heard in the case on 12 November 1986. That same year, in *Lockhart v. McCree,* the Court had held that it was allowable to remove jurors from the jury panel if they were opposed to capital punishment.

Yet, on 18 May 1987, the Court, voting 5–4 (Chief Justice William Rehnquist was joined in dissent by Justices Antonin Scalia, Byron White, and Sandra Day O'Connor), held that the "exclusion of a juror for cause, in [a] capital prosecution, who is not irrevocably committed to vote against the death penalty regardless of facts and circumstances that might emerge in [the] course of [the] proceedings, is reversible constitutional error." Speaking for the majority, Justice Harry Blackmun wrote, "As was stated in *Witherspoon,* a capital defendant's constitutional right not to be sentenced by a 'tribunal organized to return a verdict of death' surely equates with a criminal defendant's right not to have his culpability determined by a 'tribunal organized to convict.'" See *Davis v. Georgia* for the principle on which *Gray* was decided.

**See also:** *Lockhart v. McCree.*

## *Gregg v. Georgia* (428 U.S. 153, 49 L.Ed. 2d 859, 96 S.Ct. 2909 [1976])

Landmark American court case in which the United States Supreme Court, just four years after finding that the death penalty as it was then applied in the United States was violative of the Eighth Amendment to the Constitution, held that the new schemes devised by the states to sentence persons convicted of murder to death were constitutional.

In 1972, in the landmark decision of *Furman v. Georgia,* the Supreme Court had struck down state schemes for sentencing persons to death, particularly those of Georgia and Texas, as arbitrary—some persons were sentenced to death for a particular crime while others might not be. The Georgia legislature established new guidelines, which called for a bifurcated trial, that is a trial separated into two portions: the trial phase and the sentencing phase. The minitrial in the sentencing phase allowed the state to prove aggravating circumstances and the defense to show mitigating circumstances.

In 1974 Troy Leon Gregg was convicted in a Georgia state court of two counts of armed robbery and two counts of murder in the deaths of two men who had offered him a ride in November 1973. After Gregg was convicted, a jury sat through the sentencing phase and pronounced a death sentence on him for the murders and the two counts of robbery. On appeal, the Georgia Supreme Court affirmed the death sentences for murder but struck down those for robbery, holding that death had never been an accepted form of punishment for that offense. Gregg then appealed the remaining death sentences to the U.S.

Supreme Court. His case was argued the same day (31 March 1976) as another death penalty case, *Proffitt v. Florida*, and one day after a third, *Jurek v. Texas*, was heard by the Court.

Decisions in all three cases were handed down on 2 July 1976. On that date, seven justices, unable to agree on a common opinion, nonetheless held that Georgia's new death sentencing scheme did not violate the cruel and unusual punishments prohibitions in both the Eighth and Fourteenth Amendments to the Constitution. Justices Potter Stewart, Lewis Powell, and John Paul Stevens announced the judgment of the Court, with Justice Stewart reading the joint opinion of the three men. Chief Justice Warren Burger was joined by Justices Byron White and William H. Rehnquist in arguing that the minority argument—that a death sentence constituted cruel and unusual punishment—was "without merit." Justice Harry Blackmun merely concurred in the majority's findings, leaving his minority opinion in *Furman* four years earlier to stand as his reasoning in this case. Justices William Brennan and Thurgood Marshall dissented from the entirety of the opinion, claiming that under any statutory scheme the death penalty constituted cruel and unusual punishment, a violation of the Eighth Amendment. The Court held to the same decision in two companion cases, *Proffitt v. Florida* and *Jurek v. Texas*.

As to Troy Gregg, he escaped from prison in 1980, but before he could be recaptured he was found beaten to death, thus escaping the punishment that his case had made legal.

## Grey, Lady Jane (c.1537–1554)

Known as the "Nine Days' Queen," Lady Jane Grey of England was overthrown by her cousin, Mary I ("Bloody Mary") and put to death at the age of 16.

A great-granddaughter of King Henry VII, Jane was the daughter of Henry Grey, Earl of Dorset and Duke of Suffolk. With the aid of private tutors, she learned to speak Greek and Latin at an early age, and before the end of her short life became proficient in French and Italian, and could speak some Hebrew, Chaldee (the Aramaic vernacular that was the original language of some parts of the Bible, and which superseded Hebrew in Palestine), and Arabic.

In 1553, Henry VIII's son, Edward VI, was slowly dying. John Dudley, the Duke of Northumberland, conspired to strike Mary, Henry's Catholic daughter, from the line of succession, and replace her with the Protestant Jane. To further this plot, Northumberland had Jane marry the Duke's youngest son, Lord Guildford Dudley, and after Edward's death installed the two, on 10 July 1553, as queen of England and her regent. For nine days, Jane ruled over England while Mary formed an army to take by force her rightful place as head of the nation. Nine days after taking power, Jane was arrested and committed to the Tower of London, and the Catholic Mary was proclaimed Queen.

Although Mary at first decided to take pity on Jane, her cousin, for her indiscretion in participating in the plot against her, she turned against the young princess when Earl Grey launched an abortive attempt to bring his daughter back to power. He was caught (and later beheaded), and Mary demanded that Jane renounce her Protestantism in exchange for her life. The young Jane refused, and on 12 February 1554 she faced the headsman's axe on the green within the grounds at the Tower of London, "her countenance nothing abashed, neither her eyes anything moistened with tears."

Historian Alison Plowden relates Jane's final moments:

> Nurse Ellen and Elizabeth Tylney helped her to undress and gave her "a fair handkercher to knit about her eyes." Now the hangman was kneeling for the ritual asking and receiving of forgiveness. He told her to stand upon the straw and in doing so she saw the block for the first time. There was nothing left to do but make an end. Whispering, "I pray you despatch me quickly," she tied the blindfold over her eyes. The world vanished and she was alone, groping in the darkness, crying shockingly, "What shall I do? Where is it?" Someone stepped forward to guide her and she laid her down upon the block and stretched forth her body and said, "Lord into thy hands I commend my spirit." The axe swung and blood spouted obscenely over the scaffold, soaking the straw and spattering the standers-by.

Later that day, Jane's bloodied and headless corpse was laid under the stones of the St. Peter-ad-Vincula, a small abbey just a few yards from where she was beheaded, next to her young husband of less than a year. There her body rests to this day.

**References:** Bourke-Jones, Derek, *Brief Candle: A Poetic Study of Lady Jane Grey, 1537–1554* (Eastbourne, England: Downlander, 1991); Chapman, Hester Wolferstan, *Lady Jane Grey, October 1537-February 1554* (London, England: Cape, 1962; reprint, London: Grafton, 1985); Davey, Richard Patrick Doyle (Martin Hume, ed.), *The Nine Days' Queen. Lady Jane Grey and Her Times* (London: Methuen & Co., 1909); Hudson, M. E., and Mary Clark, *Crown of a Thousand Years: A Millennium of British History Presented as a Pageant of Kings and Queens* (New York: Crown Publishers, Inc., 1978), 83–85; Lee, Sidney L., "Dudley, Lady Jane" in Sir Leslie Stephens and Sir Sidney Lee, eds., *The Dictionary of National Biography,* 10 vols., 12 supplements (Oxford, England: Oxford University Press, 1917–1993), 6:105–07; Plowden, Alison, *Lady Jane Grey and the House of Suffolk* (New York: Franklin Watts, 1986), 125–26; Strickland, Agnes, *Lives of the Tudor Princesses, Including Lady Jane Grey and Her Sisters* (London: Longmans & Co., 1868).

## Guillotine

Method of capital punishment utilized almost exclusively in Europe. A heavy blade, placed between two slats, is allowed (usually by way of a pulley) to fall down and slice off the head of a person placed inside its lock. Its invention was brought about by the onset of the French Revolution. In 1791, the French National Assembly's legislation committee approached Dr. Antoine Louis (1723–1792), a surgeon, to design a mode of capital punishment that could be used on a massive scale while preserving precious materials such as bullets, which were wasted with a firing squad. Louis turned to Dr. Joseph Ignace Guillotin (1738–1814), like himself a physician, who two years earlier had proposed a machine based on the Halifax Gibbet and the Scottish Maiden, two other beheading machines, as well as a machine called the *mannaja,* used in Italy and France in the sixteenth century. Guillotin's effort had been to establish a system for humane executions; yet when Louis adopted the Guillotin model and designed his machine, he foresaw its use on a widespread basis.

The French Assembly embraced the machine, accepting it on 20 March 1792. Revolutionary Jean-Paul Marat called it the "louisette," after its inventor, but after its first use, on Nicholas-Jacques Pelletier, a highwayman, on 25 April 1792, it assumed the name of the man who had come up with the idea and was called the guillotine.

Among the famous persons beheaded by the guillotine during the French Revolution were King Louis XVI, Queen Marie Antoinette, Georges-Jacques Danton, Marie-Anne Charlotte Corday (the assassin of Marat), Lucie-Camille Simplice Desmoulins, and Maximilien François Marie Isidore de Robespierre. The instrument has been used almost exclusively in France (other forms of a guillotine were used in Scotland); thus

France became the last nation in the world to utilize the guillotine, officially ending its use in 1981, when it abolished capital punishment.

**See also:** Halifax Gibbet; Scottish Maiden.
**References:** Arasse, Daniel (Christopher Miller, trans.), *The Guillotine and the Terror* (Paris: Flammarion, 1987; translation, London: Allen Lane, 1987); Laurence, John, *A History of Capital Punishment* (New York: The Citadel Press, 1960), 38–40; Nash, Jay Robert, *Encyclopedia of World Crime,* 4 vols. (Wilmette, IL: CrimeBooks, Inc., 1990), 4:3284.

## Guiteau, Charles Julius (1841–1882)

American assassin hanged for the murder of President James A. Garfield in 1881.

Born in Freeport, Illinois, on 8 September 1841, Guiteau (pronounced Git-toe), was orphaned by his mother's death when he was seven and by the insanity of his father. (Guiteau later claimed that insanity ran in his family, and some evidence points to this possibility). He married but abandoned his wife, a 16-year-old girl, and moved to Washington, D.C., where he styled himself as an important operative for the Republican party. (He did some work for the party, but it was minor at best). When Rep. James A. Garfield of Ohio won the Republican presidential nomination in 1880, Guiteau went to New York and delivered a speech, "Garfield against Hancock" (Winfield Scott Hancock was the Democratic presidential candidate), and, because he felt it was important, had the speech privately published in pamphlet form and distributed to the few people who paid attention to him.

After Garfield was elected, Guiteau seemed to believe that his speech had helped the new president win. Guiteau set out for Washington, D.C., where friends of the incoming chief executive were already swamping him with requests for offices. Guiteau went to the White House and demanded that the president appoint him ambassador to France. When the president did not return his messages, Guiteau went back to the White House, demanding to see Garfield. He was rebuffed and decided to punish the president by killing him.

For three days, beginning on 30 June 1881, he followed Garfield. He also visited the District of Columbia jail, where he knew he would be incarcerated after killing the president, and wrote that it was "an excellent jail." On 2 July, Guiteau read in the newspapers that Garfield was heading off on vacation; at the Washington, D.C., railroad station he walked up to president and fired off two shots. The first missed; but the second hit the president in the back and lodged behind his pancreas. A policeman knocked Guiteau to the ground before he could do further damage, and he was hauled away to jail.

Garfield was taken back to the White House where doctors attempted to treat his wound. Slipping into periods of fever and unconsciousness, the president was removed during the stifling summer to the cooler coastal village of Elberon, New Jersey. He seemed to rally, but finally, on 19 September 1881, after being in office less than a year, he succumbed to his wound.

Authorities did not try Guiteau for attempted murder; instead he was jailed while they waited on Garfield's condition to improve before proceeding. Guiteau wrote many notes to the press and the public while in the D.C. prison, including what he called his "Address to the American People." Editors H. G. and C. J. Hayes wrote of Guiteau's demeanor, as he dictated to them while in prison: "His vanity is literally nauseating. Guiteau has an idea that the civilized world is holding its breath waiting to hear of the minutest details of his career. He thinks the people have an especially acute desire to be fully informed concerning his conduct during confinement in jail, and he has frequently urged visiting correspondents to describe his dress and demeanor."

When the president died, Guiteau was charged with murder. His trial opened on 14 November 1881, with his lawyers attempting to show that their client was hopelessly insane. The judge allowed Guiteau to argue to the jury that it was not he who had killed Garfield, but God, who told him in a vision that the president was destroying the Republican party and the nation had to be saved from the Democrats.

In his closing argument, a defense attorney told the court that such an obviously insane man could not be responsible for his actions. The judge, however, instructed the jury members that if they felt Guiteau had any understanding about what he was doing, they must convict. On 13 January 1882, they returned with a guilty verdict. Guiteau immediately rose to his feet and said "You are all low, consummate jackasses."

Judge Cox sentenced Guiteau to death, and he was taken to his cell in the "excellent jail" to await execution. On 30 June 1882, he was led up the stairs of the gallows. He wept for a moment, then asked to recite a small prayer he had composed that same morning, entitled, "I Am Going to the Lordy." Guiteau finished his poem and was summarily hanged. He was 41 years old.

**References:** Christianson, Stephen G., "Charles Guiteau Trial: 1881" in Edward W. Knappman, ed., *Great American Trials* (Detroit: Visible Ink Press, 1994), 187–91; "Expiation: Charles Guiteau Hanged for the Murder of the President," *The Washington Post,* 1 July 1882, 1; "Extra! An Avenger! Attempt to Kill Guiteau. The Assassin Shot at While on His Way to Jail," *The Chicago Evening Critic,* 19 November 1881, 1; "Guiteau Trial: Closing Speech to the Jury of John K. Porter of New York, in the case of Charles J. Guiteau, the assassin of President Garfield, Washington, Jan. 23, 1882" (New York: J. Polhemus, Printer, 1882); Hayes, H. G., and C. J., eds., *A Complete History of the Trial of Guiteau, Assassin of President Garfield, to Which is Added a Graphic Sketch of His Life as Detailed (Expressly for this Work) by his Former Wife, Mrs. Dunmire; Also, an Autobiography, as Dictated by Himself Since the Shooting, the History of the Trial (in Many Respects, the Most Remarkable of the Present Century), gives All of the most Important and Interesting Portions of the Testimony, the Startling Interruptions by the Prisoner, Incidents, Arguments of Counsel, Charge by the Judge, Sentence, &c., &c.* (Philadelphia: Hubbard Brothers, Publishers, 1882); "The Life and Trial of Guiteau the Assassin" in John Clark Ridpath, *The Life and Work of James A. Garfield, embracing an Account of the Scenes and Incidents of his Boyhood; the Struggles of his Youth; his Valor as a Soldier; his Career as a Statesman; his election to the Presidency; and the Tragic Story of his Death* (Cincinnati: Jones Bros. & Company, 1881); Sifakis, Carl, *The Encyclopedia of American Crime* (New York: Facts on File, 1982), 302–03; Taylor, John M., "Charles J. Guiteau: Assassin on Trial" *American Heritage, 32:4* (June/July 1981), 30–39; *U.S. v. Guiteau,* Criminal Case #14056, Boxes 1 & 2, Records of the District Courts of the United States, RG 21, Papers of the Supreme Court of the District of Columbia, National Archives.

## Gunpowder Plot

See Fawkes, Guy or Guido

## Hale, Nathan (1755–1776)

American teacher and patriot put to death by the British in New York for spying; he remains perhaps the most famous American ever executed by a foreign power.

Born in Coventry, Connecticut, on 6 June 1755, Hale graduated from Yale University in 1773 and became a schoolteacher, teaching at East Haddam and later New London, Connecticut. He also spoke out on behalf of liberty and independence for the American colonies, and when the first shots were fired at Lexington and Concord, Hale volunteered for service in the infant American army. He was made a lieutenant by the General Assembly of Connecticut on 1 July 1775 and was sent to Cambridge, Massachusetts, to be stationed with the Continental Army. Six months later, he was promoted to captain. While in New York in May 1776, he assisted in the uncover operation to destroy a British man-o-war carrying supplies for the British army. When the American army was defeated at the battle of Long Island that August, Gen. George Washington needed a spy to go behind enemy lines and find out the strength of the British army and its capacity to prosecute the war. Hale volunteered for this dangerous mission, although he was warned against it by a friend. Hale replied, "I wish to be useful, and every kind of service, necessary to the public good, becomes honorable by being necessary."

Dressed in civilian clothes, Hale crossed by ferry from Norwalk, Connecticut, to Long Island. There he found out the needed information. Before he could return to the colonial lines, however, he was arrested, taken before General William Howe (1729–1814), the commander in chief of British land forces in North America. He was exposed, and his notes and maps of the British were confiscated. Without hesitation, Hale "at once declared his name, his rank in the American army, and his object in coming within the British lines." Although there is no evidence, many in Hale's family believe that his uncle, the Tory sympathizer Samuel Hale (who was also Howe's deputy commissioner of prisoners), exposed him. Howe, without benefit of trial, ordered Hale's immediate execution.

The following day, 22 September 1776, the 21-year-old Hale went to his death with more bravery than perhaps has ever been shown in the history of capital punishment, save the death of Socrates. As he faced the hangman's noose, Hale gave an impassioned speech in his defense; at its conclusion, he spoke words that have become immortal: "I regret that I have but one life to lose for my country." His remark is similar to one found in Joseph Addison's play, *Cato,* and there has been speculation, though no proof, that he read the play at Yale and was able to quote it.

**See also:** André, John.

**References:** "All Honor to Martyr Hale, in Bronze the Patriot Stands where he Gave His Life for his Country," *The New York Herald,* 26 November 1893, 1; Goetz, Philip W., ed.-in-Chief, *The New Encyclopedia Britannica,* 22 vols. (Chicago: Encyclopedia Britannica, Inc., 1995); Lossing, Benson John, *The Two Spies: Nathan Hale and John André, by Benson John Lossing, LL.D. Illustrated with pen-and-ink sketches by H. Rosa. Anna Seward's Menody on Major André* (New

York: D. Appleton & Company, 1886); Malone, Dumas, et al., eds., *Dictionary of American Biography,* 10 vols., 10 supplements (New York: Charles Scribner's Sons, 1930–95), IV:107–09; Stuart, Isaac William, *Life of Captain Hale, the Martyr-Spy of the American Revolution* (Hartford, CT: F. A. Brown, 1856).

## Halifax Gibbet

Method of execution, called the English guillotine; it operated on the same principle as the French model, with a larger base and a pin instead of pulley to release the large blade. Crime historian Oliver Cyriax wrote of it, "The gibbet incorporated a highly idiosyncratic communal release mechanism, triggered by removal of a pin attached to a rope pulled by 'every man there present'—except in cases involving the theft of animals, when the creatures themselves were roped up and herded away from the gibbet to pull out the pin."

English historian Raphael Holinshed described the Halifax gibbet in his famed *Chronicles:*

> The engine wherewith the execution is done is a square block of wood, of the length of four feet and a half, which doth ride up and down in a slot, rabet or regall, of five yards in height. In the nether end of a sliding block is an axe, keyed or fastened with an iron into the wood, which being drawn up to the top of the frame, is there fastened by a wooden pin (with a notch made in the same, after the manner of Samson's post), into the middest of which pin also there is a long rope fastened, that cometh down among the people, so that when the offender hath made his confession, and hath laid his neck over the nethermost block, every man there present doth either take hold of the rope (or putteth forth his arm so near to the same as he can get, in token that he is willing to see justice executed), and pulling out the pin in this manner, the head block wherein the axe is fastened doth fall down with such violence, that if the neck of the transsgressor were so big as that of a bull, it should be cut asunder at a stroke, and roll from the body by a huge distance.

When the Earl of Morton first saw the machine used, he was so impressed by its efficiency that he had a similar instrument constructed in Edinburgh in 1565. Known as the Scottish Maiden, it severed some 120 heads, including, ironically, the Earl of Morton's, on 2 June 1581.

**See also:** Scottish Maiden.
**References:** Cyriax, Oliver, *Crime: An Encyclopedia* (London: André Deutsch Ltd., 1993), 157–58; Holinshed, Raphael, *Holinshed's Chronicles of England, Scotland and Ireland,* 6 vols. (London: Imprinted for George Bishop, 1587).

## Hamilton, Patrick (c.1503–1528)

Protomartyr of the Scottish Reformation born in either 1503 or 1504 at his father's estate at Stanehouse, Scotland. Hamilton attended the University of Paris, where he embraced Lutheran doctrines, and graduated in 1520. He then returned to Scotland and entered St. Andrew's University, where he began to spread his Lutheran teachings. Hearing of this, the Archbishop of St. Andrews, James Beaton, began a campaign to sweep such thoughts from his campus—a heresy hunt. Hamilton fled to Germany, where he met and became friends with Martin Luther, the originator of the Lutheran faith.

Convinced of the need to further Lutheranism, Hamilton returned to Scotland in 1527. The following February he was arrested, tried, convicted, and condemned to be burned at the stake for heresy. On 29 February 1528 he was brought to the place of execution. According to his biographer, Aeneas J. G. McKay:

> Vain attempts were made to get him to repeat the Ave Maria, to which his only

reply was to ask his accusers to prove the truth of their religion "by putting a little finger into the fire with which I am burning my whole body." To the taunt of heresy addressed to him . . . he answered calmly, "Brother, you do not in your heart believe that I am a heretic." His death was slow. According to Alesius, it was six o'clock before the body was reduced to ashes. Hamilton was, according to one account, only twenty-four years old, certainly under thirty, when he suffered. His youth, his noble blood, his recent marriage, and his unflinching courage moved the hearts of the spectators; "the reek of Patrick Hamilton infected all it blew on."

**Reference:** McKay, Aeneas James George, "Hamilton, Patrick" in Sir Leslie Stephens and Sir Sidney Lee, eds., *The Dictionary of National Biography,* 10 vols., 12 supplements (Oxford, England: Oxford University Press; 1917–1993), 8:1085–87.

## Hammurabi's Code

The first set arrangement of the rules of law ever established, especially before Biblical times, codified in the seventeenth century B.C.E.

Although firm proof is lacking, the code is credited to Hammurabi (reigned c.1792–1750 B.C.E.), a Babylonian king and lawmaker, the sixth ruler of the first, or Amorite, dynasty of Babylon. Set into a stela (a slab or pillar of stone usually inscribed for commemorative purposes) in Akkadian, or Semitic, text, the code was exhibited in Babylon's Temple of Marduk. The code covered economic, family, criminal, and civil law, and was the first set of laws to mention death as a penalty for certain offenses. The most famous of its tenets is "an eye for an eye, a tooth for a tooth." The code was also the first to dictate:

- If a man has stolen an ox or sheep or an ass or a pig or a boat, the property of a god or a palace, he shall repay thirtyfold; of an aristocrat, he shall replace it tenfold. If the thief lacks the means of repayment, he shall be put to death.
- If a man has broken into a house, he shall be put to death and hanged before the breach he made.
- If a woman has caused her husband's death because of another man, she shall be impaled.
- If a man strikes a free man's daughter, causing her to miscarry, he shall pay two shekels for the fruit of her womb.
- If that woman dies, his daughter shall be put to death.

The code remained in the Temple of Marduk until Babylon was sacked about 1158 B.C.E. by the Elamites, who removed many famous Babylonian monuments to Susa, including the famous Law Code stela of Hammurabi; in 1901 the French Orientalist Jean-Vincent Scheil discovered it there and moved it to France for study. It now sits in the Louvre in Paris.

**References:** Goetz, Philip W., ed.-in-Chief, *The New Encyclopedia Britannica,* 22 vols. (Chicago: Encyclopedia Britannica, Inc., 1995), 5:668–69; Wigoder, Geoffrey, *They Made History: A Biographical Dictionary* (New York: Simon & Schuster, 1993), 259–60.

## Hanging

Method of execution in which the condemned is hanged by the neck with a rope or other cord from a gallows or, in the case of lynching, from a tree or lamppost.

Hanging has always been considered a lowly form of punishment, a death reserved for cowards, because the Bible says, in Deuteronomy 22–23, "And if a man have committed a sin worthy of death, and he be put to death; and thou hang him on a tree; his body shall not remain all night upon the tree; but thou shalt in any wise bury him that day; (for he that is hanged *is* accursed of God;) that thy land be not defiled, which the LORD thy God giveth thee for an inheritance."

In a hanging, the victim walks onto a gallows, a platform, usually constructed from wood, with a trapdoor where the victim stands. (The earliest hangings involved having the victim hang from a tree or jump from a cart into the air.) The victim's hands are tied behind the back (the legs are usually also tied together to avoid kicking after the victim drops), and a noose, a thick rope with several knots, is placed around the neck, with one knot situated behind the left ear. Then a black hood is placed over the head. At a signal, the hangman pulls a cord, and the trap door swings open, allowing the victim to fall straight down. In the best of situations, the knot breaks several bones in the cervical vertebrae, thus collapsing it onto the spinal column and causing instant death. In some botched executions, the head is ripped off—as it was with Black Jack Ketchum in New Mexico in 1901, which left the spectators in the front row splattered with blood, and in 1931, when West Virginia murderer Frank Myer was decapitated. In others, instead of dying quickly, the victim slowly strangles to death.

Some famous persons hanged include British spy John André, American spy Nathan Hale, scholar Eugene Aram, and Pakistan president Zulfikar Ali Bhutto. Presently in the United States, only two states, Montana and Washington, utilize this form of capital punishment.

**See also:** André, John; Aram, Eugene; Bhutto, Zulfikar Ali; Hale, Nathan.

**References:** Nash, Jay Robert, *Encyclopedia of World Crime,* 4 vols. (Wilmette, IL: CrimeBooks, Inc., 1990), 4:3284–85; Sifakis, Carl, *The Encyclopedia of American Crime* (New York: Facts on File, 1982), 236–37.

## Hanging, not Punishment Enough for Murtherers, High-Way Men, and House-breakers

Influential English pamphlet printed in 1701 by one A. Baldwin, which expressed the pro–death penalty sentiment in England during that period. Baldwin submitted the tract to Parliament, but there is no record if anything came of it.

> I am sensible, That the *English* Clemency and Mildness appear eminently in our Laws and Constitutions; but since it is found that *Ill* Men are grown so much more incorrigible, than in our fore-fathers Days, it is not fit that *Good* Men should grow less merciful to them, since gentler methods are ineffectual? . . .
>
> I acknowledge also, That the Spirit of Christianity disposes us to Patience and Forebearance. . . . And I acknowledge with the Wise Quintilian, *That if Ill men could be made Good, as, it must be granted, they sometimes may, it is for the Interest of the Commonwealth, that they should rather be spared than punished.* And I know, this 'tis frequently alledg'd, That you take away a Better thing, and that is a Man's Life, for that which is worse, and that is, your Money and Goods; but tho' this be speciously enough urged, yet I doubt not, but the Publick Safety and Happiness may lawfully and reasonable be secured by this way, if it can by no other. No doubt, if other Methods would do, there had never been recourse to *Death,* since *that* was questionless reserv'd as the *last* Refuge. But even *that* now fails, and so fails, that if some Remedy be not found to stop this growing Evil, we shall shortly dare not Travel to *England,* unless, as in the Desarts of *Arabia,* it be in large Companies, and Arm'd.

**Reference:** Baldwin, A., *Hanging, not Punishment Enough for Murtherers, High-Way Men, and House-breakers. Offered to the Consideration of the Two HOUSES OF PARLIAMENT* (London: Printed for A. Baldwin in Warwicklane, 1701).

## Hanratty, James (1937–1962)

He was known as the A-6 Murderer, executed for a roadside attack committed in 1961, yet some believe that James Hanratty, a lifelong criminal, was innocent of the crime for which he was put to death.

In 1961, Michael Gregsten, a married 36-year-old research physicist, was having an affair with his lab assistant, Valerie Storie. After leaving a London pub on the night of 22 August 1961, the two drove to a lover's lane. There they were interrupted by a man who held them at gunpoint, ordered Gregsten to buy him some food, then shot him somewhere along the route known as the A-6 Highway. Ms. Storie was then brutally raped and shot. She survived but was paralyzed from the waist down. She identified her assailant as a young man with brown hair; police at first narrowed their search to Peter Louis Alphon, who fit the description and whose movements that night could not be accounted for. However, slugs matching the gun were found in the hotel room of James Hanratty, a small time burglar who went by the alias James Ryan. When Hanratty was asked to repeat the phrase the killer spoke in the car, "Be quiet, will you, I am thinking," Storie picked Hanratty as the killer.

Many people, however, argue that Hanratty could not have been the killer. While the assailant asked Gregsten how to drive, Hanratty was known to be a good driver. There was no forensic evidence tying the 24-year-old Hanratty to the crimes, and he had no apparent motive to commit them. Yet Valerie Storie picked him out of a line-up, and Hanratty had no alibi. At trial, the mildly-retarded Hanratty pled his innocence, but to no avail. He was convicted of Gregsten's murder, and on 4 April 1962, he was hanged in Bedford Prison in London. From his cell shortly before his death, he wrote: "Dear Mum and Dad, Though I will never see you again, I will know in my own mind that as my love for you is very strong, your love for me will be just as strong. I promise you that I will face it like a man just the way you and Dad would want it, and I hope this will open the eyes of many people. And what I have said before, will one day be proved to the world. . . . From your ever loving son, Jim."

In the years after the execution, many who think Hanratty was innocent believe that he was in another city, Rhyl, during the crimes, but this theory cannot be proven. The papers on the case, held by Scotland Yard, are closed, and the British government hopes to retain the closure seal well into the twenty-first century. As to Peter Alphon, he gave an interview in 1967 to a journalist in which he claimed to be the killer, but he has since retracted the confession. In 1969, John Lennon of the Beatles and his wife Yoko Ono presented a petition to the British government asking for Hanratty to be posthumously pardoned, but there had never been action on the request.

On 28 January 1997, Reuters reported that British justice officials, after studying the Hanratty case, became convinced that Hanratty was in fact not guilty of the crime for which he was put to death. "Yes, we are considering the case but we don't have a date for a decision. We do, however, hope it will be soon," a spokeswoman for the Home Office in London said. A decision on the ultimate disposition of his case, including the possibility of a posthumous pardon, may come in 1998.

**References:** Cyriax, Oliver, *Crime: An Encyclopedia* (London: André Deutsch Ltd., 1993), 1–2; Nash, Jay Robert, *Encyclopedia of World Crime,* 4 vols. (Wilmette, IL: CrimeBooks, Inc., 1990), 2:1444; Terror on Dead Man's Hill" in *Crime and Punishment: The Illustrated Crime Encyclopedia,* 28 vols. (Westport, CT: H. S. Stuttman, 1994), 11:1360–68.

## Harris, Robert Alton

See *Pulley v. Harris*

## *Harris v. Alabama* (504 U.S. -, 130 L.Ed. 2d 1004, 115 S.Ct.—[1995])

U.S. Supreme Court decision in which it was held that where a state allows for a jury's sentencing recommendation in a capital case, such a decision was not binding upon the judge in his final disposition as to sentence.

Petitioner Louise Harris asked her lover to hire someone to help murder her husband, a deputy sheriff in Alabama, and the murder was carried out. Harris was tried and found guilty, and the jury recommended life imprisonment. State law, however, allowed the judge to override the recommendation. With that statute in mind, the judge sentenced Harris to death. The Alabama Court of Criminal Appeals rejected Harris's contention that the state statute allowing the judge not to give "great weight" to the jury's recommendation was in violation of her constitutional rights; the Alabama Supreme Court affirmed this decision. The U.S. Supreme Court heard arguments in the case on 5 December 1994.

On 22 February 1995, Justice Sandra Day O'Connor spoke for an 8–1 Court (Justice John Paul Stevens dissented) in upholding Harris's death sentence and finding that the state statute allowing the judge to effectively override the jury's sentencing recommendation was constitutional. Justice O'Connor stated simply: "The Constitution permits the trial judge, acting alone, to impose a capital sentence. It is thus not offended when a State further requires the sentencing judge to consider a jury's recommendation and trusts the judge to give it the proper weight."

## Hauptmann, Bruno Richard (1899–1936)

German-American immigrant who was executed in the electric chair for his role in the Lindbergh baby kidnapping and murder.

Born in Kamenz, Germany, just before the start of the twentieth century, Hauptmann was the youngest of three boys, all of whom would fight in World War I on the side of Germany. Only Bruno survived and became a carpenter's apprentice in depression-ridden postwar Germany. On 15 March 1919, Hauptmann was convicted of breaking and entering with the intent to rob the home of the mayor of Kamenz, Germany, for which he was sent to jail for a short time. (He did steal about 100 German marks and a gold watch.) Beginning in 1919, Hauptmann and his cohort Fritz Petzold committed several burglaries, using a ladder to enter second-floor windows. During one burglary, Hauptmann threatened the women of the household to "keep quiet or get a bullet." Sent to prison for five years, he tried to get the radical German communists, known as the Spartacists, to intercede on his behalf and release him, but they did not act. Hauptmann was paroled in 1923.

He tried to emigrate to the United States by stowing away on a vessel but was caught and sent back to Germany. After several further attempts, he boarded a ship using a disguise and forged papers and made it to New York. After getting a job, he met Anna Schoeffler, also a German immigrant. He and Anna worked, putting away some money. In 1931 they were able to purchase a green Dodge sedan. The Depression, however, knocked Hauptmann out of work. Still, he told Anna that he had ways of making money, and when the statute of limitations on his crimes back in Germany elapsed, he decided to go back to his homeland.

On the evening of 1 March 1932, kidnappers sneaked into the second floor nursery of Charles Lindbergh, Jr., son of the aviator who in 1927 thrilled the world by flying across the Atlantic Ocean solo from America to France. The abduction set off a nationwide frenzy to find the young child, including $50,000 in ransom left in a cemetery. On 12 May 1932, less than six weeks after being taken, the body of the little boy was found in the woods two miles from his home. His skull had been crushed.

Now the search for the child became a hunt for his killers. The first clue was the wooden ladder, which had been made with some care by a man who had some carpentry training. But there the trail grew cold. In September 1934, just before he planned to leave for Germany, Hauptmann paid for some gas at a service station with a $10 dollar gold certificate. The station attendant, who had been alerted to look for gold certificates, noted the bill, the license number of the car the man drove, and took the bill to the police, who confirmed it as part of the $50,000 in ransom paid by Lindbergh. After Hauptmann was arrested, his home was searched; floorboards matching those used to construct the ladder were found to be missing from his attic, $14,590 in gold certificates from the ransom were secreted in his closet and, written on a wall, was the number of Dr. John Condon, the self-appointed mediator between the kidnappers and Lindbergh.

When Hauptmann's trial opened in the small courthouse in Flemington, New Jersey, the press across America was calling it "the trial of the century." Condon testified that Hauptmann's voice was identical to the one he heard the night he paid the kidnapper in the cemetery; handwriting specimens of Hauptmann's were compared to the kidnapper's ransom note and found to be the same; a wood expert showed how the ladder used in the kidnapping fit into Hauptmann's attic perfectly. Hauptmann himself took the stand, denying that he was involved, and claiming that a friend, Isidor Fisch, who had since gone back to Germany and died, had given him the money to hold until he returned to the United States. The prosecutor, state attorney general David T. Wilentz, exposed Hauptmann as a liar on the stand. All of Hauptmann's witnesses, trying to hold to the Fisch story, were impeached by Wilentz.

The jury returned after one day of deliberations with a verdict of guilty, and Judge Thomas Trenchard sentenced him to death. Unsuccessful appeals followed. Prosecutors offered to spare his life if he confessed, but he refused. Bruno Richard Hauptmann went to the electric chair on 3 April 1936. His case, however, continues to haunt American justice. Was he innocent as some of his supporters claim? Did the state of New Jersey, seeking to get someone for the murder of the famed aviator's son, railroad an innocent man to his death by electrocution? Or did Hauptmann get what he deserved?

In 1985, British author Ludovic Kennedy published *The Airman and the Carpenter: The Lindbergh Kidnapping and the Framing of Richard Hauptmann,* which by its title claims the former scenario. Yet historians looking at the evidence conclude that Hauptmann was involved to some degree, if he was not the kidnapper himself. Hauptmann's wife, Anna, spent the rest of her life trying to clear her husband's name and died in 1994 at the age of 95.

As well, the controversy over cameras in the courtroom led them to be barred for twenty years, until 1955, when they were allowed to witness a felony case in Waco, Texas.

**References:** Bedau, Hugo Adam, and Michael L. Radelet, "Miscarriages of Justice in Potentially Capital Cases" *Stanford Law Review, 40* (November 1987), 124–25; Kennedy, Ludovic, *The Airman and the Carpenter: The Lindbergh Kidnapping and* *the Framing of Richard Hauptmann* (New York: Viking, 1985); Nash, Jay Robert, *Encyclopedia of World Crime,* 4 vols. (Wilmette, IL: CrimeBooks, Inc., 1990), 2:1485–90; Oxford, Edward, "The Other Trial of the Century," *American History,* 30:3 (July 1995), 18–26, 66–69; Ryan, Bernard, Jr., "Bruno Richard Hauptmann Trial: 1935" in Edward W. Knappman, ed., *Great American Trials* (Detroit: Visible Ink Press, 1994), 386–91.

## Haymarket Martyrs Case

The four men who paid with their lives on the gallows for killing a policeman during a labor rally in Haymarket Square in Chicago in 1886 died controversial deaths and their executions, with those of Sacco and Vanzetti and the Rosenbergs, remain the most debatable in the history of American jurisprudence.

The events of 4 May 1886 constitute what many historians consider to have been the most violent event in American labor relations history. On that day, a call to assemble at the Haymarket, a square at Desplaines and Randolph streets, was issued to workers in the Chicago area protesting for an eight-hour day and recent labor unrest at the McCormick Reaper plant in Chicago. After listening to several incendiary speeches, police attempted to break up the gathering; at that point, someone threw an explosive device at the police lines, killing one officer immediately and injuring 70. Six of those later died, leaving the city in a panic against anarchists.

Several leaders of the anarchist movement who were present at the Haymarket riot were arrested: George Engel, a noted anarchist born in 1836; Adolph Fischer (1858–1887), August Vincenz Theodor Spies (1855–1887), Louis Lingg (1870?–1887), a professional bombmaker, Michael Schwab, Oscar Neebe, and Samuel Fielden.

Immediately missing from the group was the leading anarchist spokesman, Albert Richard Parsons (1848–1887), a radical who had once been a soldier in the Confederate army before turning to anarchism after the Civil War. Born in Montgomery, Alabama, Parsons, orphaned at an early age and raised by an older brother, seemed destined for life as a printer in the South, probably in Texas, after the war. Yet after he married and moved to Chicago, he joined the Typographical Union and slowly drifted toward anarchism. He became the editor of the anarchist journal *The Alarm,* which developed into perhaps the most radical and incendiary newspaper in the nation at that time. He was the chief speaker at a rally at the Haymarket on the night of the explosion and was thus the key target of the police investigation. When Parsons heard that his comrades were being imprisoned, he returned to Chicago and surrendered to authorities.

The trial that opened in Chicago was, even by the accounts of those opposed to the anarchists, not a model of American jurisprudence. From the beginning, the prosecution aimed to have the defendants sentenced to death, even though they agreed that none of them had actually thrown the bomb that killed the policemen. The prosecutors' argument, in the end, was that the group had incited an atmosphere that allowed the bomb to be made and thrown.

The defendants mistakenly believed that their own martyrdom would somehow hasten the onset of the socialist government they desired. Their closing arguments, as well as their appeals to the jury, were laden with socialist and anarchist propaganda, labeling their deaths as noble experiments on the road toward a socialist paradise. The time between trial and execution allowed the men to broadcast their appeals to the world, and voices rose demanding clemency. Unfortunately for the Haymarket defendants, their crime came at a time of increased hatred of the labor movement, and their cries went unheeded.

At the end, a few of the condemned asked for mercy and received it from Illinois governor Richard J. Oglesby: those pardoned to a term of life included Samuel Fielden, Oscar Neebe, and Michael Schwab. Defendant Louis Lingg, whom some historians believe was as young as 17 but was an experienced bombmaker (and whom, others believe, did build the bomb that was thrown at the Haymarket), built a device inside his cell and blew off his face the night before the execution, dying in horrible pain a few hours later. Defendants Spies (whose challenge to the convictions went all the way to the U.S. Supreme Court), Parsons, Engel, and Fischer all were hanged on 11 November 1887. According to a contemporary account by the *Chicago Journal:*

> On the Scaffold. They died Bravely.
> There is a whisper of "hats off" from the bailiff, and on the instant, and in utter silence, every head is uncovered. There is heard, indistinct but sure, the sound of slowly approaching footsteps on the flagging, and a long line of deputies range themselves along the western wall.
>
> The footsteps grow nearer, are heard ascending the iron stairway, and in the midst of a stony silence, they come out upon the scaffold. First Spies, then Fischer, Engel and Parsons, in the order named, walk slowly out upon the deadly platform, arrayed in shrouds of snowy whiteness. All are pale, but there is not observable the ghost of a tremor or the inclination to die otherwise than as brave men should. Spies' features are simply ashen in their pallor; Fischer is not so pale, and smiles slightly as he stands with pinioned arms awaiting their end. Upon the homely features of Engel there suddenly breaks a broad smile, and he turns squarely around and addresses an evidently jocular remark to the solemn-visaged bailiff who is busily pinioning his limbs. The face of Parsons, as he stands to the right of his three companions in doom, is as fixed and inscrutable as marble. There is no expression there whatever, save that of a supreme resignation.
>
> THE AWFUL PRELIMINARIES appear terribly slow. The adjustment of the deadly noose must be made by an experienced hand, and this necessitates the placing of the coil of the rope upon the necks of each in turn. Spies is the first to feel the touch of the cord, but he does not wince under it. Fischer next, and he simply stretches his full, white throat slightly as though to make the noose rest more easily. Engel again smiles when his turn comes, and Parsons is still erect, stern and defiant.
>
> Now there is a pause, for the most ardent preliminary act is accomplished. The next sends a perceptible shudder through the now thoroughly awe-struck spectators. The deputy again steps forward, and one by one places upon the head of each victim of the law's vengeance the ominous cap of white lawn. The pinioning is finished. They step forward upon the fatal trap. The moment has arrived.
>
> Mark! From the throat of one of the motionless white-robed forms upon the trap comes the sound of a voice. It is muffled and indistinct, but it can still be recognized as the voice of the dauntless Spies. The voice says:
>
> "There will come a time when our silence now will be more powerful than the voices you are strangling to death now!"
>
> The audience is breathless, but before it can realize the sense of the words the silence is broken again. It is Fischer who speaks, and he cries, in accents loud, clear and bell-like:
>
> "This is the happiest moment of my life!"
>
> Still another pause, and then there rings forth in defiant tones that fairly ring through the vaulted corridors—tones that could well befit the man who could sing the "Marseillaise" in broad, open voice, at the very moment of starting upon the march to his doom. "Hurrah for Anarchy," cries Engel, and is silent.

Parsons, too, it seems, must speak. His accents breathe much less of defiance than those of the other three; they speak more of pleading, entreaty, despair.

"May I be allowed to speak, Sheriff Matson? You promised me that I should speak. The voice of the people must be heard . . ."

The words are yet on his lips when there is harsh, grating sound, a mulled gasp, and it is over. Sheriff Matson has given the signal and, like so many blocks of metal, the four white-robed bodies shoot down through the fatal trap, and the haymarket massacre is avenged.

**See also:** *Ex parte Spies* for the background behind the Supreme Court's intervention in this case.

**References:** Kebabian, John S., *The Haymarket Affair and the Trial of the Chicago Anarchists 1886* (New York: H. P. Kraus, 1970); "Law Supreme: Spies, Parsons, Engel, and Fischer Expiate Their Crimes Upon the Gallows," *The Times* (Chicago), 12 November 1887, 2; "On the Gallows: Spies, Parsons, Engel and Fischer Meet Their Doom on the Gallows," *Chicago Journal,* 11 November 1887, 1.

## Hébert, Jacques-René (1757–1794)

French journalist and revolutionary leader guillotined for his opposition to the government of Robespierre.

The leader of the radical revolutionary group known as the *sansculottes* (French: "without breeches") or Hébertists, he was born into a prosperous family in Alençon, France, on 15 November 1757. Little is known of his life before 1780, when he relocated to Paris. Until the start of the revolution ten years later he lived virtually in poverty.

When the revolution began, he started the radical newspaper *Le Père Duchesne* (Father Duchesne), named after a popular comical figure of the time, and adopted the same name as his pseudonym. Soon, under this name, bawdy and potentially libelous articles began to appear, first against the aristocracy and the clergy, and then, in 1792, against King Louis XVI. He soon attained a wide following among the Parisian working class, becoming a leading demagogue. One source writes of him, "Hébert became an influential member of the Club of the Cordeliers, and as a representative to the Revolutionary Commune he helped plan the popular insurrection that overthrew the monarchy on 10 August 1792. In the ensuing autumn the Hébertists had the Cathedral of Notre Dame turned into a Temple of Reason and had some 2,000 other churches converted to the worship of Reason."

In his newspaper, he called for the destruction of religion, the execution of the king, and the institution of revolutionary government. After the king's death, Hébert inspired his supporters to incite anti-Christian riots and the destruction of established religion. For Robespierre and the rest of the Committee of Public Safety, the radical governmental body, Hébert and his left-wing followers had become a dangerous and volatile contingent that needed to be done away with. His call on 4 March 1794 for a popular rising against the revolutionary government led to his arrest. On 24 March, he and 17 of his followers were led to the guillotine in Paris and beheaded. Few people today remember his name as part of the story of the French Revolution's violent days.

**Reference:** Goetz, Philip W., ed.-in-Chief, *The New Encyclopedia Britannica,* 22 vols. (Chicago: Encyclopedia Britannica, Inc., 1995), 5:790.

## *Herrera v. Collins* (122 L.Ed. 2d 203, 113 S.Ct. 853 [1993])

U.S. Supreme Court decision in which the Court held that a "claim of actual innocence based on newly discovered evidence is not ground for federal habeas corpus relief." (Habeas corpus, literally "You have the body"; the name given to a number of writs having as their object to bring a person into court. In this case, it is used to decide whether a person's liberties have been violated.)

Petitioner Leonel Torres Herrera was convicted in 1982 for the 1981 murders of two Texas police officers. (He was found guilty of one killing and pleaded guilty to the second.) At the first trial, evidence was introduced from a witness who saw Herrera fire, and from the deceased police officer, who identified Herrera as the shooter before he succumbed to his wounds nine days after being shot. For both convictions, Herrera was sentenced to death. He appealed his conviction on the grounds that both eyewitness accounts were unreliable. The Texas Court of Criminal Appeals affirmed the conviction and sentences, and the U.S. Supreme Court refused to hear the case in 1985.

Then, Herrera turned to a new appeal. He claimed that his brother, before dying in 1984, had told his lawyer and his son that he—and not his brother Leonel—actually murdered the two officers. The state district court denied relief, holding that no evidence was presented at the trial that remotely suggested that anyone other than Leonel Herrera had committed the crime. The Texas Court of Criminal Appeals affirmed this ruling, and again the U.S. Supreme Court refused to hear the case.

In 1992, Herrera appealed again, arguing that because he was innocent of the crimes, executing him would violate his civil rights under the Eighth and Fourteenth amendments to the Constitution. He produced an affadavit from his brother's son, who claimed that his father had told him in 1983 that he had committed the two murders. Further, claimed Herrera, the police had known of this and covered it up, a further violation of his rights. Although the district court that heard the appeal found the evidence failing, it nonetheless issued a stay of execution to allow Herrera to appeal to a higher court. This court, the Court of Appeals for the Fifth Circuit, vacated the stay on the grounds that Herrera had failed to prove his innocence; this decision was supported by the Texas Court of Criminal Appeals. The U.S. Supreme Court agreed to hear arguments in the case on 7 October 1992.

On 25 January 1993, Chief Justice William H. Rehnquist spoke for a 6–3 Court (Justice Harry Blackmun was joined by justices John Paul Stevens and David Souter in dissent) in holding that Herrera's claim was not valid in federal courts. It also affirmed the lifting of the stay of execution.

Chief Justice Rehnquist wrote:

> Petitioner's newly discovered evidence consists of affidavits. In the new trial context, motions based solely on affidavits are disfavored because the affiants' statements are obtained without the benefit of a cross-examination and an opportunity to make credibility determinations. . . . Petitioner's affidavits are particularly suspect in this regard because, with the exception of Raul Herrera, Jr.,'s, affidavit, they consist of hearsay.

After arguing that the affidavits were loaded with inconsistencies, Rehnquist added,

> This is not to say that petitioner's affidavits are without probative value. Had this sort of testimony been offered at trial, it could have been weighed by the jury, along with the evidence offered by the State and petitioner, in deliberating upon its verdict. Since the statements in the affidavits contradict the evidence received at trial, the jury would have had to decide important issues of credibility. But coming 10 years after petitioner's trial, this showing of innocence falls far short of that which would have to be

> made in order to trigger the sort of constitutional claim which we have assumed . . . to exist.

On 12 May 1993, Leonel Herrera was put to death by lethal injection in Huntsville Prison in Texas, the 202nd inmate executed in the United States since the Court found in the 1976 decision *Gregg v. Georgia* that capital punishment was constitutional. Herrera's last words were: "I am innocent, innocent, innocent. Make no mistake about this. I owe society nothing. I am an innocent man and something very wrong is taking place tonight."

**Reference:** Definition of *habeas corpus* in Henry Campbell (Joseph R. Nolan and Jacqueline M. Nolan-Haley, editors), *Black's Law Dictionary: Definitions of the Terms and Phrases of American and English Jurisprudence, Ancient and Modern* (St. Paul, MN: West Publishing Company, 1990), 709.

## Hickock, Richard Eugene (1932–1965), and Perry Smith (1929–1965)

Infamous American murderers whose crime of slaughtering an entire family was portrayed in the bestseller *In Cold Blood,* murders for which both men were executed.

Hickock and Smith were lifelong thieves; while in the Kansas State Penitentiary, they overheard a cellmate, Floyd Wells, say that a man he had worked for in Holcomb, Kansas, kept a large amount of money around his home. That man was Herbert Clutter, who lived with his wife and two of his children (an older daughter lived alone), Kenyon and Nancy. Hickock and Smith decided that when they were paroled, they would go to Clutter's house and ransack it for the loot they figured was there.

On the night of 15 November 1959, the two men invaded the Clutter home to find only $50; Wells had been horribly wrong. Demanding the money they knew had to be in the house, the two convicts terrorized the entire family, tied them up, then decided to murder them all and leave. All were either shot, or shot and stabbed to death; the two mass murderers picked up bullet shells, cleaned up, then fled the farm.

Wells heard of the multiple murders and told the warden at the prison that Hickock and Smith had shown an interest in the Clutter house and had just been paroled. The two men were targeted for arrest, which came in Las Vegas, Nevada, where they were picked up for passing bad checks. Hickock denied being in the Clutter home, but under pressure Smith admitted to the murders. Hickock soon broke down and confessed to his role as well, and both men were returned to Kansas for trial.

The lawyers for the two began a defense claiming that their clients were insane. However, the evidence that they had cleaned up the shells and slit the throat of Herbert Clutter lent weight to proving that Hickock and Smith knew full well what they were doing. The jury returned after 40 minutes with a guilty verdict, and Judge Roland Tate sentenced both men to death. The failure of Tate to allow for an intensive psychiatric examination prior to the trial, a shoddy defense, and the seating of a juror who may have been biased led to a series of appeals that lasted five years—at that time a long wait for an execution.

While on death row, the men were interviewed by author Truman Capote, who became interested in the case after reading about the murders in *The New York Times.* Capote's work, *In Cold Blood,* while criticized for many factual errors and its humanization of the two killers, nonetheless has become perhaps the most widely read fictionalized crime biography ever. By examining the pathetic and morally bankrupt lives of Hickock and Smith, Capote came to be opposed to capital punishment. He described the lives of the two men on death row, as they appealed their convictions and sentences.

On 14 April 1965, both men were led to a vacant storehouse on the grounds of the Kansas State Penitentiary and hanged. Smith spoke some final words to the witnesses (including Capote): "I think it is a hell of a thing that a life had to be taken in this manner. I say this especially because there's a great deal I could have offered society. I certainly think capital punishment is legally and morally wrong. Any apology for what I have done would be meaningless at this time. I don't have any animosities toward anyone involved in this matter."

*In Cold Blood* appeared that same year, and a motion picture version was released in 1967. The Clutter homestead, now owned by a different family, remains a major tourist site in Kansas.

**References:** Nash, Jay Robert, *Encyclopedia of World Crime*, 4 vols. (Wilmette, IL: CrimeBooks, Inc., 1990), 2:1534–35; Smith, Thomas C., "Richard Hickock and Perry Smith Trial: 1960" in Edward W. Knappman, ed., *Great American Trials* (Detroit: Visible Ink Press, 1994), 487–90.

## Hicks, Albert E. (?–1860)

American mass murderer put to death on Bedloe's Island (now the site of the Statue of Liberty) for the slaughter of the entire crew of the oyster sloop *Edwin A. Johnson*.

Little is known of Hicks's life before he went aboard the sloop using the alias William Johnson. The sloop sailed from Virginia on 16 March 1860 to New York Harbor, where the captain intended to pick up a shipment of oysters. On 21 March, the boat was found in New York Harbor, virtually abandoned. The bodies of the captain, a man named Burr, and his crew were never found, but bloody trails around the ship, as well as the apparent launching of a small boat used to go to shore indicated that someone had left alive.

Johnson, it was discovered, had arrived home soon after with a large sum of money in his possession. The police followed his trail, which led to a small house on the outskirts of Providence, Rhode Island, where Johnson had holed up with his wife and child. Captured and taken back to New York, he identified himself as Albert Hicks and maintained that he had never been aboard the sloop. Found in his possession, however, was a watch belonging to Captain Burr as well as a daguerreotype belonging to one of the crew. Hicks was quickly put on trial (18 May) and found guilty five days later. The judge quickly sentenced him to death.

The judgment against Hicks was carried out on 13 July 1860, four months after the murders. In the time between trial and execution, Hicks, jailed in the New York prison known as the Tombs, confessed to the murders—he admitted that while the crew was sleeping he had bashed in their heads with a coffee pot (which had been found by the police with blood and human hair on it) and then dumped their bodies overboard. He stole ashore in a small lifeboat with the money that was to be used for purchasing the oysters.

On 13 July 1860, Hicks was taken aboard a ship called the *Red Jacket* to Bedloe's Island, where a scaffold for a public execution had been erected. Countless boats sailed into New York Harbor to witness the execution; the *New York Herald* estimated the crowd to number about 10,000. *The New-York Times* for 14 July 1860 covered Hicks's execution:

> On reaching the gallows, Hicks knelt beside the priest, Father Duranquet, and prayed, with every appearance of real devotion, for some minutes. He then

> stood up, while Assistant-Marshal De Angelis and Mr. Isaacs, the executioner, adjusted the rope around his neck. The shouts from the boats of "Stand away in front!" were at this time perfectly deafening; the troops, in forming one side of the square, having shut out the view from the water. At a signal from one of their officers, they moved aside, and then the noise comparatively subsided. The executioner, whose province it was to test the rope, retired to his box. Mr. De Angelis gave the signal, and Hicks was hung. He died very easily, the third cervical vertebra being at once broken. There were no struggles, and there was scarcely a muscular twitch. So he expiated, on this earth, [for] the great crimes he had committed.

According to the *Times,* Hicks's last words were: "Hang me quick—make haste." After Hicks was cut down, his body vanished. Many speculate that it was sold to a medical school for use in experiments.

**References:** "Execution of Hicks, the Pirate. Twelve Thousand People at Bedloe's Island. Scenes at the Tombs, in the Bay, and at the Place of Execution. His Confession," *The New-York Times,* 14 July 1860, 1, 2; *The Life, Trial, Confession and Execution of Albert W. Hicks, the Pirate and Murderer, Executed on Bedloe's Island, New York Bay, on the 13th of July, 1860, for the Murder of Capt. Burr, Smith and Oliver Watts, on Board the Oyster Sloop E. A. Johnson* (New York: Robert M. DeWitt, Publisher, 1860); "The Pirate Hicks. His Execution at Bedloe's Island. Ten Thousand Persons Present. Exciting Scenes at the Gallows. The Bay Covered with Steamers and Boats. Conduct of the Culprit. His Extraordinary Indifference," *New York Herald,* 14 July 1860, 3, 6; "The Trial of Albert W. Hicks, For Piracy, New York City, 1860" in Lawson, John D., ed., *American State Trials: A Collection of the Important and Interesting Criminal Trials Which Have Taken Place in the United States, from the Beginning of our Government to the Present Day,* 17 vols. (St. Louis, MO: F. H. Thomas Law Book Company, 1914–36), 14:625–56.

## Hill, Joe (1879–1916)

Swedish-American labor leader, whom writer Joyce Kornbluh called the "Wobbly Bard," put to death for being involved in a labor-inspired murder.

Hill was born Joel Emanuel Hägglund on 7 October 1879 on Gävle, Sweden, the son of a railroad conductor who was killed in an accident when his son was seven. It was Joel who went to work to support his large family (he was one of nine children), and when his mother died in 1902 he emigrated to the United States. He immediately got caught up in the growing American labor movement as it fought for the right to form unions. The nearly illiterate Swede worked in a factory but was fired when he tried to organize his coworkers. He then changed his name to Joseph Hillstrom to avoid being blacklisted, but he would come to be known as Joe Hill.

Hill became famous for writing labor songs, including "Casey Jones, the Union Scab" and "The Preacher and the Slave." He came to believe that labor rights would come only with violence, and through his songs he seemed to preach that doctrine. In 1910, he joined the Industrial Workers of the World (IWW), also known as the Wobblies, a radical labor union. Many speculate that Hill was deeply involved in the demolition of the *Times* building in Los Angeles that same year, but there is no proof. Hill fled California after the explosion, and two IWW workers, the McNamara brothers, were ultimately convicted of the act.

In 1913, Hill wound up in Utah, a conservative state where Wobbly activity was rife. When he got close to the labor leadership there, he was given a list of business owners who opposed the IWW and were slated for execution. Among these was John Morrison, a former policeman who had antagonized the IWW by breaking strikes. Now a store owner, he was near the top of the "hit list." On the night of 10 January 1914, Hill and a fellow Wobbly, Otto Applequist, went to Murray, Utah, where Morrison's store was located. That night, two masked and armed men broke into Morrison's home, yelling, "We've got you now!" The men exchanged shots with Morrison and his son, killing both; in the fray, however, the son had gotten off a single shot, striking one of the culprits. Later that night, Hill showed up at a local doctor with a gunshot wound, claiming that a friend had shot him in a fight. When the doctor heard of the Morrison killings, he informed the authorities. The police went to a house where Hill was holed up; when asked to surrender, he reached for an object (later deemed to be a handkerchief) and was shot in the hand. Applequist, the man he had been seen with, had disappeared and was never seen again.

Hill was put on trial. With his mysterious wound, his unknown whereabouts on the night of the crime, and his connections with the IWW, the jury convicted him outright. His lawyer begged him to explain where and when he was shot, but Hill refused. He was convicted of the Morrison killings and, on 18 July 1914, sentenced to death. His case then became a *cause célèbre* in the labor movement. IWW president William "Big Bill" Haywood was joined by President Woodrow Wilson and Helen Keller in calling for the commutation of Hill's sentence, but for naught. To Haywood, Hill wrote, "Don't waste any time mourning—organize!"

On 19 November 1915, as the warden came for him on his final day, Hill had barricaded his cell with a mopstick and his mattress. The guards had to batter down the obstructions as Hill threw objects at them. Captured, he sheepishly said, "Well, I'm through. You can't blame a man for fighting for his life." He was led to a courtyard and strapped into a chair, a paper target pinned over his heart. He yelled to the firing squad members, "Fire! Go on and fire!" The shots rang out, with five hitting him in his heart and killing him instantly. Hill was 36 years old.

In his letter to Haywood, Hill had written: "It is a hundred miles from here to Wyoming. Could you arrange to have my body hauled to the state line to be buried? I don't want to be found dead in Utah." Instead, his body was taken to Chicago, where over 30,000 people attended his funeral. He was cremated, and his ashes were spread across every state in the Union—except Utah. Many in the labor movement, and those to the left politically, believe that Hill was framed—that he was martyred in order to preserve capitalism. Anti–death penalty activists Hugo Adam Bedau and Michael Radelet have added Hill to their list of people whom they believe have been wrongly executed, calling him "an innocent victim of politics, finance, and organized religion" and his case "one of the worst travesties of justice." On the other hand, crime historian Jay Robert Nash argues that "he was unmistakably a killer who deserved his grim fate."

**References:** Bedau, Hugo Adam, and Michael L. Radelet, "Miscarriages of Justice in Potentially Capital Cases" *Stanford Law Review, 40* (November 1987), 125–26; Gillespie, L. Kay, *The Unforgiven: Utah's Executed Men* (Salt Lake City, UT: Signature Books, 1991), 79–83; Kornbluh, Joyce L., ed., *Rebel Voices: An IWW Anthology* (Ann Arbor: University of Michigan Press, 1964), 412; Nash, Jay Robert, *Encyclopedia of World Crime,* 4 vols. (Wilmette, IL: CrimeBooks, Inc., 1990), 2:1552; Ryan, Bernard, Jr., "Joe Hill Trial: 1914" in Edward W. Knappman, ed., *Great American Trials* (Detroit: Visible Ink Press, 1994), 273–75; Sifakis, Carl, *The Encyclopedia of American Crime* (New York: Facts on File, 1982), 335; Smith, Gibbs M., *Joe Hill* (Salt Lake City, UT: Peregrine Smith Books, 1984).

## Horn, Tom (1860–1903)

American lawman put to death on the gallows for a number of murders that he carried out while serving as a hired killer in the American West.

Horn was born near Memphis, Missouri, on November 21, 1860. At 14, after being punished by his father, he ran away and headed west. He became a scout for the U.S. Army at age 16 and for more than a decade took part in many of the army's campaigns against the Indians, including that against Geronimo in 1886. He then wandered the American West in search of adventure and became an expert cowboy and ranch hand. In 1890, he joined the Pinkerton Detective Agency, considered one of the world's finest investigative firms, and for several years was on the side of the law, hunting down bank robbers and other assorted criminals. He is said to have killed 17 men as part of his job.

When he left Pinkerton's, he joined the Wyoming Cattle Growers' Association as a hired gunman to stop homesteaders and protect the rights of cattlemen. For several years, he swept down on unsuspecting homesteaders and killed them and their families, reportedly earning $600 for each person he murdered. His undoing was the murder of Willie Nickell. Hired to kill Kels Nickell, a rancher whom other ranchers wanted dead, Horn crept up to the Nickell property and shot and killed a person he thought was Nickell. It was, in fact, Nickell's 14-year-old son, Willie. The murder remained unsolved for a time, but lawman Joe Lefors eventually tracked Horn down and through a ruse (getting Horn drunk and asking him for the details of the Nickell killing) got a confession. Taken to Cheyenne, Horn was put on trial for the murder, found guilty, and sentenced to death. Although his "boss" (the man who had hired him for the Nickell murder), John Coble, tried to get commutation, there was little sympathy for the hired killer. After an unsuccessful breakout attempt, Horn became resigned to his death, and in the months leading up to his execution wrote his memoirs and wove the rope that was used to hang him.

Biographer Doyce Nunis, Jr., writes of Horn's last day just as he was put to death:

> November 20 was Horn's final mortal day. He faced it calmly and serenely. Not once was there any hint or trace of anxiety, fear or nervousness. His deportment was cool and dignified. He was a man of steel, not to be bent or dented by the prospect of death. As he approached the gallows, he had requested that two of his stalwart friends sing a popular range song, "Life Like a Mountain Railroad," in sonorous tenor voices. When asked if he had anything to say, "No" was the quiet answer. As a clergyman read prayers for the dying, "Horn, standing relaxed, listened without a tremor." His coolness caused others to tremble. With a black hood over his head, standing on the trap, the water trickling away his life in seconds, his last words were to a friend who had recently gotten married. "I hope you're doing well. Treat her right." The trap parted with a crash at 11:00 A.M., 31 seconds from the time Horn was placed on it. Unfortunately, the drop was too short to break the neck, but, mercifully, the heavy-knotted noose knocked him unconscious. His pulse continued to beat for 17 minutes before death, at last, claimed him.

Buried in the Columbia Cemetery in Boulder, Colorado, Horn suffered the final indignity of having the date of his birth imprinted improperly on his tombstone (it reads 1861). Horn was the subject of *Tom Horn,* a 1980 motion picture with Steve McQueen in the starring role. Some have described the film as a half-baked attempt to rehabilitate Horn, whom crime historian Carl Sifakis has called "probably the most callous hired gun and bushwacker the Old West ever saw."

**See also:** Motion Pictures, Capital Punishment as Depicted in.
**References:** Carlson, Chip, *Tom Horn: The Definitive History of the Notorious Wyoming Stock Detective* (Cheyenne, WY: Beartooth Corral, 1991), 220–21; Horn, Tom, *Life of Tom Horn, Government Scout and Interpreter, Written by Himself, Together with His Letters and Statements by his Friends: A Vindication* (Denver: Published [for John C. Coble] by The Louthan Books Company, 1904), 17; Nunis, Doyce B., Jr., *The Life of Tom Horn Revisited* (Los Angeles: The Westerners Los Angeles Corral, 1992), 88–90; Sifakis, Carl, *The Encyclopedia of American Crime* (New York: Facts on File, 1982), 347–48.

## Howard, Catherine (1520?–1542)

English queen, the fifth wife of King Henry VIII of England, put to death, according to history, for alleged affairs that she had before marrying Henry.

Born about 1520, Catherine was the daughter of Lord Edmund Howard and a niece of Thomas Howard, the third duke of Norfolk. Little in her life prepared her to be queen; yet three weeks following Henry's divorce from Anne of Cleves, Catherine secretly wed the king at Oatlands on 28 July 1540. Because she was unable to bear Henry the son and heir that he craved, her days, like those of her predecessor, Anne Boleyn, were numbered. In 1542 she was accused by Archbishop Thomas Cranmer of having premarital affairs with several men, including her cousin, Thomas Culpepper. Catherine confessed to the affairs, and the men, including Culpepper, were beheaded; Catherine herself was released, but she was soon imprisoned in the Tower of London. Parliament enacted a law declaring that an unchaste woman could not be queen, and just two days later, on 13 February 1542, when she was about 22 years old, she was taken to a site inside the Tower and beheaded. Alexandre Dumas Père dramatized her story in his 1834 play *Catherine Howard.*

**References:** Bailey, Thomas, *The Life and Death of the Renowned John Fisher, Bishop of Rochester, who was Beheaded on Tower-Hill, the 22nd of June 1535, and in the 27th Year of the Reign of King Henry VII, Comprising the Highest and Hidden Transactions of Church and State in the Reign of King Henry the Eighth; with divers Moral, Historical and Political Animadversions upon Cardinal Wolsey, Sir Thomas More, and Martin Luther; with a Full Relation of Queen Katherine's Divorce, Carefully Selected from Several antient Records* (Dublin, Ireland: Printed for P. Lord, R. Fitzsimmons, and D. Kylly, Booksellers, 1765); Delderfield, Eric R., *Kings & Queens of England & Great Britain* (London, England: David & Charles, 1994); Gascoigne, Bamber, *Encyclopedia of Britain* (New York: Macmillan, 1993), 118–19; Hudson, M. E., and Mary Clark, *Crown of a Thousand Years: A Millenium of British History Presented as a Pageant of Kings and Queens* (New York: Crown, 1978); Roper, Thomas, and Thomas Bailey, *The Lives and Deaths of Sir Thomas More, KNT. Lord High Chancellor of England. And of John Fisher, Bishop of Rochester; who were both Beheaded in the Reign of H. VIII. Comprising the Highest and Hidden Transactions of Church and State, in the Reign of Henry the Eighth; with divers Moral, Historical, and Political Animadversions upon Cardinal Wolsey, Sir Thomas More, and Martin Luther; with a Full Relation of Queen Catherine's Divorce, and the Will of Henry the VIII; to which are added, Some Original Letters, refer'd to in the Work* (Dublin, Ireland: P. Lord, R. Fitzsimmons, and D. Kylly, Booksellers, 1765).

## Howells, William Dean (1837–1920)

American writer noted for his opposition to slavery and, to a degree, capital punishment, exemplified in his writings during the 19th and 20th centuries.

In 1904, Howells wrote a piece called "State Manslaughter" that appeared in the magazine *Harper's Weekly* on 6 February 1904. His work differs from that of most reformers in that he accepts the fact that capital punishment will not be abolished and focuses, instead, on the horrors of the electric chair.

What the advocates of the chair . . . implied if they did not express, was that killing by electricity was almost the same as not killing at all. It would remove with dignity and decorum the offender who had forfeited his life, and not be attended by the depraving incidents inseparable from guillotining, garroting, or even hanging, and of course not by the cruel accidents to which the art of the headsman was subject. . . .

It was not imagined that electricity could fail to kill instantly, much less that the criminal, who had become the State's peculiar care, could be so ineffectually tortured as to froth at the mouth, and strain at his bonds with writhings of agony which almost burst them, or give out the smell of his burning flesh so that the invited guest was often made sick at his stomach by the loathsome and atrocious fact. Yet all this has happened again and again. . . .

[According to "eminent authority" Dr. Allen McLane Hamilton,] killing does not kill when done by electricity in the hands of the official homicides. He declared that in the case of a murderer whose life was lately attempted by the appointed agency, six "shocks" so failed of their due effect, that the examining doctor "collapsed from sheer horror when he found that his stethoscope still carried the heart beats of the victim to his ear." He . . . suggests something like "poisoning with carbonic dioxide" would be "an effective and painless" method, which might be properly substituted for the very fallible means of happy despatch that electricity has shown to be. . . .

If electricity has proved not merely appalling and disgusting, but ineffective, by all means let us have carbonic dioxide, and if that fails, too, let us keep on trying till we get the perfect agency of painless homicide. But let the State never corrupt the potential private murderer by ceasing to kill with accumulated terrors such as he never dreamt of.

**Reference:** Howells, William Dean, "State Manslaughter," *Harper's Weekly,* 6 February 1904, 196–98.

## Hus[s], John (1372? or 1373?–1415)

Bohemian religious reformer and activist burned at the stake by orders of the Council of Constance for his heretical teachings.

Born in Husinec, a village in southern Bohemia (now located in the Czech Republic), of poor parents, he studied at the University of Prague. In 1398, he began to teach theology. Soon he became the rector of the university (1400) and then dean of the faculty of philosophy (1401). In his youth, he had become acquainted with the writings of John Wyclif (also Wycliffe), a religious writer and lecturer whose railings against certain church doctrines, including the selling of indulgences and masses for the dead, led to his writings being publicly burned by Stynko, the archbishop of Prague, in 1410. Hus sent a letter to Pope John XXII (considered by history to be an antipope, or unofficial pope) asking that the archbishop's work be terminated. Instead, the pope demanded that Hus appear before him and recant; when Hus refused, the pope ordered an interdict, or religious ban, placed on Prague as long as Hus remained in that city. Hus recanted for a time, but the fervor was stirred up again when the pope granted further indulgences. Excommunicated, Hus retired to his home in Husinec and there wrote two antipapal pamphlets, "On the Six Errors" and "On the Church."

In 1413, Pope John XXII convened the Council of Constance to discuss the problem of the schism between popes in Rome and Avignon. Hus, who had angered many at the conference, was called before it to explain his actions and writings. The Holy Roman Emperor Sigismund promised Hus safe passage to and from the meeting, but when Hus arrived and refused to recant his writings, he was arrested, taken to a court, and sentenced to death. He was burned at the stake on 6 July 1415. According to a work from 1653, his last words as the flames rose about him were "O Sancta Simplicitas!" ("O Holy Simplicity!").

Seventy years later, in 1485, tolerance toward the teachings of those outside the church was finally assented to. Four years after Hus's death, his followers, called Hussites, began a series of wars against the Holy Roman Empire, the Hussite Wars, which lasted for 17 years. The Hussites invaded Silesia in 1425–1426 and Franconia in 1429–1430. In 1434, the group split into two factions: the Utraquists and the Taborites, the latter being the more radical assemblage. Although the group as a whole accepted the Compactata in 1433, the Taborites fought on, and were finally routed at Lipany in 1434.

**References:** Spinka, Matthew, *John Hus: A Biography* (Princeton: Princeton University Press, 1968); Spinka, Matthew, *John Hus' Concept of the Church* (Princeton: Princeton University Press, 1966); Spinka, Matthew, trans. and ed., *John Hus at the Council of Constance* (New York: Columbia University Press, 1965).

### *In Cold Blood*

See Hickock, Richard Eugene, and Perry Smith

### Innocent, Potential for the Execution of the

One of the main arguments of those opposed to the imposition of capital punishment is that there may be a chance that an innocent person may be put to death. The history of the argument is compelling and deserves close examination.

Two of the leading opponents of capital punishment in the United States today, professors Hugo Adam Bedau and Michael L. Radelet, concluded in a 1987 study that 23 innocent persons have been put to death in the United States since 1900. However, they list among this group Charles Becker, whom many historians consider to have been guilty of the crime for which he was executed, and Sacco and Vanzetti, whose innocence has never been convincingly shown. Missing from their list, which starts in 1900, are James Halligan and Dominic Bailey, hanged in Massachusetts in 1806 (another person later confessed to the crime for which they were put to death) and William Jackson Marion, hanged in March 1887 for the murder of a person who reappeared—alive—four years later.

Today's courts commit vast resources to avoid miscarriages of justice like these and to see that innocent persons are not put to death. But as late as 1962, James Hanratty, considered innocent, was hanged in England for a crime committed on an English road named A-6. Another man may have confessed to the offense, and Hanratty pleaded his innocence before his execution. In 1997, a British commission concluded that Hanratty may have been innocent. In 1998 they considered pardoning Derek

Bentley, a youth hanged in 1953, although not the triggerman in the murder of a policeman.

In 1996, a national poll in the United States showed that Americans continued to support capital punishment overwhelmingly even if "1 out of 100" persons put to death was innocent.

**See also:** Becker, Charles; Hanratty, James; Sacco, Nicola, and Bartolomeo Vanzetti.
**Reference:** Bedau, Hugo Adam, and Michael L. Radelet, "Miscarriages of Justice in Potentially Capital Cases" *Stanford Law Review, 40* (November 1987), 21–172.

### *In re Kemmler* (136 U.S. 436 [1890])

The first U.S. Supreme Court case to address the ability of states to execute persons with electricity, the Court held in *Kemmler* that such an execution was not cruel and unusual punishment. (The facts behind the Kemmler case can be found in the entry on William Kemmler.) As he neared the date of his execution for murder, William Kemmler appealed his conviction to the U.S. Supreme Court, claiming that death in the electric chair constituted cruel and unusual punishment. On 19 May 1890, Chief Justice Melville Weston Fuller held for a unanimous court in denying the appeal: "Punishments are cruel when they involve torture or a lingering death; but the punishment of death is not cruel within the meaning of that word as used in the constitution. It implies there is something inhuman and barbarous—something more than the mere extinguishment of life."

**See also:** Kemmler, William Francis; *Wilkerson v. Utah.*

## Internet, Use of in the Capital Punishment Debate

The Internet, one of the most influential public communications devices in history, is being utilized by both sides in the capital punishment debate. Sites dedicated to upcoming executions, to groups with arguments for and against the use of capital punishment, and to discussions on the subject permeate the World Wide Web. A search of the term "death penalty" yields more than 1.7 million web sites.

Such groups as Amnesty International, Hands Off Cain: The Citizens' and Parliamentarians' League for the Abolition of the Death Penalty Worldwide by 2000, and the Friends Committee to Abolish the Death Penalty (the Quakers) use their web sites to call attention to their opposition to the death penalty. Lawyers for Illinois death-row inmate Girvies Davis used a web site with information about their client to try to get public opinion on his side, but the effort failed, and Davis was put to death on 16 May 1995. Condemned killer Michael Sharp, before being put to death by the state of Texas on 19 November 1997, published his last words in a three-page statement that appeared on the Internet. He wrote, "I became a new creature in Christ and turned away from my sins, and now I have tasted the sweet going away," begging for "forgiveness from those I have sinned against." To the state, which was about to put him to death, he said, "Yes, I was once a reflection of you—blind, wicked, and a taker of life."

### Jesus Christ

Religious figure crucified on the cross for opposing the Roman government in Israel.

Jesus was born in Bethlehem, located perhaps five to six miles south of the city of Jerusalem, sometime around 4 B.C.E. (he may have been born as early as 25 B.C.E.), the son of Joseph, a carpenter, and his wife, Mary, known to Christian worshipers as the Virgin Mary or simply the Virgin. The name Jesus is a latinized form of Iesous, a translation of the Hebrew Joshua, which means "Jehovah is salvation." Christ comes from the Latin *Christos* and the Hebrew *Messiah*, meaning "one who is anointed." Jesus lived what could be considered an obscure life, learning the trade of his father, until he was approximately 30 years of age.

At that time, Jesus went out among the people in at least nine separate journeys in Galilee and Judea, preaching. The Bible relates several miracles he performed: he restored the sight of two blind men by touching their eyes, he helped feed 5,000 people with five loaves of bread and two small fishes, and he raised a man named Lazarus from the dead. Betrayed by his own follower Judas, Jesus was arrested and tried for blasphemy before the Sanhedrin, or Jewish court of law. The two judges, Annas and Caiphas, found him guilty and ordered him to be crucified on the cross until dead. The court then handed Jesus over to Pontius Pilate, the Roman procurator of Israel, for execution.

On the day of his death, Jesus was forced to carry the heavy wooden cross to Calvary Hill while wearing a painful crown made of thorns. At Calvary, the cross was erected between the crosses of two thieves known to history as Dismas and Gestas, and Jesus was nailed to it through his wrists and his feet. Upon an order by Pilate, a sign was put on top of the cross: I.N.R.I., which read (in Greek, Hebrew, and Latin), *Iesus Nazarenus Rex Iudeorum* (Jesus of Nazareth King of the Jews).

The Bible describes this event:

> And he bearing the cross went forth into a place called the place of a skull, which is called in the Hebrew Golgotha: Where they crucified him, and two others with him, on either side one, and Jesus in the midst. And Pilate wrote a title, and put it on the cross. And the writing was of JESUS OF NAZARETH THE KING OF THE JEWS. This title then read many of the Jews: for the place where Jesus was crucified was nigh to the city: and it was written in Hebrew, and Greek, and Latin. Then said the chief priests of the Jews to Pilate, Write not, The King of the Jews; but that he said, I am King of the Jews. Pilate answered, What I have written I have written. Then the soldiers, when they had crucified Jesus, took his garments, and made four parts, to every soldier a part; and also his coat; now the coat was without seam, woven from the top throughout. They said therefore among themselves, Let us not rend it, but cast lots for it, whose it shall be; that the scripture might be filled, which saith, They parted my raiment among them, and for my vesture they did cast lots. These things therefore the soldiers did. Now there stood by the cross of Jesus his mother, and his mother's sister, Mary the wife of Cleophas, and Mary Magdalene. When Jesus saw his mother, and the disciple standing by, whom he loved, he saith unto his mother, Woman, behold

thy son! Then saith he to the disciple, Behold thy Mother! And from that hour that disciple took her unto his own home. After this, Jesus, knowing that all things were not accomplished, that the scripture might be fulfilled, saith, I thirst. Now there was set a vessel full of vinegar: and they fulled a sponge with vinegar, and put it upon hyssop, and put it to his mouth. When Jesus therefore had received the vinegar, he said, It is finished: and he bowed his head, and gave up the ghost.

After he was dead, the body of Jesus was taken down by Joseph of Arimathea and Nicodemus, placed in a shroud (which many believe to be cloth now known as the Shroud of Turin), and left in a catacomb, a sepulchre belonging to Joseph. When several women returned to the tomb to anoint the body with spices, they discovered that the tomb's seal had been broken and that the body was missing. The women were then told by an angel that Jesus had come to life and had risen to Heaven.

Historian James Hastings explores the various meaning that have been applied to the execution of Jesus Christ in the *Encyclopedia of Religion and Ethics:*

> The atonement of Christ is conceived of as a sacrifice, and His personality as fully representative.
>
> According to the Western [Catholic] Church, Christ discharged his punishment due to the sins of mankind, and propitiated the justice of his Father, in his capacity of a man, as a representative of the human race; whereas in the East, where it was maintained that the *deity* suffered (though he suffered through the human nature which he had made his own), the idea of substitution could hardly take root, since, as Harnack remarks, "the dying *God*-man really represented no one." The Greek [Orthodox] Church regarded the death of Christ as a ransom for mankind paid to the devil, and this doctrine as also accepted by the most important of the Western Fathers, although it flatly contradicted their own theory of atonement.

In the eleventh century Margaret, the queen of Malcolm III of Scotland, brought to that nation what has been called the Black Rood of Scotland, a cross of gold in the form of a casket, which contains what is believed to be a portion of the true cross. It was captured by the British in 1346 and hung in a church in Durham; it disappeared soon after.

**See also:** Dismas and Gestas.

**References:** Bunyan, John, *The Advocateship of Jesus Christ: Clearly Explained, and Largely Improved, for the Benefit of All Believers, By John Bunyan* (London: Printed for Dorman Newman, 1688); Hastings, James, *Encyclopedia of Religion and Ethics,* 13 vols. (Edinburgh, Scotland: T. & T. Clark, 1908–27), 6:842; Owen, John, *Salus Electorum, Sanguis Jesu. The Death of death in the death of Christ: Being a treatise of the redemption and reconciliation that is in the blood of Christ, Wherein the whole Controversy about Universal Redemption, is fully discussed: in four parts. By John Owen, D.D.* (Carlisle, PA: Printed by George Kline, M,DCC,XCII [1792]); Sherman, Josiah, *Christ the True Victim and Conqueror: A History of the War, in which the Son of God engaged with all the powers of darkness, concerning the righteousness of God as moral Governor—how it commenced; and how he decided it, by being made a victim and sacrifice to the Devil's kingdom; by means of which, he conquered and destroyed God's enemies—made atonement for his sin—paid the price of our ransom—merited the kingdom of the universe to himself—and redeemed multitudes to God out of every Nation. By Josiah Sherman, A.M.; published at the desire of the hearers* (Litchfield, CT: Printed by T. Collier, in the south end of the court-house, 1787).

## Joan of Arc, Saint (1412–1431)

French heroine and savior of her nation, known as the "Maid of Orleans," put to death by the English for trying to rescue her homeland from the invading armies of King Henry V.

Born Jeanne D'Arc in the village of Domrémy en Barrois, in the Meuse Valley between Champagne and Lorraine, on 6 January 1412, she was the daughter of Jacques D'Arc, a farmer, and his wife Isabelle. Deeply religious from her upbringing, Joan became a shepherdess and would have remained unknown but for her devotion to her faith. While she was growing up, France was occupied by English forces, prohibiting Prince Charles, the heir to the French throne, from taking his rightful place as sovereign. Joan apparently heard voices that told her she must lead a mission to expel the English from France and make Charles the monarch. The prince armed Joan with 10,000 troops; she then marched at the head of the legion to Orleans, where she defeated the English army led by Lord John Talbot and reinforcements under Sir John Fastolf at the battle of Patay. On 17 July 1429 she was at Charles's side as he was crowned Charles VII of France. But when Joan attempted to take Paris, Charles withheld military support for some unknown reason. Joan was then captured by English forces at Compiègne, put on trial for her life before a tribunal overseen by Bishop Pierre Cauchon, and sentenced to death for sorcery.

W. P. Barrett, writing in his *The Trial of Jeanne d'Arc,* translated from the French, writes of Joan's last act, her refusal to recant her beliefs, as a disavowal of all that her accusers stood for.

> And Joan was required and admonished to speak the truth on many different points contained in her trial which she had denied or to which she had given false replies, whereas we possessed certain information, proofs, and vehement presumptions upon them. Many of the points were read and explained to her, and she was told that if she did not confess them truthfully she would be put to the torture. . . .
>
> To which the said Joan answered in this manner: "Truly if you were to tear me limb from limb and separate my soul from my body, I would not tell you anything more: and if I did say anything, I should afterwards declare that you had compelled me to say it by force." . . . She asked her voices if she would be burned and they answered that she must wait upon God, and He would aid her.

Vita Sackville-West, another biographer, wrote of these last moments:

> Instead of a crown of thorns, a tall paper cap, like a mitre, was set upon her head, bearing the words: "Heretic, relapsed, apostate, idolatress" . . . [Frère Isambard] de la Pierre [a priest who was a close friend], at her request, and sent by Massieu, fetched the crucifix from the neighboring church of Saint Sauveur, and, mounting the scaffold, held it up before her. She told him to get down when the fire should be lighted, but to continue holding the crucifix up so that she might see it. . . . Then as the flames crackled and rose, she called loudly and repeatedly upon Jesus; her head sank forward, and it was the last word she was heard to pronounce.
>
> Many wept; John Tressart, secretary to the King of England, exclaimed, "We are lost; we have burnt a saint."

After she was found to have expired, Joan's ashes were thrown into the Seine, but almost from the moment that she was dead the people began to realize that she may have had divine powers; her last prophecy, that the English would be expelled from her homeland, came true soon after. Twenty-five years after her execution, on 7 July 1456, she was declared to be innocent of the charges against her. In 1902 the Catholic Church declared her to be "venerable," seven years later had her beatified, and, on 9 May 1920, Pope Benedict XV canonized her. On 10 July 1920, the French government declared her execution day to be a national holiday. Her story was told in Carl Dreyer's 1928 silent masterpiece *The Passion of Joan of Arc* with Maria Falconetti in the leading role.

**References:** Barrett, Wilfred Phillips, trans., "The Trial of Jeanne D'Arc: Translated into English from the Original Latin and French Documents by W. P. Barrett; with an essay, *On the Trial of Jeanne d'Arc, and Dramatis Personae, Biographical Sketches of the Trials and Other Persons Involved in the Maid's Career, Trial and Death,* by Pierre Champion; Translated from the French by Coley Taylor and Ruth H. Kerr" (New York: Gotham House, 1932), 303–04; Sackville-West, Vita, *Saint Joan of Arc* (New York: Image Books, 1991), 23–50; Thurston, Herbert J., and Donald Attwater, eds., *Butler's Lives of the Saints,* 4 vols. (Westminster, MD: Christian Classics, 1988), 2:427–31;

## Jodl, Alfred Josef Ferdinand

See Nuremberg War Crimes Defendants

## John of Leiden (1509? or 1510?–1536)

Dutch martyr executed for his role in a religious uprising in Germany in the first half of the 16th century.

His real name was either Johann Bockoldt, Jan Bockelson, or Johann Beuckelson, and he was a Dutch Melchiorite Anabaptist fundamentalist. He was born near Leiden, where he was a tailor, merchant, and innkeeper before leading the Anabaptist movement in its revolution to establish a religious theocracy at Münster, Germany, in 1534. During his short reign as king of the "Kingdom of Zion," John introduced the tenets of polygamy, which was made legal, and the community ownership of goods. After the collapse of the Münster revolt, he was imprisoned by the bishop of Münster, where along with the other leaders of the revolt he was tortured and burned at the stake. He is the subject of Giacomo Meyerbeer's 1849 opera *La Prophète* ("The Prophet").

**References:** Barnhart, Clarence C., ed., *The New Century Cyclopedia of Names,* 3 vols. (New York: Appleton-Century-Crofts, 1954), 2:2201, 2733; Goetz, Philip W., ed.-in-Chief, *The New Encyclopedia Britannica,* 22 vols. (Chicago: Encyclopedia Britannica, Inc., 1995), 7:252.

## Jon, Gee (?–1924)

Chinese American murderer famed as the first man to die in the gas chamber.

Little is known of Jon, an American of Chinese descent who became mixed up in a tong (a Chinese gang that used terror to get its way) and was convicted of helping to murder an old Chinese man (although there was evidence that Jon was not the killer, but merely the accomplice to the killing). Sentenced to death in Nevada in the early 1920s, he originally was set to die by the noose. By this time, however, the reformist tide was beginning to turn against the noose and the electric chair; both were seen as cruel and inhuman methods of punishment. As a result, Nevada authorities turned to a new method, poison gas. At first, it was supposed that the criminal would be gassed while asleep, the gas pumped into the cell. But because of the difficulty of containing the gas, this method was rejected in favor of a closed room in which the condemned, seated, would be gassed. This room was the birth of the modern gas chamber, used in no other nation but the United States.

Gee Jon went to his death, according to witnesses, in a calm and gentle manner and was dead "ten seconds after the gas was turned on." In an editorial, the *Mountain Democrat* of Placerville, California, wrote enthusiastically:

> It will be a source of unlimited satisfaction to those who believe in capital punishment to know that henceforth the

victims will not be compelled to endure any physical pain but can be bumped off in a gentle manner. It will also take much of the sting out of death for the criminal to know that he will not be harmed and will look perfectly natural when laid out for burial. We congratulate the great State of Nevada on the success of their experiment and proof that a legal death can be painless as modern chemistry.

**References:** "Chinese Killer Executed by Gas At State Prison," *Las Vegas Review,* 15 February 1924, 4; "Making Light of Lethal Gas," *Mountain Democrat,* quoted in the *Las Vegas Review,* 29 February 1924, 2; Sifakis, Carl, *The Encyclopedia of American Crime* (New York: Facts on File, 1982), 377.

## Joyce, William (1906–1946)

Irish-American-German propagandist known as "Lord Haw Haw" for his zealous radio broadcasts from inside Nazi Germany during World War II, which led the British authorities to put him to death after the war.

Born in New York City on 24 April 1906, he was the son of Irish immigrants. Three years after the birth of their son, the Joyces returned to Ireland, and their son attended schools there. He later moved to London, maintaining his U.S. citizenship. In 1933, he joined the movement known as the British Union of Fascists (BUF), led by British reactionary Sir Oswald Mosley. Here, Joyce received all of his training in fascism, and when Hitler's Nazi movement took over in Germany that same year, Joyce saw an opportunity for the growth of his kind of thinking. Joyce fraudulently obtained British citizenship in 1939 so that he could go to Germany, which he did on 26 August of that same year.

Less than a month later, on 18 September 1939, just after German armies overran Poland, Joyce was hired to head up anti-British radio broadcasts on Radio Germany. On 26 September 1940 he officially became a German citizen. During the run of his program, he began his broadcasts with the haunting exchange, "Germany calling, Germany calling, Germany calling" in a nasal, artificial British tongue, and then would dive into his propaganda, usually stories of German victories that did not exist, of falling British civilian morale, of massive Allied casualties. Although German bombs began to rain down on Britain causing massive civilian casualties, Joyce was immensely popular in England, with an audience estimated at 50 percent of the British listening audience. But from this audience Joyce earned the name of "Lord Haw Haw," an indication of how seriously they took his broadcasts.

On 28 May 1945, he was captured by a British patrol in western Germany while trying to escape. Taken back to Britain, he claimed that as a citizen of Germany he was beyond the reach of British justice. However, his fraudulent British passport from 1939 proved to be his undoing. Taken to London, he was quickly tried in 1945 and convicted of aiding the enemy (his prosecutor was Attorney General Sir Hartley Shawcross, who was the next year Great Britain's representative before the Nuremburg War Crimes Tribunal), and sentenced to death. His appeal denied by the House of Lords, Joyce faced the hangman's noose in London's Wandsworth Prison on 3 January 1946. An estimated 300 people waited outside the jail, cheering when word of his death was announced.

**References:** "Crime File: William Joyce" in *Crime and Punishment: The Illustrated Crime Encyclopedia,* 28 vols. (Westport, CT: H. S. Stuttman, 1994), 7:824; Snyder, Louis L., *Encyclopedia of the Third Reich* (New York: McGraw-Hill, 1976), 183–84; Zentner, Christian, and Friedemann Bedüftig, eds., *Encyclopedia of the Third Reich,* 2 vols. (New York: Macmillan, 1991), 1:476.

## Juveniles, Execution of

Perhaps the most controversial aspect of the death penalty, particularly in the United States and in recent years, has been the subject of the execution of juveniles and exactly what age should be considered a "cutoff" at which the state must decide whether to imprison a defendant for life or put him to death. As late as 1970, when Associate Professor Martin Frey wrote a major article on the disposition of juvenile murderers, he spent much of the piece reflecting on the ability of the state to merely *prosecute* for the crime of murder (and finding the age in some states to be as low as seven) but not even discussing a cutoff age for persons convicted of murder who could legally be put to death.

Until recent times, the death penalty has been reserved for adults who committed adult crimes. Helene Greenwald, writing in the *Supreme Court Review* in 1982, explained that "the juvenile court system [was] the product of an early nineteenth century movement which advocated that juvenile offenders be treated differently than adults, and that these youths be rehabilitated rather than punished." However, as death-penalty historian Victor Streib points out, between 1642 and 1986, approximately 281 persons under the age of 18, considered by the law to be juveniles, were put to death in the United States. (The term *juvenile* is by law considered to represent an offender under the age of 18.) In two cases decided in two consecutive terms, *Thompson v. Oklahoma* (1988) and *Stanford v. Kentucky* (1989), the Court held that persons under the age of 16 could not be executed without violating the Eighth Amendment to the U.S. Constitution. In *Thompson,* a 15-year-old who was sentenced to death for murder had his sentence struck down. In 1946, in *Francis v. Louisiana ex rel. Resweber,* the Court held that it was constitutional to execute a 15-year-old black boy, Willie Francis, even though a previous attempt to execute him had failed.

Under Article 6(5) of the International Covenant on Civil and Political Rights (ICCPR), as well as Article 37(a) of the United Nations Convention on the Rights of the Child, the execution of juvenile offenders is prohibited. The United States, a signatory to both documents, has declared a reservation regarding the articles in question, claiming that they infringe on a nation's right to conduct proper law enforcement.

Among anti–death penalty forces, Amnesty International ranks highest in its condemnation of the execution of juveniles or of persons convicted of crimes committed when they were juveniles. The group reports that "since 1990, only four countries worldwide are reported to have executed juvenile offenders: one was executed in Saudi Arabia, and one in Pakistan, in 1992; one in Yemen in 1993; and six in the United States. A total of nine juvenile offenders have been exe-

**Executions since 1977 of Those Committing Crimes as Juveniles**

| *Name* | *Date Executed* | *State* | *Race* | *Age at Crime* | *Age at Execution* |
|---|---|---|---|---|---|
| Charles Rumbaugh | 9/11/85 | Texas | White | 17 | 28 |
| J. Terry Roach | 1/10/86 | South Carolina | White | 17 | 25 |
| Jay Pinkerton | 5/15/86 | Texas | White | 17 | 24 |
| Dalton Prejean | 5/18/90 | Louisiana | Black | 17 | 30 |
| Johnny Garrett | 2/11/92 | Texas | White | 17 | 28 |
| Curtis Harris | 7/1/93 | Texas | Black | 17 | 31 |
| Frederick Lashley | 7/28/93 | Missouri | Black | 17 | 29 |
| Ruben Cantu | 8/24/93 | Texas | Latino | 17 | 26 |
| Chris Burger | 12/7/93 | Georgia | White | 17 | 33 |
| Joseph J. Cannon | 4/22/98 | Texas | White | 17 | 38 |

cuted in the United States since 1985 and over 35 remain under sentence of death."

**See also:** *Thompson v. Oklahoma.*

**References:** Amnesty International USA, "Amnesty International Country Report 1996" (New York: Amnesty International, 1996); Amnesty International USA, "The Death Penalty and Juvenile Offenders" (New York: Amnesty International, 1991); Frey, Martin A., "The Criminal Responsibility of the Juvenile Murderer," *Washington University Law Quarterly,* 1970:2 (Spring 1970), 113-33; Greenwald, Helene B., "Eighth Amendment—Minors and the Death Penalty: Decision and Avoidance," *Supreme Court Review,* 73 (1982), 1525; Streib, Victor L., "Death Penalty for Children: The American Experience with Capital Punishment for Crimes Committed While under Age Eighteen," *Oklahoma Law Review,* 36:3 (Summer 1983), 613–41; Streib, Victor L., "The Eighth Amendment and Capital Punishment of Juveniles," *Cleveland State Law Review,* 34:3 (1985–86), 363–99.

## Keitel, Wilhelm

See Nuremberg War Crimes Defendants

## Kelly, Ned (1854–1880)

Australian "bushranger" (an outlaw in the Australian bush) hanged for his illegal actions in the Outback.

Just as the American West has its Jesse James, a criminal who has become myth, legend, and hero rolled into one, Australia has Ned Kelly, a noted outlaw remembered perhaps more for his costume than his crimes. Kelly lived only 26 years, but in that short time he became one of the most famous criminals in Australian history.

Kelly was born in the village of Beveridge, north of Melbourne, New South Wales, into a poor family. His parents, John and Ellen Kelly, both from Tasmania, moved their family when Ned was 16 to the village of Avenel, where Ned attended school. Little else is known of his early life, but he began his short life of crime when, at just 24 years of age, he was arrested on charges of assault and sentenced to six months in the local jail. In early 1878 he attacked a policeman and began a crime wave that lasted for almost two years. He assembled a gang, known as "the Kelly Gang," made up of Ned, his brother Dan, Steve Hart, and Joe Byrne. The gang then proceeded to go on a crime spree that culminated in October 1878 in the murders of three policemen, Sergeants Kennedy and Scanlon and Constable Lonigan, who were trying to arrest Kelly for stealing horses. After this crime, authorities put a reward on Kelly's head. The gang also held up the National Bank in Euroa and the Bank of New South Wales in Jerilderie. The area where the Kelly Gang committed these crimes is now known as "Kelly country." On 24 June 1880, the gang was ambushed by police in the inn in the village of Glenrowan. Ned was captured, his brother Dan and Steve Hart committed suicide during the siege, and Joe Byrne was shot and killed by police.

Kelly was tried in Melbourne. His unique mask and suit of armor, made from stolen ploughshares, were introduced as evidence against him. The defense mounted by Kelly's attorney was ineffective. According to historian Robert Melville, "No witnesses were called for the defence. The defending counsel, appointed by the Crown because Ned had no funds, relied on an address to the jury, pointing out a few discrepancies in the evidence." The jury was out only a half hour before returning with a verdict of guilty. Thereafter, Kelly made this statement to the court.

> Well, it is rather too late for me to speak now. I thought of speaking this morning and all day, but there was little use, and there is little use blaming any one now. Nobody knew about my case except myself, and I wish I had insisted on being allowed to examine the witnesses myself. I am confident I would have thrown a different light on the case. It is not that I fear death; I fear it as little as to drink a cup of tea. On the evidence that has been given, no juryman could have given any other verdict. . . . I lay blame on myself that I did not get up yesterday and examine the witnesses, but I thought that if I did so it would look like bravado and flashiness.

The judge then sentenced Kelly to death, and after he concluded, "May the Lord have mercy on your soul," Kelly turned to him and replied, "I will go a little further than that, and say that I will see you there where I go." He was hanged at Melbourne jail less than two weeks later, on 11 November 1880.

British historian Francis Hare reported that days after Kelly's execution, "a show was opened in Melbourne, with Kate Kelly, one of the sisters of the dead bushrangers, 'mounted on Ned Kelly's celebrated grey mare.'" After his death, his armor, death mask, and the gallows on which he was hung were put on exhibit at the Melbourne jail. In 1970, the English film *Ned Kelly* was released, directed by Tony Richardson and starring Mick Jagger; another production, a miniseries entitled *The Last Outlaw* starring Australian actor John Jarratt as Ned, appeared on Australian television in 1980. In 1992, Kelly's boyhood home in Beveridge was designated a historical landmark and added to Australia's Register of Historical Buildings.

**References:** Barry, Redmond, "The Sentencing of Ned Kelly" in Alan Lindsey McLeod, ed., *Australia Speaks: An Anthology of Australian Speeches* (Sydney, New South Wales, Australia: Wentworth Press, 1969), 74–77; Cave, Colin F., *Ned Kelly, Man and Myth* (North Melbourne: Cassell Australia, 1968); "Famed Australian Bushranger Dead," *Victoria Daily Times* [New South Wales, Australia], 19 December 1946, 18; Hare, Francis Augustus, *The Last of the Bushrangers: An Account of the Capture of the Kelly Gang* (London: Hurst and Blackett, Limited, 1892), 341, 384; McQuilton, John, *The Kelly Outbreak, 1878–1880: The Geographical Dimension of Social Banditry* (Carlton, Victoria: Melbourne University Press, 1979); Melville, Robert, *The Legend of Ned Kelly* (New York: The Viking Press, 1964), 27; Sayers, Andrew, *Sidney Nolan: The Ned Kelly Story* (New York: Metropolitan Museum of Art, 1994); Seal, Graham, *Ned Kelly in Popular Tradition* (Melbourne: Hyland House, 1980).

## Kemmler, William Francis (1861–1890)

The first man put to death by electricity, executed for the brutal murder of a woman.

Little is known of him, except that his alias was John Hart and that he was having an affair with a woman named Tillie Zeigler when he murdered her with a hatchet in Buffalo, New York, on 29 March 1889. Brought to trial, he was quickly convicted and sentenced to death. A year earlier, Kemmler would have been hanged. However, his death sentence came at the same time that New York was replacing the noose and hangman with the electric chair, a newfangled method of capital punishment that promised more humane executions than had occurred on the scaffold.

After his appeals were exhausted, Kemmler was taken on the morning of 6 August 1890 by Auburn prison warden Charles F. Durston from his cell to the death chamber, where a crowd had gathered around the new wooden electric chair. Electrodes were fastened to his back and head, and a leather mask lowered on his face. To Durston, he said, "Now take your time and do it all right, Warden. There is no rush. I don't want to take any chances on this thing, you know." When everything was set, Durston said to him, "Good-bye, William." Before Kemmler could reply, the executioner turned on the current of 1,000 volts, which was enough to stun, but not kill, Kemmler. For seventeen seconds the power raged, as Kemmler fought against the straps. A second shock was ended, and Kemmler sank into the seat. A doctor rushed over, as witnesses saw the condemned was still alive. To shouts of "Great God, he is alive!" and "Turn on the current!" the electricity flowed again. By now, however, the wet sponges around the electrodes had dried, and the new electric surge started to burn the skin. The cap of Kemmler's head began to turn purple, and smoke started to rise from his spine. This third shock lasted anywhere from one minute to four and a half—none of the observers looked at their watches. After eight minutes Warden Durston stopped the dynamo controlling the electricity, and Kemmler's body sagged. He was finally dead.

At the autopsy, held three hours after death to allow the body to cool down, doctors found that while Kemmler had struggled against the straps after the first current hit and later exhibited signs of life, he had been knocked unconscious by the first shock and had not felt any further pain. His blood had turned to carbon, and the areas where his skin burned resembled badly cooked beef.

The local New York newspapers blasted the execution as nothing short of torture, even for a murderer like Kemmler. "Kemmler's Death by Torture" wrote the *Herald*. "Far Worse Than Hanging" wrote *The Times*. The *World* labeled Kemmler "The First Electrocide." The pressure mounted to do away with the chair, but Governor David Hill allowed more executions to proceed. When four men were put to death on one single day with no problems, the cruelty of Kemmler's death vanished from the front pages.

**See also:** *In re Kemmler.*

**References:** Beichman, Arnold, "The First Electrocution," *Commentary,* 35:5 (May 1963), 410–419; "Far Worse Than Hanging: Kemmler's Death Proves an Awful Spectacle," *New-York Times,* 7 August 1890, 1, 2; "The First Electrocide: How Brutal Murderer Kemmler Was Killed at Auburn," *World* (New York), 7 August 1890, 1; *In re Kemmler* (opinion) (136 U.S. 436 [1890]); "Kemmler's Death by Torture," *New York Herald,* 7 August 1890, 3; Sifakis, Carl, *The Encyclopedia of American Crime* (New York: Facts on File, 1982), 392.

## Kidd, William (c.1655–1701)

Scottish pirate executed for crimes committed on the high seas, although many historians now believe that he should not have suffered the penalty that he did.

Also known as Robert Kidd, he was born in Greenock, Scotland, the son of the Reverend John Kidd. He was interested in the sea from his youth, and by 1695 was considered to be one of the finest sea captains in the world. When piracy on the seas started, Kidd accepted a commission from King William III of England to captain an armed vessel, the *Adventure Galley,* and capture the pirates—he was even allowed a share of the recovered wealth. He left Plymouth, England, in April 1696, and sailed along the east coast of what is now the United States for several months but came across no pirate activity. Apparently, during this time, he turned to pirating himself, beginning the period of pillage and plunder that made his name famous.

After collecting an enormous fortune off the coast of Africa, Kidd and his crew returned to New York, then New Amsterdam, sometime in 1698. He buried some of his treasure on Gardiner's Island, north of what is now Long Island, before sailing into Boston Harbor and settling down to enjoy his new-found wealth. But reports of his activities had reached England, and the governor of New York and Massachusetts, the Earl of Beilamont, arrested Kidd on a charge of piracy and sent him back to England in chains.

Instead of piracy, however, Kidd was tried on a charge of having murdered one of his crew, and after a short trial that many historians have called unfair, he was convicted and sentenced to death. On 24 May 1701, he was taken to the area known as the Execution Dock in London and hanged in a gibbet until dead. At the time of his death, Kidd was in his late 40s, and while he was probably guilty of piracy, his name has lived on throughout history as a victim of injustice.

**References:** "The Arraignment, Tryal, and Condemnation of Captain William Kidd, for Murther and Piracy, at the Old-Bailey, the 8th and the 9th of May, 1701, as also the tryals of Nicholas Churchill, James Howe, and Darby Mullins for Piracy to which are added Captain Kidd's commissions, etc." (London: J. Nutt, 1701); *Captain Kidd, a Noted Pirate Who was Hanged at Execution Dock, in England* (Boston: L. Deming, 1840?); Gosse, Philip, *"The Pirate's Who's Who, Giving Particulars of the Lives & Deaths of the Pirates and Buccaneers"* (London: Dulau, 1924), 180–184; Knapp, Andrew, and William Baldwin, "The New Newgate Calendar; Being Interesting Memoirs of Notorious Characters, Who have Been Convicted of Outrages on the Laws of England, During the Seventeenth Century, Brought Down to the Present Time. Chronologically Arranged," 5 vols. (London: Printed by and for J. and J. Cundee, Ivy-Lane, 1826), 1:31–36; Teach, Edward, "He Was Just a Kidd; Only His Enemies Called Him a Pirate," *Sky,* June 1996, 92–94.

## Kolbe, Father Maximilian (or Maksymilian) Maria (1894–1941)

Polish priest who lost his life by lethal injection at the hands of the Nazis in order to save the life of another concentration camp inmate, an act for which he was made a saint.

Born in the village of Zduñska Wola, in the Lòdz district of Poland, on 8 January 1894, he was christened Raymond Maria Kolbe (Kol-bay), but at the age of 13, when he entered the Franciscan order, he changed his name to Maximilian. Kolbe told of having a dream: that he was asked by the Virgin Mary to choose either a white crown for purity or a red one for martyrdom, and he related that he chose both. In 1912, after five years in the Franciscan movement, he went to Rome to study theology at the Pontifican Gregorian University. In 1917 he helped to found the Order of the Knights of the Immaculata, a sodality, or devotional association. A year later, he was ordained as a priest.

Returning to Poland, Kolbe began to publish the journal of the sodality, *Rycerz Niepokalanej* (The Knights of the Mary Immaculate), and eventually founded, in 1927, the Niepolkalanow, or City of Mary Immaculate, a religious community located near Warsaw that used the image of the Virgin Mary to spread the gospel. In 1939, shortly before the outbreak of World War II, the community had more than 700 followers. In 1930, sick with tuberculosis, Kolbe nonetheless traveled to Nagasaki, Japan, to found a Catholic mission there, which he called Mugenzai no Sono (Japanese for Garden of the Immaculate). In 1936 he returned to Poland, where he took control of the operations of Niepolkalanow and began the publication of a newspaper, *Maly Dziennik* (Small Daily). Historians have noted, however, that while Kolbe used the pages of this and other religious publications to advance his religious views, he also expressed virulent anti-Semitic views, at times using the discounted Protocols of the Elders of Zion, an anti-Semitic tract, as a chief source of his quotations. Critics of Kolbe's eventual sainthood pointed to these writings and views.

With the start of World War II, Kolbe was arrested by German occupation troops but was later allowed to return to Niepokalanow, where he helped to shield refugees, including many Jews. For this work, in February 1941, he was again arrested and deported to Pawiak prison in Poland. Later, he was transferred to Auschwitz, the most infamous of the German concentration camps. When a prisoner escaped from Kolbe's cell block, the SS troops in charge of the camp decreed that one of every ten persons in the block would be put to death in retaliation. When a married man with children named Franciszek Gajowniczek was selected, Kolbe stepped forward and offered his life for that of the condemned man. Kolbe was taken to a starvation cell, where he lingered for ten days. On 14 August 1941, he was finally injected with phenol or carbolic acid and died a painful death; thereafter his remains were cremated. According to historians, when approached by a Nazi officer with the injection, Kolbe, in his last act, raised his arm so that he could die as quickly as possible.

Although the Church has strict rules declaring that a saint must have performed at least two miracles, in 1982 Kolbe became the first person declared a saint under a new code allowing those martyred in the name of the Church to be so venerated.

**References:** Briggs, Kenneth A., "New Saint Is Inspiration for the Message of Hope," *New York Times,* 11 October 1982, A8; Dewar, Diana, *All for Christ: Some Twentieth Century Martyrs* (Oxford, England: Oxford University Press, 1980), 147–167; Fiske, Edward B., "Auschwitz Friar Beatified by Pope," *New York Times,* 18 October 1971, 7; Goetz, Philip W., ed.-in-Chief, *The New Encyclopædia Britannica,* 22 vols. (Chicago: Encyclopædia Britannica, Inc., 1995), Micropædia 6:938; Gutman, Israel, "Kolbe, Maximilian" in Israel Gutman, ed., *Encyclopedia of the Holocaust,* 4 vols. (New York: Macmillan, 1990), 4:811–12; Kamm, Henry, "The Saint of Auschwitz Is Canonized by Pope," *New York Times,* 11 October 1982, A1, A8; "Wartime Priest Will Become a Saint," *New York Times,* 3 March 1981, A8; Winowska, Maria, *"The Death Camp Proved Him Real: The Life of Blessed Maximilian Kolbe, Franciscan"* (Libertyville, IL: Prow Books/Franciscan Marytown Press, 1971).

## *KQED, Inc. v. Vasquez* (U.S. Dist. Court, Northern. Dist. of California, 1991)

Little-known but important capital punishment decision that held that while "paper and pencils" may be brought in by reporters to witness executions, cameras may be excluded.

In February 1990, San Quentin Prison in California had published a revised policy regarding witnesses and the items they could bring with them to observe executions. It prohibited the use of "cameras, recording equipment, sketch pads, note pads, pens or pencils." On 15 March 1990, radio station KQED in San Francisco asked the prison warden, Daniel B. Vasquez, for permission to being cameras in to videotape the execution of Robert Alton Harris. The prison denied the request. Harris's execution was eventually stayed (he was not put to death until 21 April 1992, the first man to be executed in California since 1967), and in that time KQED sued to have the execution videotaped.

A trial began on 25 March 1991 in the U.S. District Court in San Francisco, with Judge Robert H. Schnacke presiding. On 7 June Judge Schnacke held that (1) the plaintiff, KQED, would be enjoined from bringing cameras into an execution; (2) the defendant's "method and procedure for selecting media representatives" was not unconstitutional; (3) that plaintiff KQED and other media representatives could not be stopped using paper and pencils; and (4) that the defendant, Warden Vasquez, could "not exclude all representatives of media from the witness area." The judgment was never appealed to a higher court and remains the lone decision in the United States regarding the use of cameras by the media in witnessing an execution.

**References:** Text of "Amended Judgment" in *KQED, Inc., Plaintiff, vs. Daniel B. Vasquez, Warden of San Quentin Prison, Defendant,* C-90–1383, U.S. District Court for the Northern District of California, 1 August 1991.

## Kürten, Peter (1883–1931)

Known as "The Vampire of Düsseldorf," he remains one of the least known but most vicious murderers of the twentieth century, a man for whom the title "serial killer" would have been appropriate, but the term had not yet been invented when he committed his series of brutal crimes.

One of thirteen children, he was born in 1883 in the village of Cologne-Mülheim, Germany. His father abused alcohol, brutally beat his wife, and sexually molested his children. Like most serial killers, Kürten began to appease his growing pleasure for pain and blood by torturing and killing animals. In 1894, he and his family moved to Düsseldorf, and within three years he satisfied his deviant sexual fantasies by assaulting and nearly strangling his young girlfriend. He discovered that the experience excited him. At seventeen he was sent to prison for two years for theft; but while there, he began to fantasize more and more about violent torture and perverted sex acts. As he told the court after his arrest, "I thought of myself causing accidents affecting thousands of people and invented a number of crazy fantasies such as smashing bridges and boring through the bridge piers. Then I spun a number of fantasies with regard to bacilli which I might be able to introduce into the drinking water and so cause great calamity. I imagined myself using schools or orphanages for the purpose, where I could carry out murders by giving away chocolate samples containing arsenic which I could have obtained through housebreaking. I derived the sort of pleasure from these visions that other people would get from thinking about a naked woman."

Excited by fire, Kürten began a spree as an arsonist in 1904 but was arrested a year later and spent seven years at hard labor. This interval left him more time to think up brutal torments. When released in 1913, he turned for the second time to murder. Staying at an inn in the city of Cologne-Mülheim, Kürten suffocated and then cut the throat of his first official victim, 13-year-old Christine Klein, and, for the excitement, returned to the scene the next day to watch the police investigate. The experience left Kürten wanting more and more blood. He later told the court that the sight of his victims' blood drove him to orgasm. In a park, he severed the head of a swan and sucked the blood from the wound. In 1923, Kürten married a former prostitute, but his deviance did not subside. He changed implements, moving from a pocketknife to a pair of scissors to a hammer. His viciousness grew in intensity. His last victim was a 5-year-old child, Gertrud Albermann, whom he stabbed with scissors 36 times. He was now being called the "Vampire of Düsseldorf."

In 1930, Kürten slipped up. He invited an unemployed maid, 21-year-old Maria Büdlick, to his loft for a warm meal. Instead, he took her to some woods near his home and tried to rape her. When he could not, he asked her if she could recognize where she was. When she could not, he turned and left her. Dazed, she made her way off but later wrote the details of her encounter in a letter to a friend. But she put the wrong address on the letter, and it wound up being read by a stranger in Düsseldorf who recognized the Vampire's modus operandi and directed the correspondence to the police. They tracked down Maria Büdlick, and she told them what the man looked like and where he lived. Kürten was then picked up.

When he finally stood trial for the spree, Kürten was found to be shy, soft-spoken, unassuming and seemingly harmless. At his trial in the Düsseldorf drill-hall in April 1931, where he was forced to sit in a wooden cage to prevent his lynching by an angered crowd that taunted him from outside, he calmly cataloged his crimes for the court, 68 in all, including nine murders and seven attempted murders. The judges and jury were amazed at his sanity, his vision for every detail of each crime, his unwillingness to see the sickness in what he had done. In the end, the jury took an hour and a half to find him guilty. On 2 July 1931, he faced the guillotine. As he approached the instrument, the blade shining, he asked the executioner if, at the moment his head was cut off, he could hear the blood spew forth from his neck. The thought, he said, excited him more than anything else.

That same year, German film director Fritz Lang released *M,* starring Peter Lorre and based on the Kürten case.

**See also:** Motion Pictures, Capital Punishment as Depicted in.

**References:** Keith, W. Barrington, *The World's Greatest Crimes: Murder, Robbery and Mayhem from 1900 to the Present Day* (London: Hamden, 1990), 54–59; Nash, Jay Robert, *Encyclopedia of World Crime,* 4 vols. (Wilmette, IL: CrimeBooks, Inc. 1990), 2:1862–1863; "The Vampire of Dusseldorf" in John Paton, ed., *Crimes and Punishment: A Pictorial Encyclopedia of Aberrant Behavior,* 19 vols. (London: Symphonette Press, 1973–1974), 7:45–52.

## Lapidation

See Stoning to Death

## Last Words of the Condemned

In their last moments on earth, many of the condemned, when allowed to speak, have made comments that carry with them the weight of their final moments on earth. These comments range from anger to philosophical musings. A selection of the most historical or interesting follows.

"Sanson, thou wilt show my head to the people; it is worth showing." George Jacques Danton, beheaded 5 April 1794.

"Hang me quick—make haste." Albert Hicks, executed 13 July 1860.

"Center on my heart, boys. Don't mangle my body!" John Doyle Lee, to the firing squad that executed him, 23 March 1877.

"God help me." Martha Place, executed 20 March 1899.

"Standing, as I do, in the view of God and eternity, I realize that patriotism is not enough. I must have no hatred or bitterness towards anyone." Nurse Edith Cavell, executed 12 October 1915.

"Fire! Go on and Fire!" Joe Hill, to the firing squad that executed him on 19 November 1915.

"Take a step or two forward, lads. It will be easier that way." Erskine Childers, to the firing squad that executed him on 24 November 1922.

"I think it is a hell of a thing that a life had to be taken in this manner. I say this especially because there's a great deal I could have offered society. I certainly think capital punishment is legally and morally wrong. Any apology for what I have done would be meaningless at this time. I don't have any animosities toward anyone involved in this matter." Perry Smith, hanged in Kansas on 14 April 1965.

"Let's do it." Gary Gilmore, executed by firing squad on 17 January 1977.

"Capital punishment—them without the capital get the punishment." John Spenkelink, executed 25 May 1979.

"Commute me or execute me. Don't drag it out." Jesse Bishop, while sitting in the gas chamber, 22 October 1979.

"I guess nobody is going to call." Edward Earl Johnson, executed 20 May 1987.

"That's it. Let's go." Johnny Taylor, Jr., executed 29 February 1984.

"Don't feel bad, Mama. I deserve this." Charles Bass, executed 12 March 1986.

"I'm sorry for what I done. I deserve it. I hope Jesus forgives me. I'm tingling all over." Jeffrey Barney, executed 16 April 1986.

"Yeah, I think I'd rather be fishing." Jimmy Glass, executed 12 June 1987.

"No, sir." Robert Streetman, executed 7 January 1988.

"Give my love to my family and friends." Ted Bundy, executed 24 January 1989.

"I wish everybody a good life." Jerome Butler, executed 21 April 1990.

"I still proclaim that I am innocent and that's all I have to say." Johnny Anderson, executed 17 May 1990.

"OK." Michael Van McDougall, executed 18 October 1991.

"Lock and load. Let's do it, man." G. W. Green, executed 12 November 1991.

"I'd like to thank my family for loving me and taking care of me. And the rest of the world can kiss my ass." Johnny Frank Garrett, executed 11 February 1992.

"I just want everyone to know I think the prosecutor and Bill Scott are some sorry sons of bitches." Edward Ellis, executed 3 March 1992.

"You can be a king or a street sweeper, but everybody dances with the Grim Reaper." Robert Alton Harris, executed 21 April 1992.

[After injection] "I'm still awake. . . ." Robyn Leroy Parks, executed 10 March 1992.

"I look stretched out like a cooked goose." Robert Black, executed 22 May 1992.

"I am the low sinner of sinners." Markham Duff-Smith, executed 29 June 1993,

"I'm an African warrior born to breathe and born to die." Carl Kelly, executed 20 August 1993.

"Remember, the death penalty is murder." Robert Drew, executed 2 August 1994.

"See ya." Warren Bridge, executed 22 November 1994.

"There is not going to be an execution. This is premeditated murder by the appointed district attorney and the State of Texas. I am not guilty of this crime." Jesse DeWayne Jacobs, executed 5 January 1995.

"The state of Missouri is committing as premeditated a murder as possible." Alan J. Bannister, executed 22 October 1997.

"I am going to be face to face with Jesus now. . . . I will see you all when you get there. I will wait for you." Karla Faye Tucker, executed by lethal injection on 3 February 1998.

Convicted serial killer Michael Sharp put his last words on the Internet shortly before being executed by lethal injection by the state of Texas on 19 November 1997. Prison officials in Texas said they believe this was the first time a condemned prisoner used the Internet to make his final statement, which is generally heard only by execution witnesses.

## Laval, Pierre-Jean-Marie (1883–1945)

French politician and prime minister (1931–32, 1935–36, 1942), shot by a firing squad following the end of World War II for collaborating with the Germans.

Born in Châteldon, France, on 28 June 1883, Laval was the son of Baptiste Laval, a middle-class innkeeper, and his wife Claudine. Pierre left school at the age of 12 to drive a cart for his father's meat business. As a result, he was mostly self-educated. However, he did eventually get jobs teaching at the schools of Saint-Etienne, Lyons, and the Paris Law School, where he was awarded degrees in natural history and law.

After a short time practicing the law, he ran for a seat in the national legislature on the Socialist ticket. During World War I, he was among a number of deputies who urged a pacifist line against the Germans, even a negotiated peace to end the war as quickly as possible. In 1919, he was among the group that opposed the Treaty of Versailles because its terms were too harsh for Germany. Prime Minister Georges Clemenceau regarded him as perhaps the most dangerous man in France and many times unsuccessfully demanded his arrest. However, Laval's stands cost him his legislative seat in 1919.

This loss, however, allowed Laval to enter the business world, and he soon amassed a large fortune from various investments. In 1923, he was elected mayor of Aubervilliers, although he ran as an independent, and not mainline, Socialist, and was reelected the following year. During the next decade he held a number of political offices, including prime minister in 1931 and 1935. This second ministry, however, was racked by a scandal when it was discovered that together with British Foreign Minister Sir Samuel Hoare, Laval had appeased Italy by allowing it to take over Ethiopia; the revelation brought down Laval's government.

In 1940, the Germans occupied France and set up the Vichy government, a puppet government in full collaboration with the Germans, under Henri Pétain. Laval was named vice premier and eventually succeeded the elderly Pétain as premier. Laval soon became the most despised man in France, and in 1941 the French Resistance, an underground group bent on destroying the German war machine in France, attempted to assassinate him. He was deposed for a time, but Hitler pressured Pétain to return him to the government.

After the Allies invaded France in June 1944, Laval panicked and fled to Germany. He was tried in absentia and sentenced to death for collaboration. He was discovered in Barcelona, Spain, with his wife on 2 May 1945 but fled to Austria, where he was picked up by American troops near the city of Linz. While in Fresnes Prison awaiting trial, he began work on his autobiography; he completed the text just days before he was shot by a firing squad, and it was subsequently published under the title "The Unpublished Diary of Pierre Laval." His trial opened on 4 October 1945, and he was tried on a single charge of treason. Justice for Laval was quick: just five days later, the French High Court of Justice found him guilty and sentenced him to death. On 15 October he tried to kill himself with poison but succeeded only in making himself sick. Taken to a courtyard in the prison, Laval was shot by firing squad.

**References:** Chambrun, Rene de (Elly Stein, trans.), *Pierre Laval: Traitor or Patriot?* (New York: Scribner's, 1984); Cole, Hubert, *Laval: A Biography* (London: Heinemann, 1963); Doenecke, Justus D., "Pierre Laval" in Anne Commire, ed., *Historic World Leaders,* 5 vols. (Detroit: Gale Research, 1994), 3:760–65; Laval, Pierre, *The Unpublished Diary of Pierre Laval* (Falcon Press, 1948); Thomson, David, *Two Frenchmen: Pierre Laval and Charles de Gaulle* (London: Cresset Press, 1951); Torrés, Henry, *Pierre Laval* (New York & Toronto: Oxford University Press, 1941); Warner, Geoffrey, *Pierre Laval and the Eclipse of France* (London: Eyre & Spottiswoode, 1968); Whitcomb, Philip W., trans., *"France during the German Occupation, 1940–1944: A Collection of 292 Statements on the Government of Marshal Pétain and Pierre Laval"* (Stanford, CA: Distributed by Stanford University Press for the Hoover Institution on War, Revolution and Peace, 1957).

## Lawes, Lewis Edward (1883–1947)

American prison administrator and death penalty reformer noted for his opposition in the 1920s and 1930s to capital punishment.

Born in Elmira, New York, on 13 September 1883, he was the son of Harry Lewis Lawes, a British expatriate, and Sarah Lawes. He grew up a mile from the Elmira State Reformatory, where his father worked as a guard, and was thus exposed to the American penal system from an early age. He attended the Elmira Free Academy, as well as other local schools, and at the same time worked for the city newspaper, the *Elmira Telegram.* He served in the United States Army from 1901 to 1904. After that he took a position as a guard at New York's Clinton penitentiary but was transferred to Auburn prison, in the same state, and then to the Elmira facility where he had grown up.

In the intervening years his service in the area of social work and his work to improve conditions in the New York City Reformatory for male juvenile delinquents on Hart's Island made him a respected figure in the penal reform movement. On 1 January 1920, Lawes was named warden of New York's Sing Sing prison in Ossining, the site at that time of that state's electric chair, and in this position Lawes oversaw 302 executions. In the 21 years he served as warden, Lawes gradually became a staunch opponent of capital punishment and an important writer on penal reform and anti–death penalty sentiment in the 1920s and 1930s. His works during this period include *Life and Death in Sing Sing* (1928), *Twenty Thousand Years in Sing Sing* (1932), *Cell 202 Sing Sing* (1935), *Invisible Stripes* (1938), and *Meet the Murderer* (1940).

In his famous 1924 work, *Man's Judgment of Death: An Analysis of the Operation and Effect of Capital Punishment Based on Facts, Not on Sentiment,* Lawes wrote:

> I have come to this very definite conclusion. There has been in the past and there is to a greater degree today a general trend toward a lessening in the severity of punishment. . . . so that the logical goal must be the complete elimination of the death penalty from our system of punishment. The death penalty rests upon wrong basic principles. It conforms to none of our ideas of modern criminology. It is impossible of scientific application. As a punishment it lacks celerity and certainty of execution. It fails as a deterrent measure. . . . I do believe that life imprisonment with a long unavoidable minimum provides a form of punishment that is more certain of application than the death penalty can ever be made, that is more scientific in its application because with its long but variable minimum it presents a possibility for individualization and differentiation of treatment; that by reason of these qualities its universal adoption will provide a more effective deterrent.

Biographer W. David Lewis writes, "Lawes trenchantly analyzed society's involvement in the responsibility for crime through its toleration of poverty, outmoded educational practices, formalistic religion, parental neglect, and unethical tactics which were condoned in business life but harshly punished in other contexts. He called for judicial reforms such as the indeterminate sentence, urged a thorough revamping of the criminal law, and criticized police conduct that was predicated upon inspiring fear rather than respect."

Lawes spent his final years trying to reform criminal laws that favored capital punishment; he even wrote a prison play, *Chalked Out,* which appeared on Broadway for a short time in 1937. Four years later, he retired. On 23 April 1947, Lawes died at his home in Garrison, New York, of a cerebral hemorrhage and was buried in Tarrytown, New York.

**References:** Lawes, Lewis E., "*Man's Judgment of Death: An Analysis of the Operation and Effect of Capital Punishment Based on Facts, Not on Sentiment*" (New York: G. P. Putnam's Sons, 1924), 78–79; "Lawes, Lewis Edward" in *National Cyclopedia of American Biography,* 57 vols., supplements A-L (New York: James T. White, 1898–1977), F:314–315; Lewis, W. David, "Lawes, Lewis Edward" in Dumas Malone, et al., eds., *Dictionary of American Biography,* 10 vols., 10 supplements (New York: Charles Scribner's Sons, 1930–1995), 4:471–473.

## Lee, John Doyle (1812–1877)

Mormon leader put to death for his alleged role in Utah's Mountain Meadow Massacre of 1857. He remains to this day perhaps the most controversial person in Mormon history.

Born on 12 September 1812 near St. Louis, Missouri, John Doyle Lee was the son of Ralph Lee, a carpenter, and Elizabeth (nee Doyle) Lee. Ralph Lee was a relative of the famed Lee family of Virginia (which included as its members Robert E. Lee and "Lighthorse Harry" Lee of Revolutionary War fame); Elizabeth Doyle Lee's father, John Doyle, was himself a Revolutionary War veteran.

Lee worked as a mail carrier, on a steamboat, and in a grocery store in Galena, Illinois. There he met Aggatha Ann Woolsey, and the two were married on 24 July 1833. While in Vandalia, Lee and his wife became interested in the Mormon faith then being preached in Illinois by the Mormon activist Joseph Smith. Both were baptized on 17 June 1838 after they met Smith for the first time. Lee became one of Mormonism's earliest and most devout followers. In the following years, he married 18 other woman and fathered a total of 60 children; he also became a secret member of the Danites, a radical Mormon group that defended the rights of Mormons, then under attack in Missouri and Illinois. When on Election day 1838 Mormons were prohibited from voting, Lee and other Danites took up arms and began looting. They were joined by anti-Mormons, and the chaos forced Missouri Governor Lilburn Boggs to issue an "Extermination Order" against Mormons for "the public good."

Fleeing for their lives, Lee and his wife headed to the Mormon headquarters at Nauvoo, Illinois, where Lee became a bodyguard to Smith and his brother Hyrum, as well as a traveling preacher. In this latter capacity, he was in Kentucky in June 1844 when the Smiths were murdered during Joseph Smith's presidential campaign. Lee then joined the new Mormon leader, Brigham Young, and with the "Council of Fifty," proposed leaving Illinois for safer and freer lands further west. When he finally reached the Great Basin, now called the Great Salt Lake in Utah, Lee's status as a mentor and advisor to the Mormon leadership resulted in his being chosen to open the Iron Mission (now Iron County). In January 1856, the U.S. government named Lee as the area Indian Agent to deal with the local Paiute Indians and help them with agricultural techniques. It was in this capacity that he became involved in the act that would later cost him his life.

In September 1857, a group of about 125 emigrants bound for California (the numbers reported range from 90 to 150) from Arkansas and Missouri, known to history as the Fancher party, crossed into Utah and settled for a time at a place called Mountain Meadows. There they were attacked by the Paiutes, and a number of them were killed. Lee and another Mormon, William Bateman, met with the survivors and agreed to help them move away under a truce flag. Lee separated the men from the women and children, then confiscated the weapons of the group. At his urging, the Mormons then opened fire, cutting down the male members of the party; the women and children were then butchered by the Indians.

Why the Mormons opened fire has remained unclear to this day. Some historians believe that Lee had heard a rumor that the members of the Fancher party were spies for a federal party that was coming west to round up the Mormons for deportation or mass murder. Others surmise that some of those in the party had boasted of helping to murder Joseph Smith. To this day, Lee's family denies that he was a party to the murders and claims that he was merely made a scapegoat.

After the massacre, Lee returned to his normal life, and for several years, no one questioned his role in it. A letter from Lee to Brigham Young placed the blame for the killings directly on the Paiutes, but even among the Mormons it was widely known that Lee was the leader of the guilty party. By the end of the 1860s, many were questioning Brigham Young's role in the cover-up of the Mountain Massacre. Young, to placate authorities looking into the matter, excommunicated Lee from the Mormon

Church. To avoid arrest, Lee removed himself and his extended family to a remote outpost on the Colorado River in New Mexico Territory that later became Lee's Ferry, Arizona. Young wrote to Lee, advising him to "make yourself scarce and keep out of the way."

Lee remained at Lee's Ferry (even at one point hosting explorer John Wesley Powell in Powell's successful journey down the Colorado River), but his health declined and his family broke apart. In November 1874, while Lee was visiting Panguitch, Utah, a local sheriff arrested him, and he was charged with multiple counts of murder. In his first trial, in 1875, a jury consisting of eight Mormons and four non-Mormons deadlocked; in a retrial in 1876, an all-Mormon jury found him guilty and Lee was sentenced to death. In the first trial, the prosecutors pointed to Brigham Young as the mastermind of the massacre; in the second, responsibility for the crime was placed squarely on Lee.

On 23 March 1877, John Doyle Lee was taken by his jailers to the spot where the massacre had occurred 20 years previously. In the wagon with Lee was the coffin in which his body would be placed. As he was forced to sit on his coffin before the firing squad, he said: "Center on my heart, boys. Don't mangle my body!" The deadly shots rang out, Lee tumbled over, and his lifeless body was then lifted into the casket. Lee's body was returned to Panguitch, Utah.

In 1961, Church of Latter Day Saints (LDS) president David O. McKay, acting on the request of Lee's granddaughter, Ettie Lee, and Lee biographer Juanita Brooks, reinstated John Doyle Lee to full membership in the Mormon Church.

**References:** Bishop, William W., ed., "Mormonism Revealed: Including the Remarkable Life and Confessions of the late Mormon bishop, John D. Lee (written by himself) and complete Life of Brigham Young, embracing a history of Mormonism from its inception down to the present time, with an exposition of the secret history, signs, symbols and crimes of the Mormon Church. Also the true history of the horrible butchery known as the Mountain Meadows Massacre" (St. Louis, MO: Excelsior, 1882); Brooks, Juanita, *John Doyle Lee: Zealot—Pioneer Builder—Scapegoat* (Glendale, CA: Arthur H. Clark, 1962); Cleland, Robert Glass, and Juanita Brooks, eds., *A Mormon Chronicle: The Diaries of John D. Lee, 1848–1876* (Salt Lake City: University of Utah Press, 1983); Gillespie, L. Kay, *The Unforgiven: Utah's Executed Men* (Salt Lake City, UT: Signature Books, 1991), 44–47; Lee, John Doyle, *The Life and Confession of John D. Lee, the Mormon. With a Full Account of the Mountain Meadows Massacre and Execution of Lee* (Philadelphia: Barclay, 1877).

## Leisler, Jacob (1640?–1691)

Confrontational German political figure put to death in the colony of New Amsterdam (now New York) for treason.

Born in Frankfurt, Germany, about 1640, Leisler was the son of a Calvinist pastor, Jacob Victorius Leyssler, and his wife Susanna. When he was about 20, Jacob Leisler came to the colony of New Amsterdam, where, after marrying a rich woman, he entered the fur and tobacco trade and became a prosperous merchant.

Leisler's problems arose when William III assumed the English throne in 1689. William, a Protestant like Leisler, had overthrown James II, a Catholic, and the change encouraged Leisler to refuse to pay the Catholic port-collector dues for merchandise he was importing. When the city council met and decided to keep imposing the customs duties, Leisler refused to pay and led a revolt against Governor Francis Nicholson. Seizing English documents and Nicholson's office, Leisler named himself lieutenant-governor of New Amsterdam. Meanwhile, the ousted governor, Nicholson, had arrived back in England and relayed news of Leisler's rebellion to the Crown. A new governor, Sir Henry Sloughter, was sent to replace Nicholson, while a military officer, Major Richard Ingoldesby, was sent ahead to arrest Leisler and his cohorts and end the insurrection.

When Ingoldesby arrived, he found that Leisler had established an assembly of politicians to oversee the colony and instituted a series of laws governing the same. The English officer's demand that Leisler surrender was met with refusals, and Leisler was tried for treason. At trial, ten men, including Leisler and his son-in-law, Jacob Milborne, were accused of treason. Leisler and Milborne refused to plead, arguing that the court, overseen by Thomas Newton (who had presided over the Salem witch trials), had no legal authority from King William. Eight of the ten were found guilty, but Sloughter asked the king to pardon all but Leisler and Milborne. The new governor did not wait for orders from London. On 16 May 1691, Leisler and his son-in-law were taken from their prison cells to a gallows and hanged. According to eyewitness reports, the two men sang the Seventy-ninth Psalm before they were executed.

In Boston, Increase Mather wrote that "these men were not only murdered, they were barbarously murdered." Leisler's biographer, Teddi DiCanio, offers a mixed review of Leisler's deeds: "Some of Leisler's actions were laudable, such as strengthening the province's defenses. Others are subject to interpretation. Leisler held a convention of delegates from the counties and towns. (Not everyone came.) Later, based on writs he issued, an assembly was elected. Some historians praise this as the first representative body for the province. Others believe Leisler manipulated both convention and assembly, often by threat of arms."

**References:** Andrews, Charles McLean, *Narratives of the Insurrections: 1675–1690* (New York: Charles Scribner, 1915); DiCanio, Teddi, "Jacob Leisler Trial: 1691" in Edward W. Knappman, ed., *Great American Trials* (Detroit: Visible Ink Press, 1994), 15–17; McCormick, Charles Howard, *Leisler's Rebellion* (New York: Garland, 1989), 123–125; Pargellis, Stanley M., "Leisler, Jacob" in Dumas Malone, et al., eds., *Dictionary of American Biography,* 10 vols., 10 suppl. (New York: Charles Scribner's Sons, 1930–1995), VI:156–157; Reich, Jerome R., *Leisler's Rebellion: A Study of Democracy in New York, 1664–1720* (Chicago: University of Chicago Press, 1953).

## Lethal Injection

Method of capital punishment first instituted in 1982 and used exclusively in the United States, in which a condemned prisoner is laid upon a hospital gurney or stretcher, given an intravenous (I.V.) solution of three lethal chemicals, and allowed to die.

Although use of this method began relatively recently, it has been considered for more than a hundred years. In 1886, as a commission in New York state convened by Governor David Hill debated how to replace the hangman's noose, lethal injection was considered but ultimately rejected in place of the electric chair, then a new-fangled mechanism. In 1953, the Royal Commission Inquiry on Capital Punishment, a British panel assembled by King George VI four years earlier, excluded lethal injection as a proper form of capital punishment to replace the noose.

After a prisoner is strapped down in a gurney, he is wheeled into the death chamber, in some cases the compartment where the electric chair or the gas chamber used to be situated. After the execution order is read, an intravenous needle is inserted into a vein, preferably in the arm, but if necessary—as often is the case with former drug users—in other veins. The tube connected to the needle is hooked up to a small machine containing three vials of solution. These chemicals are sodium pentothal (the trade name for thiopental), a barbiturate that renders the condemned unconscious; pancuronium chloride (brand name: Pavulon), which induces neuromuscular paralysis; and potassium chloride (chemical name: KCl), which, in the prescribed dose, stops the heart muscle. To ease the injection of the chemicals, a solution of sodium chloride, ordinary saline solution, is introduced. Death is usually instantaneous.

However, there have been botched lethal injections. On 23 January 1996, the state of Virginia set out to execute Richard Townes, Jr. According to persons who witnessed the execution, the executioner could not find a suitable vein in the arms or legs of Townes, a life-long drug abuser, delaying the execution for 22 minutes. Finally, claims the Reuters News Service (though the claim was not confirmed by the prison), a vein was found in the top of his right foot, and he was put to death.

Currently, 27 states utilize lethal injection; they include Arizona, California, Illinois, Louisiana, New Jersey, Ohio, Pennsylvania, Texas, Virginia, and Wyoming.

**References:** Richard J. Lewis, Sr., *Hawley's Condensed Chemical Dictionary* (New York: Van Nostrand Reinhold, 1993), 1145; Trombley, Stephen, *The Execution Protocol: Inside America's Capital Punishment Industry* (New York: Crown, 1992), 74–80. For information on the chemicals used in a lethal injection execution, consult Susan Budavari, ed., *The Merck Index: An Encyclopedia of Chemicals, Drugs, and Biologicals* (Whitehouse Station, NJ: Merck, 1996), 1313, 1474, 1595.

## Lincoln Conspirators, Execution of

For the first time in the history of the United States, citizens of the nation stood trial for conspiring to assassinate the President of the United States, Abraham Lincoln. Among them was the first woman ever to be put to death by the United States, Mrs. Mary Elizabeth Jenkins Surratt, a saloon owner; George Atzerodt, a German carriage maker; David Herrold or Herold; and Lewis Paine or Payne, the son of a minister and attempted assassin of Secretary of State William Seward.

Assassination as a tool to change the U.S. government was unknown in 1865, when a diverse group of southern sympathizers gathered together in Washington, DC, and Virginia to plot first the kidnapping, and then the murder, of President Abraham Lincoln, who had been elected in 1860. Even in the northern states that comprised the Union after southern states, trying to preserve the institution of slavery, broke away to form the Confederate States of America, Lincoln was not a particularly popular figure. He was regularly castigated in the northern press, Democrats in Congress berated his war policy, and he was opposed even by some in his own party (the so-called Radical Republicans, who demanded an even stricter line toward the seceding states).

In the South, at the end of the war, the conspirators had been plotting to kidnap Lincoln to force the North to end the war with the South remaining independent. Instead their plan turned to assassination. John Wilkes Booth, a young Shakespearean actor whose father (Junius Brutus Booth) and brother (Edwin Booth) were well-known stage performers at the time, headed the ring, which also included Atzerodt, Paine, and Herold. Mary Jenkins Surratt, a saloon owner from Maryland, was a supplier to the group. Surratt, born on a Maryland farm about 1823, ran a tavern with her husband John H. Surratt in the small village of Surrattsville (now Clinton), Maryland, and a boardinghouse in Washington, DC, where her son, John, a Confederate courier during the Civil War, hung around with fellow southern sympathizers Booth and Paine.

After Lincoln was shot on the night of 14 April 1865, Booth escaped from Washington with Herold at his side. Atzerodt fumbled his mission, the assassination of Vice President Andrew Johnson, but Paine did attack and badly wound his target, Secretary of State William H. Seward. Testimony later showed that Surratt had left carbines and whiskey for Booth and Herold at her tavern. During the investigation, her boardinghouse was raided and Paine was found there. Booth and Herold were followed to a barn in Virginia, where Booth was shot and killed. Herold was brought back to Washington to stand trial with Paine and Atzerodt, who had both been captured, and Surratt.

Secretary of War Edwin M. Stanton convened a military tribunal to hear the trial against the living conspirators, which started on 10 May 1865 and ended on 29 June. Atzerodt, Herold, Paine, and Mrs. Surratt were all found guilty of conspiring to murder the president and sentenced to death. Mary Surratt's daughter Anna tried to get an audience with President Andrew Johnson to ask him to spare her mother's life, but the request was turned down. On 7 July 1865, the four were taken from the cells at the Old Capitol Prison in Washington, DC, into the sweltering summer heat to the gallows, and hanged. Surratt, the oldest, was 42 years old.

Today, the names of all but Surratt and John Wilkes Booth have been forgotten. Surratt's home in Surrattsville was targeted for demolition but saved by a group called the Surratt Society. The home, as well as a museum dedicated to Surratt, is located in Clinton, Maryland.

**References:** Hanchett, William, "The Lincoln Murder Conspiracies: Being an Account of the Hatred Felt by Many Americans for President Abraham Lincoln during the Civil War and the First Complete Examination and Refutation of the Many Theories, Hypotheses, and Speculations Put Forward since 1865 Concerning Those Presumed to Have Aided, Abetted, Controlled, or Directed the Murderous Act of John Wilkes Booth in Ford's Theater the Night of April 14" (Urbana: University of Illinois Press, 1983); Stanchak, John E., "Surratt, Mary Elizabeth Jenkins" in Patricia L. Faust, ed., *Historical Times Illustrated Encyclopedia of the Civil War* (New York: Harper & Row, 1986), 735. Statements of those conspirators put to death can be found in the Investigation and Trial Papers Relating to the Assassination of President Lincoln, Microcopy 599, National Archives.

## Lisle, Alice Beckenshaw (1614?–1685)

English martyr executed for her role in hiding John Hicks, who had tried to topple the English crown.

Little is known of Lisle's life. Her biographer, Sir Sidney Lee, reports that she was born Alice Beckenshaw, daughter of Sir White Beckenshaw, in Moyles Court, Ellingham, near Ringwood, Hampshire. She was the widow of John Lisle, who had sat in judgment of King Charles I in 1649, a trial that resulted in the execution of the king and, ultimately, in Lisle's own execution as a "regicide." During Monmouth's rebellion, she was contacted by the dissident minister John Hicks (also spelled Hickes), who, having fought with Monmouth at the battle of Sedgemoor (6 July 1685), asked for shelter from the English authorities. Without question, Lisle took him and several accompanying guests in. A spy living nearby saw the mysterious figures and reported the action to the authorities. Lisle and the guests were arrested.

When she was interrogated—by a man whose father had been sentenced to death by John Lisle—Alice Lisle denied knowing Hicks's crime. She was quickly placed on trial before Lord

Chief Justice George Jeffreys on a charge of harboring a traitor. Although no evidence was presented that Lisle knew of Hicks's activities (she thought he was merely hiding because he was a dissenter) or that she cooperated in any way with the rebels, she was browbeaten by Jeffreys, who declared before the trial that he would make an example of her no matter what the evidence. (It is also rumored that he obtained from the king a promise that she would be shown no mercy.) The jury was charged; it returned with an acquittal because Hicks had not been convicted of being a traitor. Angered, Jeffreys told them to reconsider their verdict. When they returned three more times with an acquittal, Jeffreys threatened all of them with a charge of treason if they failed to convict. With this, they returned with a verdict of guilty. Jeffreys ordered that Lisle be burned at the stake; when Lisle asked mercy of the king, he changed her sentence to beheading.

On 2 September 1685, Lisle was taken to the marketplace at Winchester and beheaded. Before she mounted the scaffold, she presented a petition to the sheriff in charge claiming innocence. Four years after her death, on the application of her two daughters, the English Parliament reversed her conviction and sentence because under English law she could not be convicted of harboring someone who had yet to be charged with a crime. The Parliament edict also condemned Jeffreys, claiming that "the verdict was injuriously exhorted and procured by the menaces and violences and other illegal practices" of the Lord Chief Justice.

**References:** Lee, Sidney, "Lisle, Alice" in Sir Leslie Stephens and Sir Sidney Lee, eds., *The Dictionary of National Biography,* 10 vols., 12 suppl. (Oxford, England: Oxford University Press, 1917–1993), 11:1218–219; Raby, R. Cornelius, *Fifty Famous Trials* (Washington, DC: Washington Law Book Company, 1937), 47–54.

## Literature, Capital Punishment Reflected in

Much of the writings dealing with the subject of the death penalty have been broken down into four categories: criminality studies and law books explaining the laws dealing with the subject of capital punishment; pamphlets written hundreds of years ago; first-hand accounts of "true-crime" events; and fictionalized works.

The leading authority on capital punishment in the last half of the twentieth century is Professor Hugo Adam Bedau of Tufts University in Massachusetts. Professor Bedau, a visible and vehement opponent of capital punishment, has contributed greatly to the study of the death penalty in the United States. His numerous works include *The Death Penalty in America: An Anthology* (1964), *The Case against the Death Penalty* (1973), *Capital Punishment in the United States* (1976), and *The Courts, the Constitution, and Capital Punishment* (1980). Another American writer who has written about capital punishment and the law is Thorsten Sellin. He has argued, through such works as *The Death Penalty* (1959) and *Capital Punishment* (1967), that homicide rates are lower in states that do not have capital punishment than in those that use it. A leading British writer on the laws of England and the death penalty is Dr. Leon Radzinowicz, a member of the British Royal Commission Inquiry on Capital Punishment. His major work, *A History of English Criminal Law and Its Administration from 1750,* should be considered the preeminent treatise on the hangman and headsman in England.

Hundreds of years ago, when executions were daily events (particularly in

England), colorful and illustrative pamphlets were issued commemorating the event, discussing the crime of the accused, and reporting the condemned person's last words on the scaffold. These pamphlets had such lengthy titles as "The Arraignment and Conviction of Mervin Lord Avdley, Earle of Castlehaven, who by 26 peers of the realm found guilty for committing rapine and sodomy at Westminister on Monday, April 25, 1631: by virtue of a commission of oyer and terminer directed to Sir Thomas Coventry, Lord Keeper of the great seale of England, Lord High Steward for that day accompanied with the judges: as also the beheading of the said Earle shortly after on Tower Hill." Many of these tracts were anonymously printed, or written by eyewitnesses to public executions, thus adding to the spectacle of the event. Several are reprinted in this work as separate entries.

In the early part of the twentieth century, such works as *An American Tragedy* fictionalized famous American criminal cases resulting in the death penalty. In the last 40 years, however, "true crime" books have become all the rage. Beginning most notably with Truman Capote's engrossing true story of the murder of the Clutter family in Kansas, *In Cold Blood,* which became both a literary and film classic, the demand for such works seemed to be insatiable. After Capote, however, there was a wave of reform in the nation; the genre was resurrected in 1989 with Ann Rule's classic thriller, *The Stranger Beside Me,* about her experiences with serial murderer Ted Bundy. William B. Huie's 1971 investigative essay "The Execution of Private Slovik" opened for further scrutiny the case of a World War II soldier executed for desertion. Sister Helen Prejean's recent autobiographical work on her life among the condemned of Louisiana's death row, *Dead Man Walking,* became a major motion picture in 1995.

A fourth, and neglected, category of death penalty writings is fiction, little explored by scholars. Perhaps the most powerful work of this genre is Shirley Jackson's masterpiece, *The Lottery,* a tale of a small town's execution by stoning to death one of its citizens, chosen by lottery. After *The Lottery* appeared in *The New Yorker,* the magazine received more letters on that piece than it had ever received.

**See also:** *An American Tragedy;* "The Manner of the Death and Execution of Arnold Cosbie, for Murthering the Lord Boorke"; Motion Pictures, Capital Punishment as Depicted in.

**References:** Bedau, Hugo Adam, *The Case against the Death Penalty* (New York: American Civil Liberties Union, 1973); ———, *The Courts, the Constitution, and Capital Punishment* (Lexington, MA: D.C. Heath, 1977); ———, ed., *The Death Penalty in America: An Anthology* (New York: Oxford University Press, 1982); Jackson, Shirley, *The Lottery and Other Stories* (New York: Noonday Press, 1989); Larson, Richard W., *Bundy: the Deliberate Stranger* (New York: Pocket Books, 1986); Sellin, Thorsten, *Capital Punishment* (New York: Harper & Row, 1967); ———, *The Penalty of Death* (Beverly Hills, CA: Sage, 1980); ———, ed., *The Death Penalty* (Philadelphia: American Law Institute, 1959).

## Livingston, Edward (1764–1836)

American politician whom historian Philip Mackey calls "the most influential and renowned opponent of the gallows in American history."

The son of Robert R. Livingston, a jurist and Revolutionary War patriot, and Margaret (nee Beekman) Livingston, Edward Livingston was born at his father's estate, Clermont, in Columbia County, New York, on 28 May 1764. Edward attended local schools in Albany, then graduated from the College of New Jersey (now Princeton University) in 1781. He studied the law in Albany under John Lansing and had as his fellow students Alexander Hamilton and Aaron Burr. He was admitted to the state bar in 1785, and practiced law for the next nine years. In that time he married and had three children; his wife, Mary McEvers, died of scarlet fever in 1801. In 1794, Livingston was elected to the U.S. House of Representatives and served for three terms before leaving in 1801. His main focus was penal reform, but his only success seems to have been his support of a bill to provide relief for sailors impressed (kidnapped) by foreign navies.

In 1800 Livingston refused to run for a fourth term, and after he left office was appointed U.S. Attorney for the District of New York and, at the same time, was appointed mayor of the city. A bout of yellow fever caused him to give up both offices that same year, but after he recovered he moved to New Orleans and began the practice of law there. When the War of 1812 broke out, he joined the military and served as an aide-de-camp, military secretary, and interpreter for General Andrew Jackson. After the battle, he was put in charge of negotiating with the British for the exchange of prisoners of war. In debt, he spent the next several years attempting to rebuild his fortune. In 1820 he was elected to the Louisiana legislature, and, because of his interest in the reform of the penal laws (which by this time had also become a desire to end capital punishment), he was assigned to report to the legislature on a means to do just that, which had been ordered by Governor Thomas B. Robertson.

In his report to the Louisiana legislature, delivered to them on 13 March 1822, Livingston wrote:

> A great part of my task is rendered unnecessary, by the general acknowledgment, universal, I may say, in the United States, that this punishment ought to be abolished in all cases, excepting those of treason, murder and rape. . . . Let us have constantly before us, when we reason on the subject, the great principle, that the end of punishment is the prevention of crime. Death, indeed, operates this end most effectually, as respects the delinquent; but the great object of inflicting it is the force of the example on others. . . . If it were proved, that the fruit in a garden could not be preserved without punishing the boys who stole it with death, the evil to be apprehended from the offence is so much less than that produced by the punishment, that it ought never to be inflicted by the law, much less . . . by the party injured; but on the contrary, it is a less evil to destroy the life of an assassin, than to permit him to take of a man, whose existence is useful to his country, and necessary to his family. The burthen of argument rests here on those who advocate this punishment; they must show that it is the only means of repressing the offence; they must show, that in the cases to which they mean to apply it, the evil of the offence is greater than the punishment. . . . I [have come] to the conclusion, that the punishment of death should find no place in the code which you have directed me to present.

For this work, Sir Henry Maine called Livingston "the first legal genius of modern times." He was named secretary of state by President Andrew Jackson on 24 May 1831, resigning two years later, on 29 May 1833, to become the American minister plenipotentiary to France. He retired to his home, Montgomery Place, bequeathed to him by his sister. He died at Rhinebeck, New York, on 23 May 1836, and was buried in the family crypt at Clermont, although his remains were eventually removed and placed next to those of his second wife at Rhinebeck.

**References:** Carpenter, William S., "Livingston, Edward" in Dumas Malone, et al., eds., *Dictionary of American Biography,* 10 vols., 10 suppl. (New York: Charles

Scribner's Sons, 1930–1995), VI:309–312; Franklin, Mitchell, "Concerning the Historic Importance of Edward Livingston," *Tulane Law Review* 11:2 (February 1937), 163–212; Harris, Rufus C., "The Edward Livingston Centennial," *Tulane Law Review* 11:1 (December 1936), 1–3; "Livingston, Edward" in Robert Sobel, ed., *Biographical Directory of the United States Executive Branch, 1774–1989* (Westport, CT: Greenwood Press, 1990), 234–235; Livingston, Edward, "Report on the Plan of a Penal Code" in *The Complete Works of Edward Livingston on Criminal Jurisprudence*, 2 vols. (New York: National Prison Association, 1873), 1:35–59; Mackey, Philip English, "Edward Livingston and the Origins of the Movement to Abolish Capital Punishment in America," *Louisiana History* 16:2 (Spring 1975), 145–166; ———, ed., *Voices against Death: American Opposition to Capital Punishment, 1787–1975* (New York: Burt Franklin, 1976),14–33.

## *Lockett v. Ohio* (438 U.S. 586, 98 S.Ct. 2954, 57 L.Ed. 2d 973 [1978])

U.S. Supreme Court case in which it was held that a state death penalty statute that did not allow for the consideration of a "wide range" of mitigating factors as to capital punishment's infliction was constitutionally invalid.

Sandra Lockett was charged with aggravated murder after she participated in the robbery and murder of a pawn shop owner. She was the driver, the person who waited in the car with the engine running while her accomplices committed the robbery and murder. Although she was convicted of aggravated murder, it was felt that because of her limited role, she deserved less than a sentence of death. The Ohio statute declared that upon such conviction, the trial judge must consider "the nature and character of the offense" as well as the defendant's "history, character, and condition." The judge ordered a psychiatric report, which claimed that while Lockett had had a history of minor juvenile offenses, she had not been involved in any major crimes, was free of psychosis, but had used heroin at one time. The judge, saying that he had "no alternative, whether [he] like[d] the law or not," sentenced Lockett to death. The Court of Appeals of Summit County, Ohio, affirmed, as did the Supreme Court of Ohio. The United States Supreme Court heard arguments on 17 January 1978.

On 3 July of that same year, Chief Justice Warren Burger spoke for a divided Court that agreed and disagreed on various points but declared in a majority opinion that Lockett's death sentence was invalid on constitutional grounds. Chief Justice Burger wrote: "The limited range of mitigating circumstances which may be considered by the sentencer under the Ohio statute is incompatible with the Eighth and Fourteenth Amendments. To meet constitutional requirements, a death penalty statute must not preclude consideration of relevant mitigating factors." Justices Harry Blackmun and Thurgood Marshall concurred; Blackmun argued that the Ohio statute was invalid because it "authoriz[ed] the death sentence for a defendant who only aided and abetted a murder, without permitting any consideration by the sentencing authority of the extent of the defendant's involvement." Marshall declared that "the death penalty was, under all circumstances, a cruel and unusual punishment prohibited by the Eight Amendment." Justice Byron White concurred in part and dissented in part, claiming that

> although it did not violate the Eighth Amendment for a state to impose the death penalty on a mandatory basis when the defendant was found guilty of committing a deliberate, unjustified killing, nevertheless, the death penalty should not, consistent with the Eighth Amendment, be inflicted without a finding that the defendant had engaged in conduct with the conscious purpose of producing death, the infliction of death upon those

> who had no intent to bring about the death of the victim not only being grossly out of proportion to the severity of the crime, but also failing to significantly contribute to any perceptible goals of punishment.

Justice William H. Rehnquist concurred in part and dissented in part; he wrote that the statute was not invalid because it allowed the trial judge to "dismiss the specifications of aggravating circumstances, thus precluding the imposition of the death penalty only when a defendant pleaded guilty or no contest." Justice William Brennan did not participate.

A companion case, *Bell v. Ohio,* was decided the same day.

**See also:** *Bell v. Ohio.*

## *Lockhart v. McCree* (476 U.S. 162, 90 L.Ed. 2d 137, 106 S.Ct. 1758 [1986])

U.S. Supreme Court decision holding that the removal of potential jurors during the *voir dire* phase of juror selection who had a moral objection to capital punishment was not an unconstitutional violation of a defendant's rights to a fair trial under the Sixth Amendment to the U.S. Constitution.

Andria McCree was charged in an Arkansas court with the robbery and murder of a store owner. During the voir dire process (in which prospective jurors are questioned), the judge, over defense counsel's objections, removed several jurors because they expressed moral opposition to capital punishment. McCree was then convicted and sentenced to death. McCree's first appeals were denied; he then turned to appealing his sentence on the grounds that so-called "Witherspoon excludables" were exempted from the jury. (In 1968, in *Witherspoon v. Illinois,* the U.S. Supreme Court held that persons could not be removed from juries even if they had a moral opposition to capital punishment and that such removals were a violation of a defendant's right to a fair trial under the Sixth Amendment to the U.S. Constitution.) The U.S. District Court for the Eastern District of Arkansas held that McCree's sentence violated the *Witherspoon* doctrine, and the U.S. Court of Appeals for the Eighth Circuit affirmed this decision. A. L. Lockhart, the director of the Arkansas State Department of Correction, which had custody of McCree, then appealed to the U.S. Supreme Court for relief, and the Court heard arguments on 13 January 1986.

On 5 May 1986, in a 6–3 decision (Justices Thurgood Marshall, William Brennan, and John Paul Stevens dissenting), the Court overturned the *Witherspoon* doctrine and held that the exclusion from juries of persons with a moral opposition to capital punishment was not an unconstitutional violation of the Sixth Amendment guarantee to a fair trial. Speaking for the majority, Justice William H. Rehnquist wrote:

> In our view, it is simply not possible to define jury impartiality, for constitutional purposes, by reference to some hypothetical mix of individual viewpoints. Prospective jurors come from many different backgrounds, and have many different attitudes and predispositions. But the Constitution presupposes that a jury selected from a fair cross section of the community is impartial, regardless of the mix of individual viewpoints actually represented on the jury, so long as the jurors can conscientiously and properly carry out their sworn duty to apply the law to the facts of the particular case. We hold that McCree's jury satisfied both aspects of this constitutional standard. The judgment of the Court of Appeals is therefore reversed.

**See also:** *Witherspoon v. Illinois.*

## "Lord Haw Haw"

See Joyce, William

## Louis-August (Capet) XVI, King of France (1754–1793)

French monarch, only the second sovereign of a nation (Charles I of England was the first) to be put to death by his people, guillotined by French revolutionaries.

The third son of Louis and his wife Marie Josepha, the daughter of Frederic Augustus, king of Poland and elector of Saxony, Louis himself was born at the grand palace of Versailles on 23 August 1754. He was the great great-grandson of the Sun King, Louis XIV, and until he took the throne from his grandfather, Louis XV, in 1774, he was known as the Duke of Berri. He grew up in the indulgent world of French royalty and when only 16 married Marie Antoinette, the archduchess of Austria, daughter of Holy Roman Emperor Francis I and his wife, Maria Theresa, as well as the sister of Emperor Joseph of that nation. Four years later Louis succeeded to the French throne.

Louis XVI began his reign with several steps that seemed to ensure his viability: he named the popular Anne Robert Jacques Turgot, Baron de L'Aulne (1727–1781), as the minister of finance, and convened Parliament to do the nation's business. However, his decision to side with the American colonists against England forced France to fight in other areas and slowly drove the country into bankruptcy. Furthermore, Queen Marie Antoinette lived in an opulent manner, flaunting her jewels, which by 1785 led to increased public dissatisfaction. An attempt to raise higher taxes from the nobles failed, and Louis was forced to disband a meeting of the Estates-General.

The situation among France's peasant population became crushing. The economy declined, and Louis was forced to recall the Estates-General, which finally met at Versailles on 5 May 1789. Even as they were meeting, the king angered the group by firing his minister of finance, the popular Jacques Necker, and then deciding to call out the army to subdue the hostile conference. The people in the streets rose up and confronted government troops, first at the Hôtel de Ville in Paris on 12 July; two days later, the crowd stormed and took the Bastille, a prison in Paris. Across the French countryside an attitude known as the Great Panic spread; on 4 August, the French Assembly banned the privileges of the upper classes. The people rioted, and at Versailles the king was taken prisoner and brought to Paris in chains on 6 October 1789.

Louis began secretly to plot to have European troops enter France, defeat the insurrectionists, and reestablish him as monarch. In furtherance of this plan, he was aided in his escape from Paris on 20 June 1791. While Louis was eating dinner in an inn at Sainte-Menenhould during his flight, a waiter, Jean Baptiste Drouet, compared the king's face to a coin with Louis's likeness, saw that they were one and the same, and reported that the fleeing king was at the inn. Louis was apprehended by the revolutionaries, returned to Paris, and Louis and the royal family were imprisoned in an ancient fortress known as the Temple.

After Louis's capture, Leopold II of Germany and William (Wilhelm) II of Prussia met and signed the Declaration of Pillnitz, in which they pledged to use their troops to invade France and restore Louis to the throne. On 20 April 1792, war was declared against the insurgent French government. Angered by Louis's treasonous correspondence with these leaders, as well as the lightning-quick victories of the European allies against hapless French forces, the National Convention, made up of antimonarchial radicals, demanded that Louis relinquish the throne. The French victory against the Germans at Valmy, 20 September 1792, sealed Louis's fate. On 21 September the convention proclaimed the French Republic and then demanded on 3 December the appearance of the king to hear charges of treason. On 20 January 1793, Louis was found guilty on four separate votes and sentenced to death, with the judgment to be carried out within 24 hours. The final vote for death was 361 to 360, while a vote for a reprieve strangely was 380 to 310.

Marie Antoinette faced the guillotine herself less than a year after her husband, on 16 October 1793. His son, Louis-Charles Capet (1785–1795), unofficially became King Louis XVII on his father's death but was never crowned. He died in a dungeon at the age of ten. Over the next thirty years, several people stepped forward to claim they were Louis, but none of the claims was proven.

**See also:** Malesherbes, Chrétien Guillaume de Lamoignon de.

**References:** Carol, R. L., "Louis XVI" in Samuel F. Scott and Barry Rothaus, eds., *Historical Dictionary of the French Revolution, 1789–1799,* 2 vols. (Westport, CT: Greenwood Press, 1985), 2:599–602; Donaldson, Norman, and Betty Donaldson, *How Did They Die?* (New York: St. Martin's Press, 1980), 237–238; Laurence, John, *A History of Capital Punishment* (New York: Citadel Press, 1960), 81; "Massacre of the French King. View of la Guillotine; or, the Modern Beheading Machine, at Paris, by which the unfortunate Louis XVI. (late King of France) suffered on the scaffold, January 21st, 1793" (London: Printed at the Minerva Office, for William Lane, 1793).

## Loving v. United States (116 S.Ct. 1737 [1996])

U.S. Supreme Court decision holding that Congress has the power to delegate to the President the right to set the guidelines for capital punishment as prescribed in the Uniform Code of Military Justice (UCMJ).

Dwight J. Loving, an army private, was found guilty under Article 118 of the UCMJ (also located at 10 U.S.C. 918[1], [4]) of premeditated murder and felony murder for his role in the slaying of two taxicab drivers in Killeen, Texas, near where he was stationed. Loving was then sentenced to death. He appealed on the grounds that his crime did not call for a death sentence. In 1983, the Supreme Court found in *United States v. Matthews* that the UCMJ did not specify the death penalty for certain aggravating factors. Congress, in an attempt to remedy this flaw, passed a law giving the president exclusive authority to change the code. President Ronald Reagan, with an executive order, changed the Rules for Court Martial (RCM) to stipulate that a unanimous finding would allow for a death sentence with (a) a list of prescribed aggravating circumstances, and (b) the allowance of mitigating circumstances, if any exist, and that (c) the court martial would weigh these factors to determine sentence. Loving's appeal was based solely on this question: Did Congress have the right to delegate such wide authority to the president? The U.S. Army Court of Military Review denied Loving's appeal, as did the U.S. Court of Appeals for the Armed Forces. The U.S. Supreme Court agreed to hear the case, and arguments were heard on 9 January 1996.

On 3 June of that same year, the Court held 9–0 that Congress had the power to delegate authority to the president to write and maintain rules of order in the military. Justice Anthony Kennedy wrote:

> It is hard to deem lawless a delegation giving the President broad discretion to prescribe rules. From the early days of the Republic, the President has had congressional authorization to intervene in

> cases where courts-martial decreed death. . . . It would be contradictory to say that Congress cannot further empower him to limit by prospective regulation the circumstances in which courts-martial can impose a death sentence. Specific authority to make rules for the limitation of capital punishment contributes more towards principled and uniform military sentencing regimes that does case-by-case intervention, and provides greater opportunity for congressional oversight and revision. . . . Separation-of-powers principles are vindicated, not disserved, by measured cooperation between the two branches of the Government, each contributing to a lawful objective through its own processes. . . . Loving's sentence was lawful, and the judgment of the Court of Appeals for the Armed Forces is affirmed.

Dwight Loving, as of this writing, is one of only 10 men who sit on death row under federal, and not state, jurisdiction.

### *Lowenfield v. Phelps* (484 U.S. 232, 98 L.Ed. 2d 568, 108 S.Ct. 546 [1988])

U.S. Supreme Court decision in which it was held that a "polling" of the jury, and the sending of the jury back for further deliberations in the penalty phase of a trial, did not constitute reversible error, and that a death sentence may stand.

Leslie Lowenfield was convicted of five murders. During the sentencing phase, the jurors sent the judge several notes saying that they were unable to reach a unanimous recommendation. Twice, the judge asked them if further deliberations might help, and they answered in the affirmative. After the second poll, which showed that the jury was still deadlocked, the judge told them that if they did not unanimously agree to the death sentence he would be forced to sentence Lowenfield to life in prison. Defense attorneys did not object to the polls or the instruction from the judge. Thirty minutes after this last exchange, the jury returned with a recommendation of death, and the judge sentenced Lowenfield accordingly. The Louisiana Supreme Court upheld the sentence, as did the U.S. District Court for the Eastern District of Louisiana and the U.S. Circuit Court of Appeals for the Fifth Circuit. The U.S. Supreme Court heard arguments in the case on 14 October 1987.

Chief Justice William H. Rehnquist spoke for the Court (Justices Thurgood Marshall, William Brennan, and John Paul Stevens dissented) on 13 January 1988 in upholding Lowenfield's death sentence:

> Our review of petitioner's contention that the jury was improperly coerced requires that we consider the supplemental charge given by the trial court in its context and under all the circumstances. . . . Surely if the jury had returned from its deliberations after only one hour and informed the court that it had failed to achieve unanimity on the first ballot, the court would incontestably have had the authority to insist that they deliberate further. This is true even in capital cases such as this one . . ., even though we are naturally mindful in such cases that the "qualitative difference between death and other penalties calls for a greater degree of reliability when the death sentence is imposed."

In his strong dissent, Justice Marshall explained, "Adhering to my view that the death penalty is in all circumstances cruel and unusual punishment prohibited by the Eighth and Fourteenth Amendments, I would vacate the decision below insofar as it left undisturbed the death sentence imposed in this case."

On 13 April 1988, Leslie Lowenfield was put to death by a lethal injection in Louisiana's execution chamber in the state prison at Angola.

## Lynching

Form of justice usually utilized by mobs out to avenge a lack of equity in the courts.

The origin of the practice of lynching is unknown. Some attribute it to the form of justice in England in the Middle Ages known as the Lydford Law, some to the so-called "Jeddart Justice" in Scotland, and some even to James Lynch Fitz-Stephen of Galway, Ireland, who helped hang his own son for murder. The term *lynching* comes from Charles Lynch (1736–1796), an American soldier and judge, who during the American Revolution persecuted Tories in the colonies by stringing them up by their thumbs until they cried "Liberty forever!" Even though the "court," composed of Lynch, Thomas Calloway, and Robert Adams, never imposed the death penalty on any of the persons brought before it, the name stuck to the term "lynch law," and when illegal hangings began they simply took on the name lynchings.

Punishing criminals outside the court system, originally called "regulating," was well known before Lynch's time, however. In the western United States, so-called regulators punished persons before the courts were established, but they did not put anyone to death.

The first true cases of persons being put to death may have come in California in the Gold Rush of the 1850s, when many persons accused of illegal behavior went before a lynch court (with a person in charge named "Judge Lynch"), were sentenced to death, and were executed soon after by a mob. After the Civil War, the Ku Klux Klan used lynchings, as well as mob terror, to threaten and intimidate free blacks and former slaves in the South. This practice soon spread to the northern states as well, and between 1882 and 1950, 4,729 persons were lynched in the United States; of these 3,436 were black. In this period, one of the most notable victims was Jewish factory owner Leo Frank, convicted of murdering a young girl in Atlanta; after the governor commuted Frank's death sentence, a mob calling itself the "Knights of Mary Phagan" (named after the victim) abducted Frank from jail and lynched him. He remains perhaps the most famous white victim of lynch justice. As governor of Virginia, Charles Triplett O'Ferrall (1840–1905) made a persistent and determined attempt to wipe out lynching in his state, but failed.

Lynching as a device of white mobs died out in the 1950s; there is no record when the last lynching occurred. According to capital punishment historian William J. Bowers, there were about 3,498 lynchings in the United States from the 1890s until 1956. His numbers are broken down in the following table.

**Lynchings from 1890s through 1960s**

| *Decades* | *Lynchings* | *Legal Executions* |
|---|---|---|
| 1890s | 1,540 | 1,215 |
| 1900s | 885 | 1,192 |
| 1910s | 621 | 1,039 |
| 1920s | 315 | 1,169 |
| 1930s | 130 | 1,670 |
| 1940s | 5 | 1,288 |
| 1950s | 2 | 716 |
| 1960s[1] | — | 191 |

1. Executions up to 1967, when a national moratorium went into effect.

**References:** Barber, Henry Eugene, *The Association of Southern Women for the Prevention of Lynching, 1930–1942* (Master's thesis, University of Georgia, 1967); Hall, Jacquelyn Dowd, *Revolt against Chivalry: Jessie Daniel Ames and the Women's Campaign Against Lynching* (New York: Columbia University Press, 1979); Higgins, Ray E., Jr., *Strange Fruit: Lynching in South Carolina, 1900–1914* (Master's thesis, University of South Carolina, 1961); Mounger, Dwyn M., *Lynching in Mississippi, 1830–1930* (Master's thesis, Mississippi State University, 1961); O'Malley, Stephen, *The Salisbury Lynching, 1906* (Master's thesis,

University of North Carolina, 1977); Zangrando, Robert L., *The NAACP Crusade against Lynching, 1909–1950* (Philadelphia: Temple University Press, 1980). Graph from Bowers, William J., with Glenn L. Pierce and John F. McDevitt, "*Legal Homicide: Death as Punishment in America, 1864–1982*" (Boston: Northeastern University Press, 1984), 54. See also *Historical Statistics of the United States from Colonial Times to 1957* (Washington, D.C.: Government Printing Office, 1960), 218.

**McCleskey v. Kemp (481 U.S. 279, 95 L.Ed. 2d 262, 107 S.Ct. 1756 [1987])**

Landmark U.S. Supreme Court decision, in which the court held that "statistics indicating that race bias affects Georgia's capital sentencing [is] held [to be] insufficient to prove that imposition of [the] death penalty on [a] black man for murdering [a] white man violated the Eighth or Fourteenth Amendment."

Warren McCleskey, a black man, was convicted and sentenced to death in the Superior Court of Fulton County, Georgia, in 1978 for the murder of a white police officer during a robbery. McCleskey appealed the conviction and sentence, but they were upheld by the Supreme Court of Georgia (*McCleskey v. State*), and, in 1980, the U.S. Supreme Court declined to hear the case. McCleskey sued in the Fulton County Court to have a new trial, but that too was denied. He then filed a motion in the Superior Court of Butts County, Georgia, for a new trial, which was also denied (*McCleskey v. Zant, 1981*). The Supreme Court of Georgia upheld this decision, and once again the U.S. Supreme Court declined to hear the case.

After this last defeat, McCleskey filed a petition claiming that Georgia's sentencing process is administered in a racially biased way in violation of the Eighth and Fourteenth amendments to the Constitution. To support his claim, McCleskey submitted a study done by professors David C. Baldus, Charles Pulanski, and George Woodworth (a report known as the Baldus Study), which claimed that black defendants who killed whites received the death sentence more often than whites who murdered blacks. The District Court for the Northern District of Georgia, hearing McCleskey's appeal, examined the Baldus Study and, while finding that it was an important document, held that the "statistics do not demonstrate a prima facie case in support of the contention

that the death penalty [in McCleskey's case] was imposed upon him because of his race, because of the race of the victim, or because of any Eighth Amendment concern" (*McCleskey v. Zant, 1984*). The Court of Appeals for the Eleventh Circuit upheld the district court's denial of McCleskey's writ of habeas corpus, and, on appeal, the U.S. Supreme Court agreed to consider the case. Arguments on this single matter, in which McCleskey sued Ralph Kemp, the superintendent of the Georgia Diagnostic and Classification Center where he was being imprisoned, were heard on 15 October 1986.

On 22 April 1987, Justice Lewis Powell spoke for a 5–4 Court (Justices William Brennan, Thurgood Marshall, Harry Blackmun, and John Paul Stevens dissented) in finding that although the statistics showed a pattern of racial bias, there was no proof that McCleskey's jury sentenced him to death because of his race or the race of his victim, and thus upheld both the conviction and sentence. Justice Powell wrote:

> Apparent disparities in sentencing are an inevitable part of our criminal justice system. . . . Two additional concerns inform our decision in this case. First, McCleskey's claim, taken to its logical conclusion, throws into serious question the principles that underlie our entire criminal justice system. The Eighth Amendment is not limited in application to capi-

tal punishment, but applies to all penalties. . . . Thus, if we accepted McCleskey's claim that racial bias has impermissibly tainted the capital sentencing decision, we could soon be faced with similar claims as to other types of penalty. Moreover, the claim that his sentence rests on the irrelevant factor of race easily could be extended to apply to claims based on unexplained discrepancies that correlate to membership in other minority groups, and even to gender. Similarly, since McCleskey's claim relates to the race of his victim, other claims could apply with equally logical force to statistical disparities that correlate with the race or sex of other actors in the criminal justice system, such as defense attorneys or judges. Also, there is no logical reason that such a claim need be limited to racial or sexual bias. If arbitrary and capricious punishment is the touchstone under the Eighth Amendment, such a claim could—at least in theory—be based upon any arbitrary variable, such as the defendant's facial characteristics, or the physical attractiveness of the defendant or the victim, that some statistical study indicates may be influential, in jury decisionmaking. As these examples illustrate, there is no limiting principle to the type of challenge brought by McCleskey. The Constitution does not require that a State eliminate any demonstrable disparity that correlates with a potentially irrelevant factor in order to operate a criminal justice system that includes capital punishment. As we have stated specifically in the context of capital punishment, the Constitution does not "plac[e] totally unrealistic conditions on its use." . . . Second, McCleskey's arguments are best presented to the legislative bodies. It is not the responsibility—or indeed even the right—of this Court to determine the appropriate punishment for particular crimes. . . . Despite McCleskey's wide-ranging arguments that basically challenge the validity of capital punishment in our multiracial society, the only question before us is whether in his case, the law of Georgia was properly applied. We agree with the District Court and the Court of Appeals for the Eleventh Circuit that this was carefully and correctly done in this case."

On 25 September 1991 Warren McCleskey was executed in Georgia's electric chair.

**See also:** Blackmun, Harry Andrew; Race, Issue of in Capital Punishment.

## *McGautha v. California* (402 U.S. 183 [1971])

Dual U.S. Supreme Court decisions, which was combined with *Crampton v. Ohio,* in which the court held that a defendant could be sentenced to death by a jury that had sole penalty discretion and that a defendant could be sentenced to death following a guilt and sentencing proceeding.

In the first case, *McGautha,* Dennis Councle McGautha was convicted of two armed robberies and a murder in 1967 and sentenced to death. California law at the time specified that following the guilt phase of the trial, a separate sentencing stage would take place. In this second phase, the state presented evidence of the defendant's prior criminal record, then allowed one of his accomplices in the robbery and murder to testify that McGautha was the individual responsible for the spree. Although the defendant testified that he was not to blame for the murder, the jury nonetheless held him responsible and recommended that he be sentenced to death. After a probation report was prepared, the judge agreed with the jury's recommendation and sentenced him to die. McGautha ultimately appealed his case on the grounds that the jury had not been issued standards as to what sentence they could recommend. The California Supreme Court upheld both the sentence and conviction, and McGautha appealed to the U.S. Supreme Court.

In the companion case, *Crampton v. Ohio*, James Edward Crampton was convicted of the murder of his wife. The jury convicted him after over four hours of deliberations, and at the same time recommended that he be sentenced to death. The judge followed this recommendation. Crampton appealed his case to the Ohio Supreme Court, which found the sentencing scheme to be constitutional. The United States Supreme Court, combining the cases, heard arguments in both matters on 9 November 1970.

On 3 May 1971, Justice Hugo L. Black held that both schemes were constitutional. Opposed by dissenting justices William Brennan and Thurgood Marshall, Black explained in a lengthy opinion why both sentencing plans met constitutional muster.

> We consider McGautha's and Crampton's common claim: that the absence of standards to guide the jury's discretion on the punishment issue is constitutionally intolerable. To fit their arguments within a constitutional frame of reference petitioners contend that to leave the jury completely at large to impose or withhold the death penalty as it sees fit is fundamentally lawless and therefore violates the Fourteenth Amendment that no State shall deprive a person of his life without due process of law. Despite the undeniable surface appeal of the proposition, we conclude that the courts below correctly rejected it. . . . Certainly the facts of these gruesome murders bespeak no miscarriage of justice. The ability of juries, unassisted by standards to distinguish between those defendants for whom the death penalty is appropriate punishment and those for whom imprisonment is sufficient is indeed illustrated by the discriminating verdict of the jury in McGautha's case. . . . The procedures which petitioners challenge are those by which most capital trials in this country are conducted, and by which all were conducted until a few years ago. We have determined that these procedures are consistent with the rights to which petitioners were constitutionally entitled, and that their trials were entirely fair. Having reached these conclusions we have performed our task of measuring the States' process by federal constitutional standards, and according the judgment in each of these cases is affirmed.

## Malesherbes, Chrétien Guillaume de Lamoignon de (1721–1784)

French statesman, a leading figure of the pre-Revolutionary era of reform in France, executed for his role as legal counsel to King Louis XVI during his trial.

Malesherbes, born in Paris on 6 December 1721, was educated in that city and soon thereafter studied the law and became a lawyer. In 1745, when only 24, he became the counsel to the French Parliament, and within five years was named president of the Court of Aids and director of the national press—in essence, he became a national censor. However, he was known for his liberal attitude toward publication, which allowed the printing of Denis Diderot's *Encyclopédie* from 1751 to 1772 as well as the writings of the theorists known as the *Philosophes*. Opposed to the dictatorial powers of Louis XV, he was removed from office in 1771 and exiled from Paris.

When Louis XVI ascended the throne, he recalled Malesherbes from abroad and named him minister of the interior in 1775. Yet Malesherbes's support for royal reform of taxes and his own opposition to the king's tax plan led to his resignation. He then left France and spent several years traveling and writing. One of his essays led to the recognition of Protestant marriages in France. In 1787 Louis recalled him as minister of the interior, but he resigned two years later just as the French Revolution began. Called into service as defense counsel for Louis during the trial in which the monarch was found guilty of treason and sentenced to death, Malesherbes was arrested himself after the king's conviction and imprisoned. Two years later, on 22 April 1794, he was sent to the guillotine.

**References:** Merrick, J., "Malesherbes, Chrétien Guillaume de Lamoignon de" in Samuel F. Scott and Barry Rothaus, eds., *Historical Dictionary of the French Revolution, 1789–1799,* 2 vols. (Westport, CT: Greenwood Press, 1985), 2:620–622; Paxton, John, *Companion to the French Revolution* (New York: Facts on File, 1988).

## "The Manner of the Death and Execution of Arnold Cosbie, for Murthering the Lord Boorke"

A 1591 English tract detailing the execution of one Arnold Cosbie on 27 January 1591. The pamphlet reads, in part:

> Imediately after that Arnold Cosbie had receaved iudgment, . . . he had his hands fast bound, and by the knight Marshals men was committed unto the Mashalsey, where he had learned preachers came and conferred with him, shewing him that this life was but fraile and transitorie, and in no sort comparable unto the life to come. . . . By meanes of which godly conferences, the said Arnold Cosby, . . . [s]eeing his sodaine downefall through his pride and folly before committed, he [wept?] bitter teares and grievously lamented both his follie and his fall. . . . Wednesday about nine of the clocke in the morning, . . . he was conveyed from the Marshalsey in a cart unto Wansworth townes end, where uppon a high hill a gibbet was set up, and being brought thither by the knight Marshals men he was taken from the cart, and placed at the foot of the said hill, where at his comming he found the Earl of Druiond, with manie knightes, captaines and Gentlemen, who came to see him suffer death. . . . Then after praiers which the prisoner seemed to pure foorth from a penitent heart, confessing that he before committed sundry hainous offences, stil calling upon God to forgive him even to the last gaspe, he was turned off from the ladder and there hanged till he was dead, and nowe remaineth in the placed hanged up in chaines, according to his former iudgement.

**Reference:** "The Manner of the Death and Execution of Arnold Cosbie, for Murthering the Lord Boorke, who was Executed at Wanswoorth townes end on the 27. Of Ianuarie 1591. With Certaine verses written by the said Cosby in the time of his imprisonment, containing matter of great effect, as well touching his life, as also his Penitencie before his Death" (London: Imprinted for William Wright, 1591).

## Marie Antoinette, Queen of France

**See** Louis-August (Capet) XVI, King of France

## Marshall, Thurgood (1908–1993)

Black American lawyer, advocate for civil rights for black Americans, Associate Justice of the United States Supreme Court (1967–1990), and firm advocate that the death penalty was, in any case, a violation of the Eighth Amendment's ban on cruel and unusual punishments.

Born in Baltimore, Maryland, on 2 July 1908, Marshall was the son of William Canfield Marshall and Norma (nee Williams) Marshall. Brought up in the segregated world of the early twentieth-century (his father was a steward at a country club and his mother was a teacher at a segregated school for black children), Thurgood Marshall nonetheless graduated with honors from Douglas High School in Baltimore before attending Lincoln University in Chester County, Pennsylvania. He then attended the Howard University Law School in Washington, D.C., where he graduated magna cum laude in 1933 and was admitted to the Maryland bar that same year.

Marshall opened a law office in Baltimore, and he served as the counsel to the Baltimore branch of the National Association for the Advancement of Colored People (NAACP), but he soon found that most of his clients were poor blacks—a situation that earned him great respect but little money. One of his cases at this time was *Missouri ex rel. Gaines v. Canada,* an important case in which a black student, Lloyd Gaines, successfully sued to be admitted to the University of Missouri Law School. In 1938, Marshall succeeded Charles Hamilton Houston, a revered black civil rights attorney, as the NAACP special counsel. Two years later, in 1940, when the NAACP Legal Defense and Education Fund was established, he was named as its first director-counsel. As the head of the NAACP's legal defense team, Marshall spearheaded a national campaign to tear down segregation in the schools through the courts. In the 1950s, these efforts came to fruition as the NAACP sponsored four cases that came before the Supreme Court in *Brown v. Board of Education.* This landmark 1954 decision allowed the courts to strike down segregation in the nation's schools and order its destruction "with all deliberate speed."

If Thurgood Marshall's career had ended right there, he would have been considered one of the greatest champions of civil rights in the history of the United States. But he continued to fight for civil rights throughout the 1950s, representing hundreds of clients on behalf of the NAACP Legal Defense and Education Fund. He appeared before the U.S. Supreme Court 32 times and won 27 of those cases. On 23 September 1961, President John F. Kennedy nominated Marshall to a seat on the U.S. Court of Appeals for the Second Circuit. Opposed strenuously by Senator James O. Eastland of Mississippi, Marshall's appointment went through rigorous hearings before he was finally confirmed by a vote of 54 to 16, with all opposition coming from southern Democrats. Although he did not spend enough time on the bench—less than four years—to create a long record, the opinions he did write established him as a leading liberal jurist. In July 1965, President Lyndon B. Johnson named Marshall as the first black solicitor general, in which capacity he argued cases on behalf of the government before the Supreme Court. His most notable achievement in this position was his argument, and the Court's agreement, that the 1965 Voting Rights Act was constitutional.

On 13 June 1967, Johnson nominated Marshall as an associate justice on the Supreme Court to replace the retiring Tom Clark. Johnson said of the appointment, "[It was] the right thing to do, the right time to do it, the right man and the right place." The Senate confirmed the appointment on 30 August by a vote of 69 to 11; of the 11 who voted against his confirmation, 10 were from the South and one was a Republican (Strom Thurmond of South Carolina).

In what would become a 24-year career as a Supreme Court justice, Marshall was identified with the liberal wing of the Court. A staunch supporter of all civil rights initiatives, including affirmative action, he was equally determined in his opposition to capital punishment. In such cases as *McGautha v. California* (1971), *Gregg v. Georgia* (1976), *Coker v. Georgia* (1977), *Gardner v. Florida* (1977), *Lockett v. Ohio* (1978), *Skipper v. South Carolina* (1986), *Lowenfield v. Phelps* (1988), *Mills v. Maryland* (1988), *Walton v. Arizona* (1990), and *Payne v. Tennessee* (1991), Justice Marshall consistently held that the death penalty *in any form,* regardless of the crime committed, was a violation of the cruel and unusual punishments clause of the Eighth Amendment to the Constitution. In most of these cases he was joined by his fellow liberal, Justice William Brennan. (In his later years, Marshall was also joined in opposing capital punishment by Justice Harry Blackmun, who had earlier been a defender of the death penalty.)

When Marshall retired from the Court in 1991, Richard Lacayo called him "a lawyer who changed America." He was replaced by Clarence Thomas, a conservative black jurist with a record of supporting capital punishment. On 24 January 1993, Thurgood Marshall succumbed to heart failure while hospitalized at the Bethesda Naval Medical Center in Maryland. See Marshall's comments in *Lowenfield v. Phelps*.

**See also:** Blackmun, Harry Andrew; Brennan, William Joseph, Jr.; *Coker v. Georgia; Gardner v. Florida; Gregg v. Georgia; Lockett v. Ohio; Lowenfield v. Phelps; McGautha v. California; Mills v. Maryland; Payne v. Tennessee; Skipper v. South Carolina; Walton v. Arizona.*

**References:** Albright, Robert C., "Senate Confirms Marshall, 69–11, for High Court," *Washington Post,* 31 August 1967, 1; Greenhouse, Linda, "Ex-Justice Thurgood Marshall Dies at 84," *New York Times,* 25 January 1993, 1; Lacayo, Richard, "Marshall's Legacy: A Lawyer Who Changed America," *Time,* 8 July 1991, 24–25; MacKenzie, John P., "LBJ Names Marshall to Court; Would Be First Negro on Tribunal," *Washington Post,* 14 June 1967, 1; "Marshall, Thurgood" in Charles Moritz, ed., *Current Biography 1954* (New York: H. W. Wilson, 1955), 441–442; Mello, Michael, "Against the Death Penalty: The Relentless Dissents of Justices Brennan and Marshall" (Boston: Northeastern University Press, 1996).

## Martyrs

Although defined as "those in the Christian Church who voluntarily accept the penalty of death for refusing to renounce his or her faith," the actual meaning of a martyr is one who endures death or "great suffering" to realize a cause or maintain his or her beliefs.

The history Christian martyrs is long and heralded. Apparently the first was Stephen I, who was stoned to death and whose life is detailed in the Bible in Acts 7. Other Christian martyrs include St. Laurence, who was burned alive on a gridiron in 258; Arnold of Brescia, hanged in 1155; Edward Campion, the Roman Catholic protomartyr; and the German revolutionary John of Leiden, tortured and executed in 1536.

The veneration of relics—the remains of saints and martyrs or articles from their martyrdom—has long been approved by the Roman Catholic Church; on 3 December 1563, the Council of Trent condemned those persons who believed that "the veneration and honor are not due to the relics of the saints." The Bible itself speaks of the reverence for such relics. Acts 19:12, which describes the acts of those who witnessed the execution of Paul the Apostle, reports, "From his body were brought unto the sick handkerchiefs or aprons, and the diseases parted from them, and the evil spirits went out of them." In II Kings 13:21, a man is lowered into the tomb of Elisha, "and when the man was let down, and touched the bones of the Elisha, he revived, and stood up on his feet." History records that when St. Cyprian was about to be put to death by beheading in 258 C.E., Christian followers cast their handkerchiefs before his face so that they could be soaked in the blood of his martyrdom.

**See also:** Campion, Edmund, Blessed; Stephen, Saint.

## Mary Stuart, Queen of Scots (1542–1587)

Scottish queen put to death for opposing England's Queen Elizabeth, who was both her enemy and cousin.

The daughter of James V of Scotland and Mary of Guise, Mary was born on 8

December 1542, just days before her father was killed after suffering a defeat at the Battle of Solway Moss. She was betrothed to marry Prince Edward of England, later King Edward IV, but Scots feared that Edward's father, Henry VIII, desired to annex Scotland, so the young princess was sent to live with her mother's relative in France. There she was betrothed to the dauphin, Francis (later King Francis II), whom she eventually married when she turned 15. The same year, 1558, Mary's cousin Elizabeth, Henry VIII's daughter, became the queen of England, but many considered the Catholic Mary as the rightful monarch. Francis succeeded his father, Henry II, as king of France, in 1559, but he died the following year and left the 18-year-old Mary a widow.

Mary returned to Scotland, where her mother, who had served as regent until her return, had recently died. Because she stood to gain the throne of England in a power struggle, Mary married Henry Stuart, Lord Darnley, who was distantly related to the Stuart family of which Elizabeth was a part. But Darnley was a weak man who could never rule side by side with his ambitious wife. When Darnley's associates feared that Mary was having an affair with her Italian secretary, David Rizzio, they conspired to murder him. Mary suspected that her pompous husband was behind the murder, but she waited to act until after her son and only child, James (later James VI of Scotland and James I of England), was born; then she conspired to have Darnley strangled.

Mary then married James Hepburn, the Earl of Bothwell (1536?–1578), a Scottish nobleman who many of Mary's enemies suspected was involved in Darnley's murder. Anti-Catholic forces rose up against Mary, defeating her army at Carberry Hill near Edinburgh. She was forced to abdicate the Scottish throne in favor of her son, who was named James VI of Scotland. Imprisoned, Mary escaped and joined with her forces to retake the Scottish throne, but she was defeated by troops under the Earl of Moray (or Murray) at Langside, south of Glasgow, in 1568. She then fled to England and threw herself on the mercy of her cousin, Elizabeth, who wanted revenge for the murder of her other cousin, Darnley. Evidence in the form of letters written in French from Mary to Bothwell detailing the Darnley murder plot convicted Mary, but Elizabeth decided to spare her from the ax. She was imprisoned at Fotheringhay Castle and remained there for 19 years.

During that time, a number of Mary's Catholic supporters, including the Englishman Anthony Babington, plotted to murder Elizabeth and install Mary on the English throne. When the so-called Babington Plot was exposed in 1585, Elizabeth put Mary on trial. But even after the conviction, Elizabeth was reluctant to sign the death warrant of her royal cousin. However, Elizabeth realized that so long as Mary lived, she herself was not safe. On 8 February 1587, Mary was led before the block at Fotheringhay and beheaded. Her chief biographer, Antonia Fraser, writes of her execution:

> When the queen's prayers were finished, the executioners asked her as was customary, to forgive them in advance for bringing about her death. Mary answered immediately: "I forgive you with all my heart, for now I hope you shall make an end of all my troubles." Then the executioners, helped by Jane Kennedy and Elizabeth Curle, assisted the queen to undress—Robert Wise noticed that she undressed so quickly that it seemed as if she was in haste to be gone out of the world. Stripped of her black, she stood in her red petticoat and it was seen that above it she wore a red satin bodice, trimmed with lace, the neckline cut low at the back; one of the women handed

her a pair of red sleeves, and it was thus wearing all red, the colour of blood, and the liturgical colour of martyrdom in the Catholic Church, that the Queen of Scots died.

Yet all the time her belongings were being stripped from her, it was notable that the queen neither wept nor changed her calm and almost happy expression of what one observer called "smiling cheer"; she even retained her composure sufficiently to remark wryly of the executioners that she had never before had such grooms of the chamber to make her ready. It was the queen's women who could not contain their lamentations as they wept and crossed themselves and muttered snatches of Latin prayers. . . . [T]turning to her menservants, standing on a bench, close by the scaffold, who also had tears pouring down their faces, and were calling out prayers in French and Scots and Latin, and crossing themselves again and again, she told them to be comforted, with a smile on her lips to reassure them. . . .

The time had come for Jane Kennedy to bind the queen's eyes with the white cloth embroidered in gold which Mary had herself chosen for the purpose the night before. Jane Kennedy first kissed the cloth and then wrapped it gently round her mistress' eyes, and over her head so that her hair was covered as by a white turban and only the neck left completely bare. The two women then withdrew from the stage. The queen without even now the faintest sign of fear, knelt down once more on the cushion in front of the block. . . . The queen stretched out her arms and legs and cried: "In manus teus, Domine, confide spiritum meum"—"Into your hands O Lord I commend my spirit."—three or four times. When the queen was lying there quite motionless, Bull's assistant put his hand on her body to steady it for the blow. Even so, the first blow, as it fell, missed the neck, and cut into back of the head. The queen's lips moved, and her servants thought they head the whispered words: "Sweet Jesus." The second blow severed the neck, all but the smallest sinew, and this was severed by using the axe as a saw. It was about 10 o'-clock in the morning of 8 February, the Queen of Scots being then aged forty-four years old, and in the nineteenth year of her English captivity.

After her death, her son, James I of England, had the castle where his mother was executed demolished. Mary's grandson, Charles I of England, was to die in a similar manner, the only British monarch put to death.

**See also:** Babington, Anthony.

**References:** Fraser, Antonia, *Mary Queen of Scots* (New York: Dell, 1969), 622–623; Wigoder, Geoffrey, *They Made History: A Biographical Dictionary* (New York: Simon & Schuster, 1993), 422–424.

## Mata Hari (1876–1917)

Dutch courtesan and spy for the Germans during World War I who may have been responsible for more deaths than any spy in modern history, and who was executed by the French for this treachery.

Margaretha Geertruida Zelle, the daughter of a Dutch businessman, was born in Leeuwarden, the Netherlands, on 7 August 1876. Convent-educated, at age 18 she naively married a 40-year-old Scottish soldier, Capt. Campbell MacLeod, who was a member of the Dutch colonial army. While the couple lived in a fashionable apartment in Amsterdam, Margaretha gave birth to a son and then a daughter before they moved on to Java. The marriage seemed happy, but the pleasant public facade masked MacLeod's gambling, alcoholism, and violence against his wife. When they returned to Holland, Margaretha sued for divorce. But at that time the courts did not look kindly on such proceedings instituted by women and only gave her husband the decree after many years of bitterness.

It was about this time, in 1903, that Margaretha went to Paris, where she became a nude dancer. She told people in the French capital that she was from Java, that her name was Mata Hari (apparently meaning Child of the Dawn), and that she knew how to perform exotic Indian dances. For the next decade, she used her body to entertain in the dance clubs of Paris, to seduce her countless lovers, and to gather information. When World War I broke out in August 1914, she was in Berlin, where she was seen with the chief of police. Her French citizenship, however (as well as her contacts with high members of the French government), allowed her to return to Paris without question.

Her return to France, however, did not go unnoticed. The French secret police had a thick file on her German contacts, including several members of the German High Command who were her lovers. At the same time she was passing French secrets to the Germans, she was also passing German secrets to the French. For three years, she was able to avoid falling into the many traps laid by the French police, but that all ended on 13 February 1917 in a Paris hotel, when she was arrested after meeting with several German naval and intelligence officers. At last, the information tying her to the Germans could be used, and it was employed to great effect: one document, possibly the one that spelled Mata Hari's doom, was an intercepted telegram from German headquarters in Berlin to its embassy in Madrid, directing Agent H21 (known to be Mata Hari's code with the German High Command) to return to Paris, where a check for 15,000 pesetas for previous work done would be waiting for her. Her other activities (for one service she was paid 30,000 marks) were estimated to have cost 50,000 French lives.

Conviction was a formality; but how would the court deal with a female defendant? The court could not be lenient; after all, French and other Allied soldiers were dying in massive numbers on the front lines (more than a million at the Somme alone in 1916), and anything short of a death sentence for one who had helped betray them would be folly. Mata Hari was sentenced to death by firing squad. Historian Robert Hendrickson wrote,

> It was 4 A.M. on 15 October 1917 when Mata Hari was awakened in cell # 12 at St. Lazare and prepared for the firing squad . . . hope still prevailed as she drank the traditional last glass of rum prescribed by law for all prisoners sentenced to death. Even as she was taken out into the chill morning to the rifle range at Vincennes, her supreme ego must have asserted itself. She was tied to a young tree stripped of its leaves and branches. She faced her firing squad as the death warrant was read, refused a blindfold, and no witness saw any sign of fear on her face. Then this woman who had rarely been known to show any outward emotion, neither laughter nor tears, smiled toward the rifles gleaming in the early light. . . . Mata Hari stood straight up, and did not flinch as Major Massard barked his terse final command. She didn't cry out when the rifles cracked and smoked. Her several lovers, watching among the witnesses—perhaps some in the firing squad itself—knew that she had died only by the crimson ropes that held her slumped body.

Mata Hari, perhaps one of the greatest courtesans in history, was only 41 years old.

**References:** Howe, Russell Warren, *Mata Hari: The True Story* (New York: Dodd, Mead, 1986); Huebsch, Edward, *The Last Summer of Mata Hari* (New York: Crown Books, 1979); Ostrovsky, Erika, *Eye of Dawn: The Rise and Fall of Mata Hari* (New York: Macmillan, 1978); Wallechinsky, David, and Irving Wallace, *The People's Almanac* (Garden City, NY: Doubleday, 1975), 648, 999–1000; Wheelwright, Julie,

*The Fatal Lover: Mata Hari and the Myth of Women in Espionage* (London: Collins and Brown, 1992).

## Maximilian I of Mexico (1832–1867)

Emperor of Mexico, put to death by forces in that nation for his despotic activities.

Born Archduke Ferdinand Maximilian Joseph, the younger brother of Austrian emperor Franz (or Francis) Joseph I, on 6 July 1832, in Vienna, Maximilian grew up in the shadow of his older brother and entered the Austrian navy in 1846. Eight years later he was awarded the rank of rear admiral and served as the head of his nation's marine force. After marrying Princess Marie Charlotte Amélie Augustine Victoire Clémentine Léopoldine, the daughter of King Leopold I of Belgium, in 1857, Maximilian was named viceroy of the Lombardo-Venetian kingdom, serving for two years. After a scientific voyage to Brazil, he and his wife settled in the Italian village of Miramar, near Trieste.

On 3 October 1863, after the French had partially conquered Mexico, an assembly of Mexican notables in exile sent Maximilian a message offering him the throne. He accepted the crown on 10 April 1864 and traveled with his wife to Vera Cruz. As monarch, he established a program to advance education and protect worship. However, he came between the independence forces of Benito Juarez and the French troops of Napoleon II. The Empress Charlotte went to Europe to raise funds for her husband, but the French withdrew, leaving Maximilian without an army. Yet he stayed on to try to unite the country to his way of thinking. At the battle of Querétaro, he was betrayed by one General Lopez. Tried by the Juarez forces, he was convicted and sentenced to be shot. On 19 June 1867, Maximilian faced the firing squad with his principal officers, generals Tomás Mejía and Miguel Miramón. Jasper Ridley, a biographer of the emperor, writes of his last moments:

> The execution took place early in the morning of June 19 on the outskirts of Querétaro, on the Cerro de las Campanas, the hill where Maximilian had surrendered on May 15. . . .
>
> Maximilian made a short speech in Spanish. "Mexicans! Men of my class and race are created by God to be the happiness of nations or their martyrs." Then he said, "I forgive everybody. I pray that everyone may also forgive me, and I wish that my blood which is now to be shed may be for the good of the country. Long live Mexico, long live independence!"
>
> . . . . The officer gave the order to fire. Six bullets hit Maximilian, and three of them inflicted fatal wounds. He died instantly, as did Miramón and Mejía. It was all over by 6:40 A.M."

Maximilian's body was returned to his relatives in Vienna, where it was received with a flourish on 18 January 1868. After the execution, Maximilian's widow drifted into insanity. She went into exile at the Chateau de Bouchot in Belgium, where she died in 1927 at the age of 86.

**References:** Ridley, Jasper, *Maximilian and Juarez* (New York: Ticknor & Fields, 1992), 276–77; Wigoder, Geoffrey, *They Made History: A Biographical Dictionary* (New York: Simon & Schuster, 1993), 427.

## *Maynard v. Cartwright* (486 U.S. 356, 100 L.Ed. 2d 372, 108 S.Ct. 1853 [1988])

U.S. Supreme Court decision in which it was held that a state statute that allowed a jury to sentence to death a defendant who was convicted of a crime that was "especially heinous, atrocious, or cruel" was unconstitutional.

Respondent William T. Cartwright worked for a couple in Muskogee, Oklahoma. After being dismissed, the disgruntled former employee broke into their home, shot the wife with a shotgun, slit her throat, then shot the husband to death as well. When Cartwright was convicted of two counts of first degree murder, the jury followed the state's sentencing guidelines, which allowed them to recommend a sentence of death for anyone convicted of a crime that was "especially heinous, atrocious, or cruel." Cartwright appealed; the Oklahoma Court of Criminal Appeals affirmed the sentence, but the U.S. Court of Appeals for the Tenth Circuit overturned the death sentence, holding that the state statute was "unconstitutionally vague." Gary D. Maynard, the warden of the prison where Cartwright was being held, appealed the reversal to the U.S. Supreme Court, which heard arguments in the case on 19 April 1988.

Four weeks later, on 6 June 1988, a unanimous Court upheld the court of appeals' reversal that struck down the state statute and Cartwright's death sentence. Speaking for the Court, Justice Byron White wrote:

> The State complains . . . that the Court of Appeals ruled that to be valid, the "especially heinous, atrocious, or cruel" aggravating circumstance must be construed to require torture or serious physical abuse and this was error. . . . We . . . do not hold that some kind of torture or serious physical abuse is the only limiting construction of the heinous, atrocious, or cruel aggravating circumstance that would be constitutionally acceptable. . . . What significance these decisions of the Court of Criminal Appeals have for the present case is a matter for the state courts to decide in the first instance. Like that of the Court of Appeals, our judgment is without prejudice to further proceedings in the state courts to redetermination of the appropriate sentence. A check of death row inventories for 1996 and executions carried out since the Supreme Court okayed capital punishment in *Furman* in 1976 shows that Cartwright was neither put to death nor on Oklahoma's death row, meaning that he probably received life sentences upon resentencing.

## Mazzatello

Method of capital punishment, utilized to a small degree in Italy during the era of the Papal States, which lasted from 756 to 1870 C.E. Crime historian Jay Robert Nash reports that the name of the process comes from the Italian word for the mallet, or poleax, used in the punishment.

Historian John Laurence describes the use of the mazzatello:

> Accompanied by a priest, the criminal was led out to the public square, where a scaffold had been erected. On the platform was a coffin, and by it stood the executioner, garbed in black and masked, who leant on a heavy mallet or poleaxe. This instrument was the mazza or mazzatello.
>
> On to the scaffold the culprit was led and, after a few final prayers from the priest, he was asked if he was ready. Standing behind the condemned, the executioner then raised the awful mallet, swung it once or twice in the air, as if to test its strength, and then, with a resounding thud, brought it down with his full force on the head of the condemned man. To make his work complete the executioner drew a knife across the throat of the unconscious man. The whole method of execution was most revolting.

Nash relates that the use of the mazzatello ended with the formation of a united Italy in 1861.

**References:** Laurence, John, *A History of Capital Punishment* (New York: Citadel Press, 1960), 228; Nash, Jay Robert, *Encyclopedia of World Crime,* 4 vols. (Wilmette, IL: CrimeBooks, Inc. 1990), 2:3286–3287.

## Mencken, H(enry) L(ouis) (1880–1956)

Noted American writer and wit, editor of the influential magazine the *American Mercury* during the 1920s and 1930s, and supporter in the United States of capital punishment.

Born in Baltimore, Maryland, on 12 September 1880, he graduated from a local high school, then went to work as a police reporter for the *Baltimore Morning Herald* in 1899. Seven years later he moved over to the *Baltimore Sun,* a paper he was associated with for the rest of his life as both writer and editor. From 1914 to 1926 he edited (with George Jean Nathan) a literary magazine called *The Smart Set.* A year after that journal ceased publication, Mencken founded *The American Mercury,* which he edited until 1933. It became, from the late 1920s and through the 1940s, one of the most influential periodicals in the nation. Mencken also wrote many letters and books; from 1919 to 1927 his numerous essays were collected in six volumes entitled *Prejudices.* His other works were collected and edited by Huntington Cairns and released posthumously in the *American Scene* (1965).

Mencken was not widely known for his views on the death penalty, but he did publish, in 1949, *A Mencken Chrestomathy,* in which he included an extended essay on capital punishment called "The Penalty of Death."

> Of the arguments against capital punishment that issue from uplifters, two are commonly heard most often, to wit:
>
> 1. That hanging a man (or frying him or gassing him) is a dreadful business, degrading to those who have to do it and revolting to those who have to witness it.
> 2. That it is useless, for it does not deter others from the same crime.
>
> The first of these arguments, it seems to me, is plainly too weak to need serious refutation. All it says, in brief, is that the work of the hangman is unpleasant. Granted. But suppose it is? It may be quite necessary to society for all that. . . . Moreover, what evidence is there that any actual hangman complains of his work? I have heard none. On the contrary, I have known many who delighted in their ancient art, and practised it proudly.
>
> In the second argument of the abolitionists there is rather more force, but even here, I believe, the ground under them is shaky. Their fundamental error consists in assuming that the whole aim of punishing criminals is to deter other (potential) criminals. . . . This, I believe, is an assumption which confuses a part with the whole. Deterrence, obviously, is *one* of the aims of punishment, but it is surely not the only one. On the contrary, there are at least half a dozen, and some are probably quite as important. At least one of them, practically considered, is *more* important. Commonly, it is described as revenge, but revenge is really not the word for it. I borrow a better term from the late Aristotle: *katharsis. Katharsis,* so used, means a salubrious discharge of emotions, a healthy letting off of steam. . . . What I contend is that one of the prime objects of all judicial punishments is to afford the same grateful relief (a) to the immediate victims of the criminal punished, and (b) to the general body of moral and timorous men.
>
> These persons, and particularly the first group, are concerned only indirectly with deterring other criminals. The thing they crave primarily is the satisfaction of seeing the criminal actually before them suffer as he made them suffer. What they want is the peace of mind that goes with the feeling that accounts are squared. . . . I do not argue that this yearning is noble; I simply argue that it is almost universal among human beings. . . . It is plainly asking too much of human nature to expect it to conquer so natural an impulse.
>
> The same thing precisely takes place on a larger scale when there is a crime which destroys a whole community's

> sense of security. Every law-abiding citizen feels menaced and frustrated until the criminals have been struck down—until the communal capacity to get even with them, and more than even, has been dramatically demonstrated. Here, manifestly, the business of deterring others is no more than an afterthought. . . .
>
> The real objection to capital punishment doesn't lie against the actual extermination of the condemned, but against our brutal American habit of putting it off for so long. . . . [It] is one thing to die, and quite another thing to lie for long months and even years under the shadow of death. No sane man would choose such a finish.

Mencken, known throughout his working life as "The Sage of Baltimore," died there on 29 January 1956, but has remained one of the United States' most influential opinionmakers.

**Reference:** Mencken, H. L., "The Penalty of Death" in Mencken, ed., *A Mencken Chrestomathy* (New York: Alfred A. Knopf, 1949), 118–121.

## Mentally Ill and Retarded, Execution of the

On 24 June 1986, Jerome Bowden, a 33-year-old black man, was put to death in Georgia's electric chair for the murder of a woman during a robbery in 1976. Tests taken the day before showed that Bowden's IQ was about 65, a level considered near retarded. However, state psychologists did not feel that an IQ of 65 made Bowden unable to consider right and wrong, and the execution proceeded. In 1992, the execution of a man many abolitionists consider to have been retarded (he had had a lobotomy) was used for political purposes. As Arkansas planned to put to death Rickey Ray Rector, convicted of killing a police officer, Governor Bill Clinton, then running for president, let the execution proceed, in part to demonstrate that he was a law-and-order candidate. The Southern Center for Human Rights, an anti–death penalty advocacy group, estimates that up to 10 percent of those currently on death row suffer from some mental retardation, but that number cannot be independently verified.

The U.S. Supreme Court has spoken only once on the subject of the execution of those considered mentally ill or retarded: in 1989, in *Penry v. Lynaugh,* it held that evidence presented before a jury during a sentencing phase of a trial of mental illness or retardation must be considered by the jurors as a mitigating factor in whether or not to impose the death penalty. (The facts of that case are discussed in the *Penry v. Lynaugh* entry.) In 1994, however, in a case the Court decided not to hear, *McCollum v. North Carolina* (129 L.Ed. 895), Justice Harry Blackmun wrote in his dissent, "[Henry Lee] Buddy McCollum is mentally retarded. He has an IQ between 60 and 69 and the mental age of a 9-year-old. He reads on a second grade level. This factor alone persuades me that the death penalty in his case is unconstitutional." (McCollum was convicted of helping to rape and murder an 11-year-old girl. The jury weighed his IQ as a mitigating factor, but in the end held that the aggravating factors in the case demanded that he receive the death sentence.)

The governing legal authority in the world in such matters is the United Nations Economic and Social Council (ECOSOC). The council, in a May 1989 resolution (res. 1989/64) entitled "Safeguards Guaranteeing Protection of the Rights of Those Facing the Death Penalty," endorsed a stand toward "eliminating the death penalty for persons suffering from mental retardation or extremely limited mental competence, whether at the stage of sentence or execution."

The execution of Jerome Bowden caused the state of Georgia to outlaw the execution of those found "guilty but mentally retarded." The law took effect on 1 July 1988. Other states, including Kansas (1994) and Colorado, followed.

**See also:** *Penry v. Lynaugh.*
**References:** Amnesty International USA, "Amnesty International Country Report 1996" (New York: Amnesty International, 1996); Long, Robert Emmet, "Criminal Sentencing" (New York: H.W. Wilson, 1995), 79; text of decision in *McCollum v. North Carolina,* 129 L.Ed. 2nd 895, at 896.

## Methods of Execution

**See** Beheading; Boiling to Death; Breaking on the Wheel; Burning at the Stake; Crucifixion; Drawing and Quartering; Electric Chair; Gas Chamber; Guillotine; Halifax Gibbet; Hanging; Lethal Injection; Mazzatello; Scottish Maiden; Stoning to Death

## Mill, John Stuart (1806–1873)

English economist and social reformer noted less perhaps for his strong sentiments and writings in favor of capital punishment.

Born in London on 20 May 1806, he was the son of James Mill and his wife Harriet (nee Burrow). From the beginning, he underwent a rigorous educational regimen dictated by his father; at the age of three, he began to read Greek, at age seven Latin. He also consumed a strict "diet" of calculus, algebra, and geometry and was schooled in such classical works as Aristotle's *Logic* and David Ricardo's *Principles of Political Economy and Taxation.* In 1823 he was hired as a clerk for the East India Company in the office of the examiner of India correspondence, where he remained for the next 35 years until his retirement in 1858. During this period, he contributed articles to such magazines as *The Westminster Review* and, in 1834, he became the editor of a radical publication, the *London Review,* which then became *The London and Westminster Review.* He married in 1851, but his wife died just seven years later. In 1865, Mill entered the lower House of Parliament from Westminister, and for his entire single term worked to get reformist measures enacted. However, he was a staunch supporter of capital punishment, with the caveat that it be utilized only on the worst of criminals. During a parliamentary debate in the House of Commons on 21 April 1868, Mill spoke in opposition to a motion calling for the elimination of capital punishment in Great Britain:

> [Criminal laws] have [been] so greatly relaxed [in] their most revolting and most impolitic ferocity, that aggravated murder is now practically the only crime which is punished by death by any of our lawful tribunals; and we are now even deliberating whether the extreme penalty should be retained in that solitary case. . . . Sir, there is a point at which, I conceive, that career [of trying to end capital punishment] ought to stop. When there has been brought home to any one, by conclusive evidence, the greatest crime known to the law; and when the attendant circumstances suggest no palliation of the guilt, then I confess it appears to me that to deprive the criminal of the life of which he has proved himself to be unworthy—solemnly to blot him out from the fellowship of mankind and from the catalogue of the living—is the most appropriate as it is certainly the most impressive, mode in which society can attach to so great a crime the penal consequences which for the security of life it is indispensable to annex to it. I defend this penalty, when confined to atrocious cases, on the very ground on which it is commonly attacked—on that of humanity to the criminal. . . . Few, I think, would venture to propose, as a punishment for aggravated murder, less than imprisonment with hard labor for life;

*A drawing illustrates the painful death at the stake of one Margery Polley "at Tunbridge, in Kent."*
*(Corbis-Bettmann)*

*The so-called "Haymarket Martyrs" are put to death on 11 November 1887 for the murder of eight policemen during a labor rally. Left to right are August Spies, George Engel, Adolph Fischer, and Albert Parsons. (Corbis-Bettmann)*

*Testing of the new electric chair in New York state, 1888. (Corbis-Bettmann)*

*Emperor Maximilian I is put to death by a Mexican firing squad on 12 June 1867, along with his compatriots General Tomás Mejîa and Miguel Miramón. (Corbis-Bettmann)*

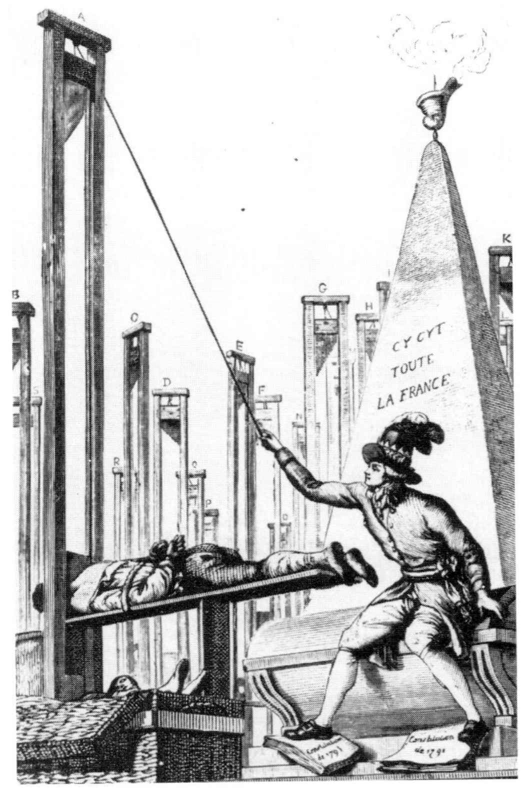


*A cartoon from the French Revolution portrays the revolution's final victim, Maximilien François Marie Isidore de Robespierre. (Corbis-Bettmann)*

*Mexican engineer Luis Segura is executed by firing squad for helping to assassinate Mexican president-elect Álvaro Obregón in 1928. (UPI/Corbis-Bettmann)*

*The mesmerizing Margaretha Geertruida Zelle, a Dutch wife, became the exotic Javanese dancer Mata Hari, dancing in the nude in Paris and commanding a minimum of $7,500 to entertain countless lovers; her spying for the Germans, however, led to her execution by firing squad on 15 October 1917.*

*Outlaw Tom Horn weaves the rope that was used to hang him on 20 November 1903 for the murder of the son of a cattleman. (American Heritage Center, University of Wyoming)*

*The gas chamber in San Quentin Prison, California: The second-to-last execution before the 1967 moratorium, that of Aaron Mitchell, took place here on 12 April 1967. (UPI/Corbis-Bettmann)*

*The electric chair in the state of Connecticut, last used in 1960. (UPI/Corbis-Bettmann)*

*The Lincoln assassination conspirators pay for their crime on the gallows. Among them is Mary Surratt, far left, the first woman put to death by the U.S. government. (Photograph by Alexander Gardner, 1865)*

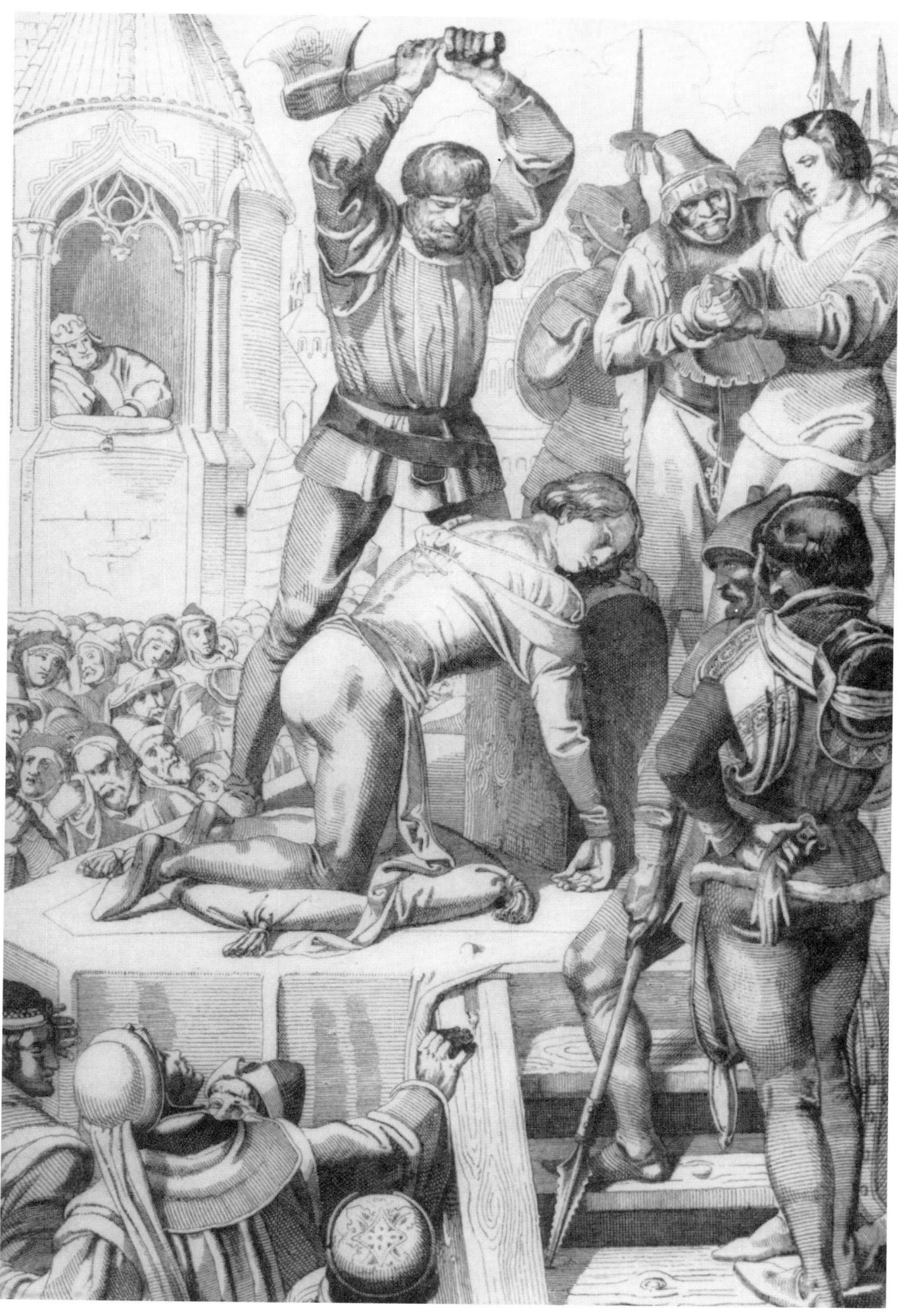

*Prince Conradin, also known as Conrad V of Swabia, is beheaded along with Prince Frederick of Baden under the orders of Charles, king of Naples and Sicily, on 29 October 1258. (Corbis-Bettmann)*

*Lynch mobs claim another "victim": Cattle rustlers "Cattle Kate" and a man named Averill are hanged by a vigilante committee in Wyoming. (Corbis-Bettmann)*

*The guillotine: Modeled on the Halifax Gibbet and the Scottish Maiden, it was used to behead most of the victims of the French Revolution, including King Louis-August XVI, Queen Marie Antoinette, and George-Jacques Danton. (Corbis)*

*An 1837 woodcut of Captain Kidd in chains. (Library of Congress)*

Sunday, 1,357,556
Daily, 1,193,297

# DAILY NEWS

NEW YORK'S PICTURE NEWSPAPER

EXTRA EDITION

Vol. 9 No. 173 56 Pages — New York, Friday, January 13, 1928 — 2 Cents

# DEAD!

Story on page 3

*In one of the most famous front pages of all time, the New York* Daily News *shows the shocking scene of the execution of Ruth Snyder, put to death in the electric chair on 12 January 1928 for the murder of her husband. A wily reporter took the shot with a camera secreted in his pants leg. (New York* Daily News*)*

*An ancient woodcut from the sixteenth century illustrates the cruel deaths of four suspected witches at the stake in Wittenburg in 1540. (Hacker Art Books)*

*The beheading of Sir Thomas Wyatt on London's Tower Hill on 11 April 1554. The death of the English soldier and conspirator, who was the son of the poet Sir Thomas Wyatt, was among one of the most gruesome on record. (Mary Evans Picture Library)*

> that is the fate to which a murderer would be consigned by the mercy which shrinks from putting him to death. . . . What comparison can there really be, in point of severity, between consigning a man to the short pang of a rapid death, and immuring him in a living tomb, there to linger out what may be a long life in the hardest and most monotonous toil, without any of its alleviations or rewards—debarred from all pleasant sights and sounds, and cut off from all earthly hope, except a slight mitigation of bodily restraint, or a small improvement in diet? . . . I think, Sir, that in the case of most offences, except those against property, there is more need of strengthening our punishments than of weakening them; . . . I shall therefore vote against the Amendment.

Defeated for reelection in 1868, Mill retired to continue work on several books. He died in Avignon, France, on 8 May 1873.

**References:** "Mill, John Stuart" in Sir Leslie Stephens and Sir Sidney Lee, eds., *The Dictionary of National Biography,* 10 vols., 12 suppl. (Oxford, England: Oxford University Press, 1917–1993), 13:390–99; Remarks of Mill in "Parliamentary Debate on Capital Punishment within Prisons Bill," Parliamentary Debates, vol. 191 (London: Her Majesty's Stationary Office, 1868), 1053–1055. Some of Mills's further thoughts on crime and capital punishment can be found in Mill, *Dissertations and Discussions; Political, Philosophical and Historical. Reprinted Chiefly From the Edinburgh and Westminster Reviews,* 4 vols. (London: J. W. Parker, 1859–1875).

## *Mills v. Maryland* (486 U.S. 367, 100 L.Ed. 2d 384, 108 S.Ct. 1860 [1988])

U.S. Supreme Court decision in which it was held that a Maryland capital sentencing instructions violated the Constitution because they could be interpreted by jurors as "requiring [a] unanimous finding as to particular mitigating circumstances."

Ralph Mills, an inmate at the Maryland Correctional Institution at Hagerstown, was convicted of the first-degree murder of his cellmate. The jurors were then handed a state-mandated form, in which they would check off aggravating circumstances that could lead to a death sentence, and mitigating circumstances that would allow for a lesser sentence. The state statute required a unanimous verdict only for aggravating circumstances, but not for mitigating ones. Mills challenged his death sentence on the grounds that the juror form violated his rights under the Eighth Amendment to the Constitution. The Maryland Court of Appeals upheld both the conviction and death sentence; the U.S. Supreme Court agreed to consider the case, and arguments were presented on 30 March 1988.

On 6 June of that same year, Justice Harry Blackmun spoke for a 5–4 Court (Chief Justice William H. Rehnquist was joined in dissent by Justices Sandra Day O'Connor, Antonin Scalia, and Anthony Kennedy) in striking down Mills's death sentence and the Maryland juror form as arbitrary and improper. Joined in his majority opinion by Justices William Brennan, Byron White, Thurgood Marshall, and John Paul Stevens, Justice Blackmun wrote:

> The decision to exercise the power of the State to execute a defendant is unlike any other decision citizens and public officials are called upon to make. Evolving standards of societal decency have imposed a correspondingly high requirement of reliability on the determination that death is the appropriate penalty in a particular case. The possibility that petitioner's jury conducted its task improperly certainly is great enough to require resentencing. We conclude that there is a substantial possibility that reasonable jurors, upon receiving the judge's instruction in this case, and in attempting to complete the verdict form as instructed, well may have

thought they were precluded from considering any mitigating evidence unless all 12 jurors agreed on the existence of a particular such circumstance. Under our cases, the sentencer must be permitted to consider all mitigating evidence. The possibility that a single juror could block such consideration, and consequently require the jury to impose the death penalty, is one we dare not risk.

## Molly (or Mollie) Maguires

Radical Irish-American group whose members were executed for their roles in violent labor activity.

Formed about 1843 at Farney, County Monaghan, Ireland, the Molly Maguires were originally a secret society named after a mythical Irish heroine who fought landlords with violence. Because it was a clandestine organization, little is known about it. In 1874 in the United States, the Maguires began a series of labor pickets against the mines and mine owners called the Long Strike, using violence to achieve their goals of better working conditions and shorter hours.

In 1874, to combat the terror of the Maguires, the president of the Philadelphia and Reading Railroad hired the Pinkerton agency to infiltrate the group and crack it. To these ends, detective Allan Pinkerton (1819–1884), head of the agency, sent to Ireland for James McParland (1844–1919), an Irish detective of whom little was known or is known today. McParland came to the United States in 1863 posing as a radical who opposed the bosses, but in fact he took a job in the early 1870s with Pinkerton. He was soon ingratiating himself inside the Maguires and acting as one of them, becoming secretary of his secret division. Gradually, he gathered evidence of the Maguires' activities and secretly reported back to Pinkerton and the authorities. McParland's information and testimony led to several trials of Maguires from 1875 to 1877, which resulted in the conviction of 60 members for various offenses, including 19 who were convicted and executed for murder. The series of executions led to the decline and ultimately to the breakup of the Maguires in 1877.

Detective Allan Pinkerton, head of the infamous Pinkerton Detective Agency, wrote of the infiltration of the Maguires in his book *The Mollie Maguires and the Detectives* (1877). Many Maguires sympathizers and labor historians believe that McParland's testimony was made up. A 1969 work by historian Charles A. McCarthy, *The Great Molly Maguire Hoax,* which implied that Maguire leader Jack Kehoe had been framed and sent wrongly to his death, led to a 1979 state pardon.

**References:** Heywood, Ezra Hervey, *The Great Strike, Its Relations to Labor, Property, and Government, Suggested by the Memorable Events Which, Originating in the Tyrranous Extortion of Railway Masters, and the Execution of Eleven Labor Reformers, called "Mollie Maguires," June 21, 1877, Culminated in Burning the Corporation Property, in Pittsburg, Pennsylvania* (Princeton, MA: Co-operative Publishing, 1878); Pinkerton, Allan, *The Mollie Maguires and the Detectives* (New York: G. W. Carleton, 1877), 13–16; Sifakis, Carl, *The Encyclopedia of American Crime* (New York: Facts on File, 1982), 493–494. For another viewpoint, see McCarthy, Charles Ambrose, *The Great Molly Maguire Hoax, Based on Information Suppressed 90 Years—The Story of John J. Kehoe* (Wyoming, PA: Cro Woods, 1969). One of the court transcripts regarding a defendant in the Molly Maguire trials can be found in Commonwealth of Pennsylvania, Court of Oyer and Terminer, "Argument of Franklin B. Gowen, Esq., of counsel for the Commonwealth, in the case of the Commonwealth vs. Thomas Munley, indicted in the Court of Oyer and Terminer of Schuykill County, Pa., for the murder of Thomas Sanger, a mining boss, at Raven Run, on September 1st, 1875" (Pottsville, PA.: Chronicle Book and Job Romms, 1876).

## Monmouth, James Scott, Duke of (1649–1685)

Pretender to the English throne beheaded for his role in the uprising against his uncle, King James II.

He was presumably born James Fitzroy on 9 April 1649 in Rotterdam, Holland, the illegitimate son of King Charles II of England and his mistress Lucy Walter. (Some historians note that Monmouth more resembles one Robert Sidney, whose mistress his mother had also been, and they presume that he was Sidney's natural son.) Placed under the supervision of Lord William Crofts, James was named James Crofts and raised in the court of Henrietta Maria of France, the empress dowager. When his father, Charles, took the English throne as Charles II, he summoned his natural son to London and betrothed him to Anne Scott, the heiress to the dukeship of Buccleuch. James took her last name and was titled James, Duke of Monmouth and of Buccleuch. The fact that James was a staunch Protestant, whose compassion toward the Protestant Scottish covenanters whom he defeated at the battle of Bothwell Bridge in 1679 made him popular with English Protestants, led to calls for Charles to make James his legal heir to the throne. But Charles could not allow a son born out of wedlock to be in line to the crown and refused to name him as his successor.

On 6 February 1685, Charles died, leaving no heir. When anti-Catholic sentiment in the English countryside demanded that the King's brother, the Catholic Duke of York, later James II, be excluded from the succession, Monmouth put himself forward as the Protestant alternative. Perceiving the menace to his brother's right to the throne, Charles had ordered Monmouth into exile in 1679. But after a few months he secretly returned and in 1682 attempted to secure support in the west. Exiled again in 1683, Monmouth returned in 1685 to make good his claims by force and at Taunton was proclaimed King James of England. Marching on London, he was assaulted at Sedgmoor by the forces of Louis Durfort, the earl of Feversham, and his troops were utterly routed. Begging James II for mercy, he was nonetheless sentenced to death and beheaded on Tower Hill in London on 25 July 1685.

In his work on the history of England, Lord Thomas Babington Macaulay wrote of Monmouth's last moments in a badly botched execution:

> He . . . accosted John Ketch the executioner, a wretch who had butchered many brave and noble victims, and whose name has, during a century and a half, been vulgarly given to all who have succeeded him in his odious office. "Here," said the Duke, "are six guineas for you. Do not hack me as you did my Lord Russell. I have heard that you struck him three or four times. My servant will give you some more gold if you do the work well." He then undressed, felt the edge of the axe, expressed some fear that it was not sharp enough, and laid his head on the block. . . .
>
> The hangman addressed himself to his office. But he had been disconcerted by what the Duke had said. The first blow inflicted only a slight wound. The Duke struggled, rose from the block, and looked reproachfully at the executioner. The head sank down once more. The stroke was repeated again and again; but still the neck was not severed, and the body continued to move. Yells of rage and horror rose from the crowd. Ketch flung down the axe with a curse. "I cannot do it," he said; "my heart fails me." "Take up the axe, man," cried the sheriff. "Fling him over the rails," roared the mob. At length the axe was taken up. Two more blows extinguished the last remains of life; but a knife was used to separate the head from the shoulders. The crowd was wrought up to such an ec-

stasy of rage that the executioner was in danger of being torn to pieces, and was conveyed away under a strong guard.

In the meantime many handkerchiefs were dipped in the Duke's blood; for by a large multitude he was regarded as a martyr who had died for the Protestant religion. The head and body were placed in a coffin covered with black velvet, and were laid privately under the communion table of Saint Peter's Chapel in the Tower.

After his death, many realized that even though he had been convicted of treason against the crown, James was nonetheless of royal blood, and his head had to be sewn back onto his body to allow for a royal portrait to be painted. A 1902 work entitled *King of Monmouth* laid out the grand scheme that Monmouth allowed a double to be executed in his place, fled England, and waited the rest of his life to return to the land of his father and claim the throne, but there is no evidence of this and it appears to be a myth.

**References:** Bevan, Bryan, *James, Duke of Monmouth* (London: Hale, 1973); "By the King: A Proclamation Against Spreading of a Trayterous Declaration Published by James Duke of Monmouth, 15 June 1685" (London: Printed by the Assigns of John Bill, 1685); Clifton, Robin, *The Last Popular Rebellion: The Western Rising of 1685* (London: Maurice Temple Smith, 1984), 76–77; D'Oylen, Elizabeth, *James, Duke of Monmouth* (London: Geoffrey Bles, 1938); Laffin, John, *Brassey's Battles: 3,500 Years of Conflict, Campaigns and Wars from A-Z* (London: Brassey's Defence Publishers, 1986), 383–384; Lodge, Richard, *The History of England, from the Restoration to the Death of William III, 1660–1702* (London: Longman's, Green, 1910); Macaulay, Lord Thomas Babington, *The History of England from the Accession of James the Second,* 3 vols. (London: Longman, Brown, Green, Longmans, and Roberts, 1858–1861), 1:625–27; Manley, Sir Roger, *The History of the Rebellions in England, Scotland and Ireland, from the Year 1640 to the Beheading of the Duke of Monmouth in 1684* (London: E. Meredith and T. Newborough, 1691); Roberts, George, of Lyme Regis, *The Life, Progresses, and Rebellion of James, Duke of Monmouth, to his Capture and Execution. With a Full Account of the Bloody Assize, and Copious Biographical Notices,* 2 vols. (London: J. R. Smith, 1844).

## Montrose, James Graham, First Marquis of (1612–1650)

Scottish general executed for his role in the support of Charles I during the English Civil War.

The son of John Graham, the fifth earl of Montrose, and Lady Margaret Ruthven, he was born in 1612, the scion of a famous family, the Clan Graham of Scotland. At the age of 12 he was sent to study in Glasgow; two years later he succeeded to his father's earldom and entered the University of St. Andrew's. At age 17 he was married, and after leaving the university decided to tour the European continent.

On his return, Graham presented himself to England's King Charles I to smooth relations between the two nations. Biographer Mark Napier reported that Charles presented a cold shoulder to the young aristocrat and may thereby have changed Scottish history. At the time, Scottish rebels were fighting for independence from England, and although Graham played no part in the early movement, his treatment at the hands of the English king turned him.

Ironically, James Graham soon found himself at war not with the English but with fellow Scots. In 1638 he signed the covenant in support of Presbyterianism in Scotland but became a rival of the antiroyalist Archibald Campbell, first marquess and eighth earl of Argyll, because deep in his heart Graham supported a constitutional monarchy that would check the power of Campbell and the so-called "covenanters." Graham on three occasions led an army into the city of Aberdeen to quell separatist riots there. Argyll had him arrested and imprisoned in Edinburgh Castle when he found evidence of correspondence between Charles and Graham. He was finally released, but kept warning Charles that a Scottish invasion of England was likely.

On 6 May 1644, with Scottish troops marching into England, the king knighted Graham as marquis of Montrose, and the Scot came to the king's defense during the English Civil War. As head of a small but powerful army, he won key victories over the covenanters at Tippermuir, Aberdeen, Inverlochy, Auldearn, Alford, and Kilsyth. For his services, the king wanted to make Graham his ambassador to France; instead, Montrose asked for reinforcements. When they did not come, his army disbanded, and Graham had to flee Scotland in 1646 to the Continent to avoid being apprehended.

Arriving in France, Graham intended to restart the war, but he had no funds to raise an army and was forced to wait in exile. When he heard of Charles's execution by the parliamentarians in 1649, he is said to have fainted and pledged to avenge him. Conferring with Charles's son, later Charles II of England, Graham was named lieutenant governor of Scotland, and, raising a 1,200-man army, sailed for Scotland. Even though more than a thousand men were killed in a shipwreck, Graham nonetheless moved on to Scotland, where his force was badly defeated at Invercarron (27 April 1650). Although he escaped, Scottish covenanters captured him and delivered him to Edinburgh on 18 May. The previous day, the Scottish parliament passed a sentence of death on Graham for treason, mandating that he be hanged and dismembered after death. In his final days, his chaplain was George Wishart, the bishop of Edinburgh, who later collected and composed Graham's memoirs in book form.

Biographer Samuel Rawson Gardiner writes:

> In a conference with some ministers on 20 May, Montrose laid down his political profession of faith. "The covenant which I took," he said, "I own it and adhere to it. Bishops, I care not for them. I never intended to advance their interest. But when the King granted you all your desires, and you were every one sitting under his vine and under his fig-tree, that then you should have taken a party in England by the hand, and entered into a league and covenant with them against the King, was the thing I judged my duty to oppose to the yondmost." On 21 May 1650 the sentence was carried out. Montrose, dressed "in his red scarlet cassock," was hanged in the Grassmarket.

As Montrose faced the ax on the gallows, a copy of Wishart's *History of the Wars of Montrose* was hung dutifully around his neck.

**See also:** Argyll, Archibald Campbell, First Marquess and Eighth Earl of.

**References:** Donnachie, Ian, and George Hewitt, *A Companion to Scottish History: From the Reformation to the Present* (New York: Facts on File, 1989), 82–83; Gardiner, Samuel Rawson, "Graham, James" in Sir Leslie Stephens and Sir Sidney Lee, eds., *The Dictionary of National Biography,* 10 vols., 12 suppl. (Oxford, England: Oxford University Press, 1917–1993), 8:316–319; Napier, Mark, *The Life and Times of Montrose: Illustrated from Original Manuscripts, including Family Papers now first published from the Montrose Charter-Chest and other private repositories; with portraits and autographs* (Edinburgh, Scotland: Oliver and Boyd, 1840), 94.

## Morant, Harry Harbord (1864–1902)

Australian soldier executed by the British in South Africa in what has been claimed was a frame, a story that was heralded in a motion picture.

Born on 9 December 1864 in Bridgewater, Somerset, England, as Edwin Henry Murrant, he was the son of Edwin Murrant, who died before his son was born, and Catherine (nee

Riely) Murrant. All that is known of his early life is that he was brought up in a poorhouse in England and that he married one Daisy May O'Dwyer, an Irish immigrant to Australia, in 1884. In 1901 he joined the British army to fight the Boers in South Africa and became a lieutenant in the Bushveldt Carbineers (BVC). In a newspaper called *The Bulletin,* a friend, A. G. Stephens, described Morant: "He was a broad, short nuggety man with a 44 inch chest and stout pair of capable arms. His whole aspect spoke courage, resolution and good fellowship. Short legged, he rode on balance and although he had been thrown [from his horse] and smashed up often, he was always ready to mount and try again."

In 1901, soon after Morant arrived in South Africa, the events that would end Morant's life occurred. A friend of Morant, Captain Hunt, was captured by the Boers and trampled to death. Morant and another soldier, Captain Peter Handcock, apparently captured some of the Boers and had them tortured and shot. For this crime against the "laws of war" (there was no Geneva Convention prohibiting such behavior), Morant and Handcock were court-martialed and found guilty. On 27 February 1902, just after the end of the trial, Morant and Handcock were shot to death by firing squad outside Pretoria Prison. Morant was 37 years old. According to fellow carbineer George Witton, who was also found guilty of the war crime and imprisoned for life (but freed in 1904 after the case of the men came to public attention in Australia), the two men went to their deaths unflinchingly. Morant was interred in the Pretoria Cemetery, in a common grave with Handcock; their shared stone reads simply, "Handcock & Morant."

Morant's case became the subject of numerous books, and his image, that of the "Breaker," remains infamous. Australian writer Frank Renar's work on Morant appeared soon after the executions; he claimed to be looking for "the sorry history of the man" who had faced the bullets of the firing squad. George Witton's account, a sympathetic account written by a comrade, was published five years later. In 1962, F. M. Cutlack's *Morant: A Horseman Who Made History* revived the heroic version of the story and romanticized the condemned prisoner. Morant was also the subject of the 1980 motion picture *Breaker Morant* (based on a play by Australian playwright Kenneth Ross), which starred Edward Woodward as Morant, Jack Thompson as Major Thomas, Bryan Brown as Handcock, and Terence Donovan as Captain Simon Hunt.

**References:** Carnegie, Margaret, and Frank Shields, *In Search of Breaker Morant: Balladist and Bushveldt Carbineer* (Armadale, Victoria, Australia: H. H. Stephenson, 1979), 6–7, 12, 140; Davey, Arthur, ed., *Breaker Morant and the Bushveldt Carbineers* (Cape Town, South Africa: Van Riebeck Society, 1987), xvii, xxiii; Renar, Frank, *Bushman and Buccaneer: Harry Morant, His Ventures and Verses, Showing the Bushveldt Carbineers' Operations* (Sydney, New South Wales: H. T. Dunn, 1902), 2–10; Witton, Lieutenant George, *Scapegoats of the Empire: The True Story of Breaker Morant's Bushveldt Carbineers* (Melbourne, New South Wales, Australia: D. W. Paterson, 1907), 153–154.

## More, Sir Thomas, Saint (1477–1535)

English lawyer, scholar, and saint, whose martyrdom for his refusal to permit the Church of England to deny the authority of the Pope and the Roman Catholic Church shocked his contemporaries for its brutality and finality at the same time that More was barely protesting the executioner's axe.

The son of John More, a lawyer and judge, Thomas More was born on 6 February 1477 (some sources give the date as 1478) in London. After serving as a page to John Morton, archbishop of Canterbury, More went to Oxford University, where he studied the law. Setting aside plans to join the Carthusians, a religious order, he instead entered the English parliament in 1505. Later elected as an undersheriff of London, he was sent by King Henry VIII, whom he had tutored as a child, on diplomatic missions to France. For this work, More was knighted by Henry in 1521. He joined the king's Privy Council in 1518 and succeeded Cardinal Wolsey as chancellor in 1529.

In order to divorce his wife, Catherine of Aragon, and marry Anne Boleyn, Henry sought an annulment, which the pope refused. Henry then separated England from the Church, establishing the Anglican Church in its stead. More refused to sign the oath declaring Henry "the supreme head of the church in England," resigned his posts, and retired to his cottage in Chelsea. Henry then called on him to officially recognize Edward, the son of Anne Boleyn, as his heir, which More refused to do. In 1534 More was imprisoned (with John Fisher, Bishop of Rochester, who also refused to recognize Henry's supremacy) after refusing to swear to the new Act of Succession because it repudiated papal authority across England. For this act he was brought to trial for treason in 1535. In spite of a brilliant self-defense, he was convicted on false evidence and, on 6 July 1535, within a week of the start of his trial, was beheaded. His execution came two weeks after his friend Fisher was decapitated on the same spot.

In a description of More's execution, historian James Harvey Robinson wrote in 1906:

> The twenty-second day of the month John Fisher, Bishop of Rochester, was beheaded, and his head set upon London Bridge. This bishop was of very many men lamented, for he was reported to be a man of great learning, and a man of very good life, but therein wonderfully deceived for he maintained the pope to be [the] supreme head of the Church and very maliciously refused the king's title of supreme head. . . .
>
> Also the sixth day of July was Sir Thomas More beheaded for the like treason before rehearsed, which, as you have heard, was for the denying of the king's Majesty's supremacy. This man was also counted [as] learned, and, as you have heard before, he was the lord chancellor of England, and in that time a great persecutor of such as detested the supremacy of the bishop of Rome, which he himself so highly favored that he stood to it until he was brought to the scaffold on the Tower Hill, where on a block his head was stricken from his shoulders and had no more harm. . . . The hangman kneeled down to him asking for forgiveness of his death (as the manner is), to whom he said, "I forgive thee, striking of my head, my neck is so short." Also even when he should lay down his head on the block, he, having a great gray beard, and said to the hangman, "I pray you let me lay my beard over the block lest ye should cut it." Thus with a mock he ended his life.

More was canonized as a saint by Pope Pius XI in 1935, 400 years after his execution, and his feast day is 9 July. His daughter, Margaret More Roper, died in 1544, and as per her wishes her father's severed head was placed in her arms in her coffin.

More's best-known scholarly work is *Utopia* (1516), in which he discussed an ideal social and political system. He also wrote an unfinished *History of King Richard III* (c.1513–18), a *Vindication of Henry against Luther* (1523), and a *Treatise on Passion* (1524).

**See also:** Fisher, John, Saint, Bishop of Rochester.

**References:** Delaney, John J., and James Edward Tobin, *Dictionary of Catholic Biography* (London: Robert Hale, 1962), 826; Robinson, James Harvey, ed., *Readings in European History,* 2 vols. (Boston: Athenaeum, 1906), 142–143; Wigoder,

Geoffrey, *They Made History: A Biographical Dictionary* (New York: Simon & Schuster, 1993), 453–454.

## Motion Pictures, Capital Punishment as Depicted in

While the American public has had a love-hate relationship with the death penalty, Hollywood has had a continuing fascination with the subject and exemplifies it in several motion pictures spread over a period that spans nearly a century. Movies made in England and France have also favored this leitmotif. These movies illustrate at first the punishing effect of the death penalty and then, later, a sense that society was paying a price for executing even its most brutal offenders. Many of these pictures also seemed to shift to the anti–death penalty stance by implying that many, if not all, of those put to death were innocent.

In the first years of the motion picture, films dealing with capital punishment were done in a documentary style, including *Execution of Mary, Queen of Scots* (1895), and *Execution of Czolgosz with Panorama of Auburn Prison* (1901). (However, the first movies to fictionally portray the carrying out of death sentences were the crime films, which would appear later in the silent era and then became prevalent in the 1930s.) Wallace Reid's 1913 anti–death penalty drama, *Thou Shalt Not Kill* (which was filmed under the same title in 1915 but with a slightly different slant), dealt with the possible execution of a woman, which was a rarity at that time.

*The Gangsters of New York* was the first to show death in the electric chair. Yet the movie to have the most impact at this time was D. W. Griffith's *Intolerance* (1916), which featured the ministory entitled "The Mother and the Law": a labor leader (Robert Harron) implicated in a riot is saved from execution by hanging. Although a financial disaster, the movie as a whole, and its four stories of history's "intolerance," today is considered a classic. Other films on this theme include *The People vs. John Doe* (1916), *The Return of Maurice Donnelly* (1914), *The Girl and the Crisis* (1917), *Who Shall Take My Life?* (1917), and *The Last Hour* (1923). B. P. Schulberg's *Capital Punishment* (1925), inspired by the Leopold-Loeb case, appeared to show that innocent people were being put to death. Herbert Hoover's documentary, *Starvation* (1919), which was filmed while he undertook famine relief in Russia following the Bolshevik Revolution, was widely criticized because it showed real executions of Bolsheviks by rebellious White soldiers.

After this short moralistic period, the crime film became the standard; it was inspired by real crime, which was rampant in cities with the onset of Prohibition, although many pictures found their plots in foreign crimes. The 1933 film *M* was based on the true case of mass murderer and child killer Peter Kürten, known as "The Vampire of Düsseldorf," who was beheaded in Germany in 1931. Directed by the brilliant German director Fritz Lang, the film stars Peter Lorre as Beckert, a normally ordinary citizen who desires to kill and commits gross crimes against children to satisfy that urge. The film is the first attempt to characterize the brutal atrocities committed by what is now known as the serial killer. Film critic Morris Dickstein comments:

> Again and again, the ordinary criminals' lives are disrupted by the forces of the law, hunting for Beckert. He is identified at his trial by a blind beggar who recognizes his whistling, who reaches in and grasps his shoulder from outside the frame. . . . When the criminals are closing

in on Beckert, we see him scurrying through the streets like a rat in a maze, and when he takes refuge in a warehouse he is lost in shadows yet they close in on him methodically. The entrapped killer becomes another victim, as he has been all along, pursued from within and without. *The Murderer among Us,* the film's original title, is also the murderer inside us, the force of the irrational, the instinctive, the obsessional, over which we have so little real influence.

The second major film to present a criminal/death penalty theme was *Angels with Dirty Faces,* starring James Cagney and Pat O'Brien, with the Dead End Kids, a group of young character actors noted for their New York accents, playing the followers of Cagney's character. Cagney, a bootlegger, is sent to the electric chair for murder, while O'Brien is a priest. As Harry Hossent wrote, "Cagney . . . is defiant almost to the end. He's not going to break down and plead for mercy. To the Dead End Kids, he's still a hero . . . which gives Father O'Brien something of a problem. Even that final chat in the Death Cell appears to leave Cagney unrepentant. Then, as he is marched to the death house, a different Cagney emerges. He collapses, he becomes a screaming coward. He goes to electrocution in abject fear."

The 1950s ushered in a new era: of films that questioned the guilt of some notorious capital punishment victims. Among these was the 1958 movie *I Want to Live!* starring Susan Hayward (for which she won the Best Actress Oscar) as murderess Barbara Graham, put to death in California's gas chamber. In this film, however, the character of Graham, who in real life had at one point confessed, is set up and sent to her death wrongly. Another film in this genre is *Tom Horn,* the 1980 film starring actor Steve McQueen (in his last performance before his death) as the cowboy murderer who was hanged in 1900 for killing a rancher's son. The 1975 movie *The Man in the Glass Booth* is in part based on the trial of Nazi war criminal Adolf Eichmann.

Recent American made-for-television movies that had capital punishment as their main theme include *The Execution of Private Slovik* (1982), starring Martin Sheen and based on William Bradford Huie's 1954 work of the same name, and *The Executioner's Song,* a 1977 work by Norman Mailer that dealt with the life and execution of killer Gary Gilmore, the first man put to death after the U.S. Supreme Court found in *Gregg v. Georgia* that the death penalty was constitutional under the Eighth Amendment. In 1996, the book *Dead Man Walking* was made into a major motion picture.

Films made outside the United States have also shown a fascination with the death penalty. The story of Nurse Edith Cavell, put to death by the occupying Germans in Belgium in 1915 for helping Allied soldiers escape, has been told twice: in the 1930 English film *Dawn,* starring Sybil Thorndike as Cavell, and in *Nurse Edith Cavell,* 1939, which starred Anna Neagle. The cases of Timothy Evans, executed for the murder of his daughter in 1950, and John Christie, put to death in 1953 for seven other murders, led to the 1961 book *10 Rillington Place* by Ludovic Kennedy, which demonstrated that Christie was responsible for the murder of Evans's daughter and that an innocent man had been put to death. The story was brought to the screen in the 1970 film of the same name, starring John Hurt as Evans and Richard Attenborough as Christie.

Murderer Ruth Ellis's story was told in the 1985 British film *Dance with a Stranger,* with Miranda Richardson in the starring role and Rupert Everett as her lover and victim, David Blakely. The 1991 movie *Let Him Have It* dealt with the controversial hanging of Derek Bentley, a 15-year-old youth who had been involved in the murder of a policeman but had not been the shooter; his crime was telling a friend to "let the cop have it"—the gun—but the meaning of his words was unclear and led to the policeman's death. The 1963 French film *Landru* brought the case of the famed French murderer to the silver screen. The 1971 Swedish film *Joe Hill* fictionalized the life of the Swedish-American labor leader put to death by firing squad in Utah in 1915 for the murder of a business owner and his son. The 1995 film *Der Totmacher* (The Death-Maker), directed by German director Romuald Karmaker and starring German actor Götz George, centers on the case of German serial killer Fritz Haarmann, a pedophile and vampire known as the "Butcher of Hannover," who killed 27 boys in a sexual fit and sold their bodies as meat in his butcher shop in the 1920s. The picture, which won George the Best Actor award at the 1995 Venice Film Festival, revolves around Haarmann's interrogation in the asylum at Göttingen, where, through the use of actual transcripts, Haarmann confessed to brutal and shocking crimes before he was beheaded by guillotine in 1928.

**See also:** Gilmore, Gary Mark; Kürten, Peter; Literature, Capital Punishment Reflected in; Slovik, Edward Donald.

**References:** Brownlow, Kevin, *Behind the Mask of Innocence* (New York: Alfred A. Knopf, 1990), 255–261; Dickstein, Morris, "Fritz Lang: Metropolis (1927) [and] M (1931)" in Kathy Schulz Huffhines, ed., *Foreign Affairs: The National Society of Film Critics' Video Guide to Foreign Films* (San Francisco: Mercury House, 1991), 35–36; Hossent, Harry, *The Movie Treasury: Gangster Movies—Gangsters, Hoodlums and Tough Guys of the Screen* (London: Octopus Books, 1974), 27; Maltin, Leonard, ed., *Leonard Maltin's 1996 Movie and Video Guide* (New York: Plume Books, 1995); Musser, Charles, *The Emergence of Cinema: The American Screen to 1907* (New York: Charles Scribner's Sons, 1990), 320–321.

## Murder Rates, Capital Punishment's Effect on

There has been a long-standing argument over what effect the use of the death penalty has on murder rates. The effect of the abolition of capital punishment in a particular state or nation may be negligible. Many who advocate an end to the death penalty in the United States argue that states where there is no death statute have lower murder rates than those with such laws. Yet, as jurist Bernard Lande Cohen found, Canada, after the *de facto* end of capital punishment in 1957, saw its murder rate increase from 129 for every 100,000 of the population in that year to 314 per 100,000 in 1968, a more than 150 percent increase. Pro–death punishment advocates argue that while the death penalty *may not* be a deterrent, it does allow society to do away with a particular murderer who is beyond rehabilitation.

## Musmanno, Michael Angelo (1897–1968)

Judge and advocate against the death penalty, particularly in his writings in which he felt that Sacco and Vanzetti were innocent of the crime for which they were put to death.

The son of Italian immigrants, Antonio and Maddelena (nee Castelluci) Musmanno, Michael Musmanno was born in McKee's Rocks, Pennsylvania, on 7 April 1897. He attended local schools, then worked during the day while taking law classes at night. He eventually entered Georgetown University in Washington, D.C., where he earned bachelor's and master's degrees. After serving as an infantryman during World War I, he completed his law studies and was awarded an LL.B. degree.

Starting off as a journeyman attorney, Musmanno lost his first five cases. Convinced that he should not be a lawyer, he went to Europe and studied Roman law at the University of Rome, even working at one point as an extra in the 1925 silent version of the motion picture *Ben Hur.* Returning to the Pittsburgh area, he took on several indigent clients and became known as a defender of the underprivileged. It was in this work that he came to the defense of noted anarchists Nicola Sacco and Bartolomeo Vanzetti, accused of killing a paymaster and a guard during a holdup in Massachusetts in 1920. After they were convicted and sentenced to death, their case became the cause célèbre of the decade. Believing that the two men were convicted and sentenced to die on the basis of their radical political views rather than any evidence against them, Musmanno, along with other leading national attorneys, demanded to review the evidence used against them. Musmanno and the other critics remained unconvinced of the two men's guilt, but Sacco and Vanzetti were executed anyway. Musmanno believed a great injustice had been committed; in 1939 he published *After Twelve Years,* a critique of the case.

Elected in 1930 to the Pennsylvania House of Representatives, Musmanno campaigned for a law to end the use of police in coal and iron mine disputes. He claimed they were used to intimidate workers. Although the bill was vetoed by the governor, Musmanno's book on the subject, *Jan Volkanik* (named after a miner he claimed had been beaten to death by such police), became a minor success and was made into the 1935 motion picture *Black Fury,* starring Paul Muni. In 1932 Musmanno was elected judge of the Allegheny County Court, then two years later to the Court of Common Pleas, where he served for 16 years. During World War II, he served in the U.S. Navy as a lieutenant (his ship was sunk), then on the staff of General Mark Clark in Italy. After the war, he worked to stop the forced repatriation of Austrian refugees to Soviet control and worked for President Truman to discover if Adolf Hitler had really died. He was also a judge at the Nuremberg War Crimes Trials, sitting in judgment of some of the minor Nazi officials. In 1951, he was elected to the Pennsylvania Supreme Court. Two failed bids for Lieutenant Governor (1950) and U.S. Senate (1964) were bracketed by an appointment from President John F. Kennedy to the Commission on International Rules of Judicial Procedure.

An avowed anti-Communist, Musmanno helped to write the Communist Control Act of 1954, and he spoke out that all Communists should be sent to prison. Musmanno died on 12 October 1968. His published works, in addition to his autobiography, *Verdict!* (1958), include *Musmanno Dissents* (1955) and *That's My Opinion* (1966), the latter published posthumously.

**See also:** Sacco, Nicola, and Bartolomeo Vanzetti.

**References:** "Michael A. Musmanno, 72, Dies; Defender of Sacco and Vanzetti," *New York Times,* 13 October 1968, 84; Musmanno, Michael, *Verdict! The Adventures of the Young Lawyer in the Brown Suit* (Garden City, NY: Doubleday, 1958); Urofsky, Melvin I., "Musmanno, Michael Angelo" in Dumas Malone, et al., eds., *Dictionary of American Biography,* 10 vols. 10 suppl. (New York: Charles Scribner's Sons, 1930–1995), 8:455–457.

## NAACP Legal Defense and Educational Fund

Leading civil rights organization committed to obtaining equal opportunities for black Americans as well as ending capital punishment in the United States.

Founded in 1940 by the late Supreme Court Justice Thurgood Marshall, then lead attorney for the National Association for the Advancement of Colored People (NAACP), the Legal Defense and Educational Fund (LDEF) was declared a separate organization in 1957. While it maintains its affiliation with the NAACP as a civil rights organization, it has its own funding and staff.

The LDEF has a long history of securing civil rights victories in the courts. In the area of capital punishment, its achievements have been less exemplary. It does provide briefs to courts on death penalty issues, but in the anti–death penalty arena it takes a decided backseat to the American Civil Liberties Union. In 1972, the LDEF was instrumental in helping to prepare briefs in the famous case of *Furman v. Georgia,* in which the U.S. Supreme Court declared capital punishment, as it was then applied by the states, unconstitutional.

Today the LDEF is headed by black attorney Elaine R. Jones; its death penalty counsel, George Kendall, also sits on the board of directors of the Death Penalty Information Center. The fund's national headquarters is in New York City, and it has offices in Washington, D.C., and Los Angeles.

**Reference:** "Death Row U.S.A.," a publication of the NAACP Legal Defense and Education Fund, Summer 1996.

## Nagy, Imre (1896–1958)

Hungarian Communist leader executed for his role in fomenting the failed Hun-

garian uprising against Soviet forces in 1956.

Born in Kaposvár, Hungary, on 7 June 1896, Imre Nagy (pronounced "Eem-ray Naj") was the son of poor Hungarian peasants. After being apprenticed as a locksmith, he enlisted in the Hungarian army and saw action during World War I before being captured by Russian troops. But Nagy sympathized with the Bolshevik Revolution, which occurred while he was a captive. Indoctrinated by Marxist ideology, he returned to Hungary after the war and participated in the short-lived Marxist government of Communist revolutionary Béla Kun. After 1929 Nagy lived in Moscow, became a Soviet citizen and, during World War I, delivered propagandistic radio broadcasts to Budapest.

Nagy followed the advancing Soviet Army that occupied Budapest and the rest of Hungary after the defeat of the Germans at the end of World War II. Because of his experience in Moscow, the Soviets installed him as the minister of agriculture (1945–1946) and minister for internal affairs (1946). Nagy also served as speaker of the Hungarian National Assembly (1946–1949). Because he was considered a nationalist desirous of loosening Soviet control over Hungarian affairs, Moscow did not allow him to hold major government posts, although he served as minister of agriculture from 1952 to 1953. With the death of Josef Stalin, Nagy became the premier of Hungary on 4 July 1953. For almost two years, Nagy embarked on a program of liberalization of Communist policies: he ended collectivization on farms and released political prisoners. But Moscow did not appreciate Nagy's nationalist line and again dismissed him from government.

During the October 1956 Revolution that swept Hungary, Nagy appealed to the West for aid in defeating the Soviet plan to make Hungary a satellite of Moscow. When the revolution collapsed with the arrival of Russian tanks, Nagy went to the Yugoslavian embassy for protection. But he was tricked by the Soviets into leaving when they promised safe passage out of the country and was deported to Romania. He was smuggled back inside Hungary, found guilty of treason against the state, and executed by firing squad with his associates, Miklós Gimes, Pál Maléter, and Géza Losonczy.

Nagy historian Alajos Dornbach writes:

> The executions [of Nagy, Gimes, Losonczy, and Maléter] were carried out in the early hours of June 16, 1958, in a section of the largest Budapest prison, the so-called Transit Detention House, where all executions in Budapest at the time took place. Before the execution, strict regulations were introduced in order to limit to an absolute minimum the number of people who would know what was happening. The bodies of the executed were placed in primitive coffins and buried at the scene, next to the gallows, in the yard of the so-called Small Detention House.

The bodies of the three men were later buried in pauper's plots in Budapest's Kozma Street Cemetery, in Lot 301, which over the years became a garbage dump. In 1989, the Hungarian Supreme Court posthumously "rehabilitated" Nagy. On 16 June of that year, after the bodies of the men were exhumed and positively identified, Nagy's remains were given a state funeral through the streets of Budapest.

**References:** Dornbach, Alajos, *The Secret Trial of Imre Nagy* (Westport, CT: Praeger, 1994), 13–14; Goetz, Philip W., ed.-in-Chief, *The New Encyclopædia Britannica,* 22 vols. (Chicago: Encyclopædia Britannica, Inc., 1995), 8:484; Haag, John, "Imre Nagy" in Anne Commire, ed., *Historic World Leaders,* 5 vols. (Detroit: Gale Research, 1994), 3:962–965; "The Truth about the Nagy Affair: Facts, Documents, Comments" (London: Secker & Warburg, 1959); Unwin, Peter, *Voice in the Wilderness: Imre Nagy and the Hungarian Revolution* (London: Macdonald, 1991).

## National Coalition to Abolish the Death Penalty

American anti–capital punishment group consisting of an umbrella of more than 120 national, state, and private organizations determined to abolish the death penalty in the United States.

The NCADP was founded in 1976 by several anti–death penalty activists as part of the American Civil Liberties Union's attempt to fight the Supreme Court's ruling in *Gregg v. Georgia,* which held that capital punishment was not an unconstitutional violation of the Eighth and Fourteenth Amendments. The NCADP works through seven standing committees, including the religious community committee and the litigation committee, to devise strategies that will delay or overturn death sentences. Their state affiliates (such as the Texas Coalition to Abolish the Death Penalty) send religious persons to pray at executions when they occur.

The NCADP separated from the American Civil Liberties Union since 1982, when it became a nonprofit organization. The group's national headquarters are located at 918 F Street, N.W., in Washington, D.C., and it has a field office in Liberty Mills, Indiana.

The executive director is Steven Hawkins, who also sits on the board of directors of the Death Penalty Information Center. The NCADP publishes two periodicals: "Lifelines," an information newsletter, and "Executions Alerts," which highlights and discusses upcoming executions.

## Newton, Thomas (1660–1721)

See Leisler, Jacob; Salem Witch Trials

## Ney, Marshal Peter Michel, Duke of Elchingen and Prince of Moscow (1769–1815?)

He was called "the bravest of the brave" by Napoleon but apparently that could not save him from the firing squad, although there have been many rumors that he escaped death and spent his last years in America.

The son of a cooper, he was born in Saarlouis, France, on 10 January 1769. His military training came early, and he became a noncommissioned officer of hussars in 1787. Napoleon saw great promise in him and made Ney one of his leading commanders. Ney did not disappoint. His bravery and his accomplished victory at Mannheim in 1799 led Napoleon to name him general of division. He also contributed greatly to the French triumph at Hohenlinden on 3 December 1800, which led to the collapse of the second allied coalition against Napoleon. After his own victory over the Austrians at Elchingen in 1805, Napoleon named Ney Duc d'Elchingen. Further victories at Jena, 1806, and at Friedland, 1807, and an indecisive battle at Eylau (also known as Bagrationovsk), 1807, led Napoleon to label Ney as "le brave des braves" (the bravest of the brave).

When Napoleon decided to invade Russia, he turned to Ney to command the Third Corps of the French Army. Ney fought with distinction at Borodino and Smolensk, and for his valor was given the title Prince de la Moskova (Moscow), even though that city never fell to French forces. Ney commanded the French troops at the battle of Dennewitz, 6 September 1813, against the machinations of the Prussians under Baron Count Friedrich Wilhelm von Bülow (also known as Count Bülow von Dennewitz, 1755–1816). Ney's forces were routed and forced to flee from the field of battle, leaving some 15,000 dead on the field.

In 1814, he was forced to command Napoleon's rear guard as the French army retreated in defeat from Russia, and he succeeded in keeping up the morale of the troops under his command despite the horrible weather and disastrous reverses in their fortunes. Back in France, as Paris was falling to the coalition, it was he who went to Napoleon and told him that abdication was a necessity. With Napoleon's resignation, Ney swore allegiance to the new French king, Louis XVIII, who in turn made Ney a peer and conferred upon him the Cross of St. Louis. For his oath of loyalty to the king, he was made a member of the royal court and once again enjoyed the privileges of aristocracy.

Yet when Napoleon escaped from Elba and landed in France, the king sent Ney to arrest the former French leader. Instead Ney joined Napoleon at Lyon to once again conquer Europe. This regime lasted only one hundred days, but in that time Ney was placed in charge of the 1st and 2nd French corps. At Waterloo, the first major test of Napoleon's worthiness to again be the leader of France, he made Ney his battlefield commander and placed most of the responsibility for the continuation of his empire at the feet of his friend. During the bitter fighting, particularly at Quatre Bras, Ney exhibited great fortitude and bravery, even though three horses were shot from under him. His clothes full of gunshot holes although he himself was unhurt, Ney fought for the losing French cause until long after darkness had settled on the battlefield. With the cause hopeless, and Paris again fallen to its enemies, Ney set out for exile in Switzerland, but he was captured by the king's soldiers.

The French House of Peers found Ney guilty of treason against the French state, and condemned him to be shot by a firing squad. However, rumors circulated for many years that Ney was saved from the firing squad by loyal soldiers who refused to kill their old commander and helped him escape to the United States in 1816 to live the rest of his life in North Carolina under the name of Peter Stewart Ney. Papers at one time in the possession of a history teacher in North Carolina were compared to those in Ney's handwriting in France, and they were identical. Marshal Ney was known to have had a large gash across his forehead, and the teacher Ney was noted for combing his hair low on his forehead to mask a large scar. The teacher Ney died in 1846, and was buried in the Third Creek churchyard in Rowan County, North Carolina.

**References:** "Marshal Ney in America: Did He Escape Death and Teach School in North Carolina?" *World* (New York), 11 May 1884, 10; Keegan, John, *The Face of Battle: A Study of Agincourt, Waterloo and the Somme* (London, England: Jonathan Cape, 1976), 127.

## Norris, Kathleen Thompson (1880–1966)

American novelist and short story author who wrote about her opposition to capital punishment.

Born in San Francisco, California, on 16 July 1880, she was the second of six children of James Alden Thompson and Josephine (nee Moroney) Thompson. When she was 19, both her parents died within a month, and she had to work at odd jobs to support her siblings. In 1909 she married American writer Charles Gilman Norris (1881–1945), and her career prospered after the union. Charles Norris had his wife contribute articles to his journal, *American Magazine,* and she also sent small pieces of fiction to the *New York Telegram.* Her first work, *Mother,* which was printed serially in the *American Magazine,* appeared in 1911.

A militant feminist who supported prohibition, the cessation of child labor, and the ending of capital punishment, Norris joined the American League to Abolish Capital Punishment in the 1920s and became one of its more outspoken speakers. Her article "Our Jungle Passions," which appeared in the 8 October 1927 issue of *Collier's* magazine, expressed her ideas on the subject.

> And so for capital punishment. "Would you fill the world with murderers?" the complacent voice asks triumphantly. And usually the word "hysterical" is introduced.
>
> Strangely enough, this primitive attitude has at last made clear to me the truth regarding the Spanish Inquisition, the burning alive or hanging of innocent old "witches" in Scotland and Massachusetts, the fate of Jeanne the Maid, and all the other cruelties formally enacted in the name of Him who said, "Judge not." . . .
>
> Those of us whose loyalty to the Christian ideal has made the history of religious persecutions hard to understand need search no further. It is all explained fully by the exactly similar condition that exists today: the great public unseeing and unhearing, the great machinery of stupid punishment moving almost automatically, and the occasional fanatic—Nero, Torquemada, Jeffries'—gladly seizing upon the two for a more than ordinary atrocious abuse of power.
>
> But, incidentally, cruelty is inherent in human nature, and these things have nothing to do with religion, fundamen-

> tally. Too many latter-day essayists and commentators fall into the error of thinking the two things are allied. They love to remember the old story of the shipwrecked mariner who, staggering exhausted upon an unknown shore, beheld a gibbet [gallows], with a corpse swinging from it in the wind, and gasped fervently: "Thank God, I'm in a Christian country, at least!"

Norris died in San Francisco on 18 January 1966.

**References:** Kunitz, Stanley J., and Howard Haycraft, eds., *Twentieth Century Authors: A Biographical Dictionary of Modern Literature* (New York: H. W. Wilson, 1942), 1032–1033; McCarthy, Joanne, "Kathleen Thompson Norris" in Lina Mainiero, ed., *American Women Writers: A Critical Reference Guide from Colonial Times to the Present*, 5 vols. (New York: Frederick Ungar, 1979–1994), 3:276–78; Mackey, Philip English, ed., *Voices against Death: American Opposition to Capital Punishment, 1787–1975* (New York: Burt Franklin, 1976), 180–190.

## Nuremberg War Crimes Defendants

Perhaps the most famous set of trials in history, this entry focuses on the defendants who led Nazi Germany in the years before and during World War II, including Hans Frank, Wilhelm Frick, Alfred Josef Ferdinand Jodl, Ernst Kaltenbrunner, Wilhelm Keitel, Joachim von Ribbentrop, Alfred Rosenberg, Hermann Goering, and Fritz Saukel.

Nuremberg, the site of the trial, is a city in Bavaria on the Pegnitz River. The birthplace of German artists Albrecht Dürer and Hans Sachs, Nuremberg was a center of trade and artistry during medieval times and subsequently became the nucleus of the German Renaissance. From 1933 to 1938, Hitler held Nazi party congresses and immense rallies there, and the laws that stripped German Jews of all civil and political rights were called the Nuremberg Laws. During the war the city was heavily bombarded by the Allies.

The procedure that allowed the Allies to hold a war crimes trial was outlined in a report dated 7 June 1945 and written by Robert Houghwout Jackson, associate justice of the U.S. Supreme Court. Jackson was then named by President Harry S Truman to negotiate with the other allied nations. The resulting agreement, the London Agreement of 1945, established the International Military Tribunal. It was signed in that city by Jackson as well as representatives of the USSR, Great Britain, and France. The tribunal was then created with Lord Justice Geoffrey Lawrence of the British Court of Appeals as president. Judges were Francis Biddle, former attorney general of the United States; Major General I. T. Nikitchenko, vice chairman of the Soviet Supreme Court; and Donedieu de Vabres, professor of law at the University of Paris. Alternates were Sir Norman Birkett, chief of the High Court of England; Judge John J. Parker of the United States Court of Appeals; Judge A. F. Volchkov of the Moscow District Court, and Judge Robert Falco of France's Court of Cassation. The chief prosecutors were Jackson for the United States, Sir Hartley Shawcross and Sir David Maxwell Fyfe for Great Britain, François de Menthon for France, and Roman Rudenko for the Soviets.

The indictment held that the Nazis on trial (1) had a "common plan" or had conspired to commit war crimes; (2) had committed crimes against peace, including waging aggressive war against innocent nations; (3) had committed gross war crimes, including violating the laws and customs of warfare; and (4) had committed crimes against humanity. The defendants, except one, pleaded not guilty. (The only defendant to plead guilty was Albert Speer (1905–1981), Nazi minister of armaments and ammunition, who received a 20 year sentence for his part in the Holocaust.) The defense attorneys for the defendants argued that the trial was unfair based on the theory of *nullem crimen sine lege, nulla peona sine lege praevia:* "[there can be] no crime and no punishment without existing law." They maintained that since the men were being judged as war criminals on statutes that did not exist when their "crimes" were committed, they could not be held responsible. But with the four judges facing a world that wanted revenge, this argument held little weight.

The trial began on 20 November 1945 in courtroom 600 of Nuremberg's Palace of Justice and lasted until 1 October 1946. Most of the men who had run the Nazi war and death machine were found guilty and sentenced to death, including Frank, Frick, Goering, Jodl, Kaltenbrunner, Keitel, von Ribbentrop, Rosenberg, and Saukel, as well as Julius Streicher, and Artur Seyss-Inquart. (Martin Bormann, who had disappeared following the collapse of Nazi Germany and was tried at Nuremberg in absentia, was also found guilty on counts 3 and 4 and sentenced to death, a sentence that remains to be carried out as of this writing.) Three men—Hjalmar Schact, Franz von Papen, and Hans Fritzche—were found not guilty on all counts. Seven others, including Speer and Rudolf Hess, were found guilty on some counts and sentenced to various terms in prison.

On 16 October, those sentenced to death, except for Bormann, who had not been found, and Goering, who swallowed poison smuggled to him in his cell, were all executed on the gallows at the Nuremberg prison in less than an hour and a half. The men were photographed after death, with the ropes still around their necks; they were then cremated (probably in the ovens at the Dachau concentration camp, which, if true, lends rich irony to this story), and their ashes dumped into the Isar River near Munich.

**References:** Cooper, R. W., *The Nuremberg Trial* (Harmondsworth, England: Penguin Books, 1947); Davidson, Eugene, *The Trial of the Germans: Nuremberg, 1945–1946* (New York: Macmillan, 1966); Hockett, Jeffrey D., "Justice Robert H. Jackson, the Supreme Court, and the Nuremberg Trial," *Supreme Court Review 1990* (1990), 257–299; Robert Jackson Oral History, Robert H. Jackson Papers, Box 191, Manuscript Division, Library of Congress; Taylor, James, and Warren Shaw, *The Third Reich Almanac* (New York: World Almanac, 1987); Tusa, Ann, and John Tusa, *The Nuremberg Trial* (New York: Atheneum, 1986); Taylor, Telford, *The Anatomy of the Nuremberg Trials: A Personal Memoir* (New York: Alfred A. Knopf, 1992).

### O'Sullivan, John Louis (1813–1895)

American reformer and activist, a stalwart in the effort during the nineteenth century to end capital punishment.

O'Sullivan was born on a British ship in the harbor of Gibraltar sometime in November 1813, the son of John O'Sullivan, a sea captain and later consul for the island of Teneriffe (now the Canary Islands). He received his education at a military school in France, at the Westminister School in England, and at Columbia College (now Columbia University) in New York, the latter institution awarding his two degrees in 1831 and 1834. Although he began the practice of law, he soon joined Samuel Langtree in founding the *United States Magazine and Democratic Review* in 1837, established as a literary journal to highlight the writings of "the democratic genius of the age." In the July-August 1845 edition, O'Sullivan personally wrote of the right of the American people to move further west, beyond established borders, and take possession of lands belonging to other countries—and, with this article, he coined a phrase that has become part of the lexicon of American history: "manifest destiny."

In 1841, O'Sullivan was elected to the New York state legislature, where he served for a single term. It was during this time that he forcefully advocated the complete abolition of capital punishment in his "Report in Favor of the Abolition of the Punishment of Death by Law."

O'Sullivan never wrote about capital punishment again. He sold his interest in the magazine in 1846 and founded a newspaper with future presidential candidate Samuel Tilden. Later in life, he was named U.S. chargé d'affairs to Portugal by President Franklin Pierce, where he served from 1854 to 1858. After living in Europe for several years, he returned to New York where he died on 24 February 1895.

**References:** "Obituary: John Louis O'Sullivan," *New-York Daily Tribune,* 26 March 1895, 7; O'Sullivan, John Louis, "Report in Favor of the Abolition of the Punishment of Death by Law, Made to the Legislature of the State of New York, April 14, 1841, by John L. O'Sullivan, Member of the Assembly, From the City of New York" (New York: J. & H. G. Langley, 1841), 9–10; "O'Sullivan, John Louis" in *National Cyclopedia of American Biography,* 57 vols. suppl. M–Z (New York: James T. White, 1898–1977), 12:337; Pratt, Jules W., "O'Sullivan, John Louis" in Dumas Malone, et al., eds., *Dictionary of American Biography,* 10 vols. 10 suppl. (New York: Charles Scribner's Sons, 1930–1995), VII:89.

## Parker, Isaac Charles (1838–1896)

American magistrate known as "The Hanging Judge" for his brand of Western American justice in which he sent 79 men to their deaths.

Of English ancestry, Parker was born in a log cabin on 15 October 1838. He settled in Ohio as a young man and was admitted to the Ohio bar in 1859. He then moved to St. Joseph, Missouri, where he married and practiced law for 14 years. During the Civil War he served two terms as St. Joseph city attorney and as the assistant provost marshal in the state militia. In 1864, after serving as an elector for Abraham Lincoln, Parker was elected state's attorney for the Twelfth Judicial Circuit of Missouri. Elected to congress in 1870, he served for two years and became interested in Indian land issues. In 1875 President Ulysses S Grant appointed him judge in the Federal Court for the Western District of Arkansas, located at Fort Smith. Parker, at only thirty-six, thus became the youngest man ever to serve on the federal bench.

As a member of the Committee on Territories in Congress, Parker had become acutely aware of the problems of law and order in areas where the federal government had little or no reach. Finding the court where he was to sit in a shambles, he set about naming new clerks and establishing a network of honest attorneys to stand before him. Parker named George Maledon as his court-appointed executioner, and through his work, Maledon would become almost as famous as Parker.

During Parker's first eight weeks on the bench, eighteen people were tried for murder, fifteen were convicted, and of those six were sentenced to death. During his tenure, Parker sentenced 160 men to death, of which 79 were actually hanged. Under Maledon's guidance, multiple public executions were not rare, and for this Parker's court became

known as the "Court of the Damned." When the U.S. Supreme Court struck down several convictions from his courtroom, Parker criticized its "laxity." After murderer Henry Starr was convicted, he interrupted Parker as the judge was sentencing him to death, exclaiming, "If I am a monster, you are a fiend, for I have put only one man to death, while almost as many men have been slaughtered by your jawbone as Samson slew with the jawbone of that other historic ass." (Starr's death sentence was thrown out by the U.S. Supreme Court on appeal in 1895; he was later sentenced to only five years in prison.)

By 1895, many in the American justice system had come to question Parker's tactics. Congress removed Indian Territory from his docket, but still men were sentenced to death. Parker himself died on 17 November 1896 after a lengthy illness. As for George Maledon, he lived until 1911, dying at the age of 77. When asked if he had any regrets, he said, "No, I simply did my duty. I never hanged a man who came back to have the job done over."

**References:** Nash, Jay Robert, *Encyclopedia of Western Lawmen and Outlaws* (New York: Da Capo Press, 1994), 225, 252; ———, *Encyclopedia of World Crime,* 4 vols. (Wilmette, IL: CrimeBooks, Inc.,1990), 3:2411; Shirley, Glenn, *Law West of Fort Smith: A History of Frontier Justice in the Indian Territory, 1834–1896* (Lincoln: University of Nebraska Press, 1971), 26–40.

## Parsons, Albert Richard

See Haymarket Martyrs Case

## *Payne v. Tennessee* (501 U.S. 808, 111 S.Ct. 2597, 115 L.Ed. 2d 720 [1991])

This landmark case overturned the precedent established in *Booth v. Maryland* (1987) and *South Carolina v. Gathers* (1989), in which the court had held that victim impact statements (VISs) were an unconstitutional violation of the Eighth Amendment of the Constitution; in *Payne v. Tennessee,* the Court reversed course and held that such statements were permissible under the Eighth Amendment.

Pervis Tyrone Payne was convicted in the Shelby Criminal Court in Tennessee for the first-degree murder of a woman named Charisse Christopher and her two-year-old daughter, and first-degree assault on her three-year-old son, Nicholas—crimes Payne committed after Christopher spurned his advances. During the sentencing phase of the trial, Payne was allowed to have friends and relatives explain the "mitigating aspects" of his life and character, while the prosecution called Nicholas's grandmother to testify that the boy missed his mother and sister and that the murders had a continuing effect on his life. The jury then sentenced Payne to death on both murder counts. He appealed, claiming that the grandmother's testimony violated his Eighth Amendment rights as established under *Booth v. Maryland,* a 1987 case in which the high court struck down such statements as violating the Eighth Amendment. The Tennessee Supreme Court affirmed the lower court's decision, and Payne appealed to the U.S. Supreme Court.

The case was argued on 24 April 1991, and the Court handed down a decision two months later, on 27 June 1991. Speaking for a 6–3 court (Justices Thurgood Marshall, Harry Blackmun, and John Paul Stevens dissented), Chief Justice William H. Rehnquist held that the Eighth Amendment "erects no per se bar prohibiting a capital sentencing jury from considering 'victim impact' evidence relating to the victim's personal characteristics and the emotional impact of the murder on the victim's family, or precluding a prosecutor from arguing such evidence at a capital sentencing hearing." In his dissent, Justice Marshall wrote, "Where, as is ordinarily the case, the defendant was unaware of the personal circumstances of his victim, admitting evidence of the victim's character and the impact of the murder upon the victim's family predicates the sentencing determination on 'factors . . . wholly unrelated to the blameworthiness of (the) particular defendant.'"

**See also:** *Booth v. Maryland; South Carolina v. Gathers.*

## Pearse, Padraic (Patrick) Henry (1879–1916)

Irish nationalist and martyr, considered the first "President" of the Irish Republic, put to death by firing squad for his role in the Easter Uprising of 1916.

Born in Dublin in 1879 as Padraic Henry Pearse (named after the American patriot Patrick Henry), Pearse was the son, ironically, of an English father, James Pierce (who changed his name to the more Irish "Pearse" after moving to Ireland), and an Irish mother, Margaret (nee Brady) Pearse, whose family, from County Heath, had been victims of the Irish Potato Famine of the 1840s. Patrick attended a local school, the Westland Row Christian Brothers School, and after graduating became a member of the nationalistic Gaelic League. He later entered the Royal University and the King's Inns of Court in London to study the law, and though he was called to the bar he never practiced law. Starting in 1903 and continuing for six years, Pearse edited the Gaelic League's publication, *An Claideamh Solius* (The Sword of Light). Eventually, he returned to Ireland and founded a school of higher education, St. Enda's, where he attempted to put the ideals of the league and the concept of Irish nationality into action. He was assisted in this undertaking by his brother, William Pearse, and fellow Irish nationalists Thomas MacDonagh and Con Colbert.

After leaving *An Claideamh Solius,* Pearse's politics became more radical. He became a leading member of Sinn Fein (Ourselves), a radical group established by Arthur Griffiths in 1911 to protest the English Parliament's failure to pass a Home Rule law and establish Irish independence. Pearse contributed to Griffith's newspaper, *The United Irishman,* established two short-lived publications, and created an unsuccessful association, *Cumann na Sairu* (The Society for Freedom). Eventually, Pearse turned from Sinn Fein and opted for more radicalism: he joined the Irish Republican Brotherhood and read its newspaper, *Irish Freedom,* edited by Bulmer Hobson; he later became a contributor to its pages. In 1913, Pearse reached the end against British rule in Ireland and founded the Irish Volunteers, who pledged violence against the English if they did not leave Ireland.

In 1915, the year before his own death, Pearse stood before the grave of fellow Irish revolutionary O'Donovan Rossa in Dublin's Glasneven Cemetery and proclaimed that an unfree Ireland would never be at peace. In the next year, he planned an armed uprising against the English authorities that he felt would become a revolution. He wrote: "We may make mistakes in the beginning and shoot the wrong people, but bloodshed is a cleansing and a sanctifying thing, and the nation which regards it as the final horror has lost its manhood. There are many things more horrible than bloodshed; and slavery is one of them."

On Easter Sunday, 24 April 1916, Pearse and 1,400 volunteers from the radical Irish Republican Brotherhood stormed and occupied the Dublin General Post Office and other vital buildings in Dublin in an attempt to found an Irish Republic. From the GPO he read aloud the Irish Proclamation of Independence and declared himself the first president of a free Irish Republic. For six days the lightly-armed Irish rebels held out against the British forces, suffering heavy casualties. On 29 April, Pearse surrendered unconditionally to the British commander, Brigadier General Lowe. Within days the rebellion had collapsed; following a quick court-martial, Pearse was convicted and sentenced to death. At 3:30 A.M. on the morning of 3 May 1916, he was led from his cell at the Dublin Military Prison into a courtyard and executed by firing squad. The following morning, his brother Willie met the same fate.

The fight for which Pearse gave his life, that of a free Ireland, goes on today. His eldest sister, Margaret Pearse, ran St. Enda's after her brother's execution; she became an Irish Senator, and upon her death in 1932 the school became a national museum to Patrick Pearse and is today a leading tourism site.

**References:** Carty, Xavier, *In Bloody Protest: The Tragedy of Patrick Pearse* (Dublin: Able Press, 1978), 10–20; De Rosa, Peter, *Rebels: The Irish Rising of 1916* (New York: Doubleday, 1990), 507; Edwards, Ruth Dudley, *Patrick Pearse and the Triumph of Failure* (London: Gollancz, 1977), 52–54; Hickey, D. J., and J. E. Doherty, *A Dictionary of Irish History Since 1800* (Dublin: Gill and Macmillan, 1980), 467–468; McCay, Hedley, *Padraic Pearse: A New Biography* (Cork, Ireland: Mercier Press, 1966); Moran, Seán Farrell, *Patrick Pearse and the Politics of Redemption: The Mind of the Easter Rising, 1916* (Washington, D.C.: Catholic University of America Press, 1994); Murphy, Brian P.,

*Patrick Pearse and the Lost Republican Ideal* (Dublin: James Duffy, 1991); Pearse, Patrick (Séamas Buachalla, ed.), *The Letters of P. H. Pearse* (Gerrards Crossing, England: C. Smythe, 1979).

## *Penry v. Lynaugh* (492 U.S. 302, 106 L.Ed. 2d 256, 109 S.Ct. 2934 [1989])

In this landmark case, the United States Supreme Court held that "executing mentally retarded people convicted of capital offenses is not categorically prohibited by the Eighth Amendment" to the United States Constitution, although in this case it struck down the death sentence of a mentally retarded man.

That man, Johnny Paul Penry, was charged, for the rape and murder of a woman, with capital murder in a Texas state court; however, a psychologist testified that he was retarded to the point that he had the mental capacity of a 6-year-old. His attorney pleaded that he was not guilty by reason of insanity. The jury, however, did not believe that Penry's retardation had anything to do with the crime and found him guilty. In the sentencing phase, the jury was asked to consider three "special issues": (1) whether Penry's action was deliberate and undertaken with the reasonable expectation that death would result; (2) whether there was a probability that he would be a continuing threat to society; and (3) whether the killing was unreasonable in response to any provocation by the victim. The defense requested that the terms set out in the special issue be relayed to the jury and that the jury be allowed to consider mercy in answering any one of the three questions. The jury returned and answered yes to all three issues, whereupon the judge sentenced Penry to death (a single "no" answer would have mandated a life sentence). On appeal, the Texas Court of Criminal Appeals upheld the sentence, and the district court as well as the U.S. Court of Appeals for the Fifth Circuit followed suit.

Penry appealed to the U.S. Supreme Court, which heard arguments in the case on 11 January 1989. Five months later, on 26 June 1989, Justice Sandra Day O'Connor spoke for a divided Court in striking down Penry's death sentence but upholding the doctrine that mentally retarded persons could be sentenced to death. In a decision in which all of the justices concurred in part and dissented in part, Justice O'-Connor based her decision on two prior cases, *Lockett v. Ohio* and *Eddings v. Oklahoma:*

> Mental retardation is a factor that may well lessen a defendant's culpability for a capital offense. But we cannot conclude today that the Eighth Amendment precludes the execution of any mentally retarded persons of Penry's ability convicted of a capital offense simply by virtue of his or her mental retardation alone. So long as sentencers can consider and give effect to mitigating evidence of mental retardation in imposing sentence, an individualized determination whether "death is the appropriate punishment" can be made in each particular case. While a national consensus against execution of the mentally retarded may someday emerge reflecting the "evolving standards of decency that mark the progress of a maturing society," there is insufficient evidence of such a consensus today.

**See also:** Mentally Ill and Retarded, Execution of the.

## Petiot, Dr. Marcel (1897–1946)

French mass murderer beheaded by guillotine for his role in the murders of at least 27 people during World War II.

Born in Auxerre, in the Yonne region of France, on 17 January 1897, Petiot was sent to live with an aunt who was unmarried. Bored by his colorless childhood and convinced that his parents did not want him (he wrote in prison later that he surmised that he had been conceived because a condom his father wore had "blown out"), he started down the trail that most serial killers head down, namely, torturing small animals. Before he was grown, he visited his parents and privately boasted that he would be more important than they, including his father, who had been elected mayor of Auxerre.

During World War I, Petiot served in the French army but was court-martialed for stealing drugs. Although he never spent any time in jail, he underwent psychiatric treatment. After the war, he attended medical school, and in 1921, though still considered a mental deficient, was able to obtain his medical degree and set up a practice in the village where he grew up, Villeneuve-Yonne. He became a leading member of the village and was even elected its mayor. He married and had a son. And there, it seemed, the life of Dr. Marcel Petiot could end, happily.

Instead, a housekeeper vanished, and he was accused of stealing. In 1930, a patient, a Mademoiselle Debauve, also vanished, but because the chief witness against Petiot also disappeared mysteriously, charges were never filed. In 1936, Petiot moved to Paris, but within months was arrested for stealing from a bookstore. However, it was agreed that the charges would be dropped if he underwent psychiatric counseling. Still he retained his medical license, and opened shop in Paris. After a short stay at a small office, he moved to a larger one located at 21 rue Le Sueur, in the Etoile district of the city, part of a 15-room house.

As World War II started (1940), Jews, and particularly French Jews, sought any way possible to get out of the country to escape the threat of Nazi persecution. Petiot saw an opportunity to amass a large fortune. Advertising his services, he convinced wealthy Jews to bring their cash and jewels to 21 rue Le Sueur, and he would spirit them out of the country. Instead, he strangled them, stripped them of all valuables, and then disposed of their bodies in an iron stove in the residence. The plan was perfect: these people would not be missed, since they were voluntarily "disappearing" anyway. At least 27 people vanished in this way.

Petiot's downfall came from murdering so many people so fast. On 11 March 1944, as the war entered its final year, neighbors on rue Le Sueur complained to police that the chimney from Petiot's house was emitting smoke that had a foul odor. Firemen arrived, fearing a conflagration, but once inside found a chimney loaded with burning corpses, as well as a boiler room filled with the parts of bodies. Once on the scene, Petiot admitted to the killings but claimed that they were "Germans and traitors." A policeman who shared Petiot's sentiments about punishing these groups of people allowed Petiot to go off, and he promptly escaped, not to be found until that November. By then, the police had reasoned that all of the people were in fact Jews or others trying to get out of Nazi-occupied France. When questioned, Petiot admitted to killing 63 people, all "traitors."

At the trial, Petiot and his lawyers knew that if he convinced a jury that the people whose corpses were found were indeed traitors, he would easily be found not guilty. For some of Petiot's victims, the prosecution had no evidence to the contrary. Numerous suitcases, jewels and other valuables did not prove otherwise. The court, however, did not believe Petiot. He was found guilty on 24 of the 27 counts of murder. After being sentenced to death, he yelled to his wife in the courtroom, "You must avenge me!"

On 26 May 1946, Petiot faced the guillotine, cocky and joking to the end. According to his biographer, John V. Grombach, Petiot smoked a cigarette and then told his jailers that he was ready to face *Madame Guillotine.* As Grombach relates:

> Before leaving his cell, Petiot was offered the traditional glass of rum provided for all condemned prisoners in France just before execution. He quietly refused this final kindness. Then the group, led by one of the prison officials, walked with measured step out through the hallways and into the cobbled courtyard where the guillotine stood. "M. Paris," the executioner, gently asked Petiot to loosen his collar. Then Petiot smoked his final cigarette. Now, if ever, was the time for an ultimate confession or revelation of what had gone on behind the doors at 21 rue le Sueur. [Pierre] Dupin [the "Advocat General" who prosecuted Petiot] asked Petiot if he had any final remarks to make. The answer was published all over the world: "AUCUNE. Je suis un voyageur qui emporte tous ses bagages avec lui!" ("None. I am a traveler who is taking all his baggage with him!")
>
> Petiot's hands were tied behind his back. He was led toward the guillotine. His smile was now contemptuous and his eyes still showed no fear. The guards of the execution detail seized him roughly and seated him, tied in place, and shoved his head into the lunette [the metal bar that holds the condemned in place]. At precisely five minutes past five, the weighted blade and block fell with a peculiar thud. Dark-red blood from the several arteries spurted in several directions for as far as six feet. The head had tumbled into a large basket and the stub of the neck, slipping out of the lunette, still pumped out quantities of darker and thicker blood. Some witnesses said that when the head fell into the basket, it still wore a contemptuous smile. It was certain that Petiot remained cool and disdainful to the very end. Said Dr. Paul, who had seen many men die: "In my forty years, I never before saw a condemned man with so much scorn and indifference to death."

**References:** "Doctor Death" in *Crime and Punishment: The Illustrated Crime Encyclopedia,* 28 vols. (Westport, CT: H. S. Stuttman, 1994), 19:2346–2352; Grombach, John V., *The Great Liquidator* (Garden City, NY: Doubleday, 1980), 31–37, 394–395; Maeder, Thomas, *Dr. Petiot: The True Story of France's Most Diabolical Killer* (New York: Penguin Books, 1992); ———, *The Unspeakable Crimes of Dr. Petiot* (Boston: Little, Brown, 1980).

## Place, Martha Garretson Savacoli (?–1899)

American murderer, the first woman to die in the electric chair.

Little is known of Place, except that her maiden name was Garretson, that she lived until age 46 with her mother, and that her first husband, who died sometime in the 1890s, was named Savacoli. Sometime around 1898 she became the housekeeper for one William W. Place, a widower with a daughter, Ida, about 22 years old, and married him soon after. After an argument about finances with her husband on 7 February 1898, Martha Place murdered her step-daughter by smothering her with a pillow, and then tried to kill her husband with an ax when he returned home. Although she claimed that another had killed the young girl, Place was found guilty and sentenced to be executed in New York's electric chair, the first woman to be sentenced to die by the new method of capital punishment.

Responding to critics who felt that only a cold-blooded murderer should die in the chair, Governor Theodore Roosevelt asked a panel of experts whether Place fit that category; when they reported back that she did, Roosevelt allowed her execution to continue. On 20 March 1899, a year after her brutal crime, Martha Place walked to the death chamber in New York's Auburn Prison with the aid of a matron, and, holding her Bible, was executed. Reporting on the execution, the *New Haven Evening Register* said, "Mrs. Place was calm beyond expectation. No one has walked into the death chamber as serenely as she. Death came with less struggle than was ever witnessed here before. . . . The first shock lasted four seconds. The voltage was 1,760. It was then reduced to 200 for 56 seconds. A second shock was then given. . . . Death was instantaneous. Just as she sat down in the chair she said, 'God help me.'"

**References:** "Mrs. Place Electrocuted: Brooklyn Murderess Put to Death at Sing Sing Today," *New Haven Evening Register,* 20 March 1899, 1; "Mrs. Place Put to Death," *New York Times,* 21 March 1899, 5; Nash, Jay Robert, *Encyclopedia of World Crime,* 4 vols. (Wilmette, IL: CrimeBooks, Inc. 1990), 3:2473.

## *Poland et al. v. Arizona* (476 U.S. 147, 90 L.Ed. 2d 123, 106 S.Ct. 1749 [1986])

U.S. Supreme Court decision holding that it was not to be considered double jeopardy when a defendant or defendants were resentenced to death utilizing an aggravating factor once rejected by a higher court.

Petitioners Patrick Gene Poland and Michael Kent Poland, disguised as police officers, stopped a Purolator bank truck making money deliveries to banks in northern Arizona. After removing some $281,000 from the truck, the Polands took the two bank guards to a lake and dumped their weighted bodies into the water. (Autopsies later showed that one died from drowning, while the other probably succumbed from a heart attack.) The men were arrested, but pleaded that they had an alibi at the time of the robbery and killings. The jury did not believe them and convicted them both of first-degree murder.

On appeal, the petitioners argued that their crime did not fit the state's definition of "especially heinous, cruel, or depraved" and thus should not merit the death penalty. The Arizona Supreme Court struck down the two death sentences, finding that the evidence admitted at trial by the state did not meet the criteria for such a finding, and ordered a new trial. Again, the defendants were convicted of first-degree murder. The prosecutors then introduced at the sentencing hearing not only evidence shown at the first trial but additional evidence that they felt proved more clearly the charge that the crime committed was "especially heinous, cruel, or depraved." The jury agreed and sentenced the brothers to death. They then appealed, claiming that the reimposition of a sentence of death violated the double jeopardy clause (the prohibition against charging a person twice with the same crime). This time, the Arizona Supreme Court rejected their claim, holding that the first death sentence could not be supported by the evidence introduced at the first trial, but it could with the additional evidence offered at the second.

The U.S. Supreme Court then decided to hear the issue in the case of whether the reimposition of a death sentence after it had been originally struck down by a higher court was a violation of the double jeopardy clause. Arguments in the case were presented before the Court on 24 February 1986. A little more than two months later, on 5 May 1986, the Court held 6–3 (Justice Thurgood Marshall was joined by Justices William Brennan and Harry Blackmun in dissent) that since additional evidence was presented at the second trial, a death sentence could stand judicial scrutiny; and, further, that a court is not barred from seeking a second capital sentence if it has originally been struck down by a higher court because the defendant has not been acquitted but merely had a sentence or conviction overturned.

Speaking for the majority, Justice Byron White wrote:

> At no point during petitioners' first capital sentencing hearing and appeal did either the sentencer or the reviewing court hold that the prosecution had "failed to prove its case" that petitioners deserved the death penalty. Plainly, the sentencing judge did not acquit, for he imposed the death penalty. While the Arizona Supreme Court held that the sentencing judge erred in relying on the "especially heinous, cruel, or depraved" aggravating circumstance, it did not hold that the prosecution had failed to prove its case for the death penalty. . . . Petitioners argue, however, that the Arizona Supreme Court "acquitted" them of the death penalty by finding the "evidence [insufficient] to support the sole aggravating circumstances found by the sentencer" . . . We reject the fundamental premise of petitioners' argument. . . . Because the reviewing court did not find the evidence legally insufficient to justify imposition of the death penalty, there was no death penalty "acquittal" by that court. The Double Jeopardy clause, therefore, did not foreclose a second sentencing hearing at which the "clean slate" rule applied.

As of this writing, the Poland brothers remain on Arizona's death row.

## Pope John Paul II, Statement against Capital Punishment of

On 25 March 1995, Pope John Paul II released his encyclical entitled "Evangelium Vitae" (The Gospel of Life), in which he condemned the use of capital punishment except "in cases of absolute necessity[;] in other words, when it would not be possible otherwise to defend society." In paragraph 56 of the encyclical is this passage:

> Public authority must redress the violation of personal and social rights by imposing on the offender an adequate punishment for the crime, as a condition for the offender to regain the exercise of his or her freedom. In this way authority also fulfills the purpose of defending public order and ensuring people's safety, while at the same time offering an incentive and help to change his or her behaviour and be rehabilitated. . . .
>
> [T]he principle set forth in the new *Catechism of the Catholic Church* remains valid: "If bloodless means are sufficient to defend human lives against an aggressor and to protect public order and the safety of persons, public authority must limit itself to such means, because they better correspond to the concrete conditions of the common good and are more in conformity to the dignity of the human person."

## Pressing to Death

**See** Stoning to Death

## Protopopov, Aleksandr Dmitriyevich (1866–1918)

Russian statesman, his nation's last Minister of the Interior (1916–17), put to death by the Soviets.

Born in Moscow on 30 December (18 December, Old Style) 1866, Protopopov was a wealthy landowner when he was elected to the third Duma (Parliament) from the Simbirsk region in 1907. Elected to the Fourth Duma five years later, he became a leading spokesman for military readiness and, when it began, Russian participation in World War I. He journeyed to Britain to appeal for aid, then to Stockholm to meet with representatives of the German government to sound out the possibility a Russo-German peace. These actions led Czar Nicholas II to name Protopopov Russia's minister of the interior.

Though Protopopov had been a respected politician in the Duma, many of his former colleagues saw his joining the government as an act of betrayal. Furthermore, he was a weak administrator; he ignored the staggering food shortages in the outlying villages and underestimated the Communists, led by Vladimir Lenin. When the shortages led some to protest, Protopopov called out the secret police to arrest the demonstrators. Serious riots and strikes broke out in March 1917, aimed at the government in general and Protopopov in particular. The Communist Revolution surprised him, and he was arrested and thrown into the Peter-Paul Fortress in Moscow. He had no trial; the newly-created Cheka (secret police) desired to be rid of him, and on 1 January 1918, the day after his fifty-third birthday, he was taken to the fortress yard and executed with a single shot to the back of the head.

**References:** Cockfield, Jamie, "Protopopov, Aleksandr Dmitrievich" in Joseph L. Wieczynski, ed., *The Modern Encyclopædia of Russian and Soviet History,* 58 vols. 1 suppl. (Gulf Breeze, FL: Academic International Press, 1977–1995), 30:39–41; Goetz, Philip W., ed.-in-Chief, *The New Encyclopædia Britannica,* 22 vols. (Chicago: Encyclopædia Britannica, Inc., 1995), 9:743.

## Public Executions

From the beginning of history, executions were considered to be public events, part of the "ceremony" for society to see punishment inflicted properly; at the same time, it was also a mawkish ritual in which spectators showed great emotion (either cries of sorrow or cheers for the death of the victim), and some businessmen found a chance to hawk their wares, and even some trinkets dealing with the execution itself.

From the first public execution in the United States in 1630 until the last, that of murderer Rainey Bethea in Kentucky in 1936, Americans have had a great fascination with public executions. The death of John Billington, the first man to be executed in the colonies, was used to admonish others to follow society's laws. In 1860, pirate/murderer Albert E. Hicks was hanged on New York's Bedloe's Island (now the site of the Statue of Liberty), and the newspapers of the day trumpeted the fact that not only did thousands of people flock to the island to see Hicks hang, but that shiploads of people sat in the surrounding waters to see the sight as well.

England and France had a long history of public executions before their abolition, with the former allowing the public to witness beheadings near the Tower of London, and the latter having murderer Eugen Wiedemann beheaded before a crowd of spectators, an act that ended public executions in France. In other nations, even to this day, public executions remain the norm rather than the exception, especially Middle Eastern countries, where public beheadings are considered a lesson to the general populace.

**Reference:** Sifakis, Carl, *The Encyclopedia of American Crime* (New York: Facts on File, 1982), 240–241.

## Pugachev (or Pugachov), Emel'ian Ivanovich (c.1742–1775)

Russian Cossack soldier and leader of a major peasant uprising against Catherine the Great, 1773–74, for which he was put to death by beheading.

A nomadic adventurer of an undetermined ancestry, Pugachev was apparently born in an unnamed Cossack settlement on the Don River in the Urals in southern Russia. He was sent to Prussia sometime in the 1750s and subsequently served as a soldier in the Seven Years' War, the Polish war of 1764, and the first Russo-Turkish War (1768–1774), until he was struck by an unknown illness in 1770. In 1773 he returned to the Urals and witnessed firsthand the sufferings of the native peoples then occurring under the reign of Catherine II. Pugachev took advantage of the extent of this peasant discontent, assumed the name of Peter III, the murdered husband of Catherine, and raised the banner of rebellion among the Ural Cossacks to call for better living conditions.

With the rebel Pugachev as its head, the rebellion soon expanded to the fugitive serfs who were trying to get more land, to laborers forced to work in the deadly Russian mines, to the large sect of dissenters from the Russian church known as the Old Believers, and to Russia's numerous oppressed minorities. Soon he had amassed a ragtag army of some 30,000, and they advanced on the cities of Kazan and Nizhi Novgorod. Soon the entire Volga River region was in the hands of Pugachev's discontented horde.

Queen Catherine, who at first had ignored the calls for reforms from the Volga region and took little notice of Pugachev's rebellion, became alarmed, particularly when Kazan fell in July 1774. Then she became convinced that the movement was a threat to her reign as well as the stability of the nation, and she assembled an army to put down the insurrection. The loyalists marched toward the rebels, who were situated at Tsaritsyn and, wresting the betrayal of their leader from some of his weaker supporters, captured Pugachev in September 1774 and put down the revolt. Pugachev was brought to Moscow in an iron cage, tried by a court of high government officials, and beheaded on 10 January 1775.

**References:** Alexander, John T., "Pugachev, Emel'ian Ivanovich" in Joseph L. Wieczynski, ed., *The Modern Encyclopædia of Russian and Soviet History,* 58 vols. 1 suppl. (Gulf Breeze, FL: Academic International Press, 1977–1995), 40:72–79; Florinsky, Michael T., ed., *McGraw-Hill Encyclopedia of Russia and the Soviet Union* (New York: McGraw-Hill, 1961), 464.

## *Pulley v. Harris* (465 U.S. 37, 79 L.Ed. 2d 29, 104 S.Ct. 871 [1984])

U.S. Supreme Court decision, in which it was held that the theory of "comparative proportionality" of death sentences was held not to be constitutionally required in every capital sentencing review.

Robert Alton Harris was convicted in a California court of killing two young boys after holding up a bank. It was, as many agreed, a cruel and vicious crime for which Harris was justifiably sentenced to death in California's gas chamber. Harris appealed the sentence, however, under the theory of "comparative proportionality"—that is, that Harris could only be sentenced to death if other criminals who had committed comparable crimes had also been sentenced to death, and that the absence of a review to see if this was true was a violation of his rights under the Constitution. After the California state courts refused to grant him a new trial, he sought relief from the U.S. District Court for the Southern District of California, which upheld the lower courts; however, the U.S. Court of Appeals for the Ninth Circuit, sitting in San Francisco, vacated the two death sentences because the failure to proportionally examine such a death sentence violated the Constitution. The warden of San Quentin Prison, R. Pulley, then sued in the U.S. Supreme Court to overturn the judgment. The Court granted certiorari, and arguments were heard on 7 November 1983.

On 23 January 1984, the Court struck down the Court of Appeals' judgment and remanded the case back to the lower court, where Harris could be resentenced to death. In an opinion by

Justice Byron White (Justices William Brennan and Thurgood Marshall dissented), the Court held that "comparative proportionality" was not a "constitutionally required element of the capital sentencing system." Justice White spoke for the Court's majority of 7–2: "Traditionally, 'proportionality' had been used with reference to an abstract evaluation of the appropriateness of a sentence for a particular crime. Looking to the gravity of the offense and the severity of the penalty, to sentences imposed for other crimes, and to sentencing practices in other jurisdictions, this Court has occasionally struck down punishments as inherently disproportionate, and therefore cruel and unusual, when imposed for a particular crime or category or crime."

On 21 April 1992, after a series of delays between the Ninth Circuit and the Supreme Court, Robert Alton Harris died in the gas chamber, the first man to be executed in California since 1967.

## Purge Trials

Particular to the Soviet Union, as well as other Communist countries, purges (from the Russian "chistka") have been used to eliminate and eradicate political enemies by show trials and mass executions.

The first victim of the Soviet government was Aleksandr Vasilyevich Kolchak (1873–1920), leader of the "White" forces against the Bolsheviks during the Russian civil war, who was shot in 1920. Other victims of the Soviet purges who were also shot were Yakov Ivanovich Alksnis (1897–1938), commander of the Soviet air forces after 1931; Vasily Konstantinovich Blücher (1890–1938), commander of the Far East Military District; the Bulgarian Communist leaders Blagoi Popov (1902–?) and Vasil Tanev (1898–?), both of whom disappeared into Siberia and were executed there; Latvian Communist leader Robert Indrikovich Eikhe (1890–1940); Yiddish writer David Bérgelson (1884–1952); former Soviet premier Aleksei Ivanovich Rykov (1881–1938), shot soon after his show trial in 1938; Nikolai Ivanovich Bukharin, editor of the Soviet newspaper *Pravda,* shot on 13 March 1938 for allegedly supporting Trotsky against Stalin; as well as countless *millions* who disappeared in the prisons of the Gulag.

On 13 August 1990, Soviet President Mikhail Gorbachev signed a decree posthumously rehabilitating all of the victims of Stalin's purges.

**See also:** Zinoviev, Grigori Yevseyevich.

**References:** Salisbury, Harrison E., "Stalinist Purges Left Wide Mark in Soviet," *The New York Times,* 3 October 1967, 1, 18; Solzhenitsyn, Aleksandr I., *The Gulag Archipelago, 1918–1956: An Experiment in Literary Investigation, Parts I and II* (New York: Harper & Row, 1974); ———, *The Gulag Archipelago, 1918–1956: An Experiment in Literary Investigation, Parts III and IV* (New York: Harper & Row, 1975).

## Quelch, John (c.1665–1704)

American pirate put to death by the Massachusetts colonial authorities for his crimes. Unlawfully in command of the Boston brigantine *Charles,* Quelch plundered a number of Portuguese ships off the coast of Brazil between November 1703 and February 1704. On the return of the *Charles* to Marblehead, Massachusetts, Quelch and a number of his crewmen were arrested, tried, and hanged on 30 June 1704. The speed and questionable procedures of the trial, together with the eagerness of the Boston authorities to confiscate and divide the plunder of Quelch's forays, have caused some to characterize the case as "judicial murder."

## Quisling, Lauritz Vidkun Abraham (1887–1945)

Norwegian dictator put to death for his cooperation with the Nazi regime during the occupation of his country.

Born in Fyresdal, Norway, on 18 July 1887, Quisling was trained at Norway's military academy, entering the Norwegian army in 1911. From 1922 to 1926 he worked with Fridtjof Nansen (winner of the 1922 Nobel Peace Prize) in lending aid to starving Soviet citizens, and then as legation secretary to the Norwegian Embassy in Moscow from 1927 to 1928. By 1931 he had attained the rank of major of field artillery, and as a loyal member of the Norwegian Agrarian party was named Norway's minister of defense. Although he had sympathized with the Bolsheviks while in Moscow, he became a rabid anti-Communist after returning to Oslo. In 1933 he helped found the anti-Communist party called the Norwegian Popular Awakening, later renamed the National Unity (*Nasjonal Samling*) party. But the founding of the party did not help him win a seat in the Norwegian parliament.

When Adolf Hitler began his drive to take over Europe, Quisling went to Berlin, warned the German leader that Britain was the real threat to European hegemony, and helped plan a Nazi invasion of his homeland. After the Germans landed in Norway on 9 April 1940, Quisling called for all resistance against the aggressors to end. Although Quisling was more than subservient to the German leadership, Hitler did not trust him and made him answerable to Josef Terboven, the Reich Commissioner. In 1942, however, Hitler turned to Quisling to form a national government and made him premier. Quisling ruled the one-party state from Oslo's high-walled medieval palace known as the *Akershus,* which also served as his headquarters during the war.

On 9 May 1945, as Allied troops swept through Norway, Quisling turned himself in to the new government that had been in exile. He was brought to trial in the Freemasons' Hall in Oslo on August 22 on charges of betraying his country, causing the deaths of uncounted Norwegians, and inciting mutiny. Found guilty on 10 September, he appealed for mercy during an eight-hour speech in which he called himself "the Saviour of Norway." Nonetheless, he was sentenced to death; his appeal was denied, and on 24 October 1945 he was shot within the walls of the *Askershus*. Before his death, he told the members of the firing squad, "Don't let your conscience trouble you in later years. . . . You are acting under orders and are only doing your duty like myself." After he was executed, his body was cremated; years later his remains were handed over to his widow, taken to the village of Gjerpen, and buried beside his mother. Today, his name is remembered in history as synonymous with the word "traitor."

**References:** *Crime and Punishment: The Illustrated Crime Encyclopedia,* 28 vols. (Westport, CT: H. S. Stuttman, 1994), 14:131–32; Donaldson, Norman, and Betty Donaldson, *How Did They Die?* (New York: St. Martin's Press, 1980), 307–308; Hewins, Ralph, *Quisling: Prophet without Honor* (London: W. H. Allen, 1965); Taylor, James, and Warren Shaw, *The Third Reich Almanac* (New York: World Almanac, 1987), 261; Zentner, Christian, and Friedmann Bedüftig, eds. (Amy Hackett, trans.), *The Encyclopedia of the Third Reich,* 2 vols. (New York: Macmillan, 1991), 2:744.

## Race, Issue of in Capital Punishment

In the landmark U.S. Supreme Court decision *McCleskey v. Kemp,* the leading case in the United States in which racial statistics were used to show a pattern of bias in capital punishment, Justice Lewis Powell wrote, "The Constitution does not require that a State eliminate any demonstrable disparity that correlates with a potentially irrelevant factor in order to operate a criminal justice system that includes capital punishment."

Many have considered the issue of race a major problem in the application of capital punishment in the United States. Opponents of the death penalty argue that racial minorities suffer the death penalty far in excess of their proportion in the population at large. Supporters, on the other hand, claim that there is no way to show that minorities are targeted for execution more than any group. In the 1970s, a study by Professor David Baldus seemed to show that minorities were being targeted, and the study was used by death row inmate Warren McCleskey in his appeals. However, according to the U.S. District Court for the Northern District of Georgia, which heard McCleskey's appeal before it went to the court of appeals and then the Supreme Court, the Baldus Study was "flawed in several respects." Among these, the court noted, was the fact that the authors of the study did not consider mitigating and aggravating factors in each case, which might draw a clearer picture of how the death penalty was utilized. The U.S. Supreme Court upheld McCleskey's conviction, and he was ultimately put to death. The Court may yet revisit the issue in future decisions.

The numerical count of whites and minorities on death rows across the United States comes under constant scrutiny. In the summer of 1996, there were 1,509 whites, 1,291 blacks, 235 Latinos (men and women), 49 Native Americans, 23 Asians, and 47 of unknown ethnic background. Drawing

**Prisoners Executed in the United States, Total and by Race, 1930–1996**

| *Year(s)* | *Total* | *White* | *percent*[1] | *Black* | *percent* |
|---|---|---|---|---|---|
| 1930–67[2] | 3,859 | 1,751 | 45.4 | 2,066 | 53.5 |
| 1977 | 1 | 1 | 100.0 | 0 | 0 |
| 1978 | 0 | 0 | 0 | 0 | 0 |
| 1979 | 2 | 2 | 100.0 | 0 | 0 |
| 1980 | 0 | 0 | 0 | 0 | 0 |
| 1981 | 1 | 1 | 100.0 | 0 | 0 |
| 1982 | 2 | 1 | 50.0 | 1 | 50.0 |
| 1983 | 5 | 4 | 80.0 | 1 | 20.0 |
| 1984 | 21 | 13 | 62.0 | 8 | 38.0 |
| 1985 | 18 | 11 | 61.0 | 7 | 39.0 |
| 1986 | 18 | 11 | 61.0 | 7 | 39.0 |
| 1987 | 25 | 13 | 52.0 | 12 | 48.0 |
| 1988 | 11 | 6 | 55.0 | 6 | 45.0 |
| 1989 | 16 | 7 | 44.0 | 8 | 50.0 |
| 1990 | 23 | 16 | 70.0 | 7 | 30.0 |
| 1991 | 14 | 5 | 36.0 | 8 | 57.0 |
| 1992 | 31 | 18 | 58.0 | 11 | 35.0 |
| 1993 | 38 | 20 | 53.0 | 13 | 34.0 |
| 1994 | 31 | 19 | 61.0 | 11 | 35.0 |
| 1995 | 56 | 30 | 54.0 | 22 | 39.0 |
| 1996 | 22 | 15 | 68.0 | 6 | 27.0 |
| 1977–96: | 335 | 187 | 56.0 | 128 | 38.0 |

Race of others executed, from 1977 through the end of 1996:[3]

Latino: 17 (5 percent)
Native American: 2 (1 percent)
Asian: 1 (0.5 percent)

1. As a percentage of total executions. Numbers have been rounded up to the nearest percentile, because others of other races were also executed. For instance, in 1989, one Latino was executed, accounting for 16 total executions. In 1993, there were four Latinos and one Native American executed.
2. The last year executions were conducted; moratorium lasted until 1977.
3. Numbers rounded to the nearest higher percentile, accounting for more than 100 percent total.

upon Justice Department statistics, the numbers of executed have been broken down by race, first during the period 1930–1967, and then from 1977 to the present.

**See also:** Lynching; *McCleskey v. Kemp;* NAACP Legal Defense and Educational Fund.
**References:** Graph statistics from Bureau of Justice Statistics, *Sourcebook of Criminal Justices Statistics, 1988* (Washington, D.C.: Government Printing Office, 1989) and *Death Row U.S.A.*, a publication of the NAACP Legal Defense and Education Fund, Summer 1996. Text of *McClesky v. Kemp,* 481 U.S. 279.

## Rais (or Retz) Gilles de Laval, Baron de (1404–1440)

French satanist and devil worshipper, also known as "Bluebeard," burned at the stake for his role in the murders of hundreds of children. Crime historian Jay Robert Nash says of him, "The complete transformation of Gilles de Rais from idealist and most able supporter of Joan of Arc to the slaughterhouse killer of 140 children is one of the most chilling stories in the annals of crime."

De Rais, or de Retz, was born in the village of Champtocé, France, sometime in the year 1404. A man of noble blood, he married Catherine de Thonars on 30 November 1420, thus becoming one of the wealthiest men in Europe. When he heard that Joan of Arc was assembling an army to drive the English from France, his devout Christianity impelled him to offer his support. Joan agreed, and with his riches Gilles funded her small but powerful force; he was largely responsible for her dramatic victory at Orléans. Complete victory, however, was denied Joan. She was betrayed to the English and burned at the stake.

Joan of Arc's death left de Rais disheartened and alone. He retreated to his magnificent chateau, known as Gilles de Rais a Tiffauges, in the Vendee region of France (still a tourist attraction today). There he lived lavishly and began to drink. In order to pay for his lifestyle of debauchery, he sold much of his land. Also at this time, he began to abduct small children, rape and sodomize them, and dispose of their bodies. Using brutal methods to torture them, de Rais killed at least 140 children, though many historians believe the number to be nearer to 800, making him perhaps the worst serial murderer in the history of the world.

Finally, de Rais was captured by agents of the Inquisition, and, under extreme torture (including the threat of excommunication, which to him was more intolerable than death), he confessed to his crimes. On 29 July 1440, the Bishop of Nantes published the results of the secret inquest, making public for the first time the charges that de Rais murdered at least 140 children and made pacts with demons. Further, he was accused of cannibalism, sorcery, and necrophilia. There is no record of general public reaction, although the parents of some of his victims demanded his immediate death. Quickly tried and condemned to death for his barbarous rampage, de Rais was taken on 26 October 1440 to a field in the city of Nantes and raised aloft on a scaffold. As he was being strangled slowly by a cord but kept alive, a bonfire was lit beneath him and he was burned to death. What little wealth remained in his name, as well as numerous manuscripts and expensive works of art, was seized by the Church; to this day his effects remain locked away in the vaults of the Church in Rome.

**See also:** Joan of Arc, Saint.
**References:** Bataille, Georges, *The Trial of Gilles de Rais: Documents Presented by Georges Bataille and Translated by Richard Robinson* (Los Angeles: Amok, 1991); Lewis, Dominic Bevan Wyndham, *The Soul of Marshal Gilles de Raiz, with Some Account of*

*His Life and Times, His Abominable Crimes, and His Expiation* (London: Eyre & Spottiswoode, 1952); Nash, Jay Robert, *Encyclopedia of World Crime,* 4 vols. (Wilmette, IL: CrimeBooks, Inc. 1990), 4:2530; Schechter, Harold, and David Everitt, *The A-Z Encyclopedia of Serial Killers* (New York: Pocket Books, 1996), 13; Winwar, Frances, *The Saint and the Devil: Joan of Arc and Gilles de Rais, a Biographical Study in Good and Evil* (New York: Harper, 1948).

## Raleigh, Sir Walter (1552? or 1554?–1618)

English military commander beheaded for his alleged role as an "agent of Spain" against the English crown. There is some dispute as to the proper spelling of Raleigh's name; many historians list him as "Ralegh." In fact, he himself used more than 40 different spellings in his lifetime, including "Rawleigh" and "Rawley."

He was born about 1552 or 1554 in the village of Hayes Barton, in Devonshire. He attended Oriel College in Oxford from 1566 to 1569, after which he became a soldier of fortune. His pairing with his famous half-brother, Sir Humphrey Gilbert, during Gilbert's expedition in 1678, led to his service for the Queen, Elizabeth I, in Ireland against the Dormond rebellion there. Raleigh gained the favor of the queen, and became a prized member of her royal court. (There is no evidence to support the story that he gained her favor by spreading his cloak over a muddy puddle so that her royal feet would not touch the dirty water.) Because of this favoritism, the queen would not allow him to go off on expeditions to bring riches back to England. In 1584, the queen knighted him Sir Walter Raleigh, and a year later he was appointed as lord warden of the Stannaries and vice-admiral of Devon and Cornwall. Under his command, a ship called the *Raleigh* sailed to the New World; there, a new colony was founded and named "Virginia" after the Virgin Queen. For this he was named the Lord of Virginia. The remains of this first settlement by Europeans in North America, which did not last long, are preserved at the Fort Raleigh National Historic Site.

During the war against Spain, Raleigh constructed a ship called the *Ark Royal,* and she led the outnumbered English forces to victory against the Armada. Once again, Raleigh had proven his worth to the crown. Yet when Elizabeth discovered that Raleigh was having an affair with one of her maids of honour, Bessie Throckmorton, she grew angry and had him imprisoned for a time in the Tower of London; he was released only after one of his exploring ships, the *Madre de Dios,* returned with treasure from a captured Spanish ship. He then married Throckmorton and retired to his estate.

In 1603, when Elizabeth died and was replaced by James I (James VI of Scotland), the new king accepted the word of his counselors (who disliked the adventurous Raleigh) that Raleigh was an "agent of Spain" involved in some sort of plot to overthrow him. The king had Raleigh thrown into the Tower of London. James commuted Raleigh's death sentence to life, and he was forced to live in the Tower. There, where Raleigh lived for 13 years with his family, he studied and wrote, completing his masterpiece, *History of the World,* which reached a total of five volumes but ended with the second Macedonian War in 130 B.C.E. The five volumes were published in 1614; in the preface to the first volume, Raleigh thanked those who conspired against him, forcing him to be interned in one place so that he had the time to compose such a work.

In 1616, two years after his *History* was first published, Raleigh was released, but not pardoned, by James, who wanted the former naval commander to go to Guiana (now in South America), then a Spanish colony, to find gold without drawing the Spanish into a war. Raleigh could not locate a mine, however, and instead destroyed a Spanish fort in the battle of Cadiz, then returned to England empty-handed. The Spanish branded him a warmonger and demanded either his head or war with England. James rearrested Raleigh, and reinstated the death sentence that he had once commuted. On 28 October 1618, Raleigh faced the headsman on Tower Hill just outside the Tower of London. Historians Jack H. Adamson and Harold F. Folland write of Raleigh's final moments:

> He ascended the scaffold and the crowd had their first view of him. In his younger days he had always overdressed; bravery of apparel was the principal sign of his "damnable pride." He had worn his hair curled like an Italian, with pearls in his ears and shoes, emeralds and rubies sewed into his coat and diamonds flashing from the fingers of both hands. Now the effect was stark. He was dressed in a black waistcoat and breeches and was wearing a black velvet gown and cap. The only relief from the sombre black was the ash-colour of his silk stockings. He had recently suffered a second stroke; there was still some paralysis in the left side that now caused a leg to drag, the same leg that had been torn by a Cadiz; even his slight deformity seemed heroic.
>
> . . . [After speaking to the crowd,] he turned to the hooded headsman who knelt to him and asked his forgiveness. Sir Walter placed both hands on the man's shoulders and forgave him, he said, with all his heart. Then quite unexpectedly he continued, "Show me thine axe." The headsman was confused; it was not proper to show a man the weapon that would kill him. But Ralegh had his reasons, and he repeated the request firmly. This time the headsman held out the axe and Ralegh put the edge of his finger against the blade. "This blade gives me no fear," he said. "It is sharp and fair medicine to cure me of all my diseases." There was a slight smile again, the superb poise, the immaculate manliness.
>
> . . . The executioner, as though Shakespeare had written his part, then took off his cloak and spread it for Sir Walter to kneel on. And everyone suddenly remembered that this was the way Ralegh had first won favour with the Queen. Then the headsman asked Sir Walter if he didn't wish to kneel facing the east. . . . Ralegh knelt, prayed briefly and said to the headsman, "When I stretch forth my hands despatch me." He then placed his head upon the block and stretched forth his hands. [The headsman hesitated.] Again Ralegh waited a moment, then spoke sharply, "What dost thou fear? Strike man, strike." . . . The axe fell, raised, and fell again. The body never moved, never twitched; only the lips kept moving in prayer.

Historian Geoffrey Abbott, who once worked as a Yeoman Warder at the Tower of London, wrote in 1991, "After the axe had done its work, it was reported by the historian Arthur Cayle that 'the head, after being shown on either side of the scaffold, was put into a leather bag, over which Sir Walter's gown was thrown, and the whole conveyed away in a mourning coach by Lady Raleigh.' It was preserved by her in a case during the twenty-nine years by which she survived her husband, and afterwards with less piety by their affectionate son Carew, with whom it was supposed to have been buried at West Horsely, Surrey." In fact, report biographers Norman and Betty Donaldson, the head vanished during Carew's lifetime and has never been recovered.

**References:** Abbott, Geoffrey, *Lords of the Scaffold: A History of the Executioner* (London: Robert Hale, 1991), 19; Adamson, Jack H., and Harold F. Folland, *The Shepherd of the Ocean: An Account of Sir Walter*

*Ralegh and His Times* (Boston: Gambit, 1969), 444–446; Donaldson, Norman, and Betty Donaldson, *How Did They Die?* (New York: St. Martin's Press, 1980), 309–310; Latham, Agnes M. C., "Sir Walter Ralegh" in Ian Scott-Kilvert, ed., *British Writers,* 7 vols. 2 suppl. (New York: Charles Scribner's Sons, 1979–1987), 1:145–59; Patrides, Constantinos Apostolos, "Ralegh, Sir Walter" in James Vinson, ed., *St. James Reference Guide to English Literature: The Beginnings and the Renaissance* (Chicago: St. James Press, 1985), 234–27; "Ralegh and His Circle Seen in Vivid Close Up," *The Times* (London), 5 April 1962, 13; Salgado, Gamini, "Christopher Marlowe" in Christopher Ricks, ed., *English Drama to 1710* (New York: Peter Bedrick Books, 1987), 108–109.

## Rantoul, Robert, Jr. (1805–1852)

American politician and reformist noted for his opposition to capital punishment in the first half of the nineteenth century.

Rantoul was born in Beverly, Massachusetts, on 13 August 1805, the son of Robert Rantoul, Sr. (1778–1858), a reformer in his own right, and his wife Joanna (nee Lovett) Rantoul. Both parents were liberal Unitarians and instilled in their son a reformist spirit. Robert Junior graduated from Harvard in 1826; he subsequently studied the law in Salem and was admitted to the state bar in 1827. He practiced in Gloucester, which he represented in the state legislature from 1834 to 1837, distinguishing himself as an advocate of the common man and of ending capital punishment and slavery. Historian Philip English Mackey calls him "America's most active and renowned opponent of capital punishment in the late 1830s."

In 1843 Rantoul was named collector of the port of Boston, and two years later was appointed U.S. District Attorney for that city. In 1851 he was elected to fill the U.S. Senate seat of the deceased Daniel Webster, while at the same time winning a U.S. House seat with the backing of the Free Soil Party. But Rantoul did not live long enough to make an imprint in the Congress. On 7 August 1852 he died suddenly of a heart attack. His death was a great shock to death penalty opponents and to the antislavery activists who had taken to his side in the last months of his life as he opposed the Fugitive Slave Act. In 1854, a memorial volume of his speeches and writings, accompanied by a memoir, was published under the editorship of Luther Hamilton.

**References:** Bulkley, Robert DeGroff, Jr., *Robert Rantoul, Jr., 1805–1852: Politics and Reform in Antebellum Massachusetts* (Ph.D. dissertation, Princeton University, 1971); Curti, Merle E., "Rantoul, Robert" in Dumas Malone et al., eds., *Dictionary of American Biography,* 10 vols. 10 suppl. (New York: Charles Scribner's Sons, 1930–1995), VIII:381–82; Hamilton, Luther, ed., *Memoirs, Speeches and Writings of Robert Rantoul, Jr.* (Boston: Jewett, 1854), 436–438; Mackey, Philip English, ed., *Voices against Death: American Opposition to Capital Punishment, 1787–1975* (New York: Burt Franklin, 1976), 34; Massachusetts State Legislature, House of Representatives, "Report Relating to Capital Punishment," House Report No. 32, 1836, 5–6.

## Razin, Stepan Timofeyevich (?–1671)

Russian Cossack revolutionary put to death for his rebellion against the Russian government.

Little is known of Razin's early life. He gained much of his reputation as the leader of a Cossack gang that plundered trade caravans and fisheries along the Volga River. Popularly known as Stenka Razin, he was pardoned by Czar Alexis in 1669. Soon, however, he returned to his old profession, and this time he attracted disenchanted elements of Russian society and raised a ragtag army to take over the Russian countryside. Like other rebellions that have occurred in Russia, this one was directed primarily against the wealthy landlords. But at the same time it was an expression of both religious and social dissatisfaction, uniting the religious sect known as the Old Believers with landless peasants eager to gain revenge against the nobility. Razin's army captured Astrakhan, which he made his capital, and soon the entire Volga and Don basins were under his control up to Nizhni Novgorod. Eventually, however, he was defeated by the Russian army and brought to Moscow, where he was publicly executed. In Russian ballads and songs he is extolled as hero, a sort of Russian Robin Hood, for his promises to deliver the peasants from the throes of poverty.

**Reference:** Florinsky, Michael T., ed., *McGraw-Hill Encyclopedia of Russia and the Soviet Union* (New York: McGraw-Hill Book Company, Inc., 1961), 470.

## Rehnquist, William Hubbs (1924– )

American jurist, Associate Justice (1971–86) and Chief Justice (1986– ) of the United States Supreme Court, and noted supporter of capital punishment.

Born in Milwaukee, Wisconsin, on 1 October 1924, Rehnquist was the son of William Benjamin Rehnquist and Margery (nee Peck) Rehnquist. He attended local Milwaukee schools, then entered Stanford University in California, where he received his bachelor's degree in 1948, after spending some time in the air force. In 1949 he was awarded a master's degree from Harvard University in political science, and, in 1952, a law degree from Stanford.

Rehnquist began his law career as a clerk for Robert H. Jackson, associate justice of the U.S. Supreme Court. He then joined a prestigious law firm in Phoenix, Arizona, and became immersed in the conservative politics of Arizona, a state that boasted Barry Goldwater, the 1964 Republican presidential candidate, as its senator. Richard Kleindienst, an aide to Richard Nixon, was a close friend of Rehnquist. After Kleindienst helped Nixon win the presidency in 1968, he took Rehnquist to Washington, where he was named as the assistant attorney general in charge of the Justice Department's Office of Legal Counsel. On 21 October 1971, following the resignations of Supreme Court Justices Hugo Black and John Marshall Harlan, Nixon named Rehnquist and Lewis F. Powell, Jr., to fill the vacant seats. Charged with blocking certain black and Hispanic citizens from voting in Phoenix, Rehnquist handled himself well in his Senate hearings, and on 10 December 1971 the Senate confirmed him 68–26.

On the Supreme Court, Rehnquist was a strong advocate for smaller government and an expanded death penalty. In case after case, he voted to uphold the state's right to carry out the death penalty: these cases include *Bell v. Ohio, Booth v. Maryland, Coker v. Georgia, Furman v. Georgia,* and *Gregg v. Georgia.* In 1986, Rehnquist was chosen by President Ronald Reagan to succeed retiring Chief Justice Warren Burger. Although the same charges of voter intimidation resurfaced, Rehnquist denied them, and he was confirmed.

In Rehnquist's first decade as chief justice, his Court has been one of the most conservative in history. Joined by fellow conservatives Antonin Scalia, Clarence Thomas, Sandra Day O'Connor, and Anthony Kennedy, Rehnquist has shaped the Court by narrowing the scope of its constitutional reach. And although he is nearly 75 years old, he remains one of the most prolific justices in our time. The Rehnquist Award for Judicial Excellence, bestowed on state judges, is handed out annually by the National Center for State Courts.

**See also:** Scalia, Antonin.

**References:** Garrow, David J., "The Rehnquist Reins," *New York Times Magazine,* 6 October 1996, 65–71; "More

Death, Less Justice," *New York Times,* 21 May 1990, A20; "Rehnquist, William H(ubbs)" in Charles Moritz, ed., *Current Biography 1972* (New York: H. W. Wilson, 1972), 359–362; "Rights Leaders Set to Oppose Poff for Court," *Washington Post,* 22 September 1971, A4.

## Reign of Terror (Revolutionary France)

See Danton, Georges Jacques; Desmoulins, Lucie Simplice Camille Benoist; Hébert, Jacques-René; Louis-August (Capet) XVI, King of France; Malesherbes, Chrétien Guillaume de Lamoignon de; Robespierre, Maximilien François Marie Isidore de

## Retribution and Deterrence, Theory of

In his spirited opinion that reflected the will of the majority in the landmark American death-penalty decision *Gregg v. Georgia* (428 U.S. 153, at 183, 49 L.Ed. 2d 859, 96 S.Ct. 2909 [1976]), Justice Potter Stewart wrote, "The death penalty is said to serve two principal social purposes: retribution and deterrence of capital crimes by prospective offenders. In part, capital punishment is an expression of society's moral outrage at particularly offensive conduct. This function may be unappealing to many, but it is essential in an ordered society that asks its citizens to rely on legal processes rather than self-help to vindicate their wrongs."

In the 1970s, 1980s, and 1990s, while the rest of the world came to see the usage of capital punishment as cruel and inhuman, the United States saw it both as a tool of punishment and as a reflection of the will of the people to impose some semblance of retribution on the condemned while at the same time establishing a system of deterrence for future criminals. For many who oppose the death penalty, the opinion is that society does not have the right to visit retribution on convicts in the form of capital punishment, and furthermore that the death penalty is in no way a deterrent to further crime.

Justice Stewart added in his opinion from *Gregg,* "The instinct for retribution is part of the nature of man, and channeling that instinct in the administration of criminal justice serves an important purpose in promoting the stability of a society governed by law. When people begin to believe that organized society is unwilling or unable to impose upon criminal offenders the punishment they 'deserve,' then there are sown the seeds of anarchy—of self-help, vigilante justice, and lynch law." In part quoting historian Thorstein Sellin, Justice William Brennan penned in his concurring opinion in *Furman v. Georgia* (1972),

> The country has debated whether a society for which the dignity of the individual is the supreme value can, without a fundamental inconsistency, follow the practice of deliberately putting some of its members to death. In the United States, as in other nations of the western world, "the struggle about this punishment has been one between ancient and deeply rooted beliefs in retribution, atonement or vengeance on the one hand, beliefs in the personal value and dignity of the common man that were born of the democratic movement of the eighteenth century, as well as beliefs in the scientific approach to an understanding of the motive forces of human conduct, which are the result of the growth of the sciences of behavior during the nineteenth and twentieth centuries." It is this essentially moral conflict that forms the backdrop for the past changes in and the present operation of our system of imposing death as a punishment for crime.

Professor Hans Zeisel of the University of Chicago wrote in 1976, "All studies that explore the possible deterrent effect of capital punishment are efforts to simulate the conditions of what is conceded to be an impossible controlled experiment. . . . In the end one must remain skeptical as to the power of evidence to change ancient beliefs and sentiments."

**References:** Brennan opinion in *Furman v. Georgia,* 408 U.S. 238, at 296, 33 L.Ed. 2d 346, 92 S.Ct. 2726 (1972); Gardner, Romaine L., "Capital Punishment: The Philosophers and the Court," *Syracuse Law Review,* 24 (1978), 1177; Stewart majority opinion in *Gregg v. Georgia,* 428 U.S. 153, at 183, 49 L.Ed. 2d 859, 96 S.Ct. 2909 (1976); Zeisel, Hans, "The Deterrent Effect of the Death Penalty: Facts v. Faith," *Supreme Court Review,* 67 (1976), 317–43.

## Ribbentrop, Joachim von

See Nuremberg War Crimes Defendants

## *Roberts (Stanislaus) v. Louisiana* (428 U.S. 325, 49 L.Ed. 2d 974, 96 S.Ct. 3001 [1976])

U.S. Supreme Court decision that held that mandatory death sentences for first degree murder convictions were a violation of the cruel and unusual punishment doctrine enunciated under the Eighth and Fourteenth Amendments to the U.S. Constitution.

Stanislaus Roberts was indicted, convicted, and sentenced to death in Lake Charles, Louisiana, for the murder of a gas station attendant. Roberts's three accomplices turned state's evidence against him and testified for the prosecution. The judge sentenced Roberts to death on the basis of a 1973 state statute that ordered a mandatory death sentence for a conviction of first degree murder. The Supreme Court of Louisiana affirmed the verdict and the sentence; however, the U.S. Supreme Court decided to hear the issues raised in the case, and arguments were presented on 30 and 31 March 1976.

On 2 July, the Court held 5–4 (Chief Justice Warren Burger was joined in dissent by Justices Byron White, Harry Blackmun, and William H. Rehnquist) that the state scheme mandating a death sentence for first degree murder was unconstitutional. Writing for the majority, Justice John Paul Stevens found that such mandatory sentences "were unconstitutional as failing to focus on the circumstances of the particular offense and the character and propensities of the offender." Justice Stevens explained:

> The futility of attempting to solve the problems of mandatory death penalty statutes by narrowing the scope of the capital offense stems from our society's rejection of the belief that "every offense in a like legal category calls for an identical punishment without regard to the past life and habits of a particular offender." . . . As the dissenting justices in Furman [*Furman v. Georgia*] noted, the nineteenth century movement away from mandatory death sentences was rooted in the recognition that "individual culpability is not always measured by the category of the crime committed." . . . Louisiana's mandatory death sentence law employs a procedure that was rejected by that State's legislature 130 years ago [in 1846] and that subsequently has been renounced by legislatures and juries in every jurisdiction in this Nation. . . . The Eighth Amendment, which draws much of its meaning from "the evolving standards of decency that mark the progress of a maturing society," simply cannot tolerate the reintroduction of a practice so thoroughly discredited. Accordingly, we find that the death sentence imposed upon the petitioner under Louisiana's mandatory death sentence statute violates the Eighth and Fourteenth Amendments and must be set aside.

## Robespierre, Maximilien François Marie Isidore de (1758–1794)

French revolutionary, leader of the Committee of Public Safety, and the last of the major revolutionaries to be put to death by beheading.

Robespierre was born in Arras, France, on 6 May 1758, the son of an attorney. He was raised by his grandfather when orphaned at an early age and attended the Collège Louis-le-Grand in Paris. Later, he studied the law and was admitted to practice. In 1781 he returned to his hometown, where he became a prominent lawyer known for his integrity. Robespierre read voraciously, particularly the writings of Jean Jacques Rousseau, the French philosopher who dreamed of the ideal society. He later applied these teaching in his grab for power during the French Revolution. An essay that he wrote at this time carried the ominous title—"Memoire su les peines infamantes" (Commentary on Degrading Punishments).

When the monarchy of King Louis XVI was overthrown in 1789, Robespierre stepped forward to fill the vacuum, along with such notable leaders as Georges Jacques Danton, Jean-Paul Marat, Camille Desmoulins, Jacques-René Hébert, and others. He was selected speaker of the National Assembly, speaking first on 18 May 1789. The king attempted to flee France, but he was captured; Robespierre helped the prosecution attain a guilty verdict, and the king was beheaded.

In 1793, Robespierre became the head of the radical Committee of Public Safety, which helped institute the so-called Reign of Terror. At first, Robespierre seemed to be the perfect reformer: he embraced the principles embodied in the Declaration of the Rights of Man and of the Citizen, adopted in 1791, which called for the vote for all persons, the right to petition the government for a redress of grievances, legislative reform, and rights for French minorities. Yet as the Terror grew and thousands of people were beheaded by "Madame Guillotine," Robespierre became a recluse, turning against the men he had once conspired with to bring down a king. He ordered the execution of Hébert and, to consolidate power, had Danton and Desmoulins arrested for plotting against the government. At their trial, which became a circus, they demanded that Robespierre be forced to defend his crimes against the people. In the end, the men were convicted, and on 5 April 1794 Danton and Desmoulins went to their deaths along with 14 others.

Robespierre's aloof manner had bought him numerous enemies, and the Terror's widespread impact on French society lost him the confidence of the French people. On 26 July 1794, he gave a speech at the assembly but received a cold, rude reception where before he had been embraced. As soon as he left, the members voted to arrest the leader on charges of betraying the revolution. When the guards tried to break down his door to apprehend him, Robespierre took out a pistol and shot himself, but he merely wounded himself in the jaw. He was carried, bloodied, to trial, where he was found guilty and sentenced to be beheaded on the same machine to which he had sent some 30,000 people to their deaths. On 28 July 1794, he was taken to the Place de la Concorde along with 100 others and beheaded.

**See also:** Danton, Georges Jacques.

**References:** Bienvenu, Richard, *The Ninth of Thermidor: The Fall of Robespierre* (New York: Oxford University Press, 1968); Cleugh, A., *A Complete History of the Invasions of England, including the most memorable battles and sea-fights from Julius Caesar, down to the French landing in Wales in 1796: the calamities of France, being a catalogue of French cruelties, with a complete abstract from [Abbé Augustin] Barruel's History of the French Clergy, detailing the refined system of murder pursued by the notorious Jourdan, Carrier, Marrat, General Duquesnoy, and Robespierre; the ejectment of the priesthood, and total abolition of religion and humanity in France* (London: Printed by J. Skirven for A. Cleugh, 1801); Coleridge, Samuel Taylor, *The Fall of Robespierre* (Cambridge, England: W. H. Lunn and J. and J. Merrill, 1794; reprint, Oxford, England: Wood Stock Books, 1991); Morton, John Bingham, *The Bastille Falls, and Other Studies of the French Revolution* (London: Longmans, Green, 1936); Nash, Jay Robert, *Encyclopedia of World Crime,* 4 vols. (Wilmette, IL: CrimeBooks, Inc., 1990), 3:2595; O'Brien, James Bronterre, *The Life and Character of Maximilen Robespierre. Proving by Facts and Arguments, that that much-calumniated Person was one of the Greatest Men, and one of the Purest and Most Enlightened Reformers, that ever existed in the world: also, containing Robespierre's Principal Discourses, Addresses, Reports, and Projects of Law, &c., in the National Assembly, National Convention, Commune of Paris, and the Popular Societies; with the author's reflections on the principles events and leading men of the French Revolution, etc., etc., etc.* (London: Printed by J. Watson, 1837?); Thompson, James Matthew, *Leaders of the French Revolution* (Oxford, England: Blackwell, 1929).

## *Romano v. Oklahoma* (512 U.S. 1, 114 S. Ct. 2004, 129 L. Ed. 2d 1 [1994])

Supreme Court decision that held that "the admission of evidence regarding" a defendant's "prior death sentence did not amount to constitutional error." John Joseph Romano killed two people, one in 1985 and another in 1986. He was tried first for the second murder, convicted, and sentenced to death. He was then tried and convicted for the first murder. During the sentencing phase of the second trial, the state introduced the death sentence obtained during the first trial as an aggravating factor in determining a second death sentence. Romano's attorneys objected to the introduction, but it was allowed, and Romano was sentenced to death a second time. Romano then appealed on the grounds that "the admission of evidence regarding his prior death sentence undermined the . . . jury's sense of responsibility for determining the appropriateness of the death penalty, in violation of the Eighth and Fourteenth Amendments." The Oklahoma Court of Criminal Appeals then held that while "the evidence of petitioner's prior death sentence was irrelevant to determining the appropriateness of the second death sentence," the admission did not violate the defendant's rights under the Eighth or Fourteenth Amendments. Romano then sued to the U.S. Supreme Court, which agreed to hear the case. Arguments were heard on 22 March 1994.

On 13 June 1994, Chief Justice William H. Rehnquist represented a 5–4 court (Justices Harry Blackmun, Ruth Bader Ginsburg, John Paul Stevens, and David Souter dissented) in holding that the admission was not a violation of Romano's Eighth and Fourteenth Amendment rights. Rehnquist wrote, "Even assuming that the jury disregarded the trial court's instructions and allowed the evidence of petitioner's prior death sentence to influence its decision, it is impossible to know how this evidence might have affected the jury. It seems equally plausible that the evidence could have made the jurors more inclined to impose a death sentence, or it could have made them less inclined to do so. Either conclusion necessarily rests upon one's intuition. To hold on the basis of this record that the admission of evidence relating to petitioner's sentence in [one] case rendered petitioner's sentencing proceeding for the [second] murder fundamentally unfair would thus be an exercise in speculation, rather than reasoned judgment."

## Rosenberg, Alfred

See Nuremberg War Crimes Defendants.

## Rosenberg, Julius (1918–1953), and Ethel Greenglass Rosenberg (1915–1953)

American spies executed at the height of the Cold War for conspiring to steal the secrets of the American atomic bomb and send them to the Soviet Union.

Both Ethel and Julius, a weak-eyed man who suffered from poor health from the start of his life, were born to poor Jewish parents on New York's Lower East Side; at an early age, they were converted to radicalism by the Great Depression, when the ability of capitalism to solve the problems of common people came into question. Julius, who attended the City College of New York, earned an electrical engineering degree in 1939. By then, he was an active member of the Communist party and, at some point, convinced his wife, whom he met and married in 1935, to become a member. Starting in 1940, when he began working for the U.S. Army Signal Corps, Julius used his technical skills to help the Soviet Union by stealing small pieces of military information that came before him and sending them on to the Russians. Eventually, many historians surmise, the Rosenbergs had a contact in New York who reported directly to the Soviets; also, and more importantly, they began to assemble a cell of sympathizers around them, directly answerable to their Soviet contacts, to aid their effort.

Among the members of the Rosenberg cell were Ethel's younger brother, David Greenglass, and his wife, Ruth. David Greenglass, a sergeant in the U.S. Army, was sent just after the start of World War II to Los Alamos, New Mexico, as a guard on the Manhattan Project to build an atomic bomb. Julius, instructed by his superiors in Moscow to obtain vital information on the project, directed his brother-in-law to steal vital documents on what was the proximity fuse to set off an atomic weapon. The information was sent to the Soviets using several drop locations in New York and Connecticut.

By the late 1940s, however, through the use of cable codes that had been broken in the now-famous "Venona" program, the U.S. government was sure of the spy ring's existence. The Soviets used nicknames in their cables; however, in one slip, a cable dated 27 November 1944 and decoded by Venona identified the leader of the New York ring as "Liberal," and Liberal's wife as "Surname that of her husband, first name ETHEL, 29 years old. Married five years. Finished secondary school."

In 1950, former Communist party member Elizabeth Bentley, who had turned against her friends, told a grand jury in New York that a spy named Harry Gold had once told her that he had received information on the atomic bomb from a soldier at Los Alamos. Arrested, Gold confessed that the soldier was Greenglass; Greenglass then turned in his brother-in-law, Julius, and later his own sister, in exchange for leniency for his wife. The FBI arrested two of Rosenberg's college classmates, Max Elitcher and Morton Sobell, as members of the ring; in a deal, Elitcher confessed that Rosenberg was the head of the spy cell and that Greenglass, Gold, and Sobell were active members.

The trial of the ring members started in New York on 6 March 1951 and ended on 29 March. Ethel's brother accused the Rosenbergs of aiding in the effort to type up handwritten notes and of conspiring during wartime to aid the Soviet Union. But Ethel and Julius Rosenberg, on taking the stand, denied being involved at all and refused to answer any questions dealing with their Communist affiliations. On 29 March the jury convicted all of the defendants; a week later, on 5 April, Judge Irving H. Saypol accused the couple of collaborating in helping the Soviets kill thousands of Americans then at war in Korea and sentenced them to death.

For the next two and a half years, the couple struggled to avoid the electric chair by telling a detailed story of their innocence. In June 1953, U.S. Supreme Court Justice William O. Douglas offered a stay on the proposition that the couple had been sentenced under a law enacted in 1946—which decreed a jury recommendation of death—over a 1917 statute that allowed sentencing by the judge. In a landmark hearing before the full Court after its term had expired, lawyers for the couple and the government argued whether acts that were committed during World War II but not discovered until after the passage of the 1946 act fell under it or the 1917 law; in the end, the Court held that since the acts occurred under the 1917 act, it was proper for the judge alone to sentence them, and Douglas's stay was vacated. A final appeal for clemency to President Dwight Eisenhower was ignored, and the Rosenbergs were put to death just after sundown on 19 June 1953.

According to eyewitnesses, Julius's last words, as he was led to the chair, were, "We are innocent. That is the whole truth. To forsake this truth is to pay too high a price even for the priceless gift of life. For life thus purchased we could not live out in dignity." After his body was removed from the death chamber, Ethel was brought in with the assistance of a matron. Her last words were, "We are the first victims of American fascism!" After death, their bodies were taken for burial to Pinelawn Cemetery in Farmingdale, New York.

Since the Rosenbergs' death, the group once known as the National Committee to Secure Justice in the Rosenberg Case has worked tirelessly to clear the names of the couple, with little success. Their sole accomplishment—having the government release once classified documents—has made the Rosenbergs appear even guiltier. The so-called Venona cables, recently decoded secret messages from the Soviets to a ring of spies in the New York area, were released in July 1995 and show Julius Rosenberg first as agent "Antenna," then later as agent "Liberal." Liberal's wife is also cited, showing the depth of Ethel's involvement in the spy ring. The cable alleges that Liberal was paid $4,000 for his activities in 1944.

**References:** "The Atom Spies" in *Crime and Punishment: The Illustrated Crime Encyclopedia,* 28 vols. (Westport, CT: H. S. Stuttman, 1994), 21:2569–2576; Garber, Marjorie, and Rebecca L. Walkowitz, eds., *Secret Agents: The Rosenberg Case, McCarthyism, and Fifties America* (New York: Routledge, 1995); Neville, John, *The Press, the Rosenbergs, and the Cold War* (Westport, CT: Praeger, 1995); O'Toole, George J. A., *The Encyclopedia of American Intelligence and Espionage from the Revolutionary War to the Present* (New York: Facts on File, 1988), 395–396; Ryan, Bernard, Jr., "Trial of Julius and Ethel Rosenberg and Morton Sobell: 1951" in Edward W. Knappman, ed., *Great American Trials* (Detroit: Visible Ink Press, 1994), 452–456; Schneir, Walter, and Miriam Schneir, "Rosenberg Case" in Mari Jo Buhle, Paul Buhle and Dan Georgakas, eds., *Encyclopedia of the American Left* (New York: Garland, 1990), 658–661. Much of the material on the earlier years of the Rosenbergs comes from Nizer, Louis, *The Implosion Conspiracy* (Greenwich, CT: Fawcett,1973).

## Royal Commission Inquiry on Capital Punishment

In 1949 King George VI of England appointed a commission headed by Sir Ernest Arthur Gowers to investigate whether Great Britain should retain the death penalty as a tool of punishment. From their appointment in 1949 until 1953, the commission members heard from 118 witnesses, visited prisons, and received research papers from other nations, including the United States. For a time, the commission members debated ending hanging, an increasingly unpopular form of capital punishment, by substituting lethal injection, but anti–death penalty advocates and the British medical community defeated that idea. Although the commission's final report, released in 1953, did not mention the word "abolition," many persons agreed that that was the direction the commission wanted the nation to go.

In this excerpt from the final report, the commission members discussed capital punishment as retribution:

> Discussion of the principle of *retribution* is apt to be confused because the word is not always used in the same sense. Sometimes it is intended to mean vengeance, sometimes reprobation. In the first sense the idea is that of satisfaction by the State of a wronged individual's desire to be avenged; in the second it is that of the State's marking its disapproval of the breaking of its laws by a punishment proportionate to the gravity of the offence. . . .
>
> There is no longer in our regard of the criminal law any recognition of such primitive concepts as atonement or retribution. We have, over the years, fortunately succeeded to a very large extent, if not entirely, in relegating the purely punitive aspect of our criminal law to the background.
>
> . . . But in another sense retribution must always be an essential element in any form of punishment; punishment presupposes an offence and the measure of the punishment must not be greater than the offence deserves. Moreover, we think it must be recognised that there is a strong and widespread demand for retribution in the sense of reprobation—not always unmixed in the popular mind with that of atonement and expiation. . . . The ultimate justification of any punishment is not that it is a deterrent, but that it is the emphatic denunciation by the community of a crime; and from this point of view, there are some murders which, in the present state of public opinion, demand the most emphatic denunciation of all, namely the death penalty.
>
> [T]he law cannot ignore the public demand for retribution which heinous crimes undoubtedly provoke; it would be generally agreed that, though reform of the criminal law ought sometimes to give a lead to public opinion, it is dangerous to move too far in advance of it.

In 1965, twelve years after the report was released, Great Britain abolished capital punishment.

**References:** "Final Report of the Royal Commission on Capital Punishment, 1949–1953" (London: Her Majesty's Stationary Office, 1953), 17–18. Refer also to Christoph, James Bernard, *Capital Punishment and British Politics: The British Movement to Abolish the Death Penalty, 1945–57* (Chicago: University of Chicago Press, 1962).

## Rush, Benjamin (1745–1813)

American physician, scientist, educator, and social reformer noted for his opposition in the eighteenth century to capital punishment.

Born in the village of Byberry, near Philadelphia, on 24 December 1745, Rush was the son of John Rush, a farmer, and Susanna Hall (nee Harvey) Rush. He attended the College of New Jersey (now Princeton University) and graduated in 1760, then served as an apprentice to Dr. John Shippen, a Philadelphia physician. From 1766 to 1768 he attended Edinburgh University in Scotland, where he was awarded an M.D. degree. After a year of study in London, he returned to his native state and was accepted as the first professor of chemistry at the College of Philadelphia. He later served as a professor of medicine and clinical practice at the University of Pennsylvania. In this period he became one of the nation's best known authorities on disease and physical health. Besides numerous medical articles, Rush wrote pamphlets denouncing slavery and calling for its abolition. His marriage to Julia Stockton of New Jersey led to a dynasty of sorts; his father-in-law, Richard Stockton, was, with Rush, a member of the Continental Congress and likewise one of the signers of the Declaration of Independence.

In the field of prison reform and opposition to capital punishment, Rush's was one of the leading voices of the late eighteenth century. His spirited advocacy led to a 1794 law in Pennsylvania abolishing the death penalty for all crimes except first-degree murder. He also wrote several works on the subject. In his 1787 work, *An Enquiry into the Effects of Public Punishments upon Criminals and upon Society,* Rush wrote: "I have said nothing upon the manner of inflicting death as a punishment for crimes, because I consider it as an improper punishment for *any* crime. Even murder itself is propagated by the punishment of death for murder."

John Adams wrote of Rush in a letter to Thomas Jefferson that he knew of "no Character living or dead, who has done more real good in America." Dr. Benjamin Rush died in Philadelphia on 19 April 1813 at the age of 67.

**References:** Hawke, David Freeman, *Benjamin Rush: Revolutionary Gadfly* (Indianapolis, IN: Bobbs-Merrill, 1971); Masur, Louis P., "Benjamin Rush" in Emory Elliott, ed., *American Writers of the Early Republic* (Detroit: Bruccoli Clark, 1985), 259–265; Rush, Benjamin, *Considerations on the Injustice and Impolicy of Punishing Murder by Death. Extracted from the American Museum. With Additions* (Philadelphia: Matthew Carey, 1792); ———, *An Enquiry into the Effects of Public Punishments Upon Criminals and Upon Society. Read in the Society for Promoting Political Enquiries, Convened at the House of His Excellency Benjamin Franklin, Esquire, in Philadelphia, March 9th, 1787* (Philadelphia: Printed by Joseph James, 1787), 15–16; ———, *Essays, Literary, Moral and Philosophical* (Philadelphia: Printed by Thomas & Samuel F. Bradford, 1798; reprint, Philadelphia: Printed by Thomas and William Bradford, 1806). ———; *On the Punishment of Murder by Death* (London: Sold by J. Johnson and J. Phillips, 1793).

## Ryan, Ronald Joseph (1925–1967)

Australian murderer hanged in the D Division of Melbourne's Pentridge Prison on 3 February 1967 for killing a prison guard, noted as being the last execution in Australia before a moratorium was imposed.

What little is known of Ryan's life comes from Australian author Barry Dickins, who has taken up Ryan's cause. Born in the village of Mitcham, in Victoria, Australia, in 1925, Ryan was the product of two drunken parents and soon became a thief. In a piece called "Front the Hangman," Ryan himself wrote, "I used to call in and tell my Mobil superiors [at his job for Mobil Oil] I was crook. And I was crook. I was addicted to horseracing. And forging cheques. I was called the Rembrandt of Warrnambool Racetrack, at the height of my fame." After serving a number of prison terms for petty offenses (and constantly watched to prevent his escape), he was finally convicted in 1964 of a series of robberies and sentenced to 14 years at hard labor in prison.

On 19 December 1965, Ryan and fellow inmate Peter Walker, 24 years old, who himself was serving a 13-year sentence, used knotted towels and a handmade hook to escape over the walls of Melbourne's Pentridge Prison. After overpowering a warder (guard) and taking his rifle, they stole a car and made their getaway. Later, on Sydney Road, Warder George Hodson tried to capture the two men. According to witnesses, the escaped convict bent down, aimed at Hodson, and fired between one and three shots, striking Hodson and killing him instantly. Ryan and Walker were eventually apprehended on 5 January 1966, but Ryan alone was charged with murder. On 3 March 1966, after a two-week trial in which 17 independent witnesses testified that he shot Hodson in cold blood, Ryan was found guilty of the killing of the warder and sentenced by the judge to death.

For the next 10 months, a legal battle raged unlike any seen in Australia since. In June the Court of Appeals upheld Ryan's conviction and sentence; the Australia Supreme Court refused in November to hear Ryan's appeal. Appeals went out to Queen Elizabeth of England, but she did not intervene. Finally, Sir Henry Bolte, the Premier of Victoria state, decided against clemency and allowed the execution to proceed. A national debate raged: Should Ryan be put to death? Regardless of public opinion, however, Bolte refused to budge and set the date of execution for 3 February 1967. At 8 A.M. on that morning, Ryan walked to the gallows in Pentridge and was put to death. The *Australian,* the newspaper of Canberra, the Australian Capital Territory, wrote, "He died silently. His face [was] white but impassive. His thin lips [were clasped] together, but not clenched. . . . The trap door was opened efficiently at eight."

According to the *Herald* of Melbourne, 31 July 1985 edition, Ryan's last words were, "God bless you. Whatever you do, do it quickly." (Peter Walker was released from prison in 1985 after serving two terms for manslaughter, a crime committed during the escape for which Ryan was not charged.) Soon after Ryan's execution, public opinion swung against the practice, and no one has been put to death in Australia since.

Ryan's case has received new attention in the years since his death; one newspaper interviewed a warder who admitted that he may have shot Hodson by accident. In an interview in 1986 in the Melbourne *Sun,* Sister Margaret Kingston, a friend of the Ryan family, quoted Ryan in one of his last interviews as saying, "I shot to wing; I didn't shoot to kill." Barry Dickins's play, *Remembering Ronald Ryan,* premiered at Melbourne's Playbox Theatre Company in 1994 and in 1995 was awarded the Louis Esson Prize for Drama by Victorian Premier's Literary Awards selection committee.

**References:** Bates, Nicholas, et al., *Ronald Ryan: A Case Study in Criminal Proceedings* (Fitzroy, Victoria, Australia: VCTA Publishing, 1976); "Death of Ronald Ryan," *Australian* (Canberra, Australian Capital Territory), 4 February 1967, 1; Dickins, Barry, *Guts and Pity: The Hanging That Ended Capital Punishment in Australia* (Sydney, New South Wales: Currency Press, 1996), 70–71; "Hanging Law Stays, Says Bolte; Ryan is Hanged," *Melbourne Herald,* 3 February 1967, 1.

## Sacco, Nicola (1891–1927), and Bartolomeo Vanzetti (1888–1927)

Italian-American anarchists executed for their role in the murder of a paymaster and a bank guard in 1920. The period of U.S. history during which the crime occurred was known as the "Red Terror"—a period of relentless attacks by the U.S. government, including Attorney General A. Mitchell Palmer, on all those labeled "Reds" and "Anarchists."

On 15 April 1920, two men, Frederick A. Parmenter, the paymaster, and Alessandro Berardelli, the guard, employed by a shoe factory in South Braintree, Massachusetts, were taking that day's payroll to the local bank when they were gunned down by several men in a car and robbed of $16,000. Three weeks later, on 5 May, two men answering the description of two of the suspects were arrested; one, Nicola Sacco, who had been employed at a shoe factory in nearby Medford for 11 years (excluding a year in which he went to Mexico to avoid the draft during World War I), was attempting to pick up from the garage a car that looked like the one used in the robbery. The other suspect, Bartolomeo Vanzetti, the older of the two, was a fish peddler. Both men had emigrated to the United States in 1908 and had been caught up in anarchist activities.

Their trial opened in Dedham on 31 May 1921 and ended on 14 July. The case of the Commonwealth of Massachusetts rested on two pieces of evidence: that the men were arrested trying to claim from a garage an automobile that witnesses placed at the scene of the crime, and that a pistol found on Sacco when he was arrested matched that used to kill the two men. Some contradictory evidence from witnesses and an alleged alibi for Vanzetti failed to convince the jury, which returned a verdict of guilty against the two men. The judge, Webster Thayer, hated anarchists with a particular passion and sentenced the two men to death in the electric chair.

For the next six years, the case of Sacco and Vanzetti became a cause célèbre around the world, rallying socialists and anarchists in a futile effort to save their lives. Vain attempts to appeal the convictions were denied by higher courts. In 1925, a two-bit hoodlum, Celestine Madeiros, already on death row for another murder, claimed that he was the triggerman at the South Braintree holdup (done, according to him, by a gang from Providence, Rhode Island) and that Sacco and Vanzetti were completely innocent. Many holes in his story made Sacco and Vanzetti's chances for clemency all the more remote.

Responding to the cries of injustice and political persecution, Massachusetts governor Alvan Tufts Fuller asked a commission, headed by Harvard president Abbott Lawrence Lowell, and including Samuel Wesley Stratton, the president of the Massachusetts Institute of Technology, and Robert Grant, a former judge, to investigate the claims and decide whether the evidence justified the guilty verdict and sentence of death. On 3 August 1927, Governor Fuller announced that the Lowell Committee had found the two men to have received a fair trial, that their guilt was evident, and that the sentence of death was fair. Several stays followed, but on 23 August 1927, Sacco and Vanzetti and, ironically, Madeiros, sat down in the electric chair. Madeiros went first, declaring "in a stupor" that Sacco and Vanzetti were entirely innocent of the crime. Following him, Sacco and then Vanzetti calmly faced the executioner. Their attorney, William G. Thompson, having visited them prior to the executions, told the newspapers that Vanzetti stated: "No lawyer who has ever been concerned in my defense has any right to say or hint that I, in any form of words whatever, said anything which could possibly be interpreted as an admission of any guilt whatever."

On 23 August 1987, the fiftieth anniversary of the executions, Massachusetts governor Michael S. Dukakis signed unconditional pardons for the two men.

**See also:** Musmanno, Michael Angelo.
**References:** Ehrman, Herbert B., *The Case That Will Not Die: Commonwealth v. Sacco and Vanzetti* (Boston: Little, Brown, 1964); "Madeiros, Sacco, Vanzetti Died in Chair This Morning," *Boston Daily Globe,* 23 August 1927, 1; Musmanno, Michael A., *Verdict! The Adventures of the Young Lawyer in the Brown Suit* (Garden City, New York: Doubleday, 1958), 267–283; Ryan, Bernard, Jr., "Sacco-Vanzetti Trial: 1923" in Edward W. Knappman, ed., *Great American Trials* (Detroit: Visible Ink Press, 1994), 289–293; "Sacco and Vanzetti: The Italian Anarchist Background" in Paul Avrich, *Anarchist Portraits* (Princeton, NJ: Princeton University Press, 1988), 162–175; *The Sacco-Vanzetti Case: Transcript of the Record of the Trial of Nicola Sacco and Bartolomeo Vanzetti in the Courts of Massachusetts and Subsequent Proceedings, 1920–7,* 4 vols. (New York: Henry Holt, 1928).

## Salem Witch Trials

Series of prosecutions against supposed witches in the English colonies of America that took place during the late seventeenth century and resulted in the deaths of 20 people, including one who was pressed to death.

The first work to detail witchery was Jacob Sprenger's *Malleus Maleficarum* (Hammer of Evildoers), a 1489 work. Sprenger, a German Dominican friar, succeeded in spreading the word about witchcraft to such an extent that the manuscript was used for more than 200 years as a "manual" to identify and punish untold numbers of people as witches. In Cologne, Germany, from 1625 to 1636, numerous women were accused of being witches and burned at the stake—and their families were charged the expense of the trial and execution. After Pope Urban VIII sent various dignitaries to Cologne to instill education and call for a termination to the executions in 1636, they largely ended, although the last witch was burned in Cologne as late as 1655.

Yet the most famous incident of witchcraft phobia occurred in Salem, Massachusetts. Starting in 1692, a total of 19 people were executed for corrupting the youth of village with witchcraft. Governor William Stoughton appointed a commission, under the direction of the Reverend Samuel Parris, to investigate charges against several well-known members of the Salem community. Among these were Sarah Bishop, Rebecca Nurse, Sarah Good, and Giles Corey. One Sarah Osborne, also accused, was jailed but died there. The judge overseeing the trials was Thomas Newton (1660–1721), whom historians have accused of presiding in a "morally criminal" manner.

The first person tried, Bridget Bishop, was accused by her husband; her sentence, death by hanging, was carried out on Salem's Gallows Hill (also called Witch's Hill) on 10 June 1692. Other women followed. Finally, the first man, Giles Corey, who had accused his own wife, fell under suspicion himself. In front of the court, he refused to plead or answer the charges, claiming that he was "a poor man." Because Salem was still under English colonial law, Corey was forced to suffer *peine forte et dure* ("duration of punishment"), in which large stones were placed on his chest until his ribs cracked or he spoke.

In 1711, the families of those put to death were awarded monies by the Commonwealth for their suffering. On the 300th anniversary of the trials in 1992, a monument was erected on Gallows Hill in Salem with the names of those put to death.

**References:** DiCanio, Teddi, "Salem Witchcraft Trials: 1692" in Edward W. Knappman, ed., *Great American Trials* (Detroit: Visible Ink Press, 1994), 18–22; Nash, Jay Robert, *Encyclopedia of World Crime,* 4 vols. (Wilmette, IL: CrimeBooks, Inc. 1990), 2:754; Weatherford, Doris, *American Women's History* (New York: Prentice Hall General Reference, 1994), 304–305; "Witch-Hunt" in *Crime and Punishment: The Illustrated Crime Encyclopedia,* 28 vols. (Westport, CT: H. S. Stuttman, 1994), 22:2709–2716.

## Saro-Wiwa, Kenule Beeson (1941–1995)

Ogoni Nigerian human rights and environmental activist executed, despite worldwide appeals, for conspiring to murder a rival.

Born on 10 October 1941, in Bori, Rivers State, Nigeria, Saro-Wiwa was the son of J. B. Saro and Widu Wiwa, and took both their names. Educated at the University of Ibadan (Nigeria's premier school of higher learning), he became a teacher at Government College in Umuahia in southeastern Nigeria when only 21, and later taught at Stella Maris College in Part Harcourt, Nigeria, and at the University of Lagos. Interested in governmental affairs, he served in several Nigerian ministries. He also became a significant writer whose work discussed life in Nigeria for the common man, using humor and satire. His most popular character, Basi, also known as Mr. B, appeared in several of his works, and his soap opera, "Basi & Co.," was one of the most popular programs on Nigerian state-run television.

In later years, Saro-Wiwa wrote treatises on unrest and civil war in his homeland. His *Nigeria: The Brink of Disaster* (1991) called attention to the growing crisis there. Yet his most passionate work may have been *Genocide in Nigeria: The Ogoni Tragedy* (1992), which explained the misfortune of the Ogoni people, an ethnic minority in Nigeria of which Saro-Wiwa was a member. Saro-Wiwa and others have urged political autonomy for and self-sufficiency of the Ogonis, who live in an oil-rich area that has been exploited by others. Yet the Nigerian government, and its leader Sani Abacha, turned a deaf ear to these pleas.

In 1990, Saro-Wiwa founded the Movement for the Survival of the Ogoni Peoples (MOSOP), which used passive resistance and declarations to make the Ogoni voice heard. In response, Abacha sealed off Ogoniland, placed the area under martial law, and banned rallies by MOSOP members. When Shell Oil, which had been drilling on Ogoni land, felt pressed by world pressure to come to the aid of the Ogonis, the Nigerian government dealt with the threat to its livelihood by arresting Saro-Wiwa on 22 May 1994 and accusing him of helping to murder four Ogoni leaders who were killed after a rally that Saro-Wiwa had attended. Held without trial and allegedly tortured, he was declared a prisoner of conscience by Amnesty International. Saro-Wiwa and eight so-called conspirators were tried, convicted, and sentenced to death on 31 October 1995.

In his final statement to the military tribunal that was sending him to his death, Saro-Wiwa said:

> I am a man of peace, of ideas. Appalled by the denigrating poverty of my people who live on a richly endowed land, distressed by their political marginalization

> and economic strangulation, angered by the devastation of their land, their ultimate heritage, anxious to preserve their right to life and to a decent living, and determined to usher to this country as a whole a fair and just democratic system which protects everyone and every ethnic group and gives us all a valid claim to human civilization. I have devoted my intellectual and material resources, my very life, to a cause in which I have total belief and from which I cannot be blackmailed or intimidated. I have no doubt at all about the ultimate success of my cause, no matter the trials and tribulations which I and those who believe with me may encounter on our journey. Nor imprisonment nor death can stop our ultimate victory.

On 10 November 1995, Saro-Wiwa was taken with the eight men condemned with him to the prison in Port Harcourt and hanged. The News Agency of Nigeria reported that hundreds of Ogonis lined the streets to the prison, weeping uncontrollably after hearing word of Saro-Wiwa's execution. He had been awarded the 1995 Goldman Environmental Prize, bestowed by the Goldman Foundation in San Francisco for work in environmental affairs.

On 20 December 1995, the heads of major environmental organizations in the United States sent an open letter to American President Bill Clinton, calling on him to institute sanctions against Nigeria for putting Saro-Wiwa to death. Ultimately, the United States did nothing to punish Abacha or Nigeria.

**References:** "Letter by Environmental Organizations on Nigerian Executions, 20 December 1995," courtesy of the Sierra Club; "Nigeria: The Making of a Legend," *Newsweek*, 18 December 1995, 47; Saro-Wiwa, Ken, *Genocide in Nigeria: The Ogoni Tragedy* (Port Harcourt, Nigeria: Saros Press, 1992); "Saro-Wiwa, Ken(ule Beeson)" in Donna Elendorf, ed., *Contemporary Authors: A Bio-Bibliographical Guide to Current Writers in Fiction, General Nonfiction, Poetry, Journalism, Drama, Motion Pictures, Television, and Other Fields*, 151 vols. (Detroit: Gale Research, 1962–1996), 142:389–390.

## Saukel, Fritz

See Nuremberg War Crimes Defendants

## Savonarola, Girolamo (1452–1498)

Italian religious reformer put to death for heresy against the Catholic Church.

He was born the son of Italian nobles in Ferrara, Italy, on 21 September 1452. His parents wanted him to become a doctor, but instead he turned to the Church and religion, leaving home in 1475 and joining a Dominican order. After undergoing a strenuous novitiate at the monastery at Bologna, he became a teacher there.

Savonarola would have remained a little-known educator had he not moved to St. Mark's monastery in Florence, where he soon became involved in a movement to end corrupt practices in the Church. Soon he used sermons to denounce church elders for their wicked ways and demand reforms. Coincidentally, his lectures began at Brescia, the birthplace of another heretic who had been put to death for his outspoken views three hundred years earlier, in 1155. Savonarola returned to Florence, where he became prior of St. Mark's in 1491.

Savonarola came into conflict with Lorenzo de' Medici, a member of a powerful and wealthy Florentine family, refusing to pay homage to him, as was customary. When Charles VIII of France invaded Italy, there was political bedlam in Florence, and when Lorenzo died, Savonarola opposed the formation of a government composed of nobles. Savonarola himself assumed dictatorial powers over the city, calling on a rebirth of spiritualism and remained in control of it for three years. He oversaw the public burning of works of art and literature that he felt to be irreligious, acts that earned the title of the "bonfire of the vanities." With these acts, as well as others, Savonarola came into conflict with Pope Alexander VI, who called many of his actions against the Church heresy, and demanded a cessation of his preaching.

Refusal brought excommunication, the strongest penalty the Church can dispense, in 1497, and Florence was threatened with an interdict if it continued to allow Savonarola to preach there. Florence remained silent, but Savonarola decried the excommunication and called for a Church council to assemble and remove Alexander from the papacy. Savonarola assumed that the citizens of Florence supported him; when they did not (his severity had made him many enemies), he was arrested, tried on a charge of heresy against the Church, and after six days of horrendous torture and a trial many historians have found to be unjust, he was found guilty. He was then condemned to be hanged and, before succumbing, to be burned at the stake. The execution, which is described herewith, remains one of history's most cruel and unusual.

> On 23 May 1498, the parricide Republic executed its founder and his comrades. Unfrocked and barefoot, they were led to the same Piazza della Signoria where twice they had burned the "vanities." As then, and as for the trial by ordeal, a great crowd gathered for the sight; but now the government supplied it with food and drink. . . . The three men were hanged from a gibbet, and the boys were allowed to stone them as they choked. A great fire was lit under them, and burned them to ashes. The ashes were thrown into the Arno [river], lest they be worshipped as relics of saints. Some *Piagnoni* [Italian, "weepers"; supporters of Savonarola], braving incrimination, knelt in the square and wept and prayed. Every year until 1703, on the morning after the 23rd of May, flowers were strewn on the spot where the hot blood of the friars fell. Today a plaque in the pavement marks the site of the most famous crime in Florentine history.

**See also:** Arnold of Brescia.

**References:** Clark, William Robinson, *Savonarola: His Life and Times* (Chicago: A. C. McClurg, 1890); De la Bedoyne, Michael, *The Meddlesome Friar and the Wayward Pope: The Story of the Conflict Between Savonarola and Alexander VI* (Garden City, NY: Hanover House, 1958); Durant, Will, *The Renaissance: A History of Civilization in Italy from 1304–1576 A.D.* (New York: Simon & Schuster, 1953), 161; Erlanger, Rachel, *The Unarmed Prophet: Savonarola in Florence* (New York: McGraw-Hill, 1988); Misciattelli, Piero, *Savonarola* (New York: D. Appleton & Co., 1930); "'We Shall Make a Good Bonfire of Him'" in *Crime and Punishment: The Illustrated Crime Encyclopedia,* 28 vols. (Westport, CT: H. S. Stuttman, 1994), 22:2725–2732.

## Scalia, Antonin (1936– )

American jurist, associate justice on the United States Supreme Court (1986– ), and a firm supporter of capital punishment.

Born in the Italian section of Trenton, New Jersey, on 11 March 1936, Scalia is the son of Eugene Scalia, a Sicilian immigrant who became a professor of romance languages at Brooklyn College, and Catherine Louise (nee Panaro) Scalia, an elementary school teacher. He attended local schools then went to Georgetown University and the University of Fribourg, Switzerland, where he was awarded a bachelor's degree in 1957. After attending Harvard University Law School, he was awarded a law degree in 1960. Admitted to the Ohio bar, he went into private law practice from 1961 to 1967 and taught law at the University of Virginia from 1967 to

1974. He also served as general counsel of the Office of Telecommunications Policy in the Nixon administration from 1971 to 1972, chairman of the Administrative Conference of the United States from 1972 to 1974, and assistant attorney general in the Department of Justice's Office of Legal Counsel from 1974 to 1977. Between 1977 and 1982, Scalia was a professor of law at Georgetown University (1977) and the University of Chicago (1977–1982), and visiting professor of law at Stanford University (1980–1981).

His conservative viewpoint, expressed in his writings, led President Ronald Reagan to name Scalia in 1982 to a vacant seat on the U.S. Circuit Court of Appeals for the District of Columbia. In his four years on that court, Scalia cast his conservative viewpoint into legal concrete. In a minority opinion for one death penalty case, he mocked the majority's finding that drugs used in lethal injection executions had to meet Food and Drug Administration standards. When Chief Justice Warren Burger resigned from the Supreme Court in 1986, Associate Justice William H. Rehnquist was elevated to Chief Justice, allowing President Reagan to name Scalia to the Court. Although several civil rights and feminist organizations opposed his nomination, Scalia was approved both by the Senate Judiciary Committee (unanimously) and the full Senate (by a vote of 98–0). On 26 September 1986, he took the oath of office as the first Italian-American ever to sit on the High Court.

Scalia was and continues to be a supporter of capital punishment. In his ten years on the court, he has not shied away from adamantly upholding death sentences and denying appeals. For instance, in his dissent in *Booth v. Maryland,* a case in which victim impact statements were held to be a violation of the Constitution (the doctrine was later reversed), Scalia wrote:

> Recent years have seen an outpouring of popular concern for what has come to be known as "victims' rights"—a phrase that describes what its proponents feel is the failure of the courts of justice to take into account in their sentencing decisions not only the factors mitigating the defendant's moral guilt, but also the amount of harm he has caused to innocent members of society. Many citizens have found one-sided and hence unjust the criminal trial in which a parade of witnesses comes forth to testify to the pressures beyond normal human experience that drove the defendant to commit his crime, with no one to lay before the sentencing authority the full reality of the human suffering the defendant has produced—which (and *not* moral guilt alone) is one of the reasons society deems his act worthy of the prescribed penalty. Perhaps these sentiments do not sufficiently temper justice with mercy, but that is a question to be decided through the democratic processes of a free people, and not by the decrees of this Court.

His dissent in *South Carolina v. Gathers,* a case involving the *Booth* doctrine, is noted for its ferocity.

By 1996, Scalia remained perhaps the most conservative justice in the history of the Court, joined in most of his dissenting opinions by fellow conservatives Chief Justice Rehnquist and Justice Clarence Thomas.

**See also:** Rehnquist, William Hubbs.

**References:** Biskupic, Joan, "In Terms of Moral Indignation, Justice Scalia Is a Majority of One," *Washington Post,* 30 June 1996, A3; Bronner, Ethan, "Combative Justice Scalia Moves into Ascendancy," *Boston Globe,* 29 April 1990, 1; Fein, Bruce, "Scalia's Way," *ABA Journal* 76:2 (February 1990), 38–41; "Scalia, Antonin" in Charles Moritz, ed., *Current Biography Yearbook* 1986 (New York: H. W. Wilson, 1986), 502–505; "That's Skul-LEE-Yuh: An editorial 'Asides' about the Proper Pronunciation of Antonin Scalia's Name," *Wall Street Journal,* 19 June 1986, 30.

## Scholl, Hans (1918–1943), and Sophie Scholl (1921–1943)

German dissidents, beheaded by the Nazi regime for handing out leaflets denouncing Hitler.

The second (Hans) and fourth (Sophie) of the five children of Robert Scholl, the mayor of the German village of Forchtenberg, they apparently grew up in a prosperous and loving family with little contact with the outside world. In 1935, however, the children in the family became firm supporters of Adolf Hitler, whose rise to power two years earlier ushered in, at least at the beginning, a flush of pride for the German homeland and an attempt to end staggering unemployment. That same year Hans went to Nuremberg to carry a flag at a Nazi rally and saw firsthand the Nazi plans for the conquest of Europe, the end of civil liberties in Germany, and the eventual mass murder of the Jews. With his sister Sophie, who had been an unenthusiastic supporter of the Hitler Youth, Hans began to read banned literature. This activity, along with participation in illegal groups, such as the *Deutsche Jugend* (German Youth), led to a brief arrest in 1937. Even Robert Scholl was arrested.

As the growing totalitarianism of the 1930s in Germany turned into increased hatred toward Jews—displayed in the *Kristallnacht* ("Crystal Night"; also known as "the Night of the Broken Glass") in which Jewish businesses and houses of worship were invaded and ransacked—as well as the start of World War II on 1 September 1939, Hans and Sophie Scholl gradually realized that opposition to the regime was their moral duty.

Soon after her twenty-first birthday Sophie was able to enter Munich University, where Hans was also enrolled to study medicine. There the two—joined by several other like-minded German students, including Willi Graf, Christoph Probst and Alexander Schmorell—decided to establish a campaign of resistance to the Nazi regime using leaflets calling for an end to Hitler's rule and to the war. Calling themselves "The White Rose," they secretly disseminated the first of the leaflets in June and July 1942. However, their failure to understand the grip that Nazism had on German society would prove fatal.

On 18 February 1943, as the group was distributing a leaflet in the main court of the University of Munich, a janitor saw them and reported their activities to the authorities. The Scholls and Christoph Probst were quickly put on trial before the infamous Roland Freisler, known as "Hitler's Hanging Judge." The main evidence against them: the 18 February leaflet denouncing the regime for the horrendous German losses against the Russians at Stalingrad. Addressed to "Fellow Students," it claimed that "the day of reckoning is come, the reckoning of German youth with the most appalling tyranny that our people has ever endured." A short trial followed; the outcome was predetermined, and yet they refused to allow for mercy when the sentence of death by guillotine was announced. Taken to Standheim Prison in Munich, they, along with Probst, 24, were executed under the blade of the Nazi guillotine on 22 February. Hans was 24, while his sister was only 21.

The Scholls were buried two days later in Perlach cemetery in Munich, and their funeral was protested with grafitti around town: "Their spirit lives." Today, the main square of the University of Munich, where their courage was betrayed, is called Geschwister-Scholl Platz. Their story, as well as others involved in the dissident movement that opposed the Nazis, was highlighted in Hava Kohav Beller's Oscar-nominated 1991 documentary *The Restless Conscience.*

**References:** Gill, Anton, *An Honourable Defeat* (New York: Henry Holt & Co., 1994),

183–95; Hanser, Richard, *A Noble Treason: The Revolt of the Munich Students Against Hitler* (New York: Putnam, 1979); Jens, Inge Scholl (Cyrus Brooks, trans.), *Six Against Tyranny* (London: Murray, 1955); Jens, Inge Scholl (J. Maxwell Brownjohn, trans.), *At the Heart of the White Rose: Letters and Diaries of Hans and Sophie Scholl* (New York: Harper & Row, 1987); Zentner, Christian, and Friedemann Bedüftig, eds., *Encyclopedia of the Third Reich*, 2 vols. (New York: Macmillan, 1991), 2:841.

## Schwarzchild, Henry (1925–1996)

German-American anti–capital punishment activist, founding member (1976) of the National Coalition to Abolish the Death Penalty (NCADP).

Born in Wiesbaden, Germany, in 1925, he was raised in Berlin until 1939, when he and his family fled the rising anti-Jewish persecution in that nation and came to the United States. He later said of this early experience with Nazism, "It was impossible to avoid being made enormously, prematurely conscious of the world around one." He grew up in New York City and eventually served in the U.S. Army's Counterintelligence Corps. He graduated from the City College of New York and later did some graduate work at Columbia University. Starting in the 1950s, Schwarzchild worked with the Anti-Defamation League of the B'nai B'rith, a Jewish charitable organization, as well as the American Committee for Cultural Freedom. In the early 1960s he participated in the freedom rides in the American South that called attention to the lack of civil rights for black Americans. Jailed in Mississippi, he was commended for his work by the Rev. Dr. Martin Luther King, Jr.

In the 1960s, Schwarzchild turned his attention to the fight to abolish capital punishment in the United States. For more than half of that decade he was the executive director of the Lawyers' Constitutional Defense Committee, a civil rights group. According to death penalty historian Herbert Haines, Schwarzchild "emerged as the major architect" of the anti–death penalty movement in the 1960s and 1970s, and it was only natural that Schwarzchild should become the director of the American Civil Liberties Union's Capital Punishment Project (CPP) in 1975, a position he held for 15 years until his retirement. In 1976, Schwarzchild was a founding member of the National Coalition to Abolish the Death Penalty (NCADP), an umbrella group of nationwide organizations committed to ending capital punishment in the United States.

In 1996, shortly before his death, Schwarzchild contributed an article to *The Machinery of Death: A Shocking Indictment of Capital Punishment in the United States,* compiled and published by Amnesty International USA. He wrote:

> When the issue is whether the government may kill a human being, there is no reliability sufficient to justify that. I would not find it justifiable if that reliability were available, because I believe that no society can truly call itself civilized that uses premeditated violent homicide as an instrument of social policy; but it seems to me useless to talk about a hypothetical society in which the death penalty is applied rationally, predictably, fairly, without error, without discrimination. Such a society does not exist here and is unlikely ever to exist. In any real society, the death penalty ought to be eliminated because human beings are fallible.

Henry Schwarzchild died in a hospital in White Plains, New York, on 1 June 1996, of cancer.

**See also:** American Civil Liberties Union Capital Punishment Project; National Coalition to Abolish the Death Penalty.

**References:** Haines, Herbert H., *Against Capital Punishment: The Anti–Death Penalty*

*Movement in America, 1972–1994* (New York: Oxford University Press, 1996); "Henry Schwarzchild, 70, Opponent of Death Penalty," *New York Times*, 4 June 1996, B8; *The Machinery of Death: A Shocking Indictment of Capital Punishment in the United States* (New York: Amnesty International USA, 1997), 5.

## Scottish Maiden

Mode of capital punishment similar to the guillotine, except that it originated in Scotland instead of France and became less famous (or infamous) than its French cousin.

Originally constructed as the Halifax Gibbet, it became famous when the Earl of Morton saw it in operation and had a similar machine built in Edinburgh in 1565, where it was named the Scottish Maiden. Among its estimated 120 victims were Sir John Gordon of Haddo, the Marquis of Argyle, and, ironically, the Earl of Morton, who met his fate on the Maiden on 2 June 1581. Its use was discontinued in 1710, and, according to crime historian John Laurence, it is now located in the museum of the Society of Antiquaries in Edinburgh.

In their *Complete Newgate Calendar,* a record of those hanged at the Newgate in London, historians J. L. Radner and G. T. Crook write of "The Maiden: Origin of the Guillotine":

> Mr. Pennant gives the following account of the Maiden:
>
> The Maiden seems to have been confined to the limits of the forest of Hardwicke, or the eighteen towns and hamlets within its precincts. . . .
>
> The offender had always a fair trial, for as soon as he was taken he was brought to the lord's bailiff at Halifax; he was then exposed on the three markets, which here were held thrice in a week, placed in the stocks with the goods stolen on his back, or if the theft was of the cattle kind they were placed by him; and this was done both to strike terror into others and to produce new informations against him. The bailiff then summoned four freeholders of each town within the forest to form a jury. The felon and prosecutors were brought face to face, and the goods, the cow or horse, or whatsoever was stolen, produced. If he was found guilty he was remanded to prison, had a week's time allowed for preparation, and then was conveyed to the spot where his head was struck off by this machine. I should have premised that if the criminal, either after apprehension or on the way to execution, could escape out of the limits of the forest (part being close to the town), the bailiff had no further power over him; but if he should be caught within the precincts at any time after, he was immediately executed on his former sentence.
>
> . . . It is in form of a painter's easel and about ten feet high; at four feet from the bottom is a cross bar, on which the felon lays his head, which is kept down by another placed above. In the inner edges of the frame are grooves; in these is placed a sharp axe, with a vast weight of lead, supported at the very summit by a peg; to that peg is fastened a cord, which the executioner cutting, the axe falls, and does the affair effectually, without suffering the unhappy criminal to undergo a repetition of strokes, as has been the case in the common method. I must add that if the sufferer is condemned for stealing a horse or a cow, the string is tied to the beast, which, upon being whipped, pulls out the peg and becomes the executioner.

**References:** Abbott, Geoffrey, *The Book of Execution: An Encyclopedia of Methods of Judicial Execution* (London: Headline, 1995); Laurence, John, *A History of Capital Punishment* (New York: Citadel, 1960), 38; Rayner, John L., and G. T. Crook, eds., *The Complete Newgate Calendar,* 5 vols. (London: Privately Printed for the Navarre Society, 1926), 2:320–322.

## Seyss-Inquart, Artur

See Nuremberg War Crimes Defendants

### *Skipper v. South Carolina* (476 U.S. 1, 90 L.Ed. 2d 1, 106 S.Ct. 1669 [1986])

A state court's exclusion from a sentencing hearing of a defendant's record of good behavior while in jail violated the Eighth Amendment's ban on cruel and unusual punishment—so held the U.S. Supreme Court in this little-known landmark case decided in 1986. Chief Justice Warren Burger, joined by Justices Lewis Powell and William H. Rehnquist, argued that the sentencer also violated the due process clause of the Fourteenth Amendment.

Ronald Ray Skipper was convicted in a South Carolina court of rape and murder; during the sentencing hearing, even though he was allowed to introduce evidence that he was a model prisoner in the time between his arrest and trial, other persons who could back up his testimony were excluded because their testimony was considered by the court to be irrelevant. Skipper was then sentenced to death. On appeal, the defendant argued that the court committed a constitutional error by not allowing what he considered to be mitigating evidence. On appeal, the South Carolina Supreme Court upheld the sentence, asserting that evidence of Skipper's "adaptability to prison" was properly excluded. On certiorari, the U.S. Supreme Court agreed to hear the appeal, and arguments were heard on 24 February 1986.

Two months later, on 29 April 1986, the Court struck down Skipper's death sentence and remanded the case back to the lower court for further proceedings. In an opinion by Justice Byron White, joined by Justices Thurgood Marshall, Harry Blackmun, John Paul Stevens, and Sandra Day O'Connor, the Court held that "a defendant's disposition to make a well-behaved and peaceful adjustment to life in prison is an aspect of his character" and that an exclusion of such evidence was a violation of the cruel and unusual punishments clause of the Eighth Amendment to the Constitution. Justice White wrote:

> We think, however, that characterizing the excluded evidence as cumulative and its exclusion as harmless is implausible on the facts before us. The evidence petitioner was allowed to present on the issue of his conduct in jail was the sort of evidence that a jury naturally would tend to discount as self-serving. The testimony of more disinterested witnesses—and, in particular, of jailers who would have had no particular reason to be favorably predisposed toward one of their charges—would quite naturally be given much greater weight by the jury. Nor can we confidently conclude that credible evidence that petitioner was a good prisoner would have had no effect upon the jury's deliberations. The prosecutor himself, in closing argument, made much of the dangers petitioner would pose if sentenced to prison, and went so far as to assert that petitioner could be expected to rape other inmates. Under these circumstances, it appears reasonably likely that the exclusion of evidence bearing upon petitioner's behavior in jail (and hence, upon his likely future behavior in prison) may have affected the jury's decision to impose the death sentence. Thus, under any standard, the exclusion of the evidence was sufficiently prejudicial to constitute reversible error.

### Slovik, Edward Donald (1920–1945)

American soldier executed by the U.S. Army in France for desertion, the first man since 1864 to be executed for that offense.

Born in 1920 in Hamtramck, Michigan, he became involved in a series of petty offenses between 1932 and 1937 that earned him some jail time. The final black mark on his record—a record that would come back to haunt him—was a five-year term for embezzlement in 1937, two months before he turned 18.

(He had stolen some gum and small change from his employer, a drug store, in Detroit, valued at $59.60.) Paroled in 1942, he married a girl named Antoinette Wisniewski, took honest employment, and seemed to have settled down.

Just two years after being paroled, however, Slovik was drafted into the U.S. Army, which was looking for every man possible to send to the front against the Nazis and Japanese in World War II. In spite of a 4-F classification because of poor feeling in his legs, Slovik was shipped off to training camp, first in Illinois, then Texas. Assigned to the 109th Infantry Regiment of the 28th Army Division, he was shipped to France on 7 August 1944 on board the troopship *Aquitania.* As soon as he landed in France, however, Slovik began to have second thoughts about fighting, desiring instead to be safely behind the lines where there was no shooting. Two weeks after joining his outfit, he and another soldier, Private John P. Tankey, either were separated from or deserted their fellow American soldiers and became attached to a Canadian cooking unit. There Slovik worked for two months, until he returned for some unknown reason to his outfit. After only a few hours, he again went AWOL (absent without leave). When he surrendered, he was thrown into the stockade. The judge-advocate overseeing his case made him a deal: charges resulting in court-martial would be dropped if Slovik would return to the front lines. Slovik refused, and, on 11 November 1944, was brought before a formal court martial, accused of desertion.

Slovik's contention that he wanted a safer position was never defended by his court-appointed counsel, Capt. Edward P. Woods. Instead, the army brought forward witnesses who testified that Slovik alone deserted. As the trial proceeded, guns outside pounded home to the small courtroom the testimony of the 109th's death struggle against the Germans. Slovik remained silent, refusing to take the stand. The nine-member panel returned from deliberations with a verdict of guilty and, upon further reflection, sentenced Slovik to death.

The decision was appealed automatically to the division commander, Major General Norman "Dutch" Cota, an FBI background check was done on Slovik, and his lengthy criminal record was found. Cota agreed with the sentence, as did others. When higher-ups reviewed Slovik's record, they saw a former convict who refused to fight for his country in time of war, and they felt that if such feelings spread, the fight against the Nazis would collapse just as it was nearing its victorious conclusion. One judge advocate wrote that "if the death penalty is ever to be imposed for desertion it should be imposed in this case." The final decision rested with the Allied field commander, Gen. Dwight D. Eisenhower. Slovik wrote an apologetic, error-filled note to the general, asking for a pardon:

> Dear General Eisenhower:
>
> I Private Eddie D. Slovik ASN 36896415 was convicted on the 11th day of November Armistic Day by General Court Martial to be shot to death for desertion of the United States Army.
>
> The time of conviction or before my conviction I had no intentions of deserting the army whatsoever. For if I intended too I wouldn't have given or surrendered myself as I did. I have nothing against the United States army whatsoever, I merely wanted a transfer from the line. . . ..
>
> I don't believe I ran away the first time as I stated in my first confession. I came over to France as a replacement, and when the enemy started to shelling us I got scared and nerves and I couldn't move out of my fox hole. I guess I never did give myself the chance to get over my

first fear of shelling. The next day their wasn't any American troops around so I turned myself over to the Canadian MPs. They in turn were trying to get in touch with my outfit about me. I guess it must have taken them six weeks to catch up with the American troops. Well sir, when I was turned over to my outfit I tried to explain to my CO just what took place, and what had happened to me. Then I asked for a transfer. Which was refused. Then I wrote my confession. I was then told that if I would go back to the line they would destroy my confession, however, if I refused to go back on the line they would half to hold it against me which they did.

How can I tell you how humbley sorry I am for the sins Ive committed. I didn't realize at the time what I was doing, or what the word desertion meant. What it is like to be condemned to die. I beg of you deeply and sincerely for the sake of my dear wife and mother back home to have mercy on me. To my knowledge I have a good record since my marriage and as a soldier. I'd like to continue to be a good soldier.

Anxiously awaiting your reply, which I earnestly pray is favorable. God bless you and your Work for victory:

I remain Yours for Victory,

Pvt. Eddie B. Slovik

With a war raging and thousands of young men just as scared as Slovik being slaughtered, Eisenhower had no sympathy for a man who did not want to fight for his nation. He issued an order confirming the sentence, and Slovik's superiors set 31 January 1945 as the date of execution. Taken to a small chateau in the French village of St. Marie aux Mines, Slovik was tied to a stake on the morning of 31 January and executed by firing squad. His body was conveyed to the Oise-Aisne American Cemetery at Fère-en-Tardenois, where other Americans who had been put to death in the European Theater for such crimes as rape and murder were buried. His widow was not told of her husband's execution until 1953 (she had been informed that he had been killed in the war), when author William Bradford Huie, investigating the case for a book he was writing, discovered Slovik's fate. Although she spent the next 20 years trying to clear his name, the army would have none of it. After her death, the army had Slovik's remains exhumed and, in July 1987, returned to the United States for reburial. In 1974, Martin Sheen played Slovik in the television movie based on Huie's book, entitled *The Execution of Private Slovik.*

**References:** Drimmer, Frederick, *Until You Are Dead: The Book of Executions in America* (New York: Windsor, 1990), 160–163; Huie, William Bradford, *The Execution of Private Slovik* (New York: Dell, 1970); Nash, Jay Robert, *Encyclopedia of World Crime,* 4 vols. (Wilmette, IL: CrimeBooks, Inc., 1990), 4:2778–2779; Ryan, Bernard, Jr., "Eddie Slovik Court-Martial: 1944" in Edward W. Knappman, ed., *Great American Trials* (Detroit: Visible Ink Press, 1994), 413–416.

## Snyder, Ruth May Brown (1895–1927)

American housewife put to death in New York's electric chair (along with her lover Henry Judd Gray) for the brutal murder of her husband, Albert Snyder.

Ruth Snyder was born Ruth Brown in New York City in 1895. In 1915 she married 32-year-old Albert Snyder, an art editor for *Motor Boating* magazine. But Ruth soon tired of Albert. Rumors are that she took several lovers; in 1925 she met and fell for Henry Judd Gray, a brassiere salesman who was also married. Gray seemed to be the polar opposite of Ruth Snyder: he was short, stiffly attired, and wore thick, steel-rimmed glasses. Yet the two became passionate lovers.

By 1926, Ruth had decided to kill Albert; in fact, she had insured his life for

$96,000 and that year had tried seven times, unsuccessfully, to murder him. When she asked Gray to help her, he shied away at first; finally, Ruth's imploring convinced him that in order for them to be together, Albert Snyder must be killed. On the night of 19 March 1927, while Ruth slept upstairs with the unsuspecting Albert, Gray slipped in through the unlocked back door. Ruth had arranged the murder weapon, a heavy dumbbell, and rubber gloves, for him to use in the deed. He crept into their bedroom and hit Snyder in the head as instructed, but the force was not enough to kill. Ruth Snyder took the weight from her lover's hands and hit Albert Snyder until his skull was crushed. A wire from a picture frame was then wrapped around his neck, and a bottle of chloroform was dumped into a rag and placed on his face (so much that Snyder's face was burned from the chemical).

The next morning, a tied and gagged Ruth made her way into her daughter's room; her daughter summoned the neighbors. The police were called to the grisly scene: Albert Snyder was dead, but his wife was uninjured, and, as they noted, bound so loosely that she could have untied herself. She told the police that a man with a large mustache attacked the pair in their bed and then robbed the house, killing Albert Snyder before they left. No evidence of forced entry was found, Ruth was untouched, and her jewelry, which she claimed to have been part of the take, was found underneath her mattress. A button with the initials "J. G." found on the floor near the bed, an entry in Ruth's address book for a "Gray, Judd" on the G page, and a check from Ruth to Gray, made the police suspicious. Was this Judd Gray involved? they asked. Ruth blurted out, "Has he confessed?" They claimed that he had, at which point Ruth admitted murdering her husband. Gray was found in a hotel in Syracuse, New York, waiting for news from his lover. When he was picked up by the police, he told them that he had been in Syracuse the night of the murder. But when confronted by Ruth's confession, Gray admitted his and claimed that the murder was all Ruth's idea.

Writer Damon Runyon, who covered the double trial for the New York *American,* dubbed the crime "The Dumbbell Murder." Others in the press called Ruth "the Marble Woman" for her expressionless face in court and Gray "the Putty Man" for being so pliable under Ruth's bidding. On 9 May 1927, the jury, after one hour and forty minutes, accepted Gray's version of events but convicted both of first-degree murder; both were then sentenced to death. The two appealed, but to no avail.

On the night of 12 January 1928, both were put to death in the electric chair in New York's Sing Sing Prison. As the electricity surged through Ruth's body, Thomas Howard, a cameraman for the *New York Daily News,* pressed a small plunger in his hand, setting off a camera on his ankle, which took a picture of Ruth Snyder as she died. Six minutes after her body was removed, Judd Gray was seated in the same chair, having been forgiven by his wife for sleeping with Ruth. The snapshot of Ruth's death appeared the following morning on the cover of the *Daily News,* perhaps the most famous newspaper cover photo in the history of photojournalism. It has outlived the names of Ruth Snyder and Judd Gray.

The sordid story became the inspiration for James M. Cain's classic work, *Double Indemnity,* which itself became the basis for the 1944 film starring Fred MacMurray and Barbara Stanwyck.

**References:** Sann, Paul, *The Lawless Decade: A Pictorial History of a Great American Transition: From the World War I Armistice and Prohibition to Repeal and the New Deal*

(New York: Bonanza Books, 1972), 158–161; Jones, Ann, "She Had to Die!" *American Heritage* 31:6 (October/November 1980), 20–31; Ryan, Bernard, Jr., "Ruth Snyder-Judd Gray Trial: 1927" in Edward W. Knappman, ed., *Great American Trials* (Detroit: Visible Ink Press, 1994), 338–341.

## Socrates (470–399 B.C.E.)

Plato said of him, "He was the wisest, most just and best of all the men I have ever known." Socrates, Greek philosopher and moralist, was put to death for refusing to bow to the authority of the leaders of Greece.

Socrates was the son of Sophroniscus and Phaenarete, both Athenian citizens; because of his social status, he served as a hoplite, or infantry foot soldier, in the Athenian army during the Pelopponesian War (a hoplite had to purchase his own equipment, a huge expense). He then became a tutor who fed his students' minds for free and thus suffered poverty, surviving on a small stipend from his father, by then deceased. As a tutor, he called upon the youth of Athens to challenge, to question, and to analyze the government and its policies. For many years, he got away with this sort of teaching in clear defiance of the authorities; however, by 399 B.C.E., as he approached his seventieth birthday and the city-state of Athens closed in on itself after badly losing the Pelopponesian War, the regime saw in him not a nuisance but a real threat.

An era of free speech and freedom ended when Socrates was accused of corrupting the city's youth and failing to properly worship the Athenian gods. Arrested, he faced a jury of his peers but treated the affair as a joke by refusing to defend himself against the charges. Plato, who witnessed the miscarriage of justice, quoted Socrates as warning the jurors: "If you kill me, you will not easily find a successor to me who will be, if I may use such a ludicrous figure of speech, a sort of gadfly attached to the state by God. The state is a great and noble horse who is rather sluggish, owing to his very size, and needs to be stirred into life. I am that gadfly . . . and all day long and in all places, I am always fastening upon you, arousing and persuading and reproaching you." Goading the jurors, he insisted that instead of executing him, the state should richly reward him for his services. Disgusted at his attitude, the jurors found him guilty and sentenced him to death. Allowed to escape execution if he agreed to go into exile, Socrates decided to abide by the jury's decision and accept his punishment. Forced by his jailers to drink poison hemlock (*Conium maculatum*), a poisonous biennial plant of the parsley or carrot family, he lay down and waited to die, chiding his friends and compatriots for their unmanliness while they watched him die.

In his work entitled *Phaedo,* Plato described Socrates' death scene:

> All broke down in sobbing and grief, except only Socrates himself. What are you doing, my friends? he exclaimed. I sent away the women chiefly that they not offend in this way, for I have heard that a man should die in silence. So calm yourselves and bear up. He walked about until his legs were getting heavy and then he lay down on his back. The man who gave the poison began to examine his feet and legs from time to time; he pressed his foot hard and asked if there was any feeling in it and Socrates said No, and then his legs, and so higher and higher, and showed us that he was cold and stiff. And Socrates felt himself and said that when it came to his heart he would be done. He was already growing cold about the groin, when he uncovered his face which had been covered and spoke for the last time. Crito, he said, I owe a cock to Asclepius; do not forget to pay it. It shall be done, replied Crito. Is there anything else you wish? He made no answer to this question; but after a short in-

> terval there was a movement, and the man uncovered him and his eyes were fixed. Then Crito closed his mouth and eyes.

His death scene, captured in the painting *The Death of Socrates* by French painter Jacques Louis David, has become better known than Socrates' life and work. Socrates' contemporaries, including the playwright Aristophanes, the soldier Xenophon, and Plato, remembered him chiefly for his wisdom; Aristophanes satirized him in his work *The Clouds*.

**References:** Durant, Will, *The Life of Greece* (New York: Simon & Schuster, 1939); Wigoder, Geoffrey, *They Made History: A Biographical Dictionary* (New York: Simon & Schuster, 1993), 607–608.

## Somerset, Edward Seymour, Duke of (c.1506–1552)

English statesman. As protector during the minority of Edward VI, Somerset sought peaceful union with Scotland, offering trade and other advantages and a marriage between Mary, Queen of Scots, and King Edward. Only when those overtures failed did he go to war, winning the Battle of Pinkie in 1547. His religious policy, enshrined in the Act of Conformity, 1549, introduced the Book of Common Prayer and brought a body of moderate Protestantism into the Church of England. Somerset's economic and social views, which favored the peasantry in its protests against enclosure of common lands by the propertied class, led to his overthrow in 1549 following Kett's rebellion. The Duke of Northumberland seized power in England, and, after a show of friendship toward Somerset, had him executed.

## Sorge, Richard (1895–1944)

Russian-Azerbaijani spy put to death by the Japanese shortly before the conclusion of World War II for his spying activities.

He was born in the village of Adjikent, near Baku, Russia (in the area that is now Azerbaijan), on 4 October 1895, the youngest of nine children. His father, Adolf Sorge, was a German petroleum engineer who lived and worked in Azerbaijan, and his mother, Nina Semionova Kobieleva Sorge, was an Azerbaijani housewife. Three years after Richard's birth, Adolf Sorge returned to Germany.

Richard Sorge grew up in his father's homeland, and saw action with the German army during World War I. After the conflict ended, Sorge earned a doctorate in political science at the University of Hamburg. A socialist since 1917, Sorge joined the German Communist party in 1919 and served (1920–1921) as editor of the party journal, *Bergische Arbeiterstimme* (The Mine Workers' Voice). By 1924, however, the Communist movement in Germany had been put down, and Sorge headed back to Russia, where the government there saw his Asian features as an asset; he was sent to China to start a Communist ring there. While in China, under cover as a journalist for the German newspaper *Frankfurter Zeitung*, Sorge spied for the Russians. In 1933, to enhance his cover, he joined the Nazi party and was sent to Japan to work for the German ambassador to Japan, Major General Eugen Ott.

Although in 1939 the Germans and Russians signed a pact that called for a peace between them, Sorge discovered through the German Embassy in Tokyo that Hitler was planning to abrogate the treaty by invading Russia. In Moscow, Josef Stalin, in the midst of a massive purge of his military, ignored Sorge's warnings and did not prepare for an invasion. On 12 May 1941 Sorge learned that Hitler intended to launch Operation Barbarossa, the invasion of Russia, on 20 June utilizing 170 German divisions. Again, Sorge's forewarning was disregarded. On 22 June, two days later than Sorge's sources reported, German troops instituted a massive assault on Russia. The Russians were ill-prepared. When Sorge, spying directly on the Imperial Japanese Army, reported that the Japanese army was moving against southern Pacific targets rather than the easternmost portions of the USSR, Stalin made use of that intelligence to free up troops from the east to battle the Germans in the West.

The movement of Soviet troops, however, telegraphed to the Japanese that there was a spy in their midst. On 18 October 1941, Sorge, along with his fellow spy Ozaki Hotzumi, also in the employ of Russia, were arrested and charged with spying. Sentenced to death, the two men languished in Japanese jails and Stalin refused to lift a finger to help them. Three years after their arrests, on 7 November 1944, Sorge and Hotzumi were executed by hanging, Hotzumi suffering his fate first. After he was dead, Sorge was brought into the execution chamber.

> Like Ozaki, [Sorge] remained calm, dignified, a gentleman to the last. With sincerity he thanked Ichijima [the Governor of Sugamo Prison] and other prison officials for all they had done for him. Then with composure he walked into that bare, sunlit room that had already claimed Ozaki. From death he feared nothing and expected nothing. Once again the functionaries left the anteroom and took their places in the death chamber.
>
> The attendants bound his arms and legs, then melted into the background. In that precise moment, Sorge spoke clearly and distinctly. His words tolled in the taut silence like funeral bells:
>
> "Sakigun [The Red Army]!"
>
> "Kokusai Kyosanto [The International Communist Party]!"
>
> "Soviet Kyosant [The Soviet Communist Party]!"
>
> Man must worship as he must eat and drink and breath. Let him deny there is a God, and he will invest with divinity some force within his understanding. So Sorge had set up his own trinity and called upon it in his last hour. Yet he spoke neither in German, the language of his boyhood, nor in the broken Russian of his adopted tongue; he spoke in Japanese, which always came haltingly to his lips. Thus Sorge's last words did not well up spontaneously; he had carefully selected them. He had to be sure that his audience understood, that they would report his words correctly, so that all would know that he had died in his faith.
>
> A second time Sorge intoned his litany. The words, the dedication with which Sorge uttered them, his whole attitude impressed Yuda [an official witness to the executions] to his very soul. "There was no show-off in his manner," said Yuda in retrospect. "Sorge was loyal and faithful to his cause to the end. He repeated his words like a person saying a prayer."
>
> For the third time Sorge spoke his farewell salute to the outside world. Then he snapped to attention. Instinctively recognizing the sure moment, the executioners sprang the trap. It was exactly 10:20 A.M.
>
> Yuda's eyes moved irresistibly to Sorge's hands—much bigger than Ozaki's, hands that quivered in the death struggle. Watching them, Yuda asked himself, "What are we accomplishing by executing these two men? Will it be a plus for us or a minus?"
>
> Ozaki's body, submissive to fate, had released his spirit willingly. Sorge's body had always kept his spirit earthbound; now it clung fiercely to life. Sorge took nineteen minutes to die.

In 1964 Sorge was declared a Hero of the Soviet Union, but his name has since been forgotten.

**References:** Goetz, Philip W., ed.-in-Chief, *The New Encyclopædia Britannica,* 22 vols. (Chicago: Encyclopædia Britannica, Inc., 1995), 21:20; Johnson, Chalmers A., *An Instance of Treason: Ozaki Hotsumi and the*

*Sorge Spy Ring* (Stanford, CA: Stanford University Press, 1990); Prange, Gordon W., *Target Tokyo: The Story of the Sorge Spy Ring* (New York: McGraw-Hill, 1984), 510–511; van Sweringen, Bryan T., *The Case of Richard Sorge* (New York: Garland, 1989); Taylor, James, and Warren Shaw, *The Third Reich Almanac* (New York: World Almanac, 1987), 303; Zentner, Christian, and Friedemann Bedüftig, eds., *Encyclopedia of the Third Reich,* 2 vols. (New York: Macmillan, 1991), 2:888.

## *South Carolina v. Gathers* (490 U.S. 805. 109 S.Ct. 2207, 104 L.Ed. 2d 876 [1989])

U.S. Supreme Court case in which the court held that using information about the characteristics of the victim during closing arguments and sentencing in a capital case violated the Eighth Amendment to the United States Constitution.

Demetrius Gathers was tried and convicted of murdering a man he and other youths killed in a park. The victim, a preacher, dropped several articles on the ground during the attack. The prosecutor made reference to these and to the victim's personal characteristics in final arguments and sentencing: namely, that the preacher had been "a religious man"; that a prayer was printed on one of the cards he had with him, and that he carried a voter registration card, which "indicat[ed] the victim's belief in his community and his country." The defendant's attorney did not object to the introduction of this evidence; Gathers was convicted of first-degree murder and sentenced to death.

In 1987, in *Booth v. Maryland,* the Court had held that victim impact statements (VISs), reports presented during sentencing that show the impact of the crime on the victim's family, were a violation of the Eighth Amendment to the Constitution. Using this guideline, the South Carolina Supreme Court, finding the statements of the prosecutor in Gathers's case "unnecessary to an understanding of the circumstances of the crime" and concluding that they "conveyed the suggestion appellant deserved a death sentence because the victim was a religious man and a registered voter," struck down Gathers's death sentence and remanded the case back to the trial court for another sentencing hearing. The state of South Carolina appealed to the U.S. Supreme Court, which granted certiorari. Arguments in the case were heard on 28 March 1989.

Two and a half months later, on 12 June 1989, the Court, voting 5–4, upheld the South Carolina Supreme Court's finding that the statements violated Gathers's Eighth Amendment rights. Speaking for the majority (Chief Justice William H. Rehnquist was joined in dissent by Justices Sandra Day O'-Connor, Anthony Kennedy, and Antonin Scalia), Justice William Brennan wrote:

> Our opinion in Booth . . . left open the possibility that the kind of information contained in victim impact statements could be admissible if it "relate[d] directly to the crime." . . . South Carolina asserts that such is the case here . . . It contends that the various personal effects which were "maliciously strewn around [the victim's] body during the event" were "relevant to the circumstances of the crime or reveal certain personal characteristics of the defendant." We disagree. The fact that Gathers scattered [the victim's] personal papers around his body while going through them looking for something to steal was certainly a relevant circumstance of the crime, and this is a proper subject for comment. But the prosecutor's argument in this case went well beyond that fact: he read to the jury at length from the religious tract the victim was carrying and commented on the personal qualities he inferred from [the victim's] possession of [his prayer] and the voter registration card. The *content* of these cards, however, cannot possibly have been relevant to the "circumstances of the crime." There is no evidence whatever

> that the defendant read anything that was printed on either the tract or the voter card. Indeed, it is extremely unlikely that he did so. The testimony at trial was that Gathers went through [the victim's] bags very quickly, "just throwing [his belongings] everywhere, looking through things," and that he spent not more than a minute doing so . . . The crime took place, moreover, at night, along a dark path through a wooded area. . . . Nor did the assailants have flashlights. . . . Under these circumstances, the content of the various papers the victim happened to be carrying when he was attacked was purely fortuitous and cannot provide any information relevant to the defendant's moral culpability. Notwithstanding that the papers had been admitted into evidence for another purpose, their content cannot be said to relate directly to the circumstances of the crime. The judgement of the Supreme Court of South Carolina is therefore affirmed.

Justice Byron White voted with the majority, stating that "unless *Booth v. Maryland* . . . is to be overruled, the judgment below must be affirmed."

**See also:** *Booth v. Maryland; Payne v. Tennessee.*

## *Spaziano v. Florida* (468 U.S. 447, 82 L.Ed. 2d 340, 104 S.Ct. 3154 [1984])

U.S. Supreme Court decision that held that a "trial judge's imposing [of a] death sentence despite [the] jury's life sentence recommendation" was held to be constitutional.

Petitioner Joseph Robert Spaziano was convicted in a Florida court of first-degree murder. Two years and one month earlier, he had allegedly kidnapped and tortured a young woman, Laura Harberts; he later showed her mutilated body to a friend, Tony DiLisio, who led the police to the grave and testified against Spaziano. Because of the statute of limitations on such noncapital offenses as kidnapping and assault, the defendant could not be tried for these. The jury, deadlocked after six hours of deliberations, was given additional instructions by the judge to help arrive at a verdict. Finally, they returned with a guilty verdict on the charge of first-degree murder. In the sentencing phase, a majority of the jurors recommended life. But Florida law makes the jury recommendation only advisory, so the judge overruled it and sentenced Spaziano to death.

On appeal, the Florida Supreme Court upheld the conviction but struck down the death sentence, sending the sentencing phase back to the lower trial court. The court found in striking down the death sentence that the trial judge had erred in examining a portion of the presentence report that discussed Spaziano's previous criminal career as well as crimes of which he was accused but had not yet stood trial. On remand, the trial court ordered a new presentence report to be prepared; the prosecutor was also allowed to introduce the defendant's subsequent convictions for forcible carnal knowledge and aggravated battery. The judge reiterated his original finding that the murder of which Spaziano had been convicted was "especially heinous, atrocious, and cruel" and resentenced him to death. Spaziano appealed, claiming that the use of the two prior convictions tainted the court's death sentence; the Florida State Supreme Court upheld the sentence, holding that since the accusation had properly been excluded from the first trial but introduced once Spaziano had been convicted, it was appropriate. The U.S. Supreme Court agreed to hear the case, and arguments were presented on 17 April 1984.

A month and a half later, Justice Harry Blackmun held for a 6-3 court (Justices John Paul Stevens, William Brennan, and Thurgood Marshall dissenting) that the judge's overriding of the jury's recommendation was not unconstitutional, and that the state statute that allowed for such an override was not "so broad and vague as to violate the constitutional requirements of reliability in capital sentencing." Justice Blackmun wrote:

> We see nothing that suggests that the application of the jury-override procedure has resulted in arbitrary or discriminatory application of the death penalty, either in general or in this particular case. Regardless of the jury's recommendation, the trial judge is required to conduct an independent review of the evidence and to make his own findings regarding aggravating and mitigating factors . . . In this case, the trial judge based his decision on the presence of two statutory aggravating circumstances. The first, that the defendant had previously been convicted of another capital felony or of a felony involving the use of threat of violence to the person . . . was based on evidence not available to the advisory jury but, under Florida law, was properly considered by the trial judge . . . Petitioner's prior conviction was for rape and aggravated battery. The trial judge also found that the murder in this case was heinous, atrocious, and cruel. The witness who accompanied petitioner to the dump site where the victim's body was found testified that the body was covered with blood and that there were cuts on the breasts, stomach, and chest. The witness also testified that petitioner had recounted the torture of the victim while she was still living. The trial judge found no mitigating circumstances. . . . Whether or not "reasonable people" could differ over the result here, we see nothing irrational or arbitrary about the imposition of the death penalty in this case.

In 1994, Tony DiLisio gave an interview to *The Miami Herald* in which he claimed that he had been pressured by police and his abusive father to say that Spaziano, a member of the Outlaws motorcycle gang, was the killer. In January 1996, a trial judge, O. H. Eaton, Jr., heard evidence that DiLisio was threatened by the Outlaws to recant because, after 20 years on death row, Spaziano's time was running out. DiLisio denied this, and, on 22 January 1996, Judge Eaton ruled that Spaziano deserved a new trial.

## Spear, the Rev. Charles (1801–1863)

American prison reformer and prisoner rights advocate, noted for his opposition to capital punishment in the nineteenth century.

Born in Boston, Massachusetts, on 1 May 1801, he grew up in a religious atmosphere, and after studying theology, became a Universalist minister at Brewster and Rockport, both in Massachusetts. In 1839, he settled in Boston, where he began his crusade against prison abuses. He soon became well known for his advocacy of state legislation to aid and reform prisoners. His visits to prisons, his insistence on the humane treatment of all prisoners regardless of their crime, and his attempts to secure employment for released convicts made him a leading spokesman for prison reform in the years before the Civil War. He also led a spiritual movement for reform; in 1845 he began the publication of *The Hangman,* the first journal in the United States to *strictly* advocate an end to capital punishment. Spear's most important work, *Essays on the Punishment of Death,* appeared in 1844.

With the outbreak of the Civil War, Spear established himself in a number of hospitals as a traveling minister for the amelioration of conditions for wounded prisoners of war. On this mission, he contracted an infectious disease and died in a Washington, D.C., hospital on 18 April 1863.

**References:** McKelvey, Blake, "Spear, Charles" in Dumas Malone et al., eds.,

*Dictionary of American Biography,* 10 vols. 10 suppl. (New York: Charles Scribner's Sons, 1930–1995), 9:438–439; Spear, Charles, *Essays on the Punishment of Death* (Boston: Privately Published, 1844), 127–128.

## Spies, August Vincenz Theodor

See Haymarket Martyrs Case

## Stephen, Saint (?–30 C.E.?)

Considered by some historians to be the protomartyr (defined as the first martyr in any cause) of the Catholic Church, Stephen was stoned to death, an act described in the Bible.

Little is known of Stephen, whom historian Herbert Lockyer says was "one of the seven primitive disciples." In the Bible (Acts), he is described as "a man full of faith and of the Holy Ghost," as "having the face of an angel," and as one "who did great wonders and miracles among the people." He is alleged to have spoken profane words against Moses and God, and when those of the synagogue called him before their council and found him guilty of blasphemy, they had him stoned to death. Afterwards, they carried him to be buried, and "made great lamentations over him" (Acts). Saul of Tarsus, who later became Paul the Apostle, said, "and when the blood of thy martyr Stephen was shed, I also was standing by, and consenting unto his death, and kept the raiment of them that slew him." Paul himself was beheaded by the Roman forces of Nero. Stephen's feast days are 3 August and 26 December.

**Reference:** Lockyer, Herbert, *All The Men of the Bible* (Grand Rapids, MI: Zondervan, 1958), 321–322.

## Stephen I, Saint, Pope (d.257)

Born in Rome, Stephen was elected pope on 12 May 254, and he served for about three years. His papacy was marked by a raucous dispute with African bishops over the issue of the validity of the baptism by heretics, an issue Stephen supported. Although history says that he was beheaded in the catacombs while praying, many sources report that no proof has been found supporting the story. His feast day is 2 August.

**Reference:** Delaney, John J., and James Edward Tobin, "Dictionary of Catholic Biography" (London, England: Robert Hale Limited, 1962), 1080.

## Stoning to Death

Method of capital punishment, where a victim was chosen, trapped in a corner, and pelted with heavy rocks and stones until his or her skull was crushed.

This punishment was specified in the Mosaic Code, the laws of the Jews promulgated in the name of Moses. In references to biblical times, this process is called lapidation, and perhaps the most important instances come from Numbers 15:32–36 and Joshua 7:25–26:

> Numbers: And while the children of Israel were in the wilderness, they found a man that gathered sticks upon the Sabbath day. And they that found him gathering sticks brought him unto Moses and Aaron, and unto all the congregation. And they put him in ward [prison], because it was not declared what should be done to him. And the LORD said unto Moses, The man shall surely be put to death: all the congregation should stone him with stones without the camp. And all the congregation brought him without the camp, and stoned him with stones, and he died; as the LORD commanded Moses. . . .

Another form of stoning was also called pressing. Large stones were placed on the victims until their ribs broke or their chest collapsed, killing them, but not before they had suffered great agony. In 1426, the English instituted the law called *peine forte et dure* ("duration of punishment"). As the weights crushed his chest, a prisoner was fed bad bread on the first day of the torture, foul water the second, and "so shall he continue till he die."

Never really utilized to a great degree, stoning now occurs only in extremist Muslim countries, such as Afghanistan, where a 1996 stoning took place because of a couple's adultery, and Iran, where laws promulgated on stoning prohibit the use of large stones because death might occur too quickly.

**References:** Laurence, John, *A History of Capital Punishment* (New York: Citadel, 1960), 221; Peters, Edward M., "Prison Before the Prison: The Ancient and Medieval Worlds" in Norval Morris and David J. Rothman, eds., *The Oxford History of the Prison: The Practice of Punishment in Western Society* (New York: Oxford University Press, 1995), 12. For a work on stoning in modern Iran, see Sahebjam, Friedoune (Richard Seaver, trans.), *The Stoning of Soroya M.* (New York: Arcade, 1994).

## Streicher, Julius

See Nuremberg War Crimes Defendants

## Thackeray, William Makepeace (1811–1863)

British writer famed for his essay "Going to See a Man Hanged," which spurred the abolitionist movement against capital punishment in the nineteenth century in both England and abroad.

One of the leading English writers of the Victorian era, Thackeray was born in Calcutta, India, on 18 July 1811, the son of Richmond Makepeace Thackeray, an official of the British East Indian Company in India, and his wife Anne (nee Beecher or Becher) Thackeray. Richmond Thackeray died when his son was only three years old, at the age of 33; before his mother remarried a little more than a year later, William was sent to England for his education. He went to school at Chiswick, and many of his experiences there found their way into his later classic work, *Vanity Fair.* After finishing his primary education at an exclusive private school, the Charterhouse, Thackeray attended Cambridge but left without a degree after only two years.

Thackeray traveled across Europe in 1830 and 1831, then returned to England to study law. Yet writing was more appealing to him than the study of law. In 1833 Thackeray used his father's endowment to purchase a magazine, *National Standard,* and began to contribute articles to it. The enterprise soon failed, and the young writer was forced to find new ways of earning a living. His first published work, *Flore et Zéphyre,* appeared in 1836.

In July 1840, Thackeray was in London and decided to attend the public hanging of François Courvoisier, a Swiss servant who had been sentenced to death for the murder of his master, Lord William Russell. Until that time, there is no evidence of Thackeray's opinions of capital punishment; after the hanging, however, he was so incensed at what he perceived to be the great injustice of the

act that he wrote "Going To See a Man Hanged," which appeared in *Fraser's Magazine for Town and Country* in August of that year and is excerpted here.

> The sight has left on my mind an extraordinary feeling of terror and shame. It seems to me that I have been abetting an act of frightful wickedness and violence performed by a set of men against one of their fellows; and I pray God that it may soon be out of the power of any man in England to witness such a hideous and degrading sight. . . . [A Christian government] agrees, that is to say, a majority in the two houses agree, that for certain crimes it is necessary that a man should be hanged by the neck. Government commits the criminal's soul to the mercy of God, stating that here on earth he is to look for no mercy; keeps him for a fortnight to prepare, provides him with a clergyman to settle his religious matters (if there be time enough, but government can't wait); and on a Monday morning, the bell tolling, the clergyman read[s]out the word of God, "I am the resurrection and the life," "The Lord giveth, and the Lord taketh away." . . . [A]t eight o'clock, this man is placed under a beam, with a rope connecting it and him; a plank disappears from under him, and those who have paid for good places may see the hands of the government agent, Jack Ketch, coming up from his black hole, and seizing the prisoner's legs, and pulling them, until he is quite dead—strangled.

**See also:** Courvoisier, Benjamin.

**References:** Harden, Edgar F., "William Makepeace Thackeray" in Ira B. Nadel and William E. Fredeman, eds., *Victorian Novelists before 1885* (Detroit, Michigan: Bruccoli Clark, 1983), 258–293; Thackeray, William Makepeace, "Going to See a Man Hanged," *Fraser's Magazine for Town and Country,* 22:127 (August 1840), 156–157.

## *Thompson v. Oklahoma* (487 U.S. 815, 101 L.Ed. 2d 702, 108 S.Ct. 2687 [1988])

U.S. Supreme Court decision in which it was held that a defendant could not be legally executed for a crime committed when he or she was below the age of 16.

In 1983, William Wayne Thompson, who was 15 then and acting with three other people, brutally killed his former brother-in-law. Each of the defendants was arrested, tried, convicted, and sentenced to death. Only Thompson was below the age of 16 and thus considered a "child" under Oklahoma law. The prosecutor filed a petition stating that "the said child is competent and had the mental capacity to know and appreciate the wrongfulness of his [conduct]." The court of criminal appeals found that since Thompson was tried and convicted as an adult, he should be sentenced as an adult.

The case was argued before the U.S. Supreme Court on 9 November 1987, and it was not until 29 June 1988 that the justices handed down their decision. Writing for a 5–3 majority (Chief Justice William H. Rehnquist was joined by Justices Antonin Scalia and Byron White in dissent, and Justice Anthony Kennedy did not participate), Justice John Paul Stevens struck down Thompson's death sentence as violating the cruel and unusual punishments clause of the Eighth Amendment:

> The Court has already endorsed the proposition that less culpability should attach to a crime committed by a juvenile than to a comparable crime committed by an adult. The basis for this conclusion is too obvious to require extended explanation. Inexperience, less education, and less intelligence make the teenager less able to evaluate the consequences of his or her conduct while at the same time he or she is much more apt to be motivated by mere emotion or peer pressure than is an adult. The reasons why juveniles are not trusted with the privileges and responsibilities of an adult also explain why their irresponsible conduct is not as morally reprehensible as that of an adult. "The death penalty is said to serve two principal social purposes: retribution and deterrence of capital crimes by prospective offenders." *Gregg v. Georgia* . . . (joint opinion of Stewart, Powell, and Stevens, JJ.) In *Gregg* we concluded that as "an expression of society's moral outrage at particularly offensive conduct," retribution was not "inconsistent with our respect for the dignity of men." *Ibid.* Given the less culpability of the juvenile offender, the teenager's capacity for growth, and society's fiduciary obligations to its children, this conclusion is simply inapplicable to the execution of a 15-year-old offender.

**Reference:** Streib, Victor L., *Death Penalty for Juveniles* (Bloomington: Indiana University Press, 987).

## Tojo, Hideki (1884–1948)

Japanese soldier and politician, Prime Minister (1941–1945), put to death for war crimes—his own and his government's—committed during World War II.

Born in Tokyo, the son of an army officer, on 30 December 1884, Tojo graduated from a military academy and then from the army staff college when he was 30 years old. By the time of the Japanese invasion of Manchuria (which the Japanese made into a puppet state and renamed Manchukuo) in 1937, Tojo was named to the chief of staff of the Japanese Army. The following year he was named vice minister of war (serving

1938–1939), then minister of war (1940–1941). On 16 October 1941, he was named prime minister of Japan.

Under Tojo, the Japanese used every brutality to prosecute the war against its enemies. At first, his methods seemed to work, as one dramatic Japanese military victory was followed by another. Yet as the Americans gradually took back islands in the Pacific and the tide of the war turned, Tojo was blamed by his compatriots and forced to step down as prime minister. After the Japanese surrendered, Tojo tried to commit suicide.

Along with other leading Japanese military and political leaders, Tojo was tried in the International Military Tribunal for the Near East. In his defense during his trial, Tojo said, "Never at any time did I conceive that the waging of war could be challenged by the victors as an international crime, or that regularly constituted officials of the vanquished nations would be charged individually as criminals under any recognized international agreements or under alleged violations of treaties between nations . . . I feel . . . that I did no wrong. I feel I did what was right and true."

Ultimately convicted of crimes against humanity, on 23 December 1948 Tojo and six of the most notorious collaborators of the Japanese Empire during the war were hanged at Sugamo Prison outside Tokyo.

**References:** Donaldson, Norman, and Betty Donaldson, *How Did They Die?* (New York: St. Martin's Press, 1980); Kentaro, Awaya, "Tojo Hideki" in Itasaka, Gen, ed., *Kodansha Encyclopedia of Japan,* 9 vols. (Tokyo: Kodansha, 1983), 8:39; Wigoder, Geoffrey, *They Made History: A Biographical Dictionary* (New York: Simon & Schuster, 1993), 646–647.

## Tyler, Wat (or Walter) (?–1381)

English revolutionary, whose leadership of the English Peasants' Revolt in 1381 over the imposition of a poll tax on English peasants led to his execution and the similar death of fellow conspirator John Ball.

Little if anything is known of Tyler's life, including the date and place of his birth. Even his name is uncertain; it may have been Tegheler or Helier, and history has secured it as Tyler. The reasons he rose to command the 1381 revolt also remain clouded. Tyler took advantage of the peasants' hatred of the government in general and excessive poll taxes in particular. He was chosen as the head of the Kentish rebels on 7 June 1381; after assembling the shock troops of the rebellion at Blackheath, a small village in southeast London, Tyler led them into battle to take over the city of Canterbury, John the Gaunt's Savoy Palace, and, when they seemed invincible, they marched on the capital and took over London Bridge. There they were joined by discontented clergy and craftsmen, and they occupied the Tower of London.

King Richard II met with Tyler and his rebels at Smithfield, near London, but the rebels presented the king with radical demands, including the confiscation of all church lands to pay for any tax increases on the people. During the negotiations, a fight broke out, and Tyler was wounded. He was taken to St. Bartholomew's Hospital in London, but he was seized by order of the lord mayor of London, William Walworth, and taken back to the Tower of London, where royal troops had mercilessly overthrown the insurrection. He was quickly beheaded without trial. A compatriot in the uprising, John Ball, was also taken prisoner and beheaded as well.

**See also:** Ball, John.

**Reference:** Goetz, Philip W., ed.-in-Chief, *The New Encyclopædia Britannica,* 22 vols. (Chicago: Encyclopædia Britannica, Inc., 1995), 7:84.

### Use of Capital Punishment to Keep Order

Since the beginning of time and of the use of justice to punish, societies have put people to death mainly to "keep order" among people. During the Middle Ages, and particularly the tenth century, judicial systems in Europe moved from a system of punishing crime as being against people to being against the state and the king. Criminals who had once injured individual parties discovered that their crimes now damaged the state, and with this change in emphasis a system was needed to institute order. In 1116, during the reign of Henry I of England, the Leges Henrici (Laws of Henry) were instituted: they allowed that "there shall be certain offences against the King's peace: arson, robbery, murder, false coinage, and crimes of violence." In the United States, the early application of the "lynch law" was to preserve order, not to use violence against certain minorities. Hangings of slaves involved in revolts, as well, were utilized to bring order, and to teach a lesson to other slaves.

One of the arguments of those who support the death penalty is its ability to help establish and maintain a sense of law and order. The case of Saudi Arabia is often alluded to in support of this thesis. In that Middle Eastern nation, stern punishments are handed out for even the smallest of crimes: robbery can warrant the amputation of a hand, and adulterers are often beheaded. In Singapore, those who have been convicted of

smuggling even small amounts of drugs have been hanged, despite worldwide condemnation of such a penalty. However, Singapore remains one of the safest nations on earth. Death-penalty advocate Walter Berns wrote, "A country that does not punish its grave offenses severely thereby indicates that it does not regard them as grave offenses." Those opposed to capital punishment, however, argue that order in a society is sacrificed because people have less respect for a society that executes its own citizens.

**References:** Gibbs, Jack P., "Preventive Effects of Capital Punishment Other Than Deterrence," *Criminal Law Bulletin,* 14:1 (January 1978), 34–50; Meltsner, Michael, *Cruel and Unusual: The Supreme Court and Capital Punishment* (New York: Random House, 1973); Post, Richard S., and Arthur A. Kingsbury, *Security Administration: An Introduction to the Protective Services* (Boston: Butterworth-Heineman, 1991), 34; Tushnet, Mark, *The Death Penalty: Constitutional Issues* (New York: Facts on File, 1994), 5.

## Valentine, Saint (d. c.269 C.E.)

Holy priest put to death for his religious beliefs, and whose name, blessed years after his death, is remembered because of the holiday set aside in his name commemorated by lovers.

According to an early biographer, the Reverend Alban Butler:

> Valentine was a holy priest in Rome, who, with St. Marius and his family, assisted the martyrs in the persecution under [Emperor] Claudius II. He was apprehended, and sent by the Emperor to the prefect of Rome, who, on finding all his promises to make him renounce his faith ineffectual, commanded him to be beaten with clubs, and afterwards to be beheaded, which was executed on February 14, about the year 270 [other sources report the year as 269]. Pope Julius I is said to have built a church near Ponte Mole to his memory, which for a long time gave name to the gate now called Porta del Popolo, formerly Porta Valentini.

**Reference:** Thurston, Herbert J., and Donald Attwater, eds., *Butler's Lives of the Saints,* 4 vols. (Westminster, MD: Christian Classics, 1988), 332–334.

## Van der Lubbe, Marinus (1909–1934)

Dutch Communist beheaded by the Nazis for his alleged role in the setting of the Reichstag fire, 27 February 1933.

Little is known of his life. According to one historian, van der Lubbe was born on 13 January 1909 in the Netherlands. By 1927 he was a builder's apprentice, but that same year his face was sprayed with lime, which left his eyesight permanently impaired. In the next four years, he apparently joined the Dutch Communist party, but the extent of his role as a party activist is not known. After traveling throughout Europe in 1931, he settled in Germany. (At his trial, he admitted that while he was still a Communist, he had

not belonged to the party since leaving the Netherlands.)

The Nazi party and its leader, Adolf Hitler, needed an incident they could use to destroy political opposition inside Germany. On 27 February, less than a month after the Nazis took power, a large fire broke out in the Reichstag building in Berlin, which housed the German Parliament. Hermann Goering called the conflagration "a Communist outrage," and several leading Communists were picked up, including former Reichstag deputy Ernst Torgler, Bulgarian writer Georgi Dimitrov, student Blagoi Popov, and shoemaker Vassili Tanev. Among the group was van der Lubbe. The trial of the five men began on 21 September 1933 and ended on 23 December of that same year. Although there was virtually no evidence that the men had set the fire (and it has since been determined that the Nazis themselves set the fire), van der Lubbe became the scapegoat. He was found guilty of high treason and arson, though the other men were all acquitted. The young Dutch laborer was sentenced to death; on 10 January 1934, three days before his twenty-fifth birthday, he was guillotined. His family was not allowed to claim his body, and he was buried in an unmarked grave in Leipzig.

In 1967, a West German court struck down van der Lubbe's conviction for high treason but upheld the arson conviction, reducing his sentence from death to eight years. In December 1980, shortly before the forty-seventh anniversary of his execution, van der Lubbe was completely exonerated by another West German court; the van der Lubbe family attorney, German Robert Kempner, then labeled the 1933 proceedings "a deliberate miscarriage of justice and a Nazi show trial."

**Reference:** "Executed Man Exonerated in Reichstag Fire of 1933," *Long Island Newsday* (Suffolk Co. ed.), 30 December 1980, 15; Lane, John, *The Reichstag Fire Trial: The Second Brown Book of the Hitler Terror* (London: Bodley Head, 1934); Snyder, Louis L., *Encyclopedia of the Third Reich* (New York: McGraw-Hill, 1976), 288–289; Tobias, Fritz (Arnold Pomerans, trans.), *The Reichstag Fire Trial* (New York: G. P. Putnam's Sons, 1964).

## Victim Impact Statement Cases, United States Supreme Court

See *Booth v. Maryland; Payne v. Tennessee; South Carolina v. Gathers*

## Walker, William (1824–1860)

Adventurer and filibusterer executed in Nicaragua for his part in an uprising in that country.

Walker was born in Nashville, Tennessee, on 8 May 1824, and studied law and medicine. Later he was a journalist in New Orleans and San Francisco before practicing the law for a short time in Marysville, California. Starting in 1853, however, he began to filibuster (a Spanish and English corruption of the Dutch *virjbuiter,* "freebooter," originally applied to the Pirates of the Caribbean Sea) against the authorities in lower California and northern Mexico, particularly the state of Sonora. It was apparent that his goal was spreading slavery to these areas. On 4 November 1853 he moved into La Paz with a band of supporters, took the Mexican governor there hostage, and proclaimed a new nation for slave-holding Californians to settle in. These new settlers did not appear and, as his force degenerated and the threat of Mexican reinforcements grew, Walker was forced to retreat back across the border to southern California. There he surrendered to the U.S. Army, was put on trial for violating American neutrality laws but acquitted in May 1854.

During the next year Walker decided to forgo conquering Mexican territory. Troubles among American financiers in Nicaragua were heating up, and on 11 June 1855 he landed with another band of supporters at Realejo, on the western coast, and soon was fighting the local army. He won a major victory and named one of his local supporters, one Rivas, as president and himself as generalissimo. He joined with Cornelius Garrison and Charles Morgan, officials of Accessory Transit Company, which was owned by Cornelius Vanderbilt, to take over the company's headquarters and then transfer ownership to Garrison and Morgan. On 12 July 1856, Walker

named himself president of Nicaragua. For a time he held out against the combined armies of several Central American states, but when they moved on his capital he surrendered to the U.S. Navy on 1 May 1857.

After another return to his native land, Walker decided once again to take over Nicaragua. That November he led a second incursion into the nation but was arrested and sent back to the United States a second time. In 1860, in an attempt to once again establish his government in Central America, he went to Honduras but was quickly arrested by the British navy. Turned over to the Honduran government, he was tried, convicted, and sentenced to death.

Author Robert Houston, in his fictionalized work on Walker, incorporates what he calls the "Death of William Walker, From an Eyewitness in Honduras." That account reads:

> At daylight, General Walker, surrounded by a guard of seventy unkempt ruffians, was marched past our camp across a small stream. His face was pale, as usual, and I noticed a scar on his cheek received in the fights around Trujillo. Being a Catholic, he carried a small gold crucifix in his hand, which he was normally accustomed to wear around his neck. He looked neither to the left nor right, intent only on the Psalms of David, as I was later told they were, which the priest who accompanied him never ceased to recite. When they halted, the officer command-

ing the guard read a paper in Spanish, his orders, I presume, and then General Walker spoke a few moments in Spanish. We could not hear what he said, and besides, I did not understand Spanish. We could see from where we stood a newly made grave in the sands, near the edge of which the general stood while speaking to the Spanish Guards, and those collected around it. While he was speaking there was a tap on the drum, a volley of musketry followed, and General Walker was dead.

To be sure of this, the captain of the firing party advanced, and placing the muzzle against the general's forehead, blew out his brains.

The solders then threw down their guns, and with brutal ferocity tumbled his body into this hole in the sands without a coffin or shroud. They robbed his body of its clothing, quarreling among themselves over its division, then covered him up. They picked up their guns and hurried away, apparently afraid to linger near the spot where they had killed and buried him, as if he might yet rise up against them.

Few actual American government documents seem to exist on the Walker matter. One of two reports found in the National Archives in Washington is simply titled "To Clingman on Walker's Arrest," apparently referring to the 1857 confinement. The document reads: "The Committee on Naval Affairs beg leave to submit the following report, in answer to a call of the House of Representatives, the President of the United States, did on the 11th day of January in the present year [1858] transmit to the House, reports from the Secretaries of State, of the Treasury, of the Navy and the Attorney General, which together with the accompanying documents contained the information asked for, concerning 'the late seizure of General William Walker and his followers in Nicaragua.' On the 19th of January the following resolution was adopted—'Resolved, that the President's message and accompanying documents be printed and conferred to the Committee on Foreign Affairs, except so much thereof as relates to the conduct of Commodore Paulding, or other officers of the navy.'" Little was ever resolved by the government, which allowed Walker several times to slip away from his parole and inject himself back into Latin American affairs, acts which led to his execution.

Walker was portrayed in the 1988 film (a box office flop) entitled *Walker,* by American actor Ed Harris.

**References:** Goetz, Philip W., ed.-in-Chief, *The New Encyclopædia Britannica,* 22 vols. (Chicago: Encyclopædia Britannica, Inc., 1995), 12:464; Houston, Robert, *The Nation Thief* (New York: Pantheon Books, 1984); "Papers Relating to the Seizure of William Walker and His Followers [in] Nicaragua," Committee on Foreign Affairs, 35th Congress, Records of the House of Representatives, RG 233, National Archives.

## Wallace, Sir William of Elerslie (1267?–1305)

Scottish hero, dramatically profiled in the award-winning 1995 motion picture *Braveheart,* savagely executed by King Edward Plantagenet (Edward I, also known as "Longshanks") of England for rebelling against the Crown. It was not long after his brutal execution that Wallace's life was held up as an shining example of those who defy governments in the name of freedom. A 1508 work, of which fragments exist in the library at Cambridge University and at the Mitchell Library in Glasgow, Scotland, may have been one of the first. A 1570 work, "The Actis and Deidis of . . . Schir William Wallace, Knicht of Ellerslie," was written in Latin; a copy exists in the British Museum in London. In 1594, Scottish author Henry Carteris wrote a major work on Wallace, "The Lyfe and Actis of the Maist Illuster and Vailzeand Campaign, William Wallace, Knicht of

Ellerslie, Mainteiner and Defender of the Libertie of Scotland."

Much of what little is known of Wallace's life comes from a work by a man known as "Blind Harry," who could neither read nor write. Wallace's father was Sir Malcolm Wallace, of Ellerslie, Scotland, a middle-class landowner and the scion of a family who had owned land in the area since the twelfth century through his father, Richard Wallace. Educated by his uncle at the Abbey at Paisley, William was offered the crown of Scotland but seems to have refused it.

It is apparent from all who write about him that Wallace's main wish was the independence of Scotland from England. Instead of settling down to a life of wealth, he began a series of attacks on English garrisons that earned him the love of his people and the ire of England's King Edward I. Assaults on the fortification at Lanark and at Ayr (where the English sheriff was murdered) led Edward to send a force to subdue the revolt. Edward's forces defeated Wallace's at Falkirk on 22 July 1298, and Wallace then began a guerrilla war against the English. He slipped out of the country in 1299 to ask Pope Boniface VII for aid, but, refused, returned to Scotland to continue his war. In 1305, he was betrayed to the English, who took him to London and tortured him before sentencing him to death.

A witness to Wallace's execution, a man named Matthew Paris but known as Matthew of Westminster, wrote of Wallace's death in a work originally published in 1307 and translated from the Latin in 1853: "A certain Scot, by name Wilhelmus Waleis, a man void of pity, a robber given to sacrilege, arson and homicide, . . . was seized by the King's agent, carried to London, condemned to a most cruel but justly deserved death, and suffered this . . . He was drawn through the streets of London, at the tails of horses, until he reached a gallows of unusual height, specially prepared for him; there he was suspended by a halter, but afterwards let down half-living; next his genitals were cut off and his bowels torn out and burnt in a fire; then, and not till then, his head was cut off and his trunk cut off in four pieces."

Wallace's name evokes such patriotism in his native Scotland that he is considered a saint. On 24 June 1861, 556 years after his death, more than 100,000 people showed up in the city of Stirling to commemorate him at the national monument to his exploits. Even so, few outside Scotland would know the name of Sir William Wallace were it not for a 1995 book by Scottish historian James Mckay entitled *William Wallace: Brave Heart*. It brought Wallace's story to the public for the first time in hundreds of years. American actor Mel Gibson discovered the book, a screenplay was conceived, and the resulting film, *Braveheart,* won the Best Picture Academy Award in 1996. Gibson himself won an Oscar for Best Director and a nomination for Best Actor. Wallace's direct descendants, including Wallace clan chief Seoras Wallace, aided in the compilation of information on his ancestor.

**References:** Hallam, Elizabeth, ed., *The Plantagenet Encyclopedia: An Alphabetical Guide to 400 Years of English History* (London: Tiger Books International, 1996), 67, 202; *The Lyfe and Actis of the Maist Illuster and Vailzeand Campaign, William Wallace, Knicht of Ellerslie, Mainteiner and defender of the libertie of Scotland* (Imprentit at Edinburgh be Henrie Charteris, 1594), ii–iii; Mckay, James, *William Wallace* (Edinburgh, Scotland: Mainstream, 1996); Matthew (Paris) of Westminster, *Flores Historiarum (The Flowers of History, especially as Relate to the Affairs of Britain, from the Beginning of the World to the Year 1307 . . . Collected by Matthew of Westminister; translated from the Original by C. D. Yonge),* 3 vols. (London: Bohn's Antiquarian Library, 1853), 3:452; *Westminster Abbey: Official Guide* (Norwich, England: Jarrold, 1994), 45.

## *Walton v. Arizona* (497 U.S. 639, 111 L.Ed. 2d 511, 110 S.Ct. 3047 [1990])

U.S. Supreme Court decision in which the Court held that a state statute providing for a separate sentencing hearing, in which the court hears aggravating and mitigating circumstances, is not unconstitutionally vague.

Petitioner Jeffrey Alan Walton and two friends were convicted of first degree murder in a Tucson, Arizona, court after kidnapping and robbing a Marine, shooting him in the head, then leaving him in the desert to die. As per a statute enacted by the Arizona state legislature, a separate sentencing hearing was conducted after the trial, in which the prosecution was allowed to introduce evidence of aggravating factors that could lead to a death sentence and the defense could introduce those mitigating factors that would call for a lighter sentence. The prosecution argued that the murder was committed "in an especially heinous, cruel [and] depraved manner" and that it was done "for pecuniary gain." Walton entered evidence that his youth—20 at the time of sentencing—precluded him from "appreciat[ing] the wrongfulness of his conduct," and that he may have been sexually abused as a child. The trial judge then concluded that the mitigating factors were not "sufficiently substantial" and sentenced Walton to death. The Arizona Supreme Court upheld Walton's sentence, rejecting the petitioner's challenge to the constitutionality of the state statute and concluding that his death sentence "was proportional to sentences imposed in similar cases." The U.S. Supreme Court heard arguments in the case on 17 January 1990.

On 27 June 1990, Justice Byron White delivered the majority opinion for a divided 5–4 Court (Justices Harry Blackmun, William Brennan, Thurgood Marshall, and John Paul Stevens dissented) in upholding the state sentencing scheme. He explained:

> Walton . . . contends that the heinous, cruel, or depraved factor has been applied in an arbitrary manner and, as applied, does not distinguish his case from cases in which the death sentence has not been imposed. In effect Walton challenges the proportionality review of the Arizona Supreme Court as erroneous and asks us to overturn it. This we decline to do, for we have just concluded that the challenged factor has been construed by the Arizona courts in a manner that furnishes sufficient guidance to the sentencer. This being so, proportionality review is not constitutionally required, and we "lawfully may presume that [Walton's] death sentence was not 'wantonly and freakishly' imposed and thus that the sentence is not disproportionate within any recognized meaning of the Eighth Amendment.

Justices Brennan and Marshall, in their dissent, argued that "the death penalty is in all circumstances a cruel and unusual punishment" and that "the concern for human dignity lying at the core of the Eighth Amendment requires that a decision to impose the death penalty be made only after an assessment of its propriety in each individual case." As of this writing, Jeffrey Walton remains on Arizona's death row.

## Webster, Dr. John White (c.1793–1850)

American doctor put to death in 1850 for murder in one of the most widely-followed cases of the mid-nineteenth century.

Little is known of Webster, except that he attended Harvard College and graduated in 1811; one of his fellow students, who preceded him by two years, was Dr. George Parkman, and the two became strong, loyal friends. Webster himself went on to become a professor at the Massachusetts Medical College in the fields of chemistry and mineralogy. He even produced a famed workbook, *A Manual of Chemistry.*

Webster was not a rich man. To fit into Boston's society circles he was forced to borrow large sums, including money from his friend Parkman. By 1849, this debt added up to $2,432, even though Webster's salary at the medical college was only $1,900 a year. On 23 November 1849, Parkman confronted Webster about his debt. Angered when Webster tried to delay paying his debt, Parkman reached out, but Webster struck him. Parkman fell, dead. Webster, panicked, tried to burn the body in the college's incinerator, but it was too heavy to be done at one time; after a week, he still hadn't disposed of the entire corpse, and a suspicious janitor who smelled smoke found parts of jaw and other bones unburned. Alerted to the find, Webster tried to take poison and commit suicide but was arrested and charged with the murder of Parkman.

The trial, which opened in Boston, showcased some of the great intellectual talent of the New England area. Oliver Wendell Holmes, Sr. (father of the famed Supreme Court justice), who knew both men, testified. The case came down the theory of *corpus delicti:* did the bones found in the college basement belong to Parkman? Had Webster put them there? Could they even be positively identified? The jury believed that since Webster owed Parkman money, Parkman had vanished against his will, and a body was found in the incinerator where Webster worked, the professor must be guilty. Convicted of the murder, Webster was sentenced to death.

On the last Friday of the month, 30 August 1850, Webster was taken to a gallows and hanged. According to Webster case authority Helen Thomson, "In the first seconds after the fall Dr. Webster's legs jerked spasmodically twice. There was no other outward sign of struggle. The official report of the execution states that 'within four minutes all signs of life were extinct.'" After he had dangled, dead, for a period of time, he was cut down; the *Boston Traveler* commented, "After Professor Webster was cut down and placed in a rude coffin, his features appeared as in life, without distortion, and there was nothing but the purple hue of the flesh to show that his death had been a violent one."

Although he was supposed to be buried in the Webster family crypt in Mt. Auburn Cemetery in Cambridge, he instead was secretly buried elsewhere to ward off body snatchers.

**References:** Christenson, Stephen G., "Dr. John Webster Trial: 1850" in Edward W. Knappman, ed., *Great American Trials* (Detroit: Visible Ink Press, 1994), 105–108; Cozzens, James Gould, *A Rope for Dr. Webster* (Bloomfield Hill, MI: Bruccoli Clark, 1976); Nash, Jay Robert, *Encyclopedia of World Crime,* 4 vols. (Wilmette, IL: CrimeBooks, Inc. 1990), 4:3109–3111; *Report of the Trial of Prof. John W. Webster, Indicted for the Murder of Dr. George Parkman* (Boston: Philips, Sampson, 1850); Sullivan, Robert, *The Disappearance of Dr. Parkman* (Boston: Little, Brown, 1971); Thomson, Helen, *Murder at Harvard* (Boston: Houghton Mifflin, 1971), 272–275.

## *Wilkerson v. Utah* (90 U.S. 130 [1879])

U.S. Supreme Court decision holding that capital punishment was not a violation of the Eighth Amendment to the U.S. Constitution.

Wallace Wilkerson was convicted in a Utah court of the malicious and premeditated murder of one William Baxter in a saloon argument on 11 June 1877. Sentenced to die by firing squad, Wilkerson challenged his death sentence on the grounds that the Eighth Amendment's ban on "cruel and unusual punishments" prohibited death by firing squad, the proscribed measure in Utah. The Supreme Court of the Territory of Utah denied Wilkerson's appeal, and he asked the U.S. Supreme Court to hear it. On 8 January 1879 the case was submitted to the Supreme Court without arguments being heard.

On 17 March of that same year, Justice Nathan Clifford spoke for a unanimous court in upholding Wilkerson's sentence and finding that the death penalty was not a violation of the Eighth Amendment's ban on cruel and unusual punishments:

> Cruel and unusual punishments are forbidden by the Constitution, but the authorities referred to [Clifford had cited several historical sources supporting the court's decision] are quite sufficient to show that the punishment of shooting as a mode of executing the death penalty for the crime of murder in the first degree is not included in that category, within the meaning of the Eighth Amendment. Soldiers convicted of desertion or other capital military offenses are in the great majority of cases sentenced to be shot, and the ceremony for such occasions is given in great fullness by the writers upon the subject of courts-martial . . . Where the conviction is in the civil tribunals, the rule of the common law was that the sentence or judgment must be pronounced or rendered by the court in which the prisoner was tried or finally condemned, and the rule was universal that it must be such as is annexed to the crime by law. Of these, says Blackstone, some are capital, which extend to the life of the offender, and consist generally in being hanged by the neck till dead.

On 16 May 1879, Wilkerson was put to death by firing squad in a rather messy execution. The *Daily Ogden Junction* of 17 May protested: "These disgusting scenes are invariably ascribed to accidental causes, but they have become so horrifyingly frequent that some other method of judicial murder should be adopted. The French guillotine never fails. The swift falling knife flashes in the light, a dull thud is heard and all is over. It is eminently more merciful to the victim than our bungling atrocities, and the ends of justice are fully secured."

**Reference:** Gillespie, L. Kay, *The Unforgiven: Utah's Executed Men* (Salt Lake City, Utah: Signature Books, 1991), 11–14.

## Wirz, Henry (1823–1865)

German-Swiss commandant of Andersonville, the Confederate prisoner of war internment camp during the Civil War, hanged for his treatment of Union prisoners who were held there and died in terrible numbers. Wirz was the only Confederate executed for crimes committed during the Civil War.

Born in Zurich, Switzerland, on 25 November 1823, Wirz's real name was either Heinrich Hermann Wirz or Heinrich Hartmann Wirz. His father, a tailor, discouraged his son from going to medical school after he had received a common education; later in life, however, Wirz would claim that he was trained as a physician. He was married and had three children, but his marriage ended in divorce, and he emigrated to the United States in 1849. He worked for a time in a factory in Lawrence, Massachusetts, then moved to Kentucky, where as a medical assistant he pretended to be a doctor. In Louisiana, he was addressed as "Dr. Wirz."

At the start of the American Civil War, Wirz was living in Milliken's Bend, Louisiana; he enlisted as a sergeant in the Fourth Louisiana Infantry and saw action at the Battle of Seven Pines, where he was wounded, an injury that left him in horrible pain for the rest of his short life. He was assigned to the staff of Brigadier General John H. Winder, who put him in charge of the military prison at Richmond, Virginia. For his work there, Confederate president Jefferson Davis sent him on a diplomatic mission to Europe in 1862. When he returned in February 1864, he was placed in charge of Andersonville Prison in Georgia, now considered one of the worst prisoner of war camps in the history of warfare.

Because the Confederates had few if any resources to offer their own troops, the Union prisoners, particularly at Andersonville, were treated horribly, forced to live in open tents exposed to the sun, to eat rancid food, and drink putrid and fetid water contaminated with fecal matter. And, according to former Confederate soldiers who testified at his trial, Wirz was personally merciless to the bedraggled Union captives. One soldier, in order to get some water, crossed an invisible line that prisoners were not allowed to cross. Wirz pointed to him and yelled to a sentry, "God damn your soul, why don't you kill the Yankee son of a bitch?" The sentry shot the prisoner once in the head; another prisoner, too weak to march, was set upon by Wirz himself and trampled to death.

With the end of the war, Wirz was captured by Union General Henry E. Noyes. Pleading that he had just been following orders and asking that he be allowed to return to Europe, he was instead taken in chains to Washington, D.C., where a military tribunal convened on 23 August 1865 to try him on charges of murder and the gross mistreatment of prisoners of war. Owing to the times and the stories of horrendous abuse that came out of the trial, the outcome was never in doubt. Wirz was found guilty but offered a deal if he would testify against former President Davis. He refused. On 10 November 1865, Wirz was taken to a gallows in the yard of the Old Capitol Prison. As the order was read that he be hanged until dead, he told the major in charge, "I know what orders are, Major—I am being hung for obeying them." He thus became the only Confederate executed for crimes committed during the war.

After his death, Wirz became a cause célèbre for many Confederate sympathizers who believed that the Swiss commandant had been made a scapegoat. In 1909, the Georgia division of the United Daughters of the Confederacy erected a monument to Wirz at the site of the Andersonville Prison. Its four sides were inscribed with messages regarding Wirz's case, including this statement from Jefferson Davis dated 1888: "When time shall have softened passion and prejudice, when reason shall have stripped the mask of misrepresentation, then justice holding even her scales, will require much of past censure and praise to change places."

**References:** Byrne, Frank L., "Wirz, Henry" in Richard N. Current, ed., *Encyclopedia of the Confederacy,* 4 vols. (New York: Simon & Schuster, 1993), 4:1734–1736; *The Demon of Andersonville or the Trial of Henry Wirz* (Philadelphia: Barclay, 1865); Kantor, MacKinlay, *Andersonville* (New York: Signet, 1955); Marvel, William, *Andersonville: The Last Depot* (Chapel Hill: University of North Carolina Press, 1994); Robbins, Peggy, "Wirz, Heinrich Hartmann" in Patricia L. Faust, ed., *Historical Times Illustrated Encyclopedia of the Civil War* (New York: Harper & Row, 1986), 837; Spencer, Ambrose, *A Narrative of Andersonville, Drawn From the Evidence Elicited on the Trial of Henry Wirz, the Jailer. With the Argument of Col. N. P. Chipman, Judge Advocate* (New York: Harper & Brothers, 1866); Stibbs, John Howard, *Andersonville, and the Trial of Henry Wirz* (Iowa City, IA: Clio, 1911); "The Trial of Captain Henry Wirz for Conspiracy and Murder, Washington, D.C., 1865" in Lawson, John D., ed., *American State Trials: A Collection of the Important and Interesting Criminal Trials Which Have Taken Place in the United States, from the Beginning of our Government to the Present Day,* 17 vols. (St. Louis, MO: F. H. Thomas Law Book Company, 1914–1936), 8:657–875; United States Congress, Senate, "Trial of Henry Wirz," Senate executive document no. 23, 40th Congress, 2nd session (1865).

## *Witherspoon v. Illinois* (391 U.S. 510 [1968])

Landmark U.S. Supreme Court decision, holding that the exclusion of potential jurors who "hav[e] conscientious scruples against or opposed to capital punishment, without stating that they would automatically vote against capital punishment no matter what the trial would reveal" was a violation of a defendant's right to a fair trial guaranteed under the Sixth and Fourteenth Amendments to the U.S. Constitution.

William C. Witherspoon was brought to trial in the district court of Cook County, Illinois, in 1960 for murder. A state statute allowed for challenges to be made to potential jurors who "might hesitate to return a verdict inflicting" the sentence of death. Such jurors were excluded, and Witherspoon was sentenced to death. The court rejected his petition for a writ of habeas corpus, and the Supreme Court of Illinois upheld both the conviction and death sentence. The U.S. Supreme Court heard arguments in the case on 24 April 1968.

Five weeks later, on 3 June 1968, the Court held 5–4 that the exclusion of jurors who merely said that they *might* vote against capital punishment was a violation of a defendant's right to a fair trial guaranteed by the Sixth and Fourteenth Amendments to the U.S. Constitution. Speaking for the majority, Justice Potter Stewart differentiated between jurors who declared that the death penalty violated their "conscientious scruples" and jurors who claimed that they could in no way vote for the penalty of death:

> A man who opposes the death penalty, no less than one who favors it, can make the discretionary judgment entrusted to him by the State and can thus obey the oath he takes as a juror. But a jury from which all such men have been excluded cannot perform the task demanded of it. Guided by neither rule nor standard, 'free to select or reject as it [sees] fit,' a jury [that] must choose between life imprisonment and capital punishment can do little more—and must do nothing less—than express the conscience of the community on the ultimate question of life or death. Yet, in a nation less than half of whose people believe in the death penalty [in 1966, a poll showed that 42 percent of Americans believed in capital punishment, 47 percent were opposed to it, 11 percent undecided], a jury composed exclusively of such people cannot speak for the community. Culled of all who harbor doubts about the wisdom of capital punishment—of all who would be reluctant to pronounce the extreme penalty—such a jury can speak only for a distinct and dwindling minority. . . . Whatever else might be said of capital punishment, it is at least clear that its imposition by a hanging jury cannot be squared with the Constitution. The State of Illinois has stacked the deck against the petitioner. To execute this death sentence would deprive him of his life without due process of law.

In dissent, Justice William O. Douglas found that the exclusion of any juror who was against capital punishment, even if the juror told the court that he or she could in no way vote for its infliction, violated the Constitution. Justice Hugo Black was joined in dissent by Justices John Marshall Harlan and Byron White in arguing that "the state should not be forced to accept jurors who are bound to be biased against one of the critical issues in the trial." Justice White also dissented separately that the "constitutional grounds provided in the opinion were inadequate to support the court's holding."

In 1986, the Supreme Court overturned the *Witherspoon* standard in the case of *Lockhart v. McCree.*

**See also:** *Lockhart v. McCree.*

## Women, Execution of

With the execution of Karla Faye Tucker by the state of Texas on 3 February 1998, the controversy over the execution of women took center stage. Since the days when America was merely a collection of colonies, of more than 20,000 people who have been put to death, only 400 were women, including 27 who were charged with witchcraft. And although one out of every 50 persons sentenced to death in the United States is a women, only two women have been put to death since the Supreme Court found capital punishment to be constitutional in 1976.

The execution of women has been a controversial subject throughout history. Even women as hated as Lady Jane Grey, Mary, Queen of Scots, Ruth Snyder, and Velma Barfield have obtained sympathy for their plight. In fact, however, the execution of female offenders is quite rare, particularly in the United States. Since the first such case in 1632, there are only 514 documented cases out of an estimated 20,000 executions carried out since 1608. Before Barfield was put to death in 1984, the last American woman to suffer the same fate was Elizabeth Duncan, who died in California's gas chamber on 8 August 1962. In the United States, women account for approximately one of eight murder arrests, one of 50 death sentences imposed, and one of 70 persons on death row but account for only 3 of the 440 persons executed since 1977 (Velma Barfield in 1984 and Karla Faye Tucker and Judias Buenoano in 1998).

"There's a tendency to believe in female innocence," said Cathy Young, a researcher at the Cato Institute and vice president of the conservative Women's Freedom Network who argues that female offenders are historically treated more leniently than males who have committed similar crimes. "Feminists haven't paid attention when gender bias goes in the other direction." For example, double murderer Susan Smith, convicted of killing her two children in 1995, was given a life sentence instead of death. In another case, Illinois death-row inmate Guinevere Garcia's death sentence was commuted just a few hours before her 17 January 1996 execution because of the abuse she had suffered at the hands of men, although many male inmates with similar stories have not received commutation. The case of Karla Faye Tucker, who murdered two people with a pickax, became a cause célèbre in 1998. As her execution date neared, many who had previously been considered staunch supporters of capital punishment, including prominent figures from the religious right, called for the commutation of her sentence because she claimed she had "found God." Much of her case was apparently highlighted in the 1996 film *Last Dance,* which profiled a woman on death row for killing two people. In the end, however, nothing could save her, and she was put to death by lethal injection on 3 February 1998.

**Death Sentences Imposed upon Female Offenders, 1976–1997**

| *Year* | *Total Death Sentences* | *Female Death Sentences* | *Percentage* |
|---|---|---|---|
| 1976 | 234 | 3 | 1.3 |
| 1977 | 138 | 1 | 0.7 |
| 1978 | 186 | 4 | 2.1 |
| 1979 | 154 | 4 | 2.6 |
| 1980 | 175 | 2 | 1.1 |
| 1981 | 229 | 3 | 1.3 |
| 1982 | 269 | 5 | 1.8 |
| 1983 | 254 | 4 | 1.6 |
| 1984 | 287 | 8 | 2.8 |
| 1985 | 271 | 5 | 1.8 |
| 1986 | 305 | 3 | 1.0 |
| 1987 | 290 | 5 | 1.7 |
| 1988 | 295 | 5 | 1.7 |
| 1989 | 264 | 11 | 4.2 |
| 1990 | 252 | 7 | 2.7 |
| 1991 | 271 | 6 | 2.2 |
| 1992 | 293 | 10 | 3.5 |
| 1993 | 295 | 6 | 2.0 |
| 1994 | 319 | 5 | 1.6 |
| 1995 | 310 | 7 | 2.3 |
| Total | 5,680 | 116 | 1.9 |

*Source:* U.S. Department of Justice, *Capital Punishment, 1995* (Washington, D.C.: Government Printing Office, 1996), appendix table 1.

**Women Executed in the United States under Federal and State Authority, 1865–1998**

| *Name* | *Date* | *State* | *Mode* |
|---|---|---|---|
| Mary Surratt | 7 July 1865 | Federal | Hanging |
| Emeline Meaker | 30 March 1883 | Vermont | Hanging |
| Martha Place | 20 March 1899 | New York | Electrocution |
| Mary M. Rogers | 8 December 1905 | Vermont | Hanging |
| Mary Farmer | 29 March 1909 | New York | Electrocution |
| Virginia Christian | 16 August 1912 | Virginia | Electrocution |
| Ruth Snyder | 12 January 1928 | New York | Electrocution |
| Silena Gilmore | 24 January 1930 | Alabama | Electrocution |
| Eva Dugan | 21 February 1930 | Arizona | Hanging |
| Irene Schroeder | 23 February 1931 | Pennsylvania | Electrocution |
| Anna Antonio | 9 August 1934 | New York | Electrocution |
| Eva Coo | 27 June 1935 | New York | Electrocution |
| Frances Creighton | 16 July 1936 | New York | Electrocution |
| Marie Porter | 28 January 1938 | Illinois | Electrocution |
| Anna Marie Hahn | 7 December 1938 | Ohio | Hanging |
| Ethel Spinelli | 21 November 1941 | California | Gas chamber |
| Sue Logue | 15 January 1943 | South Carolina | Electrocution |
| Helen Fowler | 16 November 1944 | New York | Electrocution |
| Bessie Mae Williams | 29 December 1944 | North Carolina | Electrocution |
| Corinne Sykes | 14 October 1946 | Pennsylvania | Electrocution |
| Louise Peete | 11 April 1947 | California | Gas chamber |
| Martha Jule Beck | 8 March 1951 | New York | Electrocution |
| Ethel Rosenberg | 19 March 1953 | New York | Electrocution |
| Earle Dennison | 4 September 1953 | Alabama | Electrocution |
| Bonnie Brown Heady | 18 December 1953 | Missouri | Gas chamber |
| Barbara Graham | 3 June 1955 | California | Gas chamber |
| Rhonda Bell Martin | 11 October 1957 | Alabama | Electrocution |
| Elizabeth Duncan | 8 August 1962 | California | Gas chamber |
| Velma Barfield | 2 November 1984 | North Carolina | Lethal injection |
| Karla Faye Tucker | 3 February 1998 | Texas | Lethal injection |
| Judias Buenoano | 30 March 1998 | Florida | Electrocution |

*Source:* Bowers, William J., *Legal Homicide: Death as Punishment in America, 1864–1982* (Boston: Northeastern University Press, 1984), 399–523.

**See also:** Cavell, Edith Louisa; Corday D'Armont (or D'Armans) Marie-Anne Charlotte; Ellis, Ruth Neilson; Graham, Barbara Elaine Wood; Mata Hari; Place, Martha Garretson Savacoli; Snyder, Ruth May Brown, as well as the biography of Edith Jessie Graydon Thompson in the entry on Bywaters, Frederick Edward Francis.
**References:** "Gender and the Death Penalty," *Washington Post,* 14 January 1998, A18; Gillespie, L. Kay., *Dancehall Ladies: The Crimes and Executions of America's Condemned Women* (Lanham, Md: University Press of America, 1997); Mansnerus, Laura, "Sometimes, the Punishment Fits the Gender," *New York Times,* 16 November 1997, B7.

## Woodson v. North Carolina (428 U.S. 280 [1976])

U.S. Supreme Court decision in which it was held that a state statute that obligated a jury to return a recommendation of death upon the conviction for first-degree murder was violative of the cruel and unusual punishments clause of the Eighth Amendment, as well as the Fourteenth Amendment.

Petitioners James Tyrone Woodson and Luby Waxton were convicted of first-degree murder for their role in the robbery of a convenience store in which a clerk was murdered and a customer seriously wounded. As required by a North Carolina state statute, the jury was obligated to return a recommendation of death if the crime committed included "any willful, deliberate, and premeditated killing and any murder committed in perpetrating or attempting to perpetrate a felony." The Supreme

Court of North Carolina affirmed the sentences of the two men, and they appealed to the U.S. Supreme Court; arguments in the case were heard on 31 March 1976.

On 2 July of that same year, the Court reversed the death sentences, struck down the state statute, and remanded the case to the trial court for resentencing. Joined in the majority by Justices Lewis Powell, John Paul Stevens, William Brennan, and Thurgood Marshall (Chief Justice Warren Burger was supported in dissent by Justices Byron White and William H. Rehnquist), Justice Potter Stewart held that the state statute violated the Eighth and Fourteenth Amendments:

> The Eighth Amendment stands to assure that the State's power to punish is "exercised within the limits of civilized standards" . . . [F]urther evidence of the incompatibility of mandatory death penalties with contemporary values is provided by the results of jury sentencing under discretionary statutes. In *Witherspoon v. Illinois*, . . . the Court observed that "one of the most important functions any jury can perform" in exercising its discretion to choose "between life imprisonment and capital punishment" is "to maintain a link between contemporary community values and the penal system." . . . Various studies indicate that even in first-degree murder cases juries with sentencing discretion do not impose the death penalty "with any great frequency."

He added, discussing *Furman v. Georgia,* the landmark death penalty case decided that same year, "A separate deficiency of North Carolina's mandatory death sentence statute is its failure to provide a constitutionally tolerable response to Furman's rejection of unbridled jury discretion in the imposition of capital sentences. Central to the limited holding in *Furman* was the conviction that the vesting of standardless sentencing power in the jury violated the Eighth and Fourteenth Amendments."

## *Yamashita v. Styer* (327 U.S. 1 [1946])

U.S. Supreme Court decision, upholding the right of the U.S. government to execute the commander of Japanese forces in the Philippines for war crimes committed during World War II.

Officially titled *Application of Yamashita: Yamashita v. Styer, Commanding General, U.S. Army Forces, Western Pacific,* the case involved General Tomoyuki Yamashita who, as the commanding general of the Fourteenth Army Group of Japanese forces in the Philippines, forced Americans and other allied soldiers to make the so-called Bataan Death March and committed other acts deemed war crimes. On 3 September 1945, he surrendered to American forces on those islands and became a prisoner of war, housed at the U.S. Army bases in Baguio in the Philippines. On 25 September, Lieutenant General Wilhelm D. Styer, commanding General of U.S. Army forces in the Western Pacific, presented Yamashita with an indictment that charged him with violations of the laws of war. Yamashita pled not guilty on 8 October 1945, then was held over for trial before five Army officers chosen by Styer. Yamashita was presented with six other army officers (which included Captain Frank Reel and Captain Milton Sandberg), all lawyers, to act as his defense counsel.

The trial began on 6 November in the ballroom of the U.S. high commissioner's residence in Manila and ended, appropriately, on 7 December 1945. After hearing 286 witnesses, who gave over 3,000 pages of testimony, the five judges found Yamashita guilty and sentenced him to be hanged. Yamashita appealed the conviction and sentence for review before the U.S. Supreme Court. Arguments were heard on 7 and 8 January 1946, but the Court did not rule on the sentence.

On 4 February of that same year, Chief Justice Harlan Fiske Stone spoke for a 6–2 Court (Justices Frank Murphy and Wiley B. Rutledge lodged vigorous dissents, while Justice Robert H. Jackson did not participate) in declining to review the military's conviction and sentence. Chief Justice Stone explained:

> We do not make the laws of war but we respect them so far as they do not conflict with the commands of Congress or the Constitution. There is no contention that the present charge, thus read, is without the support of evidence, or that the commission held petitioner responsible for failing to take measures which were beyond his control or inappropriate for a commanding officer to take in the circumstances. We do not here appraise the evidence on which petitioner was convicted. We do not consider what measures, if any, petitioner took to prevent the commission, by the troops under his command, of the plain violations of the law of war detailed in the bill of particulars, or whether such measures as he may have taken were appropriate and sufficient to discharge the duty imposed on him. These are questions within the peculiar competence of the military officers composing the commission and were for it to decide. . . . It appears that the order convening the commission was a lawful order, that the commission was lawfully constituted, that petitioner was charged with violation of the law of war, and that the commission had [the] authority to proceed with the trial, and in doing so did not violate any military, statutory or constitutional command. We have con-

sidered, but find it unnecessary to discuss other contentions which we find to be without merit. We therefore conclude that the detention of petitioner for trial and his detention upon conviction, subject to the prescribed review by the military authorities were lawful, and that the petition for certiorari, and leave to file in this Court petitions for writs of habeas corpus and prohibition should be, and they are, denied.

On 23 February 1946, Yamashita was hanged in Manila. Regarding the case, historian Robert Barr Chase wrote: "The fate of [Yamashita], a first-class fighting man, affirmed something new in the annals of war. For Yamashita did not die for murder, or for directing other men to do murder in his name. Yamashita lost his life not because he was a bad or evil commander, but simply because he was a commander, and the men he commanded had done unspeakably evil things."

**References:** Smith, Robert Barr, "Justice under the Sun: Japanese War Crime Trials," *World War II* Magazine, 11:3 (September 1996), 38; text of decision at 327 U.S. 1.

## Zangara, Guiseppe (c.1900–1933)

Italian-American assassin; a short, stubby man who nearly assassinated President-elect Franklin D. Roosevelt, and instead shot and killed the mayor of Chicago, Anton Cermak, who was traveling with Roosevelt in Miami, a crime for which Zangara paid with his life in the electric chair.

A native of Italy, Zangara emigrated to the United States nine years before he committed the crime for which he was executed. On 15 February 1933, President-elect Franklin D. Roosevelt visited Bayfront Park in Miami, Florida; Chicago Mayor Anton J. Cermak went along as part of his entourage. As Roosevelt's car drew up at the park, Zangara, a small man, came forward and aimed his snub-nosed .22 caliber pistol at the motorcade. He fired several shots, hitting Cermak and four other people but leaving Roosevelt untouched. Sitting next to Miami Mayor R. B. Gautier, the President-elect was whisked from the scene with the wounded Cermak in the car, and they were taken, with the other injured, to Jackson Memorial Hospital in Miami. Zangara was wrestled to the ground and escorted to jail. There, in an exclusive interview, he told the *Miami Herald* that "he is not an anarchist, . . . He is for the working man; he is against presidents, and kings, and all the rich people who tread the poorer classes under their feet."

Put on trial quickly after the shooting, Zangara refused legal counsel. He told the judge, "I don't want anybody to help me. You're the judge and you can do what you want to do." The judge named a public defender, but it didn't help: six days after the shooting, Zangara was convicted and sentenced to 80 years. Then, on 5 March, Cermak, who had swung between survival and death, succumbed to his wounds at the age of 59. Placed back on trial, this time for murder, Zangara was again found guilty,

this time sentenced to death. He did not appeal. On 20 March, 35 days after the shootings, Zangara sat in Florida's electric chair at Raiford.

Wrote the *Herald:*

> The little Italian, taunting, bitter to the end, died in Florida's electric chair at 9:18 a.m. today, a mocking smile on his lips . . . He walked swiftly into the execution chamber, his figure dwarfed by two towering guards. He looked startingly small, but his bravada was big as he viciously shook himself free from the guards and cried: "No, don't touch me. I go myself. I no scared of electric chair. I show you." Unaided, he seated himself in the chair. A little gnomelike figure, he stared boldly at the assembled crowd of some 30 spectators; as the electricians worked with the straps on his body, Zangara lifted his voice against the drumming of the rain on the gray windows of the gloomy room, taunting, "No movies, hey? Where the camera to take my picture?" Only silence answered him, and the steady beat of the rain. He tried again, with a faint, bitter laugh: "Nobody here, hey? You no let them. You capitalists. No chance for nobody to come here and take my picture." The electricians fumbled with the connections; carefully examining the helmet that fitted loosely upon Zangara's small, shaved head, they were worried that the contact would not be precise. Then came his muffled voice again, faint against the pounding of the rain, muffled by the straps and the helmet. Zangara gave a

last command: "Pusha the button." That was all. Sheriff Dan Hardle of Dade County pulled the switch. The assassin's body stiffened against the straps. The lethal current crashed briefly through the body, and it was still. Zangara was pronounced dead at 9:27 a.m.

**References:** "Assassin Pays with Life for Cermak Death," *Miami Herald,* 21 March 1933, 1; "Assassin Says He Does Not Want a Lawyer," *Miami Herald,* 17 February 1933, 1; "Five Wounded by Gunman at Meeting for Roosevelt," *Miami Herald,* 16 February 1933, 1; "Italian Talks Freely in Cell of Shooting," *Miami Herald,* 16 February 1933, 1; "Joe Zangara Is Sentenced to 80 years," *Miami Herald,* 21 February 1933, 1; "Mayor Anton J. Cermak Dies: Death Closes Long Battle by Executive," *Miami Herald,* 6 March 1933, 1; Ryan, Bernard, Jr., "Joseph Zangara Trial: 1933" in Edward W. Knappman, ed., *Great American Trials* (Detroit: Visible Ink Press, 1994), 366–367; "Social Misfit Is Description Given Zangara," *Miami Herald,* 19 February 1933, 1; "Zangara Dies in Chair Today," *Miami Herald,* 20 March 1933, 12.

## Zinoviev, Grigori Yevseyevich (1883–1936)

Russian revolutionary leader executed for his role in formulating the so-called "Left Opposition" to Stalin's policies.

Zinoviev was born on 23 September (11 September, Old Style) 1883 in Yelizavetgrad (now Kirovograd), the Ukraine, with the name Ovsel Gershon Aronov Radomyslsky, to lower-class Jewish parents. He received very little education, only attending law lectures at Bern University in Switzerland during his travels as a youth. Zinoviev joined the Russian Social Democratic Workers' Party in 1901 and sided with Lenin's Bolshevik faction after the split of 1903. After 1909 he was Lenin's chief collaborator, returning with him to Russia in 1917 in the famous sealed train across Germany. Zinoviev voted against the Bolshevik seizure of power in October of that year but returned to serve Lenin shortly after the coup. In 1919 he became the chairman of the newly established Communist International (Comintern) and in 1921 a member of the Communist party Politburo. When Lenin fell ill in 1922, Zinoviev joined with Leo Kamenev and Stalin to form a ruling that successfully withstood the challenge of Leon Trotsky.

After Lenin's death, Stalin turned against first Trotsky and the so-called Left Opposition, and then, once they were neutralized, against the right and Zinoviev. In 1926, Zinoviev was removed from the Politburo and the following year from his post in the Communist party. After admitting to "mistakenly" opposing Stalin, he was readmitted to the halls of power, only to once again be expelled in 1932. He was arrested soon after and, in 1935 was put on trial in secret with Kamenev. Found guilty in the first of the so-called show trials that the Stalinist regime became famous for, both men were condemned to death and later secretly executed. According to Zinoviev biographer Robert D. Warth, "Zinov'ev's [Russian spelling] fate, as that of the other [purge] victims, is known only through gossip and rumor. Most accounts agree that he collapsed as he was being led from his cell, shrieking a last appeal to the effect that Stalin had double-crossed him. The secret police officer in charge, fearing a nasty scene, had the presence of mind (for which he was later commended) to shoot him without further ceremony." Zinoviev had published such works as *The War and the Crisis of Socialism* (1920), *Against the Current* (a series of articles in book form released in 1923), *For a Third International* (1924), and *A History of the Communist Party.*

**See also:** Purge Trials.
**References:** Florinsky, Michael T., ed., *McGraw-Hill Encyclopedia of Russia and the Soviet Union* (New York: McGraw-Hill, 1961), 623; Goetz, Philip W., ed.-in-Chief,

*The New Encyclopædia Britannica,* 22 vols. (Chicago: Encyclopædia Britannica, Inc., 1995), 12:920; Hedlin, Myron W., "Zinoviev, Grigorii Evseevich" in George Jackson, ed., *Dictionary of the Russian Revolution* (Westport, CT: Greenwood Press, 1989), 644–647; Korey, William, *Zinoviev on the Problem of World Revolution, 1919–27* (Doctoral dissertation, Columbia University, 1960); Patrikeeff, Felix, "Zinoviev, Grigori Evseevich" in Harold Shukman, ed., *The Blackwell Encyclopedia of the Russian Revolution* (Oxford, England: Basil Blackwell, 1988), 399; Warth, Robert D., "Zinov'ev, Grigorii Evseevich" in Joseph L. Wieczynski, ed., *The Modern Encyclopedia of Russian and Soviet History,* 58 vols. 1 suppl. (Gulf Breeze, FL: Academic International, 1977–95), 40:98.

# BIBLIOGRAPHY

## Books, Articles, and Reports


*The Abbey of Saint Alban. Some Extracts from Its Early History and a Description of Its Conventual Church* (London: George Bell, 1851).

Abbott, Geoffrey. *The Book of Execution: An Encyclopedia of Methods of Judicial Execution* (London: Headline, 1995).

———. *Lords of the Scaffold: A History of the Executioner* (London: Robert Hale, 1991).

*Acts and Ordinances of the Interregnum, 1642–1660.* Collected and edited by Charles Harding Furth and Robert Sangster Rait for the Statute Law Committee. 3 vols. (London: Her Majesty's Stationary Office, 1911).

*Address of His Excellency Alexander H. Bullock to the Honorable Council; on the occasion of presenting the case of Edward W. Green, a convict under the sentence of death for the crime of murder in the first degree. Feb. 27, 1866* (Boston: Wright & Potter, State Printers, 1865).

Alexander, John Thorndike. *Autocratic Policies in a National Crisis: The Imperial Russian Government and Pugachev's Revolt, 1773–1775* (Bloomington: Indiana University Press, 1969).

Amnesty International USA, "The Death Penalty and Juvenile Offenders" (New York: Amnesty International, 1991).

Amos, Sheldon. *Capital Punishment in England Viewed as Operating in the Present Day* (London: William Ridgway, 1864).

Ampho. *War and Capital Punishment Opposed to Christianity. With Remarks on a tract by Walter Scott, entitled "The Punishment of Death for the Crime of Murder, Rational, Scriptural and Salutary"* (London: Jackson & Walford, 1846).

*An Agreement of the People of England, and the Places Therewith Incorporated, for a Secure and Present Peace, Upon Grounds of Common Right, Freedom and Safety* (London: John Partridge, 1649).

*Andreana: Containing the Trial, Execution, and Various Matters Connected with the History of Major John André, Adjutant General of the British Army in America, A.D. 1780* (Philadelphia: Horace W. Smith, 1865).

Andrews, Charles McLean. *Narratives of the Insurrections: 1675–1690* (New York: Charles Scribner, 1915).

Arasse, Daniel. *The Guillotine and the Terror.* Translated by Christopher Miller. (Paris: Flammarion, 1987; translation, London: Allen Lane, 1987).

*The Arraignment and Conviction of Mervin Lord Audley, Earle of Castlehaven, who by 26 peers of the realm found guilty for committing rapine and sodomy at Westminister on Monday, April 25, 1631: by virtue of a commission of oyer and terminer directed to Sir Thomas Coventry, Lord Keeper of the great seale of England, Lord High Steward for that day accompanied with the judges: as also the beheading of the said Earle shortly after on Tower Hill* (London: Printed for Tho. Thomas, 1642).

*The Arraignment of John Selman, who was executed Neere Charing-Cross the 7. Of Ianuary, 1612, for a Fellony by him committed in the Kings Chappell at White-Hall upon Christmas day last, in presence of the King and divers or the Nobility* (London: Printed by W. H. for Thomas Archer, 1612).

*The Arraignment, Tryal, and Condemnation of Captain William Kidd, for Murther and Piracy, at the Old-Bailey, the 8th and the 9th of May, 1701, as also the tryals of Nicholas Churchill, James Howe, and Darby Mullins for Piracy to which are added Captain Kidd's commissions, etc.* (London: J. Nutt, 1701).

Ashley, Maurice. *The Battle of Naseby and the Fall of King Charles I* (New York: St. Martin's Press, 1992).

Averbach, Albert, and Charles Price, eds. *The Verdicts Were Just: Eight Famous Lawyers Present Their Most Memorable Cases* (Rochester, NY: Lawyer's Cooperative Publishing, 1968).

Ayresworth, Hugh. *The Only Living Witness* (New York: Linden Press, 1983).

———, *Ted Bundy: Conversations with a Killer* (New York: New American Library, 1989).

Bailey, Thomas. *The Life and Death of the Renowned John Fisher, Bishop of Rochester, who was Beheaded on Tower-Hill, the 22nd of June 1535, and in the 27th Year of the Reign of King Henry VII, Comprising the Highest and Hidden Transactions of Church and State in the Reign of King Henry the Eighth; with divers Moral, Historical and Political Animadversions upon Cardinal Wolsey, Sir Thomas More, and Martin Luther; with a Full Relation of Queen Katherine's Divorce, Carefully Selected from Several antient Records* (Dublin, Ireland: Printed for P. Lord, R. Fitzsimmons, and D. Kylly, Booksellers, 1765).

Bainton, Roland Herbert. *Hunted Heretic: The Life and Death of Michael Servetus, 1511–1553* (Boston: Beacon Press, 1953).

Baker, Newton B., et al., eds. *The Sacco-Vanzetti Case: Transcript of the Record of the Trial of Nicola Sacco and Bartolomeo Vanzetti in the Courts of Massachusetts and Subsequent Proceedings, 1920–7*. 6 vols. (New York: Henry Holt, 1928).

Ballou, Adin. *Capital Punishment: Reasons for Its Immediate Abolition* (Hopedale, England: A. G. Spalding, 1845).

Barnhart, Clarence C., ed. *The New Century Cyclopedia of Names* (New York: Appleton-Century-Crofts; three volumes, 1954).

Barrett, W. P. *The Trial of Jeanne D'Arc,* trans. W. P. Barrett (New York: Gotham House, 1932).

Bates, Nicholas, et al. *Ronald Ryan: A Case Study in Criminal Proceedings* (Fitzroy, Victoria, Australia: VCTA Publishing, 1976).

Beccaria, Cesare. *Del delitti e delle pere* (An Essay on Crimes and Punishments), *translated from the Italian, with a commentary attributed to Mons. de Voltaire, translated from the French* (London: J. Almon, 1767).

Beck, James Montgomery, Sr. *The Case of Edith Cavell: A Study of the Rights of Combatants . . . Reprinted from "The New York Times"* (New York and London: G. P. Putnam's Sons, 1915).

Bedau, Hugo Adam. "Capital Punishment in Oregon. *Oregon Law Review* 45:1 (December 1965), 1–39.

———, ed. *The Death Penalty in America* (New York: Oxford University Press, 1982).

Bedau, Hugo Adam, and Michael L. Radelet. "Miscarriages of Justice in Potentially Capital Cases." *Stanford Law Review* 40 (November 1987), 21–172.

Beedle, Susannah. *An Essay on the Advisability of Total Abolition of Capital Punishment* (London: Nichols and Son, 1867).

Beggs, Thomas. "The Capital Punishment Commission" *Meliora: A Quarterly Review of Social Science in its Ethical, Economical, Political, and Ameliorative Aspect* 9 (1866), 125–139.

*The Behaviour of Mr. Will[iam] Staley in Newgate: after his Condemnation for high-treason: with the substance of his last speech and discourses at the usual place of execution, whither being drawn on a sledge he was hang'd and quarter'd there, on Tuesday the 26th of this instant November, 1678* (London: Printed for R. G., 1678).

Behr, Edward. *Kiss the Hand You Cannot Bite: The Rise and Fall of the Ceausescus* (New York: Villard Books, 1991).

Beichman, Arnold. "The First Electrocution" *Commentary* 35:5 (May 1963), 410–419.

Belohlavek, John Milan. *George Mifflin Dallas: Jacksonian Patrician* (University Park: Pennsylvania State University Press, 1977).

Beman, Lamar T., ed. *Selected Articles on Capital Punishment* (New York: H. W. Wilson, 1925).

Bennett, Martyn. *The English Civil War, 1640–1649* (London: Longman Group, 1995).

Bevan, Bryan. *James, Duke of Monmouth* (London: Hale, 1973).

Bienvenu, Richard. *The Ninth of Thermidor: The Fall of Robespierre* (New York: Oxford University Press, 1968).

Bishop, William W., ed. *Mormonism Revealed: Including the Remarkable Life and Confessions of the late Mormon bishop, John D. Lee (written by himself) and complete Life of Brigham Young, embracing a history of Mormonism from its inception down to the present time, with an exposition of the secret history, signs, symbols and crimes of the Mormon Church. Also the true history of the horrible butchery known as the Mountain Meadows Massacre* (St. Louis, MO: Excelsior Publishing, 1882).

Black, Henry Campbell. *Black's Law Dictionary: Definitions of the Terms and Phrases of American and English Jurisprudence, Ancient and Modern* (St. Paul, MN: West Publishing, 1990).

Blackburn, Douglas. *The Martyr Nurse: The Death and Achievement of Edith Cavell* (London: Ridd Masson, 1915).

Blackstone, Sir William. *Commentaries on the Laws of England: In Four Books; with an Analysis of the Work*. 4 vols. (New York: Harper & Brothers, 1857).

Blakley, Alan F., "The Cost of Killing Criminals," *Northern Kentucky Law Review*, 18:1 (Fall 1990), 61–79.

Borowitz, Albert. *The Woman Who Murdered Black Satin* (Columbus: Ohio State University Press, 1981).

Borrow, George Henry. *Celebrated Trials and Remarkable Cases of Criminal Jurisprudence from the earliest records to the year 1825* (London: Knight and Lacey, 1825).

Bourke-Jones, Derek. *Brief Candle: A Poetic Study of Lady Jane Grey, 1537–1554* (Eastbourne, England: Downlander, 1991).

Bovee, Marvin Henry. *Christ and Gallows; or, Reasons for the Abolition of Capital Punishment* (New York: Masonic Publishing, 1869).

Bowers, William J., with Glenn L. Pierce and John F. McDevitt. *Legal Homicide: Death as Punishment in America, 1864–1982* (Boston: Northeastern University Press, 1984).

Boyle, Andrew. *The Riddle of Erskine Childers* (London: Hutchinson, 1977).

Bremond, Marie Joseph François Regis Ignace Henri. *Sir Thomas More—the Blessed Thomas More.* Translated by Harold Child. (London: Duckworth, 1904).

Broad, Charlie Lewis. *The Innocence of Edith Thompson: A Study in Old Bailey Justice* (London: Hutchinson, 1952).

Brome, Vincent. *The Other Pepys* (London: Weidenfeld & Nicolson, 1992).

Brooks, Juanita. *John Doyle Lee: Zealot—Pioneer Builder—Scapegoat* (Glendale, CA: Arthur H. Clark, 1962).

Brown, Edmund, with Dick Adler. *Public Justice, Private Mercy: A Governor's Education on Death Row* (New York: Weidenfeld & Nicolson, 1989).

Browne, Courtney. *Tojo: The Last Banzai* (New York: Holt, Rinehart and Winston, 1967).

Bruno, Giordano. *The Expulsions of the Triumphant Beast.* Edited and translated by Arthur D. Imerti. (New Brunswick, NJ: Rutgers University Press, 1964).

Bunson, Matthew. *The Pope Encyclopedia: An A to Z of the Holy See* (New York: Crown, 1995).

Burleigh, Charles C. *Thoughts on the Death Penalty* (Philadelphia: Merrihew and Thompson, 1845).

Buxton, Sydney. *A Handbook to Political Questions of the Day, and the Arguments on Either Side, with an Introduction, by Sydney Buxton, M.P.* (London: J. Murray, 1892).

*By the King: A Proclamation Against Spreading of a Trayterous Declaration Published by James Duke of Monmouth, 15 June 1685* (London: Printed by the Assigns of John Bill, 1685).

Calvert, E. Roy. *Capital Punishment in the Twentieth Century* (London: G. P. Putnam's Sons, 1927).

*Captain Kidd, a Noted Pirate who was Hanged at Execution Dock, in England* (Boston: L. Deming, 1840?).

Carlyle, Thomas. *The French Revolution. A History* (New York: Charles Scribner's, 1837).

Carnegie, Margaret, and Frank Shields. *In Search of Breaker Morant: Balladist and Bushveldt Carbineer* (Armadale, Australia: Privately Printed, 1979).

Carrick, John Donald. *Life of Sir William Wallace* (Glascow: Richard Griffin, 1849).

———, *Life of Sir William Wallace of Elderslie* (Edinburgh: Constable's Miscellany, 1830).

Carty, Xavier. *In Bloody Protest: The Tragedy of Patrick Pearse* (Dublin: Able Press, 1978).

Cave, Colin F. *Ned Kelly, Man and Myth* (North Melbourne: Cassell Australia, 1968).

Cavell, Edith Louisa. *Nurse Cavell, Dog Lover.* Edited with an introduction by Rowland Johns (London: Methuen, 1934).

Cecil, Robert. *The Myth of the Master Race: Alfred Rosenberg and Nazi Ideology* (New York: Dodd, Mead, 1972).

Chapman, Hester Wolferstan. *Lady Jane Grey, October 1537–February 1554* (London, England: Cape, 1962; reprint, London: Grafton, 1985).

Cheever, George B. *Capital Punishment: The Argument of G. B. Cheever in Reply to J. L. O'Sullivan* (New York: John Wiley, 1843).

———. *Punishment by Death: Its Authority and Expediency* (New York: John Wiley, 1849).

Cheever, George B., and Taylor Lewis. *A Defence of Capital Punishment and An Essay on the Ground and Reason of Punishment, with special reference to the Penalty of Death* (New York: Wiley and Putnam, 1846).

Cher, Marie, pseud. [Scherr, Marie]. *Charlotte Corday and Certain Men of the Revolutionary Torment* (New York: D. Appleton, 1929).

Christmas, Henry. *Capital Punishments Unsanctioned by the Gospel and Unnecessary in a Christian State: A Letter to the Rev. Sir. John Page Wood, B.C.L.* (London: Smith, Elder, 1845).

Christoph, James Bernard. *Capital Punishment and British Politics: The British Movement to Abolish the Death Penalty, 1945–57* (Chicago, IL: University of Chicago Press, 1962).

Clark, James C. *The Murder of James A. Garfield: The President's Last Days and the Trial and Execution of his Assassin* (Jefferson, NC: McFarland, 1993).

Clark, William Robinson. *Savonarola: His Life and Times* (Chicago, IL: A. C. McClurg, 1890).

Cleland, Robert Glass, and Juanita Brooks, eds. *A Mormon Chronicle: The Diaries of John D. Lee, 1848–1876* (Salt Lake City: University of Utah Press, 1983).

Cleugh, A. *A Complete History of the Invasions of England, including the most memorable battles and sea-fights from Julius Caesar, down to the French landing in Wales in 1796: the calamities of France, being a catalogue of French cruelties, with a complete abstract from [Abbé Augustin] Barruel's History of the French Clergy, detailing the refined system of murder pursued by the notorious Jourdan, Carrier, Marrat, General Duquesnoy, and Robespierre; the ejectment of the priesthood, and total abolition of religion and humanity in France* (London: Printed by J. Skirven for A. Cleugh, 1801).

Clifton, Robin. *The Last Popular Rebellion: The Western Rising of 1685* (London: Maurice Temple Smith, 1984).

Clowes, Peter. "A Fanatically Selfless Sense of Duty Drove Nurse Edith Cavell to Harbor Allied Soldiers behind Enemy Lines." *Military History* 13:3 (August 1996), 18, 73–74.

Cogswell, Jonathan. *A Treatise on the Necessity of Capital Punishment* (Hartford, CT: Press of E. Geer, 1843).

Cohen, Bernard Lande. *Law without Order: Capital Punishment and the Liberals* (New Rochelle, NY: Arlington House, 1970).

Cohn, Harm Hermann. *The Trial and Death of Jesus* (New York: Harper & Row, 1971).

Cole, John Alfred. *Lord Haw Haw and William Joyce* (New York: Farrar, Straus & Giroux, 1965).

Coleridge, Samuel Taylor. *The Fall of Robespierre* (Cambridge, England: W. H. Lunn and J. and J. Merrill, 1794; reprint, Oxford, England: Wood Stock Books, 1991).

Colman, Benjamin. *The Rending of the Vail of the Temple at the Crucifixion of our Lord and Saviour Jesus Christ, Consider'd in a Sacramental Discourse had in Boston, N.E., December 3, 1710* (Boston: B. Green, 1717).

Colquhoun, Patrick. *A Treatise on the Police of the Metropolis, Explaining the Various Crimes and Misdemeanors which are at Present felt as a Pressure Upon the Community, and Suggesting Remedies for their Prevention, by a Magistrate* (London: Joseph Mawman, 1800).

Combe, George. *Thoughts on Capital Punishment* (Edinburgh, Scotland: Maclachlan, Stewart, 1847).

Commire, Anne, ed. *Historic World Leaders*. 5 vols. (Detroit, MI: Gale Research Inc, 1994).

*Commonwealth of Pennsylvania, Court of Oyer and Terminer, Argument of Franklin B. Gowen, Esq., of counsel for the Commonwealth, in the case of the Commonwealth vs. Thomas Munley, indicted in the Court of Oyer and Terminer of Schuykill County, Pa., for the murder of Thomas Sanger, a mining boss, at Raven Run, on September 1st, 1875* (Pottsville, PA: Chronicle Book and Job Romms, 1876).

*The Confession and Execution of the five prisoners suffering at Tyburn on Fryday the 16th of March 1676/7: viz, Thomas Sadler and William Johnson, for a burglary in the house of the Right Honourable the Lord High Chancellor of England, and stealing the mace and two purses; and Francis Webb, for a burglary, and stealing of clothes of great value, Matthew Grammond and Anthony Richoake for a burglary in Clarkenwel: together with their penitent behaviour in Newgate, since their Condemnation, and last speeches at the place of Execution* (London: Printed for D. M., 1677).

*The Confession and Execution of the seven prisoners suffering at Tyburn on Fryday the 4th of May, 1677: viz, Robert Dine, William Dine, and Margaret Dine of Enfield, for barbarously wounding of Jane King, the sweet-heart of the said Robert, Margaret Spicer for murthering her bastard-childe, David Hackley, Jeremiah Dawson, and Mary Browne, all notorious offenders, and formerly burn'd in the hand for several felonies by them committed: together with their penitent behaviour at Newgate, since their Condemnation, and last speeches at the place of Execution* (London: Printed for D. M., 1677).

*The Confession and Execution of the two prisoners that suffered at Tyburn on Munday the 16th of Decemb., 1678: viz, Nathaniel Russel, a bayley's follower, for murdering a young man in Whites-Alley: and Steven Arrowsmith, for a rape committed on a girl between eight and nine years of age: giving a tru account of their behaviour after condemnation, the substance of the discourses that past between them and Mr. Ordinary in Newgate that morning before they went into the cart, and their speeches at the place of Execution* (London: Printed for R. G., 1678).

Cooper, David D. *The Lesson of the Scaffold: The Public Execution Controversy in Victorian England* (London: Allen Lane, 1974).

Cooper, R. W. *The Nuremberg Trial* (Harmondsworth, England: Penguin Books, 1947).

Cox, Tom. *Damned Englishman: A Study of Erskine Childers (1870–1922)* (Hicksville, NY: Exposition Press, 1975).

Cozzens, James Gould. *A Rope for Dr. Webster* (Bloomfield Hill, MI: Bruccoli Clark, 1976).

*Crime and Punishment: The Illustrated Crime Encyclopedia*. 28 vols. (Westport, CT: H. S. Stuttman, 1994).

Current, Richard N., ed. *Encyclopedia of the Confederacy*. 4 vols. (New York: Simon & Schuster, 1993).

Curtis, Newton M. *To Define the Crime of Murder* (Washington, D.C.: Government Printing Office, 1892).

Cyriax, Oliver. *Crime: An Encyclopedia* (London: André Deutsch, 1993).

Davey, Arthur, ed. *Breaker Morant and the Bushveldt Carbineers* (Cape Town, South Africa: Van Riebeck Society, 1987).

Davey, Richard Patrick Doyle. *The Nine Days' Queen. Lady Jane Grey and Her Times* (London: Methuen, 1909).

Davidson, Eugene. *The Trial of the Germans: Nuremberg, 1945–1946* (New York: Macmillan, 1966).

De la Bedoyne, Michael. *The Meddlesome Friar and the Wayward Pope: The Story of the Conflict between Savonarola and Alexander VI* (Garden City, NY: Hanover House, 1958).

De Rosa, Peter. *Rebels: The Irish Rising of 1916* (New York: Doubleday, 1990).

Delaney, John J., and James Edward Tobin. *Dictionary of Catholic Biography* (London: Robert Hale, 1962).

Delderfield, Eric R. *Kings and Queens of England and Great Britain* (London: David & Charles, 1994).

Delmar, Vina. *The Becker Scandal: A Time Remembered* (New York: Harcourt, Brace & World, 1968).

*The Demon of Andersonville or the Trial of Henry Wirz* (Philadelphia: Barclay, 1865).

Dew, Walter. *I Caught Crippen: Memoirs, Etc.* (Glascow, Scotland: Blackie & Son, 1938).

Dickins, Barry. *Guts and Pity: The Hanging That Ended Capital Punishment in Australia* (Sydney, New South Wales, Australia: Currency Press, 1996).

Donaldson, Norman, and Betty Donaldson. *How Did They Die?* (New York: St. Martin's Press, 1980).

Donnachie, Ian, and George Hewitt. *A Companion to Scottish History: From the Reformation to the Present* (New York: Facts on File, 1989).

Donohue, John J., III. "*Godfrey v. Georgia:* Creative Federalism, the Eighth Amendment, and the Evolving Law of Death." *Catholic University Law Review* 30:1 (Fall 1980), 13–64.

Donohue, William A. *The Politics of the American Civil Liberties Union* (New Brunswick, NJ: Transaction Books, 1985).

Dornbach, Alajos. *The Secret Trial of Imre Nagy* (Westport, CT: Praeger, 1994).

D'Oylen, Elizabeth. *James, Duke of Monmouth* (London: Geoffrey Bles, 1938).

Drapkin, Israel. *Crime and Punishment in the Ancient World* (Lexington, MA: Lexington Books, 1989).

Drimmer, Frederick. *Until You Are Dead: The Book of Executions in America* (New York: Windsor, 1990).

Dudley, Ernest. *Bywaters and Mrs. Thompson* (London: Odhams Press, 1953).

Durant, Will. *The Life of Greece* (New York: Simon & Schuster, 1939).

———. *The Renaissance: A History of Civilization in Italy from 1304–1576 A.D.* (New York: Simon & Schuster, 1953).

*The Dying Speeches and Behaviour of the Several State Prisoners that have been Executed the Last 200 Years. With their Special Characters from the Best Historians, as Cambden, Spotswood, Clarendon, Sprat, Burnet, &c. And a table shewing how the respective sentences were Executed, and which of them were mitigated or pardon'd. Bring a Proper Supplement to the State-tryals* (London: Printed for J. Brotherton and W. Meadows, 1720).

Dymond, Alfred H. *The Law on Trial, or Personal Recollections of the Death Penalty and Its Opponents* (London: Society for the Abolition of Capital Punishment, 1865).

Edwards, Ruth Dudley. *Patrick Pearse: The Triumph of Failure* (London: Gollancz, 1977).

Ehrman, Herbert B. *The Case That Will Not Die:* Commonwealth v. Sacco and Vanzetti (Boston: Little, Brown, 1964).

Eliade, Mircea, ed. *The Encyclopedia of Religion.* 16 vols. (New York: Macmillan, 1987).

Elliott, Emory, ed. *American Writers of the Early Republic* (Detroit: Bruccoli Clark, 1985).

Erlanger, Rachel. *The Unarmed Prophet: Savonarola in Florence* (New York: McGraw-Hill, 1988).

Evans, Richard J. *Rituals of Retribution: Capital Punishment in Germany, 1600–1987* (Oxford, England: Oxford University Press, 1996).

*The Execution of Francois Courvoisier for the Murder of Lord William Russell, Opposite the Debtor's Door this Day* (London: Seven Dials, 1840).

*The Execution of Henry Berry: who was Executed at Tyburn on Fryday the 28 of this instant February, 1678, for assisting in the murther of Sir Edmund-bury Godfrey, one of his Majesties justices of peace for the county of Middlesex, late of St. Martins in the fields: with an account of his deportment in Newgate and at the place of Execution, with several other remarkable circumstances* (London: Printed for D. M., 1678).

Fanning, Clara E., ed. *Selected Articles on Capital Punishment* (New York: H. W. Wilson, 1913).

Faust, Patricia L., ed. *Historical Times Illustrated Encyclopedia of the Civil War* (New York: Harper & Row, 1986).

Ferguson, Everett, ed. *Encyclopedia of Early Christianity* (Chicago and London: St. James Press, 1990).

Fernow, Berthold. *The Records of New Amsterdam from 1653 to 1674 anno Domini.* 7 vols. (New York: Knickerbocker Press, 1897).

Fitzgerald, Percy Hetherington. *A Famous Forgery: Being the Story of the 'Unfortunate' Doctor Dodd* (London: Chapman and Hall, 1865).

Flaherty, Thomas H., ed. *World War II: The Aftermath: Asia* (New York: Time-Life Books, 1983).

Flavel, John. *The Cursed Death of the Cross Described, and Confortably Improved: Wherein is Opened, the Nature and Quality of the death Christ died upon the Cross. By John Flavel, Late Minister of the Gospel* (Boston: Printed for Benjamin Gray no. 2, at the head of the town-dock, 1732).

Flexner, James Thomas. *The Traitor and the Spy: Benedict Arnold and John André* (New York: Harcourt, Brace, 1953).

Florinsky, Michael T., ed. *McGraw-Hill Encyclopedia of Russia and the Soviet Union* (New York: McGraw-Hill, 1961).

Focault, Michel. *Discipline and the Parish: The Birth of the Prison.* Translated by Alan Sheridan. (New York: Vintage Books, 1979).

Foreman, Laura, ed. *Crimes and Punishments: The Time-Life Library of Curious and Unusual Facts* (New York: Time-Life Books, 1991).

Franklin, Mitchell. "Concerning the Historic Importance of Edward Livingston." *Tulane Law Review* 11:2 (February 1937), 163–212.

Frey, Martin A., "The Criminal Responsibility of the Juvenile Murderer," *Washington University Law Quarterly,* 1970:2 (Spring 1970), 113–33.

Friedman, Lawrence M. *Crime and Punishment in American History* (New York: Basic Books, 1993).

Furet, Françcois, and Mona Ozouf, eds. *A Critical Dictionary of the French Revolution* (Cambridge, MA: Belknap Press of Harvard University Press, 1989).

Garber, Marjorie, and Rebecca L. Walkowitz, eds. *Secret Agents: The Rosenberg Case, McCarthyism, and Fifties America* (New York: Routledge, 1995).

Gardiner, Ralph, of Chilton, Northumberland. *England's Grievance Discovered in Relation to the Coal-Trade. With the Map of the River of Tine and Situation of the Town and Corporation of Newcastle. The Tyrannical Oppression of those Magistrates, their charters and grants, the several tryals, depositions, and judgements obtained against them, etc.* (London: For R. Ibbitson and P. Stent, 1655).

Gardner, Martin R. "Executions and Indignities—An Eighth Amendment Assessment of Methods of Inflicting Capital Punishment." *Ohio State Law Journal* 39:1 (1978), 96–130.

Gardner, Romaine L. "Capital Punishment: The Philosophers and the Court." *Syracuse Law Review* 29 (1978), 1175–1216.

Garey, Margot, "The Cost of Taking a Life: Dollars and Sense of the Death Penalty," *University of California at Davis Law Review,* 18:4 (Summer 1985), 1221–70.

Garnett, Henry. *Portrait of Guy Fawkes: An Experiment in Biography* (London: Hale, 1962).

Gascoigne, Bamber. *Encyclopedia of Britain* (New York: Macmillan, 1993).

Gaute, J. H. H., and Robin Odell. *The New Murderers' Who's Who* (New York: International Polygonics, 1989).

Gerard, John, Jesuit of Stonyhurst. *The Condition of the Catholics under James I. Father Gerard's Narrative of the Gunpowder Plot* (London: Roehampton, Printer, 1871).

———. *What Was the Gunpowder Plot? The Traditional Story Tested by Original Evidence* (London: Osgood & McIlvaine, 1897).

Gerould, Daniel Charles. *Guillotine: Its Legend and Lore* (New York: Blast Books, 1992).

Gibb, Sir Hamilton Alexander Rosskeen, et al., eds. *The Encyclopedia of Islam.* 8 vols. 1 suppl. (Leiden, the Netherlands: E. J. Brill, 1960–1979).

Gill, Anton. *An Honourable Defeat* (New York: Henry Holt, 1994).

Gillespie, Charles Coulston, ed. *Dictionary of Scientific Biography.* 4 vols. (New York: Charles Scribner's Sons, 1980–1990).

Gillespie, L. Kay. *Utah's Condemned Men* (Salt Lake City, UT: Signature Books, 1991).

Goodell, Abner Cheney. *The Trial and Execution, for petit treason, of Mark and Phillis: slaves of Capt. John Codman, who murdered their master at Charlestown, Mass., in 1755; for which the man was hanged and gibbeted, and the woman burned to death; including, also, some account of other punishments by burning in Massachusetts* (Cambridge, MA: J. Wilson and Son, 1883).

Goodman, Jonathan, and Patrick Pringle, eds. *The Trial of Ruth Ellis* (Newton Abbot, England: David and Charles, 1974).

Gosse, Philip. *The Pirate's Who's Who, Giving Particulars of the Lives & Deaths of the Pirates and Buccaneers* (London: Dulau, 1924).

Gould, Lewis L. *The Presidency of William McKinley* (Lawrence, Kansas: Regents Press of Kansas, 1980).

Grant, James. *Memoirs of James, Marquis of Montrose, K. G. Captain General of Scotland* (London: G. Routledge, 1858).

Granucci, Anthony F. "'Nor Cruel and Unusual Punishments Inflicted': The Original Meaning." *California Law Review* 57:4 (October 1969), 839–865.

*A Great Plot discovered, or, The Notorious and Wicked Design upon the River of Thames put in Execution on Monday last: with a hu-and-cry after the condemned prisoners that made their escape upon their removing from Newgate to be transported to Jamaica, and the manner how they made their escape and got ashore in Essex, the killing of the steer-man, the pursuing of them by souldiers, and the names and number of those since re-taken which are now to be executed upon several gibbets: likewise, the apprehending of the wicked villians ill-affected to His Gracious Majesty and his Royal Highnesse the Duke of York* (London: Printed for G. Horton, 1661).

Greenwald, Helene B., "Eighth Amendment—Minors and the Death Penalty: Decision and Avoidance," *Supreme Court Review,* 73 (1982), 1525–52.

Gregory, Ross, *Modern America, 1914 to 1945* (New York: Facts on File, 1995).

*Guiteau Trial: Closing Speech to the Jury of John K. Porter of New York, in the case of Charles J. Guiteau, the assassin of President Garfield, Washington, Jan. 23, 1882* (New York: J. Polhemus, Printer, 1882).

Gutman, Israel, ed. *Encyclopedia of the Holocaust.* 4 vols. (New York: Macmillan, 1990).

Haines, Herbert H. *Against Capital Punishment: the Anti-Death Penalty Movement in America, 1972–1994* (New York: Oxford University Press, 1996).

Hale, Leslie. *Hanged in Error* (Baltimore, MD: Penguin Books, 1961).

Hall, Jacquelyn Dowd. *Revolt against Chivalry: Jessie Daniel Ames and the Women's Campaign against Lynching* (New York: Columbia University Press, 1979).

Hallam, Elizabeth, ed. *The Plantagenet Encyclopedia: An Alphabetical Guide to 400 Years of English History* (London: Tiger Books International, 1996).

Hamilton, Luther, ed. *Memoirs, Speeches and Writings of Robert Rantoul, Jr.* (Boston: Jewitt, 1854).

Hamilton, William Douglas, ed. *Calendar of State Papers, Domestic Series, of the Reign of Charles I. 1648–49 (including undated Petitions, etc.), Preserved in Her Majesty's Public Record Office* (London: Her Majesty's Stationary Office, 1893).

———. *A Chronicle of England During the Reigns of the Tudors.* 2 vols. (London: Camden Society,1875).

Hanchett, William. *The Lincoln Murder Conspiracies: Being an Account of the Hatred Felt by Many Americans for President Abraham Lincoln during the Civil War and the First Complete Examination and Refutation of the Many Theories, Hypotheses, and Speculations Put Forward since 1865 Concerning Those Presumed to Have Aided, Abetted, Controlled, or Directed the Murderous Act of John Wilkes Booth in Ford's Theater the Night of April 14* (Urbana: University of Illinois Press, 1983).

Hanser, Richard. *A Noble Treason: The Revolt of the Munich Students against Hitler* (New York: Putnam, 1979).

Hare, Francis Augustus. *The Last of the Bushrangers: An Account of the Capture of the Kelly Gang* (London: Hurst and Blackett, 1892).

Harris, Rufus C. "The Edward Livingston Centennial." *Tulane Law Review* 11:1 (December 1936), 1–3.

Hastings, James. *Encyclopædia of Religion and Ethics,* 13 vols. (Edinburgh, Scotland: T. & T. Clark, 1908–1927).

Hatch, Robert McConnell. *Major John André: A Gallant in Spy's Clothing* (Boston: Houghton Mifflin, 1986).

Hausner, Gideon. *Justice in Jerusalem* (New York: Harper & Row, 1966).

Hayes, H. G. and C. J., eds. *A Complete History of the Trial of Guiteau, Assassin of President Garfield, to Which is Added a Graphic Sketch of His Life as Detailed (Expressly for this Work) by his Former Wife, Mrs. Dunmire; Also, an Autobiography, as Dictated by Himself Since the Shooting, the History of the Trial (in Many Respects, the Most Remarkable of the Present Century), gives All of the most Important and Interesting Portions of the Testimony, the Startling Interruptions by the Prisoner, Incidents, Arguments of Counsel, Charge by the Judge, Sentence, &c., &c.* (Philadelphia: Hubbard Brothers, 1882).

Hengel, Martin. *Crucifixion in the Ancient World and the Folly of the Message of the Cross* (Philadelphia: Fortress Press, 1977).

Hewins, Ralph. *Quisling: Prophet without Honor* (London: W. H. Allen, 1965).

Heywood, Ezra Hervey. *The Great Strike, Its Relations to Labor, Property, and Government, Suggested by the Memorable Events Which, Originating in the Tyrranous Extortion of Railway Masters, and the Execution of Eleven Labor Reformers, called 'Mollie Maguires,' June 21, 1877, Culminated in Burning the Corporation Property, in Pittsburg, Pennsylvania* (Princeton, MA: Co-operative Publishing, 1878).

Hill, Frederic. *The Substitute for Capital Punishment* (London: Society for the Abolition of Capital Punishment, 1866).

Hinton, Richard Josiah. *John Brown and His Men* (New York: Funk and Wagnalls, 1894).

*The History of Guy Fawkes and the Torrid Conspiracy of the Gun Powder Plot* (York, England: Printed by J. Kendrew, 1815?).

*The History of Jane Shore, Concubine to King Edward VI [sic]: containing an account of her wit and beauty, her marriage with Mr. Shore, the King's visits to her, her going to court, and leaving her husband, her great distress, and misery after the King's death; to which is added, the Life and Death of Sawney Beane, the Robber* (Boston: Printed and Sold by Nathaniel Coverly, Jr., 1811).

*The History of the Life, Bloody Reign and Death of Queen Mary, eldest daughter to H.8. Containing a true account of her birth, education, coronation and marriage, the beheading the Lady Jane Gray [sic] and her husband, the Dukes of Northumberland and Suffolk, &c., with their speeches at their execution, the several imprisonments of Queen Elizabeth, and her remarkable speeches and behaviour at their confinements: Wyatt's Rebellion, the siege and taking of Calais by the French, &c.: also, an account of the martyrs that suffer'd death during her most cruel reign, illustrated with pictures of the most considerable passages, engraven on copper plates* (London: Printed for D. Browne and T. Benskin, 1682).

Hockett, Jeffrey D. "Justice Robert H. Jackson, the Supreme Court, and the Nuremberg Trial." *Supreme Court Review 1990* (1990), 257–299.

Hodges, Sir Benjamin. *An Impartial History of Michael Servetus, burnt alive at Geneva for Heresie* (London: Printed for A. Ward, 1724).

Horn, Tom. *Life of Tom Horn, Government Scout and Interpreter: A Vindication* (Denver: Published for J. C. Cole by the Louthan Book Company, 1904).

Horowitz, Irving Louis. *The Renaissance Philosophy of Giordano Bruno* (New York: Coleman-Ross, 1952).

Hossent, Harry. *The Movie Treasury: Gangster Movies—Gangsters, Hoodlums and Tough Guys of the Screen* (London, England: Octopus Books, 1974).

Houston, Robert. *The Nation Thief* (New York: Pantheon Books, 1984).

Howe, Russell Warren. *Mata Hari: The True Story* (New York: Dodd, Mead, 1986).

Hoyt, Edwin Palmer. *Warlord: Tojo against the World* (Lanham, MD: Scarborough House, 1993).

Hudson, M. E., and Mary Clark. *Crown of a Thousand Years: A Millenium of British History Presented as a Pageant of Kings and Queens* (New York: Crown, 1978).

Huebsch, Edward. *The Last Summer of Mata Hari* (New York: Crown Books, 1979).

Huffhines, Kathy Schulz, ed. *Foreign Affairs: The National Society of Film Critics' Video Guide to Foreign Films* (San Francisco: Mercury House, 1991).

Huggett, Renée, and Paul Berry. *Daughters of Cain: The Story of Eight Women Executed Since Edith Thompson in 1923, etc.* (London: George Allen & Unwin, 1956).

Huie, William Bradford. *The Execution of Private Slovik* (New York: Little, Brown, 1954).

Huxley, Aldous. *The Devils of Loudun* (New York: Harper & Brothers, 1952).

Itasaka, Gen, ed. *Kodansha Encyclopedia of Japan*, 9 vols. (Tokyo: Kodansha, 1983).

Jackson, George, ed. *Dictionary of the Russian Revolution:* (Westport, CT: Greenwood Press, 1989).

Jackson, Guida M. *Women Who Ruled* (Santa Barbara, CA: ABC-Clio, 1990).

Jackson, Shirley. *The Lottery and Other Stories* (New York: Noonday, 1989).

Jackson, William, of the Inner Temple. *The New and Complete Newgate Calendar; or, Malefactor's Universal Register. Containing, new and authentic accounts of all lives—of the most notorious criminals—who have suffered death, and other exemplary punishments for murders—Interspersed with notes, reflections, remarks, inferences, arising from all the several subjects, moral, instructive, and entertaining. Comprehending all the most material passages in the Sessions papers—together with the ordinary of Newgate's account of the capital convicts; and complete narratives of all the most remarkable trials—The whole properly arranged from the records of the courts. To which is added, a concise account of the new settlements for convicts at Paramatta, Sydney, Port Jackson in Botany Bay, New South Wales, by William Jackson* (London: Printed for Alexander Hogg, 1818?).

Jens, Inge Scholl. *At the Heart of the White Rose: Letters and Diaries of Hans and Sophie Scholl.* Translated by J. Maxwell Brownjohn (New York: Harper & Row, 1987).

———. *Six against Tyranny.* Translated by Cyrus Brooks. (London: Murray, 1955).

Johnsen, Julia E., ed. *Capital Punishment* (New York: H. W. Wilson, 1939).

Johnson, Chalmers A. *An Instance of Treason: Ozaki Hotsumi and the Sorge Spy Ring* (Stanford, CA: Stanford University Press, 1990).

Jones, Ann. *She Had to Die! American Heritage* 31:6 (October/November 1980), 20–31.

Jones, David A. *History of Criminology: A Philosophical Perspective* (Westport, CT: Greenwood Press, 1986).

Kantor, MacKinlay. *Andersonville* (New York: Signet, 1955).

Kebabian, John S. *The Haymarket Affair and the Trial of the Chicago Anarchists 1886* (New York: H. P. Kraus, 1970).

Keegan, John. *The Face of Battle: A Study of Agincourt, Waterloo and the Somme* (London: Jonathan Cape, 1976).

Keith, W. Barrington. *The World's Greatest Crimes: Murder, Robbery and Mayhem from 1900 to the Present Day* (London: Hamden, 1990).

Kelly, John Norman Davidson. *The Oxford Dictionary of Popes* (Oxford, England: Oxford University Press, 1986).

Ketch, John. *The Apologie of John Ketch Esq., the Executioner of London, in Vindication of Himself as to the Execution of the late Lord Russel* (London: J. Brown, 1683).

Kimmelman, Benedict B. "The Example of Private Slovik." *American Heritage* 38:6 (September/October 1987), 97–104.

*King Charls His Speech Made upon the Scaffold at Whitehall-Gate, Immediately Before his Execution, on Tuesday, the 30 of Ian. 1648 [Old Style]. With a Relation of the Maner of his Going to Execution* (London: Printed by Peter Cole, 1649).

*King Charls His Tryal: or, a Perfect Narrative of the Whole Proceedings of the High Court of Justice in the Tryal of the King in Westminster Hall. Corrected & Enlarged by a More Perfect Copy. With a Perfect Copy of the King's Speech Upon the Scaffold* (London: For Peter Cole, Francis Tyton, & John Playford, 1649).

Knapp, Andrew, and William Baldwin. *The New Newgate Calendar; Being Interesting Memoirs of Notorious Characters, Who have Been Convicted of Outrages on the Laws of England, During the Seventeenth Century, Brought Down to the Present Time. Chronologically Arranged.* 5 vols. (London: Printed by and for J. and J. Cundee, Ivy-Lane, 1826).

Knappman, Edward W., ed. *Great American Trials* (Detroit: Visible Ink Press, 1994).

Kornbluh, Joyce L., ed. *Rebel Voices: An IWW Anthology* (Ann Arbor: University of Michigan Press, 1964).

Kunitz, Stanley J., and Howard Haycraft, eds. *Twentieth Century Authors: A Biographical Dictionary of Modern Literature* (New York: H. W. Wilson, 1942).

Laffin, John. *Brassey's Battles: 3,500 Years of Conflict, Campaigns and Wars from A-Z* (London: Brassey's Defence, 1986).

Lane, John. *The Reichstag Fire Trial: The Second Brown Book of the Hitler Terror* (London: Bodley Head, 1934).

Larson, Richard W. *Bundy: The Deliberate Stranger* (New York: Pocket Books, 1986).

Lathbury, Thomas. *Guy Fawkes; or, A Complete History of the Gunpowder Treason, A.D. 1605* (London: L. Parker, 1839).

Laurence, John. *A History of Capital Punishment* (New York: Citadel, 1960).

Lawes, Lewis E. *Man's Judgment of Death: An Analysis of the Operation and Effect of Capital Punishment Based on Facts, Not on Sentiment* (New York: G. P. Putnam's Sons, 1924).

———. *Meet the Murderer!* (New York: Harper & Brothers, 1940).

———. *Twenty Thousand Years in Sing Sing* (New York: R. Long and R. R. Smith, 1932).

Lawson, John D., ed. *American State Trials: A Collection of the Important and Interesting Criminal Trials Which Have Taken Place in the United States, from the Beginning of our Government to the Present Day, 17 vols.* (St. Louis, MO: F. H. Thomas Law Book Company, 1916).

Leber, Annadore. *Conscience in Revolt.* Translated by Rosemary O'Neill. (London: Vallentine, Mitchell, 1957).

Lee, John Doyle. *The Life and Confession of John D. Lee, the Mormon. with a Full Account of the Mountain Meadows Massacre and Execution of Lee* (Philadelphia: Barclay, 1877).

Lemon, Robert, ed. *Calendar of State Papers, Domestic Series, of the Reigns of Edward VI., Mary, Elizabeth,*

*1547–1580. Preserved in the State Paper Department of Her Majesty's Public Record Office* (London: Longman, Brown, Green, Longmans, & Roberts, 1856).

Lieberson, Goodard, prod. *The Irish Uprising, 1916–1922* (New York: CBS Records, 1966).

*The Life, Trial, Confession and Execution of Albert W. Hicks, the Pirate and Murderer, Executed on Bedloe's Island, New York Bay, on the 13th of July, 1860, for the Murder of Capt. Burr, Smith and Oliver Watts, on Board the Oyster Sloop E. A. Johnson* (New York: Robert M. DeWitt, 1860).

Livingston, Edward. *The Complete Works of Edward Livingston on Criminal Jurisprudence,* 2 vols. (New York: National Prison Association, 1873).

Lodge, Richard. *The History of England, from the Restoration to the Death of William III, 1660–1702* (London: Longman's, Green, 1910).

Long, Robert Emmet. *Criminal Sentencing* (New York: H. W. Wilson, 1995).

Longford, Elizabeth, ed. *The Oxford Book of Royal Anecdotes* (Oxford, England: Oxford University Press, 1991).

Loomie, Albert Joseph. *Guy Fawkes in Spain: The 'Spanish Treason' in Spanish Documents* (London: University of London Institute of Historical Research, 1971).

Lossing, Benson John. *The Two Spies: Nathan Hale and John André, by Benson John Lossing, LL.D. Illustrated with pen-and-ink sketches by H. Rosa. Anna Seward's Menody on Major André* (New York: D. Appleton, 1886).

Lydgate, John. (J. E. van der Westhuizen, ed.) *The Life of Saint Alban and Saint Amphibal* (Leiden, the Netherlands: E. J. Brill, 1974).

Lyons, Douglas B. "Capital Punishment: A Selected Bibliography." *Criminal Law Bulletin* 8:9 (November 1972), 782–802.

Macaulay, Lord Thomas Babington. *The History of England from the Accession of James the Second,* 3 vols. (London: Longman, Brown, Green, Longmans, and Roberts, 1858–1861).

McCafferty, James A., ed. *Capital Punishment* (Chicago: Aldine, Atherton, 1972).

McCarthy, Charles Ambrose. *The Great Molly Maguire Hoax, Based on Information Suppressed 90 Years—The Story of John J. Kehoe* (Wyoming, PA: Cro Woods, 1969).

McCay, Hedley. *Padraic Pearse: A New Biography* (Cork, Ireland: Mercier, 1966).

McClellan, Grant S., ed. *Capital Punishment* (New York: H. W. Wilson, 1961).

McCormick, Charles Howard. *Leisler's Rebellion* (New York: Garland, 1989).

McDade, Thomas M. *The Annals of Murder: A Bibliography of Books and Pamphlets on American Murders from Colonial Times to 1900* (Norman: University of Oklahoma Press, 1961).

McGehee, Edward G., and William H. Hildebrand, eds. *The Death Penalty: A Literary and Historical Approach* (Boston: D.C. Heath, 1964).

*The Machinery of Death: A Shocking Indictment of Capital Punishment in the United States* (New York: Amnesty International USA, 1997).

McIntyre, J. Lewis. *Giordano Bruno* (London: Macmillan, 1903).

Mackey, Philip English. "Edward Livingston and the Origins of the Movement to Abolish Capital Punishment in America." *Louisiana History* 16:2 (Spring 1975), 145–166.

———. "Edward Livington on the Punishment of Death." *Tulane Law Review* 48:1 (December 1973), 25–42.

———, ed. *Voices against Death: American Opposition to Capital Punishment, 1787–1975* (New York: Burt Franklin, 1976).

McLeod, Alan Lindsey, ed. *Australia Speaks: An Anthology of Australian Speeches* (Sydney, New South Wales, Australia: Wentworth Press, 1969).

McQuilton, John. *The Kelly Outbreak, 1878–1880: The Geographical Dimension of Social Banditry* (Carlton, Victoria: Melbourne University Press, 1979).

Maestro, Marcello. *Cesare Beccaria and the Origins of Penal Reform* (Philadelphia: Temple University Press, 1973).

Malone, Dumas, et al., eds. *Dictionary of American Biography.* 10 vols. 10 suppl. (New York: Charles Scribner's Sons, 1930–1995).

Manley, Sir Roger. *The History of the Rebellions in England, Scotland and Ireland, from the Year 1640 to the Beheading of the Duke of Monmouth in 1684* (London: E. Meredith and T. Newborough, 1691).

Mann, Martha, and Victor Dowling. *Nathan Hale, Patriot* (New York: Dodd, Mead, 1944).

*The Manner of the Death and Execution of Arnold Cosbie, for Murthering the Lord Boorke, who was Executed at Wanswoorth townes end on the 27. Of Ianuarie 1591. With Certaine verses written by the said Cosby in the time of his imprisonment, containing matter of great effect, as well touching his life, as also his Penitencie before his Death* (London: Imprinted for William Wright, 1591).

Marks, Alfred. *Tyburn Tree: Its History and Annals* (London: Brown, Langham, 1988).

Marks, Laurence, and Tony van den Bergh. *Ruth Ellis: A Case of Diminished Responsibility?* (London: Macdonald and Jane's, 1977).

Marvel, William. *Andersonville: The Last Depot* (Chapel Hill: University of North Carolina Press, 1994).

*Massacre of the French King. View of la Guillotine; or, the Modern Beheading Machine, at Paris, by which the unfortunate Louis XVI. (late King of France) suffered on the scaffold, January 21st, 1793* (London: Printed at the Minerva Office, for William Lane, 1793).

Mather, Cotton. *The Wonders of the Invisible World. Observations upon the Nature, the Number and Operations of the Devils, accompany'd with Accounts of the Molestations by Daemons and Witchcrafts, which have lately annoy'd the Countrey, and the Trials of some malefactors executed upon occasion thereof. Some Counsils directing a due improvement of the things lately done by evil spirits in our Neighborhood. Conjectures upon the events, likely to befall New England. A Narrative of a late Outrage committed by witches in Swedeland. The Devil Discovered in a Discourse upon Temptations of the Wicked One* (London: John Dunton, 1693).

Mayhew, Henry. "On Capital Punishment" in *Three Papers on Capital Punishment* (London: Society for the Amendment of the Law, 1856).

Mello, Michael. *Against the Death Penalty: The Relentless Dissents of Justices Brennan and Marshall* (Boston: Northeastern University Press, 1996).

Meltsner, Michael, *Cruel and Unusual: The Supreme Court and Capital Punishment* (New York: Random House, 1973).

Melville, Robert. *The Legend of Ned Kelly* (New York: Viking, 1964).

Mencken, Henry Louis, ed. *A Mencken Chrestomathy* (New York: Alfred A. Knopf, 1949).

Michel, Paul Henri. *The Cosmology of Giordano Bruno.* Translated by R. E. W. Madison. (Paris: Hermann, 1973).

Midgley, Samuel. *Halifax and its gibbet-law placed in a true light: together with a description of the town, the nature of the soil, the temper and disposition of the people, the antiquity of its customary law, and the reasonableness thereof; with an account of the gentry, and other eminent persons born and inhabiting within the said town, and the liberties thereof; with many other matters and things of great remark never before publish'd; to which are added the tragedies committed by Sir John Eland, of Eland, and his grand antagonists* (Halifax: Printed by P. Darby for J. Bentley, 1761?).

Mill, John Stuart. *Dissertations and Discussions; Political, Philosophical and Historical. Reprinted Chiefly from the Edinburgh and Westminster Reviews.* 4 vols. (London: J. W. Parker, 1859–1875).

Miller, Arthur. *The Crucible* (New York: Viking, 1953).

Misciattelli, Piero. *Savonarola* (New York: D. Appleton, 1930).

Montagu, Basil. *An Inquiry into the Aspersions upon the late Ordinary of Newgate, with some observations upon Newgate and upon the Punishment of Death* (London: Printed by Richard and Arthur Taylor, Shoe-Lane, 1815).

———, ed. *The Opinions of Different Authors Upon the Punishment of Death, Selected By Basil Montagu, Esq. of Lincoln's Inn.* 3 vols. (London: Printed for Longman, Hurst, Rees, and Paternoster Row, 1809–1813).

Moore, Guy W. *The Case of Mrs. Surratt: Her Controversial Trial and Execution for Conspiracy in the Lincoln Assassination:* (Norman: University of Oklahoma, 1954).

Morris, Norval, and David J. Rothman, eds. *The Oxford History of the Prison: The Practice of Punishment in Western Society* (New York: Oxford University Press, 1995)

Morton, John Bingham. *The Bastille Falls, and Other Studies of the French Revolution* (London: Longmans, Green, 1936).

*A Murderer Punished and Pardoned; or, A True Relation of the Wicked Life and Shameful-happy death of Thomas Savage, imprisoned, justly condemned, and twice executed at Ratcliff for his bloody fact in killing his fellow-servant, by us who were often with him at the time of his imprisonment at Newgate and at his execution, Robert Franklin, R. A., and James Janeway, et al.; to which is annexed a sermon preached at his funeral* (London: N.p., 1668).

Murphy, Brian P. *Patrick Pearse and the Lost Republican Ideal* (Dublin: James Duffy, 1991).

Nadel, Ira B., and William E. Fredeman, eds. *Victorian Novelists before 1885* (Detroit: Bruccoli Clark, 1983).

Nakell, Barry, "The Cost of the Death Penalty," *Criminal Law Bulletin,* 14:1 (January 1978), 72–80.

Nalson, John. *A True Copy of the Journal of the High-Court of Justice for the Tryal of King Charles I. Taken by J. Nalson, LL.D., Jan. 4, 1683* (Dublin: Printed for R. Gunne, 1731).

Napier, Mark. *The Life and Times of Montrose: Illustrated from Original Manuscripts, including Family Papers now first published from the Montrose Charter-Chest and other private repositories; with portraits and autographs* (Edinburgh, Scotland: Oliver and Boyd, 1840).

Nash, Jay Robert. *Encyclopedia of Western Lawmen and Outlaws* (New York: Da Capo Press, 1994).

———. *Encyclopedia of World Crime.* 4 vols. (Wilmette, IL: CrimeBooks, Inc., 1990).

Nathan, Adele Gutman. *The Gentleman Spy* (London: Sidgwick and Jackson, 1970).

Neville, John. *The Press, the Rosenbergs, and the Cold War* (Westport, CT: Praeger, 1995).

Nicolai, Sandra, et al., eds. *The Question of Capital Punishment* (Lincoln, Nebraska: CONtact, Inc., 1981).

Nixon, Edna. *Voltaire and the Calas Case* (London: Gollancz, 1961).

"Note: The Caryl Chessman Case: A Legal Analysis." *Minnesota Law Review* 44:5 (April 1960), 941–997.

Nova, Fritz. *Alfred Rosenberg: Nazi Theorist of the Holocaust* (New York: Hippocrene Books, 1986).

O'Brien, James Bronterre. *The Life and Character of Maximilen Robespierre. Proving by Facts and Arguments, that that much-calumniated Person was one of the Greatest Men, and one of the Purest and Most Enlightened Reformers, that ever existed in the world: also, containing Robespierre's Principal Discourses, Addresses, Reports, and Projects of Law, &c., in the National Assembly, National Convention, Commune of Paris, and the Popular Societies; with the author's reflections on the principles events and leading men of the French Revolution, etc., etc., etc.* (London: Printed by J. Watson, 1837?).

Ollard, Richard. *Pepys: A Biography* (London: Hodler & Stoughton, 1974).

Ostrovsky, Erika. *Eye of Dawn: The Rise and Fall of Mata Hari* (New York: Macmillan, 1978).

O'Sullivan, John Louis. *Report in Favor of the Abolition of the Punishment of Death by Law, Made to the Legislature of the State of New York, April 14, 1841, by John L. O'Sullivan, Member of the Assembly, from the City of New York* (New York: J. & H. G. Langley, 1841).

Owen, John. *Salus Electorum, Sanguis Jesu. The Death of death in the death of Christ: Being a treatise of the redemption and reconciliation that is in the blood of Christ, Wherein the whole Controversy about Universal Redemption, is fully discussed: in four parts* (Carlisle, PA: Printed by George Kline, 1792).

Paterson, Antoinette Mann. *The Infinite Worlds of Giordano Bruno* (Springfield, IL: Charles C. Thomas, 1970).

Paton, John, ed. *Crimes and Punishment: A Pictorial Encyclopedia of Aberrant Behavior.* 19 vols. (London: Symphonette, 1973–1974).

Paxton, John. *Companion to the French Revolution* (New York: Facts on File, 1988).

Pearse, Padraic. (Séamas Buachalla, ed.), *The Letters of P. H. Pearse* (Gerrards Crossing, England: C. Smythe, 1979).

Perrinchief, Richard. *The Royal Martyr: or, the Life and Death of King Charles* (London: Printed by J. M. for R. Royston, Bookseller, 1676).

Pinkerton, Allan. *The Mollie Maguires and the Detectives* (New York: G. W. Carleton, 1877).

Plowden, Alison. *Lady Jane Grey and the House of Suffolk* (New York: Franklin Watts, 1986).

Pollen, John Hungerford. *Mary Queen of Scots and the Babington Plot* (Edinburgh, Scotland: Printed for T. and A. Constable, Ltd., for the Scottish History Society, 1922).

Post, Richard S., and Arthur A. Kingsbury. *Security Administration: An Introduction to the Protective Services* (Boston: Butterworth-Heineman, 1991).

Prange, Gordon W. *Target Tokyo: The Story of the Sorge Spy Ring* (New York: McGraw-Hill, 1984).

*Proceedings of a Board of General Officers Held By Order of his Excellency General Washington, Commander-in-Chief of the Army of the United States of America, Respecting Major John André, Adjutant General of the British Army, September 29, 1780* (Philadelphia: Printed by Francis Bailey in Market Street, 1780).

Quinby, George Washington. *The Gallows, the Prison, and the Poor-House. A Plea for Humanity; Showing the Demands of Christianity in Behalf of the Criminal and Perishing Classes* (Cincinnati: Privately Printed by the Author, 1856).

Raby, R. Cornelius. *Fifty Famous Trials* (Washington, D.C.: Washington Law Book Company, 1937).

Radzinowicz, Leon. *A History of English Criminal Law and Its Administration from 1750.* 5 vols. (London: Stevens and Sons, 1948–1986).

Rantoul, Robert, Jr. *Report Relating to Capital Punishment.* Commonwealth of Massachusetts, House Document No. 32, 22 February 1836.

Rayner, J. L., and G. T. Crook, eds. *The Complete Newgate Calendar.* 5 vols. (London: Privately Printed for the Navarre Society, 1926).

Reilly, John M., ed. *Twentieth-Century Crime and Mystery Writers* (New York: St. Martin's Press, 1985).

Renehan, Edward J., Jr. *The Secret Six: The True Tale of the Men Who Conspired with John Brown* (New York: Crown, 1990).

*Report in Favor of the Abolition of the Punishment of Death by Law, Made to the Legislature of the State of New York, April 14, 1841, by John O'Sullivan, Member of the Assembly, from the City of New York* (New York: J. & H. G. Langley, 1841).

*Report of the Trial of Courvoisier for the Murder of Lord William Russell, June 1840* (London: Chiswick, 1918).

*Report of the Trial of Prof. John W. Webster, Indicted for the Murder of Dr. George Parkman* (Boston: Philips, Sampson, 1850).

Riasanovsky, Nicholas V. *A History of Russia* (New York: Oxford University Press, 1969).

Ribbentrop, Joachim von. *The Ribbentrop Memoirs*. Translated by Oliver Watson. (London: Weidenfeld and Nicolson, 1954).

Ridley, Jasper. *Maximilian and Juarez* (New York: Ticknor & Fields, 1992).

Ridpath, John Clark. *The Life and Work of James A. Garfield, embracing an Account of the Scenes and Incidents of his Boyhood; the Struggles of his Youth; his Valor as a Soldier; his Career as a Statesman; his election to the Presidency; and the Tragic Story of his Death* (Cincinnati: Jones Bros., 1881).

Ring, Jim. *Erskine Childers* (London: John Murray, 1996),

Roberts, George, of Lyme Regis. *The Life, Progresses, and Rebellion of James, Duke of Monmouth, to his Capture and Execution. with a Full Account of the Bloody Assize, and Copious Biographical Notices* (London: J. R. Smith; two volumes, 1844).

Robinson, Franklin W., and Stephen G. Nichols, Jr., eds. *The Meaning of Mannerism* (Hanover: University Press of New England, 1972).

Robinson, James Harvey, ed. *Readings in European History.* 2 vols. (Boston: Ginn, 1906).

Roediger, Dave, and Franklin Rosemont. *Haymarket Scrapbook* (Chicago: Charles H. Kerr, 1986).

Root, Jonathan. *The Life and Times of Charlie Becker: The True Story of a Famous American Murder Trial* (London: Secker & Warburg, 1961).

Roper, Thomas, and Thomas Bailey. *The Lives and Deaths of Sir Thomas More, KNT. Lord High Chancellor of England. And of John Fisher, Bishop of Rochester; who were both Beheaded in the Reign of H. VIII. Comprising the Highest and Hidden Transactions of Church and State, in the Reign of Henry the Eighth; with divers Moral, Historical, and Political Animadversions upon Cardinal Wolsey, Sir Thomas More, and Martin Luther; with a Full Relation of Queen Catherine's Divorce, and the Will of Henry the VIII; to which are added, Some Original Letters, refer'd to in the Work* (Dublin: P. Lord, R. Fitzsimmons, and D. Kylly, Booksellers, 1765).

Rosenberg, Alfred. *Selected Writings* (London: Jonathan Cape, 1970).

Rosenberg, Charles F. *The Trial of the Assassin Guiteau: Psychiatry and Law in the Gilded Age* (Chicago: University of Chicago Press, 1968).

Rush, Benjamin. *Considerations on the Injustice and Impolicy of Punishing Murder by Death. Extracted from the American Museum. With Additions* (Philadelphia: From the Press of Matthew Carey, 1792).

———. *An Enquiry into the Effects of Public Punishments upon Criminals and upon Society. Read in the Society for Promoting Political Enquiries, Convened at the House of His Excellency Benjamin Franklin, Esquire, in Philadelphia, March 9th, 1787* (Philadelphia: Printed by Joseph James, 1787).

———. *Essays, Literary, Moral and Philosophical* (Philadelphia: Printed by Thomas & Samuel F. Bradford, 1798; reprint, Philadelphia: Printed by Thomas and William Bradford, 1806).

———. *On the Punishment of Murder by Death* (London: Sold by J. Johnson and J. Phillips, 1793). (Republication of "Considerations—," 1792.)

Rushworth, John. *Historical Collections of Private Passages of the State, Weighty Matters in Law, Remarkable Proceedings in Fine Parliaments. Beginning the Sixteenth Year of King James, anno 1618, and Ending the Fifth Year of King Charles, anno 1629.* 8 vols. (London: D. Browne, 1721).

Russell of Liverpool, Lord. *The Record: The Trial of Adolf Eichmann for the Crimes against the Jewish People and against Humanity* (New York: Alfred A. Knopf, 1963).

Russell, Right Honourable George William Erskine. *Saint Alban the Martyr, Holborn. A History of the Fifty Years* (London: George & Allen, 1913).

Ryle, John Charles. *John Hooper (Bishop and Martyr): His Times, Life, Death and Opinions* (London: William Hunt, 1868).

Sann, Paul. *The Lawless Decade: A Pictorial History of a Great American Transition: From the World War I Armistice and Prohibition to Repeal and the New Deal* (New York: Bonanza Books, 1972).

Sayers, Andrew. *Sidney Nolan: The Ned Kelly Story* (New York: Metropolitan Museum of Art, 1994).

Scott, Samuel F, and Barry Rothaus, eds. *Historical Dictionary of the French Revolution, 1789–1799*. 2 vols. (Westport, CT: Greenwood Press, 1985).

Seal, Graham. *Ned Kelly in Popular Tradition* (Melbourne: Hyland House, 1980).

Sellin, Thorsten, ed. *Capital Punishment* (New York: Harper & Row, 1967).

Sherman, Josiah. *Christ the True Victim and Conqueror: A History of the War, in which the Son of God engaged with all the powers of darkness, concerning the righteousness of God as moral Governor—how it commenced; and how he decided it, by being made a victim and sacrifice to the Devil's kingdom; by means of which, he conquered and destroyed God's enemies—made atonement for his sin—paid the price of our ransom—merited the kingdom of the universe to himself—and redeemed multitudes to God out of every Nation. By Josiah Sherman, A.M.; published at the desire of the hearers* (Litchfield, Connecticut: Printed by T. Collier, in the south end of the court-house, 1787).

Shukman, Harold, ed. *The Blackwell Encyclopedia of the Russian Revolution* (Oxford, England: Basil Blackwell, 1988).

Sifakis, Carl. *The Encyclopedia of American Crime* (New York: Facts on File, 1982).

Skelton, Sophia. *Arnold of Brescia, a Dramatic Poem* (London: Simpkin, Marshall, 1866).

Smith, Alan Gordon. *The Babington Plot* (London: Macmillan & Co., Ltd., 1936).

Smith, H. Bodell. *The State Murder of John Griffiths & the Ilford Executions, or Capital Punishment Condemned: An Appeal to Humanity and to the Churches, by H. Bodell Smith* (London: C. W. Daniel, 1923).

Smith, Horace Wernyss, ed. *Andreana. Containing the Trial, Execution and Various Matter Connected with the History of Major John André* (Philadelphia: Privately Printed, 1865).

Smith, Joshua Hett. *An Authentic Narrative of the Causes Which Led to the Death of Major André, Adjutant-General of His Majesty's Forces in North America, To Which is Added a Monody on the Death of Major André by Miss Seward* (London: Printed for Mathews and Leigh, 1808).

Smith, Lacy Baldwin. *Treason in Tudor England: Politics and Paranoia* (Princeton, NJ: Princeton University Press, 1986).

Smith, Sir William, ed. *Dictionary of Greek and Roman Biography and Mythology*. 3 vols. (London: Walton and Maberly, 1856).

Snyder, Louis L. *Encyclopedia of the Third Reich* (New York: McGraw-Hill, 1976).

Sobel, Robert, ed. *Biographical Directory of the United States Executive Branch, 1774–1989* (Westport, CT: Greenwood Press, 1990).

Solzhenitsyn, Aleksandr I. *The Gulag Archipelago, 1918–1956: An Experiment in Literary Investigation, Parts I and II* (New York: Harper & Row, 1974)

———. *The Gulag Archipelago, 1918–1956: An Experiment in Literary Investigation, Parts III and IV* (New York: Harper & Row, 1975).

Somers, John (Baron Somers). *A Collection of Scarce and Valuable Tracts. Selected from an Infinite Number in Print and Manuscript, in the Royal, Cotton, and other Public, as well as Private, Libraries; Particularly that of the Late Lord Somers*. 4 vols. (London: F. Logan, 1748).

Spear, Charles. *Essays on the Punishment of Death* (Boston: Privately Printed, 1844).

Spencer, Ambrose. *A Narrative of Andersonville, Drawn from the Evidence Elicited on the Trial of Henry Wirz, the Jailer. With the Argument of Col. N. P. Chipman, Judge Advocate* (New York: Harper & Brothers, 1866).

Spierenburg, Petrus Cornelius. *The Spectacle of Suffering: Executions and the Evolution of Repression: From a Preindustrial Metropolis to the European Experience* (Cambridge, England: Cambridge University Press, 1984).

Spinka, Matthew. *John Hus: A Biography* (Princeton, NJ: Princeton University Press, 1968).

———. *John Hus' Concept of the Church* (Princeton, NJ: Princeton University Press, 1966).

———, trans. and ed., *John Hus at the Council of Constance* (New York: Columbia University Press, 1965).

Stephens, Sir Leslie, and Sir Sidney Lee, eds. *The Dictionary of National Biography.* 10 vols. 12 suppl. (Oxford, England: Oxford University Press, 1917–1993).

Stibbs, John Howard. *Andersonville, and the Trial of Henry Wirz* (Iowa City, IA: Clio, 1911).

Streib, Victor L., "Death Penalty for Children: The American Experience with Capital Punishment for Crimes Committed While under Age Eighteen," *Oklahoma Law Review,* 36:3 (Summer 1983), 613–41.

———. *Death Penalty for Juveniles* (Bloomington: Indiana University Press, 1987).

——— "The Eighth Amendment and Capital Punishment of Juveniles," *Cleveland State Law Review,* 34:3 (1985–86), 363–99.

Strickland, Agnes. *Lives of the Tudor Princesses, Including Lady Jane Grey and Her Sisters* (London: Longmans & Co., 1868).

Stuart, Isaac William. *Life of Captain Hale, the Martyr-Spy of the American Revolution* (Hartford, CT: F. A. Brown, 1856).

Sullivan, Harold W. *Trial by Newspaper* (Hyannis, MA: Patriot, 1961).

Sullivan, Robert. *The Disappearance of Dr. Parkman* (Boston: Little, Brown, 1971).

Tambling, Jeffrey. *Dickens, Violence, and the Modern State: Dreams of the Scaffold* (New York: St. Martin's Press, 1995).

Tancred, Sir Thomas. *Suggestions on the Treatment and Disposal of Criminals* (London: T. Hatchard, 1857).

Taylor, James, and Warren Shaw. *The Third Reich Almanac* (New York: World Almanac, 1987).

Taylor, John M. "Charles J. Guiteau: Assassin on Trial." *American Heritage* 32:4 (June/July 1981), 30–39.

Taylor, John Sydney. *A Comparative View of the Punishments Annexed to Crime in the United States of America, and in England* (London: Harvey and Darton, 1831).

Teach, Edward. "He Was Just a Kidd; Only His Enemies Called Him a Pirate." *Sky* Magazine, June 1996, 92–94.

Thackeray, William Makepeace. "Going to See a Man Hanged." *Fraser's Magazine for Town and Country* 22:128 (August 1840), 150–158.

Thompson, James Matthew. *Leaders of the French Revolution* (Oxford, England: Blackwell, 1929).

Thomson, Helen. *Murder at Harvard* (Boston: Houghton Mifflin, 1971).

Thurston, Herbert J., and Donald Attwater, eds. *Butler's Lives of the Saints,* 4 vols. (Westminster, MD: Christian Classics, 1988).

Tobias, Fritz. *The Reichstag Fire Trial.* Translated by Arnold Pomerans. (New York: G. P. Putnam's Sons, 1964).

Tooke, William. *Life of Catherine II, Empress of Russia.* 2 vols. (London: T. N. Longman and O. Rees, 1800).

*Trial of Henry Fauntleroy, and Other Famous Trials for Forgery* (Toronto: Canada Law Book Company, 1924).

*The Trial of John Thurtell and Joseph Hunt for the Murder of Mr. William Weare, in Gill's Hill Lane, Herts, Before Mr. Justice Park, on Tuesday, the 6th, and Wednesday, the 7th January, 1824, with the Prayer, and the Condemned Sermon, that was Preached Before the Unhappy Culprits; Also, Full Particulars of the Execution[s]* (London: Printed by and for Hodgson, 1824).

Trombley, Stephen. *The Execution Protocol: Inside America's Capital Punishment Industry* (New York: Crown, 1992).

*A True Account of the last speeches, confessions, and execution of Christopher Vrats, George Boriskie, and John Sterne: who were tryed and found guilty of the barbarous murther of Thomas Thinn, Esq., on the 12 of February last, and executed in the Pallmall, near the place where they committed the murther on the 10th of this infant March: together with the manner of their behaviours in Newgate after their condemnations, and at the place of execution, containing several very remarkable passages that happened there* (London: Printed for E. Brooks, 1682).

*The Truth about the Nagy Affair: Facts, Documents, Comments* (London: Published for the Congress for Cultural Freedom by Secker & Warburg, 1959).

Tushnet, Mark. *The Death Penalty: Constitutional Issues* (New York: Facts on File, 1994).

Tutorow, Norman E., comp. *War Crimes, War Criminals, and War Crimes Trials* (Westport, CT: Greenwood Press, 1986).

Unwin, Peter. *Voice in the Wilderness: Imre Nagy and the Hungarian Revolution* (London: Macdonald, 1991).

van der Westhuizen, J. E., ed. *Here Begynnethe the Glorious Lyfe and Passion of Seint Albon.* Translated by John Lydgate (Leiden, the Netherlands: E. J. Brill, 1974).

Vidmar, Neil, and Phoebe Ellsworth. "Public Opinion and the Death Penalty." *Stanford Law Review* 26 (June 1974), 1245–70.

Walker, Samuel. *In Defense of American Liberties: A History of the ACLU* (New York: Oxford University Press, 1990).

Wallechinsky, David, and Irving Wallace. *The People's Almanac* (Garden City, NY: Doubleday, 1975).

Warnicke, Retha M. *The Rise and Fall of Ann Boleyn: Family Politics at the Court of Henry VIII* (New York: Cambridge University Press, 1989).

Watson, Alan. *The Law of the Ancient Romans* (Dallas, TX: Southern Methodist University Press, 1970).

Watson, Eric R. *Eugene Aram: His Life and Trial* (Glascow and Edinburgh, Scotland: William Hodge, 1913).

Weatherford, Doris. *American Women's History* (New York: Prentice Hall General Reference, 1994).

Weinberg, Arthur. *Clarence Darrow, Attorney for the Damned* (New York: Simon & Schuster, 1957).

*Westminster Abbey: Official Guide* (Norwich, England: Jarrold, 1994).

Wheelwright, Julie. *The Fatal Lover: Mata Hari and the Myth of Women in Espionage* (London: Collins and Brown, 1992).

White, Welsh S. *The Death Penalty in the Nineties: An Examination of the Modern System of Capital Punishment* (Ann Arbor: University of Michigan Press, 1991).

Whittier, John Greenleaf. *Anti-Slavery Poems: Songs of Labor and Reform* (Cambridge, MA: Riverside Press, 1888).

*The Whole Tryal of Edward Coleman, gent., at Kings-bench Bar at Westminister, on the 27th of November, 1678: dedicated to Wialliam [sic] Greg in Newgate, with original letters, written to Father Le Chese, the French King's confessor: and his last speech at the place of Execution* (London: Printed and sold by J. Bradford, 1678).

Wieczynski, Joseph L., ed. *The Modern Encyclopedia of Russian and Soviet History.* 58 vols. 1 suppl. (Gulf Breeze, FL: Academic International Press, 1977–1995).

Wigoder, Geoffrey. *They Made History: A Biographical Dictionary* (New York: Simon & Schuster, 1993).

Wilkinson, Burke. *The Zeal of the Convert* (Gerrards Cross, England: C. Smythe, 1978).

Williams, C. H., ed. *English Historical Documents, 1485–1558* (London: Eyre & Spottiswoode, 1967).

Wilson, James Grant, ed. *Appletons' Cyclopædia of American Biography.* 7 vols. (New York: D. Appleton, 1888–1901).

Winowska, Maria. *The Death Camp Proved Him Real: The Life of Blessed Maximilian Kolbe, Franciscan* (Libertyville, IL: Prow Books/Franciscan Marytown Press, 1971).

Wishart, George, Bishop of Edinburgh. *The Memoirs of James, Marquis of Montrose, 1639–1650, by the Rev. George Wishart, p.p. (Bishop of Edinburgh, 1662–1671);*

*translated with introduction, notes, appendices, and the original Latin by the Rev. Alexander D. Murdoch and H. F. Morland Simpson* (London: Longmans, Green, 1893).

Witton, Lieutenant George. *Scapegoats of the Empire: The True Story of Breaker Morant's Bushveldt Carbineers* (Melbourne, New South Wales, Australia: D. W. Paterson, 1907).

Woolrych, Humphrey William. *On the Report of the Capital Punishment Commission of 1866* (London: Society for the Abolition of Capital Punishment, 1866).

Wright, Elizur. *Performations in the 'Latter-day Pamphlets' by one of the 'eighteen millions of bores.' Edited by Elizur Wright. No. 1. Universal Suffrage, Capital Punishment, Slavery* (Boston: Phillips, Sampson, 1850).

Wriothesley, Charles, ed. *A Chronicle of England During the Reigns of the Tudors* 2 vols. (London: Camden Society, 1875).

Young, Filson, ed. *Trial of Frederick Bywaters and Edith Thompson* (Toronto: Canada Law Book Company, 1923).

———. *Trial of Hawley Harvey Crippen* (Toronto: Canada Law Book Company, 1923).

Young, John N. *Erskine H. Childers, President of Ireland: A Biography* (Gerrards Cross, England: Colin Smythe, 1985).

Young, Peter, ed. *The Marshall Cavendish Encyclopedia of World War I.* 11 vols. (New York: Marshall Cavendish; 11 volumes and one index, 1986).

Zangrando, Robert L., *The NAACP Crusade against Lynching, 1909–1950* (Philadelphia: Temple University Press, 1980).

Zentner, Christian, and Friedemann Bedüftig, eds. *Encyclopedia of the Third Reich.* 2 vols. (New York: Macmillan, 1991).

#### Dissertations and Theses

Allotta, Robert I. *Military Executions of the Union Army, 1861–1866* (Ph.D. dissertation, Temple University, 1984).

Barber, Henry Eugene. *The Association of Southern Women for the Prevention of Lynching, 1930–1942* (Master's thesis, University of Georgia, 1967).

Belohlavek, John Milan. *George Mifflin Dallas (1792–1864): A Political and Diplomatic Biography* (Master's Thesis, University of Nebraska, 1970).

Berlin, Robert H. *The Administration of Military Justice in the Continental Army during the American Revolution, 1775–1783* (Ph.D. dissertation, University of California at Santa Barbara, 1976).

Bulkley, Robert DeGroff, Jr. *Robert Rantoul, Jr., 1805–1852: Politics and Reform in Antebellum Massachusetts* (Ph.D. dissertation, Princeton University, 1971).

Crites, Laura Hardy. *A History of the Association of Southern Women for the Prevention of Lynching, 1930–1942* (Master's thesis, American University, 1965).

Hall, Jacquelyn Dowd. *Revolt against Chivalry: Jessie Daniel Ames and the Women's Campaign against Lynching* (Ph.D. dissertation, Columbia University, 1974).

Harris, Sheldon H. *The Public Career of John Louis O'Sullivan* (Ph.D. dissertation, Columbia University, 1958).

Higgins, Ray E., Jr. *Strange Fruit: Lynching in South Carolina, 1900–1914* (Master's thesis, University of South Carolina, 1961).

Korey, William. *Zinoviev on the Problem of World Revolution, 1919–27* (Doctoral dissertation, Columbia University, 1960).

Mackey, Philip English. *Anti-Gallows Activity in New York State, 1776–1861* (Ph.D. dissertation, University of Pennsylvania, 1969).

Mounger, Dwyn M. *Lynching in Mississippi, 1830–1930* (Master's thesis, Mississippi State University, 1961).

O'Malley, Stephen. *The Salisbury Lynching, 1906* (Master's thesis, University of North Carolina, 1977).

Yandle, Carolyn Devore. *A Delicate Crusade: The Association of Southern Women for the Prevention of Lynching*

(Master's thesis, University of Virginia, 1969).

Zangrando, Robert L. *The Efforts of the NAACP to Secure Passage of a Federal Anti-Lynching Law, 1920–1940* (Ph.D. dissertation, University of Pennsylvania, 1963).

Zeisel, Hans, "The Deterrent Effect of the Death Penalty: Facts v. Faith," *Supreme Court Review,* 67 (1976), 317–43.

#### Government Documents

Great Britain:

"Final Report of the Royal Commission on Capital Punishment, 1949–1953 (Chairman: Sir Ernest Gowers; 1949–53)." British Parliamentary Papers, CMD 8932 (London: Her Majesty's Stationary Office, 1953).

United States:

United States Congress, House. "Innocence and the Death Penalty: Assessing the Danger of Mistaken Executions." Staff Report by the Subcommittee on Civil and Constitutional Rights, Committee on the Judiciary, One Hundred and Third Congress, First Session, 21 October 1993.

United States Congress, Senate. "Trial of Henry Wirz." Senate Executive Document No. 23, 40th Congress, 2nd Session (1865).

#### Newspapers

*The Australian* (Canberra)
*The Boston Daily Globe*
*Boston Traveler*
*Buffalo* (New York) *Evening News*
*The Chicago Daily News*
*Chicago Evening Journal*
*Chicago Journal*
*Chicago Times*
*Chicago Tribune*
*Daily Graphic* (London)
*Daily News* (New York)
*Daily Sketch* (London)
*The Herald* (Melbourne, Australia)
*Las Vegas Review*
*Los Angeles Times*
*The Miami Herald*
*New Haven* (Connecticut) *Evening Register*
*New-York Daily Tribune*
*New York Herald*
*New York Journal*
*The New York Times*
*New York Tribune*
*The Scotsman* (Glasgow, Scotland)
*The Sun* (Melbourne, Australia)
*The Sunday Times* (London)
*The Times* (London)
*Victoria Daily Times* (New South Wales, Australia)
*Washington Evening Critic*
*The Washington Post*
*The World* (New York)

#### Manuscript Sources

Frederick Bywaters/Edith Thompson Criminal Records, Public Record Office, Kew, England

John Christie/Timothy Evans Criminal Records, Public Record Office, Kew, England

Dr. Hawley Harvey Crippen Criminal Records, Public Record Office, London, England

Investigation and Trial Papers Relating to the Assassination of President Lincoln, Microcopy 599, National Archives (on microfilm)

Robert H. Jackson Papers, Manuscript Division, Library of Congress

W. J. Maloney Historical Papers (records on Sir Roger Casement), New York Public Library

Records of the District Courts of the United States, RG 21, Papers of the Supreme Court of the District of Columbia

*U.S. v. Guiteau,* Criminal Case #14056, Boxes 1 & 2, National Archives

"Papers Relating to the Seizure of William Walker and His Followers [in] Nicaragua," Report of the Committee on Foreign Affairs, 35th Congress, Records of the House of Representatives, RG 233, National Archives

B.C.

**Seventeenth Century** The Egyptians enact Hammurabi's Code, the first code of law ever established which lays out a penalty of death for specific crimes.

**451–150** The Romans enact the Decemviri of the Twelve Tables, which recognizes such crimes punishable by death as publishing libels and insulting songs, and burning a house or a stack of corn near a house. One particular punishment was the *Culleus,* in which the condemned was placed in a sack with an ape, a dog, and a serpent, and then was thrown alive into the sea.

**553** The Roman Senate enacts the *Porcian Lex,* or Porcian Law, which prohibits the use of the death penalty on any Roman citizen, and instead calls for exile as punishment.

**497** Aristagoras of Miletus is put to death for trying to take the Aegean island of Naxos from the Persians.

**399** Socrates, the famed Greek philosopher and moralist, is put to death by being forced to drink hemlock.

**316** Eumenes, a Macedonian officer who served in the army of Alexander the Great, is betrayed by his men and handed over to his enemy Antigonus (382?–301 B.C.), who has Eumenes put to death.

**Second Century** Andriscus, a Greek adventurer, is defeated in the Fourth Macedonian War; taken in chains to Rome, he is tried and executed.

**46** Vercingetorix, the Gallic chief of the Arverni, is put to death in Rome after being captured by Caesar at Alesia and exhibited.

A.D.

**30?** St. Stephen is stoned to death for his religious beliefs.

**64?** St. Paul the Apostle, formerly Saul of Tarsus, is beheaded by Nero's soldiers in Rome.

**110–017** Exact date unknown; Christian bishop Ignatius of Antioch is martyred in Rome for his beliefs.

**226** Artabanus IV, the last of the Parthian monarchs, is put to death by the Roman army under Caracalla.

**258?** Novatian, a Stoic philosopher and priest of the Church of Rome, is put to death for his heretical thoughts; his followers, called Novatians who study the teachings called Novatianism, spread his message in secret until the 6th or 7th century. St. Cyprian is beheaded; Christian followers, who venerate him, cast handkerchiefs and other linen before his face so that they could soak up his blood and be honored as relics. St. Laurence, who as treasurer of the Catholic Church refused to hand over the keys to the treasury to the Roman Emperor Valerian, is put to death by being laid over a fire on bars of iron.

**269 (14 February)** Saint Valentine, a bishop of the Catholic Church, is put to death for his religious beliefs; strangely, the date of his death is commemorated as a memorial to lovers.

**272** St. Denis, known as the "Apostle of the French," is martyred in Paris.

**304** Saint Vincentius, a pupil of Bishop Valerius of Saragossa, is arrested during the persecution of Diocletian and put to death. Saint Alban is put to death in England for sheltering a Christian cleric; eight hundred years later, Pope Adrian IV orders that his name be considered as one of the first abbots of England. Agnes, later declared a saint, is ordered burned at the stake for her refusal to renounce Christianity; when she is not killed by the flames, she is taken from the site and beheaded.

**326** Flavius Julius Crispus, the ruler of Gaul, is put to death by his father, Constantine the Great, for treason.

**371 (1 August)** Eusebius of Vercelli, the Bishop of Vercelli (Italy), is stoned to death for his opposition to Arianism.

**998** Roman patriot Johannes Crescentius is beheaded for opposing Otto III, the Holy Roman Emperor.

**1076** The first man to suffer beheading in England, Waltheof, Earl of Northumberland, is executed in London.

**1127** King Louis the Bulky orders Bertholde, the murderer of Charles the Righteous, to be crucified before being executed.

**1222** A deacon is burned at the stake in Oxford, England, for converting to Judaism to marry a Jewish woman.

**1241** William Maurice, the son of a nobleman, is the first man to be hanged, drawn and quartered.

**1305** Sir William Wallace, Scottish patriot, is beheaded, then drawn and quartered in England for treason against the English crown.

**1351** The Statute of Treason, enacted during the reign of King Edward III, becomes the foundation of English law on the subject, and is utilized to put many persons to death. It includes offenses against the State for "bringing false money into the realm, counterfeit to the money in England"; "counterfeiting the coin of this realm"; "to compass or imagine the death of the King or Queen, or their eldest son and heir"; and "to violate the king's companion, or his eldest daughter unmarried, or the wife of the king's eldest son and heir." Further, it specifies that the method of punishment when death was decreed was to be drawing and quartering.

**1381** Wat Tyler, leader of the so-called Peasant's Revolt against the English crown's attempt to impose a poll tax on poor people, is summarily beheaded after being wounded while negotiating with the government. John Ball, an intimate of Tyler and a member of his peasant revolt, is put to death before King Richard III for his part in the rebellion.

**1415** John Hus (or Huss), a Bohemian religious reformer, is burned at the stake after refusing to recant his beliefs before the Council of Constance.

**1426** The English Parliament passes a law labeled *peine forte et dure* ("penalty of duration"), in which the condemned is tortured by having large stones piled on the chest until it collapses; in the meantime, he was fed bad bread on the first day, foul water the next, and so on, and "so shall he continue till he die."

**1440 (26 October)** Former confidante of Joan of Arc and mass child killer Gilles de Rais is slowly strangled to death and then burned publicly for at least 140 murders of children, and possibly as many as 800.

**1484–1682** Pope Innocent's bull against sorcery and witchcraft ("Summis desiderantes") sets off an orgy of executions of women across Europe; when the last is put to death almost two hundred years later, the program has claimed upwards of 300,000 people.

**1485** In response to the Pope's outcry against witchcraft, the city of Como, in Italy, burns to death 41 women.

**1489** German Dominican friars Jacob Sprenger and Neinrich Kraemer compose their *Malleus Maleficarum* ("Hammer of Evildoers"), which is used as a guidebook by local officials across Europe to put to death untold thousands of persons suspected of being witches.

**1498 (23 May)** Girolamo Savonarola, a Franciscan friar who protested church corruption, is hanged and then cremated for opposing official church doctrine.

**1499 (23 November)** Perkin Warbeck, pretender to the throne of England's Henry VII, is put to death at London's Tyburn prison.

**1502 (6 May)** Sir James Tyrrell, who is alleged to have directed the murder of Prince Edward and his brother the Duke of York in the Tower of London, is beheaded by King Henry VII of England for the crime.

**1509–97** During the reign of England's King Henry VIII, an estimated 30,000 men, women, and children are judicially executed for various criminal offenses.

**1510** 140 persons are burned to death at Brescia, in Italy, for witchcraft.

**1521 (15 February)** In response to a threat from several towns to refuse to burn those accused of witchcraft, Pope Leo X issues his bull Honestis, calling for the excommunication of any official who refused to execute a witch.

**1525 (30 May)** German religious reformer Thomas Münzer is executed along with several of his followers in Mühlhausen, Thuringia (now Germany) for leading the so-called "Peasant's Revolt."

**1531** By an act of the English Parliament, boiling to death is made legal as a mode of capital punishment.

**(19 August)** English heretic Thomas Bilney, who had denounced saint and relic worship, is burned to death at the stake.

**1534** London names one Cratwell or Gratwell as its first town executioner. Four years later, after being convicted of robbery, he himself is hanged in front of 20,000 spectators.

**1535 (22 June)** English prelate Bishop John Fisher, for refusing to sign a document which held that Henry VIII's marriage to Catherine of Aragon was invalid, is beheaded on London's Tower Hill.

**1536** Jacob Hutter, a religious zealot, is burned at the stake at Innsbruck in the Tirol (now in Austria); his religious followers, descendants of the Anabaptists, name themselves the Hutterian Brethren.

**1537** English rebel Robert Aske is hanged in York for leading the insurrection against the English crown known as "The Pilgrimage of Grace."

**(30 June)** Baron Thomas Darcy, the privy councilor of King Henry VIII, is beheaded for leading a rebellion against the King.

**1540 (30 July)** English reformer Robert Barnes is burned at the stake as a heretic for preaching Lutheranism.

**1546 (1 March)** Scottish religious reformer George Wishart is burned to death at St. Andrews for heresy.

**(16 July)** After being denounced for her religion by her Catholic husband, Protestant Anne Ascue is burned to death at the stake in Smithfield, England.

**1553 (22 August)** John Dudley, Duke of Northumberland and Earl of Warwick, is beheaded on Tower Hill in London for conspiring to establish his son, Lord Guildford Dudley, and his wife, Lady Jane Grey, as the monarchs of England despite Mary being in succession to the throne.

**1554 (12 February)** Lady Jane Grey, Queen of England for nine days, and her husband, Lord Guildford Dudley, are put to death by beheading; Grey inside the grounds of the Tower of London, and Dudley on Tower Hill.

**1555 (9 February)** Labeled as a heretic, English theologian Rowland Taylor is burned at the stake, as is English prelate John Hooper.

**(16 October)** For refusing to recant his religious beliefs, English clergyman Nicholas Ridley is burned at the stake in Oxford.

**1586** After Queen Elizabeth discovers a conspiracy to have her removed from the throne, she has Mary Stuart, Queen of Scots, and 11 of her followers, including Anthony Babington and John Ballard, put to death.

**1593 (6 April)** English nonconformist clergyman John Greenwood is hanged at Tyburn for denying the authority of the Church of England.

**(29 May)** Puritan pamphleteer John Penry is hanged in Surrey, England, for inciting rebellion.

**1602 (31 July)** French soldier Charles de Gontaut, Duc de Biron, is convicted of treason against the French crown and beheaded in Paris.

**1606 (30 & 31 January)** Guy Fawkes, Thomas Winter, Robert Keyes, Ambrose Rokewood, as well as four others implicated in the so-called "Gunpowder Plot" to blow up Parliament and murder England's King James I, are hanged, beheaded, and quartered.

**1608** George Kendall, one of the councillors of the colony of Virginia, becomes the first man executed by firing squad in the New World.

**1610 (27 May)** For assassinating King Henry IV of France, French revolutionary François Ravaillac is drawn and quartered by four horses.

**1612** By order of King James I of England, one Bartholomew Legate is burned at the stake for denying the divinity of Christ.

**1618 (29 October)** Sir Walter Raleigh is beheaded in the Old Palace Yard in London for treason against the English crown.

**1623** Eleven gypsy women are drowned in Edinburgh, Scotland.

**1628 (28 November)** English soldier John Felton is hanged at Tyburn outside of London for murdering George Villiers, the Duke of Buckingham.

**1630** John Billington, one of the original Pilgrims on the Mayflower, becomes the first person executed in the British colonies by hanging.

**1636** The Massachusetts Bay Colony establishes a code of law that punishes 13 different crimes, including witchcraft, punishable by death.

**1638** Dorothy Talbye, whose probable insanity led her to kill her child, is hanged in the Massachusetts Bay Colony.

**1640 (30 July)** Richard Fetherston, the chaplain to Catherine of Aragon, the first wife of England's Henry VIII, is hanged and, while still alive, disemboweled and beheaded, then quartered, for arguing that Henry had no right to marry his dead brother's widow.

**1641** The "Capital Lawes" of the Massachusetts Bay Colony establish the death penalty for several offenses, including: (1) If any man after legall conviction, shall have or worship any other God, but the Lord God, he shall be put to death. (2) If any man or woman be a Witch, that is, hath or consulteth with a familiar spirit, they shall be put to death. (3) If any person shall blaspheme the Name of God the Father, Sonne, or Holy Ghost, with direct, expresse, presumptuous, or high-handed blasphemy, or shall curse God in the like manner, he shall be put to death.

**1649 (30 January)** King Charles I of England becomes that nation's only monarch to be put to death when he is beheaded in London.

**1660 (1 June)** Mary Dyer, whose Quakerism conflicted with the Puritan religion of the Massachusetts Bay Colony, is hanged after being exiled from the colony but returning.

**1661 (27 May)** Archibald Campbell, eighth Earl of Argyll, is beheaded in Edinburgh, Scotland, for his role is helping to defeat King Charles I during the English Civil War.

**1663** John Reynolds' *The Triumph of God's Revenge Against the Crying and Execrable Sinne of Wilful and Premeditated Murther* is the first major work in English to discuss capital punishment.

**1676** French murderess Marie de Brivilliers is beheaded, then burned, for committing at least fifty poisoning murders.

**1683 (21 July)** Lord William Russell is beheaded for his alleged part in the so-called Rye House Plot to assassinate King Charles II of England.

**1685** Archibald Campbell, ninth Earl of Argyll, is beheaded in Edinburgh for his support of the Duke of Monmouth against the English crown.

**(11 May)** Margaret McLachlan, 63, and Margaret Wilson, 18, are drowned in Scotland for denying that James VII of England was entitled to rule the Church of England as he pleased.

**1682** The colony of Pennsylvania enacts William Penn's *Great Act,* which lists murder and treason as the only offenses punishable by death.

**1688 (17 February)** Scottish revolutionary James Renwick is beheaded in Edinburgh.

**1691 (16 May)** After insisting that his intent was to "maintaine [sic] against popery or any Schism or heresy," Jacob Leisler is hanged for treasonably holding the fort of King James II in the New York colony.

**1692** 19 out of 200 people charged with being witches are hanged in Salem Town (now Salem) in the Massachusetts Bay Colony; among these are Sarah Bishop, Rebecca Nurse, Sarah Good, and Giles Corey, the latter who suffers death by being pressed to death by stones.

**1693** Cotton Mather's *Wonders of the Invisible World,* an account of the Salem Witchcraft trials, appears.

**1697** The last official case in which ducking and drowning is utilized as a form of capital punishment occurs when a woman convicted of theft is executed in the Loch of Spyne in Scotland.

**1716 (24 February)** English Jacobite Sir James Radcliffe, the Third Earl of Derwentwater, is beheaded on London's Tower Hill for conspiring to restore the Stuart dynasty to the throne of England.

**1741** On ascending the throne of Russia, Tsarina Elizabeth Petrovna renounces the use of capital punishment within her empire.

**1746 (11 August)** Arthur Elphinstone, the Sixth Baron Balmerino, who sided with James Edward, the Old Pretender to the English throne, and his son James Edward, the Young Pretender, is captured at the Battle of Culloden by the British and beheaded for treason.

**1747** The corpse of British murderer Adam Graham, executed for beating a man to death, is hanged in chains on a gibbet with 12,000 nails driven into his body to prevent its removal. Simon Fraser, the 12th Baron Lovat, is put to death by beheading for his role against the English government at the Battle of Culloden, becoming the last man to be beheaded with an ax in England.

**1752 (6 April)** English murderess Mary Blandy is hanged at Oxford, England, for murdering her father.

**1753** Ann Williams, convicted of murdering her husband with white mercury, is publicly burned at the stake at Gloucester, England.

**1757** In perhaps one of the most revolting executions in history, executioners are forced to incise the muscles and joints of the arms and legs of one Robert-François Damiens, a Frenchman condemned for attempting to assassinate King Louis XV, because his muscular strength kept the horses from drawing and quartering him. It is the last time the method of drawing and quartering will be used in France.

**1759 (6 August)** Fourteen years after committing a heinous murder, British scholar Eugene Aram is hanged in York; his body is then gibbeted and, as a lesson to others, left to rot and mummify for many years on a road heavily traveled.

**1762 (9 March)** Frenchman Jean Calas is put to death for the murder of his son; later it is found that his son was a suicide, and that Calas had been innocent. His case leads to a rethinking of the use of capital punishment across Europe.

**1763** French writer and philosopher Voltaire documents what he considers to be a major injustice in the Calas case in his *Traité sur la tolérance* ("Treatise on Tolerance"), which leads to a French court reversing its conclusion that Calas murdered his son and the award of compensation to his family.

**1764** *Trattato del délitti è elle pèna* ("Essay on Crimes and Punishments"), by Italian criminologist Cesare Beccaria, the first major work advocating an end to capital punishment, is published.

**1776 (28 June)** Thomas Hickey, an American soldier, is put to death for conspiring to kidnap George Washington and deliver him to the British, the first military execution in the history of the American army.

**1781** Emperor Joseph II of Austria, influenced by Cesare Beccaria's writings, abolishes the death penalty in the Austro-Hungarian Empire.

**1786** Emperor Leopold II of Austria, who had succeeded Joseph II, establishes a penal code for his empire which stresses that punishment should be used for the return of criminals to society.

**1787** The Philadelphia Society for Alleviating the Miseries of Public Persons, the first group established in the United States to fight to end capital punishment as well as reform prison laws and conditions, is founded.

**1788** Sir Gilbert Elliot delivers his speech on the "Execution of [Rajah] Nundcomar."

**1790** By an act of the British Parliament, burning alive at the stake is outlawed as a "cruel and inhuman punishment," and hanging is substituted in its place.

**(30 April)** The first American Congress, with an act passed this day, enacts a national death penalty for murder, the forgery of public securities, robbery, and rape.

**1792** The French government accepts the design for a new form of capital punishment invented by Dr. Antoine Louis (1723–3792); called the "louisette" by revolutionary Jean Paul Marat, it is later named after the man who once thought of such a device: the guillotine.

**1793 (29 November)** Antoine Pierre Barnave, president of France's Constituent Assembly from its establishment in 1790 until its dissolution, is guillotined in Paris for alleged royalist sympathies.

**(4 December)** Armand Gui Simon de Coetnempren, the Comte de Kersaint, a famed French naval officer who had attempted to reform the French navy during the Revolution, is beheaded for protesting the execution of King Louis XVI.

**1793, October–1794, August** The French Revolutionary Tribunal sends 2,596 persons to the guillotine, including Georges Jacques Danton, Maximilien François Marie Isidore de Robespierre, Marie-Anne Charlotte Corday D'Armont, Lucie Simplice Camille Benoist Desmoulins, Jacques-René Hébert, and King Louis XVI and Queen Marie Antoinette.

**1794** Pennsylvania becomes the first state to end capital punishment for all crimes except first degree murder.

**(24 March)** Prussian politician Jean Baptiste du Val-de-Grâce, the Baron de Cloots, is beheaded in Paris after telling French revolutionaries, "My heart is French and my soul is sans-culotte."

**(5 April)** French revolutionary François Chabot, leader of the rabidly antimonarchial party known as the Montagnards, is guillotined in Paris.

**(8 May)** French chemist Antoine Laurent Lavoisier, who helped to discovery oxygen, is beheaded in Paris to calls of "We need no more scientists in France."

**(16 December)** Jean-Baptiste Carrier, a French revolutionary responsible for helping engineer the downfall of Maximilien Robespierre, is himself beheaded for the mass murder of 2,000 opponents that he had drowned in the city of Nantes.

**1800 (7 October)** Gabriel Prosser, a slave, is executed for plotting a slave revolt in Norfolk County, Virginia.

**1804 (21 March)** Louis Antoine Henri de Bourbon, the Duc d'Enghien, is shot by a firing squad and unceremoniously dumped into a ditch for allegedly plotting an insurrection against Napoleon.

**1808 (18 May)** British prison reformer Sir Samuel Romilly introduces in the British Parliament the first bill to repeal the death penalty for a criminal offense liable for that punishment at that time.

**1810** Tirolese patriot Andreas Hofer, who had fought the French takeover of his homeland in Europe, is betrayed to the French and shot.

**1813** Lord Ellenborough decries the possibility of the abolition of capital punishment in England, saying people should be put to death even for "the theft of a few shillings."

**1815 (7 December)** Marshal Michel Peter Ney, the Duke of Elchingen and Prince of Moscow, is put to death by firing squad for helping Napoleon return to power during the reign known as "The Hundred Days"; however, rumors persist that he was spirited out of Paris and traveled to the United States, where he was a teacher with the name Peter Stewart Ney and died there in 1846.

**1817 (12 March)** British rioter John Cashman is hanged at Snow Hill in London for his role in the Spafields Riot.

**1820** Arthur Thistlewood and four of his conspirators are executed for their role in formulating the unsuccessful Cato Street Conspiracy to murder Robert Stewart, Lord Castlereagh, the English Foreign Minister.

**1821–14** The first American periodical dedicated to the abolition of capital punishment in the United States, *The Moral Advocate,* is published in Mount Pleasant, Ohio, by Elisha Bates, a Quaker printer.

**1822** Edward Livingston addresses his "Report on the Plan of a Penal Code" to the Louisiana legislature.

**(2 July)** Denmark Vesey, a slave, is hanged along with 34 other slaves for plotting a slave revolt in Charleston, South Carolina.

**1823 (July)** Robert Ferebee, a slave, is put to death for leading a slave insurrection in Norfolk County, Virginia.

**(7 November)** Spanish revolutionary Rafael de Riego Y Nunez is executed as a traitor to his country in Madrid.

**1829 (28 January)** Multiple murderer and corpse thief William Burke is publicly hanged in Edinburgh, Scotland, for at least 15 murders; later, the phrase *to burke* is used to mean "to suffocate."

**(7 May)** Murderess Catherine Cashiere, a prostitute, is hanged on Blackwell's Island in New York.

**1831 (2 August)** Wife murderer Oliver Watkins is hanged in Sterling, Connecticut.

**(11 November)** Nat Turner, a slave, is hanged for leading a revolt against slave-owners in Virginia.

**1833** The state of Rhode Island becomes the first state to order private, instead of public, executions.

**1835** The legislature of the state of Maine enacts the so-called Maine Law, which make executions the jurisdiction of the governor and in effect makes them all but impossible to carry out.

**1840 (August)** William Makepeace Thackeray's "Going to See a Man Hanged," a retrospective of the execution of French servant François Courvoisier, appears anonymously in *Fraser's Magazine,* a British literary journal.

**1842** British murderer Daniel Good is hanged in London for the murder of his mistress.

**(15 September)** Honduran soldier Francisco Morazan is executed by a firing squad after attempting to take over the presidency of Costa Rica.

**1846** Michigan becomes the first state in the United States to abolish capital punishment for all crimes, with the exception of treason against the state.

**1851 (31 January)** Double murderer Reuben Dunbar is hanged in the courtyard of the jail in Albany, New York, for the murder of two men standing in the way of his inheritance.

**(March)** After twice being found not guilty of committing murder in two other cases, British murderess Sarah Chesham is executed for the arsenic murder of her husband. Her body vanishes before burial and is not seen again, leading many to speculate that she faked death during her execution.

**1852** The California Supreme Court, in *People v. Tanner,* finds that a state law allowing for the death penalty for grand larceny is constitutional; the subject of the case, George Tanner, is hanged on 23 July of the same year.

**1853** Wisconsin becomes the second American state to abolish state laws on capital punishment.

**1859 (7 October)** Japanese educator Sanai Hashimoto is beheaded in Edo (now Tokyo) by Japanese authorities for urging supreme power to be invested in a single leader; on the 50th anniversary of his death in 1909, he is remembered by the Japanese people as a patriot.

**(2 December)** Radical abolitionist John Brown is hanged in Virginia for fomenting a slave-led revolution at Harper's Ferry, Virginia; his death, applauded in the American South, nonetheless pushes the nation closer to civil war over the slavery issue.

**1860 (13 July)** Murderer Albert E. Hicks is hung on New York's Bedloe's Island, now the site of the Statue of Liberty, for the murder of three members of a ship's crew.

**(12 September)** American adventurer and filibusterer William Walker is shot by a firing squad for trying to establish an American slave colony in Honduras.

**1861** The English Parliament establishes that only murderers would be executed in England during peacetime.

**(December)** Private William H. Johnson of the American Union army becomes the first American soldier in the Civil War shot for desertion.

**1862 (22 February)** Captain Nathaniel Gordon of Portland, Maine, is hanged in New York for bringing slaves into the United States, the only ship captain hanged for violating the ban on slaves instituted in 1808.

**(22 October)** Catherine Williams, a nurse, is hanged in front of London's Old Bailey for poisoning seven people.

**1864** The death penalty is abolished in Romania. Japanese activist Kuniomi Hirano, after leading a peasant revolt against the Japanese government, is captured and executed.

**1865 (28 July)** Dr. Edward William Pritchard is executed in Jail Square, near Hutcheson Bridge, in Edinburgh, Scotland, in front of 100,000 people for killing his wife and mother-in-law, his being the last public execution in Scotland.

**(24 October)** Paul Bogle, a former slave, is put to death by the British authorities in Morant Bay, Jamaica.

**1867** Portugal outlaws capital punishment.

**(23 November)** British highway robbers and murderers William O'Meara Allen, William Gould, and Michael Larkin, known collectively as the Three Finians (or Fenians), are publicly hanged in Manchester before a crowd of 12,000.

**1868** British murderer Michael Barrett, who had tried to rescue the highway robbers Allen, Gould and Larkin by blowing up Clerkenwell Prison and in the process killing twelve, is hung, the last man publicly executed in Great Britain.

**1870** The death penalty is abolished in Holland.

**(17 March)** 22-year-old Elizabeth Butchill is hanged in England for murdering her own child.

**1874** Francis Stewart is hanged at London's Newgate, the first grandmother ever to be executed for murdering her grandchild.

**1877 (23 March)** Mormon leader John Doyle Lee is executed by a firing squad, 20 years after he leads the so-called Mountain Meadows Massacre of more than 100 emigrants to California.

**1880 (11 November)** 25-year-old Ned Kelly, leader of a gang of Australian bushrangers, or outlaws, is hanged in Melbourne gaol.

**1885 (16 November)** Canadian revolutionary Louis Riel is hanged in Regina, Northwest Territories.

**1890 (6 August)** Woman killer William Francis Kemmler becomes the first man to be executed by way of electricity when New York puts him to death.

**1892** The U.S. Congress reduces the 17 capital offenses imposed on prisoners to three (treason, rape, and murder).

**(23 May)** Australian mass murderer Frederick Bayley Deeming, who claimed to be Jack the Ripper, is hanged in Melbourne before a crowd of 10,000 spectators.

**(15 November)** Multiple murderer Dr. Thomas Neill Cream is hanged at London's Newgate Prison; his last words are reported to have been "I am Jack—," referring to Jack the Ripper, who many researchers have since believed him to be.

**1894 (13 July)** Patrick Eugene Prendergast, convicted of assassinating Chicago mayor Carter Henry Harrison, Sr., is hanged.

**1895 (1 July)** Dr. Robert W. Buchanan, convicted of murdering his wife with an overdose of morphine, is put to death in the electric chair in New York's Sing Sing prison.

**(18 October)** Hans Hansen and Thomas St. Clair, two sailors convicted of killing a shipmate during a botched attempt at taking over their ship, are put to death in San Quentin Prison in California.

**1898** Oscar Wilde's *Ballad of Reading Gaol* (Jail), based on the case of executed English wife murderer Charles Thomas Wooldridge, appears.

**1899 (19 July)** Mary Ansell, 22, is hanged in England's St. Alban's Prison for poisoning her sister.

**1900 (9 January)** British murderess Louise Masset is hanged in London's Newgate Prison for suffocating her three-year-old son, Manfred.

**1901 (21 March)** British murderer Herbert John Bennett is hanged at Norwich gaol for the murder of his wife; 11 years later, another body appears near where his wife's was discovered, murdered in the same fashion, leading many to believe Bennett was innocent.

**(25 April)** Murderer Thomas "Black Jack" Ketchum is hanged in New Mexico Territory; his noose, improperly placed, decapitates him as he is hanged, spilling blood on the onlookers in one of the most gruesome executions on record.

**1903 (3 March)** Edgar Edwards is hanged at England's Wandsworth Prison for killing an entire family and burying their bodies in his garden; on the scaffold, his last words to the chaplain are, "I've been looking forward to this lot!"

**(7 April)** Polish immigrant Severin Klosowski, alias George Chapman, is hanged in England's Wandsworth Prison for poisoing three women in London.

**(30 November)** Former lawman Tom Horn is hanged in Wyoming for the 1901 murder of a 14-year-old boy; Horn's last words, to hangman Joseph Cahill, are, "Ain't losing your nerve, are you, Joe?"

**1905 (23 May)** Brothers Alfred and Albert Stratton are both executed at England's Wandsworth Prison, the first men put to death on the strength of fingerprint evidence taken at the scene of a crime.

**1907** The state of Kansas abolishes capital punishment.

**1910 (23 November)** Wife murderer Dr. Hawley Harvey Crippen is hanged in London's Pentonville Prison.

**1911 (24 January)** Shusui Kotoku, a Japanese socialist, is hanged at Tokyo's Ichigaya prison for treason against the Meiji government.

**1914 (26 February)** For murdering his elderly employer, killer George Ball is hanged in Liverpool, England.

**1915 (30 July)** Police Lieutenant Charles Becker, who conspired to murder a gambler, Herman "Beansie" Rosenthal, is executed in Sing Sing in what is considered to be the most botched electrocution in history.

**(19 November)** Labor activist Joe Hill is executed by firing squad in Utah for killing a man and his son in a union-inspired murder plot.

**1916 (13 July)** Italian patriot Cesare Battisti, who had fought for many years to separate his native region of Trentino from Austrian rule, is captured by Austrian troops on the battlefield during World War I, and is hanged.

**(3 August)** Having been stripped of his knighthood for treason, Sir Roger Casement, an Irish patriot, is hanged at Pentonville Prison in Ireland for conspiring with the Germans during World War I.

**1917–1922** Historians estimate that as many as 600,000 people are executed in the struggle to establish the Soviet regime in Russia.

**1918 (16 April)** French adventurer Bolo Pasha is executed at Vincennes by the French for collaborating with the Germans during World War I.

**1919** The death penalty is abolished in Austria. "Within Our Gates," by black American filmmaker Oscar Micheaux (1884–4951), becomes the first motion picture made of the subject of lynching.

**1920 (6 December)** Chinese-American lawyer Chung Xi Miao is hanged at Manchester's Strangeways Prison for the murder of his wife while on their honeymoon.

**1921 (3 June)** The death penalty is abolished in Sweden.

**1922 (24 March)** Edward Ernest Black is hanged in Exeter gaol for the murder by arsenic of his wife.

**(31 May)** Major Herbert Rowse Armstrong is hanged in England's Gloucester Prison for the arsenic murder of his wife.

**1923 (9 January)** British murderers Frederick Edward Francis Bywaters and his mistress Edith Jessie Graydon Thompson are hanged in London for the murder of Thompson's husband.

**1924 (8 February)** Chinese murderer Gee Jon, a member of a Chinese tong, or gang, becomes the first man to be put to death in a gas chamber when Nevada executes him.

**(10 September)** In perhaps his most famous case, attorney Clarence Darrow, a leading American voice against the use of the death penalty, wins life sentences for child murderers Nathan Leopold, Jr., and Richard Loeb, after an impassioned, multihour address to the judge.

**1925** Theodore Dreiser's *An American Tragedy,* which is loosely based on the case of Chester Gillette, a New York murderer executed in 1908 for the killing of his girlfriend, is published.

**1926 (6 April)** Gerald Chapman, the original "Public Enemy No. 1," is hanged in Connecticut for the murder of a policeman during a store robbery in New Britain, Connecticut; before he is executed, Chapman declares that "death itself isn't dreadful but hanging seems an awkward way of entering the adventure."

**(26 June)** British female prostitute Louie Calvert is hanged in Manchester's Strangeways Prison for the murder of a widow.

**(23 December)** South African Petrus Stephanus Hauptfleisch, convicted of murdering his mother in a fit of rage over his alcoholism, is hanged in Cape Town.

**1927 (January)** The Labor Party of England circulates the *Manifesto on Capital Punishment,* signed by 27 distinguished Labor politicians, urging the abolition of capital punishment in England.

**(22 August)** Anarchists Nicola Sacco and Bartolomeo Vanzetti are put to death in the electric chair in Massachusetts for the murder of a paymaster and guard at a shoe factory in 1920.

**1928** French murderess Junka Kures, convicted of killing a young child, is beheaded by guillotine, the first woman in 41 years to suffer that punishment in France.

**(31 May)** British murderers Frederick Guy Browne and William Kennedy are hanged at different British prisons (Browne at Pentonville, and Kennedy at Wandsworth) for the murder of Constable George W. Gutteridge, whose eyes had been shot out. Both men are convicted with the use of forensic evidence, the first time such methods are utilized.

**1929 (17 August)** Bootlegger James Horace Alderman, convicted of murdering two Coast Guardsmen, is hanged by the federal government in a Coast Guard hangar near Fort Lauderdale, Florida.

**1930 (21 February)** Mrs. Eva Dugan is hanged at Arizona's State Prison at Florence, the first woman put to death in that state, for murdering a ranch owner.

**(28 February)** Dr. James Howard Snook, a veterinarian, is executed in Florida's electric chair for the murder of his mistress.

**1931** The United States Supreme Court, in *Aldridge v. United States,* holds that juries can be questioned as to racial bias in death penalty cases.

**(23 February)** Cop killing lovers Walter Glenn Dague and Irene Schroeder are put to death in Pennsylvania's electric chair; Schroeder becomes the first woman to be electrocuted in that state.

**(19 June)** Wife murderer Frank Myer suffers the same fate as Black Jack Ketchum (1901), as his head is ripped away after being hanged in West Virginia.

**(2 July)** Mass murderer Peter Kürten, known as "The Vampire of Düsseldorf," is beheaded in the courtyard of the Klingelputz prison in Cologne, Germany. The motion picture *M,* which appears two years later, is based on his case.

**(28 October)** Murderer Francis "Two Gun" Crowley is electrocuted in Sing Sing Prison in New York.

**1934 (20 July)** Double murderer William Alfred Bayly is hanged at New Zealand's Auckland Prison.

**1934–1945** The People's Courts of the Third Reich in Germany sentence some 7,000 of the 16,000 people brought before it to death.

**1936 (24 March)** Multiple murderer George Barrett is hanged by the federal government in the Marion County Jail (now Marion Prison) in Indiana for the murder of FBI agent Nelson B. Klein.

**(16 April)** British nurse Dorothea Nancy Waddingham is hanged at Birmingham's Winson Green Prison for the for-profit murders of a mother and daughter.

**(19 June)** Kidnapper Arthur Gooch is hanged at Macalester, Oklahoma, the first man put to death under the "Lindbergh Law," which made it a capital offense to carry an abducted person across state lines.

**(15 July)** British murderess Charlotte Bryant is hanged in England's Exeter Prison for the poisoning of her husband; she becomes the second woman hanged in Britain in three months.

**1938 (14 March)** Russian politician Aleksei Ivanovich Rykov, former president of the Soviet of People's Commissars, is put to death in the Soviet gulag.

**(1 November)** British murderer George Brain is hanged in England's Wandsworth Prison for the murder of a prostitute.

**1939 (17 June)** French murderer Eugen Weidmann becomes the last man to be publicly beheaded in France; the circus spectacle surrounding his execution, and the surreptitious film and newspaper photos taken of it, lead the French government to ban all further public executions.

**1941–1945** Between 70 and 96 Americans are executed in the European Theater of Operations (ETO) during World War II for offenses ranging from rape to murder.

**1941 (14 August)** Father Maximilian Kolbe, a Polish Roman Catholic priest interned at Auschwitz, offers to take the place of a Polish prisoner condemned to death, and is himself executed.

**1942 (8 August)** After being convicted of trying to inflict sabotage in the United States on behalf of Nazi Germany, German spies Herbert Haupt, Heinrich Heinck, Edward Kerling, Herman Neubauer, Richard Quirin, and Werner Thiel are put to death by the federal government in the electric chair at the Washington D.C. jail.

**(27 October)** Helmuth Günther Hübener, a 17-year-old German youth, is beheaded by the German government for listening to foreign broadcasts during the war.

**1943 (13 July)** Professor Kurt Huber, a member of the anti-Hitler organization known as *The White Rose,* is beheaded for opposing the German government.

**1945 (31 January)** U.S. soldier Pvt. Eddie Slovik is executed by a 12-man firing squad for desertion, the only American executed during World War II for that crime. His case remains closed until 1970, when it is exposed by journalist William Bradford Huie.

**(April)** Ewald Heinrich von Kleist-Schmenzin, a wealthy Prussian landowner whose son was involved in the plot to assassinate Adolf Hitler, is beheaded.

**(28 April)** In Italy, Italian dictator Benito Mussolini is executed by Italian Communist partisans, taken to Milan, and strung up with the bodies of his mistress, Clara Petacci, and her brother. His last words, to the Colonel named Valeria who had brandished a pistol to shoot him, were, "But, but, mister Colonel—"

**(9 April)** Lutheran theologian Dietrich Bonhoeffer is put to death in the Flossenbürg concentration camp for opposing the Nazi regime.

**(15 October)** Former French premier Pierre Laval is put to death by a French firing squad for collaborating with the Nazis during the German occupation of France.

**1946 (3 January)** American-born fascist William Joyce, convicted by an English court for conducting radio propaganda for the Nazis during World War II, is hanged in London for aiding the enemy.

**(1 June)** Romanian army officer and dictator Ion Antonescu, convicted of helping the Nazis invade Romania, is executed by firing squad.

**(17 July)** Serbia guerilla leader Draza Mihajlovic is executed in Belgrade for allegedly collaborating with the Axis powers during World War II.

**(16 October)** Two weeks after being convicted and sentenced to death for war crimes, crimes against humanity, and waging war, Nazi leaders Hans Frank, Wilhelm Frick, Alfred Josef Ferdinand Jodl, Ernst Kaltenbrunner, Wilhelm Keitel, Joachim von Ribbentrop, Alfred Rosenberg, and Fritz Saukel are hanged in the Nuremberg Prison.

**(26 October)** British serial killer Neville George Heath is hanged at Pentonville Prison in London; when offered a whiskey before his execution, he says, "Ah . . .you better make that a double."

**1947** On the order of dictator Josef Stalin, capital punishment is abolished in the Soviet Union.

**1948 (8 May)** Former Burmese Premier U Saw and five others are hanged in Rangoon for an attempted coup against the Burmese government the previous 10 August.

**(23 December)** Former Japanese Prime Minister Hideki Tojo and six other Japanese officials are hanged at Tokyo's Sagamo Prison for committing crimes against humanity during World War II.

**1949–93** The Royal Commission Inquiry on Capital Punishment meets to discuss a revision of Britain's death penalty system, and offer alternatives to hanging, which had become unpopular; although the idea of lethal injection is discussed, it is discarded, and hanging is retained.

**1949 (12 January)** British murderess Margaret Allen, after directing the police to evidence in a horrible murder she had committed, is hanged at Manchester's Strangeways Prison.

**(6 August)** English murderer John George Haigh, known for his series of slayings known as the "Acid Bath Murders," is hanged in England's Wandsworth Prison.

**(22 August)** Martha Julie Beck and Raymond Martinez Fernandez, known as "The Lonely Hearts Killers," are electrocuted in New York's Sing Sing prison.

**1950** The Soviet Union reinstates capital punishment for such crimes as treason, espionage, wrecking government property, terrorist acts, and banditry.

**(9 March)** After confessing, Englishman Timothy John Evans is hanged in London's Pentonville Prison for the double murder of his wife and infant daughter; later, another man, John Christie, is accused of the same murders. An investigation later shows that Evans was probably innocent.

**1951** German Einstazgruppe leader Heinz Maria Karl Jost becomes the last Nazi war criminal to be hanged, when the American forces occupying Germany execute him in Landsberg.

**1952 (August)** Russian Yiddish-language novelist and short story writer David Bérgelson is exterminated in the Soviet gulag.

**(12 December)** Multiple murderer William E. Cook is executed in the gas chamber in California's San Quentin Prison for the murder of a motorist who picked him up while he was hitchhiking.

**1953** Soviet NKVD head Lavrenti Beria is executed for his part in crimes committed during the Stalinist era. Details surrounding his execution, as well as the date, remain a mystery. The Royal Commission Inquiry on Capital Punishment (Gowers Commission) recommends that England abolish capital punishment.

**(2 January)** British murderer John James Alcott is put to death for the murder of a railway clerk, despite the fact that his attorneys argued that he was insane at the time of the crime.

**(28 January)** 19-year-old Derek Bentley, the accomplice of a youngster who murdered a policeman, is hanged in England despite pleas to spare his life. His execution pushes England closer to abolition.

**(15 July)** British murderer John Reginald Halliday Christie is hanged in London's Pentonville Prison, three years after another man, Timothy Evans, was put to death for the same crimes.

**(18 December)** Carl Austin Hall and Bonnie Brown Heady, convicted of kidnapping and murdering 6-year-old Bobby Greenlease, Jr., in perhaps the most infamous kidnapping case in American history, are put to death in the gas chamber at the Missouri State Penitentiary in Jefferson City.

**1954 (13 December)** Styllou Christofi, a 53-year-old Cypriot emigre to England, is hanged in the Holloway Women's Prison in North London for the murder of her daughter-in-law.

**1955–56** A major movement in England to abolish capital punishment, led by Labor member of parliament Sydney Silverman and publisher Victor Gollancz, is organized.

**1955 (3 June)** Barbara Elaine Wood Graham is put to death in California's gas chamber; her story is later told in the 1958 movie *I Want to Live!*

**(13 July)** Ruth Neilson Ellis, convicted of murder, is hanged at the Holloway Women's Prison in North London; she becomes the last woman to be executed in Great Britain before the abolition of the death penalty in that nation.

**1956** For the first time, England registers no executions.

**(10 February)** Canadian Wilbert Coffin is hanged in the Quebec City Prison for the murders of three hunters; doubts remain as to his guilt, and his executioner even remarked, "This man, I swear, was innocent."

**(24 February)** Kidnapper and murderer Arthur Ross Brown is put to death in the gas chamber at the Missouri State Prison at Jefferson City by the federal government for taking a kidnap victim across state lines.

**1957** In a compromise with anti-death penalty activists, the British Parliament enacts the Homicide Act of 1957, which allows capital punishment to be used for six specific crimes only.

**(15 March)** Child murderer Burton Abbott dies in California's gas chamber at San Quentin; his execution is nearly stayed by Governor Goodwin Knight, who decides to issue a stay just as the deadly cyanide pellets have already fallen.

**(11 June)** John Gilbert Graham, whose plot to kill his mother led to the bombing of a civilian airliner and the deaths of 44 people, is put to death in the gas chamber at the state penitentiary in Colorado.

**(21 August)** Brothers George and Michael Krull are both executed by the federal government at the Georgia State Prison at Reidsville for rape.

**1958 (17 June)** The Hungarian government announces the execution of former Premier Imre Nagy, put to death by Soviet troops occupying Hungary.

**(24 October)** Filipino houseboy Bart Caritativo is put to death in the gas chamber in San Quentin Prison in California for the murder of a man and woman he worked for.

**1959 (5 November)** Guenther Fritz Padola is executed in England's Wandsworth Prison, the last man put to death in the United Kingdom for killing a policeman.

**1960 (5 May)** In perhaps the most controversial execution since that of Sacco and Vanzetti in 1927, Red Light Bandit Caryl Chessman is put to death in California's gas chamber for rape and kidnapping.

**1961** Forty people are executed in the United States. British author Ludovic Kennedy's investigative work, "10 Rillington Place," shows that Timothy Evans, executed in 1950 for the murder of his daughter, was in fact innocent of the crime.

**(13 April)** In what has become the last military execution in the United States, pfc John Bennett is hanged by the Army for the rape and attempted murder of an 11-year-old girl.

**1962 (4 April)** Petty criminal James Hanratty, known as the "A-6 Killer" for the highway where he committed a murder, is hanged in England's Bedford Gaol; many believe that another man committed the murder.

**(8 August)** For murdering her daughter-in-law, Elizabeth Duncan, as well as the two men she hired for the job, Augustine Baldonado and Luis Moya, Jr., are executed in the gas chamber at San Quentin Prison in California.

**1964** Only 15 persons are put to death in the United States.

**(13 August)** British murderers Peter Anthony Allen and Gwynne Owen Evans (real name: John Robson Welby) are hanged, the last two persons in Britain to be put to death before the abolition of capital punishment in that nation.

**1965** With the royal assent of the Murder Act, Great Britain ends capital punishment (with a clause that it was to expire in five years if it did not work). The death penalty is also abolished in the states of Oregon, Iowa, Vermont, West Virginia, and in New York (in the latter with the exception for the murder of police officers).

**1967** Only two persons are put to death in the United States (Aaron Mitchell in California and Jose Luis Monge in Colorado), making the de facto abolition of the death penalty a reality five years before the Supreme Court makes such a ban the law of the land.

**(3 February)** Ronald Joseph Ryan is hanged in Melbourne's Pentridge Prison for the murder of a prison guard during an escape; he becomes the last person executed in Australia.

**1969** Former Beatle John Lennon and his wife, Yoko Ono, deliver a petition to the English government asking that James Hanratty, executed in 1962, be posthumously pardoned.

**(18 December)** On a motion by Home Secretary James Callaghan, the British House of Commons and House of Lords vote to remove the five-year clause from the 1965 Murder Act, and make the abolition of capital punishment permanent.

**1972 (29 June)** The U.S. Supreme Court, in *Furman v. Georgia,* holds the death penalty as it is currently applied to be unconstitutional.

**1974** The U.S. Catholic Conference votes to declare its opposition to the use of capital punishment.

**1976 (2 July)** In *Gregg v. Georgia,* the U.S. Supreme Court finds that states have changed their death penalty statutes to meet constitutional muster, and allows them to go forward in meting out death sentences.

**1977** The state of Oklahoma establishes its method of capital punishment as lethal injection, although it has no scheduled executions.

**(17 January)** Gary Mark Gilmore is executed by firing squad in Utah for two murders; he becomes the first post-*Furman* execution in the United States. His last words are, "Let's do it!"

**1979 (4 April)** Pakistani prime minister Zulfikar Ali Bhutto, accused of murder, is hanged in Pakistan.

**1980 (November)** The U.S. Catholic Bishops release a letter outlining their opposition to the use of the death penalty in the United States.

**(18 December)** Iran executes Simon Farzani, the Jewish editor of the Iranian newspaper *Journale de Tehrane,* for allegedly spying for the United States and Israel.

**1981** France abolishes capital punishment; its last execution had been in October 1977.

**(9 March)** Steven T. Judy, a triple-murderer who was the fourth man to be executed in the United States post-*Furman,* tells witnesses to his death, "I don't hold any grudges. This is my doing. Sorry it happened."

**1982 (7 December)** Charles Brooks becomes the first man to die by lethal injection when he is put to death in Texas' Huntsville Prison.

**1987 (12 June)** Jimmy Glass, convicted of gagging and murdering a young couple, is electrocuted in Louisiana's Angola Prison; his last words are, "I'd rather be fishing."

**(15 October)** Thomas Sankara, the President of the African nation of Burkina Faso, and 12 of his aides are executed by firing squad during a coup by troops loyal to Captain Blaise Compaore.

**1988** Congress enacts the Anti-Drug Abuse Act, which calls for the execution of so-called drug "kingpins."

**(10 June)** Kidnapper and murderer Arthur Gary Bishop is executed by lethal injection in Utah.

**1989 (24 January)** Multiple murderer Theodore "Ted" Bundy, after having confessed to murdering more than 50 young women in a killing spree across several western American states, is put to death in Florida's electric chair.

**1990 (4 May)** Jesse Tafero, convicted of killing two policemen, is put to death in Florida's electric chair; during the execution, the electrodes fail, Tafero bursts into flames, and is literally burned alive.

**1991 (7 June)** In a little-known but landmark ruling, Judge Robert Schnacke of the U.S. District Court for the Northern District of California holds that while witnesses to executions may have pens and paper, they cannot record executions with video or other recording devices, in *KQED, Inc., v. Daniel B. Vasquez, Warden of San Quentin Prison.*

**1992 (21 April)** California executes double murderer Robert Alton Harris in the gas chamber, the first man to die in that state since 1967; Harris' last words are, "You can be a king or a street sweeper, but everyone dances with the Grim Reaper."

**1993** Japan puts to death seven men, the most since 1976.

**1994** Amnesty International calls on the United States to convene a Commission on Capital Punishment, to decide whether the death penalty in the United States is working, and whether it should be phased out. Further, it calls for a moratorium on executions until the commission would release its report; President Bill Clinton does not respond to AI's request.

**(27 April)** Multiple murderer Timothy Spencer is put to death in Virginia's electric chair, the first man to be executed in the United States on the strength of D.N.A. evidence introduced against him at trial.

**(13 September)** President Bill Clinton signs into law the Federal Crime Control Act of 1994, which contains the Federal Death Penalty Act, a piece of legislation which mandates death sentences for 60 new crimes.

**(25 November)** The Japanese government releases the results of a nationwide poll showing that a large majority of the

Japanese people favor the retention of capital punishment.

**(December)** Japanese murderers Ajima Yukio and Sasaki Kazumi, the former having been imprisoned for 16 years, are reportedly executed in Japan. Because the government does not release news of executions, and since they are carried out in secret (per instructions from the Japanese Ministry of Justice), this information remains unconfirmed.

**1995 (7 March)** Gov. George Pataki of New York, who was elected the previous November on a platform of signing a death penalty statute for his state, reinstates capital punishment in New York.

**(17 March)** Filipino maid Flor Contemplacion is hanged in Singapore's Changi Prison for the murder of two people despite worldwide appeals for clemency.

**(17 May)** Despite a widespread appeal to save his life which included an interview with him posted on the Internet, multiple murderer Gervies Davis is put to death by lethal injection in Illinois' Joliet Prison.

**(6 June)** The South Africa Supreme Court abolishes the death penalty in that country.

**(11 August)** Murderer Robert Brecheen, scheduled to be executed, is found unconscious in his cell from an overdose of sedatives; he is rushed to a hospital, returned to consciousness by having his stomach pumped, and then brought back to the prison in Oklahoma City, Oklahoma, where he is then executed by lethal injection.

**(15 November)** The Spanish Senate votes to end the utilization of the sentence of death in its military penal code, effectively ending the use of capital punishment in Spain.

**1996 (25 January)** Double murderer Billy Bailey is hanged in Delaware.

**(26 January)** Child killer John Albert Taylor becomes the first person in 19 years to face the firing squad in the United States when he is put to death in Utah.

**(28 January)** Thai inmate Prommas Leamsai is executed by firing squad in Bangkok for the murder of a policeman; it is Thailand's first execution in nine years.

**(23 February)** William Bonin, known as the "Freeway Killer," is executed by lethal injection in San Quentin Prison in California, the first person in that state to be put to death in that manner.

**(15 March)** Singapore hangs five Thai migrant workers for a series of robberies that resulted in three murders.

**(13 September)** Roberto Girón and Pedro Castillo are executed by a firing squad in Guatemala for raping and murdering a four-year-old girl; when the men survive the first round of fire, the chief of the firing squad delivers the coup de grâce, a single shot in the face.

**1997 (April)** The state of Texas executed six prisoners, the most of any state in a 30-day period since the Supreme Court found the death penalty to be constitutional.

**(2 April)** Two days after finding Mohammed al-Nazari guilty of killing six people, a court in San'a, Yemen, sentences the killer to be executed by firing squad and have his corpse nailed to a cross and displayed for three days afterward.

**(5 April)** Yemeni killer Mohammed al-Nazari is put to death with a number of shots to the chest; however, the Yemeni Supreme Court rules that his body will not be nailed to a cross after death.

**References:** Christoph, James Bernard, *Capital Punishment and British Politics: The British Movement to Abolish the Death Penalty, 1945–57* (Chicago: University of Chicago Press, 1962); Cohen, Bernard Lande, *Law Without Order: Capital Punishment and the Liberals* (New Rochelle, New York: Arlington House, 1970); Foreman, Laura, ed.-in-chief, *Crimes and Punishments: The Time-Life Library of Curious and Unusual Facts* (New York: Time-Life Books, 1991); Gaute, J.H.H., and Robin Odell, *The New Murderers' Who's Who* (New York: International Polygonics, Ltd., 1989); Laurence, John, *A History of Capital Punishment* (New York: The Citadel Press, 1960); Nash, Jay Robert, *Encyclopedia of World Crime* (Wilmette, Illinois: CrimeBooks, Inc.; four volumes, 1990); Nicolai, Sandra, Karen Riley, Rhonda Christensen, Patrice Stych, and Leslie Greunke, eds., *The Question of Capital Punishment* (Lincoln, Nebraska: CONtact, Inc., 1981).

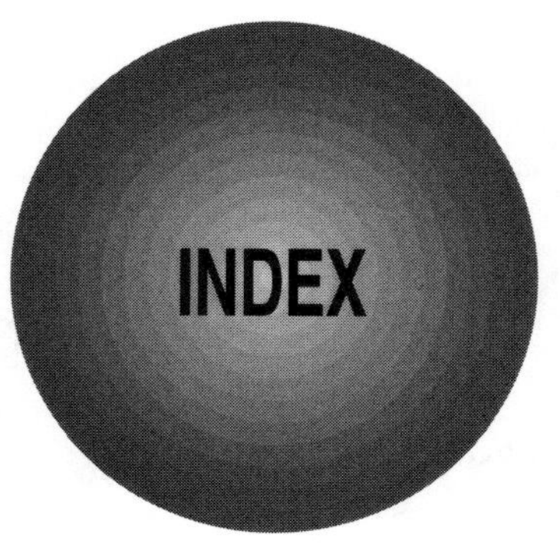
INDEX